ANTIQUES
Handbook
& Price Guide

2022~2023

Miller's Antiques Handbook & Price Guide 2022–2023
By Judith Miller

First published in Great Britain in 2022 by Miller's, a division of Mitchell Beazley,
imprints of Octopus Publishing Group Ltd., Carmelite House, 50 Victoria Embankment, London, EC4Y 0DZ
www.octopusbooks.co.uk

An Hachette UK Company
www.hachette.co.uk

Distributed in the US by Hachette Book Group, 1290 Avenue of the Americas, 4th and 5th Floors, New York, NY 10104
Distributed in Canada by Canadian Manda Group, 664 Annette St., Toronto, Ontario, Canada M6S 2C8

ISBN: 978 1 78472 830 4

Set in Frutiger

Printed and bound in China

1 3 5 7 9 10 8 6 4 2

Publisher Alison Starling
Editorial Co-ordinator Laura Meachem
Proofreader John Wainwright
Indexer Vanessa Bird
Designer Ali Scrivens, T J Graphics
Senior Production Manager Peter Hunt

Photographs of Judith Miller page 7, by Chris Terry

Page 1: A 19thC Chinese export carved hardwood display cabinet, the pierced and carved cornice centered by an armorial lion, above open shelves with pierced and carved galleries and corner brackets, over a pair of cupboard doors carved with chrysanthemums and peonies, on a separate hardwood stand. 92¼in (234cm) high $3,300-4,000 L&T

Page 3: A Tiffany Studios "Dragonfly" table lamp, of Favrile glass, leaded glass, patinated bronze, brass, and quartz pebbles, with a rare Pumpkin base with pebble decoration, marked on shade "Tiffany Studios New York." ca. 1898 18in (46cm) high $120,000-130,000 DRA

Page 4 from left to right: A Reformed Gothic brass mantel clock, designed by Bruce Talbert, probably manufactured by Cox & Co. or Hart, Son, Peard & Co.,the pinnacle set with quartz stone flower finial. 15½in (39.5cm) high $11,000-13,000 WW

A Meissen teapot, with gilt bird-head spout and wishbone handle, painted with figures beside Classical architecture, scattered ombrierte flowers, later cover. ca.1745 $1,050-1,200 CHOR

A Daum cameo glass vase, the mottled green ground overpainted with trees, signed "Daum Nancy," ground foot. 8in (20cm) high $3,300-4,000 SWO

A Victorian silver "castle-top" vinaigrette, by Nathaniel Mills, Birmingham, cover with a scene of York Minster, the underside with a vacant shield cartouche, the interior with a pierced and engraved silver-gilt grille. 1842 2in (4.8cm) wide 1.3oz $2,900-3,300 WW

A Chinese famille rose bowl, the deep rounded sides rising to a flared rim. 8in (20.3cm) diam $40,000-53,000 SWO

A William De Morgan Merton Abbey Period "Omnia Vanitas" ("Strutting Peacock") tile, impressed factory mark. 6¼in (15.5cm) wide $5,300-6,600 WW

A Clarice Cliff Lotus pitcher, "Original Bizarre," unmarked. ca. 1928 11¾in (29.5cm) high $1,300-1,800 FLD

One of a pair of Regency ebonized and parcel-gilt stools, attributed to Gillows, the top above X-frame supports. ca. 1820 24in (61cm) wide $6,000-6,600 DN

A late 19thC Black Forest carved linden wood model of a prowling bear, with glass eyes. 10¾in (27.5cm) long $850-1,000 WW

Page 7 from left to right: A Chinese Qianlong Imperial inscribed famille rose wall vase, marks reading "Qianlong chen han" (the Qianlong Emperor's own mark). 7½in (19cm) high $650,000-800,000 SWO

A pair of French Louis XVI ormolu-mounted white marble vases, after the Borghese Vase. ca. 1790 17½in (44.7cm) high $170,000-210,000 WW

A Matchbox Models of Yesteryear Y6 1916 AEC "Y"-type truck, "Osram Lamps." $7,500-8,000 VEC

ANTIQUES
Handbook
& Price Guide
2022~2023

Judith Miller

MILLER'S

Contents

LIST OF CONSULTANTS

At Miller's, we are extremely lucky to be able to call on a large number of specialists for advice. My colleagues and friends on the BBC "Antiques Roadshow" have a wealth of knowledge and their advice on the state of the market is invaluable.

It is also important to keep in touch with dealers, because they are ones dealing directly with collectors. Certain parts of the market have been extremely volatile over the past year, so up-to-date information is critical.

CERAMICS

John Axford
Woolley & Wallis
51-61 Castle Street
Salisbury SP1 3SU

Ed Crichton
Lacy Scott & Knight
10 Risbygate St
Bury St. Edmunds IP33 3AA

Nic Saintey
Bearnes Hampton &
Littlewood
St Edmund's Court
Okehampton Street
Exeter EX4 1DU

FURNITURE

Lennox Cato
1 The Square, Edenbridge
Kent TN8 5BD

Guy Schooling
Sworders
Cambridge Road
Stansted Mountfitchet
Essex CM24 8GE

ASIAN

**John Axford &
Jeremy Morgan**
Woolley & Wallis
51-61 Castle Street
Salisbury SP1 3SU

Dan Bray
Gorringes
15 North Street
Lewes
East Sussex BN7 2PE

Adrian Rathbone
Hansons
Heage Lane, Etwall,
Derbyshire DE65 6LS

Lee Young
Dore & Rees
Vicarage Street
Frome BA11 1PUA

Ling Zhu
Lyon & Turnbull
33 Broughton Place
Edinburgh EH1 3RR

CLOCKS

Paul Archard
Campbell & Archard
www.qualityantiqueclocks.com

SILVER

Duncan Campbell
Beau Nash
31 Brock Street
Bath BA1 2LN

Alastair Dickenson
128-130 High Street,
Godalming, Surrey, GU7 1AB

JEWELRY

Trevor Kyle
Lyon & Turnbull
33 Broughton Place
Edinburgh EH1 3RR

Gemma Redmond
5 Roby Mill, Wigan,
Skelmersdale WN8 0QF

SPORTING

Graham Budd
Graham Budd
PO Box 47519
London N14 6XD

TRIBAL

Alex Tweedy
Lyon & Turnbull
33 Broughton Place
Edinburgh EH1 3RR

Waddington's
275 King Street East,
Toronto, Ontario
Canada M5A 1K2

DECORATIVE ARTS

Wayne Chapman
Lynways
www.lynways.com

Will Farmer
Fieldings
Mill Race Lane
Stourbridge DY8 1JN

Michael Jeffrey
Woolley & Wallis
51-61 Castle Street
Salisbury, SP1 3SU

John Mackie
Lyon & Turnbull
33 Broughton Place
Edinburgh EH1 3RR

Mike Moir
M & D Moir
www.manddmoir.co.uk

David Rago
Rago Arts
333 North Main Street,
Lambertville, NJ 08530 USA

MODERN DESIGN

David Rago
Rago Arts
333 North Main Street,
Lambertville, NJ 08530 USA

John Mackie
Lyon & Turnbull
33 Broughton Place
Edinburgh EH1 3RR

HOW TO USE THIS BOOK

Running head Indicates the subcategory of the main heading.

Page tab It appears on every page and identifies the main category heading as identified in the Contents List on pages 4-5.

Closer look Does exactly that. We show identifying aspects of a factory or maker, point out rare colors or shapes, and explain why a particular piece is so desirable.

Essential reference Gives key facts about the factory, maker, or style, along with stylistic identification points, value tips, and advice on fakes.

Judith Picks Items chosen specially by Judith, either because they are important or interesting, or because they're good investments.

The object The antiques are shown in full color. This is a vital aid to identification and valuation. With many objects, a slight color variation can signify a large price differential.

Caption The description of the item illustrated, including when relevant, the period, the maker or factory, medium, the year it was made, dimensions, and condition. Many captions have **footnotes**, which explain terminology or give identification or valuation information.

The price guide These price ranges give a ballpark figure of what you should pay for a similar item. The great joy of antiques is that there is no recommended retail price. The price ranges in this book are based on actual prices, either what a dealer will take or the full auction price.

Source code Every item has been specially photographed at an auction house, a dealer, an antiques market, or a private collection. These are credited by code at the end of the caption, and can be checked against the Key to Illustrations on pages 588-589.

INTRODUCTION

Welcome to the 2022–2023 edition of *Miller's Antiques Handbook and Price Guide*—it is unbelievable that we published the first black-and-white edition in 1979. The BBC commissioned "Antiques Roadshow" in the same year, and now regularly receives seven million viewers.

The whole antiques market has changed substantially due to the global pandemic, and dealers and auction houses have had to change the way they operate. The Internet has become absolutely essential to sellers and collectors. Reading the reports from both auction houses and dealers, I think this change may well be permanent. Due to the pandemic and lockdowns, people have had more time to spend at home and spent less on vacations, travel, and restaurants, and therefore the desire to add antiques to the home has made the market more buoyant.

There is a certain cautious optimism about the future of the antiques trade. Some areas remain strong, such as the Asian, Russian, and Indian markets. A good example of the desirability of Chinese ceramics is found below—the Qianlong Imperial famille rose wall vase. It is obviously high quality, rare, and incorporates "Qianlong chen han," which is the Emperor's own mark (see also p. 98). This, of course, adds to its rarity and desirability.

This guide is, as always, packed with more than 8,000 images of antiques and fine decorative objects that are completely new to this edition. I am often asked if we update the prices in each edition; we don't—when we publish

A pair of French Louis XVI ormolu-mounted white marble vases, after the Borghese Vase. ca. 1790
17½in (44.7cm) high
$170,000-210,000 WW

a new edition, we start from scratch to properly reflect changes and developments in the market.

We are witnessing a transition from more traditional collecting fields to Mid-century and Modern design. Indeed, there is a shortage of good antiques—the dealers' lament today is that having made a sale, the hardest part is finding good-quality antiques to replace it.

Antiques are also green. Buying solid mahogany furniture is more ethical than buying disposable MDF pieces. A solid, plain, mahogany early- to mid-19thC chest-of-drawers will still be a practical storage piece in 200 years' time.

Any good-quality, top-end antique in original condition that is fresh to the market will excite collectors' interest. Note the beautiful pair of Louis XVI ormolu mounted marble vases, on this page and on p. 455.

We must also consider how important rarity is, particularly when it comes to collecibles. Just look at the Matchbox truck (see left and p. 487). The price achieved was solely due to its condition and the fact that it has extremely rare black solid plastic wheels. If it had the more common metal wheels it would be worth $25!

I am always asked, "What antique should I buy?," and I always answer, "Buy something you love, something that will make you smile." However, in times of economic uncertainty, top-quality antiques are often seen as a good investment, and you have the added benefit of enjoying them.

Indeed, now is a great time to be buying antiques. So please use this completely updated guide to increase your knowledge, your commercial acumen, and your enjoyment. Those hidden treasures are still out there just waiting to be discovered!

A Matchbox Models of Yesteryear Y6 1916 AEC "Y" type truck, "Osram Lamps." $7,500-8,000 VEC

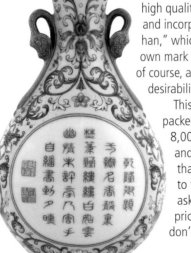

A Chinese Qianlong Imperial inscribed famille rose wall vase, marks reading "Qianlong chen han" (the Qianlong Emperor's own mark). 7½in (19cm) high
$650,000-800,000 SWO

THE PORCELAIN MARKET

The porcelain market has been affected by the global pandemic, with few collectors traveling and most using the Internet, which has proven beneficial for dealers, auction houses, and collectors. Having more time, collectors are better prepared to buy when items are rare and of excellent quality.

Chelsea pieces, particularly scent bottles, continue to excite collectors. There is also tremendous interest in rare Chelsea models, such as the owl (see page 15) and the apple box and cover (see page 16). It is the quality and rarity that excite collectors.

Worcester buyers will pay high sums for pieces with a rare early pattern and, again, of exceptional quality, for example, the wine funnel on page 39 and the mug with rare dog design on page 40, which with initials was obviously a special commission. Royal Worcester ewers and vases painted by such artists as Charles Baldwin, Harry Davis, and the Stintons still have their collectors and prices have remained steady, but the pieces have to be of a good size and preferably fresh to the market.

An area that is still struggling is British blue-and-white porcelain from both the 18th and 19th centuries. Large platters can be in demand, but not if they have a transfer-printed common pattern or any damage. Later transfer-printed blue-and-white pieces have struggled to find strong prices, with many auctioneers combining pieces in job lots. Many pieces fail to find the price levels that I was paying 30 years ago.

Lowestoft and Vauxhall prices continue to be steady, particularly when rare shapes and patterns are offered (see the tiger on page 24). Nantgarw and Swansea also remain in demand due in part to their rarity and superb quality, and unrecorded early Derby figures always excite the market.

With European porcelain, there has been little change to the market during the last few years. The market leaders—Sèvres and Meissen—have remained in demand, particularly for early 18thC examples. The "golden age" of Meissen from the factory's early years, 1710-50, is still strong, and in this area collectors are even prepared to accept some damage. One good example is the squirrel I chose as a Judith Picks (see page 28): it has extensive damage but was probably modeled by Kändler and is incredibly rare. Meissen figures from the late 19thC have to be of superb quality to attract a collector's interest. Prices remain strong for Vincennes and Sèvres, particularly for early pieces that are rare and of impressive quality—for example, the bleu celeste dish on page 34. Dresden, Vienna, and Limoges pieces have to be particularly impressive and rare to sell well. The Paris factories have struggled, and buyers are still suspicious of many so-called "Samson" pieces that do not have the quality of the true Samson copies.

In general, do your research, find a good source, either a dealer or auction house, and enjoy! It's a great time to buy.

Top Left: A 19thC porcelain figure of a greyhound, by Copeland & Garrett, with gilt border bands, green stamp on base.

11in (28cm) long

$1,300-1,800　　　　　　　**L&T**

Above: A pair of Barr Flight & Barr candlesticks, each modeled as a griffin with a bronzed mane and with a candle nozzle gilt with scrolling foliage, the pedestals painted with figures in a landscape, with impressed and script marks.

ca. 1805　　　　　　　　*7in (18cm) high*

$12,000-13,000　　　　　　　**CHEF**

PORCELAIN

A Berlin teacup and saucer, painted en grisaille, the saucer with a mother holding a young child beside two sheep, the cup with a shepherdess, blue scepter marks.

ca. 1760-70   *5¼in (13.6cm) diam*

$550-600   **WW**

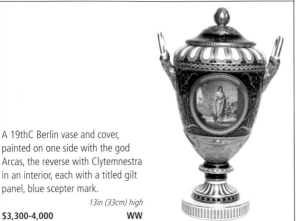

A 19thC Berlin vase and cover, painted on one side with the god Arcas, the reverse with Clytemnestra in an interior, each with a titled gilt panel, blue scepter mark.

13in (33cm) high

$3,300-4,000   **WW**

A KPM plaque, painted after Friedrich Bodenmüller with "Alms to the Poor," impressed mark and inscribed on the reverse, framed.

12½in (32cm) high

$4,000-4,600   **CHEF**

A pair of 19thC Berlin cassolettes, painted with courting couples in landscapes, applied with female mask handles, on column bases on stepped square feet, the covers reversing to form candlesticks, KPM mark, some restoration.

10¾in (27.5cm) high

$260-400   **WW**

A pair of 19thC Berlin porcelain vases, with floral sprays on a celadon ground in the Chinese style, with iron-red orb and "KPM" marks, underglaze blue scepter and eagle and circle marks.

13in (33cm) high

$1,00-1,050   **SWO**

A late-19th/early-20thC Berlin plaque, of "Das Wiener Schokoladenmädchen" or "La Belle Chocolatière," after Jean-Etienne Liotard, impressed KPM and scepter mark, with a little wear.

9¼in (23.5cm) high

$550-650   **WW**

A 19thC Continental porcelain plaque, painted after Titian's "A Woman With a Mirror," framed.

8¾in (22cm) high

$350-450   **CHEF**

A Continental porcelain plaque, painted with a fisherman sitting on the riverbank with a female nude by his side.

8½in (21.5cm) high

$750-850   **CHEF**

ESSENTIAL REFERENCE—BOW PORCELAIN

The Bow factory was founded in London ca. 1744 by Thomas Frye and Edward Heylyn. Its porcelain wares were relatively inexpensive and at first popular. However, the factory gradually declined during the 1760s and closed in 1776.

- Bow porcelain was white and chalky, with an irregular surface and granular texture, while its glassy glaze had a gray-green hue. The predominant colors in the Bow palette were blues, yellows and purples.
- Inspired by Asian designs, most early Bow wares were plain blanc-de-Chine or decorated in underglaze blue. Later enameled wares were based on the famille rose palette or Kakiemon designs.
- Bow figures were press molded instead of slip cast, making them heavier and less fine than those made by Chelsea or Derby.
- Early Bow is generally unmarked, but, from ca. 1765, an anchor-and-dagger mark was painted in red enamel.

A Bow sauceboat, painted in a bright blue with a bird perched on branches of flowering magnolia, the handles with mask head terminals.

ca. 1750-52　　　*7in (18cm) high*

$850-1,000　　　**WW**

An armorial Bow mug, painted with the arms of the Worshipful Company of Merchant Taylors, comprising a shield containing a lion above three fur-lined tents, flanked by two camels above the motto "Concordia Parva Res Crescent" (In Harmony Small Things Grow), the base broken and reattached.

The Worshipful Company of Merchant Taylors ranks sixth and seventh (on alternate years) in the Great Twelve City Livery Companies. It was founded prior to 1300 and first incorporated under a Royal Charter in 1327. Its base is the Merchant Taylor's Hall between Threadneedle Street and Cornhill, a site it has occupied since at least 1347. While initially a company for the tailoring profession, the company exists today as primarily a philanthropic association with links to a number of schools, colleges, and almshouses. Surprisingly, given its location and strong trade links, there is little tradition of armorial decoration on Bow porcelain.

ca. 1750-55　　　*6in (15.5cm) high*

$1,700-2,100　　　**WW**

A rare Bow figure of a prowling lioness, standing on a rocky base with mouth slightly agape and tail curled down between her hind legs, her coat enameled a deep orange-brown, some wear, the tail restored.

Several pairs of figures left in the white are known, including those at the National Gallery of Melbourne, Victoria, accession number 2010.10.1-2. However, only one other enameled example is recorded.

ca. 1750-52　　　*9in (23cm) wide*

$22,000-26,000　　　**WW**

A Bow shell salt, modeled with shell-encrusted base, incised arrow-and-annulet mark, cracks on the shell.

ca. 1752　　　*5¾in (14.5cm) wide*

$1,000-1,100　　　**DN**

A pair of Bow models of a lion and lioness, some spots of brown staining, minute surface chips, and light wear.

ca. 1752　　　*4in (10cm) long*

$3,300-4,000　　　**DN**

A Bow teapot and cover, painted in famille rose enamels with birds in flight above peonies and a lotus leaf, damages and restoration.

ca. 1752-54　　　*6½in (16.5cm) wide*

$260-330　　　**WW**

A white-glazed Bow Commedia dell'Arte figure of Isabella, her left hand lacking.

While a number of Italian Comedy figures produced at Bow were copied from Meissen's Weissenfels series modeled by Kändler and Reinicke, this figure of Isabella appears to be unique to the Bow factory.

ca. 1752-55　　　*6¼in (15.7cm) high*

$1,050-1,200　　　**WW**

A Bow tureen and cover, the silver shape painted with Chinese pagoda landscapes and flowering plants, with foliate scroll handles, on four scroll feet, with some firing faults and damages, the finial lacking.

ca. 1753-55　　　*15¾in (40cm) wide*

$6,000-7,500　　　**WW**

A Bow figure of Pedrolino or Pierrot from the Commedia dell'Arte, the low pad base applied with flowers and leaves, a few small chips.

The figure was first modeled by Reinicke at Meissen, using an engraving by Francois Joullain in Louis Riccobini's "Histoire du Theatre Italien," published in 1731, and was faithfully copied by Bow.

ca. 1755　　　*5¾in (14.5cm) high*

$1,300-1,800　　　**WW**

PORCELAIN

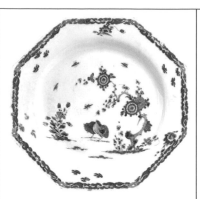

A Bow porcelain plate, painted in the Kakiemon style with the "Two Quail" pattern.

ca. 1755　　　　　*8¾in (22cm) wide*

$350-400　　　　　**BELL**

A Bow white-glazed figure of an abbess, looking down at a book.

ca. 1755　　　*6¾in (17cm) high*

$260-330　　**BELL**

A Bow white-glazed three-shell salt or sweetmeat, on rockwork applied with shells and seaweed, incised arrow and annulet, some damage.

ca. 1750-55　　　*8½in (21.5cm) wide*

$260-330　　　**BELL**

A Bow silver-shaped dish or stand, painted in the Kakiemon palette with the "Two Quail" pattern, on a low foot, red "2" mark, some wear and damages.

ca. 1755　　　*8¾in (22cm) diam*

$350-400　　**WW**

CLOSER LOOK—BOW FIGURE

This Bow figure of a lady is often with her companion, the Marquis. It is copying a model by Peter Reinicke (1715-68). He was a modeler at Meissen from 1743.

She is wearing a layered crinoline dress with a gilt locket or pocket watch suspended from her waist.

She is holding a partly folded fan in her right hand.

The model is raised on a low scroll base applied with flowers.

A Bow figure.

ca. 1758-60　　　*6¼in (15.8cm) high*

$1,500-1,800　　**WW**

A Bow figure of the Poultry Chef, with two cooked birds with slices of orange, some chipping, a repair on the plate.

ca. 1755　　　*6¾in (17.3cm) high*

$1,050-1,200　　**WW**

A Bow figure of "Smell," from the "Senses" series, modeled as a girl on a tree stump, with an apron full of flowers, bending her head to sniff the blooms, small losses to the flowers and leaves.

ca. 1756-60　　　*5in (13cm) high*

$1,600-2,100　　**WW**

A Bow figure of a girl, possibly emblematic of "Smell," a sheep at her feet, on a low pad base applied with leaves.

ca. 1756-58　　　*6in (15.2cm) high*

$750-850　　**WW**

A Bow coffeepot and cover, with pineapple molding beneath a cell diaper border, with crab-stock handle and foliate scrolls on the spout.

ca. 1758-60　　　*9½in (24cm) high*

$850-1,000　　**WW**

Two similar 18thC Bow porcelain salts, of shell form supported by dolphins spouting water, on floral and naturally modeled bases, decorated on the shells with floral work and enamel work.

6.6cm high

$15,000-18,000 ROS

A Bow "Birds in Branches" chamber candlestick, a dog lying on the ground, beneath a foliate sconce on a metal branch.

ca. 1760-65 *9in (23cm) high*

$1,000-1,100 BELL

A pair of Bow figures of dancers, raised on a pierced scrolled base with turquoise and gilt detailing, red anchor-and-dagger marks and blue crescent marks, some restoration.

ca. 1760-65 *7½in (18.9cm) high*

$900-1,050 WW

A Bow figure of the "Squire of Alsatia," his right hand in his pocket and left extended, the low scroll base picked out in penciled enamels, restored.

A Bow figure of a female musician, playing the zither, on a footed base.

ca. 1760 *7in (17.6cm) high*

$800-900 WW

ca. 1760 *6in (15.2cm) high*

$850-1,000 WW

A Bow dish, painted with a chinoiserie landscape with a figure in a boat and another on a riverbank, with fan and circular panels with landscape and flowers, six character script mark.

ca. 1765 *14¼in (36cm) wide*

$550-600 BELL

A set of four Bow porcelain figures, emblematic of the "Elements," on gilt scroll bases, red anchor-and-dagger mark and blue painted "A," some damage.

ca. 1765 *10in (25.5cm) high*

$1,800-2,400 BELL

CLOSER LOOK—BOW FIGURE

This is a previously unrecorded Bow figure.

It is probably depicting Nike, who was the winged goddess of Victory— victor both in war and peaceful competition.

Mythological figures of this type are unusual in Bow porcelain and this may be an attempt to imitate the "Muses" being produced at Chelsea.

The goddess has both arms extended and holding a flower garland before her, standing before fruiting and flowering bocage.

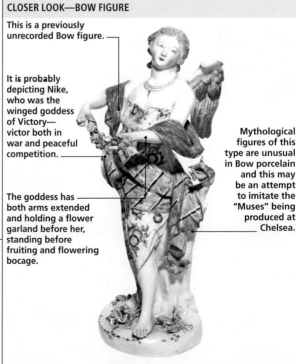

A Bow figure of "Winter," modeled as a boy standing beside a brazier before berried bocage, his hands tucked inside a fur muff.

ca. 1765 *7½in (19.2cm) high*

$600-750 WW

A Bow figure, the circular base with a gilt husk border, red anchor-and-dagger mark, some restoration.

ca. 1760-65 *14in (35.5cm) high*

$800-900 WW

ESSENTIAL REFERENCE—BRISTOL PORCELAIN

In terms of ceramics, the port city of Bristol is best- and long-known for its pottery. In contrast, porcelain production there was on a smaller scale—essentially confined to two factories—and more short-lived. The first factory was established ca. 1748-49 by, and named after, a Quaker, Benjamin Lund. It produced blue-and-white porcelain similar to that made at the Limehouse factory in London (one of whose proprietors had joined Lund in Bristol), but it was more durable due to its secret ingredient: Cornish soapstone, a substitute for petuntse (china clay). In 1752, Dr. John Wall and William Davis at Worcester, realizing the potential of soapstone, purchased Lund's factory along with its secret "hard-paste" formula, and Worcester went on to become Great Britain's most successful 18thC porcelain factory.

The second factory was originally Cookworthy's in Plymouth, but it was moved to Bristol in 1770 and its ownership subsequently transferred to Richard Champion. From 1774 to 1781, when it was sold to a number of Staffordshire potters, Champion's factory produced a harder and whiter porcelain than other 18thC English soft-paste porcelains, and its cold, glittering glaze clearly distinguished it from the wares of Bow, Chelsea, Worcester, and Derby. Early wares looked to Asian porcelain for style, but, under Champion, Meissen and French factories provided the inspiration—most notably for tea and coffee services.

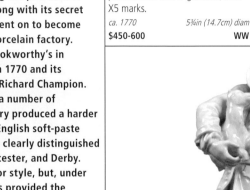

A Bristol chocolate cup and saucer, painted with flower garlands, blue X5 marks.
ca. 1770   *5¾in (14.7cm) diam*
$450-600   **WW**

A Bristol salt or sweetmeat stand, three scallop shells around a spray of coral, on a rocky base applied with small shells, coral, and seaweed, some faults.
ca. 1770-75   *8½in (21.5cm) wide*
$1,050-1,200   **WW**

A Bristol mask pitcher, with flowers, the rim with a berried garland encircling a gilt line, the spout formed as a bearded mask, blue X mark, the handle restored.
ca. 1770-72   *7¾in (19.8cm) high*
$550-650   **WW**

A Bristol Richard Champion model of a goatherd with kid, chipped hat, lamb is missing, fritting, two minor chips on corners.
ca. 1774   *11in (28cm) high*
$2,600-3,300   **DN**

A Bristol teapot and cover, painted with fuchsia and rose amid sprigs, yellow X 18 mark on the underside, chipping on the spout.
ca. 1775-80   *8½in (21.5cm) wide*
$650-800   **WW**

A Bristol teapot and cover, painted in green camaïeu with flower garlands, the spout with Rococo molding.
ca. 1775   *7in (18cm) wide*
$550-650   **WW**

A Bristol coffeepot and cover, painted with flowers, including rose and convolvulus, the rim with a leaf garland, gilt 2 mark, restoration.
ca. 1775   *9½in (24cm) high*
$1,500-1,800   **WW**

A Bristol gadrooned teapot and cover, with auricular handle and artichoke finial, blue "X" mark and "8," small cracks and rim chips, firing fault on rim.
ca. 1775   *4¼in (11cm) high*
$650-800   **DN**

A Chelsea white model of an owl, triangle-raised anchor period, naturalistically modeled in great detail, on a rocky base.

Discussed by Paul Crane, "Nature, Porcelain and Enlightenment: George Edwards and the Chelsea porcelain birds," ECC Trans, Vol. 8, 2017, this owl model is based on the image copied from George Edwards, "A Natural History of Uncommon Birds, and of Some Other Rare and Undescribed Animals," taken from Volume 2, pl. 60, "The Great Hawk or Horned Owl."

ca. 1745-49   8in (20.5cm) high

$70,000-80,000   **CHOR**

A Chelsea teapot and cover, painted with flowers in the Meissen style, one side with a tortoiseshell butterfly, cracked.

ca. 1750-54   7¼in (18.5cm) wide

$800-900   **WW**

A Chelsea teabowl and saucer, painted in the Kakiemon palette with a phoenix in flight.

ca. 1750-52   5¾in (14.8cm) diam

$2,000-2,600   **WW**

ESSENTIAL REFERENCE—CHELSEA SCENT BOTTLES

From the mid-1750s to the late 1760s, the Chelsea factory produced a wide range of small porcelain items that were highly fashionable at the time and are collectible today. Collectively known as "toys," they included bonbonnières, étuis, thimbles, seals, and scent bottles. Often given as gifts, and usually intended for carrying about the person, they were often intricately and exquisitely modeled in diverse forms—most notably bottles in baskets and human figures—and displayed styles of decoration, especially Rococo, that were often dominated by floral motifs that reflected the source of their contents. Of course, at a time when sewerage systems in villages, towns, and cities were at best seriously inadequate, and scented waters and perfumes provided some olfactory relief from the smells, these little bottles were as useful as they were decorative.

A Chelsea scent bottle, modeled as a bottle in a wicker basket, the neck painted with flowers, with a gilt metal mount and a stopper formed as a butterfly, with a bottle ticket inscribed "Eau de Senteur," restoration.

ca. 1755   3¾in (9.8cm) high

$4,600-5,300   **WW**

A Chelsea scent bottle, modeled as a bottle contained in a wicker basket, the neck painted with flowers, molded with a bottle ticket inscribed "Eau de Senteur," the stopper lacking.

ca. 1755   2½in (6.6cm) high

$2,600-3,300   **WW**

A Chelsea scent bottle, of Rococo form, painted in puce camaïeu with flower sprays and scroll detailing, with gilt metal mounts and a stopper formed as a bird, cracked.

ca. 1755   3½in (9.2cm) high

$4,600 5,300   **WW**

A Chelsea scent bottle, decorated with gilt butterflies and other flying insects, the sides with flowers and leaves, with a gilt metal mount, the stopper formed as a bird, some wear.

ca. 1756-60   3¼in (8.1cm) high

$2,200-2,600   **WW**

An English porcelain scent bottle, possibly Chelsea, in the form of a pear, the cover with a gilt metal mount.

ca. 1755-70   2in (5cm) high

$1,250-1,500   **WW**

PORCELAIN

A rare Chelsea crayfish salt, possibly modeled by Nicholas Sprimont, with a large crayfish crawling over rocks encrusted with a variety of shells and seaweed, before a large single shell applied with further small shells, red anchor mark, some restoration.

Nicholas Sprimont made this design in silver around 1742-43, transferring it to porcelain after 1745. It probably derives from a print after the French goldsmith Meissonnier. Born in 1716 in Liège, in what is now Belgium, the Huguenot Nicholas Sprimont moved to London ca. 1742, where he initially practiced as a silversmith. Working primarily in the then-fashionable Rococo style, his fine and exceptionally rare pieces included some silver shellfish salts of a striking naturalism almost certainly achieved by casting from actual seashells, crabs, and crayfish. When, ca. 1745, Sprimont went on to establish the Chelsea porcelain factory (having probably acquired knowledge of the new soft-paste porcelain from fellow Huguenots Andrew Lagrave and Thomas Briand), he adapted many of his existing and exquisite silver designs for new and highly fashionable equivalent pieces in porcelain. In 1769, prior to his death in 1771, Sprimont sold his interest in the Chelsea factory to William Duesbury, manager of the Derby factory.

ca. 1752-55   *2¾in (7.3cm) high*
$12,000-15,000   **WW**

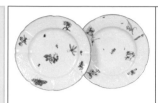

A pair of Chelsea plates, molded in the Meissen "Gotzkowsky" manner, painted with moths, a caterpillar, insects, and flower sprays, red anchor mark to one.

ca. 1755   *9½in (24cm) wide*
$650-800   **WW**

A rare Chelsea sunflower bowl or tureen and cover, with a rim of petals above sides molded with green sepals, the cover formed as the seed head, the cover heavily restored.

ca. 1755   *5¼in (13cm) diam*
$1,500-1,800   **WW**

A Chelsea saucer dish, with Meissen-style flowers, with red anchor marks, minor rubbing on brown rim.

ca. 1754-56   *8¾in (22cm) diam*
$400-550   **SWO**

A Chelsea red anchor teabowl and saucer, painted with flowers over molded and painted leaves.

ca. 1754-56   the saucer 5½in (14cm) diam
$750-850   **SWO**

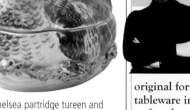

A Chelsea partridge tureen and cover, painted and modeled lain upon a nest, red anchor marks and script "33," areas of wear, small chips.

ca. 1756
$7,500-8,500   **DN**

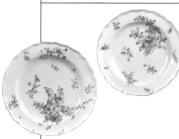

A pair of Chelsea porcelain plates, painted with flowers in the Meissen style, brown-line rims, red anchor marks, slight rubbing, one has a ¼ x ⅛-in (5 x 3-mm) shallow rim chip.

ca. 1756   *9in (23cm) diam*
$550-650   **DN**

A Chelsea "Duke of Cambridge" plate, painted with branches of peaches, persimmons, cherries, and a large butterfly, the border with fruit sprigs and molded with five cartouches painted with insects, highlighted in blue and gilt, gilt anchor mark.

ca. 1756-62   *9¼in (23.5cm) diam*
$1,300-1,600   **CHEF**

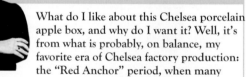

Judith Picks

What do I like about this Chelsea porcelain apple box, and why do I want it? Well, it's from what is probably, on balance, my favorite era of Chelsea factory production: the "Red Anchor" period, when many original forms of decoration were introduced, notably tableware in the form of animals, birds, fish, vegetables, and, as here, fruit. Also, this apple is so realistically modeled and painted it's almost literally three-dimensional trompe l'oeil. Beguiling realism is not, however, its only attribute: the puce and turquoise caterpillar finial on its cover is, in it's stylistic coloring, a gently amusing acknowledgment that, of course, this isn't really real.

A Chelsea porcelain apple box and cover, modeled as a russet-streaked and spotted apple with a leafy stem, the cover with a turquoise and puce caterpillar knop, cover with red anchor mark and numbered "54" in iron red, the base numbered "62."

ca. 1755   *4in (10cm) high*
$26,000-33,000   **LSK**

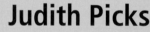
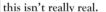

A Chelsea bowl, painted with sprays of European flowers and single scattered sprigs, red anchor mark.
ca. 1760   *7¼in (18.5cm) diam*
$600-750   **WW**

A Chelsea Gold Anchor plate, painted bird on a branch within a gilt feather and scroll border.
ca. 1760   *8¾in (22cm) diam*
$850-1,000   **CHOR**

A Chelsea leaf-shaped sauceboat, molded in relief with leaves and flowers and painted with scattered flowers and insects, raised anchor and pad mark, minute chips, occasional frits.
ca. 1760   *7in (18cm) long*
$6,500-8,000   **DN**

A Chelsea teapot and cover, painted with scattered flowers and insects, within brown-line rims, unmarked, slight fritting, slight wear on brown-line rim of the cover.
ca. 1760   *5in (12.5cm) high*
$26,000-33,000   **DN**

A Chelsea plate, painted with fruit and insects, with panels painted with fanciful birds, gilt anchor mark.
ca. 1760   *8½in (21.5cm) diam*
$800-900   **CHEF**

A Chelsea dessert dish, painted with birds, within gilt borders of spider web and flower swags.
ca. 1762   *13½in (34.3cm) wide*
$600-750   **WW**

A Chelsea botanical cabinet beaker, painted with flowers, including sweet pea, tulip, rose, and convolvulus, broken and reattached.
ca. 1765   *3½in (9cm) high*
$800-900   **WW**

A Chelsea-Derby figure of "Justice," holding a sword and on a scroll molded base.
ca. 1770   *13¼in (33.5cm) high*
$210-260   **CHEF**

A pair of late-18thC Chelsea porcelain figures of Cupid, minor losses.
the tallest 6¼in (16cm) high
$200-260   **MART**

ESSENTIAL REFERENCE—COALPORT

The Coalport factory was founded by John Rose in the 1790s, in Shropshire, England. After Rose's death in 1841, the company continued under the name John Rose & Co.

● John Rose had previously trained at Caughley, and purchased the Caughley factory in 1799. He then bought the Nantgarw factory in 1819 and took on former Nantgarw employees William Billingsley and Samuel Walker as, respectively, his chief painter and chief chemist.

● Coalport focused on table and decorative wares and, in the second half of the 19thC, also began to produce flower-encrusted Rococo pieces and Sèvres-style vases.

● Coalport's varied decorative patterns included Neoclassical designs, Imari-style decoration, landscape scenes, and bouquets of summer flowers. These were often set against a solid, dark blue ground, although green and beige grounds were also common.

A Coalport commemorative mug, painted perhaps by Charles Muss, with military motifs, including flags and a pike above drums and other military instruments, with "Success to the Bury Volunteers," the sides inscribed "In defence of our King and Country" and "To protect our Families & Property," with a rim crack.

ca. 1804   *4in (10cm) high*
$400-450   **WW**

A pair of Coalport vases, painted with flowers including rose, convolvulus, passionflower, and tulip, the handles issuing from lion head masks.

ca. 1820-30   *7in (18cm) high*
$350-400   **WW**

A Coalport garniture, comprising a cachepot, stand, and a pair of spill vases, painted probably in the workshop of Thomas Baxter, with flowers, including roses, convolvulus, and chrysanthemum, the cachepot with dolphin mask handles, the stand on three paw feet.

ca. 1820   *6¼in (15.5cm) high*
$550-600   **WW**

A Coalport Rococo cased clock, applied with flowers, the clock with an enamel face, some damages.

ca. 1840-50   *11¼in (28.5cm) high*
$450-600   **WW**

A pair of early-20thC Coalport porcelain vases with covers, painted with lake, city, and landscape scenes, marked on underside Coalport with crown - England. A.D. 1750 and further code "B 350."

8¾in (22.4cm) high
$600-650   **MART**

A limited edition Coalport Fine Bone China Limited vase and cover, with goat-head handles, to commemorate the restoration of Medeley Court, Shropshire, England, the center panel painted by Peter Gosling, certificate dated November 1, 1973, limited edition number 35/100.

9¾in (24.7cm) high
$130-200   **MART**

A limited edition Coalport Fine Bone China limited commemorative lidded vase, to commemorate The Marriage of H.R.H. The Prince of Wales and Lady Diana Spencer in 1981, limited edition number 76/250.

9½in (24.2cm) high
$150-200   **MART**

PORCELAIN

ESSENTIAL REFERENCE—DERBY

A porcelain factory was founded in Derby in ca. 1748 by Frenchman André Planché. In 1756, it was bought by John Heath and William Duesbury, previously decorators for Chelsea. In 1770, they also bought out the Chelsea factory and operated together as Chelsea-Derby until 1784. In 1811, the company was acquired by Robert Bloor, who managed the factory until its closure in 1848.

● Early Derby soft-paste porcelain is fine grained, its glaze either grayish white or grayish green. Its early wares were mostly figures—pastoral and allegorical subjects, often left in white. During the 1950s and 60s, Derby figures were typically Rococo in style and stood on scrolled bases.

● After 1756, Derby's range expanded to include tureens, baskets, and other tableware. Their tea wares often cracked with use, so examples are rarely found today.

● After the acquisition of Chelsea, the porcelain paste became a pure white and the glaze a clear blush. New designs included landscapes; detailed, naturalistic flowers; and exotic birds. Many patterns were loose copies of Chelsea or Sèvres designs.

A near pair of Derby sweetmeat figures, attributed to Andrew Planché, modeled as a gallant and his companion, some restoration.
ca. 1753-55   6½in (16.5cm) high
$1,200-1,300   WW

An early Derby figure of a Scottish dancer, some restoration to her hat.
ca. 1755-56   6¼in (15.5cm) high
$650-800   WW

A Derby dry-edge figure of a girl, some restoration.

The term "dry edge" was originally employed by Bernard Rackham, of the Victoria and Albert Museum, London, to denote a distinctive class of early porcelain figures made at Derby prior to 1756, when William Duesbury became copartner of the factory and output both increased substantially and became more commercially orientated. These early dry-edge figures are skillfully and crisply modeled and feature a distinctive soft, lustrous, and generally creamy colored glaze (not used after 1756), which, in many cases, stops short of the base of the figure, leaving a fraction of an inch of white biscuit body—a "dry edge"—exposed. Occasionally, this dry edge is also encountered on porcelain figures from other English factories—most notably the primitive "snowmen" from Longton Hall.
ca. 1755   4¾in (12.2cm) high
$900-1,050   WW

A Derby figure of Jupiter, sitting in a chariot beside a large standing eagle, holding a thunderbolt, the chariot resting on cloud scrolls, minor faults.
ca. 1760   10¼in (26.2cm) high
$1,600-2,100   WW

A pair of Derby figures of dancers, the male wearing a Pierrot-type costume, his female companion an apron, some restoration.
ca. 1755-58   6in (15.2cm) high
$1,500-2,000   WW

A Derby coffee can and stand, with a wishbone handle, enameled with birds among branches, the coffee can with a butterfly and insects.
ca. 1756-58
$800-900   CHEF

A Derby wine taster, decorated with leaf sprays, the interior painted with a peony plant, a fine, short rim crack.
ca. 1756-60   2¾in (7.1cm) wide
$750-850   WW

A Derby harvest pitcher, painted with flowers and ripe ears of corn, the reverse with a narcissus and blue flowers.
ca. 1758-60   7¼in (18.4cm) high
$650-800   WW

A Derby frill vase and cover, painted with moths and insects with flowers, the shoulders pierced with holes, with two mask head handles, the domed cover with a bird, some restoration.

ca. 1765-70   *11¼in (28.6cm) high*

$550-650   **WW**

A Derby figure of a billy goat, the base with flowers and leaves, restoration to the horns and ears.

ca. 1760-65   *4¼in (10.5cm) high*

$400-550   **WW**

A Derby model of a red squirrel, restoration to the paws.

ca. 1765   *3in (7.7cm) high*

$1,050-1,200   **WW**

A Derby figure of the "Map Seller," from the "Cris de Paris" series model at Meissen by J. J. Kändler, holding a map of Italy, a map in his left hand, a chest and other bundles strapped to his back, some restoration.

Cf. Len and Yvonne Adams, "Meissen Portrait Figures," p. 108 and p. 93 for the original drawing by Edmé Bouchardon.

ca. 1765   *6in (15.3cm) high*

$800-900   **WW**

A Derby figure of Britannia, modeled with globe, lion, and trophies of war.

ca. 1765-70   *12¾in (32.5cm) high*

$450-550   **CHEF**

A Derby figure group emblematic of Music, modeled as a flute-playing maiden with two putti holding music, instruments around them, incised no 2179.

ca. 1765-70   *10in (25cm) high*

$260-400   **CHOR**

A Derby pipe tamper, modeled as the head and shoulders of a lady with a feathered headdress.

ca. 1770   *2¼in (5.8cm) high*

$550-650   **WW**

A set of four Derby figures of the Elements, emblematic of Earth, Water, Fire, and Air, Fire with a flaming brazier and cannon, Air holding a bird with its cage in her other hand, Earth with a spade and watering can, Water holding a fish, with a creel at her feet, with restoration.

The figure of Fire is adapted from the similar Derby figure of War, while Water derives from a Bow figure of Venus with Doves.

ca. 1770   *9¾in (24.5cm) high*

$5,300-6,600   **WW**

A Derby caddy spoon, painted with flower sprays, with flat shell handle.

ca. 1770-80   *4in (10cm) long*

$350-400   **WW**

A Derby sauce tureen and cover, decorated in the Worcester manner with the "Joshua Reynolds" pattern of exotic birds, square seal mark in imitation of Worcester.

ca. 1770-80   *7½in (19cm) wide*

$550-650   **WW**

A Derby "Bute"-shaped cup and saucer, painted by Zachariah Boreman, with figures in landscapes within "pearl" band borders, puce marks, painted pattern no. 122, gilder's mark 8 for Wm. Longdon.

ca. 1790

$1,050-1,200   **DN**

A Derby coffee can, attributed to George Robertson, painted with a shipwreck, painted blue factory marks, puce numeral 2 for the gilder Joseph Stables and titled "A Shipwreck after a Storm", small rim chip.

ca. 1795

$900-1,050   **DN**

A Derby French Revolutionary Wars Naval action cabaret service, painted by George Robertson, with a tray, a sugar box and cover, a teapot and cover, and two cans and saucers, each piece with a naval scene from the engagement between the French frigate *La Loire* and the brig-sloop H.M.S. *Kangaroo* on October 18, 1798, blue scripts factory marks and titled scenes, the sugar box is damaged.

H.M.S. "Kangaroo" was an 18-gun Diligence Class brig sloop launched in 1795 and sold out of the service in 1802. This set portrays an action she was involved in following the battle of Tory Island on October 12, 1798, where a Royal Naval squadron under Sir John Borlase Warren (1753-1822) defeated a French fleet sent with reinforcements for the French army, which had landed in Mayo, Ireland, in support of the rebellion by the United Irishmen. This French fleet had sailed before the news reached France that the rebellion had been successfully crushed and the French army defeated. As the French fleet scattered after the battle, "Kangaroo," in company with the frigate H.M.S. "Mermaid," chased the French frigate "La Loire" of 44 guns. Having lost the French ship that day, they caught up the following day and after giving battle, "La Loire" was able to give them the slip. On October 18, her luck ran out when she again ran into "Kangaroo," this time in company with the razee frigate H.M.S. "Anson." She was brought to action and forced to strike her colors when she ran out of ammunition and later passed into the Royal Navy as H.M.S. "Loire."

ca. 1800   *tray 15¾in (40cm) wide*

$6,500-8,000   **DN**

A Derby botanical-shaped serving dish, attributed to William "Quaker" Pegg, painted with an iris, with blue script marks, titled verso, pattern number 212.

Initially apprenticed at 10 years old at an earthenware factory in Staffordshire, England, and then at 15 as a china and porcelain painter, William Pegg (1775-1851) joined the Nottingham Road factory at Derby in 1796. He spent the next five years working as one of Derby's top porcelain painters, before leaving due to religious reasons—having become a Quaker, it's thought he decided his craft was too frivolous an exercise and not in keeping with his new-found religious ideals. However, in 1813 he clearly had a change of heart, returned to Derby, worked there for a further seven years, and, during that time (known as his "Second Period"), he produced some of the finest floral decoration ever seen on English porcelain.

ca. 1800   *12in (30.5cm) long*

$1,500-1,800   **DN**

A Derby figure of Bonaparte.

8in (20.5cm) high

$550-650   **CHOR**

A pair of Derby tigers, both with tiny areas of restoration to extremities.

ca. 1820-30   *2½in (6cm) long*

$1,300-1,800   **DN**

A Derby bough pot and liner, painted and titled "A View in Malton."

ca. 1825   *4in (10cm) high*

$650-800   **CHOR**

A pair of Royal Crown Derby Imari pattern vases with covers, pattern number 1127, printed marks on base.

5in (12.7cm) high

$350-400   **MART**

ESSENTIAL REFERENCE—LIVERPOOL PORCELAIN

Mostly of the soft-paste type, porcelain was produced ca. 1754-1804 by a number of factories in the port city of Liverpool. A great variety of flat and hollow wares as well as some figures were made, and while most of the production was underglaze blue-and-white porcelain, some over- and underglaze transfer-printed wares and overglaze polychrome enameled pieces were also made. The Liverpool factories included:

● **Richard Chaffers & Co. (1754-65):** soapstone-type porcelain; mainly Asian designs; resembles Worcester; Philip Christian took over on Chaffers' death and produced similar design until 1778

● **Samuel Gilbody (ca. 1755-60):** enameled porcelain.

● **William Reid (1756-61):** underglaze blue Asian designs.

● **James Pennington and Co. (1769-ca. 1800):** three branches of the family, under James, John, and Seth, worked from different sites in the city; included underglaze and transfer-printed wares.

A rare Liverpool Samuel Gilbody vase, one side painted with a boy holding a parasol above a Chinese dignitary, the reverse with a willow tree.
ca. 1758-60   *5¾in (14.7cm) high*
$2,600-3,300   **WW**

A Liverpool Samuel Gilbody teabowl, painted with a Chinese figure standing beside a table with vases of flowers, beside a gnarled pine tree, the interior with a flower sprig.
ca. 1758-60   *3in (7.5cm) diam*
$450-550   **WW**

A Liverpool Richard Chaffers mug, decorated with a Chinese landscape with two figures, with a hut and a bridge, with a strap handle.
ca. 1760   *6in (15cm) high*
$850-1,000   **WW**

A Liverpool William Reid pickle dish, molded as a pointed leaf with a smaller overlapping leaf and flower sprig.
ca. 1758-60   *4¾in (12.2cm) wide*
$350-400   **WW**

A Liverpool Pennington's jug, painted with a Chinese figure in a garden with ornamental fence and hut, a small filled chip and restored crack.
ca. 1765-70   *5½in (13.7cm) high*
$450-550   **WW**

A Liverpool Philip Christian vase, painted with flowers, with blue wash ground, restoration to the rim.
ca. 1768-75   *7in (17.5cm) high*
$350-400   **WW**

A Liverpool Philip Christian vase, painted with a peacock and other colorful birds perched on leafy foliage, with other flowers on a washed blue or gros bleu ground, the cover lacking.
ca. 1768-72   *9¾in (24.5cm) high*
$550-650   **WW**

A Liverpool Seth Pennington custard cup and cover, decorated with peony and other flowering plants beneath a trellis border.
ca. 1778-90   *2¾in (7cm) high*
$750-850   **WW**

PORCELAIN

ESSENTIAL REFERENCE—LONGTON HALL

William Littler (1724-84) founded the Longton Hall factory in Staffordshire, England, ca. 1749. His first soft-paste porcelain recipe had a thick, semi-opaque white glaze that earned the nickname "snowman class" for early Longton Hall figures. However, by ca. 1752, Littler had improved the recipe to produce porcelain that could be molded thinly, making it ideal for certain forms, such as fruit, vegetables, and, especially, leaves, which dominated the factory's characteristic and brightly painted dishes, pitchers, and tureens.

- The factory's figures show the influence of Meissen and are similar to those produced at Bow and Derby.
- Meissen-style flowers in Longton Hall decoration are often attributed to an artist known as the "trembly rose painter," although many artists painted in this manner.
- The variable quality of Longton Hall porcelain—sometimes the body contains "moons" (tiny air bubbles that appear as pale spots against a strong light)—along with heavy kiln losses led to bankruptcy.
- After the factory's closure in 1760, Littler moved to Scotland, where he later opened a new porcelain works at West Pans, near Musselburgh.
- No mark was used on Longton Hall wares, and pieces marked with two crossed "L"s in blue formerly attributed to the factory are now known to come from Littler's later venture at West Pans.

A rare Longton Hall or Vauxhall model of a tiger, sitting on a scroll-molded base.
ca. 1755-60   *4in (10cm) high*
$4,000-4,600   **CHEF**

A Longton Hall mug, painted with flowers, including rose and tulip, with scattered sprigs and flower stems, the handle with a leaf thumb rest with puce detailing, some peppering.
ca. 1755   *3¾in (9.5cm) high*
$550-650   **WW**

A pair of Longton Hall sauceboats, painted with flowers, including rose and convolvulus, the interiors with further sprays, with puce detailing, some damages.
ca. 1755   *8¼in (21cm) long*
$1,000-1,100   **WW**

A Longton Hall figure of Ceres, emblematic of Summer, with a putto, holding a sheaf of corn and a sickle, some restoration.
ca. 1755   *6½in (16.3cm) high*
$850-1,000   **WW**

A Longton Hall miniature vase, painted with flowering peony, the narrow neck rising to a slightly flared rim.
ca. 1754-56   *3in (7.5cm) high*
$1,600-2,000   **WW**

A Longton Hall vase and cover, painted with butterflies within panels applied with flowers, the cover made up of a variety of different blooms, dark red C marks, a little restoration.
ca. 1758-60   *8in (20cm) high*
$350-400   **WW**

A Longton Hall armorial mug, printed by John Sadler of Liverpool, with the arms of the Stevenson of Balladoole family above a banner inscribed with the motto "Omnia Vincit Assiduitas."

This mug was probably made for Richard Ambrose Stevenson (1742-1773). The family were originally Irish (Fitzstephens) but can be traced back to the Isle of Man from the 14thC.
ca. 1758-60   *5¼in (13cm) high*
$550-650   **WW**

A Lowestoft small blue-and-white bullet-shaped "toy" teapot and cover, painted in blue with fruiting vine.

ca. 1765   *3½in (9cm) high*

$1,050-1,200   **DN**

A Lowestoft coffeepot and cover, painted with chinoiserie pagoda landscapes, a restored chip on the cover.

ca. 1765   *7in (17.8cm) high*

$850-1,000   **WW**

A Lowestoft miniature or toy teabowl and saucer, painted with boats in an Asian landscape, painter's numeral on the foot rim of the saucer.

ca. 1765-70   *3¼in (8cm) wide*

$400-450   **WW**

A Lowestoft cream pitcher, painted with a pagoda and tree behind a trellis fence, the reverse with a figure in a boat.

ca. 1765-70   *3in (7.3cm) high*

$400-550   **WW**

A Lowestoft teapot and cover, painted with a Chinese boy and his mother playing in a garden, the cover with an open flower knop, cracked.

ca. 1768-70   *7in (18.2cm) wide*

$900-1,050   **WW**

A Lowestoft punch bowl, printed on the exterior with figures in a Chinese island landscape, with further landscape vignettes, the interior with a "Pinecone" pattern and a painted trellis and husk border.

ca. 1775   *9¼in (23.5cm) diam*

$550-600   **WW**

A Lowestoft coffeepot and cover, printed with two figures before a pagoda in an island landscape, the reverse with a fisherman and cormorant in a boat.

ca. 1780-90   *9in (23cm) high*

$550-650   **WW**

PORCELAIN

ESSENTIAL REFERENCE—MEISSEN PORCELAIN

True hard-paste porcelain was first developed in Europe in 1708 by Johann Friedrich Böttger and Walther von Tschirnhausen. Böttger, an alchemist famed for his claims that he could create gold, had been ordered by Augustus the Strong, Elector Prince of Saxony and King of Poland, to assist the scientist von Tschirnhausen with his porcelain experiments. By 1710, Augustus the Strong was able to establish the Meissen factory near Dresden—it was Europe's first hard-paste porcelain factory.

● The factory prospered under J. G. Höroldt, a chemist who was also appointed chief painter in 1720. Johann Joachim Kändler joined as chief modeler in 1733 and was responsible for producing many of Meissen's most striking figures.

● Early decoration was highly influenced by Asian designs, and copies and fusions of Japanese Kakiemon and Chinese famille verte wares were produced. From these emerged a new style of exotic floral decoration known as "Indianische Blumen" (Indian flowers), so called because much Asian porcelain was imported by the East India Companies.

● From the 1730s, European themes, such as harbor scenes, cityscapes, and hunting and battle scenes, also became popular, and wares began to be made in the newly fashionable Rococo style, embellished with scrolled bases and painted in pastel colors. With this a more naturalistic floral decoration developed, known as "Deutsche Blumen" (German Flowers), which was then replaced, in turn, by a looser representations of scattered flowers known as "Manierblumen" (Mannered Flowers).

● In the 19thC, Meissen, which still produces today, made pieces in numerous diverse styles, including Neoclassical, and the Gothic, Classical, and Rococo revivals.

● Meissen's forms and decoration have been much copied by other manufacturers over the years, as have on occasions their distinctive "crossed swords" marks of identification.

A Meissen tea canister and cover, painted with panels of birds in flight and Asian plants, with a later silver-colored metal cover.
ca. 1725-28   *4¼in (11cm) high*
$850-1,000   **WW**

A Meissen chinoiserie ecuelle and stand, painted in the manner of J. G. Höroldt, with Chinese figures, cover lacking, minute rim chip on bowl.
ca. 1725   *the ecuelle 4½in (11.5cm) wide*
$750-850   **DN**

A Meissen saucer, from the "Red Dragon" service, decorated with two scaly beasts, the center with two long-tailed phoenixes, blue crossed swords mark, a chip on the foot rim.

Two services of this pattern were made for the French merchant Lemaire ca. 1730 but were confiscated and transferred to the Japanese Palace in 1733. Further wares were then produced for the exclusive use of the Saxon Court.
ca. 1740   *5¼in (13.3cm) diam*
$650-800   **WW**

CLOSER LOOK—MEISSEN CHINOISERIE

The gilt border around the internal rim of the bowl is known as "Laub-und-Bandelwerk." A particularly popular form of interwoven decoration during the 18thC, especially on rims and around cartouches, it translates from the German as "leaf and strapwork."

One of the reasons the painting is possibly by Philip Ernst Schindler, who joined Meissen in 1725, is because he is strongly associated with elaborately detailed chinoiserie scenes, distinctive headwear, and carefully delineated folds in fabric.

Inspired by those found on imported Asian porcelain, the flowers painted at Meissen during the 1720s and 30s were collectively known as "Indianische Blumen" ("Indian flowers").

From the mid-1720s onward, the earlier Meissen palette dominated by vivid colors, notably strong reds and yellows, was gradually supplanted by a more pastel palette dominated by greens, mauve, lilac, and pale yellow.

A Meissen chinoiserie porcelain bowl, with a sitting dignitary, a woman and child, an attendant reading from a tablet, and a kettle on hot coals on one side, the other side with a lady and gentleman sitting at a table taking tea with an attendant, the inner rim with gilt Laub-und Bandelwerk, small chip on rim and fine hair crack.
ca. 1725   *6¾in (17.3cm) diam*
$1,800-2,400   **DN**

A Meissen cup and saucer, painted with figures standing and on horseback beside stately buildings in European landscapes, blue crossed swords marks.
ca. 1740   5¼in (13.3cm) diam
$1,100-1,250   **WW**

A Meissen Hausmaler cup and saucer, applied with flowering prunus and possibly painted in the workshop of F. F. Meyer, Pressnitz, the saucer with travelers, a riverbank with buildings, and a mountain in the distance, the cup with figures in a landscape, blue crossed swords marks.
ca. 1740   *5¼in (13.5cm) diam*
$1,100-1,250   **WW**

An 18thC Meissen teapot and cover, decorated with the "Bird and Tree" pattern, marks in blue.

ca. 1735   *7in (17.5cm) wide*

$750-850   **CHEF**

A Meissen cup and saucer, painted with figures standing and on horseback beside stately buildings in European landscapes, with flowers and insects, blue crossed swords marks, some faults.

ca. 1740   *5¼in (13.3cm) wide*

$800-900   **WW**

A Meissen cup and a saucer decorated with harbor scenes within gilt cartouches.

ca. 1740

$260-330   **CHOR**

A Meissen ornithological soup plate, painted with a bird perched on a branch, the osier-molded rim painted with moths and other flying insects, blue crossed swords mark.

ca. 1745   *8¾in (22.5cm) diam*

$550-600   **WW**

A Meissen teapot, with gilt bird-head spout and wishbone handle, painted with figures beside Classical architecture, scattered ombrierte flowers, later cover.

ca. 1745

$1,050-1,200   **CHOR**

A Meissen porcelain figure of a street vendor, crossed swords mark in underglaze blue, handle of basket restored.

ca. 1750   *4¼in (11cm) high*

$550-650   **TEN**

A Meissen porcelain figure of a huntsman, a game bag on his back, his dog at his feet, crossed swords mark in underglaze blue, bayonet and tips of finger missing, losses to leaves.

ca. 1750   *7in (17.5cm) high*

$1,000-1,100   **TEN**

A mid-18thC Meissen figure of a ballad singer, faint blue crossed swords mark, with restoration.

5¼in (13cm) high

$260-400   **WW**

A mid-18thC Meissen tea canister, painted with moths and flying insects, blue crossed swords mark, cover lacking.

4in (10.1cm) high

$850-1,000   **WW**

Judith Picks

Why on earth would someone in their right mind pay $5,300-6,600 or more for a porcelain figure of a squirrel with its ears and part of a haunch missing, a reattached smashed base, and more damage besides? Well, first, it was produced by Meissen in the mid-18thC, so that's "blue-chip" provenance in terms of maker and when they made it. Even more significantly, it was probably modeled by Johann Joachim Kändler (1706-1775) who, during the 1730s and 40s, modeled for Meissen some of the best porcelain figures ever made. Displaying a wonderful sense of liveliness and movement, they are simply unmatched by imitators. It is also incredibly rare, and it's safe to say that without the damage, someone (in their right mind) would have paid $25,000 or more.

A mid-18thC Meissen model of a squirrel, possibly modeled by J. J. Kaendler, unmarked, extensive damage and loss, ears lacking, base smashed and glued, part of haunch missing.

8¾in (22cm) high

$5,300-6,600   **DN**

A Meissen sugar bowl and cover, with a flower finial, painted with birds and insects, faint blue mark on unglazed base.

ca. 1750-60   4¼in (10.5cm) high

$800-900   **CHOR**

A Meissen figure group of three putti beside a table, one blindfolded and drawing lots from a bowl, one sitting at the table, a third recumbent on the floor, blue crossed swords and dot mark, minor damages.

ca. 1765-70   7in (18cm) high

$1,300-1,600   **WW**

A Meissen figure of a Bolognese terrier, scratching itself under the chin with its rear paw, blue crossed swords and dot mark.

ca. 1770   7½in (19cm) high

$650-800   **WW**

A mid-18thC Meissen liquor barrel, decorated with floral vines and on a bracket support, unmarked, some chips, figural stopper and spiggot are lacking.

5¼in (13cm) long

$550-650   **DN**

Two mid-18thC Meissen figures of "Cupid in Disguise," one as a pastry seller, the other as a lady's maid, blue crossed swords marks.

4in (10.3cm) high

$400-550   **WW**

A mid-18thC Meissen figure of a young musician, modeled as a boy standing barefoot on top of a half barrel and playing the flageolet, a ewer of grapevine behind him, blue crossed swords mark on the reverse, the handle of the ewer lacking.

6in (15cm) high

$350-450   **WW**

A Meissen white-glazed figure of Bacchus, perhaps personifying Fall (Autumn), modeled by Kändler, the young man wearing a belt of grapevine, leaning against a tree trunk and raising a bunch of grapes to his mouth, a satyr or faun sitting on a barrel behind him, traces of a blue mark on the base, some faults.

ca. 1760   10¾in (27cm) high

$3,300-4,000   **WW**

An 18thC Meissen chinoiserie porcelain teapot and cover, painted in the manner of J. G. Höroldt, one side with Chinese figures taking tea and the other side fanning a tea kettle within "Laub-und-Bandelwerk" borders with Böttger luster, underglaze crossed swords mark with gilders, number "40" on the base, slight damage.

Although the chinoiserie scene of a couple taking tea is essentially painted, in terms of the composition and the style of the figures, in the manner of J. G. Höroldt, Johann Gregorius Höroldt (1696-1775) was perhaps best-known for the exquisite "Kauffahrtei" (sea-trade) scenes he painted for Meissen. A highly innovative color chemist and painter, Höroldt joined Meissen in 1720 and was esteemed for the wonderful palettes he developed—earlier, vivid reds, yellows, and black, later, more pastel colors—which were applied to the Meissen figures modeled by Johann Joachim Kändler during the 1730s and 40s, and which are widely considered among the best porcelain figures and groups ever made.

4¾in (12cm) high

$4,600-5,900   **FLD**

A late-18thC Meissen model of a leopard, painted blue crossed swords mark, a chip on the base and ear.

2½in (6.5cm) high

$1,050-1,200   DN

A late-18th/early-19thC Meissen garden figure group, modeled by Acier, with six figures around a rocaille base, blue crossed swords mark, some damages.

10¾in (27.5cm) high

$1,050-1,200   WW

ESSENTIAL REFERENCE—SCHNEEBALLEN

Translated from German as "snowball," Schneeballen is a distinctive type of porcelain decoration pioneered at Meissen in 1739 by the great modeler and decorator Johann Joachim Kändler (1706-1775). It comprises a series of bulbous, spherical, snowball-shaped forms, and it is typically applied to the bodies and covers of vases of similarly bulbous, ovoid form, the surfaces of which are then covered with hundreds of small, intricately modeled flowers— the latter traditionally, albeit not exclusively, white mayflowers. Following their introduction, Schneeballen wares continued to be made throughout the 18thC and 19thC.

An early-19thC Meissen porcelain "schneeballen" urn and cover, the domed lid with a parrot finial, with flower heads and songbirds, with blue underglaze starred crossed swords mark and incised no.1509.

32¼in (82cm) high

$6,500-8,000   L&I

A pair of 19thC Meissen figures of sweethearts, the male fastening a love letter around the neck of a carrier pigeon, his sweetheart holding the received missive in her hand and with the pigeon in a cage on her shoulder, blue crossed swords marks, with small damages.

7½in (19cm) high

$550-650   WW

A pair of Meissen salts, modeled as a lady and gentleman with a flower-encrusted basket before them, blue crossed swords mark and incised 2272 and 2875 on base.

ca. 1860   *7½in (19cm) long*

$550-650   CHOR

A large pair of 19thC Meissen figures of parrots, with colorful plumage, each perched atop a tall stump with head turned and beak slightly agape, blue crossed swords marks, incised A43.

16½in (42cm) high

$10,500-12,000   WW

A 19thC Meissen figure of an officer on horseback, the rider wearing a coat with elaborate gilt edging, blue crossed swords mark, some losses.

10in (25.5cm) high

$1,600-2,100   WW

A 19thC Meissen green mosaic pattern teacup and saucer, painted with soldiers in landscapes, blue crossed swords and impressed numbers.

$260-400   CHOR

A late-19thC Meissen gilt-metal mounted kettle and cover, typically Dresden-decorated with Watteauesque panels, blue crossed swords and cancellation mark, rim chips, old screw repair on cover finial.

9¼in (23.5cm) wide

$550-650 **DN**

A late-19thC Meissen porcelain flower encrusted bud vase, painted with insects and floral sprays, underglaze blue cross sword marks.

5in (12.7cm) high

$260-330 **MART**

A 19thC Meissen figure group of "The Good Mother," modeled by J. C. Schönheit.

8¾in (22cm) high

$750-850 **CHEF**

A 19thC Meissen figure allegorical of "Scent," from the "Five Senses," after the model by J. C. Schönheit, with blue crossed swords mark, incised "E5."

5½in (14cm) high

$450-600 **CHEF**

A Meissen porcelain figure group of lovers, the male wearing Roman armor, the female holding a billet-doux, and a dove, dog, and sheep at their feet, crossed swords mark in underglaze blue.

ca. 1880 *7in (18cm) high*

$450-600 **TEN**

A Meissen porcelain figure of Europa and the Bull, two attendants garlanding it with flowers, crossed swords mark in underglaze blue, bull lacking one horn.

ca. 1880 *8¾in (22cm) high*

$650-800 **TEN**

A 19thC Meissen "Cris de Paris" figure of a grape seller, after the model by Peter Reinicke, blue crossed swords mark, some restoration.

5¾in (14.3cm) high

$200-260 **WW**

A pair of late-19th/early-20thC Meissen porcelain figures of a Turk and companion, after the models by J. J. Kaendler, the man incised 1286, press number 147, the woman incised 1287, blue crossed swords marks.

Male 9in (22.5cm) high

$2,000-2,600 **L&T**

ESSENTIAL REFERENCE—NANTGARW PORCELAIN

In 1813, William Weston Young and William Billingsley, the latter previously a decorator at Derby, established a porcelain factory at Nantgarw, Wales. Soon after, in 1814, the company moved to Swansea and merged with Lewis Weston Dillwyn's Cambrian Pottery, but in 1817 Dillwyn left the business and Billingsley and Young returned to Nantgarw and reopened the factory there. In 1819, it was purchased by Coalport and remained open until 1823.

- Nantgarw porcelain was so fine that it was exceptionally difficult to fire and a large proportion was lost in the kiln. It is usually translucent and almost pure white when held to the light; the glaze tends to be thick and smooth.
- The factory primarily made tea wares and flatware, and large hollow wares are rare.
- Billingsley was particularly known for his flower painting.
- The factory's wares tend to be impressed "NANT-GARW C.W.", with the "C.W." standing for China Works.

A Nantgarw dish, London-decorated in the workshop of Robbins and Randall, the well with two exotic birds on and beneath a leafy branch between flowering plants, the shaped rim with a floral border, gilt dentil rim, impressed "NANT-GARW C.W." mark.

ca. 1818-20   *11¾in (29.8cm) wide*
$2,100-2,600   **WW**

A Nantgarw plate, of Brace Service type, painted in the London Bradley workshop with flowers, including rose, tulip, and auricula, the rim with panels of a finch, fruits, and further flowers, impressed "NANT-GARW C.W." mark.

ca. 1818-20   *8½in (21.5cm) diam*
$1,000-1,100   **WW**

A Nantgarw dessert dish, London-decorated with a flower spray and posies linked by gilt foliage, gilt dentil rim, cracked.

ca. 1818-20   *11¾in (29.5cm) wide*
$350-450   **WW**

A Nantgarw plate, painted with roses to the well, a moth in flight beside, the rim with roses on a gilt foliate ground, impressed mark.

ca. 1818   *9½in (24.2cm) diam*
$1,300-1,800   **WW**

A Swansea dessert dish, painted with flowers, including convolvulus, rose, and auricula, the gilt twig handles issuing from stylized leaves, iron-red factory mark.

ca. 1815-18   *11½in (28.8cm) wide*
$550-650   **WW**

A near pair of Nantgarw plates, painted with British flowers, with gilt dentil rims, impressed "NANT-GARW C.W."

ca. 1818-20   *9½in (24cm) diam*
$650-800   **WW**

A Swansea plate, painted with primrose, heather, forget-me-not, and strawberry, the well with gilt and green enamel border of leaf tendrils, gilt "Swansea" mark.

ca. 1815-18   *8½in (21.5cm) diam*
$200-330   **WW**

A Swansea porcelain part tea service, painted with panels of flowers, comprising a teapot, cover, and stand; a sugar box and cover; a milk pitcher; a slop bowl; 11 sandwich plates; 2 muffin dishes and a cover; 7 teacups and 11 saucers; and 5 coffee cups and 10 saucers; iron-red printed "SWANSEA" marks, wear throughout.

ca. 1814-26
$13,000-16,000   **DN**

PORCELAIN

A Plymouth porcelain chinoiserie teapot and cover, painted with a Chinese-style landscape with a diaper band border.

ca. 1768-70   *4¼in (11cm) high*
$2,600-3,300   **DN**

A Plymouth or Bristol William Cookworthy sauceboat, of Rococo-molded form, painted with delicate garlands of flowers within leaf-molded panels, a further flower spray beneath the spout, the shaped rim with a puce line, raised on a low scrolled foot.

ca. 1768-70   *5½in (14cm) long*
$1,300-2,000   **WW**

A Plymouth sweetmeat or pickle stand, formed of three large shells raised on a tall rocky base applied with shells and seaweed, flanking a pierced whelk shell in the center.

ca. 1768   *5½in (14cm) high*
$1,100-1,250   **WW**

A Plymouth shell salt, left in the white, on a base of further smaller shells and coral, two small restored sections.

ca. 1768-70   *5¼in (13.2cm) wide*
$1,100-1,250   **WW**

A Plymouth or Bristol hard-paste porcelain sauceboat, molded en rocaille and painted with C-scroll panels of figures and flower sprays, small firing cracks.

ca. 1768   *5½in (14cm) long*
$3,300-4,000   **DN**

A Plymouth white-glazed figure of a putto, emblematic of Fall (Autumn), holding a bunch of grapes, some bocage lacking.

ca. 1770   *5¾in (14.5cm) high*
$1,050-1,200   **WW**

A Plymouth figure group, modeled with two putti and a goat before flowering bocage, restoration to bocage, candle sconce lacking.

The original source for the model is a ca. 1640 bronze group by Jacques Sarazzin in the Louvre museum in Paris. The same group was produced at both Longton Hall and Vauxhall, and it is possible that the Plymouth example copied these instead of the original bronze.

ca. 1770   *7½in (19cm) high*
$1,050-1,200   **WW**

A set of Plymouth figures of the four Seasons, each as a putto, Spring with a bird's nest, Summer with a sheaf of corn, Fall (Autumn) holding a glass and grapes, Winter wrapping a fur-lined robe, some restoration to Fall.

ca. 1770   *4¾in (12cm) high*
$3,300-4,000   **WW**

A Plymouth or Bristol porter mug, painted with flower sprays in the Meissen style, "4" mark, a rim chip crack leading from it.

ca. 1770-75   *5½in (14cm) high*
$1,250-1,500   **DN**

ESSENTIAL REFERENCE—SAMSON, EDMÉ ET CIE

Frenchman Edmé Samson (1810-1891) began his career in the 1830s making replacements for broken pieces of porcelain dinner services. In 1845, he established the firm Samson, Edmé et Cie (Samson's son being Emile) in Paris, with the initial intention of supplying reproductions of ceramics displayed in museums and private collections. Soon the company was producing a huge range of pieces—many of which are collectible today—that either drew inspiration from other porcelain factories or directly copied them; notable examples include 18thC designs originally by Meissen, Sèvres, Chelsea, Derby, and Worcester. Samson also embraced a wide and diverse range of styles, including Italian maiolica, Persian and Hispano-Moresque, Delft, Chinese famille rose and famille verte, Japanese Imari, Rococo, and Neoclassical. It's open to doubt as to whether Samson always produced honest copies of all these wares, with no intention to deceive, because there is no doubt that in many cases marks of identification were subsequently altered in an attempt to pass the pieces off as another factory's originals. This, of course, may well have been done post factory, and, indeed, the fact that Samson wares were produced in hard-paste porcelain (while many originals were soft paste); their glazes were often glossier and glassier; the modeling stiffer or to the wrong scale; and the decoration often too heavy or the colors inaccurate has led many specialists to conclude that Samson and his firm, which eventually closed in 1969, were, in fact, enthusiastic copyists instead of forgers.

A pair of 19thC Samson famille rose wall sconces, painted with women and children playing in a garden, surrounded by figures, each mounted with a pair of silvered metal candle holders and by a figure of Budai He Shang flanked by lion dogs.

16¾in (42.5cm) high

$4,000-4,600

WW

A late-19thC Samson porcelain fishbowl, unglazed lion-head handles, decorated with exotic birds and flowers.

18in (45.5cm) diam

$4,000-5,300

L&T

A late-19thC Samson sleeve vase, painted in the Kakiemon palette with a long-tailed bird perched in a flowering tree, red horn mark in imitation of Chantilly.

17¼in (43.8cm) high

$400-450

WW

A 19thC Samson plate, after the Baltic service, the oak leaf rim with swags inscribed "Nelson San Josef 22nd April," the center with coat of arms for Nelson, coat of arms worn.

9¼in (23.5cm) diam

$160-240

CM

A late-19thC Samson Worcester-style pitcher with bearded face-mask spout, faint crossed swords mark and impressed anchor mark to underside, small chip on foot rim, crossed sword mark scratched off, some rubbing.

8¼in (20.4cm) high

$90-100

MART

A set of eight 19thC Samson of Paris porcelain cabinet cups and saucers, in a Chinese export famille rose armorial wares style.

These pieces have the pseudo-Chinese seal mark on undersides. This was the Samson factory mark for use on imitations of Chinese export porcelain.

$200-260

MART

A Samson famille verte charger, decorated in Kangxi style with fanciful birds in a garden, the border with precious objects, flowers, and mountainous landscapes, with a faux Kangxi reign mark.

15¾in (40cm) diam

$650-800

CHEF

PORCELAIN

ESSENTIAL REFERENCE—VINCENNES & SÈVRES

The French Vincennes factory was established ca. 1740, and in 1745 was granted a 20-year monopoly for the production of decorative soft-paste porcelain. The factory's "great period" began in 1751 with the appointment of Jean-Jacques Bachelier as its art director, and in 1753, after King Louis XV became its principal shareholder, it became known as the Manufacture Royale de Porcelaine and adopted the crossed Ls of the Royal cipher as its mark.

● In 1756, the Vincennes factory moved to, and became known as Sèvres, while maintaining the crossed Ls as its mark, and in 1759 Louis XV bought the factory outright. Having firmly established itself during the second half of the 18thC as one of Europe's greatest and most influential porcelain manufacturers, Sèvres lost its royal patronage during the turmoil of the French Revolution (1789-99), and neared bankruptcy at the turn of the 19thC, before recovering to produce an extensive and equally influential output throughout the 19thC. It continues to manufacture fine-quality porcelain to this day.

A Vincennes or early Sèvres wine glass cooler ("seau à verre échancré"), of six-lobed form with small scroll handles, painted in green camaïeu with flower sprays, traces of blue interlaced Ls mark, a chip on the foot rim.
ca. 1750-60   *4¼in (10.5cm) high*
$4,600-5,300   **WW**

A Vincennes sucrier and cover, painted by Jean-Louis Morin, with a putto amid flowers, with flower sprays, the cover with musical instruments and military motifs around an open flower finial, blue interlaced Ls mark and date code B, painter's mark M, date code.
ca. 1754-55   *3¼in (8.3cm) high*
$4,600-5,300   **WW**

A Vincennes tray ("plat ovale"), painted by Mutel, with figures walking in a landscape, a bridge over a river to a building beyond, blue interlaced Ls mark enclosing date letter B above a painter's mark, a date code, a restored crack.
ca. 1754-55   *9¾in (24.8cm) wide*
$1,700-2,100   **WW**

A Vincennes miniature teapot and cover ("théière calabré"), painted probably by Andre-Vincent Vielliard, with scenes of making wine, blue interlaced Ls mark enclosing date letter B, date code, broken and reattached.
ca. 1754-55   *4¼in (10.7cm) wide*
$1,050-1,200   **WW**

A Vincennes dish ("plat d'entremets"), from the first Louis XV service, painted with flowers, the molded rim with flowers reserved within gilt foliate and scroll borders.

The bleu celeste (heavenly blue) ground was created by the chemist Jean Hellot specifically for this service, and it was the first time such a color had been used on porcelain in this way. This service, the first full service delivered by Vincennes, was first used on February 4, 1754, and remained in use until the end of the Ancien regime. A first delivery of 120 components was delivered to Louis XV at the end of 1753, with a further 133 pieces being delivered a year later. Factory records detail 28 "plat d'entrées et d'entremets" delivered among the third part of the service, on December 31, 1755, each at a cost of 240 livres, and it is probable that this is one of those. Only three survivals of this shape are recorded, one in the Musée des Arts Decoratifs in Paris. Other items from the service remain in the collection at the Palace of Versailles, with a large part of the service in the collection of the Duke of Buccleuch at Boughton House.
ca. 1754-55   *12½in (31.5cm) diam*
$17,000-21.000   **WW**

A Vincennes or Sèvres pitcher ("pot à lait à trois pieds"), painted with flower sprays, blue interlaced Ls marks, and painter's mark for Tardy, a tiny chip on the rim.
ca. 1755-60   *3½in (9cm) high*
$1,050-1,200   **WW**

A Sèvres cup and saucer ("gobelet bouillard et soucoupe"), painted with flower sprays, blue interlaced Ls mark enclosing date code F above an unidentified painter's mark of the numeral 3 flanked by dots, a hairline crack on the cup.
1758   *5¼in (13.6cm) wide*
$8,000-9.000   **WW**

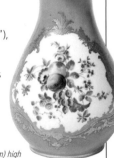

An early Sèvres water pitcher ("broc Roussel"), painted with flowers and fruit within a gilt border of foliate scrolls and trellis panels, blue interlaced Ls mark enclosing date letter F, a section of the spout broken and repaired.
ca. 1758-59   *7½in (19cm) high*
$4,600-5,300   **WW**

A Sèvres cup ("gobelet bouillard"), painted by Pierre-Antoine Méreaud, with flowers within a quatrefoil panel, traces of blue interlaced Ls mark and painter's mark.

ca. 1758   *2½in (6cm) high*

$1,700-2,100   **WW**

A Sèvres ecuelle with cover and stand, painted by Jean-Baptiste Tandart, with roses, berried laurel leaves and other flowers, reserved on a fond Taillandier ground, of bleu nouveau with an oeil de perdrix design, interlaced blue Ls marks enclosing date letter M, damages and repairs.

1765   *9in (22.6cm) wide*

$5,300-6,600   **WW**

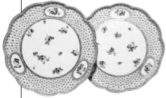

A pair of Sèvres low tazzae or stands ("soucoupes à pied"), painted by Jean-Jacques Pierre le jeune with "roses et mosaïque," with scattered pink roses on the wells, interlaced Ls marks and painter's mark.

The two stands are probably from a service produced for Simon, 1st Earl Harcourt, British Ambassador-Extraordinary Plenipotentiary to France. However, Pierre le jeune is also recorded on the piecework list for an apparently identical service for Etienne-François, duc de Choiseul-Stainville, Minister of Foreign Affairs, which was produced in the same year.

1769   *8¾in (22.5cm) diam*

$1,500-1,800   **WW**

A Sèvres vase and cover ("pot pourri Pompadour"), painted with flowers, including rose, poppy, and convolvulus, the shoulder pierced with six oval holes within foliate scrolls with gilt detailing, blue interlaced Ls mark and painter's mark for either Louis-Jean Thevenet or Charles-Louis Méreaud, restoration to the cover's knop.

ca. 1760   *7¼in (18.5cm) high*

$8,000-9.000   **WW**

A Sèvres ice cup ("tasse à glace") from an "à rubans Bleu Celeste" service, painted with flower garlands entwined with a turquoise ribbon between narrow gilt bands, unmarked

This service was ordered by Madame du Barry via her banquier, Jean-Baptiste Buffault in December 1769 and included 44 "tasses à glaces" at a cost of 24 livres each. Much of the service was passed back to Buffault in 1771 and sold by him to an English buyer. This type of decoration became popular in England, and three other services of this type were sold to England between 1770 and 1775, including one delivered to John Frederick Sackville, 3rd Duke of Dorset.

ca. 1769-70   *2½in (6.5cm) high*

$1,600-2,100   **WW**

A Sèvres stand ("plateau Bouret"), from the "attribus et groseilles" service for Louis XV, painted with three vignettes of trophies—including a rake, sickle, and cornucopia; a spade and basket of grapes; and a telescope, chart, and drawing callipers— between gilt sprays of fruiting currant.

In 1771, 1772, and 1773, Louis XV purchased a number of plateaux Bouret, compoters, and saladiers described as "attribus et groseilles," a style of decoration that was out of date at this time. The original service appears to have been ordered in 1763, but this stand was probably one of six ordered on June 13, 1772.

ca. 1770-74   *8¼in (21cm) diam*

$11,000-13,000   **WW**

A Sèvres plate ("assiette"), possibly from the Bedford Service, painted by François Binet, with a flower spray, the rim with floral panels, with a gilt vermiculé design, blue interlaced Ls mark with date letter i, some gilt wear, a reattached rim chip.

John Russell, 4th Duke of Bedford, was the British Ambassador to France between September 1762 and June 1763. An extensive dinner service was gifted to his wife, Duchess Gertrude, in recognition of the Duke's work in negotiating the end of the French and Indian War in 1763. The majority of the service is in the collection at Woburn Abbey.

1761   *9½in (24.2cm) wide*

$4,600-5,300   **WW**

A Sèvres two-handle cup with cover and stand ("gobelet à lait et soucoupe"), painted probably by Jean-Charles Sioux l'Aîné, with flower garlands above feathered, gilt floral and blue oeil de perdrix rims, crowned blue interlaced Ls mark.

ca. 1769   *7¼in (18.5cm) wide*

$3,300-4,000   **WW**

A Sèvres egg cup ("coquetier"), painted by Jean-Charles Sioux l'Aîné, with pink roses, laurel swags beneath feathered borders, and a gilt dentil rim, crowned interlaced blue Ls mark.

ca. 1770-80   *1¾in (4.5cm) high*

$750-850   **WW**

A Sèvres plate ("assiette"), for Madame du Barry, decorated with a monogram of the gilt letter D and the letter B in flowers, the rim with circlets of ivy tied with ribbon between swags of fruiting grapevine, flanking three panels with putti on clouds, blue interlaced Ls mark.

Cf. David Peters, "Sèvres Plates and Services of the 18th Century," Vol. II, pp. 495-98, for a discussion of a service similar to that produced for Maria Caroline, Queen of Naples and Sicily, which was started for Madame du Barry but never finished.

ca. 1770   9½in (24.2cm) diam
$20,000-26,000   WW

A Sèvres egg cup ("coquetier"), painted with birds perched on leafy branches, within gilt oak leaf borders, indistinct blue mark, some gilt wear.

The use of gilt oak leaves on a bleu celeste ground can be seen in the service made for Gustav III of Swede, known as the Prince of Rohan service.

ca. 1771   1½in (4cm) high
$3,300-4,000   WW

A Sèvres soup plate ("assiette à potage"), painted by Jacques-François-Louis de Laroche, gray interlaced Ls mark.

ca. 1773   9¾in (24.3cm) diam
$2,600-3,300   WW

A rare Sèvres portrait can ("gobelet litron"), painted probably by Nicolas-Pierre Pithou Jeune, with portraits of Louis XVI and Marie Antoinette, en grisaille against a brick red ground, crowned interlaced Ls mark, some retouching on the rim.

ca. 1775   3in (7.5cm) high
$5,300-6,600   WW

A Sèvres hard-paste porcelain ice pail ("seau a glace"), with liner and cover, decorated in a "roses et mosaïque" pattern with scattered pink roses and honeycomb panels of gilt dots in a stylized oeil de perdrix design, crowned puce interlaced Ls mark.

ca. 1770-86   7¾in (19.5cm) high
$1,700-2,100   WW

A Sèvres plate from the Ferdinand Service, painted by Edmé-François Bouillat, with pink roses within a border of pearls, the rim with panels of flowers within gilt borders, blue interlaced Ls mark with date letters HH on one side and painter's mark Y on the other, gilder's mark for Chauvaux.

This service was gifted to Karl Anton Joseph Johann Stanislaus, Archduke of Austria and Viceroy of Lombardy, older brother of Marie-Antoinette, by Louis XVI. He visited Paris between May and August 1786 with his consort Maria Beatrice, Duchess of Massa and Princess of Carrara, and they traveled under the assumed names of Comte and Comtesse de Nellembourg.

1785   9½in (24.2cm) diam
$12,000-15,000   WW

A Sèvres coffee can ("gobelet litron"), decorated by Louis Antoine Le Grand or Etienne-Henri Le Guay with gilded birds in flight and perched on scrollwork beside trees and fountains, gilt interlaced Ls mark enclosing date letters HH for 1785, above gilder's mark LG.

1785   2¾in (6.8cm) high
$4,600-5,300   WW

A Sèvres plate ("assiette unie"), painted by Madame Noualhier, with the initials GF, with flowers, the rim with pink rose and blue forget-me-not, blue interlaced Ls mark enclosing date letters MM.

The service was ordered by Monsieur Le Chevalier Forget on September 21, 1789. Cf. David Peters, "Sèvres Plates and Services of the 18th Century," p. 1,696, for an order of "54 assiettes unies, chiffres et fleurs."

1789   9½in (24cm) diam
$3,300-4,000   WW

A Sèvres Republican teapot and cover, painted by Jean-Jacques Dieu, with chinoiserie figure scenes in the manner of Pillement, the shoulder with scrolls linking military motifs, blue script RF monogram and Sèvres mark, blue painter's mark, repairs on the handle and cover.

ca. 1794-1800   8in (20.5cm) wide
$4,600-5,300   WW

A Sèvres cup and saucer ("gobelet bouillard et soucoupe"), painted with figures fishing and walking before buildings and trees in rural landscapes, blue interlaced Ls marks, date code.

1770   *5¼in (13.5cm) wide*
$2,600-3,300   **WW**

A Sèvres coffee can and saucer ("gobelet litron et soucoupe"), painted by Charles-Nicolas Dodin, the can with a girl and spaniel, the saucer with a basket of flowers, blue interlaced Ls marks enclosing date letter Y above painter's mark K and gilder's mark for Louis Antoine Le Grand, the can cracked.

1776
$5,300-6,600   **WW**

A Sèvres coffee can and saucer ("gobelet litron et soucoupe"), decorated by Etienne Charles Le Guay, the cup with a panel depicting the death of Cleopatra, the saucer with vignette of instruments, trophies, and flowers, puce interlaced Ls marks and blue LG painter's marks, a section of the saucer broken and reattached.

A near identical painting of Cleopatra is on an egg cup in the Louis XVI service at Buckingham Palace, England, painted in 1785. Le Guay is recorded as an artist on the Louis XVI service.

ca. 1780-85   *5¾in (14.3cm) wide*
$2,600-3,300   **WW**

A Sèvres coffee can and saucer ("gobelet litron et soucoupe"), the can painted by Jean-Louis Morin, with a harbor scene of three figures rolling barrels, the saucer by another hand with a figure, blue interlaced Ls mark, date letters dd, gilder's mark for Barré, the saucer cracked.

1781   *6in (15cm) diam*
$1,500-1,800   **WW**

A Sèvres coffee can and saucer, decorated with a formal gilt border of palmettes and tassels, printed marks, inscribed "9 D 14" on the footrims.

1814
$2,000-2,600   **WW**

A Sèvres coffee can and saucer, painted with overlapping garlands of flowers entwined around a gilt line and enclosing a green band with a border of formal palmette motifs in gilt, printed marks, inscribed "5 Mai 14" inside the foot rims.

1814
$2,600-3,300   **WW**

A Sèvres coffee can and saucer, painted in brown camaïeu with a goat and a bacchanalian figure with cymbals, with printed marks.

ca. 1814-18   *5¼in (13.3cm) wide*
$1,600-2,100   **WW**

A Sèvres coffee can and saucer, painted with bluebells and daisies with leaf husks reserved on a puce band, printed marks.

ca. 1814-18
$1,700-2,100   **WW**

A Sèvres coffee can and saucer, with flower heads and a leaf band, printed marks.

ca. 1814-18   *5¼in (13.4cm) wide*
$2,600-3,300   **WW**

A Sèvres coffee can and saucer, painted with a garden pattern of flowering plants, including tulip, rose, and poppy, printed marks.

ca. 1816
$3,300-4,000   **WW**

A Sèvres coffee can and saucer, painted with a border of bunches of grapes suspended between swags of flowers, with formal gilt borders, printed marks, inscribed "15 Jt 17" on the foot rims.

1817
$1,600 2,100   **WW**

A Sèvres coffee can and saucer, decorated with a formal gilt checkered design suspending small tassels, on a tortoiseshell ground, printed marks, inscribed "18 Avril BT 18" on the foot rims.

1818
$3,300-4,000   **WW**

A Worcester fluted cream boat, the handle with a pronounced thumb rest, the molded panels enameled with Chinese riverscapes, one with a figure fishing, the interior with four Precious Objects.
ca. 1752-53   *2in (5cm) high*
$12,000-15,000   **CHOR**

A Worcester patty pan, painted with the "Patty Pan Angler," with a figure fishing from a boat with a willow tree, the interior with flowering branches, the exterior with sprigs, workman's mark, broken and reattached.
ca. 1753-54   *5¼in (13.6cm) diam*
$1,100-1,250   **WW**

An early Worcester cream boat, of Wigornia type, with a geranium leaf molded under the lip, the handle with molded terminals, molded in relief with two Chinese buildings within a fenced enclosure, a palm tree and a curved fence on the left, the reverse with a turreted building on a slope, a bird in flight above, and a cow on the right, a flower sprig within the interior.

This example corresponds to molding F in Clarke & Riley's classification.
ca. 1752-53   *4¼in (11cm) long*
$21,000-26,000   **CHOR**

A Worcester sauceboat, of silver shape embossed with a leaf and scroll cartouches, painted with a bird on a flowering branch, the interior with a crane, trailing flowers on rim.
ca. 1753   *7¾in (19.5cm) long*
$3,300-4,000   **CHOR**

A Worcester sauceboat, the handle with a curled thumb rest, the sides molded with shells, foliage, and scrollwork, with "strutting birds" by a fence and flowering rocks.
ca. 1753   *6¼in (16cm) long*
$4,000-4,600   **CHOR**

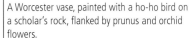

A Worcester vase, painted with a ho-ho bird on a scholar's rock, flanked by prunus and orchid flowers.
ca. 1753-54   *6¼in (16cm) high*
$7,500-8,500   **CHOR**

A Worcester mug, painted with the "Warbler" pattern, a bird perched on reeds beside a peony branch issuing from rockwork beside an ornamental fence, workman's mark.
ca. 1754-55   *3in (7.6cm) high*
$4,000-4,600   **WW**

A Worcester high-footed sauceboat, printed in the "Smoky Primitive'"manner with chinoiserie figures, the interior with bubbles, the foot and internal rim with flower sprays in the famille verte manner.
ca. 1754-55   *7½in (19cm) high*
$800-900   **WW**

A Worcester reeded coffee cup, painted with famille rose flowers with a floral swag border.
ca. 1753-54   *2in (5.2cm) high*
$550-650   **WW**

CLOSER LOOK—A WORCESTER WINE FUNNEL

The trailing floral and foliate imagery inside and outside of the funnel is of flowering peony branches, a staple of Chinese art and decoration and symbolic of prosperity, luck, love, and honor.

The color palette, originated in China and referred to there as *fencai*, meaning "pale colors," is known in Europe as famille rose, after its dominant pink-colored enamel.

Also a staple of Chinese decoration, bamboo—green shoots, which are depicted growing here—primarily signifies harmony and balance, and itis also considered lucky, particularly in relation to health.

This wine funnel may predate by 170 years or so that core tenet of Modernism, that "form should follow function," but it most certainly does, and in doing so displays a purity and elegance of line that's simply timeless.

A Worcester porcelain wine funnel with Chinese-inspired, polychrome enamel decoration.
ca. 1754   4¼in (11cm) high
$20,000-26,000   **CHOR**

A Worcester coffee can, with the "Rock Warbler" pattern, the long-tailed bird perched on tall rockwork beside an ornamental fence and flowering plants, with grooved strap handle, workman's mark.
ca. 1755-58   2½in (6.5cm) high
$750-850   **WW**

A Worcester tankard, painted with the "Beckoning Chinaman" pattern, peonies on the reverse and a prunus branch extending around the mug, anchor mark painted in red.
ca. 1755-56   3½in (9cm) high
$7,500-8,500   **CHOR**

A Worcester feather molded cup, painted in London, with flower sprays.
ca. 1755   2½in (6.2cm) high
$1,300-1,800   **CHOR**

A Worcester leaf-molded butter boat, the interior painted with Asian flower sprays, a restored rim section.
ca. 1755-56   3¼in (8.6cm) wide
$650-800   **WW**

A Worcester teabowl and saucer, painted with the "Romantic Rocks" pattern, a figure walking to the edge of a jutting precipice on an island with further rocks, a low hut, and pylon trees, another figure in a boat in the foreground, workman's marks, a short rim crack on the saucer.
ca. 1756   4¾in (12cm) wide
$1,700-2,100   **WW**

A Worcester mug, printed in black with a portrait of Frederick II of Prussia, titled "1757," the reverse printed with Fame blowing her trumpets, signed in the print "RH Worcester" for Robert Hancock, a short crack near the handle.
ca. 1757   5¾in (14.5cm) high
$550-650   **WW**

A Worcester pickle leaf dish, printed with the "Heron and Bamboo" pattern.
ca. 1757-60   3½in (8.8cm) wide
$750-850   **WW**

PORCELAIN

A Worcester Dutch pitcher, painted with flowering prunus in the "Cabbage Leaf Jug Floral" pattern, workman's mark.
ca. 1758   *7¾in (19.8cm) high*
$550-650   **WW**

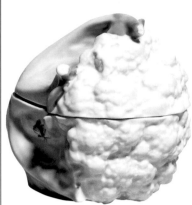

A Worcester cauliflower tureen base and associated cover, modeled with florets enclosed by leaves, the base printed with scattered butterflies.
ca. 1757-60   *4¼in (10.5cm) wide*
$1,250-1,500   **WW**

A Worcester mug, painted with tulips and other flowers tied with blue ribbon, a colorful moth and small sprigs on the reverse, grooved strap handle, a section broken and reattached.
ca. 1758   *3¼in (8.7cm) high*
$1,600-2,100   **WW**

A Worcester teabowl, coffee cup, and saucer, painted in the Chinese style with the "Hibiscus" or "Honeysuckle" pattern of flowers above a Sacred Scroll, red insects in flight.
ca. 1755-60
$2,100-2,600   **CHOR**

A Worcester partridge tureen and cover, modeled sitting on a nest, minute chips and wear.
ca. 1758   *6in (15cm) long*
$2,400-2,900   **DN**

A rare Worcester mug, with dog and flower design, initialed "J. P. W" with crescent mark.
ca. 1760   *3½in (9cm) high*
$13,000-16,000   **ROS**

A Worcester printed and hand-colored coffee cup and saucer, with "Les Garçons Chinois" pattern, one side with two Chinese figures on Rococo scrollwork, the reverse with a sitting figure.
ca. 1760   *4½in (11.7cm) wide*
$750-850   **WW**

A Worcester dish, molded with leaves within an eight-lobed rim, painted in the "Sweetmeat Stand Rose" pattern, open crescent mark.
ca. 1760-65   *10¾in (27.5cm) wide*
$2,600-3,300   **WW**

A Worcester finger bowl and stand, painted in the European style with lilies and sprigs.
ca. 1758-60   *the bowl 2¾in (7cm) high*
$1,500-2,000   **CHOR**

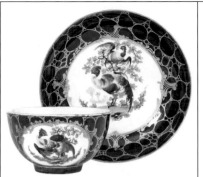

A Worcester teabowl and saucer, painted with fancy birds perched in branches, with gilt caillouté decoration.
ca. 1765   *5in (12.6cm) diam*
$800-900   **WW**

A Worcester dish, painted with flowers, within gilt scroll borders, square seal mark.
ca. 1760-70   *9¾in (24.9cm) diam*
$550-650   **WW**

A Worcester blue-and-white sauceboat, painted with the "One Porter Landscape" pattern, the lip and foot with molded gadrooning, crescent mark.
ca. 1765   *5¼in (13.5cm) long*
$600-750   **WW**

A Worcester junket dish, painted with Asian flowers, open crescent mark.
ca. 1765   *8¾in (22.3cm) wide*
$1,050-1,200   **WW**

A Worcester teacup and saucer, decorated in the London atelier of James Giles with flowers, blue crossed swords and "9" marks.
ca. 1770   *5¼in (13.7cm) wide*
$750-800   **WW**

A Worcester vase, decorated with two phoenixes or other fancy birds perched on chrysanthemum and rockwork, two panels of chrysanthemum and banded hedges in the Kakiemon palette, square seal mark.
ca. 1770   *6in (15.2cm) high*
$800-900   **WW**

A Worcester blue-scale ground tea canister, painted flowers in gilt frame cartouches and a cover, perhaps matched.
ca. 1770   *6¼in (16cm) high*
$600-650   **CHOR**

A Worcester mug, printed in the "Milkmaids" pattern.
ca. 1770   *3½in (9cm) high*
$400-450   **CHOR**

A Worcester chestnut basket, cover, and stand, pierced and applied with flowers and with crab-stock handles, some chips.
ca. 1770   *the stand 10½in (26.5cm) wide*
$1,100-1,250   **DN**

PORCELAIN

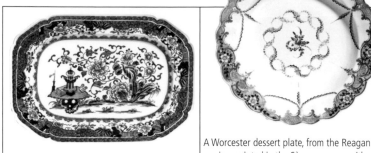

A Worcester meat dish, painted with the "Garden Table" pattern, after a Chinese design, within a Fitzhugh border.

ca. 1772   11¾in (29.5cm) wide

$2,600-3,300   **WW**

A Worcester dessert plate, from the Reagan service, painted in the Sèvres manner with a flower spray within overlapping garlands.

President and Mrs. Ronald Reagan were presented with three dishes from this service during a state visit to London.

ca. 1775   8½in (21.5cm) diam

$1,050-1,200   **WW**

A Worcester dessert plate, from the "Bishop Sumner" service, in the manner of Chinese famille verte with a kylin and a phoenix in the well, the rim with birds, flowers, and mythical beasts.

The pattern is a direct copy of a Chinese original from the Kangxi period (1662-1722), but the palette is not true to the Chinese porcelain. There are several Bishop Sumners after whom the service could be named, perhaps the most probable are the brothers John Sumner, Archbishop of Canterbury (1780-1862), and Charles Sumner, Bishop of Winchester (1790-1874). Both lived in the 19thC, so the service cannot have been originally made for them. It is possible that a link was made when the service was sold as part of one of the bishops' estates.

ca. 1775   8¾in (22cm) diam

$450-600   **WW**

A previously unrecorded Worcester slop bowl, painted with a variant of the "Formal Rose Spray" pattern, with a narcissus or passion flower, the reverse with a flying insect, the interior rim with a leaf and flower-head border, open crescent mark.

ca. 1785   4¾in (12cm) diam

$750-850   **WW**

A Worcester saucer dish, after a Chinese famille verte original, painted with a dragon chasing a flaming pearl, within a border of two dragons and two phoenixes, flowers, and foliage.

ca. 1775   6¾in (17cm) diam

$1,500-2,000   **CHOR**

A Worcester Barr period ice pail and cover, decorated with the "Royal Lily" pattern, incised "B" mark.

ca. 1800   10¾in (27cm) high

$750-850   **CHEF**

Judith Picks

One of the best-known of the early Worcester decorative designs, the "Blind Earl" pattern is certainly one of my personal favorites. Featuring rosebuds and molded leaves picked out in polychrome enamels, and painted with an insect, small sprays of flowers and leaves, and scattered flowers, all within a lobed rim with gilt C-scroll banding, it was–as legend has it—named after the earl who initially commissioned it.

Specifically, George William, the 5th Earl of Coventry, who, blinded in an hunting accident in the 1770s, ordered a raised and textured pattern that he could appreciate through touch and feel instead of sight. In recent years, some doubt has been cast on this story, relating to the pattern possibly appearing before his accident. However, the "Blind Earl" name, some 250 years on, still endures, and I for one won't be letting this possible new truth get in the way of a good story.

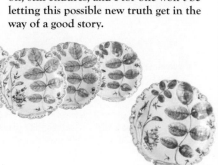

A set of six late-18thC Worcester "Blind Earl" plates, with gilt scalloped edges and decorated with single rosebuds, flower sprigs, and sprays.

7¾in (19.5cm) diam

$4,000-4,600   **L&T**

One of a pair of Barr, Flight & Barr Worcester sauce tureens and covers, decorated in the Imari manner with Chinese figures carrying parasols and catching birds amid flowering plants, ring handles with eagle masks, marks.

ca. 1805-10   6½in (16.8cm) high

$2,000-2,600 the pair   **WW**

A Worcester Barr, Flight & Barr gilt-crested cream tureen and cover, flammiform finial, cover with impressed mark, small chip on finial and, in general, some minor rubbing to the gilt.
ca. 1810 *6¾in (17cm) high*
$1,300-1,800 DN

An early-19thC Barr, Flight and Barr painted porcelain urn, painted with flowers, painted maker's marks "BARR FLIGHT & BARR/ ROYAL PORCELAIN WORKS/ WORCESTER/ LONDON ***/ NO. 1 COVENTRY STREET."
14¼in (36cm) high
$8,500-10,000 L&T

A late-19thC Royal Worcester reticulated cup and saucer, of George Owen type, with printed marks, date letter.
1881
$4,600-5,900 DN

A Royal Worcester vase, by Harry Stinton, painted with sailing boats in a choppy sea, signed, printed mark.
1903 *4¼in (10.5cm) high*
$450-600 WW

A pair of Royal Worcester Hadleigh ware vases and covers, by William Jarman, painted with roses, signed, JH monogram and printed marks, one cover restored, some wear on gilding.
ca. 1905 *12½in (32cm) high*
$1,300-1,800 TEN

A Royal Worcester vase and cover, by Frank Roberts, painted with rose sprays, signed, printed mark in puce, wear on gilding.
1909 *21¼in (54cm) high*
$650-800 TEN

A Royal Worcester vase, by Harry Stinton, painted with cattle in Highland landscape, signed, printed mark in puce, some surface wear.
1912 *8½in (21.5cm) high*
$1,700-2,100 TEN

A Royal Worcester vase and inner cover, by John Stinton, painted with Highland cattle in landscape, signed, printed mark in puce, outer cover missing, minor surface wear.
1919 *8¼in (21cm) high*
$2,000-2,600 TEN

A Royal Worcester vase and cover, by William Ricketts, painted with still lives of fruit, signed, printed mark in puce, surface wear.
1922 *6¾in (17cm) high*
$2,100-2,600 TEN

A Royal Worcester vase, by Harry Stinton, painted with Highland cattle in landscape, signed, printed mark in puce, minor wear.
1934 *6½in (16.5cm) high*
$1,100-1,250 TEN

PORCELAIN

ESSENTIAL REFERENCE—AMERICAN TEABOWL AND SAUCER

These pieces have only recently been identified as early American porcelain, believed to be part of a matched tea service that reached England in the late 1760s or 1770s. They are only the eighth and ninth recorded pieces of Bartlam porcelain. Analysis of both the glaze and the porcelain body place the teabowl and saucer within the ranges of the teapot and of sherds excavated at the site of Bartlam's factory in Cain Hoy. Little is known of John Bartlam before he traveled to North America. The UK Register of Duties Paid of Apprentice's Indentures, 1710-1811, has a record of a payment made on May 30, 1761, when one Simon Chawner is apprenticed to John Bartlam, Potter of Lane Delph, Staffordshire. Lane Delph was one of the principal areas of the ceramics industry and Bartlam would have been one of a growing number producing creamware, pearlware, and other earthenwares. He left England around 1763, possibly in some debt, to settle in South Carolina and set up business as a potter, establishing himself first in Cain Hoy about 1765. The move was a canny one—South Carolina was at the time one of the wealthiest and most fashionable, with residents vying to have the latest and finest ceramics shipped over from England. South Carolina was also part of the lucrative kaolin belt, which shipped Cherokee clay by the ton over to potters in the UK, including Josiah Wedgwood. In a May 1767 letter to his partner, Thomas Bentley, Wedgwood writes, "I am informed they have the Cherok[ee clay] to a Pottwork at Charles Town," the potter in question undoubtedly being John Bartlam. The proximity of a supply of kaolin, the wealthy local clientele, and his clear entrepreneurial spirit meant it was inevitable that Bartlam tried his hand at making porcelain to rival that being imported from England at great expense. It is almost certain that he had help from someone with knowledge of the porcelain industry, perhaps a fellow British person from one of the London factories, since not only is the Bartlam body extremely close to several of the London concerns, the decoration also bears similarities to some established patterns at both Bow and Isleworth. By 1768, it appears that Bartlam was again having financial difficulties and was looking to relocate his manufactory to Charlestown itself. This he seems to have achieved by the end of 1770, but the Charleston pottery failed and closed in 1772. Bartlam relocated farther inland to Camden, backed by a man called Joseph Kershaw, and continued to produce pottery there until his death in 1781.

An important and previously unrecorded American porcelain teabowl and saucer, attributed to John Bartlam, Cain Hoy, South Carolina, ca. 1765-69, printed with the "Man on the Bridge" pattern, a solitary figure standing on a bridge linking pagoda islands, the teabowl's interior with a small vignette of a hut beside a tree.

4½in (11.7cm) diam

$70,000-80,000   WW

A pair of Caughley custard cups and covers, printed with the "Willow Nankin" pattern, blue "S" marks.

ca. 1775-90   3¼in (8cm) high

$350-400   WW

A rare Caughley figure of a girl in Turkish dress, wearing a headdress and raised on a low scrolled base applied with flowers and leaves, detailed in blue, a little restoration.

This is one of only two Caughley figures to have been identified, after Geoffrey Godden drew attention to their existence in his book on Caughley and Worcester porcelains in the 1960s. John Sandon identified a reference to these figures in the Worcester archives—a section titled "Goods Rec'd from Tho's Turner Esq, Caughley" includes the entry "Sept. 23 '89, 6 turks white @ 9d - 4/6."

ca. 1790   4in (10.3cm) high

$7,500-8,000   WW

A rare Caughley mustard pot and cover, printed with the "Travellers" pattern, after a print by Paul Sandby, a family standing beside a donkey, the reverse with a mother and child in a rural landscape, "S" mark on the underside, restoration to the cover.

From 1775 to 1799, at Caughley near Broseley in Shropshire, England, Ambrose Gallimore and Thomas Turner produced soft-paste porcelain. They produced, in the main, useful wares, tea services, dinner services, and everyday objects that would be used in the households of the middle classes. The porcelain was decorated largely in underglaze blue, although enamel colors and gilding were also used.

ca. 1790   3½in (9cm) high

$2,100-2,600   WW

A Coalbrookdale documentary teacup and saucer, painted with birds within a puce and gilt rim, gilt conjoined "CBD" mark and dated.

1861

$650-800   CHOR

A pair of Davenport vases, painted with two named views, one with Hartlepool and Dereunurater (sic), the other with Dunstanburgh Castle and Deruenurater (sic).

19in (48cm) high

$1,600-2,100   CHEF

A Doccia leaf cream or butter boat, the stem forming the handle, the interior painted with an Asian flower spray.

ca. 1760-80   4¼in (10.9cm) wide

$600-750   WW

A Doccia cup and saucer, painted with roses on a deep blue ground.

ca. 1760-70   5½in (13.9cm) wide

$350-400   WW

A pair of late-19thC Dresden porcelain figures, modeled as a young man in 18thC dress carrying a basket of flowers, his companion holding a flower garland, with underglaze blue cross mark and incised "no.369."

19¼in (49cm) high

$1,300-1,800 **L&T**

A 19thC Dresden porcelain figure of an eagle, incised "2357" and black Dresden crown mark.

19¾in (50cm) high

$550-650 **L&T**

A Frankenthal teapot, painted with nuts and fruit, associated cover.

ca. 1765

$550-650 **CHOR**

A Fulda pitcher and associated cover, decorated with amusing scenes of family life in the manner of David Teniers, a child being spanked while others cry in the corner, blue crowned "FF" mark.

ca. 1760 *5½in (14cm) high*

$600-750 **WW**

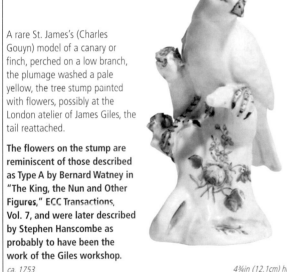

A rare St. James's (Charles Gouyn) model of a canary or finch, perched on a low branch, the plumage washed a pale yellow, the tree stump painted with flowers, possibly at the London atelier of James Giles, the tail reattached.

The flowers on the stump are reminiscent of those described as Type A by Bernard Watney in "The King, the Nun and Other Figures," ECC Transactions, Vol. 7, and were later described by Stephen Hanscombe as probably to have been the work of the Giles workshop.

ca. 1753 *4¾in (12.1cm) high*

$10,500-12,000 **WW**

A St. James's (Charles Gouyn) etui or bodkin case, painted in the atelier of James Giles, with sprays of flowers, with gilt metal mounts.

Charles Gouyn (d. 1785), a Huguenot born in Dieppe, was a jeweler with premises "at the Turk's Head," Bennett Street, St. James's, London. Gouyn helped Nicholas Sprimont (1716-1771) set up the Chelsea Porcelain Factory around 1745, but in about 1748 Gouyn left the Chelsea Porcelain Factory and set out to compete with his own "Girl-in-a-Swing" manufactory, so-called after a figure in the Victoria & Albert Museum, which has given its name to a whole class of similar porcelain figures. Gouyn's factory also made small scent bottles, etuis, etc., usually with gold or gilt metal mounts collectively known as "toys." Some "Girl-in-a-Swing" products appear to imitate Chelsea porcelain models and vice versa.

ca. 1753-55 *3¾in (9.7cm) high*

$3,300-4,000 **WW**

A Hague teabowl and saucer, decorated with hens and puce flowers, underglaze blue stork mark.

ca. 1780

$450-550 **CHOR**

An ogee cup and saucer, decorated at the Hague, with scenes of Venus and Cupid, overglaze blue stork mark.

ca. 1780

$260-330 **CHOR**

A modern Herend "Fruit and Flowers" pattern part dinner service, comprising 16 dinner plates, 14 breakfast plates, 14 soup plates, 16 side plates, a pair of oval serving dishes, a double-lipped two-handle sauceboat, and an oval serving dish or stand, with blue printed factory marks.

$6,500-8,000 **DN**

A Hoschst teacup and saucer, painted on the rim with green diaper panels suspending floral swags, scattered insects, wheel marks.
ca. 1770
$350-400   **CHOR**

A Hochst teabowl and saucer, decorated with a bullfinch perched on a branch.
ca. 1780
$400-450   **CHOR**

An Isleworth feeding cup, printed with gillyflower or carnation and other flowers and moths, the bowl halfway covered and issuing a curved spout, with two shell-shaped handles, a few small chips.

All of the known examples of Isleworth feeding cups are decorated with the same series of floral prints.
ca. 1770-85   *7in (18cm) wide*
$2,600-4,000   **WW**

An Isleworth sauceboat, molded with a floral design and painted with European flower posies, a band of daisies on a trellis ground on the rim, a foot-rim crack.

The Isleworth Porcelain Factory was established by Joseph Shore, who came to Isleworth, possibly from Worcester, in 1757. As well as making porcelain, this manufactory also made cream-color earthenware and slipware. Joseph Shore's daughters Ann and Mary married Bristol delftware potters Benjamin Quarman and Richard Goulding, who both came to Isleworth. The factory remained in the Shore, Quarman and Goulding families until its closure in 1831.
ca. 1768-75   *6¼in (16.2cm) wide*
$750-850   **WW**

A Kloster Veilsdorf teacup and saucer, painted on the rim with a trellis suspending ribbon-tied floral swags on which perch birds, with Classical urns, blue cv marks.
ca. 1770
$600-650   **CHOR**

An English porcelain pickle dish, possibly Limehouse or Pomona, painted with a flowering branch issuing from two penciled leaves.
ca. 1745   *4¾in (12cm) wide*
$2,100-2,600   **WW**

A Limehouse molded cup, with crab-stock handle molded with prunus flowers.
ca. 1746-48   *2½in (6.5cm) high*
$5,300-6,600   **CHOR**

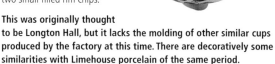

An English porcelain cup or wine taster, of peach shape, painted with a leaf spray, a sprig in the interior with flying insects, on a twig foot extending to a handle, two small filled rim chips.

This was originally thought to be Longton Hall, but it lacks the molding of other similar cups produced by the factory at this time. There are decoratively some similarities with Limehouse porcelain of the same period.
ca. 1755   *6¼in (15.6cm) wide*
$1,500-1,800   **WW**

A pair of Loosdrecht câchepots and stands, painted possibly by Fidelle Duvivier, with figures at the water's edge beneath trees, a village in the distance, the reverses with vignettes of trees and statuary, painted "M:OL" marks, some gilt wear.
ca. 1780-84   *4in (10.3cm) high*
$4,600-5,300   **WW**

A Ludwigsburg plate, painted with flowers, including rose, forget-me-not, and heartsease, blue crowned interlaced Cs mark.

ca. 1760-70   *11½in (29cm) diam*

$180-240   **WW**

A Mennecy silver-mounted snuff box or bonbonnière, modeled as a large pear, the inside cover painted with a flower spray, Paris discharge mark on the mount, restored.

Mennecy porcelain is a French soft-paste porcelain from the manufactory established under the patronage of Louis-François-Anne de Neufville, Duc de Villeroy (1695-1766) and, from 1748, housed in outbuildings ("les petites maisons") in the park of his Château de Villeroy and in the nearby village of Mennecy (Île-de-France). The history of the factory remains somewhat unclear, but it is regarded as producing between about 1738 and 1765.

ca. 1740-50   *2¾in (7cm) high*

$2,000-2,600   **WW**

An 18thC Ludwigsburg figure, modeled by Johann Christian Wilhelm Beyer, the naked fisherman standing on a rocky base, holding a net with a dolphin.

ca. 1770   *8¼in (21cm) high*

$1,600-2,100   **CHEF**

A pair of Minton vases and covers, with two panels painted with the profiles of Classical figures, with scrolling acanthus.

11¾in (30cm) high

$1,700-2,400   **CHEF**

A Mennecy silver-mounted snuff box, painted with flower sprays, the silver mount with French control marks, cracked and chipped.

ca. 1750   *2¾in (6.9cm) wide*

$160-210   **WW**

A Naples white-glazed porcelain figural group, modeled as Pan and a female nude on a seesaw made from a tree trunk, supported by two infants, with crown mark in blue.

19¼in (49cm) wide

$750-850   **CHEF**

A late-18thC Naples porcelain cream pitcher, painted on two sides with a Classical maiden wearing long diaphanous robes, the spout molded with a bearded mask, crowned blue "N" mark, with damages.

3¼in (8cm) high

$260-330   **WW**

From a set of 16 Nymphenburg plates, 5 plates printed and painted with floral bouquets.

ca. 1900   *10in (25cm) diam*

$1,300-2,000 the set   **CHOR**

A pair of early-19thC Paris porcelain gold-ground vases, in the Empire style, probably by Dartes Frères or Nast, painted with scenes of peasant life, both have gilt wear, the vase with the scene of the boy stealing washing has glued repair on the handle, base section on the other has been broken and repaired.

17in (42.8cm) high

$1,250-1,500   **MART**

A Paris porcelain cabinet cup and saucer, the cup painted en grisaille with a panel of a lion, on three paw feet, gilt CM monogram and "1815" mark.

ca. 1815　　　　　　　*6in (15.2cm) high*

$800-900　　　　　　　　　**WW**

A Saint Cloud white-glazed coffee cup and trembleuse saucer, molded in the artichoke manner with bands of overlapping petals, the cup with a molded angular handle.

ca. 1730-40　　　　*5¼in (13.1cm) diam*

$2,000-2,600　　　　　　　**WW**

A large Spode bowl, decorated in pattern 1645, with flower sprays, in the Imari palette.

ca. 1820-30　　　　*11¼in (28.5cm) wide*

$400-450　　　　　　　　　**WW**

A Joseph Hannong Strasbourg porcelain model of a pug dog, a doleful expression on his face, the base with sponged black decoration and puce sprigs, impressed "H" over "F733" and "A3" marks, a little chipping.

ca. 1770-75　　　　　*3½in (9cm) high*

$1,500-2,000　　　　　　　**WW**

A pair of Tournai plates, painted with the "Ronda" pattern of prunus and peony issuing from rockwork, the rims with sprays of Asian flowers, blue crossed swords, and + marks.

ca. 1770-80　　　　　*9½in (24cm) diam*

$350-400　　　　　　　　　**WW**

A rare Vauxhall sweetmeat stand, formed of three scallop shells, painted with chrysanthemum sprays.

Only a small number of Vauxhall pickle shells of this form are recorded, including an example from the Watney Collection of the same pattern.

ca. 1756　　　　　　*7¾in (19.5cm) wide*

$3,300-4,000　　　　　　　**WW**

A Vauxhall mug, painted with a chinoiserie scene with a figure on a bridge, with a hut before mountains, rim chip.

In 1751, a license to mine soaprock was taken out by Nicholas Crisp and John Sanders. The soft-paste porcelain was of the soapy type with some added calcium. Wares and figures were produced in underglaze blue and polychrome. John Sanders died in 1758, leaving Crisp to carry on until 1763, when he became bankrupt. The stock was finally sold in 1764.

ca. 1755-58　　　　　*4¾in (12cm) high*

$1,000-1,100　　　　　　　**WW**

A Vauxhall figure of a lady, her left arm on a stump beside her and holding an empty bowl, applied flowers and leaves before her, some repairs.

ca. 1755-58　　　　*5¾in (14.5cm) high*

$550-650　　　　　　　　　**WW**

A Vauxhall figure of a putto, emblematic of the Arts, modeled as an artist with a palette and paintbrush, sketching a portrait on a plaque, restoration to his painting.

ca. 1760   *5¼in (13.5cm) high*
$1,600-2,100   **WW**

A late-19thC Vienna-style charger, painted with the Triumph of Bacchus and Ariadne, blue shield mark.

                              14½in (36.5cm) diam
$1,300-1,800   **DN**

A Vienna hot water pitcher and cover, painted with flower sprays and scattered sprigs, the cover with a strawberry finial, blue shield mark, indistinct impressed date code.

ca. 1775   *7in (17.5cm) high*
$260-400   **WW**

A Vienna coffee cup and saucer, the cup painted with merchants unloading from a boat, the saucer with a standing figure, gilt scroll rims, blue hive marks on bases.

ca. 1760
$350-400   **CHOR**

A pair of 19thC Helena Wolfsohn porcelain-covered vases, decorated with panels of equestrian scenes after Wouwerman, and botanical studies, underglaze blue "AR" mark.

20in (51cm) high
$1,700-2,400   **L&T**

A mid-18thC London-decorated Chinese porcelain pitcher and cover, painted in the atelier of James Giles with flowers, some restoration to the cover.

5¼in (13.5cm) high
$550-650   **WW**

An 18thC London-decorated Chinese soft-paste porcelain vase, painted with flowers, including rose, heartsease, forget-me-not, and tulip, the shoulders and neck applied with squirrels, some restoration.

7in (18cm) high
$450-600   **WW**

A mid-18thC London-decorated Chinese porcelain spoon tray, with original incised anhua decoration, later decorated probably in the atelier of James Giles with "Type B" flower sprays, small sprigs, and a butterfly, brown line rim, a small rim chip.

5in (12.9cm) wide
$400-550   **WW**

THE POTTERY MARKET

Like most areas, pottery collectors have been affected by the economic climate and global pandemic. As always, when good, rare, early, and, especially, dated pieces come fresh to the market, top prices are paid. Mid-priced and low-end pieces have struggled, particularly if they were produced in large quantities, such as some of the more common transfer-printed Staffordshire patterns. Delftware has to be early and of a rare shape and decoration to achieve a strong price—the documentary Liverpool "brig" charger (see page 53) is a good example. For the more modest collector who is interested in delft and slipware, it is an excellent time to buy. There is strong competition for the top-end pieces; however, the market is generally sluggish for the more common pottery.

English Victorian pottery of the 19thC and Staffordshire figures have to be exceptionally rare and early to attract interest. A good example is the salt-glazed bear baiting pitcher (see page 69). There is still the problem of fake "Staffordshire" coming from the Far East—I have seen examples on both sides of the Atlantic. They are really easy to recognize, because they don't have the same quality of period examples, but the quality is improving.

There have been some dramatic prices paid for some early pottery, particularly the Italian maiolica istoriato ware plates, dishes, and apothecary jars created in the 16thC. A particularly good example is the maiolica winged horse Pegasus dish (see page 59). Interest in good and early (16thC) Hispano Moresque pottery remains strong, but little comes to the market. Mason's ironstone has to be an interesting shape with good strong colors to make any money. Good-quality early Wedgwood, particularly if the piece has unusual color combinations, seems to be selling better in U.S. sale rooms than in the UK.

The market for creamware, pearlware, and prattware is still sluggish, with little of real note coming onto the market. Toby jugs have to be a rare shape to attract interest.

The American market for pottery is generally stronger than the UK market. Good quality pre-1830 pottery is still in demand. Due to the pandemic, business is mainly through the Internet, and we are obviously not seeing the number of American buyers traveling around the country as in the past.

American stoneware continues to have a strong collectors' market, particularly for rare shapes and makers and the more unusual designs. Redware has seen a sluggish period where only the most unusual pieces fetch high prices. One good example is the redware bowl attributed to Henry Adam on page 71. The market for Mochaware remains strong.

In general it is a great time to buy!

Top Left: A late-19th/early-20thC French faience figure of a lion, perhaps Rouen.

28½in (72.4cm) high

$800-900 **WW**

Above: A rare Bristol delftware documentary Adam and Eve charger, the first couple depicted flanking the Tree of Knowledge, the serpent brightly enameled and entwining the tree trunk beneath sponged green foliage, the dish inscribed "John Archer 1755" in blue, broken and repaired.

1755 *10¼in (26cm) diam*

$11,000-12,000 **WW**

ESSENTIAL REFERENCE—ENGLISH DELFT

Production of tin-glazed earthenware was initiated in England ca. 1567 by two émigré Dutch potters from Antwerp. By the mid-17thC, when the town of Delft in Holland had become the leading European center of, and given its name to, such tin-glazed earthenwares, the English equivalent became best-known as "English delft."

● Like its Dutch counterpart (see pages 56-57), early English delft was largely inspired, in both form and decoration, by Chinese export blue-and-white porcelain, and then gradually acquired its own indigenous imagery and a more extensive polychrome palette.

● In general, English delft decoration is more naive, less formal, and less intricate than Dutch Delft; many aficionados think it often displays a greater freedom of artistic expression than its Dutch equivalent.

● English centers of production included: Aldgate, Southwark, Lambeth, and Vauxhall in London; Norwich; Bristol; Wincanton; and Liverpool, and there was also notable centers beyond the English borders in Glasgow, Belfast, and Dublin.

● The English delft industry thrived, as did Dutch Delft, until the mid-18thC, when it was mainly supplanted by creamware (see pages 61-62).

A Bristol delftware "Farmhouse" plate, painted with a bold peacock in yellow, blue, and red, standing between sponged manganese trees.
ca. 1720-30   8¾in (22.3cm) diam
$2,100-2,600   WW

A Bristol delftware "Farmhouse" plate, painted with a bold cockerel in yellow, blue, and red, standing between sponged manganese trees, with a flock of birds in flight above.
ca. 1720-30   8¾in (22.5cm) diam
$4,000-5,300   WW

A Bristol delft posset pot, with floral decoration, hairline crack on base, glaze wear.
ca. 1730   7¼in (18.5cm) high
$4,000-5,300   POOK

A delftware plate, possibly Bristol, painted with a Long Eliza figure holding a parasol before buildings and a figure fishing, inscribed "A V 1748."
1748   9in (22.5cm) diam
$1,700-2,100   WW

A pair of Bristol delftware chargers, with a large insect in flight above a bird perched on a flowering branch beside an ornamental fence.
ca. 1740-60   13½in (34cm) diam
$6,500-8,000   WW

A Bristol delftware plate, of Bowen type, painted with two ladies in a European landscape before a house and beneath tall sponged trees.
ca. 1760   9in (22.7cm) diam
$450-550   WW

A Bristol delftware tile, with a bird on a stump, painted in red, blue, and yellow within a manganese outline, with a floral "bianco-sopra-bianco" border.
ca. 1760   5¼in (13.2cm) high
$800-900   WW

A Bristol delftware marriage plate, painted with figures in boats and fishing from an island before buildings and a tall tree, inscribed beneath with "P R M" above the date, a 3½in (9cm) rim crack.
1770   9in (22.8cm) diam
$1,200-1,450   WW

A pair of Lambeth delftware plates, painted with a Chinese lady holding a fan, beneath curved branches.

ca. 1750-60   *8¾in (22.5cm) diam*

$750-850   **WW**

A pair of mid-18thC Lambeth delft chargers, painted with a sitting figure beside a river, with repaired chip, hairline crack, and minor glaze losses on the rim.

                                          13½in (34cm) diam

$650-800   **SWO**

A Liverpool delftware tile, decorated with a Chinese figure holding a cooking pot, with chrysanthemum corner mons in blue.

Cf. Anthony Ray, "English Delftware Tiles," p. 231, no.571 for a similar tile. A fireplace lined with these tiles can be seen at Aston Hall in Birmingham.

ca. 1750-70   *5in (12.5cm) high*

$550-650   **WW**

A Liverpool delftware ship bowl, painted with a three-masted British frigate with 16 cannons in 2 rows, the exterior with a Chinese pagoda landscape.

The majority of ships depicted on delftware relate to trading, so a warship of this type is unusual.

ca. 1750-60   *9¼in (23.3cm) diam*   **WW**

$2,000-2,600

CLOSER LOOK—LIVERPOOL DELFTWARE SHIP CHARGER

The decorative border around the rim comprises crosshatched trellising, interspersed with stylized flower heads. Although trellising—a support for garden plants—initially appeared as a motif in European decoration in the Middle Ages, the inspiration here is the Chinese vocabulary of ornament.

The attention to detail, albeit stylized, that is evident in the painting of the vessel—and extends to crew members visible on deck—suggests it may well have been by the Liverpool artist William Jackson (1730-1803).

Identification of subject (and additional provenance) is available beyond the inscription: the Lloyd's Register of Shipping in 1764 records the "John and Mary" as a single-deck brig built in 1756 at Yarmouth; sailing to Leghorn under Capt. P. Crombies; owner J. Spencer.

Blue-and-white ware bowls and, as here, chargers decorated with ships were a speciality of the port city of Liverpool's ceramic factories, especially during the 1750s and 60s.

A rare documentary Liverpool delftware charger with a two-masted brig at sail and inscription, within a floral and trellis border.

ca. 1756   *14¼in (36.2cm) diam*

$8,500-10,000   **WW**

A Liverpool delftware tile, printed by John Sadler, with a courting couple beside a pineapple plant in a formal garden setting.

This design is adapted from plate 32 of "The Ladies' Amusement," with alterations to the background. It is one of few designs of which the mirrored version is also known.

ca. 1757-61   *5in (12.8cm) high*

$350-400   **WW**

A delftware plate, possibly Liverpool, painted with bamboo and peony, the scalloped rim with four flower sprays, inscribed "I P 1757."

1757   *9in (23cm) diam*

$1,600-2,100   **WW**

A Liverpool delftware wood-block tile, printed by John Sadler, with a Dutch canal scene.
ca. 1760   *5in (12.8cm) high*
$1,700-2,200   **WW**

A Liverpool delftware tile, with a dancing Chinese figure beside another figure holding a stick.
ca. 1760-70   *5in (12.7cm) high*
$1,500-1,800   **WW**

A documentary delftware plate, possibly Liverpool, inscribed with "Success to the Old Boy at Gasting Thomas Knowles 1763," rim chipping.
1763   *9in (23cm) diam*
$4,600-5,300   **WW**

A dated London delft wine bottle, inscribed in blue "CLARET 1642," with strap handle.
1642   *7in (18cm) high*
$8,500-9,000   **DN**

A London delftware apothecary or pill slab, possibly Mortlake, painted with the arms of the Worshipful Society of Apothecaries above the motto "Opiferque Per Orbem Dicor."
ca. 1785   *12in (30.4cm) high*
$10,500-12,000   **WW**

A London delftware "Royal" dish, painted with a portrait of William and Mary, each crowned, the dish broken and riveted.

William and Mary were proclaimed King and Queen as joint sovereigns in 1689 and reigned together until Mary's death in 1694. A number of fragments found by Garner in Lambeth correspond with this design.
ca. 1690   *8¾in (22cm) diam*
$2,600-3,300   **WW**

A delftware blue dash charger, possibly Brislington, painted with three tulips and long leaves unusually issuing from a checkered vase, with a blue dash rim, the underside with a thin buff glaze.
ca. 1680   *13½in (34.5cm) diam*
$11,000-13,000   **WW**

An Irish delftware plate, possibly Dublin, painted with flowers, blue number "2" mark on the underside.
ca. 1760   *9in (23cm) diam*
$750-850   **WW**

A Dublin delftware water bottle or guglet, painted with the "Feathers in a Vase" pattern after Chinese porcelain, a chip on the rim.
ca. 1760   *10¼in (26cm) high*
$600-750   **WW**

A rare Glasgow delftware plate, painted with a boat at sail before a small building, the rim with leaves and grapes.
ca. 1760   *9¼in (23.5cm) diam*
$400-450   **WW**

An English delftware plate, inscribed with the letter "Y" over the initials "W M" above the date, all within a circlet of crossed leafy branches, plate broken and restored.
1710   *8½in (21.8cm) diam*
$1,050-1,200   **WW**

A delftware puzzle pitcher, decorated on one side with a panel of a castle flying a pennant, the other with a figure and a Chinese pagoda, the body inscribed with the traditional four-line wager above the inscription "O S M 1741," one spout broken and reattached.
1741   *6½in (16.5cm) high*
$4,600-5,300   **WW**

A delftware flower brick, painted on the longer sides with a figure in a boat before a windmill and a low hut, the shorter sides with flower sprays, with restoration.
ca. 1740   *6¼in (16.2cm) long*
$550-650   **WW**

A delftware flower brick, painted with buildings on the long sides, the short sides with a figure punting two others in a small boat, with a little chipping.
1750-60   *5¼in (13.4cm) long*
$850-1,000   **WW**

A delftware flower brick, one side painted with a pagoda landscape, the reverse with flowering peony, bamboo, and rockwork, one short side with a Chinese figure, the other with a figure crossing a bridge, the top painted with flowering plants, some faults.
ca. 1750-60   *7¼in (18.3cm) long*
$850-1,000   **WW**

A delftware flower brick, painted with landscape scenes of figures in boats beside trees and buildings, the recessed top with 18 holes flanking an opening in the center.
ca. 1760   *4¾in (12cm) wide*
$3,300-4,000   **WW**

A rare English delftware King of Prussia plate, painted with a portrait of Frederick II of Prussia between the letters "K P."
ca. 1757-60   *8¾in (22cm) diam*
$3,300-4,000   **WW**

An English delftware ointment pot, painted in manganese with "The Queen's Dentifrice."
ca. 1775   *2in (4.8cm) high*
$2,600-3,300   **WW**

ESSENTIAL REFERENCE—DUTCH DELFT

Dutch potters were making tin-glazed earthenware—originally often in imitation of maiolica from Spain and Italy—as early as the late 15thC. The attribution "Delft" derived from that city becoming the most important center of production during the second half of the 17thC, but others included Amsterdam, Delftshaven, Gouda, and Haarlem.

- The industry expanded rapidly from the mid-17thC as supply-chain problems from Asia disrupted the import of Chinese porcelain and Dutch potters looked to fill the gap in the market. One consequence of this event is that the form and decoration of earlier Dutch Delft pieces is often Chinese in style.
- Gradually, however, Dutch Delt developed a style of its own, not only in terms of imagery—such as Biblical scenes, local city and rural landscapes, and European flora and fauna—but also with the addition of colors, such as purple, red, yellow, green, and black, to the original "blue-and-white" palette.
- By the mid-18thC, many Dutch Delft factories had gone out of business, largely due to competition from rapidly expanding European porcelain production, as well as the development of more durable and refined earthenware, notably creamware (see pages 61-62).

A late-17thC Delft plate, painted in the Kraak manner, with a censer of flowering plants before a fence, within a border of flower stems and auspicious objects.

8½in (21.7cm) diam

$450-550   **WW**

A Dutch Delft portrait plate of William III, with the image in the center flanked by tulips, small rim flakes and glaze wear.

ca. 1690   *8½in (21.5cm) diam*

$2,600-4,000   **POOK**

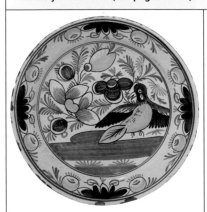

A mid-18thC Dutch Delft charger, decorated with a bird, flowers, and fruit, glaze loss on rim and chip.

13½in (34.5cm) diam

$400-550   **SWO**

An 18thC Delft marriage plate, decorated with holding hands and two love hearts, inscribed "Dirk Van der Merr and Johanna Kox," date on the reverse.

1793   *9in (23cm) diam*

$600-650   **CHEF**

A pair of mid-18thC Dutch Delft drug jars and gilt-metal covers, cartouche with peafowl and putto, reading "U MARTIAT" and "C ROS:RUB," the former with "P" mark on the base, possibly for the De Twee Scheepjes factory, with tin glaze nibbles and small chips.

14½in (37cm) and 13¾in (35cm) high

$1,500-1,800   **DN**

An 18thC Delft ring puzzle pitcher, painted with fruiting grapevine, the tall neck pierced with a scrolling floral design, the neck with three knopped spouts, the handle formed as a serpent painted with fish, with small damages.

10in (25.5cm) high

$1,300-2,000   **WW**

An 18th/19thC Delft tobacco jar, painted with a Native American sitting beside a jar inscribed "Pompadoer" [sic], marked for the Three Bells (Drie Klokken) factory, with a later brass cover.

15½in (39cm) high

$1,000-1,100   **WW**

A Delft tobacco jar and cover, decorated with a sailor smoking a pipe above the inscription "Devries Schetures Chipper," with a brass cover.

14½in (37cm) high

$750-850   **CHEF**

A small pair of 18thC Dutch Delft models of cows, bases marbled in green, yellow, and manganese, minor faults.

4½in (11.5cm) wide

$1,100-1,250   **WW**

A pair of Delft tobacco jars and covers, each decorated with an indigenous figure smoking a pipe sitting by a jar, one inscribed "Havana," the other "Pompadoe," with brass dome covers.

14½in (37cm) high

$3,300-4,000   **CHEF**

A pair of 18th/19thC Delft models of cows, their coats decorated with floral and cornucopia designs, red "APK" monogram marks after Pieter Kocx, minor restoration to three horns.

9in (23cm) long

$650-800   **WW**

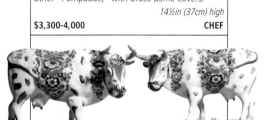

A pair of 19thC Delft models of cows, bases molded and decorated with frogs and snakes, their coats decorated in enamels with floral stripes, small damages.

9¼in (23.5cm) wide

$1,600-2,100   **WW**

A set of seventy-three 18thC Delft manganese tiles, decorated with either topographical, religious, or historical images or scenes from everyday life.

5¼in (13cm) wide each

$3,300-4,000   **CHEF**

A Delft panel of six tiles, depicting a rearing horse before a town.

15in (38cm) wide

$750-850   **CHEF**

An 18thC Delft punch bowl, De Paauw factory, painted with flowers, iron red mark.

10¼in (26cm) diam

$900-1,050   **L&T**

A pair of 19thC Delft vases and covers, painted with peacocks amid foliage, the covers with lion finials, both with restoration.

20½in (52cm) high

$6,000-6,600   **DN**

A pair of Delft gilt-metal mounted lamps, decorated with chinoiserie scenes of figures in a garden, with detachable fittings.

22½in (57cm) high

$1,700-2,100   **CHEF**

A Talavera or Puente del Arzobispo faience dish, from the "Three Color Family," painted with a profile portrait of a man wearing a hat, the rim with foliate sprays, a section of the rim broken and repaired.

ca. 1660-80   12½in (32cm) diam

$260-400   **WW**

A 17thC Birnkrug pewter-lidded tankard, painted with buildings and trees, the lid engraved "CRE/1699."

8¾in (22cm) high

$600-750   **CHEF**

An early-18thC Frankfurt-type jar and cover, painted in Chinese style, large section of foot reattached, two sections of neck restored, rim of cover restored, fritting throughout.

23¾in (60cm) high

$6,000-6,600   **DN**

A mid-18thC Brussels faience cabbage tureen and cover, probably by Philippe Mombaer, the sides applied with slugs, raised on scrolled stalk feet, with some repairs.

11in (28cm) diam

$400-450   **WW**

A pair of Spanish faience albarelli, Castille or Aragon, painted with an elephant with a castle resting on its back with the letters "FA" on each side, the letter "I" beneath, some faults.

ca. 1770   10in (25.5cm) high

$800-900   **WW**

A German faience tankard, enameled with a figure in Middle Eastern dress, flanked by trees, the hinged pewter lid inscribed "J C M 1789," the handle broken and reattached.

1789   10in (25cm) high

$260-330   **WW**

An 18thC Nevers faience jardinière, painted with landscape panels with mask handles, on a circular foot with stiff leaf design.

17¾in (45cm) high

$800-900   **WW**

An 18thC French faience portable commode or "thunderbox," possibly Lille, painted with floral swags in the Berainesque manner, with later ebonized base and round cover.

13½in (34cm) high

$1,500-1,800   **DN**

A late-18thC French faience puzzle pitcher, probably Le Croisic, the neck pierced with a stylized floral design.

7½in (19cm) high

$170-210   **WW**

A Faenza maiolica "Famiglia Gotica" albarello, inscribed in blue "DIA.CASSIA.C.MAN," with flat chips on upper rim, minor chips on foot rim, some glaze loss.

According to Drey, Cassia Lignea or Cassia Cinnamon is the bark of the tree "Cinnamomum cassia."

ca. 1480   9in (22.5cm) high

$4,600-5,300   TEN

A late-16thC Castelli D'Abruzzo maiolica blue-ground dish (piatto "alla Turchina") from the Cardinal Farnese service, with the Farnese Arms beneath galero suspending tassles, two shallow scrapes, rim chips, some surface wear.

Cardinal Alessandro Farnese (1520-89) is thought to have ordered the service referred to as "alla Turchina" from Castelli sometime between 1574 and his death in 1589. It appears as "servitio da credenza di maiolica turchina miniata d'oro con arme del Sr. cardinale Farnese" in the inventories of the Palazzo Farnese in Rome in 1643 and 1653. Other contemporaneous copies of the Farnese service also exist. There are two more elaborate plates bearing the date 1574 to be found in the Museo Nazionale di Capodimonte. The attribution of Castelli is generally based on these two plates and excavations of blue-ground material in Abruzzo.

7in (18cm) diam

$2,600-3,300   DN

A late-16thC Italian (Faenza) maiolica crespina, by Virgiliotto Calamelli, painted with an episcopal armorial of a bishop, depicting confronting lions, "VR" and "AF" monograms on the underside, with some damages.

10¼in (26.2cm) diam

$1,700-2,100   WW

A mid-17thC Montelupe maiolica dish, painted with a nobleman on horseback in landscape, two rim chips and a 6¾in (17cm) hairline crack from rim to center.

13in (33cm) diam

$2,100-2,600   TEN

A late-17thC Montelupo maiolica equestrian charger, painted with a soldier brandishing a sword as his horse gallops between trees, cracked.

12½in (32cm) diam

$550-650   WW

A late-17th/early-18thC Italian maiolica charger, probably Castelli, Abruzzo, painted with a horse boss in the center within two bands of horses and stylized foliage.

6½in (42cm) diam

$2,600-4,000   DN

Judith Picks

While unusual and striking shapes can be one of the attractions of Italian maiolica—I have in mind some coffeepot-like wet-drug jars, urnlike vases, and intricately reticulated plates—the overriding visual appeal almost invariably resides not in the form of the piece, but in the artistic skills of the decorator and the warmth and vibrancy of the palette employed. That's certainly the case with this splendid Italian maiolica dish, which probably dates from the 17thC.

Mythological figures and events were a particularly popular source of imagery on 16thC and 17thC Italian maiolica, and in this instance the winged horse Pegasus,

offspring of Olympian god Poseidon and the Gorgon Medusa in Greek mythology, provides the subject. One of the many legends associated with Pegasus—who is appealingly depicted here in a chubby, almost cherublike manner—is that, whenever his hooves struck the earth, a spring of water bursts forth, and that is probably what is being portrayed within the surrounding landscape. Pleasingly rendered in a warm, organic palette of high-fired yellow, ocher, orange, and green, contrasted with pale and lapislike blues—the latter for rocks and mountains—it's a composition that I would happily play permanent host to!

An Italian maiolica dish, with Pegasus leaping a river, a long, riveted crack.

12¼in (31cm) diam

$5,300-5,900   WW

A Naples maiolica albarello, painted with St Francis receiving the stigmata, inscribed above the foot with "Matteo Lofreda," with rim cracks.

ca. 1740   9in (22.7cm) high

$400-450   WW

A pair of late-19thC Cantagalli maiolica pedestal urns, decorated with allegorical figures, with scrolling snake handles, cockerel mark on base.

11¾in (30cm) high

$1,600-2,100   L&T

A 19thC maiolica charger, painted with a Classical scene depicting Marcus Aurelius.

16¼in (41.5cm) wide

$450-550   CHEF

An 18thC Italian maiolica albarello, probably Savona, titled "Cons di Antos" between leaf swags in blue and manganese, some glaze chipping.

7½in (18.8cm) high

$260-400   WW

A late-19thC Cantagalli Iznik-style vase, painted in typical shades of blue, red, green, and black, with flower heads under intersecting saz leaves, the shoulders with two crescent handles with a flower-head border, black cockerel mark.

16¼in (41.5cm) high

$4,600-5,300   WW

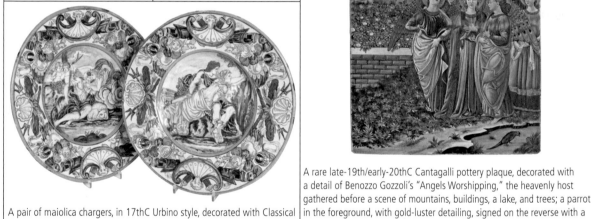

A pair of maiolica chargers, in 17thC Urbino style, decorated with Classical scenes, "GM" marks on the reverse.

15¾in (40cm) diam

$850-1,000   CHEF

A rare late-19th/early-20thC Cantagalli pottery plaque, decorated with a detail of Benozzo Gozzoli's "Angels Worshipping," the heavenly host gathered before a scene of mountains, buildings, a lake, and trees; a parrot in the foreground, with gold-luster detailing, signed on the reverse with a large cockerel.

20¾in (52.3cm) high

$18,000-21,000   WW

An Italian cylindrical drug jar, decorated in puce with a cartouche, inscribed "UNG MOND API."

9¾in (24.5cm) high

$400-550   CHEF

An Italian maiolica bulb pot, painted with birds and flowers, formed with three bulb holes and three handles, rim with 2in (5cm)-long repaired section.

ca. 1900   *7in (18cm) diam*

$200-260   DN

A pair of 20thC Italian maiolica vase-shaped table lamps, with zoomorphic masks and pierced handles, decorated with birds and animals amid foliage and grapes.

18½in (47cm) high

$3,300-4,000   CHEF

ESSENTIAL REFERENCE—CREAMWARE

Emerging in the mid-18thC, creamware was developed in Staffordshire as a more affordable alternative to expensive porcelain and as a finer and more durable alternative to tin-glazed earthenware (delft or faience).

● The initial formula for creamware is credited to Thomas Astbury, ca. 1720-40, who fired at low temperature a mix of flints and Devonshire clays covered with "smithum" (lead) powder to produce a hard, whitish earthenware with a rich, yellow-tinged glaze.

● From ca. 1740, improvements in constituents and firing were made by Enoch Booth, producing a cream-color earthenware with a lustrous glaze of uniform tint and thickness.

● Further improvements were made by the great entrepreneurial industrialist Josiah Wedgwood, with the help of potters Thomas Whieldon and William Greatbatch: in 1759, the cream color was made whiter; in 1760, a glaze was developed that concealed underlying blemishes while making it totally impervious to liquids and scratch-resistant to cutlery; and, in 1775, more purified ingredients made the body even stronger and lighter.

● Following a royal commission from Queen Charlotte in 1765, Wedgwood renamed his creamware "Queen's Ware."

● Other notable makers of creamware included: Enoch Wood, Davenport, Leeds Pottery, and Messrs Sadler & Green of Liverpool.

A pair of mid-18thC Staffordshire creamware plates, molded with swags of fruit and flowers, including pear and plum, some rim faults.

8¾in (22cm) diam

$550-650   WW

A Dutch-decorated creamware plate, painted with profile portraits of William V of Orange and Wilhelmina of Prussia beneath an orange tree, inscribed in Dutch, small rim faults.

ca. 1767-75   9¾in (24.5cm) high

$600-650   WW

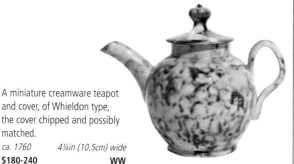

A miniature creamware teapot and cover, of Whieldon type, the cover chipped and possibly matched.

ca. 1760   4¼in (10.5cm) wide

$180-240   WW

A Leeds creamware plate, painted with a European gentleman walking across a purple-and-white checkered floor before a town house, the rim with flower sprigs in a feathered border, some restoration.

ca. 1770-75   10in (25cm) diam

$450-600   WW

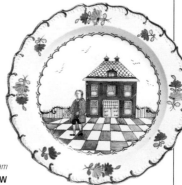

A George III Staffordshire creamware plate, painted with the inscription "Elizh, Delbeth 1782," with floral and foliate decoration, cracked with stapled repair.

9½in (24.2cm) diam

$800-850   MART

A late-18th/early-19thC creamware gelatin mold core, possibly Wilson, painted on one side with a three-masted ship at sail in a choppy sea, the sides and reverse with military trophies and motifs, the base pierced with six holes, a crack around the base.

10¼in (26cm) wide

$550-650   WW

An 18thC creamware model of a horse, by Ralph Wood, the body sponged in orange and brown, standing on a gray rectangular base.

8¾in (22cm) long

$4,000-5,300   CHEF

A late-18thC Staffordshire creamware model of a cat.

4¼in (11cm) long

$350-400   DN

A creamware pitcher, painted on one side with an anchor within a floral garland above the Isle of Man triskelion encircled by "Quocunque ieceris stabit," the other side with a lion attitude within a shield beneath a stag crest and the motto "Will God and I Shall," beneath the spout inscribed "EEK," hairline cracks, a little restoration.

The motto may relate to the Ashburnham family of West Sussex, who were linked by marriage to the Stanley family on the Isle of Man.

ca. 1800   *14¼in (36.2cm) high*
$1,300-1,800   **WW**

A creamware pitcher, possibly by John Sadler of Liverpool, printed in black and hand colored with a British sailing ship, inscribed "Success to the William & Jane, John Roberts," the reverse with the figure of Hope resting on an anchor.
ca. 1800   *9½in (24cm) high*
$750-850   **WW**

A creamware condiment stand or cruet set with a pepper shaker, sugar sifter, oil and vinegar bottles, and a mustard jar, titled in black, three covers replacements.
ca. 1800   *10in (25.5cm) high*
$210-260   **WW**

A creamware pitcher, of Masonic interest, printed in black with the Masons' Arms on one side, beneath the spout with a set square and compasses, the reverse with further Masonic symbols, with a restored crack.
ca. 1800   *7¼in (18.3cm) high*
$750-850   **WW**

A Brameld creamware figure of a deer, her coat glazed a rich brown.
ca. 1800   *6in (15.3cm) long*
$600-650   **WW**

CLOSER LOOK–CREAMWARE RHYTON

The makers of the cup, Guistiniani, were one of Naples's best-known ceramic factories from the early 17thC to the late 19thC.

Following Napoleon's Egyptian campaign in the late 1790s, Egyptian-style decoration enjoyed numerous revivals in popularity throughout the 19thC, including after the opening of the Suez Canal and the discovery of the pyramids at Giza in the 1860s and 70s.

Known in the Graeco-Roman vocabulary of ornament as "aegricanes," ram and goat heads have been a recurringly fashionable decorative motif and are often associated with Bacchus, the Roman god of wine and fertility.

Primarily used for ceremonial drinking, especially before the start of a journey or enterprise (such as hunting), animal-head rhytons (from a Greek word meaning "to flow," and also known as stirrup cups) date back to prehistoric times.

A late-18th/early-19thC creamware figure, modeled as a Medici Lion with his forepaw resting on a ball.
4¼in (11cm) high
$550-650   **WW**

A 19thC Naples (Giustiniani) creamware rhyton or stirrup cup, formed as a ram or goat head, the rim painted in Egyptian Revival style.
7¾in (19.5cm) long
$550-650   **WW**

A rare Ralph Wood pearlware figure of John Milton, standing beside a pillar molded with scenes from "Paradise Lost," leaning on a stack of books resting on the top, decorated in green, blue, black, and manganese glazes, repairs on both hands.

This apparently unrecorded figure differs from the models produced at Derby and by later Staffordshire manufacturers, but it may well still have been a companion figure to one of Shakespeare.
ca. 1790-1800   11½in (29.5cm) high
$3,300-4,000   WW

A pearlware beer pitcher and cover, painted by William Absolon of Yarmouth, with a couple riding in a pony and trap, the rim with husk swags, inscribed "A Present from Yarmouth," chipping on the cover.
ca. 1790   8in (20.5cm) high
$1,700-2,400   WW

A Ralph Wood pearlware model of St George and the Dragon, St George pushing his metal spear into the mouth of the dragon, minor faults.

The legend of St George and the Dragon tells of St George (d. AD 303) taming and slaying a dragon that demanded human sacrifices.
ca. 1780-90   11¾in (29.5cm) high
$1,500-2,000   WW

A pearlware farming or harvest pitcher, painted on one side with a shield with farming implements, the reverse with an English landscape, inscribed "R Arnold 1798," with some chipping on the spout.
1798   8in (20.3cm) high
$1,000-1,100   WW

Two pearlware models of dappled gray horses, of St. Anthony's Pottery type, painted in manganese, ocher, blue, green, and brown, with checkered saddle clothes, the smaller restored through back hocks and hooves and both ears, the larger with restored and replaced ears, cracks, and riveted repairs.
ca. 1800   7in (18cm) and 7¼in (18.5cm) high
$6,000-6,600   DN

A pair of Yorkshire pearlware sheep, on grassy bases, with ocher detailing, a little restoration on one.
ca. 1800   5¾in (14.5cm) long
$550-600   WW

A small Staffordshire pearlware figure of a leopard, repairs on his tail, right paw, and ears.

This model is based on one produced at the Derby porcelain factory.
ca. 1800   2½in (6.3cm) long
$400-450   WW

A late-18thC/early-19thC pearlware "capuchine pigeon" tureen and cover, after Derby, a little restoration.

Derby produced similar tureens of this old fancy breed from the 1760s.
6¾in (17cm) long
$600-750   WW

A pearlware pitcher, depicting John Bull "Shewing the Corsican monkey."

The satirical Napoleonic imagery is inspired by Isaac Cruikshank's original etching of ca. 1803.

7in (18cm) high

$1,100-1,250   **CHOR**

A pearlware Napoleonic pitcher, printed and hand colored with the "Cossack Mode of Attack," the mounted Russian charging at two Frenchmen, some wear.

The French defeat in Russia at the end of 1812 demonstrated that Napoleon was not invincible nor the military genius that many supposed him to be. Cf. David Drakard, "Printed English Pottery," pp. 226-228 for a discussion of wares using these prints.

ca. 1813   *6in (15cm) high*

$160-240   **WW**

A Staffordshire pearlware bust of Napoleon.

10in (25cm) high

$1,000-1,100   **CHOR**

An early-19thC English pearlware figure group "The Dandies" or "Dandy and Dandizette."

7in (18cm) high

$600-750   **CHOR**

An early-19thC miniature pearlware fish charger, molded with a flat fish, the rim with a floral design.

4¼in (10.6cm) long

$400-450   **WW**

A Swansea pearlware plate, painted with a swan swimming before mountains, within a basket-weave band glazed green, impressed Dillwyn & Co., Swansea.

ca. 1830   *7¾in (20cm) diam*

$600-650   **WW**

A pair of Yorkshire pearlware figures, the ram modeled with a shepherd, a young lamb at its feet, the ewe modeled with a shepherdess, twin lambs at its feet.

ca. 1820   *6¼in (15.5cm) high*

$4,000-5,300   **L&T**

A Staffordshire pearlware figure of a pug dog, with a green studded collar, on a tasseled cushion, the tail restored.

ca. 1820-40   *3¼in (8.3cm) high*

$260-330   **WW**

A pearlware liquor barrel, with an iron-red inscription of "JWG 1849."

1849   *6in (14.8cm) wide*

$400-450   **WW**

A Staffordshire salt-glazed stoneware "house" teapot and cover, molded on each side with a town house, one side with a coat of arms above a closed door, the reverse with a lion rampant above a fleur de lis and a figure standing in an open doorway, the handle formed as a serpent, some restoration.

ca. 1740   7in (17.7cm) wide

$1,600-2,100   **WW**

A Staffordshire salt-glazed stoneware teapot and cover, the heart or shield shape molded with a fruiting grapevine design, the spout molded as a serpent and shell motifs, minor damage on the end of the spout.

ca. 1740-45   6¾in (17cm) wide

$3,300-4,000   **WW**

A salt-glazed stoneware coffeepot and cover, painted with a Chinese lady sitting on a chair and entertaining a small child, the reverse with a Chinese man carrying small panniers on a yoke, the spout molded with C scrolls, some restoration.

ca. 1750   6½in (16.5cm) high

$1,500-1,800   **WW**

A salt-glazed stoneware plate, with a bearded beggar or fortune-teller looking at the palm of a young shepherdess, some restoration on the rim.

ca. 1750   9in (22.5cm) diam

$400-550   **WW**

A salt-glazed stoneware coffeepot and cover, enameled with a colorful bird perched on turquoise rockwork, the reverse with flowering plants, the long spout formed as a serpent, a little restoration on the spout.

ca. 1750   8¾in (22cm) high

$7,500-8,500   **WW**

A Staffordshire salt-glazed stoneware teapot and cover, painted with a rosebud and flower sprays, on an unusual black caillouté ground, with crab-stock spout, handle and finial, minor damages.

ca. 1760   7¼in (18.5cm) wide

$2,000-2,600   **WW**

A rare early-19thC Derbyshire stoneware cat, a flat chip beneath the base.

7½in (19cm) high

$400-450   **WW**

A Turner dry-bodied stoneware pitcher, molded in high relief with "The Archery Lesson," a young girl taking aim at a target while a couple stand behind her, impressed mark, a rim chip.

ca. 1800   7¾in (19.5cm) high

$130-200   **WW**

A brown stoneware commemorative pitcher, with portraits of Queen Victoria and her mother, the Duchess of Kent, with a metal cover with hinged spout.

ca. 1837-50   12¼in (31cm) high

$170-210   **WW**

A possibly 17thC stoneware Bellarmine, the neck molded with a bearded man, with a loop handle.

13½in (34cm) high

$800-900   **CHEF**

A stoneware Bellarmine pticher, the neck molded with a bearded man, with a loop handle.

11in (28cm) high

$600-650   **CHEF**

A Bayreuth brown-glazed stoneware teabowl and saucer, possibly by an Augsburg hausmaler, after Meissen's Böttger stoneware, with silberChinesen decoration, with "Laub-und-Bandelwerk" decoration, the teabowl broken and reattached.

ca. 1730-40   *4¾in (11.8cm) diam*

$1,000-1,100   **WW**

A Westerwald stoneware pitcher, applied with carnation sprays, decorated in blue on a rich manganese ground.

Westerwald Stoneware is a distinctive type of salt-glazed gray pottery from the Höhr-Grenzhausen and Ransbach-Baumbach area of Westerwaldkreis in Rheinland-Pfalz, Germany. It is typically decorated with cobalt-blue painted designs, although the more collectible items are usually multicolored.

ca. 1680   *6¼in (16cm) high*

$850-1,000   **WW**

A Westerwald stoneware Royal pitcher, with a portrait plaque of King William III, titled around the portrait with "WILHELMVS III. DG. MA BRI. FRA. ET HIB. REX" (William III, by the Grace of God, King of Great Britain, France, and Ireland), on a ground of incised and applied stylized flowers.

ca. 1690   *4¼in (10.8cm) high*

$7,500-8,500   **WW**

A Westerwald stoneware pitcher, with a heart with entwined flower stems, with further flower tendrils, a crack on the handle.

ca. 1700   *7in (17.6cm) high*

$600-750   **WW**

A Westerwald stoneware Royal pitcher, with the crowned initials "AR" for Queen Anne within a laurel wreath, broken and reattached.

ca. 1710   *7in (18cm) high*

$1,600-2,000   **WW**

A Westerwald stoneware tankard, incised with flowering tendrils and trellis panels, beneath the handle incised "1786 TG," the pewter lid with the initials "PG."

1786   *9in (23cm) high*

$260-330   **WW**

An 18thC Westerwald stoneware tankard, with a formal floral design, with a hinged pewter cover, a chip on the foot rim.

7½in (18.8cm) high

$160-240   **WW**

An early-19thC John Rogers and Son transferware meat dish, from the "Indian Views" series, printed with figures leading a laden ox before ruins, titled "Monopteros," a section broken and reattached.

The view on this charger is one of a series of engravings by Thomas and William Daniell, which were published in London in the late 18thC and early 19thC.

20¾in (52.5cm) wide.

$450-550   **WW**

A Wedgwood transferware charger, decorated with the botanical "Waterlily" pattern, broken and reattached.

This design derives from prints in the "Botanist's Repository" and the "Botanical Magazine," from 1803-6. The design was probably inspired by the interests of Josiah Wedgwood's eldest son John, who was a founder member of the Royal Horticultural Society.

ca. 1810   18½in (47cm) wide

$150-200   **WW**

CLOSER LOOK—TRANSFERWARE

The charger was made by the Don Pottery, in the Yorkshire town of Swinton. Established 1801 by John and William Green, the pottery initially made mostly good quality cream-color earthenware, and from ca. 1810-30 also produced high-quality porcelain exported worldwide. The Greens sold up in 1839.

The border decoration draws for inspiration on a number of decorative sources: the scrolling foliate forms and the ornate torchères are Classical Greco-Roman in origin, while the floral imagery is in the form of "Manierblumen" (scattered flowers) initially developed at Meissen in the second half of the 18thC.

Constructed 1609-1616 in Constantinople (now Istanbul), the 13-dome, 6-minaret, Ottoman-era mosque of Sultan Ahmet I is also and better known as the "Blue Mosque."

While the male figures on the balcony are dressed in authentic-looking early-19thC Ottoman dress, the female's A-line attire owes more to contemporary English Regency fashions.

An early-19thC Don Pottery transferware charger, from the "Ottoman Empire" series, titled "Mosque of Sultan Achmet."

18¾in (47.6cm) wide

$550-600   **WW**

An early-19thC transferware "Durham Ox" charger, printed with the bull standing beside his owner, John Day, from the print by J. Whessell after the painting by John Boultbee.

The Durham Ox was the result of an intensive breeding program and became famous after being toured around the country by his aristocratic owner. In the early 1800s, London tourists paid a total of £97 in admission fees.

19¾in (50cm) wide

$2,600-4,000   **WW**

An early-19thC Spode transferware meat dish, from the "Indian Sporting" Series, printed with "Driving a bear out of the sugar canes," a bear being chased by dogs and figures on foot, horseback, and on an elephant.

16¼in (41.5cm) wide

$1,050-1,300   **WW**

A Spode transferware cheese cradle, printed in the "Rome" or "Tiber" pattern with the "Castle and Bridge of St Angelo," with a printed mark.

This pattern was inspired by two views taken from engravings found in" Views of Rome and its Vicinity" published by J. Merigot and R. Edwards, London, 1796-98.

ca. 1820   12in (30.5cm) wide

$1,200-1,450   **WW**

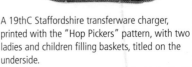

A 19thC Spode transferware soup tureen with cover and stand, printed with the "Lucano Bridge" pattern, with printed marks.

The Bridge of Lucano by James Merigot, published in 1798 in "A Select Collection of Views and Ruins in Rome and Its Vicinity - Executed from Drawings Made Upon the Spot in the Year 1791," for the source print.

16½in (42cm) wide

$600-650   **WW**

A 19thC Staffordshire transfer-printed meat platter, decorated in the "Bee Keeping" pattern with a family and courting couple in a country park landscape, within a rose border.

22in (55.5cm) wide

$850-1,000   **CHOR**

A 19thC Staffordshire transferware charger, printed with the "Hop Pickers" pattern, with two ladies and children filling baskets, titled on the underside.

19in (48.5cm) wide

$260-400   **WW**

A 19thC transferware charger, printed with figures trekking ponies through an Eastern landscape with a view of Monopteros, the rim with trailing branches, gourds, and growing plants.

20½in (52cm) wide

$350-400   **WW**

An historical Staffordshire platter, depicting the Southwest View of La Grange, Residence of the Marquis Lafayette, staining on underside, shallow chip on rim.

20½in (52cm) long

$550-650   **POOK**

A 19thC Staffordshire transfer-decorated "Gold Coast" platter, by Enoch Wood and Sons, Burslem, England, showing the famous coast of Africa, shell border.

16¾in (42.5cm) long

$400-550   **SK**

An historical Staffordshire "Landing of Lafayette" platter, rim with an area of glaze burn.

15¼in (38.5cm) long

$600-750   **POOK**

An historical Staffordshire transfer-decorated "Fair Mont Near Philadelphia" covered tureen and undertray, attributed to Enoch Wood & Sons, with scene and eagle and floral border, the lid with molded floral handle, embossed eagle and acanthus leaf, and printed eagle and floral border, the bottom of the undertray with printed title, the lid has restoration, tureen has in-painted chips on one handle.

ca. 1828   *15½in (39.5cm) wide*

$1,100-1,250   **SK**

A pair of historical Staffordshire plates, with portraits of Lafayette, light staining.

7½in (19cm) diam

$650-800   **POOK**

An historical Staffordshire transfer-decorated "Landing of Lafayette" tureen and undertray, by James and Ralph Clewes, Cobridge, England, with leafy handles, chips on handles and on the base, the lid has restoration on one corner.

ca. 1824-36   *9¾in (24.5cm) wide*

$400-450   **SK**

An historical Staffordshire transfer-decorated "Landing of Lafayette" serving bowl, by James and Ralph Clewes, Cobridge, England, professional restoration on the foot.

ca. 1824-36   *9½in (24cm) wide*

$1,050-1,200   **SK**

A Staffordshire glazed redware milk pitcher, sprigged with a flower spray in cream slip on a treacle-glaze ground.

ca. 1745   *4¼in (11cm) high*

$400-450   **WW**

A Staffordshire salt-glazed teapot and cover, painted with flower sprays beneath a trellis panel border, with crab-stock spout and handle, the cover's finial broken and reattached.

ca. 1760   *7in (17.6cm) wide*

$550-650   **WW**

A Staffordshire salt-glazed teapot and cover, painted with a lady with a washing dolly in a tub, flanked by flowering plants, the reverse with a bird perched on flowers, the cover's finial lacking.

ca. 1760   *6½in (16.4cm) wide*

$750-850   **WW**

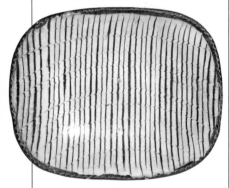

A mid-18thC Staffordshire combed slipware dish, decorated with a cream ground combed with brown stripes of slip, with piecrust indentations on the rim, some wear.

15¼in (39cm) wide

$6,500-8,000   **WW**

A mid-18thC Staffordshire salt-glazed bear-baiting pitcher and cover, the bear being baited by a dog held between its paws, the head cover with a ringed open nose, the body applied with rough grains of clay, the collar and the eyes picked out in brown slip.

10in (25.5cm) high

$4,600-5,300   **L&T**

A pair of 18thC Staffordshire cornucopia vases, of Whieldon type, the bodies resting on shells and molded with mask heads, the bases molded with foliage, with feathered rims.

6¼in (16cm) high

$1,700-2,100   **CHEF**

A Staffordshire figure group, of three children squabbling over a hat full of fruit, titled "Contest," small damages and restorations.

ca. 1800   *7¾in (19.5cm) high*

$260-330   **WW**

A late-18th/early-19thC Ralph Wood figure of "Old Age," modeled as an old man resting on a crutch with shoulders hunched.

The Wood family were Staffordshire potters. Among its members were Ralph Wood I (1715–72), his son Ralph Wood II (1748–95), and his grandson Ralph Wood III (1774–1801). The first two Ralphs were among the best modelers in Staffordshire pottery of their day, noted for their Staffordshire figures.

8¾in (22.3cm) high

$400-450   **WW**

A Staffordshire bust of Minerva, probably by Ralph Wood, wearing a plumed helmet and draped with a yellow robe over one shoulder, on a waisted socle, a few chips.

ca. 1800-10   *12¾in (32.5cm) high*

$1,600-2,100   **WW**

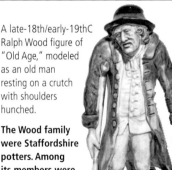

An early-19thC Staffordshire marbled figure of a dog, decorated with pale blue striations.

The modeling is similar to that of Jennings' Dog, a Roman marble sculpture now in the British Museum.

8in (20.5cm) high

$260-330 WW

An early-19thC Staffordshire pottery leech jar, decorated in cobalt blue with gilt details, labeled "LEECHES," impressed "M. TOMLINSON/ HULME" on the base.

18¼in (46cm) high

$4,000-4,600 L&T

A Staffordshire figure of a peacock, some good restoration.

ca. 1820 *4in (10.1cm) high*

$160-240 WW

An early-19thC Staffordshire drabware money box, modeled as a Georgian building, titled "Savings Bank" on the thatched roof, a coin slot flanked by chimneys on the cover, one chimney restored.

6¾in (17.1cm) high

$400-450 WW

A John Walton Staffordshire figure of the English crowned lion, with flowering bocage and on a grassy base, applied "WALTON" banner on the reverse, a chip on the base, losses on the bocage.

It is believed that the man behind the Walton mark found on many early-19thC enamel-painted figures was John Walton and that he was active in Burslem from ca. 1806 until ca. 1835.

ca. 1820 *6in (15cm) high*

$3,300-4,000 WW

A pair of 19thC Staffordshire lion and lamb groups, each lion sitting on its haunches with head turned over its shoulder, a lamb at its side.

6¾in (17cm) high

$3,300-4,000 WW

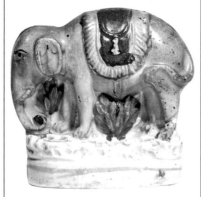

A 19thC Staffordshire figure of an elephant.

3¼in (8.5cm) high

$180-240 WW

A pair of Staffordshire pottery rabbits, each with black spotted markings eating a lettuce leaf, restored ears, repainted black area, crazed.

ca. 1870 *9¾in (25cm) long*

$6,500-8,000 TEN

A pair of 19thC Staffordshire boot flasks, in a running manganese glaze.

7¾in (19.5cm) long

$80-90 WW

ESSENTIAL REFERENCE—AMERICAN REDWARE

A utilitarian form of earthenware made from clays with a high iron content, which, when fired, turn a reddish-brown color, redware was originally made in Europe, but it became particularly popular in North America, initially during the Colonial era, because such clays were abundant there and the products were affordable.

- Being porous, redware needed to be waterproofed for food storage, cooking, dining, and drinking vessels, typically with lead-base glazes.
- Decorative imagery was either incised into the clay's surface, sometimes employing a "sgraffito" technique in a thin layer of slip to reveal the red-color clay beneath, or was applied using contrasting colors of glaze and slip.
- John Pride, of Salem, Massachusetts, is documented in the mid-17thC as the first American redware potter by name.
- Although redware was mostly supplanted by stronger and more refined stoneware and whiteware during the mid-19thC, production did continue into the 20thC, most notably in regions of North Carolina, Pennsylvania, and Virginia.

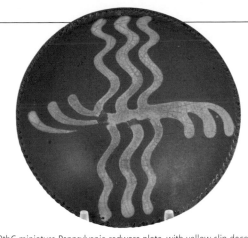

A 19thC miniature Pennsylvania redware plate, with yellow slip decoration, a couple flakes.

5¼in (13.5cm) diam

$900-1,200   POOK

An early-19thC redware bowl, Hagerstown, Maryland, attributed to Henry Adam (1782-1819).

Henry Adam is considered by some of the leading redware experts as the best in North America.

10¼in (26cm) diam

$12,000-15,000   POOK

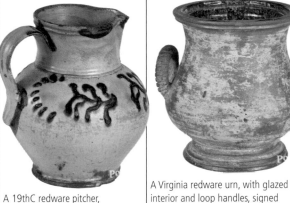

A 19thC redware pitcher, Hagerstown, Maryland, with manganese seaweed decoration, rim chip, glaze wear, old base chips.

7¼in (18.5cm) high

$4,600-5,300   POOK

A Virginia redware urn, with glazed interior and loop handles, signed Abraham Miller Winchester, one handle replaced, other handle reattached, hairline crack.

1877   *11¼in (28.5cm) high*

$2,000-2,600   POOK

A redware vase, Winchester, Virginia, with applied birds on floral sprigs, signed by potter Anthony Wise Bacher (Baecher), incised on base "A. W. Bacher," handles restored, one bird with repaired head and wing.

ca. 1880   *8½in (21.5cm) high*

$4,000-5,300   POOK

A redware vase, Winchester, Virginia, with tree decoration on opposing sides, signed by potter Anthony Wise Bacher (Baecher), one handle restored, glaze loss.

1887   *6in (15cm) high*

$4,600-5,300   POOK

A Shooner redware figure of a potter at his wheel.

7in (18cm) high

$800-1,050   POOK

A Pennsylvania redware figural whistle, of a man playing the bass, lacking bow and one tuning peg.

ca. 1900   *8in (20.5cm) high*

$2,600-3,300   POOK

ESSENTIAL REFERENCE—MOCHAWARE

A type of utilitarian, slip-decorated earthenware, Mocha or Mochaware is distinguished by its dendritic (tree-, branch-, twig-, or weedlike) decorative patterns that broadly resemble the natural geological markings on moss agate. The latter was known in Great Britain in the late-18thC as "Mocha stone," because it was imported from Arabia primarily through the port of Mocah (al Mukha) located in what is now the Yemen.

The first Mochaware was made ca. 1799 in England by William Adams of Tunstall, Staffordshire, who had discovered that by dripping a colored acidic solution into a wet alkaline slip the color would instantly reconfigure into the aforementioned dendritic patterns. While Mochaware production gradually increased in the 19thC throughout Great Britain, and also, notably, spread to France, it became especially popular in North America. Documented sales and purchases, along with archaeological finds, reveal that Mochaware was in widespread use throughout the eastern United States, in taverns and homes alike—including Thomas Jefferson's Monticello! Notable makers included the Bennet Pottery Company of Baltimore, in Maryland; the Brockville Works of Pottsville, Pennsylvania; and the Shenandoah Pottery in Virginia.

A Mocha pitcher, with marbleized decoration and molded sun at base of spout, hairline crack on base of handle, small flake on spout.

5½in (14cm) high

$1,200-1,300   **POOK**

A rare footed Mocha lidded pitcher, with marbleized glaze, a few small flakes on lid rim.

6in (15cm) high

$6,000-6,600   **POOK**

A Mocha pitcher, with unusual seaweed-over-fan decoration, a crow foot left of handle, hairline crack across base.

7½in (19cm) high

$2,000-2,600   **POOK**

A Mocha mug, with combed bands, hairline cracks around handle.

6in (15cm) high

$1,500-2,000   **POOK**

A Mocha mug, with bull's-eye design on a dark brown ground, base sprayed.

4¾in (12cm) high

$1,700-2,100   **POOK**

A Mocha lidded bowl, with engine-turned decoration, two flakes on inner rim of lid.

7½in (19cm) wide

$4,600-5,300   **POOK**

A large Mocha bowl, with twig decoration.

11¼in (28.5cm) diam

$6,000-6,600   **POOK**

A Mocha pepperpot, with fan decoration on a rust ground, repairs on raised rim, small flake on base.

5½in (14cm) high

$4,000-5,300   **POOK**

A Wood family "Thin Man" Toby jug, holding the stem of his clay pipe in his teeth, supported by his right hand, wearing a green coat, his hat and hair washed in manganese, some damages, his jug of ale lacking.

A Toby Jug is a pottery jug in the form of a sitting person. Typically, the sitting figure is a heavy-set, jovial man holding a mug of beer in one hand and a pipe of tobacco in the other. The tricorn hat forms a pouring spout, often with a removable lid, and a handle is attached at the rear. The original Toby Jug, with a brown salt glaze, was developed by Staffordshire potters in the 1760s. Similar designs were produced by other potteries, first in Staffordshire, then around England, and eventually in other countries.

ca. 1780 *10in (25cm) high*
$4,600-5,300 **WW**

A Prattware Toby jug, sitting with a foaming jug of ale on his knee, his clay pipe resting by his left foot, a wart to his nose and chin, some restoration on the hat.

ca. 1800 *9½in (24cm) high*
$850-1,000 **WW**

A Prattware Toby jug, resting a foaming jug of ale on his left knee, a line of blue dots on the handle, some restoration on the hat and handle.

ca. 1790-1800 *9½in (24.3cm) high*
$450-600 **WW**

A Prattware Toby jug, sitting and wearing a sprig-patterned coat over green breeches and striped stockings, the jug of ale on his knee overflowing down one side, some restoration on the hat.
ca. 1800 9½in (24.3cm) high
$1,600-2,000 **WW**

A Ralph Wood creamware Toby jug, of "Mold 51" type, sitting with an empty jug on his left knee, raising a cup of ale to his lips with his right hand, damages.

ca. 1790-95 *10in (25.3cm) high*
$1,000-1,100 **WW**

A late-18thC Ralph Wood-type "Ordinary" Toby jug, sitting holding a foaming jug of ale and with a barrel between his feet, restored.

10¼in (26cm) high
$400-450 **FLD**

A late-18thC Ralph Wood-type "Ordinary" Toby jug, sitting wearing a translucent blue frock coat with brown breaches holding a foaming jug of ale.
9in (23cm) high
$2,000-2,600 **FLD**

A rare Prattware "Thin Man" Toby jug, sitting with a patterned jug of ale, wearing a sponge-decorated coat over a patterned vest and yellow breeches, his cheeks rouged, damage on one foot.

ca. 1790-1800 *9in (22.7cm) high*
$6,500-8,000 **WW**

A pearlware Ralph Wood-type "Ordinary" Toby jug, sitting with a barrel between his feet and a disappointingly empty jug on one knee, some restoration to the hat.

The molding around the base of this jug is more commonly associated with the Collier Toby.

ca. 1790   *9¾in (25cm) high*

$600-750   **WW**

A Staffordshire pearlware Toby jug, a little restoration to the hat.

ca. 1790   *10in (25.5cm) high*

$550-600   **WW**

A 19thC Yorkshire pearlware Toby jug, with an empty cylindrical mug resting on his left knee, his jug and the base unusually decorated with blue shamrock, some restoration.

9¾in (25cm) high

$450-550   **WW**

A pearlware "Ordinary" Toby jug, with a replacement handle.

ca. 1800   *9¾in (24.3cm) high*

$550-650   **WW**

A "Skew Face" Toby jug, his face with a gormless expression, with restoration on his hat.

ca. 1800   *8in (20.7cm) high*

$400-550   **WW**

A Mexborough (Yorkshire) Toby jug, typically modeled with an empty jug of ale and a hexagonal goblet, with a caryatid handle.

ca. 1820-30   *9¾in (25cm) high*

$600-750   **WW**

A 19thC Yorkshire-type Toby jug, sitting holding a jug and a wine glass, the handle formed as a ship's figurehead, painted "2G1 Black" on base.

10¼in (26cm) high

$400-550   **FLD**

A 19thC "Ordinary" Toby jug and stopper, typically modeled with a jug of ale, decorated in Portobello colors, the stopper associated, some damages to the stopper.

10¼in (26.3cm) high

$200-260   **WW**

A Leonard Jarvis creamware Winston Churchill commemorative Toby jug, in the manner of Ralph Wood, one hand raised in a victory salute, incised to the base "The Rt Hon WINSTON S CHURCHILL O.M., C.H, F.R.S., M.P.," signed and numbered "301," nicks on the top of the paint brushes, hairline crack to forehead, restored hat.

ca. 1951   *7in (18cm) high*

$600-650   **TEN**

ESSENTIAL REFERENCE—WEDGWOOD

Wedgwood was founded on May 1, 1759, by the English potter and entrepreneur Josiah Wedgwood and was first incorporated in 1895 as Josiah Wedgwood and Sons Ltd. It was rapidly successful and was soon one of the largest manufacturers of Staffordshire pottery, "a firm that has done more to spread the knowledge and enhance the reputation of British ceramic art than any other manufacturer," exporting across Europe as far as Russia, and to the Americas and then worldwide. It was especially successful at producing fine stonewares that were accepted as equivalent in quality to porcelain but were considerably cheaper. Wedgwood is especially associated with the "dry-bodied" (unglazed) stoneware Jasperware in contrasting colors, and, in particular, that in "Wedgwood blue" and white, always much the most popular colors, although there are several others. Jasperware has been made continuously by the firm since 1775, and it was also much imitated due to its success.

In the 18thC, Wedgwood's table china in the refined earthenware creamware became particularly desirable, and while in the later 19thC it was both a leader in design and technical innovation, it continued to make many of the older styles that remained popular.

In 1987, Wedgwood merged with Waterford Crystal to create Waterford Wedgwood plc, an Ireland-based luxury brands group.

An early-19thC Wedgwood Jasperware jardinière or wine cooler and stand, with fruiting grapevine issuing from lion masks, the stand with palmettes, impressed mark and commas, minor faults.

14½in (36.5cm) high

$400-450   WW

An early-19thC Wedgwood Jasperware coffee can and saucer, with Classical figures and motifs between flower garlands issuing from ram heads, impressed marks.

5¼in (13.2cm) diam

$750-850   WW

A late-18th/early-19thC Wedgwood caneware miniature tea service, modeled after the Chinese as vertically banded bamboo, with a teapot and cover, a teapot and cover with overhead handle, two teabowls, two coffee cups and two saucers, impressed marks.

Wedgwood Caneware is pale yellow fine textured stoneware. Josiah Wedgwood first produced trials of this type of ware in 1771. Regular production began in 1776 and continued until 1940. A range of products, including tea wares, vases, small statues, and medallions, have been produced.

$1,600-2,100   WW

A Wedgwood creamware pitcher, printed in black, one side with the "Tithe Pig" group above lines of verse, the other with haymakers dancing before a tall rick, beneath the spout inscribed "Richard Monk, Mawdsley, 1786."

Mawdsley is a village in Lancashire, England, on the southern border of the borough of Chorley.

1786   *(22.5cm) high*

$2,400-2,900   WW

A Wedgwood caneware canopic inkwell and cover, with applied black basalt hieroglyphs in relief, fitted interior, impressed mark.

5¼in (13.5cm) high

$4,600-5,300   SK

A Wedgwood green Jasperware canopic jar and cover, with applied white bands of hieroglyphs and Zodiac signs above Egyptian motifs, impressed mark.

Canopic jars were used by the ancient Egyptians during the mummification process to store and preserve the viscera of their owner for the afterlife. They were commonly either carved from limestone or were made of pottery. Wedgwood's design of the canopic jar was based on engravings from Montfaucon. So few Egyptian antiquities existed outside of Rome, it is not surprising that almost all of Wedgwood's designs appear to have been made from prints. Montfaucon's "L' Antiquite Expliquée" was a copiously illustrated, 15-volume encyclopedia and an attempt to compile everything that European scholars knew of ancient art in the 1720s.

ca. 1876   *9¾in (24.5cm) high*

$6,000-7,500   SK

POTTERY

A Wedgwood black Jasperware Neoclassical pot-pourri vase and cover, molded with floral garlands suspended from rams heads, impressed mark, with a pair of cache pots, impressed marks.

vase 15in (38cm) high

$1,000-1,100   CHEF

A Wedgwood Jasperware vase and cover, applied lilac and green with a band of Zodiac symbols above Classical Muses below flowering festoons, impressed mark.

9in (23cm) high

$4,600-5,900   SK

A Wedgwood Jasperware urn and cover, boxed.

11¾in (30cm) high

$260-330   PSA

A 19thC Wedgwood Jasperware vase, light blue body with green and lilac acanthus and bellflowers above Classical figure groups, impressed mark.

7in (18cm) high

$850-1,000   SK

ESSENTIAL REFERENCE—PORTLAND VASE

The Portland Vase is a Roman cameo glass vase that is dated to between AD 1 and AD 25. It is the best-known piece of Roman cameo glass and has served as an inspiration to many glass and porcelain makers from about the beginning of the 18thC. It is first recorded in Rome in 1600–1. It was sold at auction in 1786 and passed into the possession of William Cavendish-Bentinck, 3rd Duke of Portland.

● **The 3rd Duke lent the vase to Josiah Wedgwood. Wedgwood devoted four years of trials to duplicating the vase—not in glass but in black and white Jasperware. He had problems with his copies, ranging from cracking and blistering to the sprigged reliefs "lifting" during the firing, He finally managed to perfect it in 1790, with the issue of the "first-edition" of copies. Wedgwood put the first edition on private show between April and May 1790, with that exhibition proving so popular that visitor numbers had to be restricted by printing only 1,900 tickets, before going on show in his public London showrooms.**

● **The Wedgwood Museum, in Barlaston, near Stoke-on-Trent, England, contains a display describing the trials of replicating the vase and several examples of the early experiments are shown.**

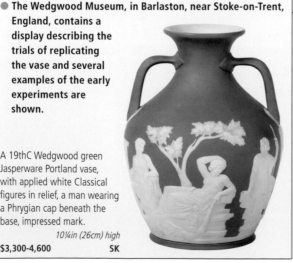

A 19thC Wedgwood green Jasperware Portland vase, with applied white Classical figures in relief, a man wearing a Phrygian cap beneath the base, impressed mark.

10¼in (26cm) high

$3,300-4,600   SK

A pair of Wedgwood black basalt wine and water ewers, the water ewer with a figure of Triton sitting atop the shoulder and holding the horns of a marine monster below the spout, aquatic festoons on each side, the wine ewer with a figure of Bacchus sitting atop the shoulder and holding the horns of a ram head below the spout, fruiting grapevine festoons on each side, impressed marks, one professionally restored on side of spout and handle, each with corner chips on plinths.

15½in (39.5cm) high

$4,000-4,600   SK

A 19thC Wedgwood "Rosso Antico" urn and cover, applied black basalt Classical figures in relief, the base with fruiting festoons between ram heads and ribbons, impressed mark.

7¾in (19.5cm) high

$1,200-1,450   SK

A Wedgwood encaustic decorated black basalt vase, iron red, black, and white decorated with figure on a chariot, impressed mark.

Josiah Wedgwood introduced into production a black stoneware body in 1768. It was made from reddish-brown clay that burned black in firing. Wedgwood's black basalt body owed its richer color to the addition of manganese. Wedgwood introduced new forms of decoration—bronzing and encaustic painting, copying the ancient Greek and Italian vases—that needed a smooth surface, and black basalt was the ideal body. Wedgwood said of his newly developed body: "Black is Sterling and will last forever."

15½in (39.5cm) high

$8,000-9,000   SK

A slipware flask, inscribed "Jno, Ashton 1795 Ies, Stingo Drink again John," chipped spout, crazed all over.

1795   *8¼in (21cm) high*

$2,600-3,300   **TEN**

A Barnstaple slipware harvest pitcher, inscribed "The ring is Round and Hath no End so is my Love unto my Friend/Evan and Elanor Dalton, Aberystwith 1826," with a broken and glued U-shape section of rim above the handle, old chips on the foot.

1826   *9½in (24cm) high*

$8,500-10,000   **CHOR**

A 19thC West Country slipware charger, decorated with Charles II standing in the Boscobel Oak with armed soldiers, inscribed "Charles Rex" and "Ye Royal Oake," broken and repaired.

19in (48cm) diam

$800-900   **WW**

A late-19thC Staffordshire slipware charger, with a mermaid, above a panel with an indistinct name, around the rim inscribed "With a comb and a glass in her hand," cracked.

16¼in (41cm) diam

$1,600-2,100   **WW**

A Duke of York Prattware pitcher, molded with profile portrait of the Duke of York, the reverse, Louis XVI, his wife and the Dauphin.

The Grand Old Duke of York – Frederick Augustus. Duke of York and Albany 1763-1827.

ca. 1793   *5¾in (14.6cm) high*

$95-100   **MART**

A Prattware figure of a young boy leaning against a branch on which perches an owl, a break at the top of the stump.

ca. 1800-10   *10in (25.2cm) high*

$550-650   **WW**

Two Yorkshire Prattware cow and calf figures, the pearlware body of each with sponged and painted decoration, modeled with a female milkmaid standing alongside and a calf lying on the grass below.

ca. 1820   *6in (15cm) high*

$2,400-2,900   **L&T**

A 19thC Prattware figure of a cat on a cushion, hollow slip cast.

3in (7.5cm) wide

$550 650   **L&T**

THE ASIAN MARKET

Asian works of art – whether ceramics, jade, metalware, furniture or textiles – have been selling well compared to other categories of antiques, and the market is becoming a lot more discerning, with top prices being reserved for rare pieces, especially those with Imperial provenance and for early pieces of exceptional quality. However, it is important to note that there has also been considerable fluctuations in price. For example, a particular lot may fetch a record price in Britain, but a similar lot may fail to meet a much lower reserve in the US or China – or the reverse.

Chinese collectors are particularly discerning, increasingly knowledgeable about fakes and reproductions, and look for pieces that are 'fresh to the market'. There is strong demand for rare and unusual Chinese snuff bottles in particular, as well as top-quality jade. Early textiles are also in demand, although condition is everything, as is furniture with good provenance. However, the problem with ivory continues, and with a ban now firmly in place on the sale of all ivory (barring a few exceptions), I have omitted ivory items from this chapter because those few exceptions are extremely difficult to value.

In contrast to the latter, Celadon porcelain continues to excite when of exceptional quality, such as the bowl on page 82 valued at $400,000-530,000. Other monochromes, especially with an Imperial connection, such as the Qianlong copper-red glazed zhadou on page 83 valued at $110,000-130,000, are also highly sought-after. Conversely, the market for blue and white Chinese wares, barring very rare pieces, has quietened. On the other hand, Transitional wares (1620-1683) have continued to stimulate buyers, particularly when beautifully painted and telling a traditional tale, such as the vase on page 87 with the God of Longevity watching a dance, valued at $80,000-90,000. Indeed, it's always important with Asian pieces to understand the symbolism of the decoration. This is exemplified in the Wanli wucai 'Zun' vase on page 106: it features prunus or plum – a symbol of purity and beauty, and a magpie – a harbinger of joy, while its leafy bamboo symbolises longevity and steadfastness. These symbols contribute significantly to its desirability and value – the latter being $200,000-260,000.

It is also worth noting this recent observation by Lee Young, Managing Director and Head of Asian Art at Dore & Rees Auctions: 'We have, over the last few years, seen a noticeable increase in the number of buyers for Japanese items, resulting in higher prices in key areas such as cloisonné and mixed-metal wares. However, the regained vigour of the Japanese market is still overshadowed by the considerable strength of the Chinese market, one consequence being European and American collectors are now often unable to compete with new and extremely affluent Chinese purchasers intent on buying back their heritage.'

Top Left: A Chinese Qianlong cloisonné weight of a mythical beast, gilt rubbed and with enameling.

3in (7.8cm) wide 12.7oz

$7,500-8,500   **SWO**

Above: A large Meiji Satsuma vase, by Kinkozan, with flora and fauna decoration, both naturalistic and formalized.

18¼in (46.5cm) high

$13,000 18,000   **WW**

CHINESE REIGN PERIODS AND MARKS

Imperial reign marks were adopted during the Ming dynasty, and some of the most common are illustrated here. Certain emperors forbade the use of their own reign mark to avoid any disrespect from a broken vessel bearing their name being thrown away. This is where the convention of using earlier reign marks comes from—a custom that was enthusiastically adopted by potters as a way of showing their respect for their predecessors.

It is worth remembering that a great deal of Imperial porcelain is marked misleadingly, and pieces bearing the reign mark for the period in which they were made are, therefore, especially sought after.

EARLY PERIODS AND DATES

Xia dynasty	ca. 2000-1500 BC	Three Kingdoms	221-280	The Five dynasties	907-960
Shang dynasty	1500-1028 BC	Jin dynasty	265-420	Song dynasty	960-1279
Zhou dynasty	1028-221 BC	Northern and Southern dynasties	420-581	Jin dynasty	1115-1234
Qin dynasty	221-206 BC	Sui dynasty	581-618	Yuan dynasty	1260-1368
Han dynasty	206 BC-AD 220	Tang dynasty	618-906		

EARLY MING DYNASTY REIGNS

Hongwu	1368-98	Zhengtong	1436-49
Jianwen	1399-1402	Jingtai	1450-57
Yongle	1403-24	Tianshun	1457-64
Hongxi	1425	Chenghua	1465-87
Xuande	1426-35		

MING DYNASTY MARKS

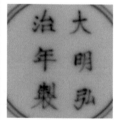
Hongzhi
1488-1505

Zhengde
1506-21

Jiajing
1522-66

Wanli
1573-1619

Chongzhen
1628-44

QING DYNASTY MARKS

Kangxi
1662-1722

Yongzheng
1723-35

Qianlong
1736-95

Jiaqing
1796-1820

Daoguang
1821-50

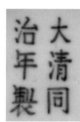
Xianfeng
1851-61

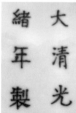
Tongzhi
1862-74

Guangxu
1875-1908

Xuantong
1909-11

Hongxian
1915-16

A large Chinese Tang pottery model of a horse, raising its front right leg dramatically, with its mouth agape and nostrils flaring, its strong body defined with its muscles, with traces of black and red pigment on the surface, its tail removable.

31½in (80cm) long

$13,000-20,000   **WW**

CLOSER LOOK—TANG FIGURES

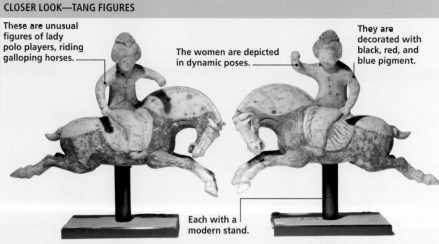

These are unusual figures of lady polo players, riding galloping horses.

The women are depicted in dynamic poses.

They are decorated with black, red, and blue pigment.

Each with a modern stand.

A pair of Chinese Tang painted pottery figures.

12¼in (31cm) and 12¾in (32.5cm) high

$8,500-10,000   **WW**

A Chinese Song Yaozhou ware vase, incised with a floral spray above a banana leaf border, glaze cracks, glaze flake on rim and another on foot rim.

7½in (19cm) high

$2,600-4,000   **SWO**

A rare Chinese Southern Song celadon bird feeder, scratches on the glaze and one firing blemish on the reverse.

2¼in (5.4cm) wide

$1,050-1,600   **DN**

A Chinese Ming Longquan celadon bowl, the body molded with stiff leaves, the shoulder with five-petal florets in relief, with a lobed rim, surface scratches.

10¼in (26cm) diam

$3,300-4,600   **SWO**

A Chinese large Longquan vase, carved with two bands of foliage beneath a stiff leaf border, and above a vertical ribbed band, the foot rim unglazed revealing the gray foot rim burned to orange in places, drilled in the base.

20¾in (52.5cm) high

$8,500-10,000   **DN**

A 13thC Chinese Southern Song Longquan celadon vase, with a bluish-green kinuta-type glaze, fitted hardwood base, with Japanese wood box, scratches in the glaze and several old chips largely on the underside of the foot rim.

6in (15cm) high

$80,000-90,000   **DN**

A Chinese Ming Longquan celadon plate, the center incised with a sprig of florets, warped, surface scratches, foot rim grounded.

10¾in (27.5cm) diam

$1,300-2,000   **SWO**

A 16thC Chinese Ming celadon garden seat, the top carved with a peony, and four further peony roundels on the trellis-incised body.

15in (38cm) high

$2,000-2,600   **CHEF**

ASIAN CERAMICS

A rare large early-18thC Chinese celadon-glazed porcelain bowl, the exterior finely carved with sprays of peony and mallow, above peach, pomegranate, and persimmon (the Suando), with clusters of swirling clouds, the foot rim with brown dressing, Yongzheng six-character seal mark in blue on the base and of the period.

13½in (34.5cm) diam

$400,000-530,000　　　　　　　　　　　　　　AB

CLOSER LOOK—GE-TYPE VASE

The vase has ram handles, "Hu."

It is decorated with pendent plantain leaves in low relief.

While the shape of this piece is familiar, it is rare to find vases with two ram-head handles; more common are those decorated with dragon handles or two zoomorphic ring handles.

All under a pale gray crackled glaze with a lattice of larger rust crackles enclosing smaller regular crackles.

A Chinese Qianlong archaistic Ge-type vase, one handle restored, the rim with one chip and restored, underglaze-blue Qianlong seal mark.

10½in (26.5cm) high

$13,000-16,000　　　　　　　　　　　　　　DN

A Chinese late Qing celadon gu-shaped vase, carved with four peony blooms among scrolling leafy tendrils, with raised flanges forming the stems of stiff pendent leaves on the flared neck and foot.

7¼in (18.6cm) high

$6,000-6,600　　　　　　WW

A Chinese Qing celadon glazed pear-shaped vase, carved with stylized lotus sprays beneath bands of ruyi-heads and upright pendent leaves, with two applied elephant head-shaped handles, the base with a six-character Qianlong mark.

11¼in (28.7cm) high

$19,000-21,000　　　　　　WW

A Chinese ge ware brush washer, with thick, opaque, crackled glaze of pale grayish-cream color.

4¾in (12cm) diam

$2,600-4,000　　　　　　SWO

A 19thC Chinese celadon vase, decorated with lotus flowers in relief, on a lotus form rosewood stand, Qianlong mark on base.

16¼in (41cm) high

$600-750　　　　　　DAWS

A mid-17thC Chinese blanc-de-Chine wine pot and cover, formed as a gourd, molded with prunus branches, the cover with a flower-shaped knop and set in silver-gilt mounts, which join to the loop handle forming a hinge.

5¼in (13cm) high

$7,500-8,000　　　　　　WW

An 18thC Chinese blanc-de-Chine figure of Guanyin, with her hair piled in a chignon and adorned with blossoming flowers, a rocky table at her feet supports a finger citron and smaller fruit.

9¼in (23.5cm) wide

$4,000-5,300　　　　　　WW

An 18th/19thC Chinese blanc-de-Chine figure of Buddha, depicted sitting in "dhyanasana," his bare chest centered by a fylfot, raised on a lotus base adorned with flowers and beads, with a six-character Wanli mark and a six-character maker's mark.

10¼in (26cm) high

$6,000-6,600 WW

A Chinese Dehua model of Guanyin, after He Chaozong, signed, with middle right hand finger tip chipped off.

13½in (34.5cm) high

$450-600 CHEF

A Chinese Kangxi langyao bottle vase, decorated with a rich red, crackled flambé glaze scattered with pale specks, the glaze draining from the rim leaving it white and pooling to a deep burgundy at the foot, with a pale mint green glaze on the base.

The term "langyao" used to describe this type of glaze derives its name from Lang Tingji, who was the director of the official kilns at Jingdezhen from 1705 to 1712. It is believed that he was responsible for the revival of monochrome glazes and that the langyao glaze developed under his supervision.

16in (40.6cm) high

$16,000-20,000 WW

A Chinese pink-enameled teabowl, the interior white and the base with a six-character Kangxi mark within double circle.

2½in (6.3cm) diam

$5,300-8,000 DN

A Chinese Qing flambé-glazed huluping gourd-shaped vase, decorated with a deep red crackled glaze draining from the rim, with vibrant lilac and purple streaks throughout the glaze, the base with a six-character Kangxi mark.

14¼in (36cm) high

$2,600-3,300 WW

A Chinese Qianlong Imperial copper-red glazed zhadou, the compressed body rising to a wide flared rim, the exterior coated in a copper-red glaze that darkens at the foot and mouth rim, the interior and base glazed white, six-character Qianlong mark.

The color of this glaze is also known as "sacrificial red." According to legend, the Xuande Emperor (r. 1426-35) wanted to use a set of bright red ceramics to make offerings to the sun, and so he instructed the workers at the Jingdezhen kilns accordingly. Despite numerous attempts, they were unable to create the red the Emperor desired, and so, unsatisfied by their work, he threatened to execute the workers. Upon hearing this news, one of the potter's daughters went to the kilns, only to find that her father had been imprisoned for failing to produce the correct color. In protest, she sacrificed herself by throwing her body into the blazing kiln. When the kiln was opened, the workers were astonished to find that all the ceramics inside were now red, supposedly having been stained by the girl's blood. This is one explanation for the origin of the term "sacrificial red."

5in (12.5cm) diam

$110,000-130,000 WW

An 18thC Chinese copper-red glazed meiping, decorated on the exterior with a mottled deep red glaze, the base and interior glazed white.

8½in (21.5cm) high

$20,000-26,000 WW

An 18thC Chinese Langyao incense burner, decorated with a rich red, crackled flambé glaze flecked with darker speckles, the color draining from the top, leaving the rim white.

8¾in (22cm) diam

$46,000-53,000 WW

A Chinese Qing copper-red glazed porcelain baluster vase, potted from a slightly flared foot rising to a bulbous body and long waisted neck.

16½in (42cm) high

$1,700-2,100 L&T

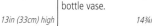

A Chinese Qianlong iron-rust glazed "Dragon" vase, decorated in relief with two applied dragons arching their backs and clutching onto the rim as their tails trail across the vase, the base unglazed.

8¾in (22cm) wide

$8,000-10,500 **WW**

An 18thC Chinese flambé-glazed bottle vase, the exterior coated in a rich red glaze with splashes of deep purple and speckles of lavender, the base drilled.

17¼in (44.2cm) high

$900-1,050 **WW**

An 18thC Chinese pomegranate flambé vase, some minor chips on base edge.

13in (33cm) high

$8,000-9,000 **PSA**

A 19thC Chinese sang-de-boeuf bottle vase.

14¾in (37.5cm) high

$2,200-2,600 **CHEF**

An 18th/19thC Chinese blue-glazed vase, the slender neck molded with four bands, some minor scratches in the glaze.

11¼in (28.5cm) high

$3,300-4,000 **DN**

A Chinese Guangxu blue-ground "Dragon" vase, painted in gilt with dragons among clouds chasing the flaming pearl, wear on gilding and small rim frits.

15in (38cm) high

$2,600-4,000 **DN**

A Chinese Kangxi powder blue-ground rouleau vase, decorated in gilt with a small figure in a sampan and others beside huts in a mountainous watery landscape.

Rouleau vases have straight cylindrical bodies with gently sloping shoulders rising to a straight, narrow neck, often with an everted rim. Well-suited to scenic decoration (painted or printed), the shape originated in Jingdezhen in the mid-17thC.

11¼in (28.5cm) high

$8,500-10,000 **WW**

A pair of 18thC Chinese ceramic foo dogs, with thick blue glaze, with scrolled foliage patterns.

6¾in (17.5cm) high

$350-450 **DAWS**

A Chinese Guangxu or Republic clair-de-lune vase, the rim glazed in brown, the base with underglaze blue six-character Qianlong seal mark, with firing blemishes.

10¾in (27cm) high

$4,600-5,300 **DN**

ESSENTIAL REFERENCE—YIXING

- Pottery has been produced in Yixing, in Jiangsu Province, since the Neolithic period. The hills are endowed with rich clay deposits, and the center of pottery making is located around the small towns of Dingshan and Shushan. This area produces dragon jars of all sizes, vessels, roof tiles, porcelains, and most important of all, the zisha (or "purple sand') teapots and objects for the scholar's table. The term "Yixing ware" generally refers to teapots and vessels of rustic elegance long sought after by tea drinkers and scholars in China. Yixing teapots have been made since the 16thC, and there has been a steady stream of known potters since the Wanli period (1573–1619).
- Yixing teapot clay would absorb the aroma and flavor of the tea over time. After many years of use, a scholar would be able to brew tea by simply poring boiling water into the empty pot.

A large 18thC Chinese porcelain "Cadogan" teapot, with a deep eggplant (aubergine) glaze, the spout and handle in the shape of gnarled branches with leaves under a turquoise glaze, one leaf with a small chip.

10in (25cm) high

$8,000-10,500   SWO

A Chinese Guangxu turquoise glazed ritual vessel and cover, decorated in relief with quatrefoil and fan-shaped panels enclosing figures by a river, the cover with a chilong holding sprigs of lingzhi and incised with the characters "zhou lu pi ka yi pan," six-character Guangxu mark.

10in (25.3cm) wide

$6,000-6,600   WW

A Chinese Qing Yixing teapot and cover, the base incised with a mark reading "Shi Da Bin yu Tian Xiang Ge zhi."

7½in (19cm) high

$15,000-17,000   WW

A Chinese dish, the exterior and interior coated in a pale pea-green glaze, the base glazed white and with six-character Qianlong mark, but probably later.

6½in (16.5cm) wide

$2,600-4,000   WW

A Chinese Kangxi Yixing hexagonal-section teapot and cover, decorated in relief with a floral spray, one side set with an auricular loop handle issuing from the mouth of a mythical beast.

5¾in (14.5cm) high

$1,300-2,000   WW

A large Chinese Qing Yixing "Phoenix" teapot and cover, the cover with a knop shaped as a lion dog with a cub, the underside of the cover and the handle with marks reading "Shao Wen Yuan."

$4,000-4,600   WW

A large late-18th/early-19thC Chinese Yixing teapot and cover.

7¾in (19.5cm) high

$1,300-2,000   WW

A large 18thC Chinese Yixing "Lion Dogs" teapot and cover, decorated in relief with two large peony sprays, the shoulder applied with four stylized archaistic mythical beasts, the domed cover with a finial formed as a large lion dog and her pup, the beasts finely incised with the details of their fur.

9in (22.5cm) high

$3,300-4,000   WW

A Chinese Qing Yixing teapot and cover, the compressed circular body with raised lips encircling the rim and foot, the base incised "yu zhen zhi wan" and with a signature reading "Dabin for Shi Dabin."

5¼in (13cm) wide

$6,000-6,600   WW

ASIAN CERAMICS

CLOSER LOOK—LANDSCAPE VASE

This is an excellent example of a Wanli (1573-1619) "Landscape" vase.

The shoulder is decorated with four cartouches containing floral sprays, the panels reserved on diaper grounds divided by ruyi motifs—ruyi being a symbol of good fortune.

It is painted with a continuous scene of houses and figures dispersed throughout a rocky mountainous landscape.

The vase has a band of lappets encircling the base and a continuous scroll on the short waisted neck.

A large Chinese blue-and-white vase.

14½in (36.8cm) high

$24,000-26,000   **WW**

A Chinese Wanli blue-and-white "Qilin" saucer dish, painted with a centered medallion enclosing a qilin supporting a lantern decorated with banners on its back, flanked by two attendants, with lanterns divided by beribboned precious objects on the reverse, six-character Wanli mark.

8in (20.5cm) diam

$15,000-18,000   **WW**

A Chinese Wanli porcelain jar, painted with deer in a landscape within paneled borders, with a restored flat chip on side of foot.

14½in (37cm) high

$6,500-8,000   **TEN**

A large Chinese "Swatow" dish, painted in turquoise and black enamels with the Eight Trigrams encircling a yin-yang symbol, the centered medallion surrounded by a scene of fishing boats, the designs divided by iron-red bands.

ca. 1600   *15½in (39.3cm) diam*

$4,000-5,300   **WW**

A Chinese Wanli blue-and-white "Fish" saucer dish, painted in the center with a mackerel, whitefish, carp, and perch swimming amid aquatic flowers.

8¾in (21.8cm) diam

$1,700-2,100   **WW**

A 16th/17thC Chinese Ming blue-and-white "Boys" jar, painted with a continuous scene of boys at play in a lush garden setting, minor scratches on the exterior and interior, with some small firing cracks.

6¾in (17cm) high

$2,100-2,600   **DN**

A Chinese Wanli blue-and-white Kraak porcelain "Klapmuts" bowl, painted in the center with a medallion enclosing pagodas in a mountainous landscape, the design encircled by four cartouches containing frogs and birds.

"Klapmuts" is Dutch and refers to a cap or a hat of a particular shape. The klapmuts was the standard 17thC headgear of the Dutch poor. The less expensive was made out of wool while the more expensive was fashioned of beaver felt. The shape of this hat is the source of the name for the typical Dutch-market soup bowl of the late Ming dynasty, typically, as in this case, in Kraak decoration.

8¾in (22.3cm) diam

$1,700-2,100   **WW**

Judith Picks

I am always in wonder at these exceptional examples of exquisite porcelain from the Ming dynasty.

During the Ming dynasty (1368-1644), the rule of the foreign Mongol invaders broke down and China was once again under the rule of ethnic Chinese, because the Ming emperors resumed control. Porcelain manufacture reached new heights as the Ming emperors established official control over the "Porcelain City" of Jindezhen. This city was located on a tributary of the Yangtze, facilitating the transfer of raw materials necessary for porcelain production, such as wood and clay, as well as the transport of finished goods to points within China, and through the port of Shanghai, to export

markets abroad. Nearby deposits of native china clay and feldspar had initially led to the establishment of porcelain production at Jingdezhen, but with imperial patronage, production expanded quickly. At this time, there was no material in the world that commanded a higher price that porcelain; even gold was not valued so highly. The Ming rulers had a veritable gold mine at their disposal in Jingdezhen, because European and Middle Eastern royalty were willing to pay any price for this precious commodity, which their own potters were unable to produce.

The Eighteen Scholars depicted here are a renowned historical group of advisors who had served the Tang emperor Taizong (reigned AD 626–49) before he assumed the imperial seat.

A Chinese 16thC/17thC Ming blue-and-white "Eighteen Scholars" stem cup, with petal lappets encircling the underside, the foot bordered with pendent leaves, the rim bordered with a geometric band, with Japanese wood box, firing frits and scratches in the glaze, a star crack on the interior, and other firing marks.

5¾in (14.5cm) diam

$17,000-21,000   **DN**

A Chinese Wanli blue-and-white Kraak porcelain bottle vase, painted with panels of flowers, hanging baskets, and tassels.
10¾in (27.5cm) high
$1,600-2,000 WW

A Chinese Transitional blue-and-white stem cup, decorated with three boys playing with a kite in a rocky setting above sprays of bamboo.
ca. 1640 4¼in (11cm) high
$9,000-10,500 WW

A large Chinese Transitional blue-and-white mug, painted with two figures in a rocky landscape beneath hanging willow tree branches, with a loop handle on one side.
ca. 1640 8in (20cm) high
$8,000-9,000 WW

A Chinese Transitional blue-and-white baluster vase, painted with a king and his attendants greeting a wise old man in a rocky landscape, all below a incised foliate band.
ca. 1640 10¼in (26cm) high
$22,000-26,000 WW

A Chinese Transitional blue-and-white ewer, decorated with mountainous wooded landscapes surrounded by floral sprays, with a band containing bearded faces on the shoulder, one side set with a large loop handle painted with dots.
ca. 1640 14in (35.5cm) high
$3,300-4,000 WW

CLOSER LOOK—TRANSITIONAL VASE

This is a fine-quality Transitional sleeve vase.

The scene is contained within finely incised foliate scrolls, with a band of pendent leaves encircling the mouth rim.

It is painted with Shoulao sitting with a deer and his attendants behind him, the God of Longevity watching a dance performance in a rocky mountain setting.

An incense burner before him emits smoke that rises in the shape of a shou character.

A Chinese Transitional vase.

For the sake of providing a working date, the Transitional period in Chinese ceramics is considered to have started with the death of the Wanli emperor in 1620. It spanned the changeover from the Ming to Qing dynasty in 1644 and extended to the arrival of Zang Yingxuan as director of the Imperial factories at Jingdezhen in 1683.
ca. 1640 17¾in (45cm) high
$80,000-90,000 WW

A near pair of 17thC Chinese Tianqi/Chongzhen dishes for the Japanese market, both decorated in underglaze blue with a buffalo herder and four oxen, one dish with a band of 10 rhomboids above following the rim, with tendrils on the undersides.
8¼in (21cm) diam
$3,300-4,000 WW

A Chinese Transitional blue-and-white bitong (brush pot), painted with a man presenting three halberds in a vase to an official, the scene divided by swirling clouds and rocky cliffs.

The image of a vase containing three halberds forms the rebus "ping sheng san ji" meaning "may you rise three ranks in quick succession" and thus expresses the wish for an imminent promotion.
ca. 1640 7¼in (18.7cm) high
$17,000-20,000 WW

ASIAN CERAMICS

A Chinese Transitional blue-and-white sleeve vase, painted with King Wen of Zhou and his attendants happening upon Jiang Ziya by the bank of a river in a rocky landscape, with plantain trees, shrubs, and swirling clouds around them, with incised lines on the rim, shoulder, and foot.

According to traditional Chinese historical records, the episode depicted occurred in the 11thC. Having become disillusioned with serving the cruel and corrupt last king of the Shang dynasty, the military strategist Jiang Ziya relinquished his duties and went into exile, living as a fisherman. When King Wen of Zhou came across Jiang Ziya while hunting, he was so impressed by his knowledge on military tactics that he appointed Jiang Ziya as his prime minister. With Jiang Ziya's assistance, the Shang dynasty was overthrown and the Zhou dynasty was founded.

ca. 1640 *19in (48.5cm) high*

$26,000-33,000 **WW**

A Chinese mid-17thC Transitional blue-and-white jar, painted with birds in a flower garden with rose and magnolia, two faults on the rim possibly from firing, several star cracks on the interior but not visible from the outside, scratches in the glaze.

10¾in (27.5cm) high

$6,500-8,000 **DN**

A Chinese Transitional blue-and-white sleeve vase, painted on the exterior with figures welcoming a deity and her attendants as they arrive on a phoenix, all in a rocky wooded landscape, with wispy clouds on the reverse, the scene contained within incised floral and geometric bands.

Provenance: from the collection of Professor Ronald N. Arnold (1908-63) and thence by descent. Professor Arnold was Regius Professor of Engineering at Edinburgh University, Scotland, from 1947 until his death. Following ill health, in 1953 he began to collect Chinese porcelain in his free time, buying most of his pieces from small antique stores and auctioneers in Edinburgh and London. Through the art historian David Talbot-Rice, Professor Arnold became acquainted with several experts in the field of East Asian ceramics, including Sir Harry Garner and Soame Jenyns.

17¼in (43.8cm) high

$70,000-90,000 **WW**

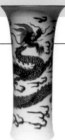

A Chinese Shunzhi blue-and-white "Dragon" sleeve vase, painted with a large four-clawed dragon in pursuit of a sacred pearl amid stylized flames.

The Shunzhi period ran from 1644-61.

16¾in (42.5cm) high

$8,000-10,500 **WW**

A Chinese Shunzhi blue-and-white "Qilin" sleeve vase, the tall cylindrical body flaring at the rim, painted with a qilin sitting in a landscape amid rockwork and plantain, with pendant leaves and sprays of pomegranate and magnolia below.

1644-61 *6in (40.6cm) high*

$7,500-8,500 **WW**

A rare Chinese early Kangxi blue-and-white dish, painted with a lady standing in a garden, she holds a fan in one hand and a sprig of osmanthus held to the sun, presenting the flower to a young boy.

The Chinese word for osmanthus is "guihua," which is homophonous with "guizi," meaning "your honorable son." The image of a lady pointing osmanthus toward the sun therefore expresses the wish for a son to be a scholar official holding a high position in court. The bamboo in the background is emblematic of the scholar's upright character, because it is a tough plant that bends in the storm but never breaks. The plum blossom is also symbolic of the moral strength required to be an official, because they are hardy plants that can survive the winter.

14in (35.8cm) diam

$24,000-29,000 **WW**

A Chinese Shunzhi blue-and-white "Qilin" dish, painted with the scaly mythical beast sitting in a landscape with a plantain tree and rocks in the background, the underside decorated with three precious objects, the base with a four-character mark reading "Zhi Lan Zhai zhi."

1644-61 *11¼in (28.5cm) diam*

$7,500-8,500 **WW**

A Chinese Kangxi blue-and-white "Baxian" Yen Yen vase, painted with cartouches, each enclosing one of the Eight Immortals standing in a fenced garden holding their attributes, the panels reserved on a carved ground of peony flower heads blooming amid scrolling foliage, with a wood stand.

17¼in (43.8cm) high

$26,000-32,000 **WW**

A Chinese Kangxi blue-and-white molded four-piece garniture, decorated with horizontal bands of molded ogee petal panels enclosing white sprays of potted peony blooms.

tallest 21in (53.5cm) high

$18,000-21,000   **WW**

A Chinese Kangxi blue-and-white triple gourd vase, painted with two literati in a rocky landscape with precious objects, minute chips on glaze around foot rim.

9¼in (23.5cm) high

$6,000-7,500   **SWO**

A Chinese Kangxi blue-and-white charger, painted with phoenixes standing on rocks among peony, chips on rim and foot rim.

13¼in (33.8cm) diam

$2,600-3,300   **SWO**

A Chinese Kangxi blue-and-white box and cover, the cover painted with a roundel containing archaistic vessels among beribboned precious objects, with blossoming peony and chrysanthemum blooms growing amid rockwork.

7¼in (18.5cm) diam

$7,500-9,000   **WW**

A Chinese Kangxi blue-and-white "Master Of The Rocks" dish, painted with a landscape scene, detailed with a small dwelling by the bank of a river and with mountains in the distance.

10¾in (27.5cm) diam

$4,000-5,300   **WW**

A Chinese Kangxi blue-and-white double-walled bowl, the interior painted with three floral sprays, the outer bowl carved in openwork with three fylfot medallions set amid a honeycomb pattern, with a beribboned lingzhi on the base.

**A fylfot is a swastika. A peculiarly formed cross, each arm of which has a continuation at right angles, all in the same direction, used as a symbol or as an ornament since prehistoric times in China.
Lingzhi, or "Ganoderma lingzhi," also known as reishi, is a polypore fungus ("bracket fungus") belonging to the genus Ganoderma.**

6in (15cm) wide

$900-1,200   **WW**

A Chinese Kangxi blue-and-white gu-shaped vase, painted with attendants and an official, the centered section painted with two cartouches enclosing a pair of cranes and a horse galloping over crashing waves, with another figural scene on the foot.

18¼in (46.5cm) high

$10,500-13,000   **WW**

A near pair of Chinese Kangxi blue-and-white molded baluster vases and covers, painted with flower heads and buds, with insects in flight, one vase with a geometric band encircling the rim.

22¾in (58cm) high

$9,000-12,000   **WW**

A pair of rare Chinese Kangxi blue-and-white erotic subject vases, each vase painted with scenes from "The Romance of the Western Chamber," each painted with a couple engaged in amorous pursuits on the base.

10¼in (26cm) high

$20,000-24,000   **WW**

CLOSER LOOK—KANGXI VASE

This pattern is known as a "San tang yin yue."

It is painted with a large ship sailing toward the "Three Pools Mirroring the Moon" on Hangzhou's West Lake.

It has temples, houses, and smaller boats dispersed through the rocky mountainous setting.

The scene is contained between bands of lappets enclosing floral sprays and landscapes.

A Chinese Kangxi blue-and-white vase.

$7,500-8,500

19¼in (49cm) high

WW

A Chinese Kangxi blue-and-white "Phoenix" incense burner, painted with six phoenix medallions, the mythical birds divided by stylized clouds.

9½in (24cm) diam

$2,600-4,000

WW

A Chinese Kangxi blue-and-white "Insects and Flowers" bowl, painted with chrysanthemum, lotus, peony, prunus, and bamboo, with insects in flight, with a seal mark on the base.

7¾in (19.7cm) wide

$6,500-8,000

WW

A Chinese Kangxi Imperial blue-and-white "Palace" bowl, painted with six lotus flower heads on a scrolling branch, with a band of lappets encircling the foot, the well decorated with a medallion enclosing a single lotus bloom, six-character Kangxi mark.

6¼in (16.2cm) wide

$17,000-21,000

WW

A pair of Chinese Kangxi blue-and-white flasks, painted with alternating panels of flowers and antiques, with beribboned precious objects on the shoulders.

8¼in (21.2cm) high

$2,600-4,000

WW

A large Chinese Kangxi blue-and-white vase, painted with ladies holding flowers and parasols in a garden as pairs of birds fly above.

18¼in (46.7cm) high

$6,500-8,000

WW

A Chinese Kangxi blue-and-white porcelain vase, painted with two kylin among sea rocks, beneath clouds and the moon, the neck cut down with later white metal mount, scratches on glaze.

9½in (24cm) high

$4,000-5,300

CHEF

A Chinese Kangxi blue-and-white gu vase, decorated with cartouches enclosing court ladies and flowerpots on stands, the bottom drilled and the foot rim with two chips in the glaze.

This is sometimes referred to as the "Long Eliza" pattern.

16½in (42cm) high

$6,500-8,000

DN

ASIAN CERAMICS

A pair of Chinese Kangxi blue-and-white ewers, painted with scrolls in a shaped panel against a crackled-ice pattern ground, covers missing, one with chips to handle, spout and foot rim, and a hairline crack from rim to neck.

7in (17.5cm) high

$3,300-4,000 SWO

A Chinese Kangxi blue-and-white export porcelain gravy boat, after a French silver original, enriched in iron red and gilt on the scalloped rim, one frontal point chipped off.

ca. 1720-30 *9in (23cm) wide*

$200-260 CHEF

A Chinese blue-and-white "Lotus" bowl, painted with lotus flower heads and scrolling foliage above a band of ruyi heads, with a roundel enclosing a similar design in the center, six-character Yongzheng mark and of the period.

6in (15cm) wide

$60,000-70,000 WW

CLOSER LOOK—KANGXI ROULEAU VASE

This vase is painted with a scene from "The Water Margin."

It depicts a soldier lifting a bronze ding high above his head with one hand.

The three large windows behind looking out onto gusts of wind, a mountainous riverscape, and a carp leaping from crashing waves.

It is believed that, in ancient China, the act of lifting a bronze ding was a display of absolute strength and a demonstration of virility.

A Chinese Kangxi blue-and-white rouleau vase, the base with an artemisia leaf.

17½in (44.5cm) high

$33,000-40,000 WW

A pair of Chinese gilt-decorated blue-and-white "botanical" plates, after a design by Maria Sibylle Merian, each painted with caterpillars and butterflies crawling on and flying amid flag irises, all surrounded by scrolling foliate borders.

Maria Sibylla Merian (1647-1717) was a Swiss naturalist and artist living and working in the 17thC. One of her principal claims to fame is that she is one of the first naturalists to have studied insects. She recorded and illustrated the life cycles of 186 insect species.

ca. 1740 *9in (23cm) diam*

$2,200-2,600 WW

A Chinese Kangxi blue-and-white cup, painted with ladies with a tree and a planter, six-character mark, minute chip on rim.

2½in (6.1cm) diam

$6,000-6,600 SWO

A Chinese Qing blue-and-white porcelain bowl, internally painted with the bajixiang and shou, externally with the wanshou wujiang within a medallion of ruyi heads, among lotus sprays, with six-character Qianlong seal mark and of the period, small firing flaw on the double circle within the inner rim.

Painted with the stylized character "Shou," for longevity. Eight motifs surrounding the shou—the bajixiang—are attributes of the Eight Immortals, a group of immortal figures widely loved and usually associated with longevity.

7in (18cm) diam

$8,000-9,000 CHEF

A Chinese Qianlong Imperial blue-and-white "Sanxing" bowl, decorated with the Eight Immortals holding their attributes, they stand on pedestals formed from swirling clouds which float over wisps of mist, with a medallion enclosing the Fu Lu Shou standing under a pine tree in the well, with a six-character Qianlong mark.

6in (15cm) wide

$22,000-26,000   WW

An 18thC Chinese blue-and-white yuhuchun vase, painted with bamboo, flowers, and rocks by a fence in a garden, between a ruyi head and false gadroon borders, the neck with scrolls below bamboo and lingzhi, a crack on foot, minute glaze frit to rim.

15in (38cm) high

$8,000-9,000   SWO

A Chinese Qianlong underglaze-blue and red celadon-ground "Bats and Clouds" dish, the flying animals picked out in red, with a six-character Qianlong mark.

15½in (39.4cm) diam

$4,600-5,900   WW

A Chinese Qianlong blue-and-white porcelain dragon dish, with centered horned dragon pursuing a pearl among flames, the external wall with two further dragons, with a Qianlong seal mark.

6½in (16.6cm) diam

$13,000-17,000   CHEF

A Chinese 18thC Qing blue-and-white garlic-necked vase, decorated with a landscape scene, frittings and shallow glaze chips above the foot rim, rim professionally restored.

10¼in (26cm) high

$1,050-1,200   DN

A Chinese Qianlong blue-glazed "Hundred Bats" bottle vase, decorated in white slip with bats in flight amid stylized swirling clouds.

19½in (49.5cm) high

$17,000-21,000   WW

A Chinese 18th/19thC blue-and-white jar, decorated with a sitting scholar in a garden scene and an official receiving his guest, drilled in the shoulder on both sides, glaze scratches.

9½in (24cm) diam

$2,200-2,600   DN

A Chinese Jiaqing blue-and-white "Dragon" bottle vase, painted with three five-clawed dragons contesting a sacred pearl of wisdom amid swirling clouds and flames, contained between a band of ruyi heads and crashing waves.

Cf. "The Complete Collection of Treasures of the Palace Museum: Blue and White Porcelain with Underglazed Red," vol.3, p.157, no.143 for a similar Jiaqing mark and period vase in the Qing Court Collection.

12¼in (31cm) high

$8,000-10,500   WW

A Chinese Daoguang blue-and-white bowl, decorated with four characters, "Shan Gao Shui Chang" (lofty mountains, lengthy river), enclosed by ruyi heads flanked by two of the Eight Buddhist Emblems, the interior centered with a stylized shou medallion below ruyi at the rim, four-character mark "Daoguang Bingwu" on the base corresponding to 1846.

1846   6½in (16.7cm) diam

$8,500-10,000   SWO

A Chinese blue-and-white plate, painted with a dragon chasing a flaming pearl, enclosed with a scrolling lotus border, minute frits and glaze cracks on rim, chipsonto foot rim.

13½in (34.2cm) diam

$8,000-10,500   **SWO**

A Chinese Qing blue-and-white porcelain vase, painted with numerous figures among a pavilion by a lake.
ca. 1880   *11½in (29cm) high*
$850-1,000   **CHEF**

A pair of Chinese blue-and-white porcelain vases, painted with phoenixes in rocks among fowers, one badly damaged.
ca. 1880   *23¾in (60cm) high*
$1,500-1,800   **CHEF**

A Chinese blue-and-white porcelain vase, painted with six foo dogs among clouds, flames and ribbons, with four small chips on rim, small hairline crack on rim.
ca. 1880   *18¼in (46cm) high*
$1,050-1,200   **CHEF**

A Chinese blue-and-white porcelain "Yen Yen" vase, painted with two registers of pavilions in lakeland mountainous landscapes, with a hairline crack on rim.
ca. 1880   *17¼in (43.5cm) high*
$1,050-1,200   **CHEF**

A pair of 19thC Chinese Qing celadon-ground blue-and-white vases, molded and decorated in slight relief with the gathering up of the Eight Daoist Immortals in a landscape, the neck flanked with two chilong dragon handles, one vase restored on the rim, handles, and lower body.
24½in (62cm) high
$6,000-6,600   **DN**

A 19thC Chinese blue-and-white hexagonal-section garden seat, painted with lotus flower heads set amid scrolling leaves, with bands of raised bosses on each facet, decorated on the top and two sides with pierced cash motifs.
18½in (47cm) high
$2,600-3,300   **WW**

A 19thC Chinese blue-and-white vase, of gu form, decorated with figures in riverside and mountainous landscapes, fitted as a lamp, drilled in base with surface scratches.
17in (43.5cm) high
$850-1,100   **SWO**

A 19thC Chinese porcelain jar and cover, painted with river landscapes on cracked ice and prunus ground, general wear.
13¾in (35cm) high
$1,700-2,100   **TEN**

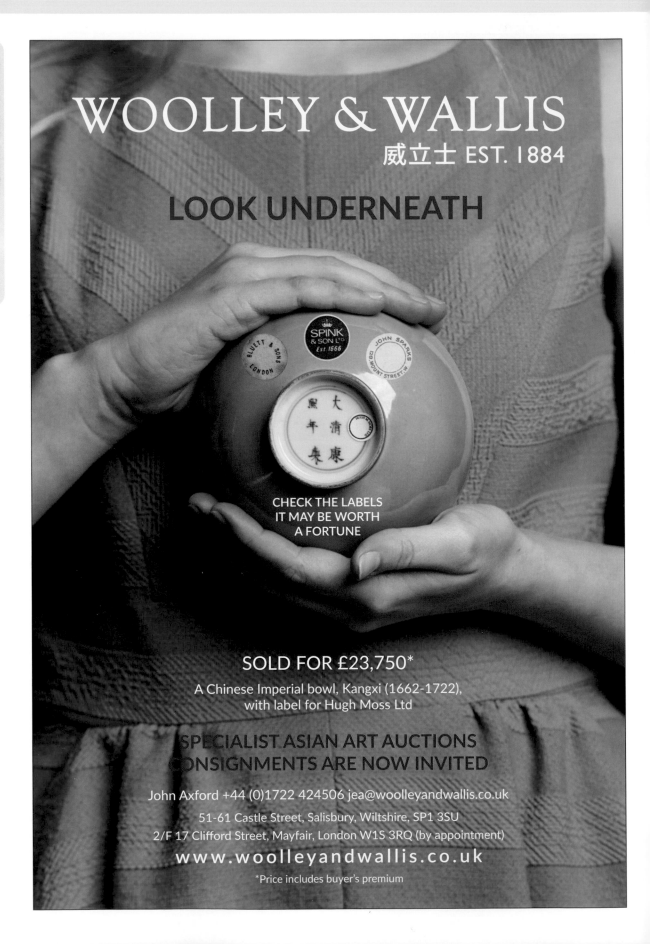

WOOLLEY & WALLIS

威立士 EST. 1884

LOOK UNDERNEATH

CHECK THE LABELS
IT MAY BE WORTH
A FORTUNE

SOLD FOR £23,750*

A Chinese Imperial bowl, Kangxi (1662-1722),
with label for Hugh Moss Ltd

SPECIALIST ASIAN ART AUCTIONS
CONSIGNMENTS ARE NOW INVITED

John Axford +44 (0)1722 424506 jea@woolleyandwallis.co.uk

51-61 Castle Street, Salisbury, Wiltshire, SP1 3SU

2/F 17 Clifford Street, Mayfair, London W1S 3RQ (by appointment)

www.woolleyandwallis.co.uk

*Price includes buyer's premium

A 19thC Chinese blue-and white export porcelain jar, painted with birds among rocks and magnolia, with a later wooden domed cover, rim possibly ground down, cracks from rim.

7½in (19cm) high

$850-1,000 **CHEF**

A pair of 19thC Chinese blue-and-white vases and covers, painted with figures in a landscape amid plantain and wutong trees, with temples and dwellings, each with a Qianlong mark on the base.

13½in (34cm) high

$3,300-4,000 **WW**

A Chinese Guangxu underglaze-blue and red vase, painted with Imperial horse trainers and two horses feeding beside a tent, inscribed with calligraphy and signed "Lin Hongqing," the base with a Kangxi mark.

8½in (21.5cm) high

$2,600-4,000 **WW**

A Chinese blue-and-white dish, in the Ming style, painted with a dragon among scrolling lotus, with a six-character Wanli mark, surface scratches, minute chips on foot rim.

8in (20.3cm) diam

$1,300-2,000 **SWO**

A pair of 19thC Chinese blue-and-white "Birds and Flowers" vases, the scenes contained between bands of lappets and ruyi heads, with applied chilong and lion dogs on the shoulders and necks.

18¼in (46cm) high

$2,600-4,000 **WW**

A 19thC Chinese blue-and-white "Temple" vase, with contemporary stand, displaying images of peasants, scholars, water buffalo, and foliage.

22in (56cm) high

$750-850 **PSA**

A Chinese blue-and-white yuhuchun vase, painted with bamboo and rocks by a fence in a garden, between a ruyi head and a false gadroon border, the neck with scrolls below banana leaves, with a six-character Guangxu mark.

11¾in (29.5cm) high

$2,600-4,000 **SWO**

A Chinese Republic period porcelain blue-and-white hu vase, of archaic bronze form, painted with stylized chilong among scrolling flowers between a banana leaf and blade border, deer-head handles, six-character Qianlong mark, foot rim chipped and three antlers from the handles missing.

A chilong is a hornless dragon or mountain demon. The Republic of China dates from 1912-49, with the early Republic from 1912-16.

20½in (52cm) high

$4,000-5,300 **SWO**

A 20thC Chinese blue-and-white porcelain vase and cover, in the Qing style, with four masks modeled on the shoulder, painted with lakeland scenes.

34¾in (88cm) high

$750-850 **CHFF**

A Chinese Kangxi famille verte barber's bowl, decorated with a quatrefoil cartouche enclosing a pair of Mandarin ducks in flight around blossoming peony, surrounded by bamboo and grapevines growing amid fencing.

A term first employed in France in the mid-19thC, "famille verte" translates as "green family" and is used to describe the polychrome enamel palette dominated by shades of green (notably apple green), which first appeared on Chinese porcelain ca. 1680 during the Kangxi period (1662-1722). Developed from the "Wucai" ("five colors") style, it typically also included less dominant reds, yellows, blues, and eggplant (or aubergine, a nonvivid purple), and sometimes also black or gold. Supplanted in popularity by the "famille rose" palette around the mid-18thC, "famille verte" wares continue to be produced in the 21stC, but the most desirable examples are from the Kangxi period.

13¾in (35cm) wide

$2,000-2,600   **WW**

A Chinese Kangxi famille verte jar and cover, decorated in enamels and gilt, with birds amid magnolia, prunus and tree peony, within dense floral borders.

6½in (16.7cm) high

$2,000-2,600   **WW**

A Chinese Kangxi famille verte tea canister and cover, painted with scenes of a lady reclining in a garden, with dwellings set amid rocks and shrubs.

5in (12.4cm) high

$5,300-5,900   **WW**

A Chinese Kangxi famille verte water cistern and cover, decorated with scruffy birds in flight and perched amid peony and chrysanthemum, the molded surmount with twin fish, the spout molded as an animal mask.

18¼in (46.5cm) high

$3,300-4,000   **WW**

A Chinese Kangxi famille verte green-ground "Three Friends of Winter" saucer dish, painted with a stylized flower surrounded by four peach-shaped panels enclosing bamboo, prunus, and pine, with a lotus mark on the base.

Provenance: Formerly the collection of the Nieuwenhuys van Hees family, one of the most famous collectors of Chinese porcelain in The Netherlands at the turn of the 20thC.

8¼in (21cm) wide

$2,000-2,600   **WW**

A Chinese Kangxi famille verte "Birds and Flowers" rouleau vase, painted with a pheasant standing on rockwork amid peony, prunus, and other flowers, with six birds in flight, the neck decorated with leafy branches.

19in (48cm) high

$16,000-20,000   **WW**

A set of three large Chinese Kangxi famille verte vases, painted with four large panels enclosing baskets containing peony, hydrangea, chrysanthemum, and lotus, with smaller cartouches depicting lion dogs and qilin.

20½in (52cm) high

$40,000-45,000   **WW**

A Chinese Kangxi famille verte charger, painted with butterflies among lotus, prunus, peony, and chrysanthemum, riveted, chips, and cracks on rim.

15in (38.2cm) diam

$800-1,050   **SWO**

A Chinese Kangxi famille verte vase, painted with scholar officials and their attendants in a pavilion, with two further figures, the scene divided by leafy trees and iron-red clouds, with panels enclosing fish, the neck decorated with precious objects, with a reticulated wood cover and stand.

13½in (34.1cm) high

$15,000-18,000   **WW**

A rare Chinese Kangxi/Yongzheng famille verte "Scholars" bowl, painted with two sitting scholars relaxing and drinking tea by rocks and shrubs, with an attendant, the reverse inscribed with a poem, with a six-character Hongzhi mark on the base.

4½in (11.5cm) wide

$20,000-24,000   **WW**

A large Chinese Kangxi/Yongzheng famille verte and Imari dish, painted with women riding on horseback, surrounded by lotus, peony, prunus, hibiscus, and daisies in enamels, underglaze blue, and gilt.

The design on this dish is known as "The Generals of the Yang Family." It depicts a scene from the Northern Song dynasty story of the Yang Family women preparing to go to war and defend the country after all the men in the family had already been wounded or killed by foreign invaders.

13½in (34.5cm) wide

$6,000-6,600   **WW**

A Chinese Qing famille verte "Immortals" jardinière, painted with figures, including the Fu Lu Shou, standing in a garden, the shoulder decorated with cartouches containing precious objects, with dragons and sprays of bamboo on the neck.

14¼in (36cm) high

$2,600-4,000   **WW**

A 19thC Chinese famille verte iron-red ground, gu-shaped vase, the neck and foot painted with various blossoming flowers, including lotus and peony, the centered section decorated with birds perched on branches and watery landscape scenes.

17¾in (45cm) high

$2,600-4,000   **WW**

A Chinese Tongzhi famille verte porcelain vase, decorated with historical figures, with inscriptions, underside with a Tongzhi mark in iron red.

11in (28cm) high

$2,600-3,300   **L&T**

ESSENTIAL REFERENCE—SANXING

The Sanxing are the gods of the three stars or constellations considered essential in Chinese astrology and mythology: Jupiter, Ursa Major, and Canopus. Fu, Lu, and Shou are also the embodiments of Fortune (Fu), presiding over planet Jupiter; Prosperity (Lu), presiding over Ursa Major; and Longevity (Shou), presiding over Canopus. They have emerged from Chinese folk religion. Their iconic representation as three old, bearded wise men dates back to the Ming dynasty, when the gods of the three stars were represented in human form for the first time. The term is commonly used in Chinese culture to denote the three attributes of a good life. Statues of these three gods are found in nearly every Chinese home with a glass of water, an orange, or other auspicious offerings, especially during Chinese New Year. Traditionally, they are arranged right to left (so Shou is on the left of the viewer, Lu in the middle, and Fu on the far right), just as Chinese characters are traditionally written from right to left.

A large 19thC Chinese famille verte, powder blue-ground vase, painted with four large cartouches enclosing scenes of figures in gardens and pavilions, one with a seal mark in gilt, decorated in gilt with butterflies and floral sprays, with a wood cover pierced with a shou medallion.

Provenance: From the collection of Sir Thomas Jackson, 1st Baronet (1841-1915). He was the third chief manager of the Hong Kong and Shanghai Banking Corporation and his influence on the company was so notable that he became known as the bank's "Great Architect." He was also one of the founding members of the Hong Kong Jockey Club. In 1866, he joined HSBC and spent several years working in Japan as the manager of the bank's Yokohama office. At the early age of 35, he was appointed as chief manager of HSBC and, under his direction, the company became the leading bank in Asia. After a successful career in Hong Kong, Jackson returned to the UK in 1891, taking charge of the company's office in London. He was knighted in 1899 and three years later he retired and received the additional title of Baronet.

15½in (39.5cm) diam

$2,600-4,000   **WW**

A 19thC Chinese famille verte "Sanxing" rouleau vase, painted with figures from Chinese mythology, including the Fu Lu Shou, the demon queler Zhong Kui, and Liu Hai holding the three-legged toad.

18in (45.5cm) high

$1,300-2,000   **WW**

ASIAN CERAMICS

ESSENTIAL REFERENCE—FAMILLE ROSE

- Famille rose (French for "pink family") is a type of Chinese porcelain first introduced in the 18thC and defined by the presence of pink color overglaze enamel. It is a Western classification for Qing dynasty porcelain known in Chinese by various terms: fencai, ruancai, yangcai, and falangcai. The color palette was introduced in China during the reign of Kangxi (1654–1722) by Western Jesuits who worked at the palace, but perfected only in the Yongzheng era, when the finest pieces were made.
- Although famille rose is named after its pink enamel, the color may actually range from pale pink to deep ruby. Apart from pink, a range of other soft colors are also used in famille rose. Famille rose was popular in the 18th and 19thC, and it continued to be made in the 20thC. Large quantities of famille rose porcelain were exported to Europe, the United States, and other countries.

A Chinese Yongzheng famille rose bowl, painted with peony, poppies, aster, and blossoming crab apple, with a single flower head and simple leaves painted in the well, the reign mark in underglaze blue on the base.

7¾in (19.5cm) wide

$6,000-6,600   **WW**

A pair of Chinese Yongzheng/Qianlong famille rose vases and covers, painted with medallions enclosing dragons and landscapes, with pink bands of further floral motifs on the shoulders and covers.

16¼in (41cm) high

$4,000-5,300   **WW**

A Chinese Kangxi famille verte wall vase, painted with two beauties standing on a balcony gazing at a gentleman below, with a crane and more ladies standing in the courtyard.

11½in (29cm) high

$2,000-2,600   **WW**

A pair of Chinese famille rose "Judgment of Paris" plates, with the shepherd prince before the three naked goddesses, offering the golden apple to the goddess of love, cartouches with Meissen-style harbor scenes on the rims.

ca. 1740   *9in (23cm) diam*

$4,600-5,300   **WW**

A Chinese famille rose "La Dame au Parasol" plate, after a design by Cornelis Pronk, enameled with a young lady and her attendant beneath a parasol, with aquatic birds and bulrushes, the border with panels of figures and birds on a bright pink cell diaper, the reverse with eight iron-red insects.

Cornelis Pronk (1691-1759) was a Dutch draftsman and painter. This design, drawn in 1734, was the first that Pronk made for the Dutch East India Company and the drawing was sent to China and Japan to be copied onto porcelain. The pattern appears on Chinese famille rose, blue-and-white, and Imari pieces.

ca. 1740   *10in (25.5cm) diam*

$9,000-13,000   **WW**

ESSENTIAL REFERENCE—WALL VASES

- Wall vases, also known as wall pockets or sedan chair vases, can be traced back to the Wanli period (1573–1620) in the Ming dynasty. During the 18thC, under the reign of the Qianlong Emperor (1735-96), government support for arts and crafts peaked, and wall vases became in particular one of the Emperor's favorite porcelain forms—their sophistication developing significantly under his patronage. There are, for example, 13 wall vases on the wall of San Xi Tang (The Hall of Three Rarities), the emperor's special study in Yang Xin Dian (Hall of Mental Cultivation) in the Forbidden City, and there are also 320 Qianlong wall vases recorded in the collection of the Palace Museum in Beijing, with 138 of them inscribed with poems by the Emperor (a few written when he was a prince).
- Enhancing the rarity of this vase, which was produced 1742-52, is its yangcai (foreign colors) decoration, which was introduced by European Jesuit craftsmen to the Qing court around 1685, adapting the European techniques of enameling on metal. This resulted not only in an enriched palette of colors, but also in a combination of European brocadelike designs, using tonal effects to appear three-dimensional, and purely Chinese elements, such as scrolling lotus motifs. Developed in the Jingdezhen Imperial workshops, this style is especially representative of the superb quality of porcelain produced during the Qianlong reign. Special orders of yangcai decoration are believed to date from only a few years in the early 1740s, which makes it more remarkable that in 2019 this vase was bought for just £1 (less than $1.50) from a Herefordshire thrift store!

A Chinese Qianlong Imperial inscribed famille rose wall vase, the form on a short splayed foot, flanked by a pair of ruyi handles on the waisted neck, the body inscribed with an Imperial poem appraising incense in a circular cartouche with a yuti mark followed by two iron-red seal marks reading "Qianlong chen han" (the Qianlong Emperor's own mark) and "Weijing weiyi" ("be precise, be undivided"), surrounded by scrolling lotus against a yellow sgraffito ground.

7½in (19cm) high

$650,000-800,000   **SWO**

A Chinese famille rose teabowl and saucer, painted with an allegorical scene, after Francesco Albani (1578-1660), representing one of the Four Elements, "Fire," depicting Jupiter with his eagle in a forge surrounded by children.

ca. 1740

$1,300-2,000   **WW**

A Chinese famille rose mythological subject plate, painted with an allegorical scene, after Francesco Albani (1578-1660) symbolizing one of the Four Elements, "Earth," with winged children playing at the foot of a lion-drawn chariot.

ca. 1740   *9in (23cm) diam*

$2,600-3,300   **WW**

A Chinese Qianlong famille rose pink-ground vase, painted with a bird perched among peony and chrysanthemum, amid rockwork, the ground incised with sgraffito scrolls.

14¾in (37.5cm) high

$2,600-3,300   **WW**

A Chinese Qianlong famille rose model of a peacock, sitting next to a prunus tree with pink flowers.

6½in (16.5cm) high

$3,300-4,000   **WW**

A Chinese Qianlong famille rose Mandarin palette "Hunting Scene" bowl, painted in enamels and gilt with huntsmen on horseback as their pack of hounds chase a fox, on a geometric ground, with a roundel enclosing a gentleman and his dogs in pursuit of a pheasant.

10in (25.5cm) wide

$4,000-5,300   **WW**

A Chinese Qianlong famille rose "Lotus" vase, painted with bats and gilt fylfots against a lemon-yellow ground on the shoulder beneath a narrow pink band of swirling designs, the neck with a band of pink spearheads enclosing beribboned precious objects and blossoms encircling the gilt rim, the interior and base glazed turquoise.

6¾in (17cm) high

$16,000-20,000   **WW**

A Chinese Qianlong famille rose European erotic subject punch bowl, the well and exterior with the initials "RW" beneath a hand clasping a blossoming branch, the base painted with a European gentleman and lady in a garden with a dog at their feet.

16in (40.5cm) diam

$4,000-4,600   **WW**

A pair of Chinese export famille rose porcelain baskets, the pierced borders painted to imitate wood grain with knots, the centers with butterflies on flowers and lychee fruits.

ca. 1780   *10¼in (26.2cm) diam*

$2,900-3,700   **CHEF**

An 18thC Chinese famille rose bowl, one side painted with floral sprays, the reverse with calligraphy.

7in (18cm) wide

$1,500-1,800   **WW**

A Chinese Qianlong famille rose porcelain "Hunting Subject" punch bowl, painted with panels of European fox-hunting scenes and exotic birds in landscape, inner rim has a restored chip, crack on the side body, some wear to the painting, small repaired chip on outer rim.

The hunting scenes on this bowl are derived from engravings by Thomas Burford and P. Canot after James Seymour.

13¼in (33.5cm) diam
$1,700-2,400   **TEN**

A Chinese famille rose vase, painted with quails next to rocks surrounded by blossoming flowers, with a six-character Qianlong mark, surface scratches.

12½in (32cm) high
$2,000-2,400   **SWO**

An 18thC Chinese famille rose European subject teabowl and saucer, painted with figures drinking and smoking as they play cards at a table in a garden, with chickens around them.

$2,200-2,600   **WW**

A Chinese Jiaqing famille rose brush rest, decorated with a boy presenting a finger citron to a sitting figure in a garden, surrounded by flowers, the base glazed turquoise, with four-character Jiaqing mark in iron red.

3½in (9cm) wide
$4,000-5,300   **WW**

A pair of large 18th/19thC Chinese famille rose ormolu-mounted vases, the porcelain 18thC, the mounts 19thC, enameled with peony and chrysanthemum, the bases drilled.

Provenance: Lionel de Rothschild (1882-1942), Edmund de Rothschild (1916-2009), the Trustees of Exbury House.

20½in (52cm) high
$6,000-7,500   **WW**

A Chinese famille rose vase, decorated with the "millefleurs" pattern, with a six-character Qianlong mark on the base, surface scratches, some flakes on enamel.

15in (38cm) high
$3,300-4,000   **SWO**

A Chinese Jiaqing famille rose and gilt "Boys" bowl, painted with boys playing in a garden rich with plantain, pine, and flowers, the interior and base glazed turquoise, one side mounted with a later metal handle, with a five-character mark reading "xie zhu zhu ren zao" on the base.

8¾in (22.4cm) diam
$4,600-5,300   **WW**

A large 18th/19thC Chinese Qing famille rose porcelain punch bowl, painted with a flower bouquet in the center, flowers further decorating the exterior.

19in (48cm) diam
$1,200-1,600   **L&T**

An 18thC Chinese famille rose chamber pot and cover, painted with peony sprays and sprigs, the handle with a heart-shaped thumbpiece.

8½in (21.5cm) high
$1,300-2,000   **WW**

CLOSER LOOK—JIAQING BOWL

This is a rare, large Jiaqing (1796-1820) famille rose bowl, decorated with archaic characters "Wanshou Wujiang" ("boundless longevity") in blue inside roundels.

Even with some damage—a small chip and a fine hairline crack on rim, the rim also with very minor fritting, water stains to interior—it is a highly desirable piece.

They are reserved on a rich yellow ground embellished with scrolling lotus on leafy tendrils and Eight Buddhist Emblems.

It has a six character Jiaqing mark in red on base.

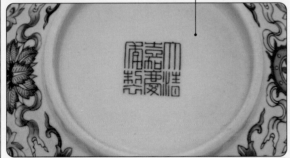

A Chinese famille rose bowl, the deep rounded sides rising to a flared rim.

8in (20.3cm) diam

$40,000-53,000 SWO

A Chinese Qianlong famille rose pseudo "Tobacco Leaf" serving dish, with flowers and floral medallions with green, iron-red, pink and brown enamel leaves heightened in gilt, with glaze chips to the rim.

16¾in (42.5cm) diam

$1,300-1,600 DN

A pair of Chinese Jiaqing famille rose lobed bowls, the interiors with a centered medallion depicting a gathering of ladies, the exteriors decorated with four ladies in landscape settings engaging into different activities, such as horse riding and laundry, the bases inscribed with a six-character Jiaqing mark, one bowl with restoration and a chip on the rim, the other bowl with one minute chip on the lobe tip and repainted.

10¾in (27cm) diam

$14,000-16,000 DN

A Chinese Daoguang coral-ground famille rose bowl, painted with butterflies, the interior glazed white, the base with a four-character mark "Shende Tang zhi" ("Made for the Hall of Prudent Virtue") in iron red, two chips each issuing a crack on the rim, and another hairline crack on rim.

5¾in (14.3cm) diam

$16,000-20,000 SWO

A Chinese famille rose bowl, painted with peony enclosed by foliage and tendrils, against a copper-red glaze, with a six-character Qianlong mark.

4¼in (11cm) diam

$2,000-2,600 SWO

A Chinese famille rose bowl, painted with roundels of precious objects surrounded by scrolling lotus against a pink ground, with a six-character Jiaqing mark.

8in (20.1cm) diam

$6,000-6,600 SWO

A pair of Chinese Daoguang famille rose bowls, painted with butterflies among endrilled gourds and leaves, against a yellow ground, six-character Daoguang mark, both with frits on rim, minute chips on foot rim.

6½in (16.5cm) diam

$9,000-10,500 SWO

ASIAN CERAMICS

CLOSER LOOK—DAOQUANG VASE

This is a well-painted example of a Daoguang (1821-50) famille rose vase of tapering square form.

The neck with shou characters, Buddhist lion, and ring handles.

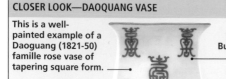

One side painted with three literati drinking below a pine tree, with their attendants, the other sides with pine trees and flowers.

Its value is affected by the fact it has been restored, but is a good example of this genre.

A Chinese vase, two-character Zaisou mark in iron red on the base, restored.

15¾in (40cm) high

$4,000-5,300   **SWO**

A pair of Chinese Qing famille rose chargers, painted with peonies, chrysanthemums, and other flowers next to a rock, surface scratches.

11¼in (28.5cm) diam

$2,600-3,300   **SWO**

A 19thC Chinese famille rose fishbowl, painted with divine figures, including Liu Hai, Daoist Immortals, and Shoulao riding a deer, standing on clouds floating over the sea and riding animals through the waters, with iron-red bats and clouds on the rim.

15¾in (40cm) high

$7,500-8,500   **WW**

A Chinese, possibly Tongzhi, famille rose vase, painted and partly gilded with two dragons and bats among scrolls and fungi, scroll pierced shoulder handles, with a six-character reign mark in underglaze blue.

6¼in (16cm) high

$2,600-3,300   **CHEF**

A mid-19thC Cantonese famille rose porcelain punch bowl, with figures in gardens and interiors and with birds and insects among foliage.

16in (40.5cm) diam

$2,900-3,700   **TEN**

A mid-19thC Cantonese famille rose porcelain punch bowl, painted with figures in gardens and interiors and with birds and insects among branches on a foliate ground.

15¾in (40cm) diam

$1,600-2,400   **TEN**

A 19thC Chinese famille rose fishbowl, painted with a scene of heavenly generals meeting around a table with crashing waves behind them, with further figures, including ladies, warriors, and martial artists, in a garden with bamboo, wutong trees, lingzhi, and rockwork.

16½in (42cm) high

$8,000-9,000   **WW**

A Chinese Xianfeng famille rose and gilt "Butterfly" teabowl, painted with butterflies amid blossoms and shrubs, inscribed in the well with three characters reading "Su Shi ju," the cavetto inscribed "san shi shi lai fen," with a four-character Xianfeng mark.

Su Shi (1037-1101) was a Chinese calligrapher, poet, and politician during the Song dynasty and he is generally regarded as one of the most accomplished and important figures in classical Chinese literature.

2½in (6.6cm) diam

$2,000-2,600   **WW**

A pair of 19thC Chinese famille rose "Taming the Tiger" vases, each with four figures, the turquoise-glazed bases with iron-red apocryphal Qianlong six-character seal mark, one vase with rim chip, the other vase with firing crack and fault on base.

16¼in (41.5cm) high

$4,600-5,900   **DN**

A 19thC Chinese Qing famille rose vase and cover, painted with magpies, pheasants, and peony, hairline crack from rim into body and two further hair cracks nearby on rim of vase, minor fritting on rims.

26in (66cm) high

$6,000-7,500 DN

A Chinese famille rose bowl, painted with a grasshopper among foliage, with a four-character Tongzhi mark, a 1¾-inch (4.5cm) hairline crack on rim.

7¼in (18.4cm) diam

$1,600-2,000 SWO

A pair of 19thC Chinese Canton famille rose "Dragon" vases, painted with blue and pink dragons in pursuit of flaming pearls, the beasts surrounded by clouds and medallions decorated with flowers, fruits, fish, and geometric designs, each with two applied handles modeled as cranes on the neck.

24¾in (63cm) high

$2,600-4,000 WW

A pair of late-19thC Chinese famille rose porcelain vases and covers, painted with equestrian figures and numerous "happy boys" playing.

17¼in (44cm) high

$750-1,000 CHEF

A Chinese famille rose bowl, painted with four pink medallions enclosing Chinese characters "Fori Changming" ("the light of Buddha shines eternally"), surrounded by scrolling lotus, hairline crack on rim, glaze frit on base, yellow enamel with crazings.

4¼in (10.7cm) diam

$2,000-2,600 SWO

A Chinese Guangxu famille rose porcelain bottle vase, painted with a bird perching on a flowering branch on one side, inscriptions on the other, a pair of elephant-head handles flanking the neck, underside with "Guan Yao Nei Zao" ("Imperial Kiln for Inner Palace") mark, the inscriptions with "Yihai year."

1899 *8¼in (21cm) high*

$1,500-2,000 L&T

A Chinese late Qing/Republic famille rose millefleurs bottle vase, decorated with flowers on a gilt ground, with a large applied iron-red and gilt-decorated dragon chasing a flaming pearl on the shoulder, the base with Qianlong mark.

15¾in (40cm) high

$4,000-5,300 WW

A Chinese Guangxu famille rose bowl, painted with floral roundels, gilt rim, with a Guangxu mark, a frit on rim, gilt rubbed, scratch marks on glaze near foot.

4¾in (11.9cm) diam

$3,300-4,000 SWO

A Chinese late-Qing/Republic period famille rose yellow-ground, beehive-shaped water pot, painted with phoenixes amid precious objects and scrolling lotus, between bands of ruyi heads and lappets, with a Qianlong mark.

3¾in (9.5cm) wide

$2,000-2,600 WW

ASIAN CERAMICS

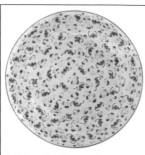

A Chinese famille rose charger, painted with bats in iron red among clouds, with a six-character Guangxu mark, surface scratches, minute chips on foot rim.

20½in (51.9cm) diam

$6,000-6,600   **SWO**

A large Chinese Qing or later famille rose pillow, modeled as a boy, the child lifts his head showing his laughing face, his tunic decorated with a dragon, butterfly, and sprays of various fruit and flowers.

15½in (39.5cm) wide

$6,000-6,600   **WW**

A large 19th/20thC Chinese Canton famille rose porcelain baluster vase, painted with noblemen in cartouches reserved on a ground with flowers and foliates, the neck flanked with two pairs of confronting mythical beasts.

24in (61cm) high

$1,300-2,000   **L&T**

A Republic period famille rose porcelain group, figurine of "He He," the scene of two boys wearing traditional robes, one sitting holding a jar and cover containing a sea creature, the other with a lotus stem and leaf across his shoulder, the base with an impressed four-character mark.

13in (33cm) high

$3,300-4,000   **JN**

A Chinese Republic period famille rose two-handle Hu "Longevity" vase, decorated on one side with narcissus and lingzhi growing around rocks and on the reverse with a crane, the neck flanked by a pair of gilt-decorated handles formed as lingzhi stems, the base inscribed with a six-character Qianlong mark, minor wear to the gilding.

9½in (24cm) high

$2,200-2,600   **DN**

A Chinese Republic period famille rose bitong, painted with figures playing drums, gongs, and cymbals, some gilding, before a window looking out onto pots of flowers.

5¼in (13.5cm) high

$2,600-4,000   **WW**

ESSENTIAL REFERENCE—REPUBLIC PERIOD (1912-49)

- After the fall of the Qing dynasty, there followed a period of great unrest in China. In spite of this turmoil, however, the porcelain industry in the Jiangxi province flourished, and a number of privately operated kilns began producing high-quality porcelain in Jingdezhen. These factories produced not only wares copying Kangxi, Yongzheng, and Qianlong-era porcelains, but there was also a revival in quality led by a number of artists, producing high quality with exquisite decoration. Many of these pieces are signed.

- The most famous artists were part of the group "The Eight Friends of Zhushan," which was comprised of the artists Wang Yi, Deng Bishan, Xu Zhongnan, Tian Hexian, Wang Dafan, Wang Yeting, Cheng Yiting, and Liu Yucen. Regarded as the finest porcelain artists of the Republic period, the group was significant in the revival of the Chinese porcelain industry.

- Buyers are attracted to the snow-white porcelain and skillful decoration. Pieces by prominent artists are desirable, and, as a result, can fetch high prices at auction.

A Chinese Republic period famille rose "Parrot" vase, painted with the bird perched among chrysanthemum blooms, the rim interior and base glazed turquoise, with a Qianlong mark in iron red.

8¾in (22.5cm) high

$8,500-10,000   **WW**

A 20thC Chinese famille rose porcelain plaque, painted with a pair of spotted deer, with a lone crane on a branch above, with an inscription describing the crane and deer together in spring, dated the Wushen year and with a signature reading "Xu Dasheng."

The image of a crane, or "he," and deer, or "lu," together forms the rebus "liuhe tongchun," which signifies the universe enjoying springtime and, by implication, prosperity and longevity.

17¼in (43.5cm) high

$4,000-5,300   **WW**

A 20thC Chinese famille rose vase, decorated with printed and painted court palace scenes and Daoist Immortals.

47¼in (120cm) high

$600-750   **CHEF**

A Chinese Kangxi doucai bitong brush pot, decorated with two panels, one depicting a scholar holding a lotus flower as he greets a gentleman and a beauty, with his attendant behind him, the other with a scholar and his attendants, one boy carrying a qin, each scene set in a fenced garden with rockwork and clouds above.

The "qin" referred to above is also known as "guqin," and is one of China's oldest and most revered instruments. Traditionally favored by scholars and literati, because of its subtlety and refinement, it most commonly has 7 strings, although ancient examples with 5, 10, or more are documented. Tuned in the base register, its lowest pitch is equivalent to that of a cello, and while its strings are mostly plucked and stopped, a sliding ("glissando") technique can produce sounds similar to a fretless bass or slide guitar.

7in (17.5cm) diam

$26,000-33,000   WW

An 18thC Chinese doucai quatrelobed "Lotus" tray or stand, the exterior decorated with four stylized flower heads growing amid winding leafy tendrils, with a scrolling band reserved on a pale green ground encircling the rim, all raised on four ruyi head-shaped feet painted with further blossoms.

8¾in (21.8cm) diam

$2,600-4,000   WW

A pair of Chinese Daoguang doucai porcelain teabowls, each decorated with stylized "honeysuckle" and leaf scrolling motifs, with a blue four-character Daoguang enamel mark.

3¾in (9.7cm) diam

$5,300-8,000   CHEF

CLOSER LOOK—DRAGON BOWL

This is a Yongzheng (1723-35) doucai "Dragon" bowl.

It is decorated with a green and purple dragon, the beast divided by stylized flames, with a further two dragons in the interior.

The dragon traditionally symbolized potent and auspicious powers, particularly control over water, rainfall, typhoons, and floods. The dragon is also a symbol of power, strength, and good luck.

The well is painted with a flaming pearl contained within a simple blue ring.

A small Chinese bowl, with the reign mark in underglaze blue to the recessed base.

$2,600-4,000   WW

A Chinese Daoguang doucai "Medallion" jar, decorated with eight double chrysanthemum roundels divided by lotus flower heads and scrolling tendrils, with a reticulated wood cover, six-character Daoguang mark.

Doucai is a technique in painted Chinese porcelain where parts of the design, and some outlines of the rest, are painted in underglaze blue before the piece is glazed and fired. The rest of the design is then added in overglaze enamels of different colors and the piece fired again at a lower temperature of 1,550°F to 1,650°F (850– 900°C.) The style began in the 15thC under the Ming dynasty in the Imperial factories at Jingdezhen, and its finest products come from a few years in the reign of the Chenghua Emperor, mostly small pieces, such as the famous Chicken cups. The style was discontinued after a few decades, when a suitable overglaze blue was developed, but it was later revived under the Qing dynasty. It is not to be confused with the wucai style, which was a related early technique for polychrome painting. Doucai can be translated as "contrasted colors," "fitted colors," or "dovetailed colors."

4¼in (11cm) high

$13,000-16,000   WW

A Chinese Qing doucai "Chicken" bowl, rising from a short straight foot to an everted rim, painted on the exterior with chickens and chicks in a rocky landscape amid plantain, peony, and other plants, with a medallion enclosing a cockerel and hen in the well, the base with a four-character mark reading "Cai Xiu Tang zhi."

6in (15.3cm) diam

$7,500-8,500   WW

ESSENTIAL REFERENCE—BOX AND COVER

Ming dynasty porcelain covered boxes of this form are exceedingly rare, and it is still unclear what their exact purpose was. It has been suggested that these boxes might have been used in pairs as containers for weiqi, also known as go, playing pieces. However, comparable jars also functioned as cricket cages. Porcelain cricket cages of this form, but with recessed covers, were first made for the Xuande Emperor (1426-35) and the popularity of the ancient sport of cricket fighting grew significantly during the Ming dynasty. The depth of this particular box would perhaps suggest that it is more likely to have functioned as a cricket cage, because it would have been somewhat impractical to pick out weiqi stones from such a tall container. It is also interesting to note that the barrel-shaped form later became popular in Japan, being utilized on mizusashi, or water vessels, used in tea ceremonies.

A rare Chinese Wanli Imperial wucai "Boys" box and cover, painted with 16 boys at play in a garden amid rockwork, plantain, pine, and willow trees, with stylized ruyi head-shaped clouds in the sky above them, the cover similarly decorated, the base with a six-character Wanli mark.

7in (18cm) high

$40,000-53,000 **WW**

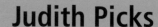

Judith Picks

It is important when looking at a piece of Chinese porcelain to investigate the history and understand the symbolism involved.

The Zun or Yi is an ancient type of bronze or ceramic vessel dating from the Shang Dynasty (1500-1028 BC). It was used in religious ceremonies to hold wine.

On this important piece from around 1600, the exquisite painted decoration has prunus, or plum, which is a symbol of beauty, purity, and longevity. The magpie is a harbinger of joy and the leafy bamboo symbolizes longevity, steadfastness, and summer.

A Chinese Wanli wucai "Zun" altar vase, the square form sides painted with panels of prunus, magpies, and leafy bamboo, applied on each side around the middle are relief-molded heads of fantastical lionlike beasts painted in underglaze blue and colored enamels, each pierced through for the attachment of a ring, six-character Wanli mark.

10¼in (26cm) high

$200,000-260,000 **DUK**

ESSENTIAL REFERENCE—WUCAI

Wucai, meaning five enamels or "five-color ware," is mostly three enamels (red, green, and yellow) within outlines in black cobalt or underglaze blue, plus the white of the porcelain body, making up five colors. The name Wucai refers to Chinese porcelain decorated in this palette dating from the Ming period, especially during the reign of Jiajing (1522-66), Longqing (1567-72), and Wanli (1573-1619) emperors. The name wu-cai, or five-color ware, may well have developed because the number five has an important symbolic significance in Chinese art. As shown by the examples on this page, the techniques were revived in the Qing dynasty.

A Chinese Shunzhi wucai "Baxian" vase and cover, decorated with the Eight Immortals in a rocky wooded landscape, watching a figure dressed in a colorful robe performing a magic trick, his breath transforming into a dragon and phoenix, the cover painted with three boys at play, with a wood stand.

19½in (49.5cm) high

$40,000-46,000 **WW**

A Chinese Transitional wucai vase, painted with officials and their attendants by a garden pavilion, the reverse with a plantain tree growing amid rockwork, the short straight neck decorated with peony blooms and encircled by a band of cracked ice.

ca. 1640 *11½in (29.5cm) high*

$6,000-6,600 **WW**

A Chinese Shunzhi porcelain wucai vase, painted with eight ruyi-head panels of animals and mythical animals, including a qilin, Buddhist lion, goat, pixie, and a horse rolling on its back, between four different landscape roundels, the biscuit base with an indistinct ink two-character mark, some wear on the surface.

The Shunzhi period covers 1644-61.

ca. 1650 *11¼in (28.5cm) high*

$3,300-4,600 **DN**

A Chinese Jiaqing Imperial wucai "Apricot Blossom" month cup, painted with a blossoming apricot tree growing amid rocks and shrubs, the reverse with a poem reading "qing xiang he su yu, jia se chu qing yan," the inscription followed by a seal reading "shang" ("to appreciate"), six-character Jiaqing mark.

Apricot blossoms are associated with the second month in the lunar calendar. Because the civil service examinations were held at this time of year, apricot blossoms are regarded as the "flowers for passing exams," and successful candidates were invited to a banquet held in the Imperial gardens called "the spring banquet in the apricot grove." The couplet is from a poem by Tang dynasty poet Qian Qi (AD 710-780) and may be translated as "Its elegant fragrance blends with the scent of overnight rain, its beautiful color stands out in the morning mist."

2½in (6.7cm) diam

$11,000-13,000   **WW**

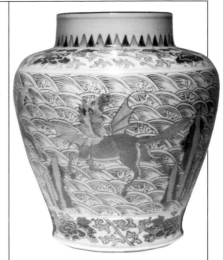

A Chinese wucai pot, painted with boys carrying a lantern in panels surrounded by flowers, between floret and false gadroon borders, six-character Jiajing mark.

16¼in (41.5cm) high

$1,050-1,200   **SWO**

A 19thC Chinese wucai vase, decorated with four mythical horses flying over iron-red crashing waves, two depicted with wings, the creatures divided by pointed rocks, with bands of peony sprays on the shoulder and encircling the foot.

11¼in (28.5cm) high

$2,600-4,000   **WW**

A near pair of 19thC Chinese wucai vases, painted with soldiers in a rocky landscape watching an archer poised to fire, set beneath cracked ice and chrysanthemum and peony, the smaller vase with a six-character Kangxi mark on the base.

12¾in (32.5cm) high

$6,000-6,600   **WW**

A pair of Chinese Qing wucai teabowls, decorated with floral motifs, Yongzheng mark on the base.

1¾in (4.3cm) diam

$2,000-2,600   **DAWS**

A Chinese Qing wucai sleeve vase, painted with a pheasant perched on rocks amid peony and magnolia branches, with many birds in flight around the flowers.

14¼in (36.4cm) high

$2,600-4,000   **WW**

An early-20thC Chinese wucai jar, painted with landscapes and mythical beasts, with an associated cover with a spear knop, surface scratches, glaze flakes, and enamel losses.

11in (28cm) high

$2,400-2,900   **SWO**

ASIAN CERAMICS

ESSENTIAL REFERENCE—ARMORIAL WARE

- Armorial ware or heraldic china (and a variety of other terms) are ceramics decorated with a coat of arms, either that of a family, an institution ,or place. Armorials have been popular on European pottery from the Middle Ages, with examples seen on Spanish Hispano-Moresque ware, Italian maiolica, slipware, English and Dutch Delft, and on porcelain from the 18thC. Earlier examples were mostly large pieces, such as pitchers or basins and ewers, but later whole table services, all painted with the arms, were produced.

- Silver tableware also often had coats of arms engraved on it, but as porcelain replaced metal as the favored material for elite tableware in the 18thC, armorial porcelain became popular. When overglaze decoration was used, the pottery could produce the glazed ware without the arms, which were then added when a commission was received.

- The term is most often associated with Chinese export porcelain, often decorated with the arms and crests of European and American families from the late-17thC through the 19thC. A painting of the arms was sent to China, and, after a considerable wait, the painted service arrived. British clients imported about 4,000 services from 1695 until 1820, when a new prohibitive tax stopped the trade, because the British government wanted to protect the domestic potteries.

- Mostly used at table on only special occasions, armorial wares are popular with collectors, albeit in terms of familial authenticity it is worth noting that many 17thC Dutch armorial plates (known as "wapenborden") were commonly sold with recurring emblems that can't be traced to any specific family!

A pair of Chinese armorial soup plates, for the Dutch market, each decorated with the arms of Adriaan or Theodorus van Reverhorst within the arms of their eight great-grandparents, the border with gilt scrolls and shells.
ca. 1745   9¼in (23.5cm) diam
$2,600-4,000   **WW**

A Chinese famille rose armorial "Marriage" dish, for the Dutch market, painted with the arms of the Zinzerling Family of Holland and the van Musschenbroek Family of Utrecht, with panels enclosing landscapes and birds.
ca. 1750   15in (38.2cm) diam
$2,000-2,600   **WW**

An 18thC Chinese export armorial dish, decorated in the center with a crest and supported by four floral sprays, the border with the initials "RG."
16½in (42cm) diam
$600-750   **CHEF**

A Chinese armorial teabowl and saucer, for the Dutch market, decorated with the arms of Adriaan or Theodorus van Reverhorst within the arms of their eight great-grandparents, the borders with gilt scrolls and shells.
ca. 1745   4¾in (12cm) diam
$1,050-1,600   **WW**

A pair of Chinese armorial dishes, the centers painted with the arms of Smith impaling Cazalet, underglaze-blue borders, with wear on interiors of both dishes and minor wear on armorials.
ca. 1795   14½in (37cm) diam
$650-900   **DN**

A rare Chinese Jiajing enameled "Deer" bowl, the exterior painted in green enamels with a continuous scene of four deer in a wooded landscape, standing amid pine and lingzhi, reserved on a red ground, the base glazed white with a six-character Jiajing mark in underglaze blue.

4¾in (12.2cm) diam

$11,000-12,000 WW

A pair of Chinese Ming figures of attendants, with removable heads, the male figure glazed in shades of green and holding a chest, the female in green and amber and holding a charger, minor wear and chips.

19in (48cm) and 19¾in (50cm) high

$1,600-2,100 CHEF

A Chinese Kangxi egglant (aubergine) and green glazed "Five Dragon" dish, the center incised and enameled with a five-clawed dragon in pursuit of a sacred pearl amid flames and stylized clouds, encircled by two dragons, with a further two dragons chasing flaming jewels above a band of lappets on the exterior, with a Kangxi mark in underglaze blue.

12¼in (31.4cm) diam

$9,000-12,000 WW

One of a pair of rare Chinese Kangxi Imperial green and yellow enameled "Dragon and Phoenix" bowls, each incised and decorated in green enamel with two dragons in pursuit of flaming pearls above phoenix medallions, all reserved on a yellow ground, with roundels enclosing stylized shou characters and clouds in the wells, with six-character Kangxi marks.

It is recorded that bowls with this design were made for guifei, the highest-ranking Imperial concubines, or fei, Imperial concubines.

$16,000-20,000 the pair

6in (15cm) diam

WW

A Chinese Kangxi Imperial yellow-ground "Dragon" saucer dish, incised with two five-clawed dragons contesting a sacred pearl amid stylized flames, one dragon picked out in green enamel, the other in eggplant (aubergine), with a six-character Kangxi mark.

5¼in (13.3cm) diam

$12,000-15,000 WW

A Chinese Kangxi Imperial porcelain saucer dish, painted on a yellow ground and incised with green and eggplant (aubergine) five-clawed dragons encircling a flaming pearl among stylized clouds and flames, the underside with eggplant-color grapes and green leaves on a yellow ground extending to the base, the base inscribed with a six-character Kangxi mark, the glaze lightly suffused with faint cracks, one hairline crack on the rim.

Provenance: Formerly in the collection of Henry Mazot (1882-1956), who lived and worked in Beijing from the 1920s for the Bank of Indochina, where he finished as chairman. The family left Beijing in 1946 to move back to France and settled in Normandy. Most of the Chinese porcelain in the family collection was left in the wooden trunks in the basement of their chateau from 1946 until Christmas 2015, when his granddaughter, who inherited the home, decided to finally open them.

5¼in (13cm) diam

$10,000-11,000 DN

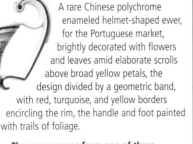

A rare Chinese polychrome enameled helmet-shaped ewer, for the Portuguese market, brightly decorated with flowers and leaves amid elaborate scrolls above broad yellow petals, the design divided by a geometric band, with red, turquoise, and yellow borders encircling the rim, the handle and foot painted with trails of foliage.

The ewer comes from one of three services made for Dom José Ribeiro da Fonseca Figueiredo (1690-1752), who was appointed as the Bishop of Porto in 1739 under the name of Dom Frei José Maria da Fonseca e Evora.

ca. 1740 *10¾in (27cm) high*

$6,500-8,000 WW

A rare Chinese Qianlong porcelain grisaille and gilt "Resurrection" plate, showing the resurrected Christ before a sunburst amid clouds, the angel sitting at his feet and the Roman soldiers in disarray in the foreground, the glaze above the foot suffused with faint cracks, the mouth rim with a minute chip.

9in (22.6cm) diam

$2,600-4,000 DN

A rare Chinese Qianlong enameled porcelain model of a lion dog, the mythical beast gazing with bulging eyes and its teeth bared, pierced with apertures in its flaring nostrils and open jaw, with gilt on its large ears.

8½in (21.5cm) long

$4,000-5,300 WW

A Chinese Qianlong Imperial iron-red altar vessel, painted with four lotus sprays between lappets and leaves, with a raised band on the neck, raised on a wide domed foot, the base concave.

8¾in (22cm) high

$6,000-7,500   WW

An 18thC Chinese black-ground vase, decorated in the manner of Cornelis Pronk, painted with a leafy branch of red currants, with a band of stylized foliage encircling the foot.

Cornelis Pronk (1691-1759) was a Dutch draftsman and painter who was employed by the Dutch East India Company from 1734 until around 1740 to create designs for porcelain. A number of Pronk's designs, including the decoration on this vase, were drawn from botanical studies and prints by the Dutch-Swiss naturalist Maria Sibylla Merian (1647-1717).

11¼in (28.7cm) high

$2,400-2,900   WW

An 18thC Chinese copper-red "Five Dragon" vase, decorated with scaly five-clawed dragons amid clouds and flames, their eyes picked out in underglaze blue, all above breaking waves, the short foot painted with a continuous leaf scroll, with gilt-metal mounts on the neck and foot, the neck reduced and the base lacking.

Provenance: Lionel de Rothschild (1882-1942), Edmund de Rothschild (1916-2009), the Trustees of Exbury House. Lionel de Rothschild, OBE (1882-1942) was the eldest son of Leopold de Rothschild and part of the prominent Rothschild banking family of England. After the death of his father in 1917, Lionel and his brother Anthony became the managing partners of N M Rothschild & Sons bank. Aside from his involvement in the family bank, Lionel was also a Conservative politician, serving as MP for the Vale of Aylesbury from 1910-23. After selling Halton House, which he had inherited from his uncle Alfred de Rothschild in 1918, the following year Lionel purchased the Mitford estate at Exbury in Hampshire. Lionel had been interested in horticulture from an early age and dedicated much time and money into creating an impressive garden at Exbury. He was also responsible for the building of Exbury House on the estate in the 1920s. Lionel passed away in 1942, and the estate was inherited by his son Edmund de Rothschild (1916-2009) who devoted himself not only to the family business but also to maintaining and developing Exbury Gardens, which had fallen into disrepair during World War II. Exbury House remains private, but the gardens are open to the public and are still regarded as some of the finest in the United Kingdom today.

$46,000-53,000

21¾in (55cm) high

WW

A pair of 18thC Chinese enameled "Ladies" dishes, painted with two ladies in a dressing room, one sits looking into a mirror as she arranges her hair in a bun, the other stands watching, holding a basket, surrounded by a white foliate scroll reserved on a diaper ground, the rim decorated with floral panels in gilt, iron red, and blue enamel against a black ground.

8¾in (22.5cm) diam

$2,600-4,000   WW

A Chinese Qianlong export porcelain Mandarin palette punch bowl, painted with hunting scenes with men on horseback with dogs, one panel hunting deer, the other birds, with buildings in the distance, the design taken from an 18thC print by Seymour, the glaze with blemishes in the interior of the bowl.

6¼in (16.2cm) diam

$2,000-2,600   DN

A Chinese Qing iron-red teabowl and cover, painted with dragons chasing flaming pearls among waves, six-character Jiaqing mark, gilt rubbed.

4¼in (10.9cm) diam

$6,000-6,600   SWO

A late-18th/early-19thC Chinese enameled porcelain imitation stone water pot, imitating agate in red and brown enamels, with gilt on the rim and turquoise in the interior, with a metal spoon terminating in a dragon's head.

2½in (6.5cm) wide

$2,400-2,900   WW

An 18th/19thC Chinese Qing export porcelain jardinière, the blind fretted "honeycomb" side panels centered by landscapes and flower specimens, with clobbered decoration throughout.

8¼in (21cm) high

$1,300-1,800   CHEF

A Chinese "Hundred Boys" vase, the boys celebrating the Spring Festival in extensive lakeside palace gardens with two separate pavilions linked by bridges over the water and set amid rocky mountains, the base with six-character Jiaqing seal mark, minor crazing in glaze.

29¼in (74cm) high

$11,000-13,000   DN

A Chinese Qing "Goldfish" bowl, painted with orange and black fish swimming among weeds, an iron-red, six-character Daoguang mark on base.

14½in (36.5cm) diam

$2,600-4,000   **DN**

A Chinese Daoguang blue-and-white puce enameled bowl, decorated with the eight Daoist immortals, the interior with a medallion enclosing Shoulao standing beside a spotted deer, Daoguang underglaze-blue seal mark, some wear and firing in interior of bowl.

8¾in (22cm) diam

$6,000-7,500   **DN**

A Chinese Daoguang Imperial green enameled "Dragon" dish, painted with a scaly five-clawed dragon chasing a sacred pearl amid flames, with two further dragons in pursuit of jewels on the reverse, the base with a six-character Daoguang seal mark in underglaze blue.

7in (17.6cm) diam

$17,000-21,000   **WW**

A Chinese Tongzhi "One Hundred Bats" yellow-ground porcelain teabowl, the bats painted in iron red and gilt, with a four-character mark in iron red, apparently made for the wedding celebration of Tongzhi Emperor Zaichun.

3½in (9cm) diam

$2,600-4,000   **CHEF**

A Chinese iron-red and blue vase, painted with bats among clouds, between a key fret and a wave border, six-character Tongzhi mark, minor surface scratches, a minute glaze chip on rim.

13¾in (35cm) high

$2,600-4,000   **SWO**

A pair of Chinese Cantonese porcelain vases, painted with dignitaries and warlords with soldiers, in pavilions with trees in a mountainous landscape, with dragon silhouette shoulder handles, restorations to both.

ca. 1850   33½in (85cm) and 33¾in (85.5cm) high

$8,000-9,000   **CHEF**

A 19thC Chinese porcelain baluster jar and cover, painted in famille noire enamels with dignitaries, attendants, and animals in landscape, on a carved hardwood stand, cover with minor chip on inner rim, restoration on rim of cover, general wear.

16½in (42cm) high

$2,000-2,600   **TEN**

A Chinese iron-red charger, painted with two dragons chasing a flaming pearl among clouds, enclosed with a ruyi-head border, the underside with scrolling lotus, with a six-character Guangxu mark, surface scratches.

15½in (39.4cm) diam

$1,700-2,100   **SWO**

A pair of 19thC Chinese iron-red rouleau vases, painted with Zhong Kui riding on horseback in a procession, the vanquisher of ghosts surrounded by his quelled demons carrying gongs, lanterns, parasols, and prisoners.

18¼in (46.5cm) high

$7,500-8,500   **WW**

A 19thC Chinese dayazhai-style green-ground baluster vase and cover, painted en grisaille with chrysanthemum and mallow blooms, with two large dragons amid the plants, the shoulder and foot encircled by yellow bands decorated with floral scrolls and cartouches enclosing magpies perched amid pink blossoms.

24¾in (63cm) high

$4,000-5,300   WW

A Chinese iron-red vase, painted with shou characters surrounded by scrolling lotus, a ruyi-head border on the shoulder, four-character "Shende Tang zhi" ("Made for the Hall of Prudent Virtue") mark in iron red, surface scratches, one handle with a small firing crack.

11¼in (28.5cm) high

$4,000-5,300   SWO

A pair of Chinese Canton porcelain vases, with foo dogs and dragons modeled on the shoulders, painted with Manchu figures in panels, possible regilding on shoulder dragons, one vase with rim chip.

ca. 1900   13¾in (35cm) high

$850-1,000   CHEF

A Chinese iron-red dou and cover, the archaic bowl decorated with dragons chasing a flaming pearl among clouds, the domed cover with a ball knop, with a six-character Guangxu mark in blue, surface scratches, gilt rubbed.

11¾in (30cm) high

$4,000-5,300   SWO

A Chinese Canton porcelain punch bowl, painted with Manchu figures in panels divided by flowers, on an associated wooden stand.

ca. 1900   14¾in (37.5cm) diam

$650-800   CHEF

A Chinese Qing porcelain bowl, painted with three butterflies on lotus leaves, with gilt rim, on a later wood stand, Jiaqing seal mark, hairline crack on rim, some enamel losses, glaze crazing, rubbing of the gilt rim.

7¼in (18.5cm) diam

$800-900   CHEF

A Chinese Qing famille noire porcelain vase, with two panels, one painted with a dragon and phoenix, the other a dragon and carp, prunus, and crackled-ice pattern basal band, the base with a six-character Kangxi mark, but later, with slight crazing in the blue enamel.

ca. 1890   19in (48.5cm) high

$600-600   CHEF

A Chinese Qing Canton vase and cover, decorated with birds and flower panels, alternating with Manchu court scenes, with a minor hairline crack in the rim, flaking of enamel, cover rim, and finial with small chips.

ca. 1890   17¾in (45cm) high

$550-650   CHEF

A Chinese blue-glazed cong vase, after an archaic jade carving, each side molded with eight raised bagua bands, covered under a sky-blue glaze, six-character Xuantong mark, surface scratches.

11½in (29cm) high

$2,000-2,600   SWO

A Chinese yellow-ground, blue and white dish, painted with gardenia blooms, encircled by pomegranate, grape, persimmon, and lotus bouquets, metal mounted rim, six-character Hongzhi mark, surface scratches, a hairline crack on rim, some areas with scratches in glaze.

10¼in (26.2cm) diam

$3,300-4,600 **SWO**

A Chinese Republic period grisaille-decorated landscape vase, decorated with a mountainous landscape with figures in dwellings near trees before a lake.

13½in (34.7cm) high

$9,000-10,500 **CHEF**

A Chinese Republic Period porcelain "Fruits" dish, enameled with pomegranates and peaches among leaves, with an apocryphal Chenghua (Ming) six-character mark in blue.

16in (40.5cm) diam

$1,500-1,800 **CHEF**

A Chinese Republic period porcelain bottle vase, painted in iron red with a pair of sky dragons, bats on the neck, basal-wave pattern banding, with a six-character Guangxu mark but considered later.

ca. 1920-30 *15¼in (38.5cm) high*

$3,300-4,000 **CHEF**

A Chinese Republic period enameled vase, painted with an old man walking by a basket of lingzhi and a burning stove, with two bats in flight among the rising smoke, inscribed with calligraphy followed by seal marks that read "Qi" and "Mi Dao," dated the renshen year and with a signature reading "Wang Qi," the base with a further "Mi Dao" seal mark.

8¾in (22cm) high

$2,000-2,600 **WW**

A Chinese Republic period enameled porcelain "Landscape" plaque, painted with pagodas, pavilions, and houses in a river landscape with mountains, with figures fishing on sampans, in a wood frame.

19¼in (49cm) wide excluding frame

$4,000-5,300 **WW**

An early-20thC Chinese polychrome enameled "Dragon" cup, painted with dragons chasing sacred pearls above waves, the flaming jewels picked out in gilt, with a four-character Daoguang mark.

2¾in (7cm) high

$400-550 **WW**

A 20thC Chinese enameled and biscuit figure, in the style of Zeng Longsheng, depicting a sitting musician.

Zeng Longsheng (1901-64) was a potter at the Jingdezhen kilns during the Republic period who specialized in figural works.

19½in (49.5cm) high

$1,050-1,300 **WW**

A Chinese porcelain large peach "Tianqiuping" vase, perhaps late Republic period, with fruiting peach branches with bats, bearing apocryphal Qianlong seal mark, with small firing blisters and tiny enamel loss.

The Republic period is generally regarded as 1912-49.

23¼in (59cm) high

$1,600 2,000 **CHEF**

A Chinese yellow-ground erotic dish, probably made by the Jiangxi Porcelain Company, the interior with centered scene with table and vases within a vivid pink and yellow ruyi-head border, the underside decorated with three erotic scenes on the rim and centered erotic scene on the base.

ca. 1950 *20in (51cm) diam*

$11,000 12,000 **DN**

ESSENTIAL REFERENCE—SATSUMA

Although Satsuma was an important center of ceramic production from the 16thC, the town is synonymous with the highly decorative export wares made there from the mid-19thC. Distinctive, cream-color earthenwares with finely crackled glazes and thickly applied enameled and gilded decoration, Satsuma wares were also produced in the town of Kyoto. Typical forms included "koro" (incense burners), vases, wine or sake ewers, bowls, covered jars, and figures; typical imagery included paneled scenes of people engaged in everyday activities, well-known landmarks, such as Mount Fuji, and indigenous Japanese flora and fauna, all surrounded by ornate borders. Displays at international fairs and exhibitions made them popular in the West, but quality of craftsmanship ranges from exceptionally high to poor—the latter often on pieces made specifically for sale in Western department stores.

A Japanese Meiji Satsuma plate, painted with ladies in three hanging scrolls, surrounded by ho-ho birds among clouds against a midnight-blue ground, with a gilt border, two Kinkozan zo marks on the base in gilt and in seal, gilt rubbed, minute chip, and crack on rim, some glaze flakes due to firing.

12¼in (31cm) diam

$4,000-5,300   **SWO**

A Japanese Satsuma vase, by Kinkozan, decorated with female figures beside a low table with a jardinière of flowers, signed within an oval on the side of the decoration, possibly Sozan, impressed mark on the base, a star crack noticable from the inside of the vase.

The Kinkozan family have been associated with pottery since 1645. They went on to become the largest producer of Satsuma ware from the end of the 19thC until 1927, after which the factory closed. Their main production period was approximately 1875-1927 under the leadership of Kinkozan V (1868-1927).

6½in (16.5cm) high

$1,200-1,450   **APAR**

A 19thC Japanese Meiji Satsuma vase, by Kinkozan, decorated in gilt and polychrome with two heart-shaped panels, one side with chickens with fruiting gourds, flowers, and scrolling tendrils, the reverse with ducks by a river, with a band of chevrons above the foot and on the rim, the base signed "Kinkozan zo."

10¼in (26cm) high

$6,000-6,600   **WW**

A Japanese Satsuma ewer and cover, by Kinkozan, decorated with trailing wisteria and detailed giltwork, signed on base, minor rubbing on the gilding.

9¼in (23.5cm) high

$6,000-6,600   **APAR**

RELEVANT JAPANESE PERIODS

Edo period
(1603-1868)

Meiji period
(1868-1912)

Taisho and Early Showa period
(1912-45)

A large Meiji Satsuma vase, by Kinkozan, with a peacock and peahen on one side, a raft of 13 ducks on the other side, with branches of flowering prunus and a couple of tits in flight above, the panels on a dark navy-blue ground with a dense pattern of stylized ginkgo leaves and brocade designs in gilt, the neck with formal roundels of birds and flowers enclosed between "shippo-tsunagi" ("jeweled cash"), the lip with flower heads between wave motifs and with a band of geometrical lappets above the foot, the base signed "Kinkozan zo."

The large dimensions of this vase suggest that it may have been made as a special commission or possibly for an international exhibition.

18¼in (46.5cm) high

$13,000-18,000   **WW**

A Meiji Satsuma pottery vase, by Kinkozan, the body divided into three panels depicting birds amid maple branches, trailing wisteria, and flowering cherry, all divided by decorative bands of tsuru, bamboo, and prunus, Kinkozan dzu seal on the base, some rubbing.

5¾in (14.5cm) high

$4,000-5,300   **DN**

A Japanese Satsuma koro, by Nakamura Beikei, with pierced white metal cover, body decorated with children playing, signature to base, one of the raised arms has been broken off and restored, minor rubbing to the gilding.

3¾in (9.5cm) wide

$3,300-4,000   **APAR**

A 19thC Japanese Meiji Satsuma vase, by Kinkozan, decorated with two panels with figures engaged in daily activities in a river landscape on one side, the reverse with two chickens in a bamboo grove, the sides painted with birds flying over trees by the riverbank in gilt, signed and impressed "Kinkozan zo" underneath.

6½in (16.5cm) high

$6,000-6,600 WW

A Japanese Meiji Satsuma plate, by Kinkozan, painted with figures in the yard of Kiyomizu-dera, among the maple and pine trees of Kyoto, Kinkozan mark on base, gilt rubbed on rim and mark.

10in (25.4cm) diam

$4,600-5,900 SWO

A Japanese Satsuma bowl, by Seikozan, internally decorated with a picnic scene, externally with floral sprays, elaborate painted mark on base.

8¾in (22cm) diam

$6,000-6,600 APAR

A 19thC Japanese Meiji Satsuma tray, by Fuzan, the well with beauties in a garden, a river on the side, and Mount Fuji in the distance, the figures in the foreground engaged in a game of kemari, with further figures observing from a veranda, the underside with further chrysanthemum blooms, signed "Fuzan" on the base.

The idea of the game of kemari is to keep the ball in the air for as long as possible.

9½in (23.9cm) wide

$3,300-4,600 WW

A 19thC Japanese Meiji Satsuma dish, by Kobayashi Keizan, decorated with birds in a river landscape, the chickens, ducks, swallows, and tits with peonies, chrysanthemum, prunus, and hibiscus, the reverse with butterflies and an elaborate signature for Kobayashi Keizan.

9¾in (24.7cm) diam

$4,600-5,300 WW

A 19thC Japanese Meiji Satsuma tray, by Tozan, decorated with butterflies, grasshoppers, beetles, fireflies and praying mantis, one small snail on one corner, the border with a band of shippo-tsunagi cash patterns, the rim with chrysanthemum, peonies, and hydrangea, the reverse with stylized flower heads and paulownia-shaped Imperial mon crests, a four-character mark on the side for Tozan.

12¼in (31.5cm) wide

$2,600-4,000 WW

A 19th/20thC Japanese Meiji Satsuma bowl, by Kinzan, the well with two rats gnawing at a feather and a third one in the distance, the rim painted with brocade patterns, the outside with branches of coral, the base signed "Kinzan" in a square reserve.

6in (15.1cm) diam

$2,100-2,600 WW

A 19thC Japanese Meiji Satsuma bowl, by Nakamura Baikei, painted with revelers on a pleasure boat, the vessel with a dragon-shaped prow and a large model of a white phoenix on the roof, the family crest for the Tokugawa clan underneath, "Maru ni Mitsuba Aoi mon," two cranes flying above, the rim with bands of chrysanthemum, the outside with many cloud-shaped panels containing figures engaged in various daily activities, the base signed "Nakamura Baikei" with a panel enclosing a long self-congratulatory inscription.

The decoration to the well may be a reference to chapter 24 of "The Tale of Genji," in which the Prince arranges for the construction of Chinese-style barges with dragon and phoenix decoration for a spring party in honor of Lady Murasaki, his favorite consort.

4¾in (12.2cm) diam

$8,000-10,500   WW

A 19thC Japanese Meiji Satsuma bowl, by Yozan, the well with butterflies above peonies, figures in a mountainous river landscape and large carp swimming in a stream, the outside with butterflies among peonies, chrysanthemum, hibiscus, and hydrangea, the base signed "Kyoto Yozan."

4in (10cm) wide

$4,000-5,300   WW

A 19thC Japanese Meiji Gosu Satsuma koro incense burner, decorated with flowering prunus and chrysanthemum, the lid in white metal, the base stamped "Satuma sshin" under the Shimazu mon.

9in (23cm) high

$1,600-2,000   WW

A 19thC Japanese Meiji Satsuma vase, decorated with a bijin standing under branches of maple, two with a small karako boy, their ornate kimonos with complex designs of geometrical patterns and flowers.

7in (17.5cm) high

$1,300-2,000   WW

A 19thC Japanese Meiji Satsuma box, by Kanzan, two sides with figures in mountainous river landscapes, the others with peonies, hydrangea, irises, and chrysanthemum, the inside painted with a still life of scholarly and Buddhist objects, painting on the back, kakemono, signed "Kanzan."

4¾in (12.1cm) wide

$4,000-5,300   WW

A 19thC Japanese Meiji Satsuma bowl, by Ryuzan, the well painted with hundreds of butterflies, the inner rim with a band of key fret and shippo-tsunagi cash on the reverse, the outside with chrysanthemum, peony, hibiscus and irises, above crickets, cicadas, flies and fireflies, the base signed "Dai Nihon Kyoro fu Ryuzan tsukuru."

9in (23cm) diam

$6,500-8,000   WW

A large 19thC Japanese Meiji Gosu Satsuma vase, decorated with flowering prunus trees and banded hedges, with gold scrolling clouds above, the neck with a band of chrysanthemum flower heads in rhomboids.

The color Gosu Blue is an on-glaze enamel found on a type of Satsuma that used to be called Imperial Satsuma in the mid-to late 19thC. Gosu Blue is distinctive and thick, and can be dark blue, green, or black, depending on the firing. "Satsuma Gosu Blue" was produced in limited quantity in Kyoto in the mid-19thC.

16¾in (42.5cm) high

$2,600-4,000   WW

A 19thC Japanese Meiji Satsuma vase, by Ryozan for the Yasuda Company, with figures in mountainous river landscapes, one side with Mount Fuji towering above revelers, some drinking sake in small thatched huts and setting up a picnic under the sakura cherry blossoms, the reverse with travelers on the shore of the Abe River, a sign on the side mentioning the Tokaido Road, with medallions on the shoulder enclosing the "Maru ni Mitsuba Aoi mon," the family crest for the Tokugawa clan, the base signed with the marks for the Yasuda Company, "Dai Nihon," and "Kyoto Ryozan" with the Shimazu mon underneath.

The elaborate decoration on one side depicts the shores of the Abe River, where the 19th station of the Tokaido Road, the main artery of Japan that connected Edo (Tokyo) to Kyoto, was located. Ryozan was the head decorator for the Yasuda Satsuma factory, and this is a telling example of his talent.

11¾in (30cm) high

$13,000-18,000   WW

ESSENTIAL REFERENCE—IMARI

Imari ware is a Western term for a brightly colored style of Arita ware Japanese export porcelain made in the area of Arita, in the former Hizen province. It was exported to Europe in large quantities, especially between the second half of the 17thC and the first half of the 18thC. Imari is typically decorated in underglaze blue, with red, gold, black for outlines, and sometimes other colors, added in overglaze. The style was so successful that Chinese and European producers began to copy it. Sometimes the different overglaze styles of Kakiemon and Kutani ware are also grouped under Imari ware. The name derives from the port of Imari, Saga, from which they were shipped to Nagasaki, where the Dutch East India Company and the Chinese had trading outposts. Blue-and-white wares were called Arita ware although in fact Imari, Kakiemon, and Arita were often produced at the same kilns. Imari ware was copied in both China and Europe, particularly in England in the 19thC by such companies as Masons Ironstone, Spode/Copeland, Hicks & Meigh, and Ridgway.

A pair of 18th/19thC Japanese Tokkeuriedo Imari sake bottles, decorated in underglaze blue, gilt, red, green, and yellow enamels, with panels showing a writhing dragon and a tiger among prunus flowers and rockwork, with figures under sakura blossoms, the shoulder with Buddhist emblems, ho-ho birds, and peonies, both with a Chinese mark for Da Ming Chenghua nian zhi.

12¼in (31cm) high

$2,600-4,000　　　**WW**

An 18thC Japanese Edo Imari vase and cover, decorated with ho-ho birds flying over paulownia, the leaves evoking the Imperial mon, on a dense background of leaves and flower heads, the neck with brocade designs, the cover with similar decoration and topped with a fierce shishi on a rocky outcrop.

36¼in (92cm) high

$6,000-7,500　　　**WW**

A pair of 18thC Japanese Edo Imari vases, decorated with ho-ho birds perched on branches of paulownia, on a deep navy-blue ground with flowering chrysanthemum among scrolling tendrils in gilt, with shaped lappets above the foot and smaller panels around the neck enclosing further birds and stylized lotus flowers, the shoulders with a band of leaping dragons on a red ground, raised on European ormolu mounts.

The ho-ho birds decorating this pair of Japanese Imari vases are essentially the equivalent in Japanese mythology of the fenghuang in Chinese mythology—the latter, images of which first appeared some 7,000 to 8,000 years ago, is commonly known in the Western world as either the Chinese phoenix or simply the phoenix. Sometimes also referred to as hoo's, foo's, ho-wo's, or just ho's, ho-ho birds—like their Chinese equivalents—symbolized good luck or fortune, as well as longevity, fidelity, and wisdom. Although often portrayed as an amalgam of several birds, including pheasants, storks, herons, and birds of paradise, they were essentially characterized by long beaks, curving necks, flowing tails, and prominent claws and crestings. As a symbolic decorative motif, they were employed not just on porcelain, as here, but throughout the decorative arts—notably, pottery, sculpture, and cabinetry and woodwork. Furthermore, the surge in popularity of Asian artifacts and decoration in Europe during the mid-18thC saw their recurring appearance in, especially, Rococo-style decoration, most notably in France and England, where they began to appear on all manner of objects and surfaces, ranging from fine-quality porcelain and furniture—notably, mirrors, and mantel clocks—to candle stands, candelabrum, and ornate plasterwork.

28in (71cm) high

$17,000-21,000　　　**WW**

One of a near pair of large late-19th/early-20thC Japanese Meiji Imari porcelain covered jars, enameled and gilded with floral and foliate imagery, the top of the lid set with shishi as a finial.

37¾in (96cm) and 38½in (98cm) high

$6,000-6,600 the pair　　**L&T**

A late-19th/early-20thC Japanese Meiji Imari porcelain covered jar, the faceted body forming hexagonal cartouches with gilt and enamel decorations.

26in (66cm) high

$1,600-2,000　　**L&T**

A late-19th/early-20thC Japanese Meiji Imari porcelain covered jar, decorated with shishi chasing brocade balls in cartouches reserved on a blue and gilded ground.

19¾in (50cm) high

$650-800　　**L&T**

A 17thC Japanese Edo Arita ewer, with three panels of chrysanthemum and peonies among rockwork and long grasses, on a dense ground of karakusa scrolls.

14¼in (36.5cm) high

$1,050-1,300 **WW**

A 17thC Japanese Edo Arita mug, decorated with panels painted with a centered figure surrounded by plantain leaves and rockwork, on a ground of karakusa scrolls.

7in (18cm) high

$1,200-1,450 **WW**

A pair of Japanese Edo Arita vases and covers, decorated with ho-ho birds in a river landscape, with hibiscus and peony flowers among rocky outcrops, with karakusa scrolls and palmettes on the shoulder and Buddhist emblems on the neck, one cover associated.

ca. 1700   26½in (67cm) and 26in (66cm) high

$13,000-16,000 **WW**

A Japanese Edo Arita dish, decorated in the Kraak style with two ho-ho birds among rockwork, pomegranates, and hibiscus flowers in the well, the rim with panels enclosing peonies and other flowers.

ca. 1700   15¼in (38.5cm) diam

$400-550 **WW**

A 17thC Japanese Tokkuri Edo Arita sake bottle, decorated with a stylized mountainous river landscape, the neck and foot with bands of lappets.

Provenance: From the collection of Richard Gordon Smith (1858-1918). Gordon Smith was an English traveler, sportsman, and naturalist who lived in Japan at the turn of the century, recording his experience in his "Ill-Spelled Diaries" and transcribing traditional myths, which he later published in "Ancient Tales and Folklore of Japan" (1908). Entries from his diaries were later published in "Travels in the Land of the Gods: The Japan Diaries of Richard Gordon Smith" (1986).

8¼in (21cm) high

$750-850 **WW**

A late-17thC Japanese Edo Arita vase, painted with flowers issuing from rockwork, with hairline crack on rim.

10in (25cm) high

$1,300-2,000 **DN**

A 17thC Japanese Edo Arita ewer, decorated with figures in mountainous river landscapes on a ground of karakusa scrolls, the neck and handle with formal flowers and further scrolling tendrils.

Cf. Gordon Lang, "The Wrestling Boys, An exhibition of Chinese and Japanese ceramics from the 16th to the 18thC in the collection at Burghley House," p. 17 no.49, for a comparable ewer. This type of pattern displays similarities with Japanese wares decorated in the "Van Frytom" style produced as export ware for the Netherlands.

9¼in (23.5cm) high

$1,300-1,800 **WW**

An 18th/19thC Japanese Tokkuri Edo or later Arita sake bottle, each side depicting a carp leaping up a waterfall, with pine and prunus above, the shoulder painted with pine needles and four chidori birds.

7¾in (20cm) high

$1,300-2,000 **WW**

A pair of 18thC Japanese Edo Arita dishes, decorated with three deer prancing among maple leaves, with brown-edged rims, the reverse with karakusa scrolls, a fuku mark on the base.

Deer and maple leaves are often depicted together in Japanese art, because they both symbolize the arrival of fall. The phrase "momiji ni shika" ("maple leaves and deer") also conveys the idea of a perfect pairing.

8¼in (21cm) diam

$2,000-2,600 **WW**

An 18thC Japanese "Blue de Hue" bottle vase, shaped as a double gourd, decorated with a continuous design of scrolling clouds and wisps of mist on a creamy-white ground.

"Blue de Hue" is Chinese blue-and-white export porcelain for the Vietnamese market. It was ordered by the Vietnamese court by way of diplomatic missions to China. Most of them were produced in Jingdezhen. Hue is the name of the old city where the Vietnamese king resided.

10¼in (26cm) high

$8,500-10,000   **WW**

A Japanese Meiji Seto porcelain vase by Kato Tomotaro, decorated with a creeper-clad, spreading pine tree, signed on the base "Yugyokuen Toju sei."

Tomotaro was a student of Gottfried Wagener (among others) and in 1877 became manager of the Edogawa Seitosho (Ceramics Manufacturing Company). In 1883, he took over a kiln set up by Wagener and renamed it Yugyokuengama, at the same time adopting the art name "Toju."

9in (22.6cm) high

$2,100-2,600   **DN**

A Japanese Meiji vase, by Makuzu Kozan, decorated with a Chinese-style mountainous river landscape, with thatched huts nestling in the shadows of the mountains, signed "Makuzu Kozan sei," with a fitted tomobako wood box inscribed "Kabin" ("vase"), "Seika iroiri sansui no zu, Makuzu Kozan saku" ("Blue landscape with color, made by Makuzu Kozan").

ca. 1900   *12½in (31.5cm) high*

$6,000-7,500   **WW**

A 20thC Japanese Meiji or Taisho vase, by Makuzu Kozan, decorated with a river landscape in underglaze blue and with a faint pink hue in the sky, with a stream and pines fading away into the mist, the base signed "Makuzu Kozan sei."

12in (30.7cm) high

$3,300-4,600   **WW**

A 20thC Japanese Taisho or Showa Fukagawa vase, decorated with a small quail hiding among sprays of millet and daisies, with a gilded rim and signed "Fukagawa sei" with the Fujiyama mark.

In 1856, Ezaiemon Fukagawa became head of his family's porcelain business and in 1875 founded Koransha (The Company of the Scented Orchid) in Arita, Japan, to produce tableware for export.

15in (38cm) high

$750-850   **WW**

A massive 18thC Japanese Edo Arita white glazed vase, the shoulders with elephant-head handles.

It is possible that this impressive vase is a blank piece meant to be enameled or lacquered at a later stage.

31½in (79.8cm) high

$7,500-8,500   **WW**

A rare Japanese Edo Arita model of a shishi lion dog, the body of the mythical beast contorted as it lands on its front paws after a jump from heaven to earth, modeled baring its fangs with a ferocious expression, a collar and bell painted around its neck.

ca. 1700   *11¾in (30.2cm) high*

$8,500-10,000   **WW**

A 17thC Japanese Edo Kakiemon dish, with two ho-ho birds in a luxuriant garden with peonies and chrysanthemum, the border on the rim with four birds flying or perched among foliage.

8½in (21.3cm) diam

$1,300-2,000   **WW**

A Japanese Edo Ko-Kutani bowl, with four large butterflies fluttering across the well, with smaller insects flying around them, the underside painted with three butterflies and red insects, with a fuku mark on the base.

Butterflies are rare as a centered motif on Ko-Kutani dishes. The design originated in the Heian period (794-1185) and was the symbol of the Taira clan.

ca. 1660   *6in (15cm) diam*

$1,050-1,300   **WW**

A rare 17thC Japanese Edo teabowl (chawan) for the tea ceremony, the tall U-shaped body of irregular shape with faint grooves on the surface and a slight depression on the side, decorated with a geometrical pattern of rhomboids, possibly inspired by textile patterns, painted in gold and silver lacquer, purple, green, and red on a black ground, the base incised with a mark for Ninsei.

Provenance: Formerly in the collection of Major William Peer Groves (1878-1946) and then Roger Soame Jenyns (1904-76). Illustrated in R. S. Jenyns, "Japanese Pottery," pl .94B, and discussed p. 214. Major Peer Groves (1878-1946) was the recipient of the Japanese Imperial Order of the Rising Sun and the Russian Imperial Orders of Vladimir and Stanislaus. A number of pieces from his collection are now at the British Museum and at the Victoria and Albert Museum in London. Roger Soame Jenyns was an important scholar and collector of Chinese and Japanese art. After working for the Hong Kong (China) civil service, where he learned Cantonese, he joined the British Museum, later becoming Deputy Keeper of the Department of Oriental Antiquities. Jenyns is also known for his seminal works on Chinese and Japanese art, including "Later Chinese Porcelain" (1951), "Ming Pottery and Porcelain" (1953), "Wares of the Transitional Period between Ming and the Ch'ing 1620-1683" (1955), "Japanese Porcelain" (1965), and "Japanese Pottery" (1971), among others. Many Japanese pieces from Soame Jenyns's personal collection are currently on display at the Fitzwilliam Museum, Cambridge, UK.

4¾in (12cm) diam

$33,000-40,000　　　WW

A pair of Japanese Meiji porcelain vases, painted with warriors, six-character marks, some surface wear.

9¾in (24.5cm) high

$1,300-1,800　　　TEN

A pair of Japanese porcelain trumpet vases, enameled with leafy bamboo stems.

ca. 1910　　14½in (37cm) high

$450-600　　　CHEF

A Japanese Meiji Kakiemon- style model of a tiger, after a 17thC Japanese model, painted in polychrome with many stripes contrasting with its lemon-yellow coat.

ca. 1900　　10¼in (26cm) high

$2,000-2,600　　　WW

A pair of Japanese late-Meiji Kutani porcelain vases, painted with a daimyo and attendants and flowers among rocks, on hardwood stands, both restored with cracks in foot rim and base.

18½in (47cm) high

$450-600　　　CHEF

A pair of Japanese late-Meiji earthenware annular vases, painted with precious Buddhist objects on one side, and with nine sparrows on the other, one with tiny hairline crack on rim, both with rubbed gilding, glued onto wooden plinths.

7½in (19cm) high

$2,600-4,000　　　CHEF

A Japanese Edo celadon-ground ewer, decorated in iron-red, cyan, cerulean, and black enamels, painted with prunus and bush clover.

It is possible that the shape originated from Middle Eastern vessels, such as kendi, and so the ewer may have been intended for that market. Enameled celadon pieces are relatively rare and were produced from an early date in Arita. Several pieces are included in the 18thC collection of King Augustus the Strong of Saxony, in Dresden.

7½in (19.2cm) high

$2,600-4,000　　　WW

A 20thC Japanese Meiji or Taisho vase, by Seifu Yohei III, with butterflies among peonies and leafy branches, the base signed "Seifu," on a wood stand and with two tomobako wooden boxes, the inner box inscribed "Hyakka nishiki botan no zu kabin" ("flower vase with hundred colorful peonies") with seal, the lid signed "Seifu tsukuru" ("made by Seifu").

10¼in (26cm) high

$2,600-4,000　　　WW

ESSENTIAL REFERENCE—CLOISONNÉ

- Cloisonné is an ancient technique for decorating metalwork objects with colored material held in place by metal strips or wire, normally of gold. The decoration is formed by first adding compartments, "cloisons" in French, to the metal object by soldering or attaching silver or gold as wires or thin strips placed on their edges. These remain visible in the finished piece, separating the different compartments of the enamel or inlays, which are often of several colors.
- The technique reached China in the 13–14thC, probably from Byzantium. The earliest datable pieces being from the reign of the Xuande Emperor (1425–35), however, show a full use of Chinese styles suggesting considerable experience in the technique. By the beginning of the 18thC, the Kangxi Emperor had a cloisonné workshop among the many Imperial factories. The most elaborate and highly valued Chinese pieces are from the early Ming dynasty, especially the reigns of the Xuande Emperor and Jingtai Emperor (1450–57). Although the Chinese craftsmen seem to have been influenced by skilled Byzantine refugees fleeing the Fall of Constantinople in 1453, it could also be argued that China obtained knowledge of the technique from the Middle East. Cobalt blue, dark green, red, yellow, white, and pink—the latter added in the 18thC—are recurring colors in Chinese cloisonné and often contrasted against a turquoise-colored ground.

A mid-16thC Chinese cloisonné tray, decorated with a stylized chrysanthemum motif, the design surrounded by flower heads amid scrolling foliage, raised on three short feet, the gilded base incised with a visvavajra.

7in (17.7cm) high 35.3oz

$12,000-15,000   WW

A 16thC Chinese cloisonné "Carp" bowl, the well with a fish leaping from crashing waves, with the eight auspicious buddhist emblems (bajixiang) and flowers on the exterior.

9½in (24cm) diam

$6,000-6,600   WW

A pair of Chinese Ming cloisonné "Lotus" bowls, decorated with six large lotus flowers on a turquoise ground, raised on short flared feet.

$3,300-4,000   WW

A Chinese Ming cloisonné "Cranes" incense burner, with later Qing mounts on the rim and foot, the base with a four-character Jingtai mark.

4½in (11.6cm) high

$17,000-21,000   WW

A Chinese Ming cloisonné bowl, with a scrolling multicolored lotus band enclosed by further floral and lappet bands, with incised six-character Wanli mark, some wear on gilding.

4in (10cm) diam

$12,000-15,000   DN

A Chinese late Ming cloisonné bowl, enameled with Buddhist lions chasing brocade balls among clouds, the interior with a carp among waves, with surface scratches and dents, both enamels and cloisons with patches of infilling and restoration.

9in (22.8cm) diam 22.2oz

$7,500-8,500   SWO

A 17thC Chinese Ming cloisonné bowl, with tall rounded sides rising to the everted rim, supported on a splayed foot, the exterior decorated with a wide register of alternating upright and pendant lotus scrolls, the interiors with birds flying above a pond, damaged with some filling repairs and losses and with replacement foot rim.

9¼in (23.5cm) diam

$4,600-5,900   DN

A Chinese Qianlong cloisonné basin, with shou characters above lotus blooms, the center with aquatic animals, including crustacea, a fish, a turtle, and a toad swimming through crashing waves, surrounded by precious objects, with winged horses flying over the sea to the cavetto, the feet possibly later.

10½in (26.5cm) high

$26,000-33,000   WW

A Chinese Qianlong cloisonné weight, of a mythical beast, its fur cast in details, its body with green and blue enamels, gilt rubbed, some enamel losses, surface scratches.

3in (7.8cm) wide 12.7oz

$7,500-8,500　　　　**SWO**

A Chinese Qianlong Imperial cloisonné jardinière, decorated with panels of stylized lotus and angular scrolls, the rim with flowers and foliage.

8in (20.5cm) diam

$6,500-8,000　　　　**WW**

CLOSER LOOK—INCENSE BURNER

This Qianlong (1736-95) cloisonné incense burner has an exterior divided into two bands of scrolling lotus.

It is enameled in vivid tones of white, red, yellow, pink, green, and blue against a turquoise ground.

Incense in China is traditionally used in a wide range of Chinese cultural activities, including religious ceremonies, ancestor veneration, traditional medicine, and in daily life.

Known as "xiang," fragrance or incense was used by the Chinese cultures starting from Neolithic times, with it coming to greater prominence in the Xia, Shang, and Zhou dynasties.

A Chinese Qianlong cloisonné incense burner, set at the shoulder with a pair of styliaed dragon handles, decorated with taotie masks surrounded by leafy scrolling lotus, the interior rim of the lid dented, knop loose and dented, surface scratches, small holes on top of handles, flanges loose, and the foot rim dented.

7in (17.5cm) high 30.6oz

$21,000-24,000　　　　**SWO**

A Chinese Qianlong cloisonné incense burner, with Qianlong mark and "wei" incised on base, enamel losses, knocks on edges.

3¾in (9.4cm) diam 15.5oz

$8,000-10,500　　　　**SWO**

A pair of 18thC Chinese cloisonné birds, their eyes picked out in dark red, the covers formed as their wings.

7½in (19cm) wide

$1,300-2,600　　　　**WW**

A 18th/19thC Chinese cloisonné incense burner, enameled with archaic scrolls and blades, the feet with taotie masks and flanges, with surface scratches and knocks on edges, enamel losses in numerous places.

13¾in (35cm) high

$6,000-6,600　　　　**SWO**

A 19thC Chinese cloisonné vase, with four panels with a dog, cat, birds, and butterflies amid trees and flowers, on a lotus-decorated ground, with bats, fruit, and precious objects on the neck.

15½in (39.5cm) high

$1,300-2,600　　　　**WW**

A 19thC Chinese Qing cloisonné box and cover, with scrolling foliage and lotus heads, with surface cracks on the interior of the base.

4in (10cm) diam

$1,700-2,100   **DN**

A pair of 19thC Chinese late Qing cloisonné vases, decorated with carp and bands of stiff leaves.

7in (18cm) high

$1,050-1,200   **CHEF**

A pair of Chinese Qing bronze cloisonné and champlevé enamel elephants, the trappings and harness detailed with champlevé enamels and inset with colored glass.

ca. 1900   *16in (41cm) high*

$6,000-6,600   **DN**

A pair of large Chinese yellow-ground cloisonné enamel vases.

21in (53cm) high

$4,000-5,300   **DRA**

A Chinese cloisonné enamel ox cart group.

15in (38cm) long

$1,300-1,800   **DRA**

A pair of Chinese cloisonné models of cranes, with archaistic motifs, with plumage in inlaid wire, their wings detachable.

ca. 1900   20¼in (51.5cm) high 70.5oz and 88.1oz

$650-1,050   **WW**

A Chinese late Qing cloisonné model of an elephant, its saddle blanket decorated with fruit and precious objects over crashing waves, with a vase decorated with antiques upon the animal's back, the ears removable, with a wood stand.

The image of an elephant carrying a vase represents the rebus "taiping youxiang," which carries the sentiment of wishing for peaceful times. An elephant with a vase is a visual embodiment of this expression, because the Chinese words for "vase" ("ping") and "elephant" ("xiang") are homophonous with two words in the saying.

ca. 1900   *13¾in (35cm) high 112.8oz*

$10,500-16,000   **WW**

A large pair of Chinese cloisonné enamel crane form candle prickets.

24in (61cm) high

$2,900-3,700   **DRA**

An 18thC Chinese Canton, famille rose enamel water pot, decorated with flowers, fruit, birds, animals, and insects, enclosed between bands of ruyi heads and lappets, with a wood stand.

2½in (6.5cm) high 2.1oz

$1,300-2,000   **WW**

ESSENTIAL REFERENCE—HAN DYNASTY

The Han dynasty (206 BC–AD 220) was one of the great dynasties of ancient China. Much of Chinese culture was established during it, and it is sometimes referred to as the "Golden Age of Ancient China." It was an era of peace, prosperity, and cultural and technological advancements, when Confucianism was established as the official state philosophy—a decision that still resonates in China 2,000 years later. In the decorative arts, the Han is especially associated with metalware and ceramics, and the dynasty's relics and artifacts have survived in considerable numbers; they can be seen in Han-era tombs, Chinese museums, such as the National Museum in Beijing and the Luoyang Ancient Tombs Museum, and in other museums around the world.

A Chinese Southern Song bronze archaistic hu-shaped vase, cast in relief with stylized birds amid rocks and crashing waves, the neck flanked by animal mask handles and decorated with bands of dragons, ruyi-shaped clouds, and other archaistic motifs reserved on a leiwen ground.

9½in (24cm) high 38.8oz

$22,000-26,000 WW

An 18thC Chinese Qing bracket-lobed bronze dish, the base impressed with a six-character Xuande mark, some scratches.

7in (17cm) diam

$12,000-15,000 DN

A Chinese Han inscribed bronze basin, the basin with flared rim and cast with band of rings and a decorative pair of taotie mask handles, the interior impressed with an auspicious line "fu gui chang yi hou wang," possibly restored.

13in (34cm) diam

$1,050-1,200 DN

A Chinese Ming bronze gu-shaped vase, cast with six petal-shaped facets, the base incised with a two character Xuande mark.

8in (20.2cm) high 26.2 oz

$9,000-12,000 WW

A Chinese Ming "Eight Trigrams" Fanghu bronze vase, a band of eight trigrams encircling the rim, the neck bordered with four medallions with lotus foliage and mythical beasts, with a pair of loop handles in the form of dragons, the base incised with two auspicious characters "fu qi," some wear.

10½in (26.5cm) high

$2,000-2,600 DN

A Chinese Ming bronze incense burner, molded with scrolling lotus in relief, the neck with Daoist emblems, dragon handles, four-character Hu Wenming mark, scratches and dents.

8¼in (21cm) wide 52.9oz

$22,000-26,000 SWO

A Chinese late Ming archaistic bronze vase, by Lei, with taotie masks and stylized beasts against a leiwen ground, with two loop handles, highlighted in gilt.

12in (30.5cm) high 130oz

$6,000-7,500 WW

A Chinese Ming parcel-gilt and silver decorated bronze "Butterfly" incense burner, with a band of auspicious beribboned objects with two loop handles emerging from stylized animal masks, the base with "Yun Jian Hu Wenming zhi."

6¾in (17cm) wide 33oz

$22,000-26,000 WW

A Chinese Ming bronze bodhisattva, sitting in "rajalilasana," the posture of royal ease, his hair swept back into a topknot beneath the crown with long braids cascading down his shoulders, wearing bracelets, earrings, and a beaded necklace, with surface scratches and dents.

11¾in (29.5cm) high 123.4oz

$26,000-33,000   **SWO**

CLOSER LOOK—BRONZE FIGURE

An impressive large 17thC Chinese parcel-gilt and lacquered bronze figure of an attendant.

He is depicted wearing a tall hat, flowing robes, and elaborate shoes.

The attendant is holding a box tied with ribbon containing an official's seal, with both hands before him.

The figure is probably the attendant of a Daoist official and would have been positioned by the side of a larger statue of his master.

A bronze figure, highlighted in gilt, raised on a stepped pedestal picked out in red lacquer.

16in (40.5cm) high 246.9oz

$13,000-16,000   **WW**

A Chinese Ming bronze figure of Guandi, sitting on a throne, robe decorated with a leaping dragon and with incised cloud decoration, with traces of old red lacquer and gilding, the back with a piece of bronze missing and further cracks, extensive on old lacquer and gilding.

18¼in (46cm) high 282.1oz

$17,000-21,000   **DN**

A Chinese Ming gilt bronze "Ram" scroll weight, with a spray of lingzhi fungus in its mouth, with wear on the gilding.

2¼in (5.4cm) wide

$1,700-2,100   **DN**

A 17thC Chinese bronze figure of Damo, standing barefoot and his right hand holding a shoe, his face framed with bushy eyebrows, curly beard, and moustache, the back of the figure incised with a four-character "qingyang shanren" mark.

10in (25.5cm) high

$21,000-24,000   **DN**

A 17thC Chinese gold-splashed Yen Yen vase, with two dragon-shaped handles, the body with three chilong on the shoulder and four shou characters.

19¼in (49.1cm) high 423oz

$8,500-10,000   **WW**

A 17thC Chinese Ming bronze figure of Damo, depicting the legend of Damo crossing the Yangtze River on a single reed, the figure possibly glued back to the base.

The Buddhist monk Bodhidharma, in Chinese Damo, was the Indian monk credited with founding the Chan (or Zen) tradition of East Asian Buddhism.

9¾in (24.5cm) high

$12,000-15,000   **DN**

A 17th/18thC Chinese bronze bombe censer, modeled with a pair of loop handles, with a six-character Xuande nianzhi mark, scratches on the surface.

15in (38.5cm) wide

$8,500-10,000   **DN**

A Chinese gilt-bronze incense burner, with a pair of faceted openwork handles projecting below the everted rim, gilt splash decoration, four-character "Shijia Guzhi" mark on the base, surface scratches.

5½in (14cm) wide 51.2oz

$180,000-210,000   SWO

A Chinese bronze censer, supported on three feet encircling the flat base bearing a crisply cast six-character Xuande mark, some marks to the old patina.

4¼in (10.7cm) wide 66.5oz

$130,000-200,000   DN

A 17th/18thC Chinese bronze pear-shaped vase, inspired by the archaic bronze zhi, the neck with two elephant-head handles, the body cast in relief with flowers and fruits.

9in (23cm) high

$4,000-5,300   DN

A Chinese bronze censer, the body flanked by a pair of angular handles, the base case with a six-character Xuande mark, the exterior polished and with minor scratches, two patches of restoration on one handle.

5¼in (13.5cm) wide 50.6oz

$80,000-90,000   DN

An 18thC Chinese bronze incense burner, on three elephant feet, molded with scrolling lotus in relief, elephant handles, four-character Xuande seal mark in zhuanshu, surface scratches, censer with small holes.

19¾in (50cm) high 234oz

$13,000-16,000   SWO

A Chinese Qing bronze "Mythical Beast" incense burner and cover, cast as a lionlike beast, the caparison cast in relief with lotus scrolls, the body inset with coral and turquoise-colored beads.

A caparison is a traditional ornamental covering for an animal.

13in (33cm) high 70.6oz

$40,000-45,000   WW

A Chinese Qing gold-splashed tripod incense burner, with two upright loop handles, the base with a six-character Xuande mark.

6¼in (15.5cm) wide 42.3oz

$12,000-15,000   WW

A Chinese Guiming Qing bronze archaistic food vessel, cast with taotie masks and other archaistic motifs against a leiwen ground, with loop handles from the mouths of mythical creatures, with a wood cover with a hardstone finial.

13½in (34cm) wide 211.6oz

$2,000-2,600   WW

A Chinese gilt-bronze hinged box, with warriors in relief in a battle outside a village gate or in a rocky landscape, with a six-character Tongzhi mark, gilt rubbed, scratches and dents, hinge missing.

6in (15.4cm) wide 46.3oz

$4,000-5,300   **SWO**

A Chinese Qing bronze figure of Dipankara, sitting in "dhyanasana," his hands held at his chest in "dharmachakra mudra," curled hair surmounted by an "ushnisha."

7¾in (19.3cm) high 70.5oz

$6,000-6,600   **WW**

A Chinese late-Qing enameled bronze vase, with bands and lappets enclosing taotie masks and other archaistic motifs, with two bird-shaped handles flanking the neck, the base with a four-character Xuande mark.

15½in (39.7cm) high 194oz

$2,000-2,600   **WW**

A 19thC Chinese Qing bronze censer, with two lion-head handles, with a bronze tripod stand, the base cast with "daoguang xuande nianzhi" mark, the base of the censer relacquered, general wear.

9½in (24cm) wide 100.4oz

$2,000-2,600   **DN**

A Chinese Qing gilt-lacquered bronze model of a canid, the beast well detailed and with a bushy tail.

2¾in (7cm) wide 7.9oz

$1,600-2,000   **WW**

A Chinese bronze incense burner, with figures holding ring handles, six-character Xuande mark, surface scratches and dents.

5¾in (14.5cm) wide

$850-1,050   **SWO**

A pair of late-19thC Chinese Qing bronze figural candle holders, modeled as Immortals, bases cast with auspicious mythical animals.

15½in (39.5cm) and 15¾in (40cm) high

$1,050-1,300   **CHEF**

A 20thC gilt-bronze "Dragon" ritual temple bell, with two dragons, cast with a handle shaped as a pair of dragons.

9½in (24cm) high 352.7oz

$1,500-1,800   **DN**

Judith Picks

Oh, the glamour of eggs for breakfast served in this egg cruet by the famous Wang Hing & Co. You can imagine the excitement when these exotic items arrived at Tiffany's and Liberty's.

Wang Hing & Co was established by the wealthy Lo family in Canton soon after the 1842 Treaty of Nanking. Having started as dealers in jade, the firm went on to become one of the most prolific and famous retail silversmiths of export silver during the late China trade period. Previously, Chinese silver had been created largely in the same style as Georgian British silverware. Suddenly, the export trade to the Western world meant that Chinese export silver began to feature traditional Chinese motifs, patterns, and symbols. This would prove to be popular with Western retailers and consumers, and the novelty of this new style of silverware made the pieces fashionable. Wang Hing & Co later opened premises in Shanghai and unveiled a flagship store in Hong Kong in the early 1920s,

which sold various luxury goods in addition to silverware. This reputation is largely due to the firm's relationship with Tiffany's. Tiffany's had an affinity for Chinese patterns and styles of silverware decoration, particularly in the mid-20thC, when Asian styles had a resurgence in popularity. In the 1940s, the invasion of Hong Kong by the Japanese lead to civil unrest and large-scale air raids and bombings, which not only saw the closure of the Wang Hing & Co. flagship storefront, but also saw the demise of the business as a whole.

A 19thC Chinese silver six-piece egg cruet, by Wang Hing, the feet with a dragon among clouds and six slots.

10¾in (27.5cm) wide 21.5oz

$2,600-4,000 SWO

A 19thC Chinese silver kettle and stand, the kettle with a scaly dragon wrapping itself around the body, cover decorated with sprays of bamboo, the handle, spout, and stand formed as bamboo branches, with a silver burner with a removable wick, the kettle and stand with punch marks reading "Cheongshin" and "Yi An."

8¾in (22cm) high 42.7oz

$2,600-4,000 WW

A late-19thC Chinese silver cup, decorated with birds in flight among prunus trees, with a shield on one side, the handles shaped as tree trunks, the foot with punch marks reading "Ti" and "WS."

10½in (26.6cm) high 24.4oz

$1,300-2,600 WW

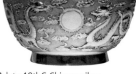

A late-19thC Chinese silver "Dragon" bowl, decorated in relief with four dragons in swirling clouds, two of the beasts contesting a pearl, another grasps a flaming jewel in its claws, while the fourth expels water from its mouth, the base with the punch marks "Bao Feng" and "WS" for Woshing, Shanghai.

9in (22.7cm) diam 30.2oz

$6,000-6,600 WW

A 19thC Chinese silver jardinière, decorated in relief with two figures in a landscape, birds, insects, and flowers, the base with punch marks reading "Yuan Ji" and "90."

7½in (19cm) diam 14.7oz

$2,600-4,000 WW

A late-19thC Chinese export silver goblet, by Wang Hing, Canton and Hong Kong, with pagodas and figures in pavilions with vacant cartouche, marked on base, and also with Fang He workshop mark.

9in (23cm) high 13.7oz

$3,300-4,000 DRA

A late-19thC Chinese export silver goblet, by Cum Wo, chased with battle scenes and vacant cartouche, the stem with circling dragons, marked on base, also marked with Quan workshop mark.

10½in (27cm) high 20.6oz

$6,000-7,500 DRA

A late-19thC Chinese silver "Dragon" punch bowl, with a scaly dragon wrapping its body around the exterior of the deep bowl, the beast depicted with a fierce expression as it pursues a large flaming pearl, the feet formed as dragon-carp, the base with three punch marks reading "WH" for Wang Hing & Co, "800," and "Kun He."

13½in (34cm) diam 9.88oz

$13,000-26,000 WW

A 19thC Chinese silver case, with figures in forest settings, marked "P.," the hinged cover initialed and inscribed "37th Reg.," the base with a presentation inscription and dated "October 24th 1895."

4½in (11.5cm) high 4.5oz

$400-550 **WW**

A late-19thC Chinese silver "Five Dragon" teapot, decorated in repoussé with two dragons in pursuit of a sacred pearl, with a handle formed as a dragon arching its back, with a further beast disgorging the spout, the cover with a finial shaped as the head of a dragon.

10in (25.5cm) wide 20.9oz

$1,800-2,100 **WW**

A Chinese silver basket, with pierced and engraved bamboo decoration, on four simulated bamboo feet, with handle, marked "95" and "WS."

8¾in (22.5cm) wide 15.1oz

$1,000-1,100 **BELL**

A Chinese silver four-piece tea and coffee service, by Wang Hing, with associated tray by Sincere Co. (1880-1940), engraved on teapot "Presented to Mr. R. Gray by the European staff of the Taikoo Dockyard on the occasion of his marriage, 1919."

ca. 1919 *7in (18cm) high 84oz*

$2,000-2,600 **DRA**

A Chinese silver box, by Wang Hing, chased with bamboo decoration, the cover with an inscription.

5¾in (14.7cm) wide 11oz

$600-750 **WW**

A Chinese silver dish, by Wang Hing, with a pierced bamboo border, chased blossom, on four dragon legs, with a later red glass liner.

ca. 1920 *19.8cm wide 21.4oz*

$4,000-5,300 **WW**

A rare Canton Chinese export gold cup, by Yuan He, chased with floral sprays, the underside stamped with retailer's mark "GEM WO" and stipple-engraved with character marks and 2nd Standard Lisbon control marks 1886-1938, visible construction seam on body.

Provenance: By repute, it was presented to Carlos Eugénio Correia da Silva, 1st Count of Paço de Arcos in 1877 on the occasion of the birth of his daughter, Jesuína Amália. Correaia da Silva was Governor of the Portuguese Colony of Macau from December 31, 1876, to November 28, 1879, living in the Santa Sancha Palace. The fact that the marks on the cup also carry Lisbon import marks used from the year 1886 concurs with historical fact, in as much as it is known that Correa da Silva returned to Lisbon at the end of 1889 to become the civil governor of Lisbon; a service to the Crown that he was rewarded for by being elevated to be "Grande do Reino"—the equivalent of a viscount. This example of a gold beaker made by the Canton goldsmith/silversmith Yuan He would appear to be the only recorded item of gold to carry a Gem Wo mark. Yuan He was located in Canton (Guangzhou) and should not be confused with another workshop in the same city at the same time, Yuan He, which was also known for producing beakers, tankards, snuff boxes, and vinaigrettes. We are grateful to Adrien von Ferscht, an expert on Chinese Export silver, for his extensive research.

A Chinese Republic silver model of a war junk, with figures and cannon on board, flying flags for the Nationalist Party, the Republic of China, and two that read "Li, Guangdong haifang jibu for the Guangdong Sea Defence Force," with a wood stand and glass display case, the ship with punch marks reading "jie" and "W0Co?."

18in (45.5cm) high 42.3oz

$6,500-9,000 **WW**

ca. 1870

$6,000-7,500

2½in (6.1cm) high 1.6oz

DN

ESSENTIAL REFERENCE—JAPANESE BRONZES

- Most Japanese sculptures are derived from the idol worship in Buddhism or animistic rites of Shinto deity. In particular, sculpture, among all the arts, came to be the one most firmly centered on Buddhism. Materials traditionally used were metal, especially bronze. The Japanese Meiji period, defined as the period between 1868 and 1912, was an era in which artists were forced to respond to these subjects and materials on a new scale.

- Meiji Japan was famously the era in which, after nearly 300 years of almost complete isolation from the globe, Japan began to trade openly with Europe and the West. Consequently, Meiji Japan saw a new flourishing in the arts, with craftsmen and artists finding their work in high demand overseas. It would lead to a vast expansion in production, and the development of a new "national" style. In bronze working, Meiji period craftsmen were newly empowered to attempt distinctive, innovative, and complex pieces. Makers were influenced less by the West than by China. Artistry in bronze work reached new heights in the Meiji period, as a number of metal-working schools developed, creating intricate pieces, including vases, sculptures, teapots, and incense burners.

- These would often take nature as their inspiration, featuring images of flora and fauna as well as mythical animals, such as dragons.

A Meiji Japanese parcel-gilt bronze figure of a man, possibly Fujiwara no Yasumasa, by Miya-O Eisuke, robes decorated in gilding with Manchurian Cranes and kiri leaves, he wears an eboshi on his head, wood stand decorated in silvered lacquer scrolling karakusa, signed in a gilt reserve "Miya-O saku," slight wear, flute and sword missing.

14¼in (36.2cm) high

$6,000-7,500 　　　　　　DN

A Japanese Meiji parcel-gilt bronze figure of a fisherman, by Miya-O Eisuke, with wood stand, lacquered on the frieze with ho-ho birds and scrolling karakusa. signed on a gilt plaque "Miya-O tsukuru," with areas on feet and belly that have been rubbed back to the raw metal.

Founded by Miya-O Eisuke, the Miyao Company of Yokohama specialized in the manufacture of bronze sculptures, embellished with gold and silver as well as patinated copper alloys, that represent generic samurai warriors as well as more precisely identifiable characters from Japanese myth and legend. In addition, the company also made a smaller number of pieces in other formats, such as incense-burners, vases, and chargers.

21¾in (55cm) high

$20,000-26,000 　　　　　DN

A Japanese Meiji bronze figure, by Miya-O Eisuke, his robes decorated in parcel gilt with Shinto symbols, signed "Miya-O," on original lacquered wood stand.

8½in (21.7cms) high

$4,600-5,300 　　　　　　DN

A Japanese Meiji parcel-gilt bronze figure of an Oni, in the style of Miya-O, standing on a modern black-lacquered wood stand, stand scuffed and with paint losses.

22in (55.5cm) high

$5,300-5,900 　　　　　　DN

A large Japanese Meiji bronze figure of a man, by Akasofu Gyokko, with a bow in one hand, a quiver of arrows on his back, and an early "dolmen"-style sword by his side, signed, repaired casting flaw on base.

37in (94cm) high

$2,600-4,000 　　　　　　DN

A Japanese Meiji parcel-gilt bronze figure of an archer, the man wearing an haori and hakama with triple tomo-e and other mons over his armor, carrying a single sword at his waist as he draws his bow, with a wood stand, signed "Gyokko" on a gilt plaque.

The haori is a traditional Japanese hip- or thigh-length jacket worn over a kimono. Hakama are the skirtlike pants that are worn over a kimono. Tomo-e is a commalike swirl symbol used in Japanese mon, roughly equivalent to a heraldic badge or charge in European heraldry.

9½in (24cm) high

$6,000-6,600 　　　　　　DN

A pair of Japanese Meiji parcel-gilt bronze figures, by Gyokko, each with a gilt signature plaque for Gyokko, each standing on a wood stand, one stand a replacement.

tallest 21in (53.4cm) high

$12,000-15,000 　　　　　DN

A Japanese Meiji parcel-gilt bronze figure of a warrior, by Gyokko, the robed and armured figure with an eboshi on his head, on original wood stand decorated with gold lacquer scrolling karakusa, signed, some scuffs on wood stand.

Eboshi was black-lacquered headgear, made of silk, cloth, or paper, originally worn by court nobles in ancient Japan.

20¼in (51.5cm) high

$6,000-6,600   DN

A Japanese Meiji parcel-gilt bronze figure of an archer, by Hidemitsu, robed and armored, his daisho at his waist, his bow with arrow ready to fire, gilt signature panel on the reverse "Hidemitsu (Shuko) saku," lacking wood stand, Tachi originally pegged but needs relocating, rubbing on face by arrows flights.

17¼in (44cm) high

$8,500-10,000   DN

A Japanese Meiji bronze group of a boy, by Miya-O Eisuke, possibly intended as Kintarō due to the peach emblem on his chest, the Oni in his hand holding a basket with a hat that acts as a tazza, with gilding, incised on the base "Tokyo (?) Miya-o sei."

Kintarō is a folk hero from Japanese folklore. A child of superhuman strength, he was raised by a yama-uba ("mountain witch") on Mount Ashigara. He became friendly with the animals of the mountain, and later, after catching Shuten-dōji, the terror of the region around Mount Ōe, he became a loyal follower of Minamoto no Yorimitsu under the new name Sakata no Kintoki.

14¼in (36.2cm) high

$4,600-5,900   DN

A Japanese Meiji parcel-gilt bronze figure of an archer, wearing an eboshi on his head and a haori over his armor, his eyes in silvering and shakudo, signed on a gilt plaque "(?)..mori," some wear, bowstring replaced.

13in (32.8cm) high

$4,600-5,900   DN

A Japanese Meiji bronze group of a sage and mule, the sage holding a ruyi scepter, decorated with kebori and gold onlay, he may have held a whip but is now missing.

23in (58.5cm) high

$4,000-5,300   DN

A Japanese Meiji-Taisho bronze figure of a boy, wearing a robe tied with an obi through which his kinchaku hangs.

24in (60cm) high

$4,600-5,900   DN

A Japanese Meiji parcel-gilt bronze figure of an archer, his armor beneath a jinbaori gilded with mon, wheels and decorative motifs, the eyes in silver and shakudo wash, signed on a gold plaque "(?) kazu saku," some wear, sword missing, no wood stand.

13½in (34cm) high

$4,600-5,300   DN

A 18thC or later Japanese Edo period gilt-bronze figure of Amida Nyorai (Amida Buddha), sitting in "dhyanasana" with his hands held before him in the "mida no join" position, raised on a lotus throne.

The "mida no join" is a Japanese variation of the "dhyana mudra" of meditation, where the index fingers are brought together with the thumbs.

17¾in (45cm) high

$6,500-8,000   **WW**

A 19th/20thC Japanese Meiji Jizai okimono bronze spiny lobster, with a fully articulated body, the surface of the exoskeleton realistically modeled.

19in (48cm) wide

$4,000-5,300   **WW**

A Japanese Meiji bronze macaque monkey, clasping an inro in his feet, holding a netsuke and inspecting it with spectacles, highlighted on the embroidered kimono with gilt foliate motifs, gilt signature plaque.

7½in (19cm) high

$8,500-10,000   **FLD**

A Japanese Meiji bronze of a carp, leaping up from waves, the eyes inlaid in gold and shakudo, with some corrosion marks.

17½in (44.6cm) high

$2,000-2,600   **DN**

ESSENTIAL REFERENCE—SHACHIHOKO

Shachihoko are sea monsters believed to cause rain. They are often used as ornaments on Japanese rooftops to protect buildings against fire. When the Meiji restoration of 1868 forbade samurai from openly wearing swords, metalwork artists had to find alternative markets to avoid bankruptcy. Some turned toward producing everyday objects for the upper classes, such as the Komai family, and others specialized in making okimono, ornaments for display. Jizai okimono are a subcategory of fully articulated metal sculptures, often depicting animals. A feat of ingenuity, this dragon fish's lifelike appearance must have made it an attractive souvenir for a wealthy tourist in Japan at the turn of the century.

An 18th/19thC Japanese Edo Jizai okimono articulated iron model of a dragon fish or shachihoko, the mythical beast with a fully articulated body constructed of hammered plates joined on the inside, its dragon head with short horns and long wavy whiskers, the eyes inlaid in gilt and shakudo.

16¾in (42.5cm) wide

$20,000-26,000   **WW**

A pair of 19thC Japanese Meiji bronze okimono shishi, the lion dogs ferocious-looking and with collars decorated with a flower head and tendrils, with bells and jewels suspended, signed Shuzan/Hideyama.

15in (38cm) high

$2,000-2,600   **WW**

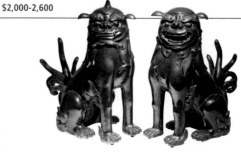

A pair of 18th/19thC Japanese Edo or Meiji bronze shishi lion dogs, one with its mouth open and baring its fangs and the other with a short horn on the top of its head, both ferocious looking and with scrolling manes.

tallest 26½in (67.5cm) high

$12,000-15,000   **WW**

A 19thC Japanese Meiji okimono mixed-metal model of a cockerel, the feathers in different colors, on a rootwood stand, signed "Ishiguro Masayoshi" with kao in a gilt cartouche.

10¼in (26cm) high

$7,500-8,500   **WW**

A 19thC Japanese Meiji okimono bronze eagle, its wings open as it prepares to take flight, the eyes inlaid in shakudo, the beak and claws in gilt, signed underneath the tail feathers.

24½in (62cm) high

$6,000-6,600   **WW**

A Japanese Meiji-Taisho bronze group of a sitting monkey, examining an inro and its accompanying manju netsuke, with gilt and silver details, some dents and wear, unsigned.

8½in (21.2cm) high

$12,000-15,000   **DN**

A pair of 20thC Japanese bronze vases, the body applied with a coiled dragon patinated green with inlaid eyes.

43in (110cm) high

$15,000-18,000   **DN**

A Japanese Meiji bronze koro and cover, the body on a base of two Oni, the shoulder with dragon handles, the cover with a knop in the form of Shoki conquering an Oni, decorated in iro-e takazogan, relief and kebori with landscape views across Edo Bay toward Fujiyama, wear to base.

An Oni is a kind of demon, ogre, or troll in Japanese folklore. They are typically portrayed as hulking figures with one or more horns growing out of their heads. Shoki is traditionally regarded as a vanquisher of ghosts and evil beings.

17in (42.4cm) high

$11,000-12,000   **DN**

A Japanese Meiji parcel-gilt bronze vase, by Miya-O Eisuke, with animal head handles, decorated on a ground of ho-ho birds amid kiri leaves and tendrils with inome-shaped panels of quail by a stream and of an incident from the "Genji Monogatari," (Tale of the Genji') gilding and iroe takazogan, the neck with a band of dragons, signed on a gilt plaque "Miya-O" with seal "Ei," some wear.

15in (37.4m) high

$13,000-15,000   **DN**

A Japanese Meiji parcel-gilt bronze Koro group, by Miya-O Eisuke, modeled as two bronze workers polishing a large amorphous object, possibly intended as a Saru Ningyo ("rag doll"), the reverse with a gilt relief poetic inscription, the cover pierced with an aperture shaped as a flaming tama, incised signature "Miya-o dzu," slight wear.

7¾in (19.5cm) high

$4,600-5,900   **DN**

A pair of Japanese Meiji-Taisho bronze vases, decorated in relief, copper, silvering, gilding, and shakudo with a row of sparrows on a branch of cherry, incised on the base "Mitsuaki," minor marks and scratches on the surface.

13¾in (35cm) high

$2,600-4,000   **DN**

A 19thC Japanese Meiji bronze jardinière, with a bale of terrapins on the body, the animals with some clambering upon others, the details of the carapaces naturalistically rendered.

13½in (34cm) high

$6,500-8,000 **WW**

A 19thC Japanese Meiji bronze jardinière, by Seiryusai, decorated with four carp among waves, signed Seiryusai chu.

14¾in (37.5cm) high

$2,600-3,300 **WW**

A late-19thC Japanese Meiji silver bowl, decorated with irises and the base marked jungin (silver), with two stamped marks.

11¾in (30cm) diam 91.4oz

$3,300-4,000 **WW**

A Japanese Meiji inlaid bronze vase, decorated in silver, gold, shibuichi, and copper "hon-zogan" with taotie masks, incised on the base with an inscription, slight loss of color, wear on foot rim.

12¼in (31cm) high

$1,500-2,000 **DN**

A pair of 19th/20thC Japanese Meiji inlaid iron vases, by Kajima Ikkoku II, decorated in gold and silver "nunome zogan" with cranes in flight above waves, the shoulders decorated with bands of lappets enclosing fireflies, the bases with pine, each with a seal mark, one for Mitsutaka and the other for Ikkoku.

Kajima Ikkoku II (1846-1925) was a famous metalworker from Kawagoe, near Tokyo. He learned traditional techniques from his father, the renowned artist Kajima Mitsuyuki (d.1882), and developed an international reputation for his mastering of "nunome zogan" (damascene work). His award-winning designs were exhibited at many important fairs, including the Japanese National Industrial Exposition (1890) and the Japan-British Exhibition in London (1910).

3¾in (9.6cm) high

$6,000-7,500 **WW**

A pair of Japanese Meiji bronze vases, with panels of the poet Narihira and of a rat eating a daikon, the usubata-style top chased and inlaid with grasses amid rocks, the sides with dragon handles, details inlaid in silver and gold.

10in (25.7cm) high

$1,300-2,000 **DN**

A pair of Japanese Meiji bronze vases, by Miyabe Atsuyoshi, decorated in iro-e takazogan, kebori, and katakiribori with plum, pine, and prunus, with cranes and distant farmers, the reverse with panels of birds, on a deeply carved diaper ground, the neck with fabulous beasts in deep relief, signed on the base "Ikkodo Miyabe Atsuyoshi" with kao, slight wear.

15¾in (39.9cm) high

$29,000-34,000 **DN**

A 19thC Japanese Meiji inlaid bronze vase, by the Kuroda workshop, the body decorated with a long-eared owl perched on a tree branch, the bird inlaid in silver with black speckles and gilt, the base inscribed Kyoto Kuroda zo.

13in (33cm) high

$8,000-10,500 **WW**

A Japanese Meiji bronze dish, by Inoue of Kyoto, decorated within a bamboo border with birds perched on a snow-covered thatched roof over a group of peonies, in kebori, katakiribori, shakudo, copper, silver, and gold takazogan, Kyoto Inoue dzu mark with seal.

12in (30.5cm) diam

$2,600-4,000 **DN**

A Japanese Meiji bronze plaque, decorated with Kintoki holding his ax and sitting astride a bear, eyes are gilt, with border of bats and reishi amid clouds, signed "Haruchika" with gold seal, slight distortion on rim.

32¾in (83cm) high

$1,600-2,400 **DN**

ESSENTIAL REFERENCE—JAPANESE CLOISONNÉ

Although Chinese cloisonné enamels had long been held in high esteem, it was not until the late-16thC that cloisonné enamels became more widely used in Japan. The development of Japanese cloisonné manufacture is credited to the former samurai, Kaji Tsunekichi (1803-83) of Nagoya in Owari province. He, like many samurai, was forced to find ways to supplement his official stipend. Around 1838, he bought a piece of Chinese cloisonné and, by examining how it was made, he produced a cloisonné enameled dish. By the mid-1850s, he took on pupils and, by the late 1850s, was appointed official cloisonné maker to the daimyō (feudal chief) of Owari. He based his designs on the motifs and color themes of Chinese cloisonné enamels and his early works are characterized by the use of a large number of wires. These were decorative, forming an integral part of the design, and practical in that they prevented the enamels from running during firing. One of Kaji's pupils was Hayashi Shōgorō (d.1896), a craftsman celebrated for the fact that his pupils were, in turn, the teachers of many of the later masters of cloisonné enameling, of whom the most important was Tsukamoto Kaisuke (1828-87). Kaisuke, in turn, taught Hayashi Kodenji (1831-1915), a craftsman who became one of the most influential of cloisonné makers. Kodenji set up an independent cloisonné workshop in Nagoya in 1862 and trained other craftsmen. He remained at the forefront of cloisonné manufacturing in Nagoya. Namikawa Sōsuke (1847-1910) was another important cloisonné artist and was also appointed Imperial Craftsman to the court of Emperor Meiji in 1896.

A 19thC Japanese Tsubameiji period Shibayama-style gold-lacquer sword guard, with a silver rim, inlays of mother-of-pearl, coral, horn, and ivory on a kinji ground, the recto with a beauty leading a deer, the verso with precious objects of the Seven Gods of Good Fortune, takaramono, including Daikoku's mallet, depicted in gold hiramaki-e.

4¼in (11cm) wide

$5,300-8,000 **WW**

A Japanese late Meiji bronze and mixed-metal inlaid page turner, the handle cast on one side with a pair of Manchurian cranes, the other with sparrows in bamboo, carved blade, signed.

12¼in (31cm) long

$200-260 **CHEF**

A pair of Meiji silver wire cloisonné enamel vases, in the manner of Namikawa Sōsuke, the rims mounted in shakudo, decorated on the toned, pale blue ground with pigeons amid the branches of a flowering cherry tree, the neck with a band of stylized floral motifs, unsigned.

14in (36.3cm) high

$40,000-45,000 **DN**

A 20thC Japanese Taisho or Showa cloisonné enamel vase, by Ando Jubei, with a band of Chinese-style archaistic designs rendered in silver wire, the foot rim stamped with the jungin silver mark and with the mark for the Ando Jubei company on the base.

10¾in (27.2cm) high

$1,300-2,000 **WW**

A Chinese, probably Ming ,celadon jade "dragon" hat finial, with a dragon amid vines, the stone with some white mottling.

2¼in (5.5cm) high

$2,600-4,000 **WW**

A Chinese Ming/Qing celadon jade carving of a cat and mouse, the stone with russet, white, and black markings.

2½in (6.6cm) wide

$3,300-4,600 **WW**

A Chinese Qianlong white jade carving of Guanyin, with a flower head in her left hand and a basket of peaches in her right, with a small boy at her side.

1736-95 *4¾in (12cm) high*

$20,000-26,000 **WW**

An 18thC Chinese pale celadon jade "horse and monkey" belt buckle, the horse, turning its head to look at the monkey, the monkey carved with a mischievous expression and clutching onto the horse's reins, the reverse with two circular loops for attachment.

The motif of a "hou," or monkey, on the back of a "ma," or horse, represents the rebus "ma shang feng hou," translated as "may you immediately be promoted to a high rank of office." Such pieces would have been used to pass on good wishes to aspiring officials.

3¼in (8.5cm) high

$6,000-7,500 **WW**

An 18thC Chinese celadon and russet jade "Yingxiong" group, carved as a lion dog with an eagle on its back, the beast in russet, the steely eyed bird of prey carved in celadon.

The imagery depicted is an interpretation of the motif "ying," or eagle, and "xiong," or bear, which together form the word "yingxiong," homophone for "hero." The theme of an eagle and bear first appeared on Western Han dynasty bronze "champion" vases.

2¾in (7cm) wide

$10,500-13,000 **WW**

An 18thC Chinese Qing pale celadon jade "horse and squirrel" belt buckle, with incised and carved details, carved wood stand, tiny chip on rear fetlock.

3½in (9cm) wide

$9,000-10,500 **DN**

An 18thC Chinese Qing pale celadon and russet jade carving of the Tian Ma, or "Heavenly Horse," a beribboned scroll tied to the back, the undulating watery ground incised with flowing lines and punctuated with plumes of sea spray.

4¾in (11.8cm) wide

$20,000-26,000 **DN**

A small 18thC Chinese spinach-green jade "Marriage" dish, the center carved with twin fish.

3¼in (8.5cm) diam

$4,000-5,300 **WW**

An 18thC Chinese Qing spinach-green jade "pine and prunus" vase, with a fitted silver metal inlaid and wave carved wood stand, some chips, the wood stand with silver work lacking at back.

jade 4¼in (10.5cm) high

$3,300-4,600 **DN**

A Chinese Western Zhou archaic celadon jade bi, the disk carved with a circular opening in the center, the celadon stone with a large dark streak and an area of calcification, raised on a wood stand.

Dr. Gordon Fryers (1922-2008) and Dr. Rosemary Fryers (1922-94), who owned this piece, moved to Singapore in 1946 after they had both qualified as doctors, and their time there introduced them to Chinese art and culture. However, the Fryers did not start collecting seriously until the 1960s, when Gordon's experiences on his many international business trips rightly led him to believe that China would one day play a crucial role in the world economy and that its art would subsequently become highly desirable. With this remarkable foresight in seeing Chinese art as an investment opportunity, Gordon and Rosemary gradually built up their collection over a fifteen-year period in the 1960s and 70s, buying from leading auction houses and dealers. Albeit a clever financial move, Gordon and Rosemary's collecting was by no means without passion, and they both developed a strong interest in the subject. While Rosemary was drawn to ceramics and various works of art, Gordon favored jades and marveled at the outstanding craftsmanship behind these pieces.

9½in (23.8cm) high

$53,000-66,000 WW

A Chinese Song-Ming Dynasty white and russet jade carving of a mythical beast, minor wear.

2in (5cm) high

$3,300-4,600 DN

A rare archaistic Chinese Song/Ming jade vase, carved with a chilong, body incised with scrolls above cicadas, the base incised with a four-character "qianlong nianzhi" mark.

5in (12.7cm) high

$9,000-10,500 DN

A Chinese Song/Ming zhi "Chicken Bone" jade pouring vessel, rim decorated with stylized dragons in pursuit of a yin-yang roundel, the body carved with chilong dragons in flight amid clouds, the stone with natural faults and cracks, minute old chips on the foot and mouth rim.

3¼in (8.5cm) high

$26,000-33,000 DN

A Chinese Ming celadon and russet jade oval plaque, with a scholar in a landscape on rocks amid pine and lingzhi, his attendant holding a tortoise, with a deer by the figure's side and a crane.

3¼in (8.5cm) high

$4,000-5,300 WW

A Chinese Ming jade cup, in the shape of a peach, on a blossoming stem that forms the handle, cracks on stone, minute chips on edges.

3¼in (8cm) wide

$2,600-4,000 SWO

A rare Chinese Ming pale celadon and russet "Fish Dragon" bi jade roundel, with incised "C" scrolls, deep natural flaws on the jade.

This auspicious imagery is symbolic of the mythical legend of the carp reaching the upper courses of the Yellow River and leaping up the rapids at Dragon Gate, where it transforms into a dragon. This feat is compared to success in the state examinations and the transformation from carp to dragon symbolizing a promotion to the highest rank as an official.

3in (7.6cm) wide

$7,500-8,500 DN

A Chinese Ming russet jade "Three Rams" group, carved as a large ram with two smaller ones.

The image of "san yang," or "three rams," is auspicious and forms the rebus "san yang kai tai," which symbolizes the New Year bringing renewal and a change of fortune.

2¼in (5.5cm) wide

$2,000-2,600 WW

A Chinese Ming jade carving, of a dog, the stone of a white tone with russet staining.

1½in (4cm) long

$600-750 SWO

A Chinese Qianlong yellow jade pendant, carved in the shape of a bell, decorated with mythical creatures, flanked by two archaistic dragons, with a hole for suspension.

2¼in (5.5cm) high

$6,000-6,600 **WW**

An 18thC Chinese Qing celadon jade water pot, carved with the leaf and stem of the water pot forming the feet.

2¾in (7cm) wide

$2,600-4,000 **DN**

A Chinese Qianlong pale celadon jade carving of pomegranates, the larger pomegranate revealing its many seeds, each fruit carved with a calyx, with a wood stand.

The pomegranate is an auspicious motif in China, because it is a symbol of fertility and abundance due to its many seeds. Pomegranates are often depicted, as on this carving, with some of their skin peeled back, showing the numerous seeds inside. This image forms the rebus "liu kai bai zi," or "the pomegranate opens revealing one hundred sons," and thus conveys the wish of producing many offspring.

3in (7.7cm) wide

$8,000-9,000 **WW**

CLOSER LOOK—MARRIAGE BOWL

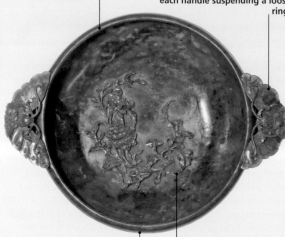

This is a good example of a Chinese 18thC spinach-green marriage bowl with many auspicious symbols.

The two handles formed as pierced butterflies with their open wings resting on the slightly incurved mouthrim, each handle suspending a loose ring.

The rounded sides are carved to the exterior with a continuous lotus scroll.

The interior is decorated in relief with a spray of peony and lingzhi, all raised on six short, ruyi head-shaped feet.

An 18thC marriage bowl, the green stone with black inclusions and areas of lighter and darker mottling.

11¾in (30cm) wide

$33,000-46,000 **WW**

A Chinese yellow jade and russet peach-form water pot, carved around the sides with a gnarled, leafy branch and a bat resting next to it, the stone with natural flaws.

4in (10cm) long

$8,000-9,000 **DN**

A Chinese Qing yellow jade plaque, one side carved with a dragon chasing a flaming pearl, the other side with two dragons surrounding a panel inscribed "Qianqing Gong," the border with two dragons.

2½in (6.5cm) long

$6,000-6,600 **SWO**

A Chinese Qing Fanggu celadon jade vase, carved with stylized banana leaves, archaistic motifs and fish, with taotie masks in the center, reserved on an incised key fret ground, the stone with some white inclusions and russet striations.

Fanggu, or Fangu, meaning "in the old style," refers to the deliberate reproduction of an old kind of glaze color, pattern, or production process.

9in (23cm) high

$15,000-21,000 **WW**

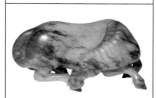

A Chinese Qing brown and white jade carving of a horse, depicted reclining with its head turned toward its back right leg, finely detailed with the hairs of its long mane and tail.

8in (20.2cm) wide

$11,000-12,000 **WW**

A 18th/19thC Chinese Qing pale celadon jade archaistic vase and cover, carved and incised with a taotie mask, the handles with pierced scrolls, the cover knop with incised details, with a silver inlaid wood stand, a crack and tiny chip on rim.

7¼in (18.5cm) high with stand

$8,500-10,000 **DN**

A celadon jade sitting figure of Buddha, shown sitting in "dhyanasana" with hands in "dhyanamudra," in flowing robes with an elaborate headdress, carved on the back with holes to simulate rocks, with traces of red pigment.

4¼in (10.5cm) high

$11,000-12,000   **DN**

An 18th/19thC Chinese white jade pendant, carved on one side with twin fish suspending from a chime, with a four-character mark reading "ji qing you yu" on the reverse.

2½in (6cm) high

$4,600-5,900   **WW**

A Chinese Qing black and celadon jade "yingxiong" group, with a single-horn mythical beast carved from the black section of the stone while an eagle is picked out in celadon, both creatures stand side by side gazing backward with well-defined bulging eyes, raised on a rocky platform, the black and celadon areas of the stone both with white and russet markings.

Like the llon dog and eagle jade carving on p. 136, this is an interpretation of the traditional Chinese "ying," or "eagle," and "xiong," or "bear," motifs, which together form the word "yingxiong" (a homophone for "hero'). After their initial appearance on Western Han bronze vases, yingxiongs gradually became more stylized during later periods, with the bear often resembling a lionlike mythical beast and the eagle a phoenix.

13½in (34.5cm) high 353oz

$40,000-45,000   **WW**

A Chinese white jade figure of Buddha, sitting in "virasana" on a raised lotus base, with natural flaws of the stone.

3¾in (9.5cm) high

$7,500-8,500   **DN**

A Chinese white jade carving, carved in the round as two boys flanking a drum, the stone of even pale tone with cloudy inclusions.

1¾in (4.5cm) high

$9,000-10,500   **DN**

A Chinese Qing white and russet jade "twin hare" group, each biting a spray of lingzhi fungus.

2¾in (7cm) long

$3,300-4,600   **DN**

A Chinese Qing yellow jade vase and cover, with C-scroll handles on the neck, the cover with an oval flattened knop, the stone with russet inclusions.

5¾in (14.5cm) high

$6,500-8,000   **WW**

A Chinese Qing archaistic celadon and russet jade rhyton, carved in relief with a bixie at the foot, the mythical beast with its large wings spread out.

A rhyton is a libation cup, a type of drinking container originally used in ancient Greece, typically having the form of an animal's head or a horn.

4½in (11.5cm) high

$7,500-8,500   **WW**

A Chinese Qing archaistic pale celadon jade Ding incense burner and cover, the body carved with taotie masks, the cover with pendant leaves and a finial shaped as a sinuous dragon, the feet emerging from the mouths of mythical beasts.

In Chinese history and culture, possession of one or more ancient Ding is often associated with power and dominion over the land.

4in (10cm) high

$3,300-4,600   **WW**

A Chinese Qing apple green jadeite pendant, carved with a boy holding a lotus and greeting a bird, reverse with a mark reading "xishi lianlian," with a hole for suspension.

The phrase "xishi lianlian" conveys the wish for happy events to occur again and again.

2¼in (5.5cm) high

$2,600-4,000   **WW**

A Chinese Qing yellow jade "squirrel and melon" carving, the rodent rests its paws on the vine from which the fruit issues, with leaves growing from the branch.

2¼in (5.5cm) high

$4,600-5,900   **WW**

A Chinese Qing white jade "abstinence" plaque, carved as a finger citron, inscribed on one side with the characters zhaijie, and repeated in Manchu on the reverse.

2½in (6.5cm) long

$3,300-4,000   **DN**

A Chinese Qing celadon jade carving of a mythical beast, the lionlike creature carved with its head turned back, grasping a sprig of lingzhi in its mouth, its bifurcated tail curling around its body, with wood stand detailed with lingzhi.

5¾in (14.5cm) long

$13,000-16,000   **WW**

A Chinese Qing pale celadon jade "wufu" ruyi scepter, the head carved in relief with peaches beneath a shou character and a qing, with five bats flying amid swirling clouds to the shaft, the reverse incised with an inscription, with an attached tassel.

14¾in (37.5cm) long

$33,000-40,000   **WW**

A Chinese Qing celadon jade brush washer, with a boy and a fish, one side with an inscription from the Song dynasty poem "Que Qiao Xian" ("Fairy on the Magpie Bridge") by Qin Guan, the seal script characters reading "rou qing si shui jia qi ru meng," with a seal mark reading "wen wan."

6¾in (17cm) wide

$2,600-4,000   **WW**

A Chinese Qing spinach-green jade bowl, incised with a four-character "jiaqing nianzhi" mark, the jade with natural flaws and inclusions.

4½in (11.2cm) diam

$1,700-2,400   **DN**

A Chinese Qing white, brown, and black jade model of a horse.

5½in (14cm) wide

$3,300-4,600   **DN**

A 19thC Chinese spinach-green jade "Dragon" brush washer, carved in relief with four scaly dragons writhing amid lingzhi-shaped clouds, with a wood stand.

9in (23cm) wide

$9,000-10,500   **WW**

A 19thC Imperial style white jade archer's ring, the script describing a hunting scene, with inscribed Yuti mark.

1in (2.7cm) high

$6,000-6,600   **DN**

A Chinese Qing or later yellow jade "Bajixiang" bowl and cover, carved as a lotus flower head, the petals enclosing the eight auspicious buddhist emblems and two Amitabha buddhas, with bats in flight.

5½in (14cm) diam

$8,500-10,000 **WW**

A 20thC Chinese yellow jade "Mythical Beast" cover and stand, the beast with pup, with wood stand.

5in (12.5cm) long

$1,300-2,000 **DN**

A Chinese Qing or later pale celadon jade "ji qing ru yi" pendant, the reverse with a poem, below ruyi head-shaped clouds.

One side of the pendant is carved in relief with two boys, one carrying a weapon suspending a lozenge and the other holding a post with two fish, together symbolizing peace and prosperity.

2¼in (5.5cm) high

$1,300-2,000 **WW**

A Chinese Qing or later white jade "zi gang" plaque, carved with figures in a mountainous landscape amid pine and rocks, one side with a poem, signed "Zi Gang."

2½in (6.5cm) high

$2,000-2,600 **WW**

A Chinese late Qing/Republic pale green jadeite carving of a sampan, formed with two elderly fishermen, with a wood stand.

2½in (6.7cm)

$3,300-4,000 **WW**

A 20thC Chinese green jadeite openwork carving of an endless knot.

With a certificate from Gemmological Certification Services, confirming natural jadeite with no indication of impregnation, report number 79230-07.

½in (1.5cm) high

$2,600-4,000 **WW**

A 20thC Chinese pale celadon jade carving of two goats.

6¼in (16cm) wide

$2,600-4,000 **WW**

A mid-20thC Chinese celadon jade figure of Budda Shakyamuni, the base possibly earlier, carved sitting in "dhyanasana" with his right hand in "bhumisparsha mudra."

The iconography depicted presents the historical Buddha in the earth-witness gesture. This refers to when Shakyamuni triumphed over the demon Mara, who was attempting to divert him from his objective of becoming enlightened through meditation. When Mara challenged Shakyamuni's right to enlightenment, Shakyamuni moved his hand from his lap to touch the ground with his middle finger, calling the earth to witness his entitlement to spiritual enlightenment. Shakyamuni's unshakable resolve forced Mara and his army of demons to flee; moments later, Shakyamuni attained enlightenment.

10½in (26.5cm) high

$13,000-20,000 **WW**

ESSENTIAL REFERENCE—PEKING GLASS

Peking glass is a form of Chinese glassware that originated in 18thC Peking, China. Originally used in the fabrication of glass snuff bottles, Peking glass has since been used for a number of objects, particularly vases. While China had long been a major producer of glassware, the introduction of European technologies to Asia in the 17thC caused a shift in the styles of Chinese glassmakers, mainly inspired by Jesuit missionaries, who introduced glassmaking methods from Italy to China. These advances led the Kangxi Emperor to establish an Imperial glassworks in 1696 to better produce the new material. Eventually, the process of creating Peking glass was spread outside of the Imperial glassworks and into the general population, leading to many artisans adopting Peking glass as a medium. The golden age of Peking glass in China is widely cited as being the reign of the Qianlong Emperor in the mid-18thC. Although the art form declined after the 19thC, the production of Peking glass continued in China through the Republic period and into the present day.

One of a pair of Chinese pink Peking glass "Phoenix" vases with turquoise overlay, with incised mark to underside.

9¾in (25cm) high

$3,300-4,000 the pair　　　**DRA**

A pair of Chinese Peking glass baluster vases, with Qianlong mark.

15in (38cm) high

$1,050-1,200　　　**DRA**

A Chinese Peking glass vase, painted with bats among peach trees, with traces of four-character Qianlong mark on base, rim chipped, mark grounded, surface scratches.

4in (10.5cm) high

$450-600　　　**SWO**

A Chinese yellow Peking glass vase.

11½in (29cm) high

$2,100-2,600　　　**DRA**

One of a pair of Chinese lemon yellow Peking glass vases.

7¾in (20cm) high

$450-600 the pair　　　**DRA**

A Chinese white Peking glass brush pot with red overlay.

5½in (14cm) high

$750-850　　　**DRA**

A Chinese Qing Beijing glass vase, with a four-character Qianlong mark.

7¼in (18.3cm) high

$2,000-2,600　　　**WW**

A pair of 19thC Chinese Beijing pink- and green-overlay glass "Phoenix" bottle vases, a standing phoenix gazing up at its partner in flight above, with peony blooms.

8¼in (21.2cm) high

$2,000-3,300　　　**WW**

A Chinese Beijing Qianlong ruby glass bowl, carved with figures in a mountainous landscape, with pine, willow, and dwellings.

7¼in (18.6cm) diam

$1,300-2,000　　　**WW**

A rare 18thC or later Chinese enameled glass "Prunus" snuff bottle, painted with branches of prunus blossoms, with gilt on the rim and foot, the base with the reign mark.

The decoration on this snuff bottle was achieved by applying each color of enamel separately to the plain glass body and firing successively at the appropriate temperature for each color. The technical process of firing painted enamels on glass was significantly more challenging than that for porcelain or metal objects. Because the melting point of glass is similar to that of enamel, accurate temperature control was crucial. If the temperature was too high, the glass body would melt; but, if it was too low, the enamel would not bond to the glass with the desired color. Enameled glass snuff bottles are, therefore, considerably rarer than their porcelain or metal-bodied counterparts.

2¼in (5.3cm) high

$20,000-26,000　　　　WW

An 18thC Chinese pale celadon jade snuff bottle, one side with a sitting figure drinking wine in a sampan, boating down a river by cliffs and beneath pine and swirling clouds, the reverse undecorated and carved following the natural shape of the stone, raised on an oval foot, the stone with some inclusions and small russet markings.

2½in (6.6cm) high

$3,300-4,600　　　　WW

An 18thC or later Chinese white jade inscribed snuff bottle, incised on each side with four lines of calligraphy, the inscriptions heightened with gilt, the stone with some pale mottling and inclusions.

One side of the snuff bottle is inscribed with the poem "Lu Zhai" ("Deer Park") by the Tang dynasty poet Wang Wei, while the poem on the other side is "Zhong Nan Wang Yu Xue" ("On Seeing the Snow Peak of Zhongnan") by the Tang poet Zu Yong.

2½in (6.3cm) high

$6,500-8,000　　　　WW

A Chinese, possibly Qianlong, famille rose enameled glass snuff bottle, painted with chicks amid rocks and blossoms, the base with Qianlong mark in iron- ed.

2in (5cm) high

$2,600-4,000　　　　WW

An 18th/19thC Chinese pale celadon and russet river pebble jade snuff bottle and stopper, with later green glass stopper.

4in (10cm) high

$11,000-13,000　　　　DN

A 19thC Chinese white jade snuff bottle, the body surmounted by a cylindrical neck and flanked by two lion masks holding rings in their mouths, the base incised with the hallmark "Xing You Heng Tang."

The hall Xing You Heng Tang is known to have been the residence of the Manchu official Zhai Quan, who was one of the great grandsons of the Qianlong Emperor. Zhai Quan was a famous collector of works of art during the Daoguang and early Xianfeng periods before his death in 1854.

2¼in (5.5cm) high

$53,000-66,000　　　　WW

A 19thC Chinese famille rose iron-red ground snuff bottle, painted on one side with two ladies welcoming a gentleman and his horse outside a garden pavilion, the reverse with a scholar and his attendant, the scenes divided by gilt floral sprays on a bright iron-red ground, the base with a four-character Qianlong mark.

1¾in (4.7cm) high

$850-1,000　　　　WW

A 19thC Chinese agate snuff bottle, carved with a monkey climbing a pine tree, and a horse below, the reverse with a precious object.

2in (5cm) high

$600-750　　　　WW

A Chinese Qing or Republic glass and enamel snuff bottle, enameled with a pink fish on each side above a yellow "basket weave," with Qianlong mark.

2¼in (5.8cm) high

$1,050-1,200　　　　DN

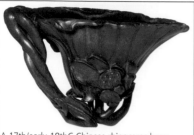

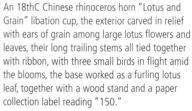

A 17th/early-18thC Chinese rhinoceros horn "Lotus" libation cup, formed as a trumpet-shaped lotus leaf, the handle shaped as stems and leaves, with seedpods and a flower on the foot.

Lotus is a popular motif on rhinoceros horn carvings, being regarded as a symbol of scholars' virtue and purity, because the beautiful flower grows from the mud, clean and unstained.

5½in (14cm) high 7oz

$40,000-53,000   **WW**

A 17th/early-18thC Chinese rhinoceros horn "Magnolia" libation cup, carved with blossoming magnolia, the branches forming a short foot, together with a wood stand carved with flowers and branches.

An export licencs will only be granted for rhinoceros horn pieces if the hammer price meet or exceed the value of 100 US dollars per gram of the item's weight.

3¾in (9.5cm) high 2.4oz

$17,000-21,000   **WW**

An 18thC Chinese rhinoceros horn "Lotus and Grain" libation cup, the exterior carved in relief with ears of grain among large lotus flowers and leaves, their long trailing stems all tied together with ribbon, with three small birds in flight amid the blooms, the base worked as a furling lotus leaf, together with a wood stand and a paper collection label reading "150."

The Chinese words for "lotus," "he," and an "ear of grain," "sui," are homophonous with the words for "harmony" and "year" respectively. Therefore, the two images together symbolize the wish of living in harmony year after year.

4¼in (11cm) wide 2.8oz

$13,000-18,000   **WW**

An 18thC Chinese rhinoceros horn libation cup, with a taotie mask reserved on a leiwen ground, the handle pierced and carved with a chilong, a smaller chilong underneath clambering on the side, with an associated wood stand, minute chips and small cracks, the smaller chilong with a split.

7in (18cm) high

$53,000-66,000   **SWO**

An 18th/19thC Chinese carved bamboo incense holder, carved and pierced with scholars, attendants, and ladies, with a pine tree growing behind a boulder, the large stone signed "Fan Bin," each end with a later wood cover.

7in (17.8cm) high

$4,600-5,900   **WW**

A Chinese Qing zitan "Bamboo" bitong brush pot, carved with bamboo branches, with a circular plug on the base, the reverse with calligraphy and signed "Wang Shixiang," dated the second month of the renchen year.

6¼in (15.5cm) high

$4,000-5,300   **WW**

A Chinese Qing or later veneered bamboo wrist rest, carved as a book tied with a bow, with geometric diaper.

10in (25.1cm) high

$850-1,000   **WW**

An 18th/19thC Chinese bamboo bitong brush pot, carved with a scene from the tale of the Red Cliff, depicting scholars sitting and drinking tea in a sampan.

6¾in (17cm) high

$1,050-1,600   **WW**

A 17th/18thC Chinese bamboo figure of Shoulao, the God of Longevity, dressed in robes with a cheerful expression, holdin a branch of lingzhi in his left hand, with three boys at his feet, with a crouching deer on the reverse.

7in (17.7cm) high

$7,500-8,500   **WW**

A 16thC Chinese lacquered and gilt-wood figure of a dignitary, his robes decorated with flower heads, the borders carved with scrolling designs.

19½in (49.5cm) high

$6,000-7,500   **WW**

CLOSER LOOK—ALOESWOOD TEAPOT

This is a rare example of a Qing aloeswood teapot and cover. Aloeswood is a fragrant dark resinous wood used in incense and small carvings. It is formed in the heartwood of aquilaria trees when they become infected with a type of mold.

It is carved in relief of varying depths—a sign of quality.

It has a landscape of rolling hills delicately detailed with a hut and figure shaded by pine trees against a backdrop of rocky mountains.

The silver metal mounts are another sign of quality.

An aloeswood teapot and cover, some wear and cracks on surface, the wood with some restoration, the area near the handle with filling.

8¼in (21cm) high 27.3oz

$7,500-8,500   **DN**

ESSENTIAL REFERENCE—HAN XIN

- Han Xin (d.196 BC) was a military general who served Liu Bang (d.195 BC), assisting him in establishing the Han dynasty. At first, Han Xin's talents were not recognized and he was merely put in charge of food supplies. Frustrated by this, Han Xin deserted, but Liu Bang's minister, Xiao He (d.193 BC), acknowledged Han Xin's competence and pursued him in the middle of the night, convincing him to continue in his service of Liu Bang's quest to unify China and in the foundation of the Han dynasty. This popular tale, recorded in Sima Qian's Shiji ("Records of the Grand Historian"), became one of the widely used designs among narrative scenes taken from historical texts, novels, and dramas reproduced on porcelain wares during the 17thC. No doubt, it would have resonated strongly with many scholar officials during the late Ming dynasty, who felt their talents to serve in the government were not being appreciated under the declining Ming empire.
- This narrative can be found on a Yuan dynasty blue-and-white meiping vase excavated from the tomb of the early Ming general Mu Ying, exhibited in "Splendors in Smalt: Art of Yuan Blue-and-white Porcelain," Shanghai Museum, 2012, Catalog, pl.64.

A 16thC or later Japanese Muromachi lacquered wood figure of Amida Nyorai (Amida Buddha), of yosegi-zukuri ("jointed") construction, the eyes inlaid in glass and downcast, his hands in a mudra representing one of the nine levels of rebirth, kubon, with remnants of gilt lacquer, with a tall mandorla, kohai, carved with a Sanskrit character.

Amida Buddha is represented performing the kubon mudra when welcoming the souls of the departed as they reach the Great Western Paradise. Sculptures and paintings depicting this subject became popular during the 12thC and were placed near the beds of dying devotees to bring them comfort.

33¼in (84.5cm) high

$6,000-6,600   **WW**

A carved Chinese Qing hardwood brush pot, possibly huanghuali, carved with Han Xin on horseback being pursued by Xiao He and his attendants from behind tall rocks, chipped on rim, drilled on base.

9in (23cm) high

$3,300-4,600   **SWO**

Two Japanese late Meiji carved wood, lacquered, and ivory-mounted figures of ladies, wearing butterfly decorated kimonos, on a wooden stand with signed red lacquer kakihan, chipped lacquer, with slight discoloration of ivory.

13½in (34.5cm) and 14½in (36.5cm) high

$3,300-4,000   **CHEF**

A small Chinese Qianlong Imperial agate "Heavenly Dove" vase, carved in relief with three doves, with archaistic scrolls dividing the birds, the base incised with the four-character Qianlong mark, the stone a dark gray color with paler areas and striations.

3½in (9.1cm) wide

$46,000-53,000   **WW**

A Chinese Qing agate carving of a mythical beast turning its head to the back with a lingzhi in its mouth, with cracks on stone.

3¼in (8.5cm) wide

$3,300-4,600   **SWO**

A Chinese Qing agate carving of a squirrel and grapes, with a white squirrel clambering over the fruit, all resting upon a large dark leaf incised with details of the veins.

2½in (6.5cm) wide

$4,000-4,600   **WW**

An 18th/19thC Chinese soapstone "toad" seal, with details of the amphibian's knobbly skin, with a band of interlocking "T" scrolls on the edge, the underside with "chen su lie zhang, han lai shu wang, qiu."

The characters form an excerpt from the "Qian Zi Wen," or "Thousand Character Classic," by Zhou Xingsi. The "Thousand Character Classic" is a poem that has been used to teach children Chinese characters since the 6thC. The poem is comprised of 1,000 characters, with each being used only once.

2¼in (5.5cm) wide

$2,600-3,300   **WW**

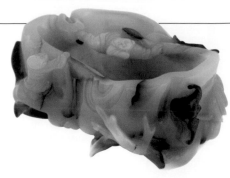

A Chinese Qing tree trunk agate washer, carved with boys climbing on the sides next to two chilong and two bats holding a string of coins.

3in (7.5cm) wide

$4,600-5,300   **SWO**

A Chinese Qing agate "Lingzhi" brush washer, carved with mushrooms growing from a gnarled branch that forms the foot.

6½in (16.5cm) wide

$6,000-7,500   **WW**

An 18thC Chinese soapstone carving of a luohan wearing a robe with cloud and wave borders, his left hand holding a hoop teasing a Buddhist lion by his feet, left earring damaged and partly missing, right-hand pinkie finger chipped.

Soapstone is a soft rock that has been carved by the Chinese for centuries, and it is still being carved today. The name derives from the soaplike feel that some of the softer grades of soapstone have. It is often possible to scratch a piece of soapstone with a fingernail or knife blade.

3¾in (9.5cm) high

$8,500-10,000   **SWO**

An 18thC Chinese soapstone figure of a luohan, with a ruyi scepter resting in his left hand, his robes incised with lotus medallions and decorated at the hem with clouds against a stylized wave ground.

3½in (9.1cm) high

$20,000-26,000   **WW**

A Chinese late Qing Furong soapstone figurine of "Guanyin and a Lion Dog," the goddess sits on the back of the beast, the details incised and gilded, the reverse signed "Yuxuan" (Yang), the oval base carved with rocks, with an inscription that reads "di zi Yuxuan xi zhu Wu Yi shan Tao Yuan dong gong feng, Kangxi ding hai jiu yue ji dan."

Furong is a town in Yongshun county, Xiangxi Prefecture, Hunan.

5¾in (14.5cm) high

$13,000-16,000 WW

A Chinese Qing soapstone "Scholars" table screen, carved on one side with three scholars standing beneath a pine tree in a mountainous river landscape, the reverse decorated with a prunus branch set between two vases.

6in (14.8cm) wide

$6,000-7,500 WW

A mid-20thC Chinese soapstone model of a pleasure boat, with a servant girl appearing from the covered section, a couple in half embrace on the open deck.

14¾in (37.5cm) wide

$550-650 CHEF

A Chinese Qing rock crystal carving of a horse, the mane, tail, and feathering delicately incised with fine hairs.

4in (10cm) wide

$8,500-10,000 WW

A Chinese Qing lapis lazuli box and cover, carved with five bats encircling a shou roundel, minute chips.

4¼in (11.2cm) diam

$3,300-4,000 SWO

A Chinese Qing amber carving of Shoulao, the God of Longevity, with a crane at his feet and Magu behind him, wood stand carved with pine, lingzhi, and shrubs.

5in (12.4cm) high

$6,000-6,600 WW

An 18thC Chinese Qing pale celadon carving of a boy holding a lotus stem.

2¾in (7cm) high

$2,600-3,300 DN

A Chinese Republic carved aquamarine seal, the top of the seal carved with a recumbent beast, turning its head backward, the stone with natural flaws and inclusions.

2in (5.2cm) high

$16,000-20,000 DN

A Chinese late Qing smoky quartz "Boys" vase, carved with five boys upon a rocky pedestal, with a wood stand pierced with pine and prunus motifs.

7½in (18.8cm) high

$2,000-2,600 WW

ESSENTIAL REFERENCE—TIXI LACQUER

The name for this type of lacquer, "tixi," literally means "carved rhinoceros," and derives from the Chinese characters most commonly used for the term, "xipi," used to describe marbled lacquer, which resembles the hide of a rhinoceros. However, although both lacquer techniques involve the application of layers of lacquer in different colors and their exposure for decorative purposes, the methods vary considerably. While the layers of differently colored lacquer are applied to a deliberately uneven surface in xipi lacquer, they are applied to a well-prepared smooth surface for tixi lacquer. While the different colors are revealed by rubbing down the surface of xipi lacquer, they are revealed by carving designs in wide U-shaped or V-shaped lines on tixi lacquers.

A rare Chinese tixi lacquer trefoil dish, the body deeply carved to the front with scrollwork, with the same design on the exterior, the patterns finely outlined in red, the base incised "jiaxu Liu Rui zao" meaning "made by Liu Rui in the jiaxu year" corresponding to 1574.

1574   *7in (17.6cm) wide*

$26,000-40,000   **WW**

A rare Chinese Qianlong Imperial two-color lacquer teabowl, carved in cinnabar lacquer with the poem "Sanqing Cha" ("Three Purity Tea") composed by the Qianlong Emperor, with bands of ruyi heads encircling the rim and foot, reserved on a black-lacquer leiwen ground, the interior in black lacquer, the verse dated to the bingyin year corresponding to 1746 and followed by the seal marks Qian and Long.

The Qianlong Emperor is believed to have written the poem "Sanqing Cha" in the bingyin year on his birthday while drinking tea on a cold day. During a visit to the sacred mountain Wutai Shan, the Qianlong Emperor drank tea brewed in snow water, which is believed to give the tea a unique flavor and purity. The poem describes this tea, which was made with prunus blossoms, finger citron and pine nut kernels. A translation of this poem by C. F. Shangraw is published in "Chinese Lacquers in the Asian Art Museum of San Francisco," Orientations, April 1986, p.41.

4¼in (11.1cm) high

$90,000-100,000   **WW**

A Chinese Yongzheng/Qianlong bamboo gilt and lacquered scholar's teapot and cover, with gilt ruyi heads centered by red lacquer encircling the rim, the cover decorated with two flowers set amid leafy tendrils and delicate scrollwork, the recessed base incised "Jiezhai zao," which can be translated as "made in the studio of restraint."

The lacquer decoration on this unusual bamboo teapot is comparable to that on Japanese lacquer pieces, particularly the delicate scrollwork on the cover and band of foliage resembling karakusa scrolls. The Yongzheng Emperor is known to have greatly admired Japanese works of art and aesthetics, and he was especially fond of Japanese maki-e lacquer with gold decoration. There were a large number of Japanese maki-e pieces in the collection of the Qing court. However, the Yongzheng Emperor's appreciation for Japanese lacquer led him not only to collect pieces made in Japan, but also to order imitation works from domestic Imperial workshops. Yongzheng is believed to have been the first Qing emperor to commission such imitation pieces, and this was to be continued by his son the Qianlong Emperor. These imitation pieces appear to have been valued as equal to rather than inferior to authentic Japanese examples. Aside from pure imitations, Yongzheng also encouraged the application of Japanese lacquerware designs on other media, including porcelain and enamel. An enameled gilt-copper inro-style case produced in the Qing court workshops and now in the National Palace Museum collection is one example of these kind of pieces produced under the Yongzheng Emperor's reign.

4¾in (12.1cm) wide

$15,000-20,000   **WW**

A Chinese Qianlong period Imperial cinnabar lacquer teabowl, carved with the four characters "wan shou wu jiang" contained within a roundel enclosed by a band of ruyi heads, the medallions set amid lotus on a ground of floral diaper, with a gilt-metal liner in the interior, four-character Qianlong mark.

Bowls with this design are believed to have been made for the Qianong Emperor's 70th birthday. The phrase "wan shou wu jiang" is used as a birthday greeting and can be translated as "may you enjoy infinite longevity." Similar patterns with these characters in medallions are also found on porcelain and cloisonné pieces.

4¾in (12cm) wide

$34,000-40,000   **WW**

A rare Chinese Qianlong two-color lacquer "Baxian Guo Hai" tray, formed as a large furling lotus leaf growing from a curved stem in dark green lacquer, one side carved with the eight immortals and their attributes in bright cinnabar lacquer, all reserved on a finely incised wave ground.

The scene depicted shows the eight immortals using their magical powers to cross the sea to attend the birthday celebrations of the Queen Mother of the West.

12½in (32cm) wide

$20,000-26,000   **WW**

A 18thC Chinese cinnabar lacquer bitong, carved over a metal base with ladies and children in gardens, set against an elaborate cell diaper ground.

6¾in (17.2cm) high

$13,000-16,000   **WW**

An 18th/early-19thC Chinese three-color cinnabar lacquer "Peaches" box and cover, carved with blossoming and fruiting peach branches, the peaches finely incised with floral diaper, the large leaves picked out in dark green, with bands of fylfots on the sides of the box and cover, the interior and base lacquered black.

4½in (11.6cm) wide

$6,500-8,000 **WW**

A pair of 18th/early-19thC Chinese cinnabar lacquer "Scholars" vases, carved with scholars and their attendants in rocky landscapes, with pine and wutong trees dispersed through the setting, the flared necks and feet decorated with lotus sprays, each together with gilt-wood mounts.

13½in (34.6cm) high excluding mounts

$2,600-4,000 **WW**

A Chinese Qing cinnabar lacquer square "Longevity" box and cover, the cover carved with a large shou character decorated with floral diaper, the sides of the box and cover incised with fylfot designs, the interior and base lacquered a dark brown.

3in (7.4cm) wide

$2,000-2,600 **WW**

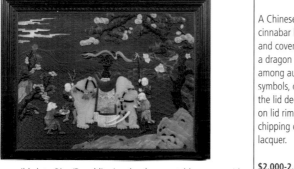

A Chinese late Qing cinnabar lacquer box and cover, carved with a dragon and phoenix among auspicious symbols, chipping on the lid decoration, crack on lid rim, rubbing and chipping of the red lacquer.

12¼in (32cm) diam

$2,000-2,600 **CHEF**

A Chinese possibly late Qing/Republic cinnabar lacquer table screen with hard stone inlay, with a caparisoned elephant supporting a vase of coral twigs and ruyi heads, attended by four figures flanked by a pine tree, rocks and hills as a backdrop, in various minerals, mother-of-pearl, bone, and ivory, and fitted into a Zitan type wooden frame, the original stand now lacking.

17¼in (44cm) wide

$3,300-4,600 **CHEF**

An 18thC or later Japanese Edo or later gold lacquer five-case inro, each side decorated with two chickens, one with the birds perched on a large war drum, together with an agate ojime bead and an ivory netsuke carved as a monkey wearing a tunic.

Inro 3¾in (9.5cm) high

$1,050-1,200 **WW**

A Japanese Edo Somada school two-case lacquer inro, decorated with iridescent shell inlays and kirikane, nashiji, and fundame, one side with a spider weaving its net and the other with a silver moon peeking from behind clouds, with a wood ojime and a netsuke shaped as a straw hat.

Inro 2¼in (5.7cm) high

$4,000-5,300 **WW**

A 19thC Japanese Meiji period Kobako lacquer incense box, tray ,and inner compartments, shaped as five volumes of the "Genji Monogatari" ("Tale of Genji"), decorated in gold and silver hiramaki-e, tamaki-e, and nashiji and with details in red lacquer, the cover bearing the tale's title, the inner tray decorated with an ornate barge on a meandering river next to a pavilion, a reference to chapter 24, the four smaller boxes underneath with symbols of the four seasons: pomegranates (winter), iris (spring), chrysanthemum (fall), and morning glory (summer), the sides with geometric brocade patterns of aogai shell inlays, attributed to the Zohiko studio, with tomobako wood box.

5¼in (13cm) wide

$11,000-12,000 **WW**

ESSENTIAL REFERENCE—NETSUKE

- Traditionally, Japanese clothing—first the kosode and later the kimono—did not have pockets. The men who wore kimono needed a large and strong container in which to store personal belongings, such as pipes, tobacco, money, and seals, resulting in the development of containers known as sagemono, which were hung by cords from the robes' sashes (obi). Netsuke emerged as a practical solution to dressing in the 17thC, when Japanese men hung stylish inro and other vessels from cords looped under and behind the wide sashes that held their kimonos in place. At the other end of those cords, men fastened small, ornamental objects as counterweights, and those objects evolved into netsuke. The carved netsuke really developed in the 18thC.

- The crafted boxes (inro) were held shut by ojime, sliding beads on cords. Whatever the form of the container, the fastener that secured the cord at the top of the sash was a carved, buttonlike toggle called a netsuke. Netsuke, like inro and ojime, evolved over time from being strictly utilitarian into objects of great artistic merit and an expression of extraordinary craftsmanship. Netsuke production was most popular during the Edo period (1615-1868). As netsuke evolved, so did the design vocabulary, encompassing mythological creatures, deities, religious subjects, zodiacal animals, common animals, masks, kabuki actors or literary heroes, crafts, plants, abstract, erotic, and social satire.

- Netsuke are a central theme in "The Hare with Amber Eyes" (much recommended), a 2010 memoir by British ceramic artist Edmund de Waal. The book traces the history of a collection of 264 netsuke—some of them by well-known craftsmen—which were taken to France in the late 19thC and purchased by a wealthy art collector who was a member of the Jewish Ephrussi family. They were then owned by the family's Vienna branch, where a family servant kept them hidden during the Holocaust, when the Nazis confiscated the family's other possessions. In 1947, the netsuke were taken back to Japan by an heir who went to live in Tokyo.

An early-20thC Japanese dark stained boxwood netsuke, mask of Okina, by Ryumin, signed "Ryumin saku."

Ryumin and Hozan have characteristics in common.

2in (5cm) high

$2,000-2,600   MAB

A 19thC Japanese Meiji wood netsuke, of a snail, emerging from its shell and bending back to the top, realistically carved with its ocular tentacles fully extended, the himotoshi underneath formed by its fleshy tail.

1½in (4cm) wide

$1,300-2,000   WW

A Japanese Meiji wood netsuke of a kirin, after a design by Tomotada of Kyoto, the mythical creature depicted sitting on its haunches, with fire wisps licking up its scaly body, a two-character mark for Gyokuseki under its hoof.

2½in (6.4cm) high

$1,300-2,000   WW

A 19thC Japanese Meiji wood netsuke of a thwarted rat catcher, the emaciated man grimacing in surprise as a rat clambers over his shoulder, a wooden box before him and with a mace in his right hand, his eyes and the rodent's inlaid.

2¼in (5.6cm) wide

$2,000-2,600   WW

An 18thC Japanese netsuke mask of a large oni, of wood with traces of red pigment in the mouth, unsigned.

2½in (6.7cm) high

$6,000-6,600   MAB

A Japanese Meiji wood netsuke of a man with an octopus on his head, holding a pipe in his right hand and one of the cephalopod's tentacles in the other, a two character mark under his left foot.

3½in (8.8cm) high

$400-450   WW

An early-20thC Japanese pale boxwood netsuke mask of a gurning ghoul, by Kokeisai Sansho, signed with "kaoō."

1½in (3.9cm) high

$4,000-4,600   MAB

A Japanese Meiji ivory netsuke, depicting the Twelve Zodiac animals compactly interwoven, some with their eyes inlaid, a two character signature underneath.

1½in (4.2cm) wide

$2,000-2,600   **WW**

A 19thC Japanese Meiji ivory netsuke, of a beauty, carved as Eguchi no Kimi sitting on an elephant, the courtesan reading a love letter, signed "Tomonobu" underneath.

Kimi was a famous prostitute from the village of Eguchi who after assiduously studying Buddhist scriptures became an incarnation of Fugen Bosatsu, the Bodhisattva of Universal Goodness, Virtue, and Worthiness.

2¾in (6.9cm) wide

$2,200-2,600   **WW**

A late-18th/early-19thC Japanese Edo ivory netsuke, of a foreigner, possibly in a Chinese outfit, tying on a mask before his face, depicted with bulging eyes and a scrolling beard, possibly the caricature of a Westerner.

6in (15cm) high

$1,050-1,200   **WW**

A 19thC Japanese Edo or Meiji ivory netsuke, of rats, gnawing on millet, realistically carved and with the eyes inlaid, signed "Okatomo" underneath.

1½in (3.9cm) high

$2,000-2,600   **WW**

An 18thC Japanese Edo ivory netsuke, of a tiger and her cub, both with long elegant tails and with their eyes inlaid, signed "Tomotada" underneath.

1½in (3.6cm) wide

$4,600-5,300   **WW**

A 19thC Japanese Meiji ivory netsuke of a rat, nibbling at a candle, its eyes and the wick inlaid in horn, signed "Okatori" on the back.

Provenance: From the collection of Collingwood "Cherry" Ingram (1880-1981) and thence by descent. Cherry Ingram was a famous British ornithologist, plant collector, and gardener who became renowned for his knowledge on Japanese cherry trees.

1½in (4.2cm) high

$6,000-7,500   **WW**

A late-19thC Japanese netsuke of a mask of Shojo, by Matsuki Hôkei, of tsuishu lacquer, signed "Hôkei."

The artist is a master of carving in solid red lacquer.

A shōjō is a kind of Japanese sea spirit with a red face and hair and a fondness for alcohol. The legend is the subject of a Noh play of the same name. There is a Noh mask for this character, as well as a type of Kabuki stage makeup.

1¾in (4.5cm) high

$4,600-5,300   **MAB**

A 19thC Japanese late Edo/Meiji Hirado porcelain netsuke, of a karako, the Chinese boy lying on his belly and smiling while holding his head in his hands, the himotoshi holes to the side.

Himotoshi are the apertures, usually in the form of drilled holes, carved in netsuke for the passage of a cord. In some instances, formations in the body of a netsuke are used for this purpose. These are known as "natural himotoshi."

2½in (6.3cm) long

$4,600-5,300   **WW**

A Japanese Meiji boxwood okimono, of a monkey, examining a hermit crab through a looking glass, his eyes inlaid with amber-color beads and with elements in ivory, signed "Saijin" ("Talented Man") underneath.

3¼in (8cm) high

$4,000-4,600   **WW**

A Chinese late-18thC or early-19thC formal chao'fu, of charcoal gray silk gauze, embroidered in silks in counted stitch and in couched gilt thread, the upper half with four five-clawed dragons amid clouds above a turbulent sea-wave border, the skirt with confronting dragons, fading throughout and some tears and holes in gauze, stitching seems missing in some places.

A chao'fu, or audience robe, featuring a fully pleated skirt was the most formal type of men's court dress. Sumptuary regulations set in the mid-18thC dictated that only the emperor and heir apparent could wear robes emblazoned with five-clawed dragons, but in the 19thC these mandates were often overlooked. Blue-black audience robes were worn by Qing nobles, high-ranking civil and military officials, and Imperial guards.

52½in (133.5cm) long
$10,500-13,000   DN

A Chinese Imperial silk-ground embroidered "Dragon" Jifu robe, worn by a high rank prince of the court of Daoguang, with coral colored bats, the nine five-clawed dragons embroidered in fine gold thread, of which seven clasp the pearl of wisdom, original neck bands extenders and horse-shoe dragon cuffs decorate the robe, wear on embroidery at the hem and other areas of wear, holes, and fraying.

The pearl of wisdom was a symbol allowed to be worn only by the close circle of the Emperor in the direct royal blood line. Clasping the pearl of wisdom added a symbol of additional power to the robe, indicating high status in the court.

ca. 1820-40   *56¾in (144cm) long*
$7,500-8,500   DN

A Chinese 19thC Qing shaded gold-thread court dragon Jifu robe, worn by a mandarin of the court who by repute became a merchant for trade in Indonesia, nine five-clawed dragons adorn the robe chasing the pearl of wisdom among clouds and auspicious symbols of good fortune.

ca. 1850   *75in (189cm) long*
$6,000-7,500   DN

A Chinese Qing kesi weave dragon Jifu robe, woven with nine five-clawed dragons, decorated with a Wan trellis pattern and large bat symbols of happiness fly among the clouds, originally tailored with matching collar edgings, sleeve insets, and cuffs, unusual green flames enhance the dragon and pearl motifs, some repair and damage to the kesi, glue has been used to repair the robe, the gold buttons are 20thC.

The lower dragons clasp the pearl of wisdom, indicating the robe was worn by a high-ranking noble mandarin.

ca. 1850   *49¼in (125cm) long*
$7,500-8,500   DN

A Chinese Qing kesi "Nine Dragon" robe, worked in gold threads with nine dragons in pursuit of flaming pearls over crashing waves and stylized rocks, the centered confronting dragon writhing above a large basket of peaches, with crested cranes and bats in flight amid ruyi head-shaped clouds and precious Daoist and Buddhist objects.

86¼in (219cm) wide
$7,500-8,500   WW

A Chinese Qing gold-work longpao Jifu "Dragon" robe, the "nine dragon pattern" in a heavenly setting surrounded by clouds and auspicious symbols of faith and power, the hem embroidered with a diagonal striped lishui border, a turbulent froth of waves surrounding four pinnacles of rocks, the ninth dragon set on the inside flap.

Dragon robes embroidered with gold and silver threads were used for only special ceremonies. The gold threads would reflect the candles or the sun at dawn, making the wearer appear even more ethereal. They were costly to make, because real silver and gold leaf was used. Usually, only the high-ranking and wealthy mandarins could afford such a garment. When a robe was put on, the person took on an immortal status, being the axis on which this heavenly world turned.

ca. 1860   *51¼in (130cm) wide*
$4,600-5,900   DN

A Chinese Qing silk chaofu, embroidered with dragons chasing flaming pearls above waves in gilt thread, loose threads, edges and button connections worn, creases, and folds.

79¼in (201cm) wide

$6,000-6,600   SWO

A Chinese 19thC Qing Guangxu Period (1875-1908) yellow silk "Imperial Court Opera" theatrical robe, embroidered with dragons, clouds, and auspicious motifs in satin stitch and with bright silk threads incorporating Pekin knot stitches, cranes symbolic of long life fly among the clouds, some wear.

These large robes were worn by an actor playing the part of an Emperor, minister, or general at the Imperial Court Opera. They are similar to the formal and semiformal Imperial robes of the Emperor.

50¾in (129cm) long

$4,000-5,300   DN

A Chinese Qing embroidered robe, with butterflies among peony and prunus, liner with stains, holes, and splits, left sleeve with discoloration, collar late, creases, and folds.

50¼in (127.5cm) wide

$2,000-2,600   SWO

A Chinese Qing embroidered kesi red robe, with butterflies between tendrilled double gourds, above rocks and precious objects among waves, creases and folds, loose threads, splits and holes, some old repairs.

78in (198cm) wide

$11,000-12,000   SWO

A Chinese late-19thC Qing Mandarin's pufu surcoat, with a pair of 5th rank badges embroidered with auspicious symbols and the pearl of wisdom, a rocky outcrop, and lishui water and wave pattern.

These surcoats were worn over the formal dragon robe on official duty within Court life.

ca. 1890   *67in (170cm) wide*

$2,600-4,000   DN

A Chinese kesi longpao "Dragon" robe, perhaps Guangxu or earlier, with eight main five-clawed dragons attempting to clutch cosmic pearls among clouds, bats, the eight Buddhist emblems, and over the terrestrial diagram, waves and lishui stripes at the hem, the cuffs and collar with further dragon motifs.

51¼in (130cm) wide

$7,500-8,500   CHEF

A Chinese late-Qing silk woman's informal robe, embroidered with medallions of cranes holding sprigs of lingzhi, the birds surrounded by butterflies in flight amid blossoming flowers.

55¼in (140.5cm) long

$11,000-13,000   WW

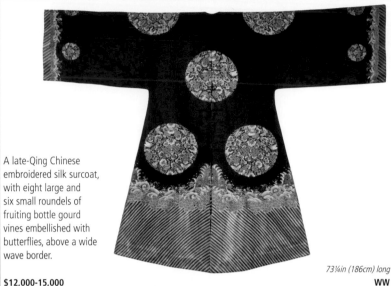

A late-Qing Chinese embroidered silk surcoat, with eight large and six small roundels of fruiting bottle gourd vines embellished with butterflies, above a wide wave border.

73¼in (186cm) long

$12,000-15,000   **WW**

A Chinese Qing embroidered summer robe, with dragons, the border with cranes and bats among clouds, with folds and creases.

46in (117cm) wide

$3,300-4,000   **SWO**

A Chinese brocade-weave robe, with eight dragons chasing flaming pearls among clouds, cranes, shou roundels, the eight Buddhist emblems, and other precious objects, above waves centered by the terrestrial diagram and lishui stripe on the hem, with creases and folding marks, stains, two burned marks on lower right.

ca. 1900   *86¼in (219cm) wide*

$2,900-3,700   **SWO**

A Chinese late-Qing embroidered silk robe, decorated with peony, lotus, orchid, prunus, magnolia, and hibiscus, with butterflies in flight, the sleeves with figures in gardens on cream silk.

51¼in (130cm) wide

$1,700-2,400   **WW**

A Chinese Qing embroidered robe, with bats holding swastika and sprigs of flowers, above waves centered by the terrestrial diagram and lishui stripe on the hem, altered at underarm to straps instead of buttons, with folds and creases.

61½in (156.5cm) wide

$750-850   **SWO**

A Chinese late-Qing embroidered silk "Nine Dragon" robe, the dragons, in gold thread, chase flaming pearls amid clouds, cranes, bats, and the Anbaxian, all above sea and lishui waves.

84¾in (215cm) wide

$4,000-4,600   **WW**

A Chinese late-Qing silk embroidered wedding jacket, embroidered in colors and gold threads with dragons above waves near cranes, phoenixes, and bats.

46in (117cm) long

$750-850   **CHEF**

An early-19thC Chinese Qing export, Hongs paper fan leaf, painted with a view of the Foreign Factories (Hongs) in Canton with flags, including the USA and Great Britain, with various watercraft in the foreground, in a modern frame, with signs of repainting.

22¼in (56.5cm) high

$3,400-4,000 CHEF

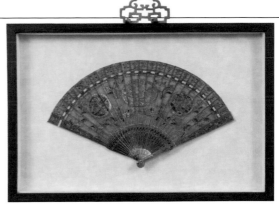

A Chinese Qing export silver-gilt filigree and enameled brisé fan, with three reserves with landscape scenes among sprigs, in modern case.

ca. 1840-50   7in (18cm) wide

$2,000-2,600 CHEF

A pair of Chinese late Qing Souchao embroidered double-sided fans, depicting auspicious birds in the heavenly gardens with various flowers, trees, and insects, stretched on a metal frame and with an inlaid ebonized wood handle, with minor staining, one wood handle repaired.

These were used by the court ladies to show modesty and hide their faces and to keep cool during the summer months.

ca. 1880   10¼in (26cm) diam

$4,000-4,600 DN

A Chinese Qing silk kesi "Peach Festival" hanging scroll, embroidered with immortals celebrating the birthday of Xiwangmu, Queen Mother of the West, of a pantheon of Daoist immortals and deities, including He He Erxian, Liu Hai, Shoulao, and the Eight Immortals, on a garden terrace with lingzhi, pine and peach trees, awaiting the arrival of Xiwangmu, who descends from the sky sitting astride her phoenix with attendants, a crane in flight above, loose threads on edges of panel, fabric stretched in numerous places, some paint faded, possible restoration on upper left corner.

The "Peach Festival," according to legend, takes place every 3,000 years at the Jade Palace in the Kunlun Mountains in the Western paradise. A traditional Daoist theme, the festival is part of the celebrations for Xiwangmu's birthday, during which she gifts Immortals with the Peaches of Eternal Life, so their immortality may continue. This scroll captures the moment the immortals wait in anticipation for Xiwangmu, who is seen making a grand entrance on the back of a phoenix. The panel's auspicious theme made it ideal to present at birthdays.

69in (175cm) high

$40,000-53,000 SWO

A 20thC Chen Zhi Chinese spotted bamboo fan, the markings of the bamboo used to depict blossoming trees, painted with a pine tree, signed and dated "wu zi year," with an artist's seal, the other side with an extensive inscription, also signed with an artist's seal.

1948   25¼in (64cm) wide

$4,600-5,300 WW

A pair of Chinese late-Qing embroidered silk bound-feet shoes, with peony blossoms, with slight fading, one side of each is darker than the other, slight deterioration of stitching at the "points" of each shoe.

ca. 1900

$350-400 CHEF

A pair of late-18thC Anglo-Chinese huanghuali and padouk open armchairs, in "French Hepplewhite" style, with oval padded back, seat, and armrests, with a molded frame and scroll arms, on turned legs.

$3,300-4,000   **WW**

A Chinese export "Brighton Pavilion" bamboo adjustable daybed, possibly Canton, decorated with pierced geometric and foliate motifs, the angle adjustable backrest above a caned rectangular seat flanked by armrests, the base incorporating a pull out footrest.

This daybed is remarkably similar, if not actually from the same source and design, as a suite of seat furniture present in the Long Gallery of the Royal Pavilion, Brighton.
ca. 1815   *37½in (95cm) long*
$6,000-6,600   **DN**

An Anglo-Indian rosewood planter's armchair, with a gadrooned and scroll carved top rail, above a tapering caned back and seat, on carved stylized pineapple front supports.
ca. 1850
$1,500-1,800   **WW**

A pair of 19thC Chinese Qing softwood armchairs, with openwork back and armrests carved in key fret patterns, the top of the back with stretched ruyi pattern.
36¾in (93cm) high
$600-750   **L&T**

A late-19thC Chinese padouk long stool, the paneled top above a scroll carved frieze and a pierced apron carved with peaches and interlocking lappets, on scroll feet.
82¾in (210.2cm) wide
$5,300-5,900   **WW**

A late-19thC Chinese hongmu double scholar's chair, carved with interlocking circles and symbols for money, of open spindle construction.
39¼in (99.5cm) wide
$3,300-4,600   **WW**

A pair of 19thC Chinese hardwood throne chairs, carved with a scholar with his pupils, pine trees, squirrels, dragon's heads, happy Buddhas, and scrolling leaves and flowers, with a later fabric padded oval back, seat, and armrests.
$2,000-2,600   **WW**

A large Chinese dreamstone-inset hardwood armchair, the seat of ruyi outline, the backrest inset with a circular dreamstone panel, carved in openwork with bats clambering amid fruit and flowers, with shou medallions dispersed throughout the design, with two smaller dreamstone panels set beneath the arms, the legs joined by stretchers shaped as two interlocking coins.

Provenance: From the collection of Sir Thomas Jackson, 1st Baronet (1841-1915). He was the third chief manager of the Hong Kong and Shanghai Banking Corporation and his influence on the company was so notable that he became known as the bank's "Great Architect." He was also one of the founding members of the Hong Kong Jockey Club. Born in County Leitrim, Ireland, Jackson joined the Belfast branch of the Bank of Ireland at the age of 19 before accepting a position in East Asia with Agra and Masterman's Bank five years later. In 1866, he joined HSBC, which had only been established the previous year. Jackson was quickly promoted to the position of an accountant in Shanghai, and he later spent several years working in Japan as the manager of the bank's Yokohama office. At the early age of 35, he was appointed as chief manager of HSBC and, under his direction, the company became the leading bank in Asia. After a successful career in Hong Kong, Jackson returned to the UK in 1891, taking charge of the company's office in London. He was knighted in 1899 and three years later he retired and received the additional title of Baronet. In 1906, a statue of Sir Thomas Jackson was unveiled in recognition of his services both to HSBC and Hong Kong. His statue still stands in Statue Square in front of the bank's Hong Kong headquarters. Jackson Road in Hong Kong was also named after him.

ca. 1900   *41in (104cm) high*
$20,000-26,000   WW

A pair of late-19thC Chinese hardwood throne armchairs, inlaid with mother-of-pearl, with scrolling leaves and auspicious shou characters with bats, the carved backs decorated with prunus trees and birds, each with a circular marble "dreamstone" panel back and seat, above a pierced frieze, on mythical beast carved legs and claw and ball feet.
$4,600-5,900   WW

A pair of late-19th/early-20thC Chinese sycamore yokeback armchairs, the serpentine top rails above curved center splats, over recessed panel seats flanked by curved open arms, on straight legs joined by peripheral stretchers, the front recess with carved panel inserts.

45¼in (115cm) high
$400-550   L&T

A 20thC Chinese huali folding chair, the horseshoe-shaped rail with a pierced and carved panel of a qilin among waves on the shaped backrest, with a woven string seat with a chilong carved top rail, sheet metal mounts throughout.
43in (109cm) high
$4,600-5,900   SWO

A pair of 20thC Chinese walnut armchairs, with upholstery.
34in (86.5cm) high
$1,200-1,450   DRA

A 19thC Chinese elm horseshoe armchair, the centered splat with two pierced and carved panels, above a panel seat and straight legs with stretchers.
36¾in (93cm) high
$550-650   L&T

ASIAN FURNITURE

A Chinese Kangxi gold and lacquer carved "Dragon" table, of lacquered and gilt wood.

45in (114cm) wide

$20,000-26,000   **DRA**

A large 18thC Chinese Ji Chi Mu stand, with a square wood top, the frieze carved with stylized bats surrounded by openwork archaistic scrolls, decorated in red, black, and gold lacquer with floral sprays and scrolls.

32in (81.5cm) high

$6,000-6,600   **WW**

A late-18thC Chinese hardwood console table, the top with molded edge, above a scroll-pierced frieze and shaped apron, on tapering cabriole legs, terminating in faceted pad feet, with knocks, scratches, and abrasions, old glued repairs on pierced scroll elements, later supporting blocks and glue residue on underside.

31¼in (79cm) wide

$2,600-3,300   **DN**

A 19thC Chinese lacquer table, decorated in gold and red lacquer with a panel enclosing a watery landscape, with birds perched on blossoming branches, the border with sprays of finger citron, orchids, lotus, and morning glory, all reserved on a black ground enhanced with diaper, with floral scrolls to the legs.

51½in (131cm) wide

$1,100-1,250   **WW**

A late-19thC Chinese hardwood table, with scrolling simulated bamboo frieze and legs, the top with dry cracking and staining.

30¼in (77cm) wide

$3,300-4,600   **CHEF**

A 19thC Chinese export eggplant (aubergine) lacquer tripod table, in gilt with a watery landscape, with pagodas, willow trees, figures, and boats, the circular tilt-top revolving on a birdcage, on a baluster-turned stem, a triform base and giltwood lion's-paw feet.

35¾in (90.8cm) diam

$6,000-7,500   **WW**

A late-19thC Chinese hardwood altar table, the rectangular paneled top above a pierced frieze, on open trestle ends and scroll feet.

60½in (153.6cm) wide

$2,100-2,600   **WW**

A large Chinese hardwood scroll table, the frieze decorated in low relief with shou characters, melons, and lotus, the spandrels carved in openwork with archaistic dragons, with four square-section legs terminating in ruyi heads.

Provenance: From the collection of Sir Thomas Jackson, 1st Baronet (1841-1915). See p. 157 for a chair from the same collection.

ca. 1900   *100¼in (254.5cm) wide*

$13,000-18,000   **WW**

A late-19th/early-20thC Chinese hardwood altar table, the paneled top with scroll ends, carved with leaves, the frieze with a pair of lovebirds perched on a prunus branch with flowers, on open trestle ends and scroll feet.

42½in (108cm) wide

$1,300-1,800   **WW**

A Chinese late Qing marble-top stand, the red and white veined marble top over a scroll pierced apron, the mask headed legs with ball-and-claw feet united by an undertier.

ca. 1900   *26¾in (68cm) diam*

$450-600   **CHEF**

A Chinese late Qing marble-top stand, the red and white veined top above a pierced and carved prunus frieze.

ca. 1900   *30in (76cm) high*

$750-850   **CHEF**

A 19th/20thC Southeast Asian hardwood stand, with five curved legs joined by stretchers, carved in relief with ferocious dragon masks.

9in (23cm) high

$200-260   **WW**

A 20thC Chinese rosewood altar table, the aprons carved with dragons chasing a flaming pearl, with pierced and carved legs terminating in key and bun feet, surface scratches.

47¾in (121.5cm) wide

$650-900   **SWO**

A 20thC Chinese burrwood drum table, the banded top on curved supports joined by peripheral stretchers.

35½in (90cm) diam

$750-850   **I&T**

An early-20thC Anglo-Indian teak camel occasional table, the circular top carved with a band of leaves and flowers.

28¼in (71.8cm) high

$2,600-3,300   **WW**

A rare 16thC or later Japanese Momoyama namban lacquer table, decorated in gold maki-e lacquer on a black urushi ground, with four shaped panels variously enclosing two monkeys, two deer, two doves, and a phoenix among branches of prunus, paulownia, maple, and wisteria, the panels divided by bands of dense geometrical patterns of diamonds and quatrefoils, with leaves and flowers picked out in mother-of-pearl, raden, each corner with copper mounts decorated with various flowering trees.

See J. Welsh, "After the Barbarians, An Exceptional Group of Namban Works of Art," pp. 78-87, where two tables are illustrated. The author suggests that they may have been used as portable altars for Jesuits missionaries. They were first recorded in Japan in 1616 in a list of goods written by Jesuit Father Manuel Bento.

19¾in (50cm) high

$70,000-80,000   **WW**

A 20thC Chinese hardwood stand, formed as twisting gnarled tree branches.

12½in (31.8cm) high

$650-800   **WW**

A 20thC Japanese Taisho red lacquer and mother-of-pearl low table, the top resting on four scrolling legs, the red lacquered surface speckled with mother-of-pearl inlays in typical wakasa-nuri style.

41¾in (106cm) wide

$550-800   **WW**

A near pair of 18thC Anglo-Chinese huanghuali and padouk bureau cabinets, with molded cornices above a pair of paneled doors with leaf-carved moldings, enclosing two adjustable shelves and two drawers, above a hinged fall revealing an arrangement of drawers and pigeonholes with a centered cupboard door, above four long graduated drawers, on bracket feet, with paktong escutcheons, hinges, and handles.

These cabinets are based on an English prototype but constructed in an entirely Chinese way, particularly with the use of solid wood.

74in (188.2cm) high

$160,000-200,000   **WW**

A Chinese Qianlong Imperial cinnabar lacquer "Dragon" cabinet, the center of the cabinet with an open compartment flanked by four drawers, incised with floral patterns and with metal handles shaped as tassels, the centered section with six hinged doors, carved with a scaly five-clawed dragon amid clouds, their handles shaped as cicadas, with two further dragon panels divided by diaper to each of the two shorter sides.

21¼in (54cm) high

$46,000-53,000   **WW**

A small 18thC Chinese polychrome lacquer display cabinet, the upper section divided into six open compartments and two drawers, the compartments set with openwork bone borders, with a pair of cabinets with hinged double doors below, the exterior decorated with lotus flowers blossoming amid scrolling leaves.

24in (61cm) high

$2,000-2,600   **WW**

An 18thC Chinese export Coromandel lacquered cabinet-on-stand, decorated with figures in traditional dress and floral motifs, the cabinet with cavetto-molded top, above a pair of panel doors opening to four drawers, the interior decorated with figures in village scenes and exotic birds, the stand with shaped tapering cabriole legs terminating in scroll feet.

44in (112cm) high

$4,000-5,300   **DN**

An 18thC Chinese Coromandel lacquer hanging corner cupboard, the twin doors decorated with Chinese figures in a landscape with a pagoda, opening to reveal shelves.

31½in (80cm) high

$1,200-1,450   **L&T**

An 18thC Chinese lacquer cabinet-on-stand, the stand later, the brass banded cornice above a pair of doors decorated with Chinese figures in a domestic scene, the top and sides with landscape scenes.

46½in (118cm) high

$2,000-2,600   **L&T**

An early-19thC Chinese export red lacquer and gilt chinoiserie chest-on-stand, decorated with foliage, the hinged domed top, front, back, and sides centered by figures in a landscape, on scroll and acanthus carved X-shaped supports centered by a reeded stretcher, on stylized paw feet, with marks, knocks, scratches, and abrasions, probably to support a tray or shelf that is now lacking, lacking key.

43in (109cm) high

$2,600-4,000   **DN**

One of a pair of Chinese Qing Jumu cabinets, the doors carved with two pairs of stylized lotus and foliate carvings, some panels with cracks.

42in (107cm) wide

$3,300-4,600 the pair   **DN**

A 19thC Chinese export carved hardwood display cabinet, the pierced and carved cornice centered by an armorial lion, above open shelves with pierced and carved galleries and corner brackets, over a pair of cupboard doors carved with chrysanthemums and peonies, on a separate hardwood stand.

Provenance: This intricately carved and detailed cabinet, formerly at Ackergill Tower, Wick, was according to family tradition purchased in India in the latter part of the 19thC by a member of the Duff-Dunbar family who was on military service with the Cameron Highlanders. It was then brought back to Scotland upon inheriting the Caithness estate.

92¼in (234cm) high

$3,300-4,000   **L&T**

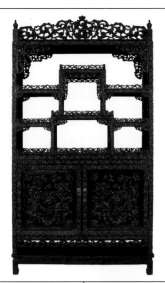

A late-19th/early-20thC Chinese Coromandel lacquer pedestal desk, the top over a long frieze drawer flanked by short drawers, on banks of four drawers, with cupboards on the reverse, on shaped plinth bases, decorated with dragons, clouds, and scrolling foliage.

59½in (151cm) wide

$8,500-10,000   **L&T**

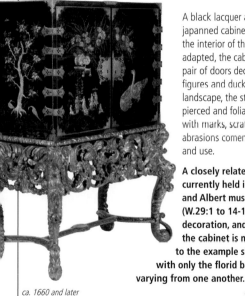

A black lacquer and gilt japanned cabinet-on-stand, the interior of the cabinet later adapted, the cabinet with a pair of doors decorated with figures and ducks in a traditional landscape, the stand with a pierced and foliate carved apron, with marks, scratches, and abrasions comensurate with age and use.

A closely related cabinet is currently held in the Victoria and Albert museum in London (W.29:1 to 14-1912). The form, decoration, and metalware of the cabinet is near identical to the example shown here with only the florid baroque stands varying from one another.

ca. 1660 and later   *61½in (156cm) high*

$26,000-33,000   **DN**

A pair of early-20thC Coromandel lacquer and gilt wood cabinets, with panels depicting Chinese figures in domestic scenes, enclosing shelves, on cabriole legs.

56¾in (144cm) high

$4,000-4,600   **L&T**

A 17thC Japanese lacquer chest-on-stand, decorated with mountainous landscapes, mounted with foliate engraved clasps and escutcheon, sides with carrying handles, the interior applied with red lacquer, on later stand.

54in (137cm) high

$6,500-9,000   **L&T**

A 17thC Japanese cabinet-on-stand, the top decorated with a mythical beast in a landscape, the sides with flowers, the door enclosing an arrangement of drawers.

49¾in (126cm) high

$4,000-5,300   **CHEF**

A Japanese Meiji cabinet, with shibayama doors, panels, and drawers with ivory, bone, and mother-of-pearl applied inlaid and carved decoration.

88¼in (224cm) high

$7,500-8,500   **CHEF**

An early-20thC Japanese wooden open display cabinet, the base simulating a tree trunk, the cabinet finished to resemble bark, with marks, knocks, abrasions, old splits, and cracks.

$1,700-2,100   **DN**

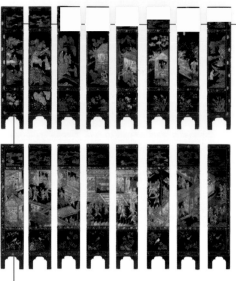

An early-18thC Chinese Coromandel lacquer eight-fold screen, with a vista of palace life to one side, and the other with a courtly battle scene, within borders of floral sprays and mountainous landscapes, raised on bracket supports.

126in (320cm) wide

$17,000-21,000   L&T

An early-19thC Chinese export black-lacquer four-fold screen, decorated in gilt with red highlights with landscape and bird panels, above a dragon border and landscape scenes with figures in various pursuits, with buildings, boats, and trees, the verso with exotic birds, trees, leaves, and flowers.

94½in (239.8cm) high

$2,600-3,300   WW

A Chinese late Qing porcelain inset 12-fold screen, 10 of the wood panels inset with polychrome, famille verte, and blue-and-white porcelain plaques depicting objects from the Hundred Antiques, figural scenes, and landscapes, the panels bordered by various fruits and flowers in mother-of-pearl, the lower sections of the wood panels carved in relief with scenes of figures amid trees and pavilions, the two outer panels decorated with dragons and figures, with bats encircling character medallions on the reverse.

Provenance: From the collection of Sir Thomas Jackson, 1st Baronet (1841-1915). See table on p. 158, which comes from the same collection.

236¼in (600cm) wide

$110,000-130,000   WW

A Chinese Qing eight-fold painted screen, oil on canvas stretched on wood frame, with figures in a garden with pavilions representing the gateway to heaven and the gateway to hell, with precious objects and dragons.

78in (199cm) high

$2,600-3,300   DN

A Chinese late-Qing celadon jade table screen, with two panels, the larger carved with turtles clambering over lotus leaves, the smaller with a group of herons under a large lotus leaf, both mounted in a hardwood frame with Qianlong poems on the reverse.

19¾in (50cm) high

$1,300-2,000   WW

An early-20thC Chinese export famille rose table screen of glazed porcelain and lacquered wood.

33in (84cm) high

$6,000-6,600   DRA

A pair of Chinese table screens, the jadeite roundels carved to one side with ducks among weeds below an inscription "Qiu Jiang Su Yan, Chen Dong Gao Fengchi Jingshu," the reverse with birds and a tree, on hardwood stands carved as buffalos below a cloud, with a Qianlong seal, one stand glued, the other stand with one horn loose, jadeite with minute chips on edges.

12¼in (31cm) diam 120oz and 124oz

$12,000-15,000　　　　SWO

A Chinese "Dragon" set of four inlay panels of porcelain and carved wood, with raised mark on each example.

32in (81.5cm) high

$1,300-1,800　　　　DRA

A Chinese early Qing lacquered tray, inlaid with mother-of-pearl figures under a willow tree by a pavilion, two-character mark on base, surface scratches and cracks to mother-of-pearl.

14¼in (36cm) wide

$3,300-4,600　　　　SWO

A 19thC Chinese hardwood cheval mirror, with carved dragon pediment and floral and fruit panel on the base, joints loose, a panel above the leg missing on the reverse.

This was acquired by Lady MacDonald while she was in China and Japan during a turbulent time between 1893 and 1912. Her husband, Sir Claude MacDonald, was in a post as the representative of the British Government, first in China and then in Japan from 1900.

78¾in (200cm) high

$1,600-2,100　　　　CHEF

A large 16thC or later Japanese Momoyama Kano school, six-fold byobu paper screen, depicting a procession in a landscape, the figures emerging from a wooden gate on the right-hand side of the composition, with a Chinese dignitary riding a horse in the center accompanied by attendants, one of them a Mongolian archer, three retainers leading a horse at the front of the procession, other men holding standards, and one with a fan made of peacock feathers, a river cascading from rocky outcrops and with palm trees on the left side.

148¾in (378cm) wide

$6,000-7,500　　　　WW

A 19thC Japanese screen of carved and painted wood and silk.

77¼in (196cm) high

$1,700-2,100　　　　DRA

A late-19th/early-20thC Anglo-Indian ebony four-fold table screen, inset with 12 miniature topographical paintings on ivory of Indian monuments, including: the Red Fort, the Taj Mahal, the Qutub Minar tower, the interior of the Red Fort, and with four portrait medallions of noble gentlemen and ladies, with later metal feet.

38in (96.5cm) high

$6,000-6,600　　　　WW

THE FURNITURE MARKET

The furniture market has continued to be very polarized. There is no doubt that the Covid-19 pandemic has encouraged people to think about their homes, and this has had some impact on the furniture market. "Brown furniture" has continued to fall in value, and most auctioneers are still reporting that the plain utilitarian 18thC and 19thC mahogany is proving difficult to sell. At the other end of the spectrum, furniture that is really top quality, fresh to the market, and "honest" continues to rise in value. It is not just age that determines the value of a piece of furniture—maker, quality, condition, and "eye appeal" are all important factors, too. This improvement can be seen in this edition in, for example, chests-of-drawers (see pages 233-36). These pieces would look particularly well in traditional settings but are of such quality they could also grace a more modern setting.

The reasons for the decline in value of midrange furniture is complex, most of it is down to fashion – this is true for all antiques. Younger buyers believe that old mahogany furniture is just not "cool" and does not fit into today's interiors. There is also a lack of good-quality examples on the market.

Pieces that are too bulky for modern interiors need to be of exceptional quality to attract buyers. There is no doubt that Georgian, and especially Regency, pieces sell better than their heavy Victorian counterparts. Also, certain pieces, such as bureaux do not have any real function in today's homes. However, while ordinary "Georgian-Victorian brown" furniture has dipped in value, 20thC, especially Mid-Century Modern, furniture has continued its renaissance. Obviously due to the pandemic, American buyers are not visiting sale rooms in their previous numbers. However, dealers and auction houses are confirming that the Internet has taken over as the major sales and buying tool.

So, has the low- to midrange furniture market reached its nadir? Some of the prices achieved at auction have been ridiculously low. However, there are signs that things are improving. I have compared prices with our previous Guide and there is a definite improvement in pieces made of solid wood by skilled craftsmen instead of MDF (medium-density fiberboard). People are coming around to the idea that "antiques are green" and that recycling or upcycling old furniture is more responsible than destroying more forests. Also, with some prices so low, younger buyers are looking at auctions to furnish their first apartment or house.

Mirrors, particularly of the 17thC and early-18thC, are selling particularly well (see pp. 268-269). Good-quality American furniture is also selling well—sturdy, good-quality, highly functional pieces are excellent value for money. These pieces could well provide good investment potential, as well as pleasing, useful home furnishings.

Top Left: A George II painted console table

ca. 1740

54in (137cm) wide

$20,000-26,000

DN

Above: An 18thC Irish George III mahogany bureau bookcase.

96in (244cm) high

$8,000-9,000

L&T

FURNITURE

UK PERIOD	USA PERIOD	FRENCH PERIOD	GERMAN PERIOD
Elizabethan *Elizabeth I (1558-1603)*		**Renaissance** *(to ca. 1610)*	**Renaissance** *(to ca. 1650)*
Jacobean *James I (1603-25)*			
Carolean *Charles I (1625-49)*	**Early Colonial** *(1620s-1700)*	**Louis XIII** *(1610-43)*	
Cromwellian *Commonwealth (1649-60)*		**Louis XIV** *(1643-1715)*	**Renaissance/ Baroque** *(ca. 1650-1700)*
Restoration *Charles II (1660-85)* *James II (1685-88)*			
William and Mary *(1689-94)*	**William and Mary** *(1690-1720)*		
William III *(1694-1702)*			
Queen Anne *(1702-14)*	**Queen Anne** *(1720-50)*	**Régence** *(1715-23)*	**Baroque** *(ca. 1700-30)*
Early Georgian *George I (1714-27)* *George II (1727-60)*	**Chippendale** *(1750-90)*	**Louis XV** *(1723-74)*	**Rococo** *(ca. 1730-60)*
Late Georgian *George III (1760-1811)*	**Early Federal** *(1790-1810)* *American Directoire (1798-1804)* *American Empire (1804-15)*	**Louis XVI** *(1774-92)*	**Neoclassicism** *(ca. 1760-1800)*
		Directoire *(1792-99)*	**Empire** *(ca. 1800-15)*
		Empire *(1799-1815)*	
Regency *George III (1812-20)*	**Later Federal** *(1810-30)*	**Restauration** *(1815-30)* *Louis XVIII (1814-24)* *Charles X (1824-30)*	**Biedermeier** *(ca. 1815-48)*
George IV *(1820-30)*			
William IV *(1830-37)*		**Louis Phillipe** *(1830-48)*	**Revivale** *(ca. 1830-80)*
Victorian *Victoria (1837-1901)*	**Victorian** *(1840-1900)*	**2nd Empire** *(1848-70)*	
Edwardian *Edward VII (1901-10)*		**3rd Republic** *(1871-1940)*	**Jugendstil** *(ca. 1880-1920)*

ESSENTIAL REFERENCE—EARLY CHAIRS

The earliest surviving antique chairs bought and sold today mostly date from the late-16thC and early 17thC. In terms of both form and methods of construction, they actually have their precedents in ancient and Classical civilizations thousands of years earlier—styles and techniques that had been largely swept away in Western Europe during the "Dark Ages" following the fall of the Roman Empire in the 5thC, but which had been gradually rediscovered and revived from the 11thC on, especially during the artistic and scientific "rebirth" of the Renaissance.

- As far as basic form is concerned, most early chairs, notably "wainscots," are essentially thronelike in appearance, recalling, for example, ancient Greek "thronos," albeit with open instead of the latter's enclosed sides.
- The most commonly used techniques for assembling the component parts—backs, seats, arms, legs, and stretchers—were pegged mortise-and-tenon joints, which, as the archaeological excavation of the Pharaoh Tutankhamun's tomb in 1922 subsequently confirmed, had also been used by the ancient Egyptians.
- Most chairs are fashioned from solid indigenous woods, notably elm, oak, and walnut. More "exotic" woods from overseas, such as mahogany, only began to be used in any quantity, and often in veneer form, in the 18thC, following considerable expansion in international trade.
- Carved decorative forms and motifs on these early chairs are primarily architectural (such as Gothic tracery), heraldic, and flora (often indigenous) and fauna (often exotic); turned decoration (shaped on a lathe), began to become fairly commonplace, especially on legs and arm supports, from the mid-16thC.

An early-17thC oak joined armchair, the high scrolled cresting carved with flowers and foliage over a back with a center lozenge carved panel.

52in (132cm) high

$2,600-3,300   L&T

A Charles II walnut open armchair, the carved cresting rail over a lattice back and seat, over barley twist supports united by stretchers, seat with later supports, heavily wormed, seat broken and repaired, legs reduced, feet replaced.

39½in (100cm) high

$750-850   SWO

A 17thC oak wainscot armchair, the arched cresting and panel back carved with flower motifs, over a plank seat flanked by open arms, raised on turned legs joined by peripheral stretchers.

48¾in (124cm) high

$2,400-2,900   L&T

A 17thC and later oak paneled-back armchair, the arched top carved with an urn issuing flowers and leaves, above a band of "S" motifs, the back carved with oak leaves and acorns, with turned supports united by peripheral stretchers.

$650-800   WW

A late Charles II oak child's highchair, the paneled back decorated with flower-head rondels, on bobbin-turned supports united by peripheral stretchers, with traces of a painted finish.

ca. 1680

$3,300-4,000   WW

A William and Mary oak child's highchair, the back carved with scrolling tulips and leaves, the scroll arms on bobbin-turned supports, with a lozenge carved apron and shaped footrest, the back branded twice with initials "T S."

ca. 1690

$1,600-2,100   WW

A 17th/18thC and later Welsh primitive elm lambing/commode chair, the hooded top above a boarded seat with an aperture and lid, the sideboards carved with the letters "WC," the front with a hinged door revealing a vacant compartment, on naive wooden casters.

55¼in (140.3cm) high

$8,000-9,000   WW

FURNITURE

A 17thC oak carved paneled settle, with a back carved with lozenge, scroll and stylized foliate motifs, above a box seat with a hinged lid and further carved panels flanked by down-sweeping arms and raised on stile feet.

71¾in (182cm) wide

$3,300-4,600   **L&T**

A late-17th/early-18thC and later carved oak settle, the back carved with lozenges and foliate scrolls, above a box seat with a hinged plank top flanked by scrolled arms with spiral carved supports.

72¾in (185cm) wide

$1,600-2,100   **L&T**

An early-18thC early Georgian oak panel back settle, the back with five arched panels, above a long seat with squab cushion and open arms.

77¼in (196cm) wide

$1,700-2,100   **L&T**

An 18thC oak and fruitwood banded three-paneled box settle, with loss of veneers, one arm broken and replaced.

48¾in (124cm) wide

$1,200-1,600   **CHEF**

An 18thC Georgian provincial elm monk's bench, the pivoting plank back lowering to form a tabletop, supported on open arms and a box seat, raised on stile legs.

A monk's bench or hutch table is a piece of furniture in which a tabletop is set onto a chest in such a way that when the table is not in use, the top pivots to an upright position and becomes the back of a settle, allowing easy access to the chest lid that forms the seat of the piece. It is debatable if monks ever used such a bench, and there does not seem to be any evidence of such furniture in monasteries. A provincial example, such as this, could have been used in a grand farmhouse kitchen.

60¾in (154cm) wide

$2,000-2,600   **L&T**

A late-18th/early-19thC George III oak settle, the back with five arched fielded panels, down-sweeping arms, on front cabriole legs.

71¼in (181cm) wide

$4,000-4,600   **L&T**

A George III mahogany and pine hall bench, with floral, foliate, and C-scroll carving throughout, the shaped back and arms above the rectangular seat and shaped apron, on tapering cabriole legs.

ca. 1775   *63¾in (162cm) wide*

$1,700-2,100   **DN**

A 17thC carved walnut high-back dining chair, the scrolled top rail above a pierced and carved back support between baluster-turned supports, on inverted turned and molded cup-and-cover forelegs joined by a turned H stretcher and an ornate pierced front rail.

50in (127cm) high

$400-500 TEN

An early-18thC ash, oak, and pine high-back Windsor armchair, the back centered by a tapering shaped splat, scratches and abrasions, some old losses.

38¼in (97cm) high

$2,000-2,600 DN

A mid-18thC George II elm, ash, and walnut comb-back Windsor armchair, from the Thames Valley region, the saddle seat flanked by horseshoe-shaped arms, on tapering cabriole legs terminating in hoof feet at the front.

40½in (103cm) high

$2,600-4,000 DN

A pair of mid-18thC yew and mahogany Gothic Windsor armchairs, with shaped seats and crinoline stretchers, one stamped "T.B" on the underside, some restoration.

38¼in (97cm) high

$17,000-21,000 CHEF

An 18thC primitive comb-back armchair, with saddle seat on turned legs, with old woodworm.

37¾in (96cm) high

$5,300-6,600 CHEF

A near pair of George III yew and elm Windsor armchairs, with hoop-stick backs centered with a pierced vase-shaped splat, above a saddle seat and front cabriole legs and pad feet united by an H stretcher.

ca. 1770-80

$4,600-5,300 WW

A George III cherry and elm Windsor armchair, Thames Valley, the wing back with an interlaced scroll-pierced splat, with bow arm supports, with a bell-shaped seat, with an applied "bob tail," on cabriole front legs united by an H stretcher.

ca. 1770

$3,300-4,000 WW

A near pair of George III yew and elm Windsor armchairs, each with a hoop-stick back centered with a pierced vase-shaped splat, above a saddle seat, on front cabriole legs and pad feet united by an H stretcher.

ca. 1770-80

$4,600-5,300 WW

A late-18thC provincial walnut "drunkard's" armchair, the pierced top rail above a spindle back and drop-in seat flanked by open arms, raised on square legs with peripheral stretchers and trestle bases.

32¾in (83cm) high

$400-500 L&T

FURNITURE

A late-18thC ash and elm comb-back Windsor chair, of West Country type, possibly Cornish, the top rail above the spindle back and curved arms, the solid seat on turned legs, marks, knocks, and abrasions.

45in (114cm) high

$5,300-5,900   **DN**

A late-18thC green-painted comb-back Windsor chair, possibly Irish, the top rail above turned spindles supports the horseshoe arms, carved with ownership initials "S*," the letter "W" has also been carved twice on one arm terminal, marks, scratches, and abrasions, fragments of a red paint are visible.

36¼in (92cm) high

$3,300-4,600   **DN**

A pair of George III fruitwood side chairs, possibly apple or pear wood.

ca. 1790   *39¾in (101cm) high*

$2,100-2,600   **DN**

A pair of late-18thC George III mahogany North Country "drunkard's" armchairs, with spindle backs and pierced top rails, with open scrolled arms, raised on low square legs with trestle bases and joined by peripheral stretchers.

31½in (80cm) high

$1,800-2,400   **L&T**

ESSENTIAL REFERENCE—WINDSOR CHAIRS

Emerging around the turn of the 18thC, Windsor chairs were made in various locations around Great Britain, including Norfolk, Lancashire, North Wales, and the West Country (and subsequently in North America), but most probably were named after the town of Windsor either because of the latter's proximity to the chair-making centers of Buckinghamshire—which had become established there because of the proliferation of beech trees in the surrounding Chiltern Hills—and/or because of Windsor's proximity to the Thames River, which made it a convenient center for the distribution of the chairs.

- **Most Windsors were made from indigenous woods, such as yew, elm, and the aforementioned beech. However, imported (and more expensive) woods, such as walnut, were also sometimes used.**
- **Aside from their carved seats and various arms and back rails, the Windsor's other structural components—legs, stretchers, arm supports—were all turned to various decorative shapes on a lathe.**
- **Variants of the Windsor are mostly named after the style of their back. Notable examples include: the comb back, one of the earliest forms and distinguished by it comblike top rail and back sticks; the hoop or bow back; and the wheel back, featuring a center, shaped splat back incorporating some two-thirds of the way up from the seat a decorative, pierced spoked wheel—a style of Windsor introduced in the 1820s, commonly used in inns, taverns, and public houses, and that survives in considerable numbers to this day.**

An 18thC and later yew and elm Gothic Windsor armchair, Thames Valley, the lancet-shaped back with three pierced fret "window" splats, with conforming arm supports, the bell-shaped saddle seat on cabriole front legs and pad feet united by a crionoline stretcher, applied with pierced brackets.

$8,000-9,000   **WW**

A George III yew, elm, and ash Windsor armchair, Thames Valley, of Goldsmith type, the comb top rail above a fan stick back, on bow arm supports, above a saddle seat and a "bob tail," on turned front legs united by an H stretcher.

ca. 1790-1800

$800-900   **WW**

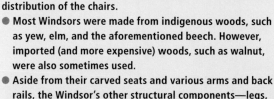

An early-19thC late George III ash and elm Windsor armchair, Thames Valley, the hoop stick back above a saddle seat, on turned legs united by an H stretcher.

$650-800   **WW**

A pair of early-19thC Georgian provincial ash side chairs, probably Staffordshire, with yoke top rails, shaped splats, framed seats, with a shaped apron on ring-turned legs on pad feet feet joined by stretchers.

36¼in (92cm) high

$650-800   **L&T**

A mid-19thC Irish sycamore and ash primitive armchair, in the manner of Gibson, with a comb top rail and a stick back, the curved arms interlocking with the outer back upright, with traces of original paint.

This type of Irish country chair is known as a "Gibson chair" and the design was most common in Northeastern Leinster. They are characterized by the "W" shape back spindles and the interlocking arms.

$1,500-1,800   **WW**

A mid-19thC matched set of six yew wood Thames Valley Windsor armchairs, the pierced splats with molded roundels above outsweeping arms and elm and ash molded seats, on turned legs joined by a crinoline stretcher, some damage.

Largest 35½in (90cm) high

$5,300-6,600   **TEN**

A set of four 19thC walnut and fruitwood wheel-back Windsor chairs, Thames Valley, with thick seats raised on turned supports united by an H stretcher, with knocks and wear, areas of repair.

34¾in (88cm) high

$1,300-1,800   **SWO**

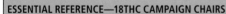

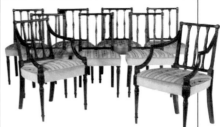

A mid-19thC Scottish darvel elm and birch comb-back Windsor armchair, the high curved back with a U-shaped midrail with baluster turned supports, on turned and tapered legs joined by a turned H stretcher.

45¼in (115cm) high

$2,600-3,300   **L&T**

Two 19thC Windsor armchairs, with pierced splats above shaped seats and U-shaped arms, one of ash and elm, the other of yew and elm.

41¾in (106cm) high

$1,700-2,100   **L&T**

A set of nine late-18thC late George III mahogany dining chairs, the square backs with foliate carved splats above wide stuffover seats covered in green needlework covers, raised on turned tapered legs, to include a pair of armchairs and seven side chairs.

Armchair 35½in (90cm) high

$1,500-2,000   **L&T**

ESSENTIAL REFERENCE—18THC CAMPAIGN CHAIRS

The design for this fashionable chair back appears in Thomas Sheraton's "Cabinet-Maker's and Upholsterer's Drawing Book" published in four parts 1791-94.

- **It is rare to find such a complete and long set of 18thC campaign or naval chairs; in fact, no other known sets of 12 are documented. The very nature of their design and use made such chairs vulnerable to wear and tear. The speed in which these chairs can be folded and packed made them ideal for use in the Navy, where it would be necessary to clear the decks quickly.**
- **There is a similar group in Nelson's cabin aboard H.M.S. "Victory," although some are reproductions.**
- **A set of four plus one armchair (although with cane seats) belonging to Admiral Boscawen are recorded in "Some aspects of 18th century Naval Furniture," by Treve Rosoman, an article published in "The Journal of The Furniture History Society," Vol. XXXIII, 1997.**
- **A similar example with a padded seat, but plain vertical bars in the back, was included in the exhibition catalog "At Ease Gentlemen: A catalogue of 18th, 19th and early-20th Century Campaign Furniture and Travel Equipment," published by Christopher Clarke (Antiques) Ltd., 2002, item 8.**

Four of a set of 12 English mahogany concertina-action campaign or naval chairs, including a pair of armchairs, each having a rectangular back with three pierced and tapering vertical bar splats headed with leaf-carved detail, the inner cross stretcher lifting out to enable each chair seat to fold away after the seat pad has been removed.

ca. 1795   *35in (89cm) high*

$17,000-21,000 the set   **CM**

A set of eight George III mahogany Hepplewhite dining chairs, each with an oval back with a pierced splat carved with leaves, drapes, and a guilloche band, on square tapering front legs with spade feet united by an H stretcher, the back rail stamped with workman's initials "I R."

$8,000-9,000   **WW**

FURNITURE

A set of six 18thC George III mahogany dining chairs, the triple-arch backs with a waisted pierced splat, above drop-in seats raised on square legs joined by stretchers, to include an armchair and five side chairs.

$1,000-1,100   **L&T**

A set of eight late-18thC George III mahogany dining chairs, in the Hepplewhite style.

40½in (103cm) high

$800-900   **L&T**

Two of a set of 14 George III mahogany and leather upholstered dining chairs, attributed to Gillows, to include two armchairs.

ca. 1810

$5,300-6,600 the set   **DN**

A set of eight early-19thC late-George III mahogany dining chairs, a pair of armchairs and six side chairs, the bar backs above X-form rails and drop-in seats, on square tapered legs joined by H stretchers.

Armchair 33in (84cm) high

$900-1,050   **L&T**

One of a pair of late Regency mahogany dining chairs.

34in (86cm) high

$260-400 the pair   **CHEF**

A set of ten Regency mahogany Grecian-style dining chairs, in the manner of George Smith, the arms carved with anthemion motifs, with reeded frames and saber legs, eight side chairs and a pair of armchairs, some rails stamped with workman's initials "I M."

ca. 1815-20

$7,500-8,500   **WW**

A set of eight early-19thC Regency mahogany dining chairs, the bar backs over pierced horizontal splats with a center roundel, the stuffover seats, raised on turned legs, with six side chairs and a pair of armchairs.

Armchair 32¾in (83cm) high

$1,000-1,100   **L&T**

A set of 10 early-19thC Scottish Regency mahogany dining chairs, the top rails carved with roses and wheat sheafs, over spiral-turned horizontal splats and stuffover seats, on lotus-carved and spiral turned legs, with two armchairs and eight side chairs.

Armchair 33in (84cm) high

$1,600-2,100   **L&T**

A set of four early-19thC late Regency mahogany dining chairs, the open backs carved with palmettes, above molded seat rails with loose cushion pads, raised on turned and reeded tapered legs.

33in (84cm) high

$600-750   **L&T**

A set of eight George IV mahogany dining chairs, with X-shaped splat backs, on turned tapered legs.

$650-800   CHOR

A set of 12 William IV rosewood dining chairs, with scrolling acanthus carved backs and splats.

$6,500-8,000   CHOR

A set of late-19thC Chippendale-style mahogany dining chairs, the shell and foliate carved backs with pierced interlaced splats, the fluted seat rails on fluted square legs with pierced scroll corner brackets and joined by pierced-fret H stretchers; to include six side chairs and a pair of armchairs of slightly different proportions.

Side chair 38¼in (97cm) high

$2,600-3,300   L&T

A set of eight 19thC Hepplewhite-style dining chairs.

36¾in (93cm) high

$650-800   L&T

A set of six early-20thC Georgian-style mahogany dining chairs, the pierced backs carved with anthemions, bell flowers, and flower heads, above wide curved seats, raised on stop-fluted square tapering legs joined by stretchers, comprising five side chairs and an armchair, with a George III mahogany armchair.

Side chair 37in (94cm) high

$650-800   L&T

A near pair of late-17thC Indian ebony side chairs, Coromandel Coast, the pierced and twist-turned backs profusely carved in low relief with flowers, each with a shaped rail and bulbous finials, above a square caned seat with a carved and pierced apron, on twist-turned supports and stretchers, seats have been recaned.

When similar pieces of this type began to be recorded in British collections in the 18thC, the prevailing thought was that they were surviving examples of early English furniture, due to their dark color, rigid square form, the use of twist-turning—which was believed to be common in Elizabethan furniture— and the often mythical decoration. Horace Walpole, who may have been responsible for this belief, asserted that this attribution, based on their physical attributes, was corroborated by the existence of such examples in houses with Tudor associations. For example, in 1748, he saw carved ebony chairs at Esher Place, Surrey, and posited that they must have belonged to Cardinal Wolsey, who had lived there after 1519.

37½in (95cm) and 35¾in (90.5cm) high

$4,000-4,600   SWO

A Queen Anne walnut side chair, on molded tapering cabriole legs, joined by a turned H-shaped stretcher and terminating in pad feet, with marks, knocks, and abrasions.

ca. 1710   *42½in (108cm) high*

$1,300-1,800   DN

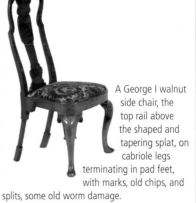

A George I walnut side chair, the top rail above the shaped and tapering splat, on cabriole legs terminating in pad feet, with marks, old chips, and splits, some old worm damage.

ca. 1720   *41¾in (106cm) high*

$1,300-1,800   DN

A pair of George II red walnut side chairs, the scrolling top rails above pierced vase-shaped splat, on acanthus and C-scroll carved tapering cabriole legs, terminating in pad feet, with marks, knocks, and abrasions.

ca. 1730

$2,600-3,300   DN

FURNITURE

A Queen Anne walnut side chair, in the manner of Giles Grendey, the shaped top rail centered by a gilt armorial, incorporating a boar's head, a stag, and an armored bust, the seat rails with a shaped apron, on cabriole legs, with marks, scratches, and abrasions, some old repairs.
ca. 1710
$650-800 DN

A Queen Anne walnut and ivory marquetry side chair, decorated with foliage, the vase-shaped splat decorated with a Classical maiden, with tapering cabriole legs, with marks, scratches, and abrasions, one side seat rail appears to be a replacement.
ca. 1715 *43in (109cm) high*
$1,000-1,100 DN

An early-18thC pair of George I mahogany side chairs, with drop-in seats, raised on cabriole legs joined by turned H stretchers.
39½in (100cm) high
$450-600 L&T

A pair of George II red walnut side chairs, with solid vase-shaped splats, above a needlework seat with petit and gros point with a shepherd and shepherdess, on front hocked cabriole legs and pad feet united by an H stretcher.
ca. 1730-40
$1,800-2,400 WW

A George II giltwood and upholstered side chair, the shield-shaped padded back above the stuffed seat, on cabriole legs terminating in scroll feet, floral motifs on the top and seat rails, some old splits and chips, the gilt surface with wear.
ca. 1740 *39¾in (101cm) high*
$1,600-2,100 DN

A pair of George II mahogany side chairs, possibly Irish, the pierced vase splats decorated with four flower head paterae, above a stuffed-over seat, and a Vitruvian scroll fret-carved frieze, on shell-capped and acanthus-carved front legs and hairy lion-paw feet.
ca. 1740-50
$7,500-8,500 WW

A set of four George II and later walnut side chairs, in the manner of William Hallett, on four shell, husk, and ribbon carved cabriole legs and claw-and-ball feet.
$7,500-8,500 WW

A George III mahogany side chair, the vase-shaped interlaced splat below a scrolled top rail with centered foliate clasp.

This chair was almost certainly supplied to Archibald Stirling of Keir (d. 1783) for Keir House, Dunblane. The parlor chair pattern with fretted vase splat incorporating addorsed and voluted ribbon scrolls issuing from the crest rail relates to patterns in Robert Manwaring's," The Cabinet and Chair-Makers Real Friend and Companion," 1765. Keir House, near Dunblane, Perthshire, was the historical seat of the Stirlings of Keir and Cawder until its sale in 1975. Keir passed down through several generations of Stirlings to the colorful James Stirling, proprietor of Keir from 1693-1715. A supporter of the Stuarts, he was tried for high treason in 1708 after the failed Jacobite invasion of that year and acquitted. Fortunately, the troubled times did not prevent the constant improvement of the house and estate. Archibald Stirling, 12th of Keir (1710-83), inherited Keir in 1757 and during the 1760s and 70s dramatically changed the use and look of the lands of Keir and Cawder. He introduced the fine up-to-date stucco work throughout the interior of Keir in the early 1760s, possibly just after his marriage to Ann Hay in 1762.
ca. 1760
$450-600 DN

A pair of Genoese cream and polychrome painted chairs, decorated with foliage, tulips, and other flowers, drop-in seats above cabriole legs and an H-shaped stretcher.
ca. 1770
$2,600-3,300 DN

A carved ash side chair, after a design by William Kent, elements possibly 18thC, the foliate scroll-molded top rail centered by a carved scallop shell, above square-sectioned supports carved with bell flowers, the scrolled legs headed by Venus masks carved with fish scales and raised on acanthus leaf-scrolling feet, marks, knocks, abrasions, the grain of a previous surface, possibly paint or gesso.

The Venus mask, scallop shell, and fish-scale decorative motifs were employed by William Kent and refer to the mythical birth of Venus and her emergence from the sea. Examples of this design of chair are present in the blue parlor room at Chiswick House.
$10,500-12,000   DN

One of a set of four George III mahogany side chairs, in the manner of Thomas Chippendale, each shaped foliate C-scroll carved top rail above a pierced vase shaped splat.
ca. 1780   38½in (98cm) high
$1,600-2,100 the set   DN

A pair of late-18thC Spanish green-painted and parcel-giltwood side chairs, each with double domed cresting rail with a pair of ducks above horizontal splats and spindles, the rush seats above turned and faceted supports joined by stretchers, marks, knocks, scratches, and abrasions.
33½in (85cm) high
$1,700-2,100   DN

A pair of 18thC Dutch marquetry single chairs, profusely inset with birds, urns, and flowers, dowels on one rear leg replaced, traces of worm.
41¾in (106cm) high
$1,500-1,800   SWO

A set of four 19thC Chinese export, padouk Chippendale side chairs, the shaped and carved top rails ending in scroll terminals above pierced and carved splats and side rails carved with oak leaves.
38½in (98cm) high
$2,900-4,000   L&T

A pair of late George III white-painted and parcel-giltwood side chairs, the turned cresting rail above the upholstered back and seat, marks, knocks, and scratches.
ca. 1810   34¼in (87cm) high
$1,000-1,100   DN

A pair of mid-19thC fruitwood stick-back correction chairs, one with old repairs to broken back.
39¾in (101cm) high
$550-650   CHEF

A George II walnut corner chair, the shaped and out-scrolling top rail above twin vase-shaped splats interspersed with turned tapering supports the shaped drop-in seat, on C-scroll molded tapering cabriole legs, terminating in pad feet, marks, scratches, and abrasions.
ca. 1730   34in (86cm) high
$2,200-2,600   DN

A George III mahogany corner chair, the curved top rail above a twin pierced splat back, on molded and chamfered legs united by an X stretcher.
ca. 1760-70
$650-800   WW

FURNITURE

ESSENTIAL REFERENCE—SGABELLO

A sgabello—the word is derived from *scabellum*, the Latin for stool—is a form of backstool or armless chair that originated in Italy during the Renaissance. Their components were essentially rudimentary: two plank-form legs united front to back by a single stretcher and supporting a wooden seat with a plank-form back. However, curvaceously shaped, often elaborately carved (with, for example, cartouches and foliate scrolls), and often additionally ornamented with family crests, sgabellos were primarily designed not for comfort (their seats were solid wood) but instead to impress guests and visitors. As such, they were usually employed in entrance halls or long, gallery-like rooms for displays, celebrations, and hospitality. Especially associated with Venice and Tuscany, their popularity gradually spread beyond Italy during the 16thC and 17thC and, indeed, in England were considered the height of fashion at the early Stuart court.

A pair of George II mahogany hall chairs, of sgabello form, with marks, knocks, scratches, and abrasions, later supporting blocks on the undersides.

ca. 1740　*39½in (100cm) high*

$1,000-1,100　　　**DN**

A set of four Regency mahogany hall chairs, attributed to Gillows, each with shell-carved backs above C-scroll supports centered by a painted armorial crest incorporating an armored arm clasping a spear with the inscription "The Fear of God and No Other."

ca. 1815　*32¾in (83cm) high*

$4,600-5,300　　　**DN**

An Irish Regency oak hall bench, the top rail with shell-carved finials, above twin X-shaped splats, the solid seat with molded edge, on tapering cabriole legs and carved lion-paw feet at the front.

ca. 1815　*83½in (212cm) wide*

$10,500-12,000　　　**DN**

A set of eight George II mahogany hall chairs, the stylized shield-shaped backs above shaped seat and supports joined by an angled stretcher, marks, knocks, and scratches.

Inspired by the Italian Renaissance sgabello (see left), this set of mahogany hall chairs was installed in Rockbeare Manor, Devon, in the mid- to late 18thC—the house having been built ca. 1769 for Sir John Duntze, an Exeter wool merchant and banker, Member of Parliament for Tiverton 1768-95, and Baronet from 1774. This style of chair is usually attributed to the London craftsman George Nix (1664-1756)—closely related sets of his can be found at Ham House and Ashdown House. However, given chairs of near-identical profile supplied by William Masters reside at Blair Castle, and by Alexander Peter at Dumfries House, it's difficult to attribute these chairs to any one maker in the absence of specific documentary provenance.

ca. 1750　*38½in (98cm) high*

$6,500-8,000　　　**DN**

A pair of Regency mahogany hall chairs, attributed to Gillows, each stylized shield-shaped back surmounted by a carved knight's helmet, flanked on each side by a griffin-head terminal, each shaped solid seat incorporating reeded detail and above a shaped and molded frieze, on turned tapering reeded legs.

ca. 1815

$1,700-2,400　　　**DN**

A Regency mahogany hall bench, in the manner of Marsh & Tatham, on reeded turned tapering legs.

The antique design and ornament of this hall bench derives from the examples in, and made fashionable by, Thomas Hope's "Household Furniture and Interior Decoration" (1807). Elements also appear in George Smith's "Collection of Designs for Household Furniture and Interior Decoration" (1808), while the style is typical of the early-19thC London Mayfair cabinetmakers and upholsters Marsh & Tatham, whose work included commissions from the Prince of Wales for the Royal Pavilion, Brighton.

ca. 1815　*71¾in (182cm) wide*

$6,500-8,000　　　**DN**

A Regency mahogany hall seat, the shaped top rail centered by an anthemion motif, above a cross splat and flanked by open scrolling arms, with turned tapering and hexagonal faceted legs.

ca. 1815　*40½in (103cm) high*

$3,300-4,000　　　**DN**

An early-19thC mahogany and simulated rosewood hall seat, attributed to Gillows, the top with turned rest on each end, on foliate-carved C scroll-shaped supports.

The form of the legs on this seat are similar to designs by Thomas King that feature on Anglo-Indian and Ceylonese furniture of the period.

54in (137cm) wide

$6,500-8,000　　　**DN**

A pair of 19thC Italian Neoclassical-style walnut hall seats, each with three caduceus splats, over solid seats and square tapering front legs, with minor wear.

In Roman mythology, a caduceus is often depicted in the left hand of Mercury, the messenger of the gods.

61¾in (157cm) wide

$4,600-5,300　　　**SWO**

A Charles I oak joint stool, the top above bicuspid-shaped rails, on ring-turned column legs, united by peripheral stretchers, branded initials "EP and DP."

ca. 1630 *20½in (52.1cm) high*
$1,100-1,250 **WW**

A rare Charles I oak child's joint stool, the top with molded edge, above the molded and shaped frieze, on turned baluster legs, joined by a peripheral stretcher, marks, knocks and abrasions.

ca. 1640 *16¼in (41cm) wide*
$1,050-1,200 **DN**

A pair of 17thC oak joint stools, tops with ovolo-molded edges, raised on ring-turned stretchered supports, split top on one stool, tops have been off and reglued.

21¼in (54cm) high
$1,600-2,100 **SWO**

A 17thC jointed oak stool, with carved inscription "WI," on turned legs united by a stretcher, some wear.

22in (56cm) high
$400-450 **CHEF**

A Queen Anne oak joint stool, with a later needlework drop-in seat, on ring-turned baluster legs with stretchers.

ca. 1705 *18in (45.5cm) wide*
$550-650 **WW**

An early-20thC pegged oak joint stool, on double-spiral twist legs.

20½in (52cm) high
$450-600 **CHEF**

A Queen Anne beech stool, the top above four collared tapering cabriole legs, joined by a turned X-shaped stretcher centered by a turned terminal, terminating in pad feet, with marks and abrasions, old worm holes.

ca. 1710 *17¼in (44cm) high*
$2,100-2,600 **DN**

A George II walnut stool, with a later needlework drop-in seat, on cabriole legs and pad feet.

ca. 1730-40 *21in (53.5cm) wide*
$2,600-4,000 **WW**

An Irish George II walnut stool, the top on scroll molded, hipped tapering cabriole legs, on faceted pad feet, minor marks, scratches and abrasions, one foot possibly had a detached fragment that is neatly reglued back into position.

ca. 1740 *19in (48cm) wide*
$3,300-4,000 **DN**

FURNITURE

A George II mahogany stool, possibly Irish, the needlework top decorated with a parrot in a verdure setting, on three acanthus-carved tapering cabriole legs, terminating in hairy claw-and-ball feet, marks, knocks, abrasions, old worm in underside, casters are later but have some age.

ca. 1750　　　　15in (38cm) diam
$1,600-2,100　　　　DN

A George II walnut stool, the later stuffed-over seat, on cabriole legs and trefid feet.

ca. 1730-40　　　　22½in (57cm) wide
$1,600-2,100　　　　WW

An early-19thC Regency rosewood X-frame stool, on scrolled and leaf-carved X supports joined by turned stretchers.

25¼in (64cm) wide
$650-800　　　　L&T

A Regency mahogany center stool, by George Rickword, the upholstered top above X-frame supports and turned stretcher, one rail with old paper label for the maker "GEORGE RICKWOOD/ CABINET MAKER, UPHOLSTERER/PAPER HANGER/AND UNDERTAKER/99, HIGH STREET COLCHESTER/HOUSE AGENT AND APPRAISER," marks, knocks, and abrasions.

ca. 1820　　　　36¼in (92cm) wide
$2,600-4,000　　　　DN

A pair of Regency simulated rosewood window seats, attributed to Gillows, of X-frame form, each with scrolls with turned rails above the caned seat and outsweeping legs terminating in scrolls and ball feet, each stamped "H H" on the undersides of the rails, with marks, knocks, and abrasions, one leg with a filled channel where some previous repair has taken place, this repair is almost certainly professionally carried out.

The attribution of Gillows workshops as the origin of these stools is based on the stretcher rails of both stools being stamped "H H" twice. According to Susan Stuart's book "H H" is one of the most common initial stamps on Gillows' chairs made during the first half of the 19thC. One set of 24 chairs sold at Mere Hall, Cheshire, were inscribed with the firms name and in particular one chair inscribed "H Howard W Yates Brook/ Mere" in addition to the "H H" stamp, suggesting that "H H" could be Henry Howard. See Susan E. Stuart, "Gillows of Lancaster and London 1730-1840," Antique Collectors Club, 2008 (vol. II, page 244).

ca. 1820　　　　43¼in (110cm) wide
$9,000-10,500　　　　DN

A pair of Regency ebonized and parcel-gilt stools, attributed to Gillows, the top above the X-frame supports.

Stools of this design were executed by Gillows for a number of known collections, including Tatton Park, Cheshire.

ca. 1820　　　　24in (61cm) wide
$6,000-6,600　　　　DN

A William IV mahogany and needlework upholstered long stool, with a pierced and scroll-carved frieze, on molded outsweeping tapering legs, terminating in scroll feet and casters.

ca. 1825　　　　48½in (123cm) wide
$1,300-1,700　　　　DN

A George IV mahogany stool, the swept drop-in seat above a molded frieze and reeded legs, marks, knocks, and abrasions, overall with a varnished appearance.

ca. 1825　　　　15in (38cm) wide
$600-750　　　　DN

A George IV rosewood stool, in the manner of Gillows, the top above lappet-molded X-shaped supports, joined by a turned stretcher and terminating in scroll feet, with marks, knocks, and abrasions, old worm in underside of rails.

ca. 1825　　　　15¾in (40cm) wide
$1,050-1,200　　　　DN

An early-19thC William IV rosewood footrest, the top with a ratchet adjustment.

18½in (47cm) wide
$1,500-1,800　　　　L&T

FURNITURE

A William IV carved rosewood stool, on cabriole shaped legs, on scroll feet.

ca. 1835 *35½in (90cm) wide*

$1,300-1,600 **DN**

A mid-19thC Victorian giltwood-framed center stool, on molded giltwood frame with cabriole legs and casters.

48¾in (124cm) wide

$1,250-1,450 **L&T**

A 19thC Irish carved mahogany stool, in George II style, the top, on lion mask-carved tapering cabriole legs, terminating in hairy claw-and-ball feet, marks, knocks, and abrasions.

29¼in (74cm) wide

$3,300-4,000 **DN**

A late-19thC rosewood stool, with turned supports and a cross stretcher.

$80-90 **WHP**

A late-19thC George II-style mahogany-framed stool, with a shaped drop-in seat, raised on shell-carved cabriole legs ending in trifid feet.

28¾in (73cm) wide

$1,300-1,800 **L&T**

A 19thC George II-style mahogany and parcel-gilt stool, with a gadroon-carved seat rail, raised on shell-carved cabriole legs ending in claw-and-ball feet.

25½in (65cm) wide

$600-750 **L&T**

A late-19th/early-20thC walnut and upholstered stool, in George II style.

30¾in (78cm) wide

$1,050-1,300 **DN**

An early-20thC George II-style mahogany stool, on acanthus-carved cabriole legs ending in pad feet.

26½in (67cm) wide

$450-600 **L&T**

An early-19thC George IV oak window seat, with scrolled arm rests, on lobed and fluted tapered legs.

26in (66cm) wide

$1,700-2,400 **L&T**

A Victorian walnut long fender stool, on turned legs.

ca. 1880 *54¼in (138cm) wide*

$850-1,000 **WW**

FURNITURE

A late-17thC William and Mary walnut-framed open armchair, on block and baluster legs joined by an H stretcher.

44in (112cm) high

$1,100-1,250   **L&T**

A George II walnut open armchair, in the manner of Giles Grendey, the shaped top rail and supports centered by a vase-shaped splat, flanked by open "shepherd's crook" arms, on shell-carved tapering cabriole legs, terminating in claw-and-ball feet, marks, knocks, and abrasions, evidence of old worm.

ca. 1740   *39½in (100cm) high*

$10,000-11,000   **DN**

CLOSER LOOK—GEORGE II ARMCHAIR

The stepped and arched top rail features a painted tribute to the creative benefits of drinking alcohol, and comprises a mask with the Latin motto "Nunc Est Bibendum" ("Now is the time for drinking"), beneath a banner "Foecundi Calices Quem Non Fecere Disertum" ("Whom has not the inspiring bowl made eloquent").

A painted cartouche between the shoulders of the vase-shaped splat back frames the chair owner's shield of arms, above the inscription "Thos. Cholmondeley of Vale Royal Esq Mayor Anno Domini 1750"— the latter above further painted foliate decoration.

The front cabriole legs, which terminate in pad feet, each feature a carved scallop shell on the knee—a particularly popular furniture motif during the 18thC and 19thC, it's shape being well suited to the curve of the cabriole leg.

Below molded out-scrolling arms, the contoured seat rails accommodate an upholstered drop-in seat pad.

A George II walnut high-backed armchair with painted coat of arms, mask and motto decoration, and later needlework seat cover.

ca. 1750   *54in (5.5cm) high*

$5,300-6,600   **DN**

An Irish George II mahogany armchair, the shaped and carved top rail cornered by shell terminals, above the pierced vase-shaped splat, flanked by scrolling outsweeping arms modeled as the necks and heads of birds, the padded drop-in seat above a shaped apron centered by a carved shell motif, on shell-carved tapering cabriole legs at the front, joined by an H-shaped stretcher, terminating in carved lion-paw feet and brass casters, with marks, knocks, and abrasions, later casters and blocks, some old veneer repairs.

ca. 1750   *41¾in (106cm) high*

$5,300-6,600   **DN**

A pair of mid-18thC Italian carved-wood, painted, and parcel-gilt armchairs, carved with stylized foliate details, with cartouche-shaped backs, above a pair of padded arms with scroll terminals, each serpentine fronted seat above a shaped apron and tapering cabriole legs terminating in scroll-carved feet, with marks, scratches, and abrasions, some old repairs, the painted and gilded surfaces refreshed.

43in (109cm) high

$2,600-3,300   **DN**

A matched pair of George III mahogany and upholstered open armchairs, the serpentine-fronted seat above a fluted frieze and square-section tapering legs at the front terminating in spade feet and surmounted by patera terminals.

These chairs have some distinctive features of the later work of Thomas Chippendale, ca. 1773-75. The scrolls of the arm terminals are seen in various forms on many of his later "salon" chairs. There are not many examples of his output that we know of that have square-tapering legs and spade feet, however they do exist. The seat rail cramp cuts are also an interesting feature to note regarding these chairs.

ca. 1770   *34¼in (87cm) high*

$3,300-4,000   **DN**

A George III mahogany open armchair, the cabochon and leaf scroll arms above a frieze and front legs carved with Chinese Chippendale-style fret decoration.

ca. 1770

$1,050-1,200   **WW**

A pair of George III mahogany and button upholstered library armchairs, of Gainsborough type, with marks, scratches, and abrasions consistent with age and use.

ca. 1780   *39½in (100cm) high*

$10,500-12,000   **DN**

A 18thC Portuguese hardwood and upholstered armchair, the back with shell carving and scrolled open arms above the seat and cabriole legs, marks, knocks, scratches, one rear leg with old spliced repair.

46in (117cm) high

$4,600-5,300   **DN**

A George III mahogany open armchair, the ladder back with four pierced and molded cross stretchers, each centered by a twist terminal.
ca. 1780   *39¾in (101cm) high*
$2,000-2,600   **DN**

A George III mahogany open armchair, the top rail above the pierced vase-shaped splat, marks, scratches, and abrasions.
ca. 1780   *37½in (95cm) high*
$1,300-1,700   **DN**

A George III mahogany and upholstered open armchair, in the manner of George Hepplewhite, the seat on turned tapering stop-fluted legs, headed by patera terminals and terminating in arrow feet.
ca. 1780   *37in (94cm) high*
$3,300-4,000   **DN**

An 18thC rosewood fauteuil, in Louis XV style, the serpentine top rail carved with flowers and scrolling foliage, above a scroll and arcaded-pierced splat back, on flower and leaf-carved cabriole legs, possibly Portuguese.
$650-800   **WW**

A pair of late-18thC Georgian mahogany-framed armchairs, in the Hepplewhite style, on channel molded square tapered legs ending in spade feet.
36¼in (92cm) high
$1,300-1,800   **L&T**

A pair of late-18thC Louis XV carve- beech fauteuil, the foliate and ribbon-molded backs flanked by outsweeping scrolling arms, the cushion seat above a foliate swag-carved apron, on molded tapering cabriole legs, on acanthus-carved scroll feet.
41¼in (105cm) high
$3,300-4,000   **DN**

A George III mahogany and upholstered open armchair, with marks and abrasions, old chips, and splits.
ca. 1790   *36¼in (92cm) high*
$3,300-4,000   **DN**

An 18thC George III mahogany library armchair, the serpentine crest rail above a padded back and seat flanked by part padded arms with scrolled supports, on square tapered legs with leather casters.
38½in (98cm) high
$2,100-2,600   **L&T**

A pair of late-18thC George III mahogany open armchairs, in the Hepplewhite French style, raised on molded cabriole legs.
37½in (95cm) high
$2,900-3,700   **L&T**

Two George III mahogany open armchairs, in French Hepplewhite style, on paterae headed fluted tapering legs.

ca. 1790

$1,300–1,800   **WW**

A late-18thC George III stained-mahogany armchair, in the Sheraton style, on leaf-carved tapered legs ending in brass caps and casters.

35¾in (91cm) high

$800–900   **L&T**

A pair of 18thC Italian Rococo carved-giltwood armchairs, the cartouche-shaped backs in foliate and channel molded frames with flower cresting, with scrolled and acanthus-carved arms, on cabriole legs with scrolled toes.

42½in (108cm) high

$2,600–3,300   **L&T**

A George III mahogany Gainsborough library armchair, raised on brass casters, with spliced repairs on back legs and doweled in arms.

38½in (98cm) high

$1,050–1,200   **CHEF**

A pair of George III stained-oak armchairs, in Gothic taste, each back pierced with tracery above the open arms and seat, on square-section legs joined by stretchers, both with marks, knocks, scratches.

ca. 1800   *44in (112cm) high*

$4,000–5,300   **DN**

A pair of possibly 18thC Italian walnut open armchairs, in Renaissance style, each with carved gargoyle finials, the front stretcher carved with a pair of angels flanking a grotesque mask.

$1,050–1,200   **WW**

A pair of early-19thC French Empire mahogany armchairs, the square-framed and padded backs above stuffover seats, flanked by lotus-carved open arms and raised on saber legs.

35¾in (91cm) high

$2,000–2,600   **L&T**

A pair of Regency mahogany open armchairs, the molded frames carved with scrolls.

ca. 1815

$1,600–1,800   **WW**

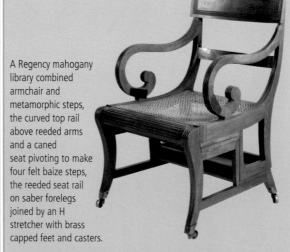

A Regency mahogany library combined armchair and metamorphic steps, the curved top rail above reeded arms and a caned seat pivoting to make four felt baize steps, the reeded seat rail on saber forelegs joined by an H stretcher with brass capped feet and casters.

This armchair is based on a design in Ackermann's "1811 Repository of Art," where it is described as "the best and handsomest article ever invented, where two complete pieces of furniture are combined in one - an elegant and truly comfortable armchair and a set of library steps."

33½in (85cm) high

$2,600–4,000   **TEN**

An early-19thC Regency rosewood library armchair, raised on X supports with brass casters.

39½in (100cm) high

$1,000-1,100   **L&T**

A pair of early-19thC Regency mahogany upholstered armchairs, raised on ring-turned tapering legs with brass caps and casters stamped "COPE & COLLINSON PATENT."

38½in (98cm) high

$3,300-4,000   **L&T**

A Regency mahogany Daws patent adjustable armchair, on carved foliate legs with large brass casters, in need of recovering, carved section above one front leg missing.

Robert Daws is recorded as being active 1820-39 at 17 Margaret Street, Cavendish Square, London, and patented his improved recumbent chair in 1827, C. Gilbert and G. Beard, "Dictionary of English Furniture Makers 1660-1840," Leeds, 1986, p. 282.

41in (104cm) high

$550-650   **CHEF**

A mid-19thC George IV laburnum and upholstered armchair, in Gothic taste, almost certainly Scottish, the pierced cresting rail above the padded back and further tracery, open arms, and faceted tapering legs, marks, knocks, scratches.

43in (109cm) high

$900-1,050   **DN**

A pair of 19thC mahogany and brass-studded leather upholstered armchairs, in George III style, a pair of padded arms with foliate-carved terminals, on square-section legs and stretchers.

$3,400-4,000   **DN**

A mid-19thC Victorian mahogany-framed upholstered armchair, the padded arms on turned spindle supports, the front rail centered by roundels, raised on ring-turned legs, the seat rail with brass plaque "J. SHOOLBRED, TOTTENHAM HOUSE, LONDON," the rear leg stamped "4092."

35¾in (91cm) high

$1,000-1,100   **L&T**

A pair of 19thC Louis XIV-style giltwood-framed open armchairs, with padded arms on scrolled supports, on carved legs joined by a center stretcher.

47¾in (121cm) high

$1,300-1,800   **L&T**

A pair of mid-19thC maple and bird's-eye maple armchairs, in the manner of Gillows, with bobbin-turned frames overall and beaded capitals on the uprights, the arms stuffed and with removable upholstered back and seat cushions, above the rattan seat panel, on conforming supports and stretchers, marks, knocks, scratches.

45in (114cm) high

$5,300-6,600   **DN**

A mid-19thC Gothic Revival beech open armchair, the arched top rail above the pierced lancet back, knocks, scratches, and abrasions, center tip of the apron is a replacement.

42¼in (107cm) high

$2,600-3,300   **DN**

FURNITURE

A pair of early-Victorian oak Gothic Revival open armchairs, after a design by William Smee.

ca. 1850

$550-650   WW

A set of eight mid-19thC French giltwood fauteuils, in Louis XVI style, after Georges Jacob, covered with mid-18thC Beauvais tapestry depicting scenes from the fables of Jean de la Fontaine, with leaf, bead, and guilloche carved frames, the underside of two applied with a metal label inscribed "HALTON COLLECTION."

"The Fables" by Jean de la Fontaine (1621-1755), many of which were taken from Aesop, made popular and suitable subjects for tapestry seat covers. They were probably woven after designs by the painter Jean-Baptiste Oudry (1686-1755) who was court painter to Louis XV and was made Director of Tapestry at Beauvais in 1734. The scenes illustrated include the cat and the thrush; the fox and the stork; the wolf and the lamb; the frog and the ox; the two doves and the heiffer; and the kid and sheep with the lion.

$20,000-26,000   WW

A pair of Gothic Revival cream-painted, parcel-giltwood and crimson-upholstered salon chairs, the turned and faceted legs on caster feet, with tracery spandrels, marks, knocks, scratches, the painted surface refreshed overall.

ca. 1854   35¾in (91cm) high

$4,000-5,300   DN

A pair of 19thC giltwood and tapestry-upholstered fauteuil, in Louis XV style, the frames carved with foliage and scrolls, each shaped and padded back flanked by padded open arms, the shaped tapering padded seat on tapering cabriole legs terminating in scroll feet.

40¼in (102cm) high

$7,500-8,500   DN

A Victorian satinwood, boxwood, and parcel-gilt armchair, the button upholstered spoon-shaped back above open arms and seat, on turned front legs and outsweeping back legs all terminating in brass caps and casters, stamped by the makers on the front seat rail "JOHNSTONE & JEANS,/67 NEW BOND ST./LONDON 55948," and by the chair maker "T.E.," marks, knocks, scratches, abrasions.

ca. 1860   35¾in (91cm) high

$2,000-2,600   DN

An early-Victorian rosewood armchair, with scroll-end arms, turned legs, and brass casters, repaired break on one arm.

46½in (118cm) high

$550-600   CHEF

A pair of 19thC Louis XVI-style giltwood fauteuils, the arms with acanthus-carved scrolled terminals, raised on fluted tapered legs.

36¾in (93cm) high

$3,300-4,000   L&T

A 19thC French walnut and tapestry-upholstered open armchair, in Louis XV style, the high arched back above the arms, bowfront seat, shell-carved apron, and cabriole legs, marks, knocks, scratches, abrasions, signs of old woodworm.

44½in (113cm) high

$1,500-1,800   DN

A pair of 19thC Louis XV style French fauteuils, wear and fading to tapestry, need reupholstering.

35½in (90cm) high

$2,200-2,600   CHEF

A 19thC mahogany leather-upholstered library chair, in the manner of Gillows, the shaped button upholstered back and padded scrolled arms over a padded seat, on shell-carved cabriole legs ending in dolphin's-head feet.

35½in (90cm) high

$2,600-3,300   **L&T**

A 19thC Anglo-Indian brass inlaid carved rosewood upholstered armchair, the carved frame surmounted by a shell motif above interlaced flowers and scrolling foliage, the padded back with brass inlaid details above a serpentine padded seat flanked by part-padded arms.

48¾in (124cm) high

$2,900-3,700   **L&T**

A pair of late-19thC Victorian carved oak armchairs, with padded back support, arms, and seat, with spiral-turned supports, leopard-mask handles, and stuffover seats, the front rails joined by turned stretchers, block feet, and casters.

51½in (131cm) high

$1,050-1,200   **TEN**

A late-19thC French walnut salon open armchair, the shield-shaped back painted with a scene of lovers in a garden, rose decoration on the arms and legs, with cracking on the back, wear to paintwork.

41in (104cm) high

$260-330   **CHEF**

A 19thC early-Victorian leather-upholstered reading chair, on turned legs ending in brass caps and ceramic casters.

30¾in (78cm) high

$1,800-2,400   **L&T**

A 19thC Louis XIV-style walnut upholstered open armchair.

52¾in (134cm) high

$650-800   **L&T**

A late-19thC Scottish oak armchair, Edinburgh, the tapered legs with a crinoline stretcher and brass caps and casters.

38½in (98cm) high

$450-600   **L&T**

A pair of early-20thC carved-mahogany high-back fauteuils, in the Louis XIV manner.

$1,300-1,800   **WHP**

A pair of 20thC oak armchairs, in 17thC style, the carved crest rails above panel backs carved with lunettes, foliate scrolls, and a flowering vase, the seats flanked by leaf-carved scrolling arms, on turned and block legs.

47¼in (120cm) high

$650-800   **L&T**

FURNITURE

An 18thC Louis XV beech, cane, and leather bergère, with a molded frame with close nail trim, raised on cabriole legs.

36¼in (92cm) high

$650-800   L&T

Two of a matched set of 10 mahogany library bergère chairs, in the manner of Gillows, each curved top rail carved with a center stylized carved foliate terminal, above down-sweeping sides incorporating molded detail, each caned seat with a loose cushion, on turned tapering and reeded legs, comprising eight of Regency period, ca. 1815, together with a pair of 20thC examples made to match.

This form of chair was named a "curricle," after the Roman magistrate or consul's seat, by Thomas Sheraton in his "Cabinet Dictionary," London, 1803 and the name was adopted by Gillows of London and Lancaster. Five chairs of this model were supplied by Gillows between 1811 and 1812 to Wilbraham Egerton for Tatton Park, Cheshire, intended for bedrooms or dressing rooms N. Goodison and J. Hardy, "Gillows at Tatton park," Furniture History, 1970, pl. 16A.

$7,500-8,000 the set   DN

A Regency mahogany bergère library armchair, in the manner of Gillows, the caned rectangular back and seat flanked by padded armrests above turned and reeded supports at the front, terminating in brass caps and casters.

ca. 1815

$4,600-5,300   DN

A pair of Regency mahogany library bergères, attributed to Gillows, the top rail above the reeded back and down-sweeping molded supports, with reeded turned tapering legs terminating in tapering feet at the front, the seat rail of a chair stamped with workman's initials, with marks, scratches and abrasions, caning is an old replacement, one back leg with spliced repair.

The stamp to the seat rail of one chairs appears to read "H H" indistinctly and may possibly be a workman's stamp. According to Susan Stuart, "HH" is one of the most common initial stamps recorded on chairs made by Gillows in the first half of the 19thC. In Stuart's book it is explained with known examples that the stamp may belong to Henry Howard, however that Henry Holmes might be a better candidate as he was a known Gillows journeyman. (Susan E. Stuart, Gillows of Lancaster & London, Antique Collectors Club, 2008, vol.II, page 244).

ca. 1815   *33½in (85cm) high*

$5,300-6,600   DN

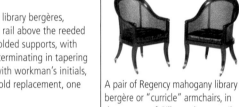

A pair of Regency mahogany library bergère or "curricle" armchairs, in the manner of Gillows, the top rail and arms centered by a roundel motif, on molded, tapering saber legs at the front, terminating in brass caps and casters, with marks, knocks, scratches, and abrasions, caning is an old replacement.

A remarkably similar pair of chairs are present as part of the furnishings of Tatton Park, Cheshire (see N. Goodison and J. Hardy, "Gillows at Tatton Park," Furniture History, 1970, pl. 16A). Gillows supplied five chairs of this model between 1811 and 1812 to Wilbraham Egerton for Tatton Park.

ca. 1815   *34¾in (88cm) high*

$13,000-18,000   DN

An early-19thC French Empire mahogany-framed hide-upholstered bergère, with revolving seat and applied brass mounts, on square section legs and brass caps.

36¾in (93cm) high

$2,600-4,000   L&T

An early-19thC Regency mahogany-framed bergère, the square back and panel sides with cane inserts, the scrolled arms with hairy paw supports, on reeded legs, brass caps, and casters.

38¼in (97cm) high

$4,600-5,300   L&T

An early-19thC Regency mahogany-framed bergère, with caned back and sides, leather cushions, on square legs with brass caps and casters.

35¾in (91cm) high

$1,600-2,100   L&T

A George IV mahogany library bergère, with loose cushion squab seat, on partly reeded turned legs and brass casters, with reinforcement on the underside of seat.

38½in (98cm) high

$2,000-2,600   CHEF

A George IV mahogany bergère library armchair, in the manner of Gillows, the shaped and scrolling back incorporating down-sweeping scrolling lappet-carved arms, with serpentine fronted seat, each reeded and turned leg at the front surmounted by a carved patera terminal and terminating in brass caps and casters.

ca. 1825   *37¾in (96cm) high*

$2,100-2,600   DN

A William and Mary silvered-gesso wing armchair, the molded apron centered by a shell terminal, on acanthus-molded tapering cabriole legs, joined by an H-shaped stretcher centered by a turned terminal.

A set of chairs of similar age and design elements are part of the furnishings of Canons Ashby, Warwickshire. This model of chair represents the earliest examples of the use of the cabriole leg in English furniture, having been inspired by the designs of André Charles Boulle.

ca. 1690
47¼in (120cm) high
$5,300-6,600
DN

A George I walnut wing armchair, later upholstered, scrolling leaves and flowers, with scroll arms, on leaf-capped cabriole front legs and hoof feet, with faceted back legs.

ca. 1725
$15,000-17,000
WW

A George II mahogany and leather-upholstered wing armchair, the shaped back and sides above the tapering seat, flanked by out-scrolling arms, on square-section legs joined by an H-shaped stretcher, terminating in brass casters.

ca. 1750
47¾in (121cm) high
$3,300-4,000
DN

A walnut wing armchair, the back flanked by out-scrolling arms, above the seat, on molded cabriole legs at the front, joined by an H-shaped stretcher, knocks, scratches, and abrasions, one front foot with section of loss.

ca. 1770 and later
49¼in (125cm) high
$4,600-5,300
DN

An early-19thC late Regency mahogany tub armchair, with lyre-outlined enclosed arms with reeded facings and flower-head carved terminals, on tapered reeded legs with ceramic casters.

40½in (103cm) high
$2,600-4,000
L&T

A Regency rosewood library armchair, on turned tapering legs, terminating in brass caps and casters.

ca. 1820
35½in (90cm) high
$5,300-6,600
DN

A George IV mahogany and leather upholstered armchair, in the manner of Gillows, on reeded turned tapering legs, terminating in brass caps and casters, marks, knocks, and abrasions.

ca. 1825
41¾in (106cm) high
$7,500-8,500
DN

A 19thC mahogany wing armchair, in George III style.

$1,000-1,100
WW

A late-Victorian walnut easy armchair, on turned front legs and brass casters, stamped "HOWARD & SONS LTD LONDON," the back left leg stamped "17742 9990 HOWARD & SONS LTD BERNERS ST."

$5,500-6,600
WW

FURNITURE

A Victorian walnut armchair.

$550-650 WHP

A late-19thC mahogany library armchair, in George II style, the arms carved with eagle heads with fish in their beaks, above husks and with a Vitruvian scroll frieze, on eagle-head, leaf, and cabochon legs and feathery claw-and-ball feet.

$2,600-3,300 WW

A late-19thC George I-style wing armchair, the arched back with scrolled wings over a loose cushion seat and wide out-scrolling arms, with a painted carved frame, raised on carved cabriole legs with ball-and-claw feet.

55¼in (140cm) high

$800-900 L&T

A late-19thC Georgian-style wing armchair.

42¼in (107cm) high

$1,300-2,000 L&T

Two late-19th/early-20thC George II-style ebonized mahogany and parcel-gilt wing armchairs, the first with squared back and wings continuing to out-scrolling arms, the seat rails carved with shells, acanthus scrolls, and satyr masks, raised on cabriole legs ending in carved paw feet, stenciled "D&P 3298," the second with similar back, wings, and cushion, raised on acanthus carved cabriole legs ending in foliate scroll-carved feet.

The wing armchair with the carved satyr mask seat rail is a near identical copy of a chair in the Cabinet Room of Houghton Hall, Norfolk. The original was part of a suite of furniture supplied ca. 1730. It is believed to have been made by Thomas Roberts Jr, who produced other seat furniture for the State Rooms at Houghton. The other armchair is derived from the celebrated suite of furniture at Chatsworth, Derbyshire, dated ca. 1740, assumed to have been commissioned by William Cavendish, 3rd Duke of Devonshire. Later copies of seat furniture from the suite have been attributed to the Edwardian furniture maker Lenygon and Morant, when there was a strong interest in Queen Anne and early Georgian furniture.

larger 44in (112cm) high

$6,000-7,500 L&T

An early-20thC mahogany upholstered armchair, the slightly arched back above rounded arms and a stuffover seat, raised on square tapering legs, the rear leg stamped "4131/4116," the casters stamped "HOWARD & SONS, LONDON," covered in Howard & Sons monogram fabric.

40¼in (102cm) high

$3,300-4,000 L&T

An early-20thC wing armchair, in George II style.

$650-800 WW

An upholstered armchair, stamped on casters "Howard & Sons, London" and number "17450 6097" stamped on one rear leg.

35½in (90cm) high

$2,000-2,600 CHEF

A pair of 20thC leather club armchairs, the low backs above deep loose cushion seats and wide scroll arms, covered in leather with brass close nail trim, raised on stylized hairy paw feet.

35¾in (91cm) high

$4,600-5,300 L&T

A mid-19thC mahogany and leather-upholstered porter's chair, in the George II style, of typical design, the hooded back above a cushion seat.

$4,600-5,900 DN

A George III green and cream-painted sofa, attributed to Ince and Mayhew, the back with beaded top rail, flanked by padded and down-sweeping arms decorated with anthemion and bell flowers, the serpentine fronted seat with fluted seat rail, on turned tapering, fluted and spirally reeded legs, terminating in gadrooned feet and leather casters, the underside of the front rail stamped "CLAREMONT."

This sofa was possibly supplied by Mayhew and Ince to King George III (d.1820), then by descent to, or acquired by, Queen Victoria (d.1901), then almost certainly moved to Claremont (the name of the house being stamped on the underside of the front rail) during a refurnishing. Subsequent occupiers of the house and users of the sofa would have included the youngest son of Queen Victoria, H.R.H. Price Leopold (d.1884), his wife H.R.H. Princess Helen (d.1922), and her daughter H.R.H. Princess Alice, Countess of Athlone (d.1981). The celebrated partnership of Ince and Mayhew endured from 1759-1803. Furniture designers, cabinetmakers, and upholsterers, their clientele comprised the nobility and gentry of the time, and their volume of engraved designs "The Universal System of Household Furniture" rivaled in influence Chippendale's "The Gentleman and Cabinet-Maker's Director."

ca. 1770   71¼in (181cm) wide
$11,000-13,000   DN

A Louis XV carved, giltwood, and painted sofa, on cabriole legs. marks, abrasions, some metal bracing, signs of old, filled, woodworm.
ca. 1760-80   75¼in (191cm) wide
$2,600-3,300   DN

An 18thC settee with needlework upholstery, on carved walnut cabriole legs.
67in (170cm) wide
$1,600-2,100   CHOR

An Italian walnut and upholstered sofa, guilloche carved throughout, the shaped top rail with swags, padded seat above turned tapering fluted legs, marks, knocks, scratches, and abrasions.
ca. 1800   77¼in (196cm) wide
$1,600-2,000   DN

An early-19thC Regency mahogany framed settee, on reeded tapered legs, the rear legs with casters.
61½in (156cm) wide
$2,400-2,900   L&T

An early-19thC French Empire mahogany-framed sofa, on square-tapered legs with brass caps and casters.
68½in (174cm) wide
$2,600-4,000   L&T

A Regency hardwood carved and caned scroll-end sofa, West Indies, the back support centered by C scrolls and a flower head, on carved legs with claw-and ball-feet, joints are loose and timber is dry, in need of recaning.
82¾in (210cm) wide
$1,100-1,250   TEN

An early-19thC gilt frame sofa, on casters, stamped "T.H Seymour" on calico base, needs total restoration.
77½in (197cm) wide
$1,500-1,800   CHEF

An early-19thC Regency mahogany sofa, the low button-upholstered back flanked by scroll arms with carved lotus facings, on carved lobed legs with brass caps and casters stamped "J.W. LEWTY/ PATENT."
92½in (235cm) wide
$4,600-5,900   L&T

A pair of 19thC late-Regency rosewood-framed sofas, on turned and tapering molded legs terminating in brass caps and casters, stamped "J.W. LEWTY'S/ PATENT."
88½in (225cm) wide
$20,000-26,000   L&T

FURNITURE

A Victorian mahogany and upholstered sofa, the padded back and arms above a loose cushion seat, on square-section tapering legs, terminating in brass caps and casters, one rear leg stamped "HOWARD & SONS LTD BERNERS ST. " and with adjacent stamped numbers "2289 2438."

ca. 1890   *64½in (164cm) wide*

$11,000-13,000   **DN**

A late-19thC Louis XV-style "Duchesse Brisée," the molded frame with carved hand grips and two squab cushions, on stop-fluted legs.

72in (183cm) long

$1,300-1,800   **TEN**

A late-19thC Victorian oak-framed humpback sofa, the serpentine back enclosed by high scrolled arms, on turned and tapering molded legs terminating in brass caps and casters, the rear leg stamped "3(?)612."

84¾in (215cm) wide

$3,300-4,000   **L&T**

A pair of late-19thC William and Mary-style sofas, the tall shaped backs above stuffover seats flanked by scrolled arms, raised on turned legs joined by trestle bases and stretchers.

60¼in (153cm) wide

$4,600-5,900   **L&T**

A late19thC/early-20thC mahogany two seater settee, in George II style, with scroll arms, on shell-capped cabriole legs and claw-and-ball front feet.

59in (149.5cm) wide

$650-800   **WW**

A late-19th/early-20thC William and Mary-style parcel-gilt walnut double chairback settee, on carved and scrolled legs joined by scroll-carved and pierced stretcher with putti masks.

62¼in (158cm) wide

$1,300-2,000   **L&T**

An early-20thC Edwardian leather-upholstered Chesterfield sofa, on bun feet with later casters.

82¾in (210cm) wide

$5,300-6,600   **L&T**

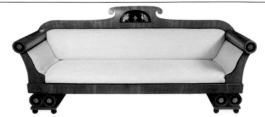

An early-20thC mahogany framed sofa, by Howard & Sons, in the George III style, low back and out-scrolling arms raised on acanthus and scroll-carved parcel-gilt cabriole legs ending in scroll toes, stamped "7960/3292" on the rear leg and with a partial trade label.

82¼in (209cm) wide

$3,300-4,000   **L&T**

An early-20thC Biedermeier-style ebonized, gilt metal-mounted satin birch sofa, the back with a scrolled crest and recess ebonized panel with gryphon mounts, with high enclosed scrolled arms terminating with center rosettes, on twin-cylinder legs and ebonized ball feet.

100¾in (256cm) wide

$1,600-2,100   **L&T**

An early-19thC Continental Grecian Revival lyre-form mahogany settee, with stiff leave-carved frame, on cornucopia-carved legs with reeded paw feet with casters.

60¾in (154cm) wide

$3,300-4,000 **L&T**

A William IV mahogany scroll-end sofa, the reeded frame carved with leaf scrolls, on leaf-carved scroll legs terminating in cast foliate and ribbed sabot and casters.

84in (212.5cm) wide

$1,500-1,800 **WW**

An early-19thC George IV rosewood sofa, in the manner of Gillows, the frame carved with urns, scrolls, and paterae, on ribbed front legs and brass casters.

72¾in (185cm) wide

$2,100-2,600 **WW**

An early-19thC late George III mahogany-framed sofa, the needlework 20thC, on tapered legs with spade feet joined by stretchers, brass plaque on the rear inscribed "WORKED BY HELEN MARTIN MACKENNA, COMPLETED 25TH AUGUST, 1940."

82in (208cm) wide

$6,000-7,500 **L&T**

A mid-19thC William IV mahogany-framed sofa, with outsweeping arms with reeded facings, on bulbous turned legs with brass caps and casters.

68½in (174cm) wide

$1,800-2,400 **L&T**

An early-Victorian Gothic Revival sofa, the design attributed to A.W.N. Pugin, and probably made by J. G. Crace, for Sir James Watts of Abney Hall, Cheadle, on Gothic chamfered giltwood legs, carved with Tudor-style rosettes and bands of laurel leaves, on sunken brass casters.

Sir James Watts (1804 1878) of Abney Hall, Cheadle, Cheshire, was a Manchester-based textile merchant who owned S & J Watts Ltd. He was Mayor of Manchester from 1855-57 and became High Sheriff of Lancashire. He had a passion for the arts and, after Prince Albert stayed with him at Abney Hall to open the Art Treasures Exhibition in 1857, Queen Victoria awarded him a knighthood. Abney Hall was originally built in 1847 for Alfred Orrell, but after his death in 1849, it was acquired by Sir James Watts and in the early 1850s he employed A. W. N. Pugin and J. G. Crace to remodel the interiors.

71in (181cm) wide

$1,700-2,600 **WW**

A Victorian black-lacquer and gilt chinoiserie-decorated settee, decorated with figures in village scenes and scrolling foliage, minor marks and abrasions.

ca. 1860 *78in (198cm) wide*

$2,600-3,300 **DN**

A 19thC early George III-style mahogany sofa, on acanthus-carved cabriole legs ending in scrolled toes.

71¼in (181cm) wide

$2,600-3,300 **L&T**

A 19thC walnut chair-back settee, the backs with shell and foliate carved top rails above solid vase splats, the drop-in seat and molded rails on shell-carved cabriole legs with claw-and-ball feet.

$6,500-8,000 **CHOR**

FURNITURE

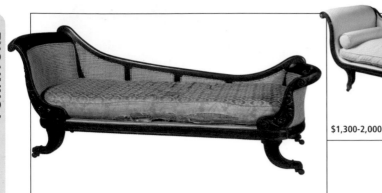

A Regency ebonized and upholstered daybed, with scroll ends and backrest transferable to either side, on brass casters.

84¼in (214cm) wide

$1,300-2,000　　**CHEF**

An early-19thC Regency mahogany bergère daybed, the foliate-carved frame with scrolled ends and a shaped back panel, all with caned double walls, with a loose cushion seat raised on removable splay legs ending in brass caps and casters.

This impressive daybed once belonged to the famed early-Victorian British photographer Julia Margaret Cameron. It descended in the family to the artist Juliet Lister, who was the second wife of John Bellany, the Scottish artist.

96½in (245cm) long

$4,600-5,900　　**L&T**

A Victorian mahogany military campaign bed, attributed to Robinsons & Sons of Ilkley, the caned base/back support with adjustable positions to form a chaise longue or daybed, with removable turned legs, brass-capped feet, and pivoting ceramic casters stamped "Parrys Patent."

ca. 1870　　*84in (213cm) long*

$850-1,000　　**TEN**

A Victorian chaise longue, the walnut frame well carved with scrolls, flowers, and foliage.

67in (170cm) long

$550-650　　**SWO**

A late-19thC mahogany and gilt metal-mounted chaise longue, in Empire style, the frieze decorated with cast laurel mounts, on molded outsweeping legs terminating in cast lion-paw cappings.

63¾in (162cm) wide

$1,600-2,100　　**DN**

A late-19thC Victorian walnut chaise longue, by Howard & Sons, the button upholstered back flanked by scrolling side rests, on turned tapering legs, terminating in brass caps and casters, one rear leg stamped "4114/9647," the underside with the remains of a paper label and ivorine plaque for "H.F THOMAS/ EASTGATE STREET/ CHESTER."

86¼in (219cm) wide

$4,000-4,600　　**DN**

A George III cream-painted and parcel-gilt window seat, the seat flanked by out-scrolling end supports, above a molded frieze, on turned tapering legs headed by acanthus-carved terminals.

ca. 1780　　*38¼in (97cm) wide*

$1,800-2,400　　**DN**

A 19thC three piece suite of Louis XVI giltwood furniture, comprising a settee and two chairs, the frames carved with flower crestings, all covered in Aubusson tapestry with center floral bouquet panels and scrolling foliate borders.

An upholstered wing back daybed, on ring turned walnut legs, the brass casters stamped "Howard & Sons, London" and stamped "1917 3673" on one leg.

58in (147cm) long

$4,600-5,300　　**CHEF**

settee 65½in (166cm) wide

$2,900-3,700　　**L&T**

A Charles I oak refectory table, the top above a fruiting vine-carved frieze, on bobbin turned legs joined by arch and foliate-carved peripheral stretchers, on square feet.

ca. 1630   *91¼in (232cm) long*

$7,500-8,500   **DN**

A 17thC English elm refectory table, the top above X-shaped trestle ends joined by a center stretcher.

90½in (230cm) long

$7,500-8,000   **DN**

An 18thC large oak and two-plank top refectory table, with leaf and lunette-carved frieze on turned heavy cup-and-cover legs, reduced in size, one frieze with average Victorian carving, Victorian brackets on inner legs, top with center dry crack.

89in (226cm) wide

$1,700-2,400   **CHEF**

A 19thC Elizabethan-style carved oak refectory dining table, the two-plank top on carved and gadrooned bulbous legs with block feet joined by a peripheral stretcher, tabletop with various later carvings of initials, figures, and names.

82¾in (210cm) long

$1,600-2,100   **TEN**

A 19thC French rustic chestnut farmhouse table, with a drawer on one end and a slide to the other, on square legs joined by an H stretcher.

73¼in (186cm) long

$2,000-2,600   **L&T**

A 20thC oak refectory table, in 17thC style, the three-board top with cleated ends above an arch carved frieze with initials "WY," "NF," "RT," and dated 1661, on heavy ring-turned baluster legs joined by peripheral stretchers.

83½in (212cm) wide

$4,000-4,600   **L&T**

A William and Mary solid cedar, gate-leg dining table, the top, above a frieze drawer on one end, on spirally turned legs, joined by peripheral stretchers and terminating in squat, turned bun feet.

ca. 1690   *48in (122cm) wide when extended*

$3,300-4,000   **DN**

An early-18thC oak gate-leg table, the hinged top above a plain frieze and a small end drawer, on four baluster legs, two hinged and opening to support the top, marks, knocks, and abrasions, later supporting blocks and drawer runners on the interior of carcass, frieze section on top of one hinged leg is detached but present.

32in (81cm) wide

$3,300-4,000   **DN**

FURNITURE

An early-18thC William and Mary oak gate-leg table, the top with drop sides, above a frieze drawer on one end, raised on egg-and-fillet turned baluster legs joined by stretchers and a pair of conforming gate-leg supports.

48¾in (124cm) wide

$650-900 **L&T**

A George II oak gate-leg dining table.

ca. 1740 *59½in (151cm) diam*

$2,000-2,600 **DN**

A mid-18thC 10 to 12-seater oak gate-leg dining table, with two rounded drop leaves to form an oval above a single frieze drawer, on cabriole legs with pad feet, the tabletop has had restoration many years ago, the center section has an old split, some old decay and repair around the cabriole legs and pad feet.

74¾in (190cm) long

$1,700-2,400 **TEN**

A 19thC 10-seat oak double gate-leg table, in the 17thC style.

71in (180cm) diam

$1,500-2,000 **SWO**

An early-19thC Regency mahogany drop-leaf dining table, the top with a reeded edge and drop-leaf sides, on ring-turned and reeded tapered legs ending in brass caps and casters.

52½in (133.5cm) wide

$1,200-1,600 **L&T**

A George II twin-pillar extending dining table, probably Irish, with two additional leaf insertions, the rectangular top with rounded corners, each turned stem above triple down-sweeping legs terminating in pad feet on brass casters, with marks, knocks, and abrasions, all clips present and probably later replacements.

ca. 1760 *116½in (296cm) long extended*

$13,000-20,000 **DN**

A George III and later mahogany triple-pillar dining table, the reeded edge top with later rosewood and parquetry crossbanding, above turned stems, reeded scroll legs, and brass paw sabot and casters, comprising a pair of D ends and four leaves, supported by a concertina action.

138in (351.5cm) long

$2,600-4,000 **WW**

A George III mahogany triple-pedestal dining table, with two additional leaf insertions, each turned pillar incorporating reeded collars, on molded down-sweeping legs on brass caps and casters, marks and abrasions.

ca. 1800 *130¾in (332cm) long extended*

$10,000-10,500 **DN**

An early-19thC mahogany and boxwood-strung twin-pedestal dining table, with demilune ends raised on plain ring-turned supports on four down-scrolling legs ending in casters, with a center leaf extension and a narrower additional leaf.

87½in (222cm) wide

$1,500-2,000   **L&T**

An early-19thC triple-pedestal mahogany dining table, three ring-turned column supports, the center pedestal with four outsweeping legs, the end pedestals with three, with brass hairy paw feet with casters.

71¼in (181cm) long

$1,600-2,100   **L&T**

A Regency figured mahogany twin-pedestal dining table, with one additional leaf, the top with molded edge, above turned stems and molded outsweeping tapering legs, on lion-paw feet and casters.

ca. 1815   *103¼in (262cm) long extended*

$1,300-2,000   **DN**

A Regency mahogany twin-pedestal dining table, with three additional leaf insertions, with "beehive" turned stems, on outsweeping tapering legs, on brass "dolphin" caps and casters.

ca. 1815   *128in (325cm) long extended*

$4,600-5,900   **DN**

A Regency mahogany triple-pedestal dining table, probably Irish, with two additional leaf insertions, pedestals on four scroll-molded down-sweeping cabriole legs, with brass caps and casters.

ca. 1815   *136¾in (347cm) long extended*

$10,000-10,500   **DN**

An early-19thC Regency mahogany twin pedestal drop-leaf dining table, each end with a drop leaf over a frieze drawer on one side and a dummy drawer opposing, raised on turned column supports ending on four outsweeping legs on brass caps and casters, with one leaf extension.

The table was previously in Somerville College, Oxford. Founded in 1879, Somerville College, Oxford, was among the first colleges in the country to be created to allow women to benefit from higher education. It was named after Mary Somerville, an important scientist of the 19thC and also an author, mathematician, astronomer, landscape artist, and suffragette. Illustrious alumnae include Dorothy Hodgkin, the only British woman to win a Nobel Prize in science, Indira Gandhi, and Margaret Thatcher. Male undergraduates first gained admission in 1994.

87in (221cm) long

$1,300-1,800   **L&T**

An early-19thC and later mahogany extending pedestal dining table, top on a later column, four reeded outsweeping legs and brass casters, with drop-down legs to support the top when extended, with four additional leaves in a pine stand.

110¼in (280cm) long extended

$4,000-4,600   **SWO**

An early-19thC George IV mahogany triple-pillar dining table, with a pair of D ends and a center drop-leaf section, on turned stems, molded splay legs and brass caps and casters.

112½in (285.5cm) long

$6,500-8,000   **WW**

FURNITURE

A George III mahogany extending dining table, by Thomas Butler, with four additional leaf insertions, the underlying frieze bearing inset makers plaque titled "BUTLERS PATENT No 13 & 14 CATHERINE ST. STRAND LONDON," each removable turned tapering reeded leg, terminating in brass caps and casters, with marks, knocks, scratches, and abrasions, the quality of the mahogany is excellent, the leaves are all solid mahogany.

Thomas Butler started his career prior to 1787, but in that year dissolved a partnership with Edward Johnson and the stock sold was by Christie's on March 28, 1787. After that date Thomas Butler carried on with the business. Through various changes of ownership and arrangements it is clear from insurance records that the business remained substantial. After giving up his business in 1814, Butler's great rivals Morgan & Sanders advertised that they had taken over "a considerable part of 'Mr Butler's late Ware-room' (ibid)." A specializer in producing patent and campaign furniture, Butler produced a pictorial handbill illustrating examples of the firms output. The text of the handbill states that he was "Manufacturer of the Patent Articles to the King & Queen, their Royal Highnesses the Duke of York & Princesses" and that his furniture was "calculated for the East & West Indies. Ship Cabins furnished."

ca. 1805-1810   *165.5in (420cm) long*
$8,500-9,000   **DN**

A Regency mahogany and ebony-inlaid concertina-action extending dining table, in the manner of William Trotter, with four additional leaf insertions, on turned tapering legs terminating in brass caps and casters.

ca. 1815   *106¾in (271cm) long when extended*
$6,000-7,500   **DN**

A Regency mahogany dining table, on turned tapering legs, with three fitted leaves.

110¾in (281cm) long
$3,300-4,000   **CHOR**

A Regency mahogany extending dining table, the top with molded edge and four leaves, on four reeded tapering legs and casters, with leaves holder.

123¾in (314cm) long extended
$2,200-2,600   **CHEF**

A Regency mahogany concertina-action extending dining table, in the manner of Gillows, with three additional leaf insertions, on reeded turned tapering legs, on brass caps and casters, when closed forming a side table.

ca. 1815   *125½in (319cm) wide*
$4,000-4,600   **DN**

An early-19thC and later George IV mahogany extending dining table, with three additional leaves, on a telescopic frame, on ribbed tapering legs and brass caps and casters.

126¼in (320.8cm) long extended
$2,600-3,300   **WW**

A George IV mahogany extending dining table, the top with molded edge, on ribbed tapering legs and brass casters, with a pair of D ends and a telescopic frame that extends to accommodate four leaves, but only two present.

107in (272cm) long
$3,300-4,000   **WW**

An early-19thC William IV mahogany extending dining table, the top opening with a telescopic action, on turned and reeded tapered legs with brass caps and casters, stamped "T. WILLSON 68 GREAT QUEEN ST. LONDON."

116¼in (295cm) wide
$4,000-5,300   **L&T**

An early-19thC William IV mahogany extending dining table, the rounded rectangular top with two leaf extensions, raised on foliate-carved and faceted tapering legs with replaced modern casters.

83in (211cm) long

$550-650   L&T

An early-19thC William IV mahogany extending dining table, with two additional leaves on a telescopic frame and ribbed and turned legs, on octagonal brass caps and casters.

93¾in (238cm) long extended

$1,000-1,100   WW

Judith Picks

I'm a little ashamed to admit that my initial response to learning what this table had just sold for at auction was a huge pang of regret. About 35 years ago, I had the opportunity to buy an identical example for a fraction of the price, but didn't. Aarrgghh! Purportedly, less than 50 of these technical marvels were ever made to Robert Jupe's ingenious, radially expanding design, which he patented in 1835. Hitherto, radial expansion had been achieved by laboriously clipping extension leaves to the edges of a fixed circumference, but Jupe's iron mechanism and leaf-insertion method could expand the table "immediately, and without the slightest difficulty to various sizes." For entertaining with style, that's a decidedly

elegant convenience—both then and now. The Jupe table differed from the telescoping table patented by Robert Gillow, which extended laterally and was an improvement on existing expanding dining tables that clipped extensions onto the edge of the tables. Robert Jupe and John Johnstone's partnership ended in 1842, when Johnstone formed a new firm called "Johnstone and Jeanes." The present example was obviously produced in this transitional period, because the brass boss is stamped "Johnstone & Jeanes."

A rare early-Victorian mahogany Jupe's-patent expanding dining table, by Johnstone & Jeanes, the top with a molded edge expanding to accommodate either eight small or eight large additional leaves with brass tips, housed in a fitted case, the center brass capstan boss inscribed "JOHNSTONE & JEANES PATENTEES," the center block stamped "JOHNSTONE, JUPE & CO. NEW BOND ST. LONDON 10288," the iron mechanism stamped "JUPE'S PATENT," above a substantial turned baluster and fluted stem, a platform base, and on scroll carved lion-paw feet, the leaf cabinet also stamped "JOHNSTONE & JEANES NEW BOND ST. LONDON,"

60in (152cm) diam (closed), 73in (184.5cm) diam (with smaller leaves), 84in (214cm) diam (with larger leaves)

$150,000-200,000   WW

A 20thC Jupe-style extending dining table, by Maple & Co, with eight additional leaves to make a circle, on stop-fluted legs with claw-and-ball feet, the stretchers joined by a center tapering support, stamped "Maple & Co, London & Paris," scratches, various scuffs, no leaf holder.

The table has three sizes: it can be left as just the triangular-section leaves, which are 66in (168cm) in diameter; the table can have the smaller leaves added, which are a rectangular shape, or the largest leaves can be added, which makes the table extended size to 95in (243cm).

95¾in (243cm) wide

$25,000-30,000   TEN

A 19thC Gillows-style mahogany dining table, with rounded rectangular top, one end with a gate leg, raised on reeded tapered legs and wood casters.

90½in (230cm) wide

$2,000-2,600   L&T

A late-19thC oak extending dining table, the wind-out oval top on a center pedestal with four outsweeping legs and four tapered and lobed legs on the D ends, bearing a paper maker's label "F. DANBY'S/Upholstery and Cabinet Works/LEEDS/No.41604/ Workman's Name W. Coates," including four leaf extensions.

F. Danby's was a 19thC cabinetmaker and upholster run by Francis Danby in the Upper Headrow of Leeds, West Yorkshire.

147in (373cm) long

$4,000-5,300   L&T

FURNITURE

An 18thC George III mahogany tilt-top table, the top with a molded edge, on a cannon barrel column and three molded legs with brass casters.

48in (122cm) diam

$2,600-3,300   **L&T**

An early-19thC Regency rosewood breakfast table, the tilt top with canted corners above a lotus carved frieze, on a square-paneled column with anthemions, the quadriform base on carved paw feet with brass casters.

47¾in (121cm) wide

$2,400-2,900   **L&T**

An early-19thC Regency mahogany breakfast table, the tilt top with a molded edge, on a paneled and tapered triform column with bead molding, on a triform base with carved paw feet.

52¾in (134cm) diam

$1,300-1,600   **L&T**

An early-19thC Regency mahogany breakfast table, attributed to William Trotter, the tilt top with a bead molded edge, on a tapered column and triform base outlined with bead molding, on lotus-carved ball feet with recessed brass casters.

53½in (136cm) diam

$4,000-5,300   **L&T**

A late-16th/early-17thC Italian Renaissance walnut center table, Tuscany, the top above a frieze with two short drawers, on a base fitted with drawers on both ends, and raised on foliate-carved trestle bases.

Provenance: This table has been on loan to Nunnington Hall, a National Trust property in North Yorkshire, for the last 70 years. It was recently returned, along with other furniture, to the family of the original benefactor.

57½in (146cm) wide

$9,000-10,500   **L&T**

A pair of mid-18thC Italian Venetian walnut Rococo center tables, each with a serpentine top crossbanded and inlaid with marquetry leaves, flowers and strapwork, above a scroll-carved frieze centered with a pierced and fluted shell-shaped cartouche, finely carved with leaves, with cabriole legs, on leaf-carved scroll feet and pad toes.

By family repute, from Belem Palace, Lisbon, Portugal, and Kilmory Castle, Argyle and Bute, Scotland.

42.5in (108cm) wide

$7,500-8,500   **WW**

An 18thC Georgian rosewood, parcel gilt, ebonized, and painted center table, on lobed and fluted tapered legs with traces of green paint.

37½in (95cm) wide

$2,000-2,600   **L&T**

A Regency rosewood and brass-mounted center table, the tilt top inlaid with marquetry with scrolling leaves and palmettes, with a platform base and gilt-bronze scrolled and winged lion-paw feet and casters.

58in (148cm) wide

$3,300-4,000   **WW**

A Regency mahogany center table, the rosewood crossbanded top with molded edge, above the turned tapering stem, on molded outsweeping tapering legs incorporating lappet-carved knuckles, terminating in brass lion-paw feet and casters.
ca. 1815   *47¾in (121cm) diam*
$4,000-4,600   DN

A Regency parquetry center table, in the manner of William Trotter, the top with radiating sectional specimen veneers centered by the center starburst motif, above the tripartite base and concave-sided plinth above tapering down-sweeping legs terminating in brass lion-paw caps and casters, marks, knocks, abrasions.
ca. 1815   *58¼in (148cm) diam*
$5,300-6,600   DN

A 19thC Regency rosewood and brass-inlaid center table, the crossbanded tilt top with bands of foliate brass inlay, on a lotus-carved column and quadriform concave base raised on saber legs outlined with brass inlay and ending on foliate-cast brass caps and casters.
50½in (128cm) diam
$9,000-10,500   L&T

A George IV rosewood center table, in the manner of Gillows, the top with molded edge, above a tapering hexagonal stem, on a concave-sided base and carved scroll feet, terminating in concealed casters, marks, knocks, and abrasions.
ca. 1825   *46½in (118cm) diam*
$1,500-1,800   DN

A Gothic Revival pollard oak and parcel-gilt marquetry center table, by A. W. N. Pugin for Morel & Seddon, commissioned by King George IV for Windsor Castle, the circular top with a band of shells and leaves in marquetry and pen work, the stem and triform base with recessed Gothic arched panels supporting fanned ribs in imitation of a Gothic vaulted ceiling, concealed casters, missing original frieze and with discoloration to the gilding and scuffing on the feet.

In 1827, when only 15 years old, A. W. N. Pugin received his first independent commission from the Royal cabinetmaker Morel & Seddon to design furniture for Windsor Castle. See Jeremy Cooper, "Victorian and Edwardian Furniture and Interiors," Thames & Hudson 1987, in which he illustrates this table. The Royal photographer Edward Kemp or Leopold William Cleave photographed this table in 1903, where it was displayed in the Picture Gallery, now known as the Queen's Drawing Room, Windsor Castle. Several of the photographs can be viewed on the Royal Collection Trust website RCIN 2936836. At this time, the table had an applied giltwood lambrequin apron, which is now missing and may have been branded with a Royal inventory stamp. The website states that the table is no longer in the Royal Collection.
ca. 1827   *50in (127cm) diam*
$40,000-53,000   GORL

A William IV rosewood center table, the square marble inset top with gadrooned border on four lappet-carved columns united by platform undertier on a scroll base.
23in (59cm) wide
$2,000-2,600   BELL

A William IV figured walnut, ebony, and specimen marquetry center table, in the manner of Edward Holmes Baldock, the top with radiating figured veneers, centered by marquetry flowers, the macassar ebony banding decorated throughout with scrolling branches interspersed by flowers, the tapering triangular stem and down-sweeping scrolling legs terminating in scroll feet and concealed casters.

A similar table attributed to Baldock exists in the collection of Ickworth House, Suffolk (NT 850055). The form of the base of this table relates to tables supplied by Edward Holmes Baldock, one of which was produced for the Duke of Buccleuch in 1840. It is now at Temple Newsam House, Leeds (C. Gilbert, "Furniture at Temple Newsam House and Lotherton Hall," vol. II, London, 1978, no. 395).The marquetry decoration featured on this table is executed in the Dutch fashion first adopted in the 1820s by the Tottenham Court Road "Cabinet inlayer and Buhl manufacturer" Robert Blake. The firm, which had been trading in the early 1840s as "Blake, Geo. & Brothers, inlayers, etc" in Tottenham Court Road and Mount Street, Mayfair, were renamed George Blake & Co. in the late 1840s (C. Gilbert, "Pictorial Dictionary of Marked London Furniture 1700-1840," Leeds, 1996, p.18; and M. P. Levy, Furniture History Society Newsletter, no. 158, May 2005).
ca. 1835   *39in (99cm) diam*
$6,500-8,000   DN

A William IV ebonized and specimen marble center table, the top above a C-scroll carved frieze, on a turned and lappet-carved tapering stem, the three-scroll carved legs on brass casters, marks, knocks, and abrasions.
ca. 1835   *27½in (69.5cm) diam*
$2,600-3,300   DN

FURNITURE

ESSENTIAL REFERENCE—THE FALCINI OF FLORENCE

The workshops of the Falcini family were established in the early-19thC in the small town of Campi, near Florence, by Gaetano Giuseppe Falcini (d. 1846). In the late- 820s, Luigi, the latter's eldest son (d. 1861), opened a bottega in the via del Fosso, Florence, and was later joined by his brother Angiolo (d. 1850). The first piece to be exhibited by the Falcini brothers was a prize-winning marquetry table shown at the Academy of Fine Arts in Florence in 1836, and subsequently purchased by Grand Duke Leopold II for his private collection. The firm continued to exhibit at the Academy throughout the 1840s and completed important commissions for a number of prominent patrons, among which Prince Anatole Demidoff, the Duchess of Casigliano, and Countess Borghesi. After the death of Angiolo Falcini in 1850, Luigi was joined by his two sons, Alessandro and Cesare, who continued the business until 1882.

A mid-19thC Italian ivory and specimen marquetry-inlaid ebony center table, by Luigi and Angiolo Falcini of Florence, the tilt top with shaped edge top centered by a floral spray, surrounded by eight panels, centered by marquetry portraits of great Italian artists or scholars, including Michaelangelo, Raphael, Dante, and Tasso, their names all depicted in marquetry, too, surrounded by an elaborate marquetry border with foliate motifs, above an undulating gilt frieze and acanthus-carved center baluster support, above outsweeping cabriole-shaped legs terminating in scroll feet, marks, knocks and abrasions, the top in sympathetically restored condition.

49¾in (126cm) diam

$10,500-12,000   DN

A Ceylonese hardwood center table, after a design by Thomas King, on three acanthus and scroll-carved shaped legs, the concave triform on scroll feet, marks, knocks and abrasions.

ca. 1850   *29¼in (74cm) high*

$1,300-1,800   DN

A Louis Philippe walnut center table, the radial bookmatched veneered top above a quadripartite pillar and platform base, with scrolled feet on the angles, marks, scratches, abrasions.

ca. 1850   *41¾in (106cm) diam*

$4,600-5,300   DN

A Napoleon III "Boulle" cut brass-inlaid scarlet tortoiseshell center table, with floral marquetry throughout, the top above a serpentine-shaped frieze with frieze drawer and opposing false drawer front, both centered by female mask mounts, on tapering cabriole legs, headed by female mask mounts and terminating in sabots.

ca. 1860   *58in (147cm) wide*

$1,300-1,700   DN

A mid-19thC Ceylonese ebony and specimen wood inlaid center table, the top with radiating serpentine bands of tropical wood within an ivory-inlaid and lappet-carved border, above a reeded tapering stem with scrolling lappet-carved terminals.

The table is typical of the ebony furniture made in the Galle district of Ceylon (today Sri Lanka) in the 19thC—the form being English, the carved ornament, such as the lotus motif, largely indigenous.

48in (122cm) diam

$26,000-33,000   DN

A mid-19thC French walnut, gilt metal-mounted and floral marquetry-inlaid center table, with cabriole legs with herm mounts.

50½in (128cm) wide

$7,500-8,000   DN

ESSENTIAL REFERENCE—HOLLAND & SONS

Provenance: Possibly acquired by Sir George Godolphin Osborne, 8th Duke of Leeds (1802-72), for the principal family seat, Hornby Castle, North Yorkshire. This table can be ascribed to Holland & Sons, one of the largest and most prestigious cabinetmaking firms in the 19thC, based on a number of stylistic attributes; the superb choice of wood, the figuring of the satinwood tilt top, the fine foliate giltwood carving, and the distinctive giltwood borders. Holland & Sons were known for their diversity of style—in the mid-1860s, supplying furniture in the fashionable Louis XVI style, such as this table, but also making Elizabethan furniture, neo-Gothic, and furniture inspired by Robert Adam, Sheraton, and Chippendale (S. Jervis, "Holland & Sons, and the furnishing of the Athenaeum," Furniture History, 1970, p. 46). First established in 1815 as Taprell & Holland at 25 Great Pulteney Street, London, the firm was renamed Holland & Sons in 1843 when William Holland, a founding member, and probably related to George IV's architect-designer, Henry Holland, took over the firm. In the 1850s, William was replaced by his son, James Holland, and the firm moved to 19 Marylebone Street and Ranelagh Works, Lower Belgrave Street, and from 1852, 23 Mount Street. They exhibited at all the major international exhibitions, including London 1851, Paris 1855, London 1862, and Paris 1867; for example, at the 1862 London International Exhibition, they exhibited a fine marquetry and gilt-bronze center table veneered with tulipwood, kingwood, New Zealand spicewood, boxwood, and purpleheart in a design by a "Mr. Rosenberg" that included engravings by Old Masters, all centered by a spider web in silver and ivory (J. Meyer, "Great Exhibitions: London, Paris, New York, Philadelphia 1851-1900," Woodbridge, 2006, p. 122).

A Victorian parcel-gilt satinwood center table, attributed to Holland & Sons, with a baluster stem and tripod base carved with foliage, marks, knocks, abrasions.

ca. 1860   *56in (142cm) diam*

$6,000-7,500   DN

A Victorian burl-walnut and marquetry center table, the top centered by a reserve decorated with a marquetry spray of flowers, the outer border similarly decorated.

ca. 1870   *54¼in (138cm) diam*
$2,600-3,300   **DN**

A 19thC Blue John and hardstone center table, the Derbyshire Ashford black-and-white marble top with etched leaf-scroll corners, inset with 77 BlueJjohn, fluorspar, hardstone, and fossil specimens, above a rosewood and simulated base, in the manner of Gillows, with nulled moldings and a turned acanthus-carved stem, on carved lion-paw and scroll feet and brass casters.

30½in (77.4cm) high
$5,300-5,900   **WW**

A probably 19thC Irish mahogany center table, in George II style, the apron carved with baskets of flowers, eagle heads, scrolling leaves, and rocaille, on leaf-capped legs with a grapevine, on hairy lion-paw feet.

41½in (105.5cm) wide
$3,300-4,000   **WW**

A 19thC Jacobean-style oak inlaid center table, the top with a molded edge and double chevron banding, above an acanthus-carved freize with a drawer, raised on ring-turned columnar corner supports and three center slender balusters on an H-form platform base with bun feet.

42½in (108cm) wide
$1,600-2,100   **L&T**

A George III mahogany drum library table, the top with tooled leather inset surface, above four frieze drawers interspersed by four false drawer fronts, the turned tapering stem on four reeded down-sweeping tapering legs terminating in brass caps and casters, one drawer stamped "W & C WILKINSON LUDGATEHILL 1964."

ca. 1800   *41¾in (106cm) diam*
$6,500-8,000   **DN**

An early-19thC late George III mahogany drum table, the top with a gilt-tooled leather insert, over four short and four dummy drawers, raised on a baluster-turned column and strung saber legs, with brass caps and casters.

40¼in (102cm) diam
$2,600-3,300   **L&T**

An early-19thC Regency mahogany drum table, the crossbanded top above a frieze with four drawers and four dummy drawers, on a ring and spiral carved column, on triform base with scroll feet and brass casters.

28in (71cm) diam
$4,000-4,600   **L&T**

A Regency mahogany drum library table, the top with tooled leather-inset top, above four frieze drawers interspersed by three false drawer fronts and a hinged drawer, the drawers inset with numbered ivory plaques, on a turned stem and four outsweeping reeded tapering legs, on brass lion-paw caps and casters, marks, scratches and abrasions, three Bramah locks present, the others are replacements.

ca. 1815   *48¾in (124cm) diam*
$4,000-5,300   **DN**

A Regency rosewood library drum table, in the manner of Thomas Hope, with four real and four dummy drawers, each with lift up lion-mask pull handles.

238¼in (97cm) diam
$15,000-17,000   **CHEF**

A Regency mahogany drum library table, attributed to Gillows, the top with bead molded edge, above four frieze drawers interspersed by carved patera terminals, the turned pillar with tongue and dart-carved collar, on acanthus-carved and reeded outsweeping tapering legs, terminating in brass caps and casters.

The carved bosses or patera terminals on the frieze of this table are typical of those incorporated into various form of furniture by Gillows. The overall quality, distinctive carving, and sophisticated design (including the slender frieze) also support this attribution. For examples of Gillows furniture demonstrating various similar distinctive attributes see Susan E. Stuart, "Gillows of Lancaster & London 1730-1840," Antique Collectors Club, 2008.

ca. 1815   *54in (137cm) diam*

$10,500-12,000   DN

A late George IV/Victorian solid satin birch center library table, the underside of the top and one leg stamped "VR, O, COBURG COTTAGE, MARCH, 1873," some old chips and splits, some fading.

The stamp relates to The Royal Estate of Osborne, in East Cowes, Isle of Wight. Coburg Cottage was built by H. R. H. Prince Albert for Queen Victoria as a birthday present in 1852. This table was almost certainly supplied to King George IV, and, by descent, to George VI, by whom given to the vendor's father, a landscape gardener at Royal Lodge Windsor, to replace furniture lost when his house was destroyed by bombing in 1940.

ca. 1815   *52in (132cm) diam*

$4,000-5,300   DN

A Regency mahogany and gilt metal-mounted octagonal library table, the top above four drawers and four alternate false drawers at the corners, decorated with ebonized stringing, the four pillar stem above a concave sided base and four hipped down-sweeping legs terminating in brass caps and casters.

One drawer of this table bears the inscription "This table was saved by the towns-people of Macroom, Co. Cork, when Macroom Castle was burnt by irregulars on August 19, 1922, and subsequently brought by Lady Ardilaun, of Macroom Castle to Dublin. It was in the Drawing Room of the Castle for 100 years or more."

ca. 1815   *61¾in (157cm) wide*

$7,500-8,500   DN

A Regency burl-oak and ebony library table, in the manner of George Bullock, the top with gilt-tooled leather inset and the crossbanding incorporating ebony banding cornered by marquetry acorn terminals, above a pair of drawers and an opposing pair of false drawers, the frieze cornered by a carved acorn pendant finial, above twin-turned supports carved with oak leaf and acorn collars, above turned acorn feet and brass casters, marks and abrasions.

While the table is described as being in the manner of George Bullock (d. 1818), certain elements of it—notably, its scale and the inclusion of distinctive pendant finials on the corners of the frieze—mean it could also be reasonably attributed to Richard Bridgens (d. 1846), who collaborated with Bullock on a number of projects, such as "Hastings Hall" at Battle Abbey, in Sussex.

ca. 1815   *72in (182.5cm) wide*

$15,000-17,000   DN

A late-18thC late George III mahogany library table, with a pair of short frieze drawers with the same opposing, and dummy drawers on the ends, raised on waisted trestle end supports joined by an arched stretcher and ending on saber legs with brass caps and casters.

45in (114cm) wide

$7,500-8,500   L&T

A George IV rosewood library table, in the manner of Gillows, on acanthus-carved turned baluster supports and acanthus-carved scroll legs.

ca. 1825   *46¼in (117.5cm) wide*

$3,400-4,000   DN

A George IV rosewood library table, with two blind frieze drawers and tapering rectangular supports, on turned acanthus-carved feet and concealed casters, marks and abrasions.

ca. 1825   *52¾in (134cm) wide*

$4,600-5,300   DN

A George IV mahogany library table, in the manner of Gillows, with a pair of frieze drawers on each long side, each fitted with a Bramah lock, on turned and tapering legs terminating in caps and casters, marks and abrasions.

ca. 1825   *54in (137cm) wide*

$4,600-5,900   DN

An Irish George II mahogany console table, the molded frieze centered by a carved mask of a bearded man, above a carved shell terminal, each corner of the frieze carved with a stylised "gargoyle" mask above tapering cabriole-shaped legs, terminating in stylized pad feet, no marble top present, with scratches, abrasions, some old nails in the frieze, possibly associated, small section of veneer detached but present.

There is great variety to the main carved terminals of such tables, however, the presence of those adopted for the current table appear to be rare. It seems possible that the main center bearded mask represents a religious figure such as an Apostle. The "gargoyle" masks on the corners of the frieze certainly relate closely to those adorning churches or cathedrals of a much earlier date during medieval times. It seems probable that the two types of terminal together reflect the faith of the person commissioning the table to be made originally.

ca. 1730   *74½in (189cm) wide*

$60,000-70,000   **DN**

A George II painted console table, attributed to William Jones, with original shaped marble top over shaped freize with a large carved conch shell in the center with trailing swags supported on two cabriole legs with lion masks on the knees terminating in hairy paw feet, scratches and abrasions.

William Jones was an architect and published drawings for furniture as an appendix to James Smith's "Specimens of Ancient Carpentry."

ca. 1740   *54in (137cm) wide*

$20,000-26,000   **DN**

A George II mahogany console table, possibly Irish, on shell-carved tapering cabriole legs, terminating in claw-and-ball feet, marks and abrasions, some old veneer repair/replacement on the frieze.

ca. 1740   *46in (117cm) wide*

$10,500-12,000   **DN**

A pair of George II and later carved pine eagle console tables, in the manner of Francis Brodie, each with a breche violette marble top above a Greek key and leaf-carved frieze, the eagle support with outstretched wings, probably originally painted.

The design for this type of "Roman" pier table has historically been associated with the eminent English architect and furniture designer William Kent (1685-1748), and this design was most popular during the 1730s-1750s throughout England and Scotland. A related table is illustrated in the 1739 trade sheet by the Edinburgh cabinetmaker Francis Brodie. In the same year he supplied "a marble table supported by and eagle, gilt in burnished gold" to the Duke of Gordon. See F. Bamford, "Dictionary of Edinburgh Wrights and Furniture Makers," Furniture History, vol. XIX, 1983, plate 24a.

37¾in (96cm) wide

$16,000-20,000   **WW**

A mid 18thC Louis XV giltwood console table, with serpentine-shaped variegated marble top, above a foliate scroll and pierced frieze, on scroll and floral-carved tapering cabriole legs, joined by a pierced rocaille terminal.

56in (143cm) wide

$10,500-13,000   **DN**

A late-18thC cream-painted and parcel-gilt semielliptical console table, possibly by an émigré maker, on tapering legs, each surmounted by a female term and decorated with trailing fruiting vines, with minor marks, scratches.

34¼in (87cm) wide

$4,600-5,900   **DN**

A late-18thC George III giltwood demilune table, with a molded Carrara marble top, on fluted and square tapered legs.

50in (127cm) wide

$4,000-4,600   **L&T**

A late-18thC Italian walnut console table, possibly Tuscan, the marble top with stepped molded edge, above a plain frieze, on tapering outsweeping legs, scratches and abrasions, top is later associated, old worm throughout.

71¾in (182cm) wide

$8,500-9,000   **DN**

An early-19thC Regency rosewood, grain-painted, giltwood, and brass-mounted console table, the marble top above a plain frieze decorated with brass mounts on scroll-carved front legs.

53½in (136cm) wide

$4,600-5,300 **L&T**

An early-19thC Regency rosewood marble top console table, with lotus-clad cabriole legs joined by an undertier and on a plinth base.

48in (122cm) wide

$2,000-2,600 **L&T**

An Irish William IV mahogany and ebony-inlaid console table, with a breakfront with two frieze drawers, on spiral-fluted and turned legs on lion-paw feet.

60in (152.5cm) wide

$4,000-4,600 **CHEF**

A George IV Irish mahogany console table, the top with an egg-and-dart molded edge, with a compartment on the right side, above a pair of carved lion monopodia supports, in the manner of Thomas Hope, each decorated with a palmette, reduced in width and probably originally with a marble top.

67in (170.2cm) wide

$6,000-7,500 **WW**

A William IV mahogany hall stand or console table, in the manner of Gillows, the shelved superstructure above the tabletop with apertures on each short side for sticks, the top above a blind frieze drawer and turned and lappet-carved columnar supports and shaped platform base incorporating the drip pans, with scratches, abrasions.

ca. 1835

$3,300-4,000

68¼in (173cm) wide

DN

A 19thC Continental marble-topped carved walnut console table, on a carved base on scroll carved legs.

47¾in (121cm) wide

$2,600-4,000 **L&T**

A 19thC Regency style oak, ebonized, and parcel-gilt console table, in the manner of George Bullock, possibly Holland & Sons, the marble top above a frieze with bands of rosettes and palmettes, raised on block and fluted tapered legs, with a mirror back and joined by a curved stretcher.

71¼in (181cm) wide

$5,300-6,600 **L&T**

A 19thC Italian limed-oak and pine serpentine console table, on compound C-scroll legs carved with rocaille, flower trails, and shells, above a conforming undertier raised on lobed feet.

44½in (113cm) wide

$2,400-2,900 **L&T**

ESSENTIAL REFERENCE—WILLIAM VILE

William Vile (1700-67) was one of the foremost English cabinetmakers of the mid-Georgian period. From 1761 to 1764, in partnership with fellow cabine maker John Cobb, they became Cabinetmakers and Upholsterers to His Majesty, George III. Their standard of craftmanship was rivaled only by that of Thomas Chippendale. Many parallels between known works by Vile and this table can be drawn. The gadrooned apron features to a less accentuated extent on a worktable of related form in the Royal Collection (RCIN 11109), currently in The King's Bedroom at Windsor Castle. A Jewel Cabinet with closely related legs incorporating scroll, channel, and bellflower carving is also held in the royal collection (RCIN 35487). Two bills exists from Vile to Queen Charlotte for these items (from 1761 and 1763, respectively). A cabinet attributed to William Vile incorporating closely related gadrooning and bead molding is currently in the stock of Ronald Phillips, London. Furthermore, the use of well-figured Cuban mahogany is consistent with Vile's use of materials (see Library table, Metropolitain Museum of Art, 24.103.3). Overall the quality of carving and elegance of form show this table to be the work of a craftsman of exceptional prominence. The dating and stylistic qualities strongly suggest this to be William Vile.

A George III mahogany serpentine serving table, attributed to William Vile, the figured top with triple slender banding border by broader crossbanding, the frieze with beaded borders and above a carved pagoda edge, each tapering cabriole leg surmounted by a naturalistically carved palmette leaf also issuing trailing bellflowers, on scroll and acanthus leaf-carved feet, with scratches and abrasions.

ca. 1760   *59in (150cm) wide*

$26,000-33,000   **DN**

A Regency satinwood and mahogany crossbanded side or serving table, the top above a sectional frieze, on reeded turned tapering legs.

ca. 1815   *53½in (136cm) wide*

$3,300-4,000   **DN**

A Regency mahogany breakfront serving table, the shaped top above the tablet molded frieze incorporating a drawer, on fluted tapering legs with ebonized collars and surmounted by carved lion-mask surmounts and terminating in lion-paw feet, scratches and abrasions, small old veneer and stringing repairs.

This serving table, with its fluted tapering legs headed by lion masks, is similar to the design published by Thomas Sheraton in his "Encyclopedia" of 1804. Equally, this sideboard table relates to an 1804 design published in George Smith's "Collection of Designs for Household Furniture and Interior Decoration," 1808, pl. 92.

ca. 1815   *78¾in (200cm) wide*

$22,000-26,000   **DN**

An early-19thC Regency rosewood serving table, the breakfront top over a frieze with a center drawers and inlaid with brass stringing, scrolls, and leaf motifs, on reeded tapered legs ending in ball feet.

67¾in (172cm) wide

$2,600-3,300   **L&T**

A late Regency Irish mahogany serving table, the frieze drawers on heavy carved cabriole legs and paw feet.

88½in (225cm) wide

$2,600-4,000   **CHEF**

An Anglo-Indian exotic hardwood serving table, in the manner of Scottish examples, the back with Gothic arcades and trefoils flanked by tapering tablets and further arches, the top above reeded and molded frieze and saber legs at the front, with scratches, abrasions.

ca. 1830   *71¼in (181cm) wide*

$2,600-3,300   **DN**

A Reformed Gothic oak dinner buffet or two-tier serving table, in the manner of Charles Bevan, with fan finials and waved gallery on the top above inverted Y-shaped supports and the undertier above further turned supports, scratches and abrasions.

ca. 1860   *42¼in (107cm) wide*

$3,300-4,000   **DN**

A 19thC Georgian-style mahogany serpentine serving table, in the Adam style, the top above a frieze carved with ribbon-tied swags and flower-head blocks, raised on lotus-carved stop-fluted and reeded tapering legs.

72in (183cm) wide

$2,600-3,300   **L&T**

FURNITURE

An early-17thC oak side table, the single-board top above a frieze with fielded panels and center drawer, raised on turned and block legs joined by flat stretchers.

43¼in (110cm) wide

$1,300-2,000   **L&T**

A William & Mary oak side table, the top above a frieze drawer and S-shaped supports united by an X-frame stretcher, and on pommel feet, marks, abrasions, the handle on the drawer is a replacement, one rear leg with a particularly "chewed" appearance.

ca. 1690   *33½in (85cm) wide*

$2,600-4,000   **DN**

A William & Mary walnut oyster-veneered and marquetry side table, the top decorated with scrolling foliage, with a frieze drawer, on spirally turned legs, joined by a H-shaped stretcher centered with a marquetry terminal, on turned bun feet, scratches and abrasions, handles are later replacements, one foot is a later replacement.

ca. 1690   *36¾in (93cm) wide*

$8,000-9,000   **DN**

A William & Mary oak side table, with a frieze drawer, on turned sectional legs, joined by a turned H-shaped stretcher, turned tapering feet, scratches and abrasions, handle replaced but in period taste.

ca. 1690   *29½in (75cm) wide*

$2,200-2,600   **DN**

An olivewood and walnut oyster-veneered side table, the top with center star motif, above a frieze drawer, on spirally turned ash legs, scratches and abrasions, some sections of replacement veneer on top, the top is ca. 1690 with the rest of the table probably 19thC.

ca. 1690 and later   *37½in (95cm) wide*

$7,500-8,500   **DN**

A William & Mary walnut and featherbanded side table, the quarter-veneered top with molded edge, above three frieze drawers and a shaped apron, on turned legs joined by a shaped peripheral stretcher, on turned bun feet, with scratches and abrasions, locks are 18thC.

ca. 1690   *31¼in (79cm) wide*

$8,500-9,000   **DN**

An early-18thC Queen Anne walnut side table, the quarter-veneered top with cross and featherbanding, above a frieze drawer on turned tapered legs on bun feet and united by an X stretcher.

28¼in (72cm) high

$1,300-1,800   **L&T**

A George I burl-walnut side table, the crossbanded, featherbanded, and quarter-veneered top above a frieze drawer, on tapering cabriole legs, terminating in pad feet, scratches and abrasions.

ca. 1720   *30¼in (77cm) wide*

$5,300-6,600   **DN**

A George I walnut side table, with three frieze drawers and a shaped apron on cabriole legs, on pad feet, scratches and abrasions, the top with some old staining, the handles are replacements.
ca. 1720   *37¾in (96cm) wide*
$2,600-3,300   **DN**

A George I walnut, burl-walnut and feather-banded side table, with one long and two short frieze drawers, on tapering cabriole legs terminating in pad feet.
ca. 1725   *30¾in (78cm) wide*
$3,300-4,000   **DN**

An Irish George II mahogany side table, the carved and pierced apron with floral acanthus scrolls, centered by a flowering basket motif, on acanthus-carved tapering cabriole legs, with claw-and-ball feet, scratches and abrasions, on one end half of the flower roundel is lacking.
ca. 1750   *72½in (184cm) wide*
$15,000-17,000   **DN**

A pair of George III mahogany side tables, each top above a frieze drawer, on tapering legs.
ca. 1790   *29¼in (74cm) high*
$3,300-4,000   **DN**

A George III mahogany and inlaid serpentine side table, the chevron strung top above a frieze drawer, on fluted tapering square legs headed by oval marquetry terminals, terminating in spade feet.
ca. 1790   *36¼in (92cm) wide*
$4,000-4,600   **DN**

A George III mahogany and marquetry inlaid side table, of serpentine outline, with a frieze with a satinwood drawer inlaid with husk swags and flanked by panels of "quilted" mahogany, the fluted angles inlaid with flutes flanked by oval fan paterae on slender turned line-inlaid legs, scratches, abrasions, replacements of veneers and inlays.
ca. 1790   *78in (198cm) wide*
$16,000-21,000   **DN**

An 18thC Italian provincial fruitwood demidune side table, with open scrollwork legs and lyre-shaped end supports, old worm, repairs to joints.
52¾in (134cm) wide
$850-1,000   **CHEF**

CLOSER LOOK—SIDE TABLE

This is a classic late-18thC George III design.

It has a serpentine-fronted marble top.

The table's cabriole legs are carved in deep relief with leaf motifs inspired by those of the Mediterranean species of the acanthus plant.

The legs are terminated with hairy paw feet.

A late-18thC mahogany side table.
48in (122cm) wide
$2,600-3,300   **L&T**

One of a pair of George III mahogany side tables, each with a plain frieze and square tapering legs terminating in caps and casters.

ca. 1800   *57¾in (146.5cm) wide*

$2,600-3,300 the pair   **DN**

One of a pair of George IV figured mahogany side tables, attributed to Gillows, each top with a bowfront above the tablet-molded frieze with one long drawer, on turned tapering and lappet-carved legs, surmounted by carved patera motifs.

ca. 1825   *65in (165cm) wide*

$13,000-18,000 the pair   **DN**

A Regency mahogany chamber table, attributed to Gillows, the top incorporating a hinged compartment at the rear, above a frieze drawer, on turned and reeded tapering legs, terminating in brass caps and casters.

Gillows supplied four tables of this pattern in 1811 to T. W. Egerton for Tatton Park, Cheshire.

ca. 1815   *28¾in (73cm) high*

$4,600-5,300   **DN**

A 19thC French bird's-eye maple side table, inlaid with ebonized stringing, the rectangular top with a frieze drawer, on baluster turned legs.

ca. 1850   *47½in (120.5cm) wide*

$850-1,000   **WW**

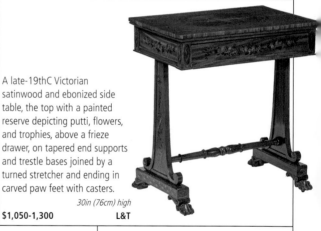

A late-19thC Victorian satinwood and ebonized side table, the top with a painted reserve depicting putti, flowers, and trophies, above a frieze drawer, on tapered end supports and trestle bases joined by a turned stretcher and ending in carved paw feet with casters.

30in (76cm) high

$1,050-1,300   **L&T**

An Italian stained softwood side table, in 18thC style, with molded frieze, above a single drawer, on six turned column legs united by an H-frame stretcher, repaired split on top.

39in (99cm) wide

$650-750   **CHEF**

A 19thC Spanish side table, with turned wooden legs, united by wrought iron stretcher, the ebonized top with walnut frieze and geometric bone inlay.

34¾in (88cm) wide

$550-650   **CHEF**

A 19thC Portuguese rosewood side table, in 17thC style, with ripple-molded decoration, with frieze drawers, on turned spiral twist legs.

38¾in (98.7cm) wide

$1,500-1,800   **WW**

A George II Irish mahogany tea table, on cabriole legs with shell-carved knees and pointed pad feet, with marks, abrasions, it was probably restored and polished recently.

ca. 1740   *35in (89cm) wide*
$4,000-5,300   **DN**

A mid-18thC George II mahogany tea table, the fold-over top opening on a gate leg, above a single frieze drawer, raised on acanthus-carved cabriole legs ending in carved claw-and-ball feet.

32¼in (82cm) wide
$1,250-1,450   **L&T**

An Irish George II mahogany silver or tea table, on acanthus-carved tapering cabriole legs, on acanthus-carved pad feet, with marks, scratches.

The carving on the table is refined for a table of this age, origin, and type and is full of character.

ca. 1750   *34¾in (88cm) wide*
$10,500-12,000   **DN**

An Irish George II mahogany tea table, with a frieze drawer, on acanthus and C scroll-carved tapering cabriole legs, with scratches and abrasions, handle is a period replacement.

ca. 1750   *32in (81cm) wide*
$2,600-3,300   **DN**

An 18thC George III mahogany tea table, on a cannon barrel column and tripod base.

31¼in (79cm) diam
$600-750   **L&T**

A mid-18thC George II mahogany tea table, on cabriole legs ending with pad feet.

32in (81cm) wide
$750-850   **L&T**

A late-18thC George III mahogany inlaid demilune tea table, on square tapered legs headed by carved sunflower motifs and ending in brass caps and casters.

33in (84cm) wide
$900-1,050   **L&T**

An early-19thC Regency rosewood tea table, on a tapered ring-turned and reeded column with a quadriform base and scrolled feet with brass casters.

36¼in (92cm) wide
$1,200-1,600   **L&T**

FURNITURE

ESSENTIAL REFERENCE—PEMBROKE TABLES

While Pembroke tables are recorded in cabinetmakers' and household accounts as early as the 1750s, the origin of why they're called Pembroke—"from the name of the lady who first gave orders for one of them"—only emerged in 1803, in the eminent cabine-maker Thomas Sheraton's pattern book "The Cabinet Dictionary."

● Elegant drop-leaf tables, Pembrokes were essentially an evolution of the breakfast table and were employed in both drawing rooms and boudoirs for not only taking meals, but also playing cards, writing, and needlework.

● The basic form, with two side flaps supported on hinged brackets, lent itself to numerous variations: they can be straight or with a bowfront, with rounded, serpentine, or D-shaped flaps, opening to form rectangular, square, oval, or even octagonal tabletops.

● Most Pembrokes have a drawer (sometimes two) in the frieze, although some have sliding sections with concealed compartments, and most have four legs of either tapering round or square section, or of cabriole form, without understretchers, and usually terminating in casters (for easy of mobility), although a few 19thC examples are supported on a center column with splayed legs (called a "pillar and claw").

● Decoration ranges from plain to simple stringing or crossbanding to sophisticated marquetry work and, sometimes, painted imagery and/or gilt-brass mounts. While notable styles include Gothic and chinoiserie, from the third quarter of the 18thC, during the late 18thC and early 19thC, Neoclassical was by far the most prominent.

A George III mahogany Pembroke table, in the manner of Thomas Chippendale, the twin-flap top with molded edge, above a frieze drawer on one end and a false frieze drawer on the other, on molded tapering legs, headed by pierced spandrels and joined by a pierced X-shaped stretcher, with leather casters.

ca. 1760   *37½in (95.5cm) wide*

$4,000-5,300   **DN**

A George III padouk Pembroke table, referred to also as a "breakfaste" or supper table, the twin hinged top with molded edge, above a frieze drawer with "ax-head" handles, the recessed gilt wirework panel inset compartment beneath, fronted by a hinged and folding door, on square-section legs, terminating in casters, with scratches and abrasions, old chips and splits, drawer lining is solid padouk.

This table relates directly to a design for a "Breakfaste Table" in Thomas Chippendale's 1st Edition of the "Gentleman and Cabinet Makers Director," (1754), plate XXXIII, and included again in the 3rd Edition of 1762 (plate LIII). The distinctive "ax-head" handles of this table are characteristic of Chippendale's output during the 1750s and 60s and feature on both a shaving table and the comparable "Breakfaste" or supper table at Dumfries House, Ayrshire, Scotland. This table is rare due to the use of exotic padouk.

ca. 1760   *41¾in (106cm) wide when open*

$15,000-20,000   **DN**

A George III mahogany Pembroke table, in the manner of Thomas Chippendale, possibly American, Rhode Island, the twin-flap top above a frieze drawer, on turned legs.

ca. 1780   *39in (99cm) wide*

$2,600-3,300   **DN**

A late-18thC George III mahogany Pembroke table, the satinwood banded top above a frieze drawer on one end with a dummy drawer opposing, on square tapered legs outlined with stringing and ending in brass caps.

27½in (70cm) high

$550-650   **L&T**

A late George III mahogany Pembroke table, on square tapered legs headed by shell motif inlay.

39¾in (101cm) wide

$750-850   **L&T**

A pair of early-19thC and later George III mahogany and satinwood Pembroke tables, the crossbanded tops, over single long frieze drawers, on square tapered legs outlined with stringing, on brass caps and casters.

39½in (100.5cm) wide

$6,000-7,500   **L&T**

A 19thC mahogany serpentine Pembroke table, on inlaid tapering legs on casters, with one drawer and a dummy drawer, repolished.

29½in (75cm) wide

$750-850   **CHEF**

A 20thC Chippendale-style mahogany two-drawer Pembroke table, with two drawers and blind fret-carved stiles, on four cluster column supports with block toes, with a pierced X stretcher.

28¼in (71.5cm) high

$450-600   **MART**

ESSENTIAL REFERENCE—SOFA TABLES

Developed during the last years of the 18thC and the first decade of the 19thC, sofa tables were in many respects an extended version of the Pembroke table (see p. 210), which they eventually supplanted in many fashionable 19thC drawing rooms. In his pattern book "The Cabinet Dictionary," published in 1803, Thomas Sheraton described them as specifically for use "before a sofa ... where the Ladies chiefly occupy them to draw, write, or read upon."

● Most sofa tables are between 5ft (150cm) and 6ft (185cm) long when fully extended, and about 2ft (60cm) wide. Their sides are always straight, their two end flaps are supported on fly brackets and have rounded or chamfered corners, and while some have sliding-top compartments (for games) or rising desks for writing and drawing, the majority have one long or two short drawers on one side of the frieze, with corresponding dummy drawers opposite.

● Sofa table bases are hugely varied. For example, the top can be set on end supports, with or without stretchers across the middle, or center supports rising from a platform base; end supports can range from simple plank shapes to lyre shapes to spindled concoctions; center supports range from turned and columnar-like to turned or carved-vase shapes.

● Splaying out from end or center supports, most legs are of tapered saber form, although cabriole legs were sometimes employed. In all instances, the legs are designed so that the feet can fit a little way under, thereby allowing the table to be pulled closer to the sitting user. In this context, tables with relatively low stretchers are often less popular than those with higher stretchers, which allow more leg room.

A Regency rosewood, inlaid, and brass-mounted sofa table, in the manner of John McLean, the top above two frieze drawers and two opposing false drawers, on squared trestle supports framing pierced trellis, on outsweeping tapering legs, terminating in brass lion-paw caps and casters, scratches and abrasions, one handle detached but present, some evidence of old worm.

ca. 1815   *57in (145cm) wide*

$1,600-2,100   **DN**

A Regency mahogany sofa table, the crossbanded top above alternate opposing drawers and dummy drawers on turned supports and out swept legs.

60¾in (154cm) wide

$260-400   **CHEF**

An early-19thC Regency mahogany sofa table, the crossbanded top with drop leaves, two frieze drawers and two dummy drawers on the reverse, on scrolled supports and outsweeping legs, brass cap,s and casters.

51½in (131cm) wide

$3,300-4,000   **L&T**

A Regency rosewood and partridgewood crossbanded sofa table, in the manner of John Mclean, attributed to Gillows, with gilt-metal bead molding throughout, with two frieze drawers, and two opposing false drawer fronts, with tapering outsweeping legs, with brass caps and casters.

ca. 1815   *62¼in (158cm) wide*

$13,000-17,000   **DN**

An George IV Irish mahogany sofa table, by Gillingtons, Dublin, the twin drop-leaf top above a pair of frieze drawers and opposing false drawers, on spiral turned legs terminating in foliate caps and casters, stamped and numbered "GILLINGTONS 3068."

ca. 1825   *59½in (151cm) wide*

$750-850   **DN**

An early-19thC Regency rosewood sofa table, the rounded rectangular top with drop-leaf ends and a bead-molded edge, above a pair of frieze drawers, raised on tapered and foliate-carved twin end supports on trestle bases with carved paw feet, the drawer with maker's stamp "WAITE."

57½in (146cm) wide

$1,100-1,300   **L&T**

FURNITURE

A George II walnut and featherbanded card table, the top, opening to a baize-inset playing surface and counter wells, on tapering cabriole legs terminating in pad feet.

ca. 1730   *32¼in (82cm) wide*

$5,300-6,600   **DN**

A George II Irish mahogany card table, the top opening to baize-inset playing surface and counter wells, above an apron centered by a carved-shell motif, on shell-carved tapering cabriole legs, with paw feet.

ca. 1750   *35½in (90cm) wide*

$4,600-5,300   **DN**

A George II mahogany folding card table, the top opening to baize-inset playing surface, on foliate carved cabriole legs, with claw-and-ball feet, scratches and abrasions, some loss of veneer at "teeth" of hinged rear frieze.

ca. 1750   *34in (86cm) wide*

$4,600-5,900   **DN**

A George II mahogany concertina-action card table, the top opening to a baize playing surface, on acanthus and cabochon-carved cabriole legs, with lion-paw feet, scratches and abrasions, larger crack running across half of the top.

ca. 1755   *35¾in (91cm) wide*

$3,300-4,000   **DN**

A late-18thC George III mahogany card table, the serpentine fold-over top with a molded edge opening to a green baize playing surface, on square tapered legs, the whole outlined with stringing.

35¾in (91cm) wide

$550-650   **L&T**

A pair of George III figured mahogany and crossbanded card tables, in the manner of Thomas Sheraton, each top opening to a baize playing surface, tapering legs, with spade feet.

ca. 1790   *36¼in (92cm) wide*

$3,300-4,000   **DN**

A pair of George III mahogany and satinwood folding card tables, each top opening to baize-inset playing surface, on square section legs, with spade feet.

ca. 1790   *35¾in (91cm) wide*

$6,500-8,000   **DN**

A pair of George III painted satinwood demilune card tables, the tops decorated with center Classical urn motif within a foliate cartouche, as well as grapes and vines, opening to a green baize lined interior, on square tapering legs, with some light scratches.

36in (91.5cm) wide

$3,300-4,000   **CHEF**

A pair of late-18thC George III mahogany and satinwood card tables, the tops with quarter veneers centered by ovals, opening to baize-lined playing surfaces, all raised on turned and tapered fluted legs.

38¼in (97cm) wide

$4,600-5,900   **L&T**

A Regency rosewood and brass marquetry card table, the hinged top, revolving and opening to a baize playing surface, above a tablet-molded frieze, the turned, reeded, and lappet-carved stem on tapering outsweeping legs, on lion-paw feet and casters.

ca. 1815   36¼in (92cm) wide

$2,000-2,600   **DN**

An early-19thC Regency rosewood card table, the top opening to a green baize-lined interior, on a turned column and four scrolled outsweeping legs with brass paw caps and casters, with gilt metal mounts.

36¼in (92cm) wide

$1,300-2,000   **L&T**

An early-19thC Regency rosewood and goncalo alves card table, the top opening to a green baize-lined interior over a gilt-metal mounted frieze, on a panel-molded column and quadriform base with scrolled gilt-metal feet with brass casters.

34in (86cm) wide

$1,300-2,000   **L&T**

An Anglo Indian carved padouk folding card table, the turned and reeded stem incorporating a flower-head motif, flanked by four molded down-sweeping pilasters, on a concave sided base with carved lion-paw feet.

ca. 1820   34¼in (87cm) wide

$5,300-5,900   **DN**

A George IV rosewood folding card table, by Johnston & Jeanes, the top rotating and opening to a baize-inset playing surface, the lappet-carved turned tapering stem on scrolling foliate carved shaped legs, on lion-paw feet, stamped "JOHNSTON & JEANES, NEW BOND ST, LONDON, 6428."

ca. 1825   34¾in (88cm) wide

$1,300-2,000   **DN**

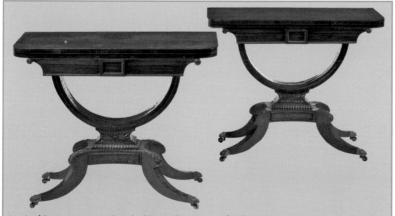

A pair of Regency rosewood card tables, in the manner of William Trotter, each top rotating and opening to a baize-inset playing surface, above a tablet-molded frieze, the U-shaped support on a patera terminal and four acanthus-carved legs, with lion-paw cast caps and casters.

William Trotter (1772-1833) was a highly respected maker of Regency furniture and is considered by many to be Scotland's greatest cabinetmaker. Working after 1805 in Princess Street, Edinburgh, he is primarily known of his distinctive, restrained, and elegant Neoclassical style, and for his use of the best-quality hardwoods. According to Thomas Dibden in his 1838 "Antiquarian and Picturesque Tour" guide, Trotter's celebrated showroom comprised "vistas filled with mahogany and rosewood objects of great temptation."

ca. 1825   35¾in (90.5cm) wide

$5,300-6,600   **DN**

A 19thC Dutch walnut and marquetry card table, the top inlaid with a flowering urn and birds, opening to a blue baize-lined surface, the counter wells inlaid with playing cards, on cabriole legs.

32¼in (82cm) wide

$1,050-1,300   **L&T**

FURNITURE

ESSENTIAL REFERENCE—JAPANNED GAMES TABLE

The Tower Family of Weald Hall is descended from Thomas Tower of Wryesdale, who died in 1659. His son Christopher went to London and prospered as a merchant, eventually becoming Deputy Collector of Customs for the Port of London. He died in 1728, leaving two sons, Christopher and Thomas. Christopher Tower (1694-1771) was a Whig politician and an MP from 1727-42, with his family seat at Huntsmoor Park, near Iver in Buckinghamshire. His brother, Thomas (1698-1778), was a lawyer and an MP who was elected to Parliament for Wareham in 1729 and bought Weald Hall in 1759. There are no written records to say who commissioned this rare triangular card table, but it was probably Thomas before he acquired Weald Hall sometime in the 1720s. The unusual triangular table top was made for the three player trick-taking card game Ombre or "hombre," which originated in Spain in the 16thC but its popularity swept through Europe at the end of the 17thC and into the 18thC. Ombre was the first card game in which a trump suit was established by bidding instead of by the random process of turning the first card of the stock, which gives this game its historical importance in the field of playing cards. Although little played today, Ombre has been described as "the most successful card game ever invented."

A rare George I japanned games table, the Chinese black-lacquer tilt top gilt-decorated with watery scenes of pagodas, bridges, and willow trees, centered with the arms of the Tower family of Weald Hall, inscribed with the motto "Love and dread," with three divided counter wells, on an English ebonized baluster stem and tripod cabriole legs and pad feet.

ca. 1720   *44in (111.5cm) wide*
$15,000-17,000   **WW**

A George II mahogany tripod games table, on a turned and gadrooned baluster stem, on shell-carved outsweeping tapering cabriole legs, with pad feet.

ca. 1750   *30¼in (76.5cm) diam*
$2,000-2,600   **DN**

A Regency rosewood games table, the figured top with brass gallery, the sliding top with an inlaid chess board, the interior with suede backgammon board, on turned end standards and outsweeping legs with brass caps and casters.

ca. 1815   *31½in (80cm) wide*
$2,000-2,600   **DN**

A George III mahogany triple folding games and tea table, the triple-hinged "eared" top opening to a plain surface, opening again to a baize playing surface and counter wells, on cabochon and C-scroll carved cabriole legs, with lion-paw feet.

ca. 1760   *33½in (85cm) wide*
$5,300-6,600   **DN**

A Regency burl-elm library games table, in the manner of William Trotter, the top with center sliding panel with birch and rosewood parquetry chessboard on one side, with a parquetry inlaid backgammon board on the recess beneath, the sections of each side with revolving lids opening by concealed push-button release, revealing divided and velvet-lined interiors, on twin-shaped and molded trestle supports incorporating roundel terminals, each on twin-hipped down-sweeping legs terminating in leaf-cast caps and casters, marks, knocks.

ca. 1815   *35½in (90cm) wide*
$7,500-8,500   **DN**

A William IV rosewood and birds-eye maple pedestal games table, the top inset with a parquetry chessboard, above four drawers and four alternate false drawers, the frieze hung with turned pendant finials, on a faceted baluster stem and concave-sided base issuing outsweeping scroll feet, on concealed casters.

ca. 1835   *28¾in (73cm) high*
$1,300-2,000   **DN**

An early-Victorian rosewood games table, with drawer over pull-out games board, on pierced end supports.

28in (71cm) wide
$450-600   **CHEF**

A late-Victorian figured walnut and floral-inlaid fold-over games table, on double gate-leg support action, the cabriole legs with stylized cloven feet, repolished, veneer repairs.

34¾in (88.5cm) wide
$800-900   **CHEF**

A George III satinwood worktable, in the manner of George Sheraton, with simulated marble top, on outsweeping square legs, joined by an X-shaped stretcher, scratches and abrasions.

ca. 1810 *29¾in (75.5cm) high*

$800-900 DN

A Regency Goncalo Alves worktable, in the manner of Gillows, scratches, abrasions, professionally restored previously.

Gonzola alves is a tree especially abundant in eastern Brazil; it yields a hard strong durable zebrawood with straight grain and dark strips on a pinkish to yellowish ground.

ca. 1820 *29¾in (75.5cm) wide*

$800-900 DN

A George IV rosewood worktable, in the manner of Gillows, the top above two frieze drawers and the sliding workbag, on an octagonal tapering stem, on scrolling feet and casters.

ca. 1825 *30in (76cm) high*

$1,500-1,800 DN

A George IV mahogany worktable, in the manner of Gillows, the satinwood top above two frieze drawers, above a slide-out tray for a bag, flanked by tablets, on scroll and shell-carved lyre supports and brass casters.

ca. 1825 *29¼in (74.5cm) high*

$550-650 WW

A mid-19thC Irish Killarney yew wood worktable, with marquetry floral decoration, the lid centered with a ruined abbey, the interior with a harp, on a faceted column to a circular base, split in top, sides, and back.

20¾in (73cm) high

$2,600-4,000 SWO

A Victorian papier-mâché and parcel-gilt decorated worktable, decorated with figures in a landscape, on cabriole legs with scrolled toes and casters.

ca. 1870 *27½in (70cm) high*

$550-650 TEN

ESSENTIAL REFERENCE—CHARLES BEVAN

Charles Bevan was born in the late 1820s and started gaining recognition for his work as a furniture designer and manufacturer in around 1865. Three London addresses are recorded from which he operated, firstly at 66 Margaret Street from 1865-6. Here, he advertised a "New Registered Reclining chair" made by Marsh and Jones of Leeds, whose London showrooms were near his own premises. In that year, with the help of Marsh and Jones, he supplied the Yorkshire mill owner Sir Titus Salt with a large group of furniture, including a bedroom suite, and in 1867 with the case of an Erard grand piano. These can all now been seen at Temple Newsam House in Leeds. In 1866, he moved to 46 Bemers Street, during which time, his fortunes improved, working with the Manchester firm of James Lamb, whose work was shown in the Paris Exposition Universelle of 1867. The following year he went into collaboration with one of the largest and most notable of 19thC furniture manufacturers, Gillows of Lancaster and London. Finally, in 1872, his works were exhibited at the International Exhibition in London with Gillows. They, in partnership, produced a pair of ebonized cabinets, decorated with Doulton stoneware plaques, which now form part of the V&A collection in London. His final move was in 1872 and coincided with a partnership with his son forming C.Bevan and Son and a move to 100 High Holborn, where the firm remained for the following 10 years. Stylistically, his furniture tends to be heavily ornamented and in the Gothic taste, elaborately decorated with geometric ornamental inlays, described at the time as in the "medieval taste," something clearly evident in this workbox.

A Reformed Gothic walnut and specimen parquetry inlaid trumpet worktable, attributed to Charles Bevan for Gillows, with internal removable tray above the trumpet paper-lined "bag," the specimen marquetry, including oak, walnut, tulipwood, and maple, scratches, abrasions, the internal tray probably originally with lids, these are all lacking.

ca. 1880 *28¼in (71.5cm) high*

$8,500-9,000 DN

A late-Victorian two-tier worktable, by the Sandringham workshop, the frieze inlaid with a continuous inscription, "ALEXANDRA/ TO. CH. KNOLLS/ SANDRINGHAM/ CHRISTMAS .1899."

Sandringham's "Technical School of Woodwork" was established by Princess Alexandra, later Queen Alexandra following her marriage in 1863 to Edward, Prince of Wales. Originally established for the children of estate workers, it later became Her Majesty Queen Mary's "Carving School" for ex-servicemen and local workers.

1899 *31½in (80cm) high*

$2,600-4,000 L&T

FURNITURE

A George II walnut lowboy, the quarter-veneered top with cross and featherbanding, with a caddy molded edge with reentrant front corners, above two short and one long drawer, the apron centered with a shell, on scroll-carved cabriole legs and pad feet.

ca. 1725-30   28½in (72.5cm) wide

$2,600-3,300   WW

A George II walnut side table or lowboy, on tapering shell-carved cabriole legs, with molded pad feet, scratches and abrasions, later blocks and drawer runners in the interior.

ca. 1740   30in (76cm) wide

$3,300-4,000   DN

A mid-18thC American black walnut lowboy, with unusual stylized leaf protruding front drawers, above three pine-lined frieze drawers, above a bat-wing and arc d'arbelete apron, on cabriole legs and pad feet.

33in (83.5cm) wide

$2,000-2,600   WW

A George II mahogany side table or lowboy, the top above three drawers centered by a fret-cut apron, on tapering cabriole legs terminating in pad feet, with scratches and abrasions, later drawer runners, old worm in back board.

ca. 1750   29½in (75cm) high

$2,100-2,600   DN

A George II burl-maple and oak lowboy, with three drawers around shaped frieze on turned legs and pad feet, usual wear.

27½in (70cm) wide

$2,600-3,300   CHEF

A late-18thC George III oak side table or lowboy, on tapering cabriole legs, with pad feet, scratches and abrasions.

28in (71cm) wide

$1,600-2,100   DN

A George III mahogany lowboy, with one long and two short drawers, water staining on the top, some cracking, replacement handles.

28¾in (73cm) wide

$1,000-1,100   CHEF

A late-18thC George III mahogany dressing table, the hinged top opening to covered compartments with metal liners, a hinged easel mirror with ratchet, and open wells, above a dummy drawer and long drawer, raised on square legs ending in leather casters.

This elegantly proportioned dressing table is nearly identical to a dressing table supplied by Thomas Chippendale in 1774 to Paxton House, Berwickshire. See Gilbert, Christopher "The Life and Work of Thomas Chippendale," pl. 425.

50in (127cm) wide

$4,600-5,300   L&T

A Regency mahogany dressing table, attributed to Gillows, the top with three-quarter gallery, above three molded frieze drawers, on turned tapering legs, with brass caps and casters, scratches and abrasions, later runners on the undersides of drawers.

Gillows supplied two related dressing tables to William Powlett, 2nd Baron Bolton (d.1850) for Hackwood Park, Hampshire in 1813.

ca. 1815   42¼in (107cm) wide

$4,600-5,300   DN

FURNITURE

A Regency mahogany dressing table, attributed to Gillows, the top with three-quarter galley, above three frieze drawers, on turned tapering legs, with brass caps and casters.
ca. 1815   *42¼in (107cm) wide*
$3,300-4,000   **DN**

An early-19thC Chinese Export black-lacquer and gilt chinoiserie dressing table, decorated with foliage, birds, and traditional village scenes, the top of the back with an enclosed shield-form mirror, two center drawers flanked by cupboard doors, each opening to reveal two short enclosed drawers, the top with a hinged compartment on each side, above three drawers, on tapering legs, scratches, abrasions, some escutcheons missing.
37in (94cm) high
$7,500-8,500   **DN**

The Scots-born cabinetmaker Ralph Turnbull emigrated to Jamaica with his brothers Cuthbert and Thomas sometime in the early-19thC. Records indicate it was probably around 1815, and, by 1819, the brothers were established enough to advertise their skills in the "Kingston Chronicle." Kingston was a thriving city built on the success of the sugar trade, and the English merchants and officials were a receptive market for locally made furniture, albeit influenced by current English prototypes. While it is believed the brothers worked together for the first years after their arrival in Jamaica, by the early 1820s, each had established his own workshop and advertised accordingly, trying to distinguish himself from other Turnbull competition. It is Ralph who was the most successful, and the only one to label his furniture, perhaps in a bid to distiguish his work from that of this brothers.

The Turnbull style is particularly idiosyncratic, not for the forms employed, but for the lavish use of exotic veneers, many of Jamaican origin, and the use of marquetry to embellish the surfaces. A number of small boxes bearing Ralph Turnbull's trade label survive, some with handwritten paper keys identifying the various specimens used in the veneers. The present table features many of the traits recognized as the work of Ralph Turnbull's workshop, and parallels can be seen between it and a labeled table currently in the collection of the Museum of Fine Arts Boston. The circular top is divided into eight panels, each containing geometric designs, tarsia geometrica, heraldic motifs, and pictorial images, enclosed by a border of doves. The pictorial elements include a cornucopia, a vase and flowers, a musical trophy, and a spray with thistles, roses, oak leaves, and clover. The concave quadriform base is decorated with floral marquetry, geometric bands, thistles, and acorns. While the individual motifs may have specific significance, some of the meanings are unknown.

A George IV mahogany dressing table, in the manner of Gillows, the top with three-quarter gallery, above three mahogany-lined drawers, on turned legs with brass caps and casters.
ca. 1825   *42½in (108cm) wide*
$1,800-2,400   **DN**

A pair of early-19thC Regency rosewood occasional tables, on ring- and baluster-turned columns and four umbrella legs.
29½in (75cm) high
$3,300-4,000   **L&T**

A late Regency rosewood occasional table, the top above a frieze drawer raised on a quatrofoil base with scroll feet and casters.
19¾in (50cm) wide
$650-800   **CHEF**

An early-19thC late-Regency mahogany occasional table, on a tapered column support with a lotus-carved collar, the concave quadriform base with corner finials and raised on foliate-carved bun feet.
30½in (77.5cm) high
$1,700-2,100   **L&T**

An early-19thC Jamaican marquetry and parquetry occasional table, attributed to the workshop of Ralph Turnbull, the top inlaid with a variety of exotic specimen wood veneers in eight sections inlaid with a cornucopia, a star motif, a heraldic shield, a vase of flowers, a musical trophy, a rose and thistle spray, and two panels of diaper pattern, within bands of flower heads and doves, on a lotus-carved column and quadriform base inlaid with a floral garland, diamond motifs, and a band of thistles and acorns, on turned bun feet.
23in (58.5cm) diam
$6,000-7,500   **L&T**

A 19thC tole tray and parcel-gilt carved occasional table, the tray painted with figures and animals, enclosed by floral panels and a pierced gallery, on an associated base with three scroll-carved painted and gilt legs.

32in (81cm) wide

$650-900 **L&T**

A 19thC Maltese olivewood occasional table, the top with sectioned veneers centered by an inlaid Maltese cross, above real and dummy drawers, on a lotus-carved column support and triform base on turned feet.

28in (71cm) high

$5,300-6,600 **L&T**

A pair of late-19thC Continental kingwood, marquetry, brass-mounted occasional tables, the tops with scrolled foliate marquetry in contrasting veneers, over a frieze with mask mounts, on turned baluster columns and bases with brass paw feet.

26¾in (68cm) high

$3,300-4,000 **L&T**

A Victorian black-marble and inlaid specimen stone-top occasional table, on a cast iron base.

21¼in (54cm) diam

$1,050-1,200 **CHEF**

An 18thC George III mahogany spider-leg drop-leaf table, on slender legs joined by peripheral stretchers and ball feet.

29¼in (74cm) wide when open

$900-1,050 **L&T**

A Regency painted occasional table, the top decorated with a river landscape with figures on a boat, within a larger floral panel, on square legs, one leg broken at the top.

28¾in (73cm) high

$1,600-2,100 **CHEF**

A Louis Philippe coromandel, satinwood banded and gilt metal-mounted occasional table.

ca. 1840 *29½in (75cm) high*

$600-750 **DN**

A late-19thC Sheraton Revival satinwood occasional table, the top painted with a portrait reserve within a band of laurel, on square legs joined by a concave undertier, the painted decoration later.

28¼in (72cm) high

$550-650 **L&T**

A 19thC Italian ebonized, ivory, and marquetry table, in the manner of Luigi and Angelo Falcini, on spiral carved legs joined by an H stretcher with conforming ivory inlay.

28¼in (72cm) high

$650-800 **L&T**

A set of early-19thC Regency rosewood brass-inlaid quartetto tables, on slender ring-turned legs joined by curved stretchers, on trestle bases.

29¼in (74cm) high

$2,000-2,600   **L&T**

A late-19thC quartetto nest of occasional tables, in Regency style.

27½in (69.7cm) high

$900-1,050   **WW**

A set of three early-20thC burl-oak, walnut, and nesting tables, the banded tops on slender supports with trestle bases and curved stretchers.

28in (71cm) high

$1,300-1,800   **L&T**

An early-19thC Regency mahogany lamp table, the top above a frieze drawer, on twin ring-turned end supports with trestle bases joined by a turned stretcher, previously fitted with a workbasket.

28in (71cm) high

$750-850   **L&T**

An early-19thC Regency mahogany lamp table, with two frieze drawers, on a baluster support and triform base with ball feet.

30in (76cm) high

$800-900   **L&T**

An early-19thC late Regency mahogany lamp table, the top with sectioned veneers, on a faceted baluster column and triform base, on bun feet.

29½in (75cm) high

$1,200-1,600   **L&T**

A mid-19thC Victorian Gothic-Revival oak lamp table, the top inset with a geometric green, black, and white marble insert, over a trefoil pierced frieze, on a faceted column and three scrolled legs.

28¼in (72cm) high

$1,700-2,100   **L&T**

A George II mahogany occasional table, the tilt top with birdcage action above a turned column and outsweeping legs.

ca. 1740   *36¼in (92cm) diam*

$650-800   **DN**

A George III mahogany tripod table, with a turned column and outsweeping legs.

ca. 1760   *33½in (85cm) diam*

$600-650   **DN**

A George III burl oak-topped tripod table, on a wrythen-turned column base.

22in (56cm) high

$1,600-2,100 **CHEF**

ESSENTIAL REFERENCE—FRANK LLOYD WRIGHT

In October 1909 Frank Lloyd Wright left the United States for Europe, in part to experience European art and architecture, and also to promote the publication of a folio of his work the following year. The folio, entitled "Ausgeführte Bauten Und Entwürfe von Frank Lloyd Wright" contained plans and perspectives of buildings from 1893-1909, and was published by the Berlin publisher Ernst Wasmuth. The folio was the first publication of Wright's work to appear anywhere in the world, and its publication had significant influence on the early Modernist architects in Europe, including Peter Behrens, Le Corbusier, and Walter Gropius. This easel, of late-19thC manufacture, is thought to have belonged to Wright at the time of his European visit and was presented to his publisher Ernst Wasmuth as an appreciation. A faint inscription on the pine board, and a brass plaque mark the presentation and a further plaque on the reverse bears an inventory number and the inscription "The Easel of Frank Lloyd Wright." In 1932, Wasmuth is thought to have lent his easel to the Werkbundsiedlung in Vienna. The Werkbundsiedlung was an exhibition involving 30 famed architects from Austria, Europe, and the USA, such as Richard Neutra, Adolf Loos, Margarete Schütte-Lihotzky, and Gerrit Rietveld, who completed 70 furnished houses for the exhibition before they were available for sale. In the 1940s, the easel was passed on to Dr. Hans Herzfeld for a postwar exhibition in Vienna. Until the mid-1980s, it was in the possession of The Westfair Estate in Malibu, a savings and loan company that had been buying architectural memorabilia from Europe. When the estate and its holdings were sold, the easel was returned to Europe.

An American Keuffel & Esser architect's easel, manufactured by Peabody of Providence R.I., of painted cast iron and pine wood, bearing later brass labels inscribed "THE EASEL/ OF/ FRANK/ LLOYD/ WRIGHT/ NR. 1898" and "TO ERNST WASMUTH BERLIN/ IN REMEMBRANCE OF KIND MEMORY/ AND WARM APPRECIATION OF...../ PAST WORK...................FRANK LLOYD WRIGHT. TALIESIN/ JUNE 1925," with faint inscription to the board "FRANK LLOYD WRIGHT/ AUSGEFÜHRTE BAUTEN UND ENTWÜRFE/ BERLIN/ FUR/ ERNST WASMUTH."

ca. 1875-85 *40½in (103cm) high*

$7,500-8,500 **L&T**

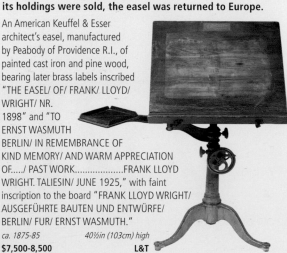

An 18thC George III oak tripod table, on a tapered and turned baluster column on cabriole legs with slipper feet.

23¾in (60cm) high

$850-1,000 **L&T**

A late-18th/early-19thC provincial oak trefoil small table, on ring-turned legs joined by peripheral stretchers.

23¾in (60cm) high

$1,100-1,250 **L&T**

A Regency black-lacquered and gilt chinoiserie tripod table, the top decorated with figures in a garden scene, above the turned tapering stem, on scrolling outsweeping legs, scratches and abrasions, decoration on top has been "touched in," gilding has been "refreshed."

ca. 1820 *24in (61cm) wide*

$1,700-2,100 **DN**

A Victorian amboyna and ebony tripod table, in the manner of Holland and Sons, the top marquetry inlaid with an outer Greek-key band and with a center leaf motif, on a fluted stem on scroll legs, with brass block feet.

16.5in (42cm) wide

$4,000-4,600 **WW**

An Edwardian mahogany and inlay heart-shaped bijouterie table.

30in (76cm) high

$850-1,000 **CHEF**

A late-19th/early-20thC Sheraton Revival painted satinwood bijouterie table, decorated with ribbon-tied leaves and other flowers.

30in (76cm) high

$1,000-1,100 **WW**

FURNITURE

A late-19th/early-20thC French giltwood table, with a marble surface, over scrolled legs with claw feet.

18¼in (46cm) diam

$400-450 WHP

A matched pair of early George III wine tables, the tops with wavy galleries above blind fret-carved friezes with cup slides.

25¼in (64cm) high

$2,600-3,300 L&T

A late-19thC French mahogany and marquetry drum table, the top with a pierced brass gallery above a gilt-bronze mounted frieze with a drawer, on cabriole legs ending in sabots.

$1,050-1,200 L&T

An early-19thC Regency mahogany washstand, in the manner of Gillows, the top with a three-quarter gallery above five drawers and an arched recess, on turned and reeded tapered legs with brass caps and casters.

48in (122cm) wide

$2,600-3,300 L&T

An early-19thC Regency mahogany washstand, by Gillows, the top with a three-quarter gallery and reeded edge, above a concave drawer and arched kneehole, with two short drawers, on ring-turned and reeded legs with brass caps and casters, stamped on the drawer "GILLOWS LANCASTER."

36¼in (92cm) wide

$7,500-8,500 L&T

A 19thC West Indian mahogany clerk's table, probably Jamaica, the back carved with stylized palm leaves, the frieze inlaid with various specimen woods and parquetry stars, with an end drawer, on turned legs.

56¾in (144.5cm) high

$800-900 WW

An 18thC Spanish walnut trestle table, on scrolled trestle ends united by iron arched supports.

82in (208cm) wide

$2,000-3,300 L&T

A late-19thC French marble-topped patisserie table, on foliate frieze cast iron and scroll base.

50½in (128cm) wide

$2,100-2,600 CHEF

A 20thC Indian carved teak occasional table, in the form of a camel.

26½in (67cm) high

$1,500-1,800 SWO

A late-17th/early-18thC William and Mary oak dresser base, the top with a molded edge above three double-panel short drawers, on tapered turned and block legs.

75½in (192cm) wide

$1,800-2,400   **L&T**

An early-18thC Queen Anne oak dresser base, the top over three molded panel short frieze drawers with lion-mask ring-pull handles, raised on turned legs ending in bun feet.

72½in (184cm) wide

$2,200-2,600   **L&T**

An 18thC George III oak inlaid dresser base, the top with a molded rim over three short inlaid drawers and a shaped apron with a center inlaid medallion, on cabriole legs.

70½in (179cm) wide

$2,200-2,600   **L&T**

An 18thC elm dresser base, the single-plank top above three drawers on shaped end supports, one foot with 19thC replacement.

73¼in (186cm) wide

$1,500-1,800   **CHEF**

A mid-18thC oak enclosed low dresser, with three deep drawers above an open shelf flanked by two molded cupboard doors, on block feet, with some old splits.

63in (160cm) wide

$2,200-2,600   **TEN**

A late-18thC George III oak enclosed dresser base, with four graduated drawers flanked by two molded cupboard doors enclosing a shelf, all between reeded stiles, on bracket feet, general bruises and scuffs, rear-right foot and front-right foot replaced.

67¼in (171cm) wide

$1,600-2,100   **TEN**

A George III oak inverted breakfront dresser, with burl crossbanding, with nine drawers surrounding a fielded panel door enclosing a shelf, flanked by fluted quarter pilasters, on bracket feet.

65in (165.2cm) wide

$1,100-1,250   **WW**

An early-19thC late-George III oak dresser base, the top above three frieze drawers and two carved-panel cupboards, flanking three false drawers flanked by column supports, on bracket feet.

65¾in (167cm) wide

$4,000-4,600   **L&T**

FURNITURE

A George III Welsh oak dresser, the plate rack with a dentil cornice, the base with a reeded edge above an arrangement of seven drawers, above a fret-carved shaped apron, on turned front legs and a potboard base.

67in (169.3cm) wide

$5,300-6,600 **WW**

A 17thC and later Welsh oak deuddarn, having a carved frieze dated "1660" above a pair of lozenge-carved doors, with further panel doors below, on stile feet, losses and chips.

57in (145cm) wide

$2,600-4,000 **SWO**

A George III oak open dresser and rack, the base of three drawers above three small drawers and an arched apron, on turned forelegs joined by a potboard.

ca. 1800 *73¾in (187cm) high*

$1,300-1,800 **TEN**

An 18thC George III oak dresser, the molded cornice with a heart-shaped cutout and wavy edge above three enclosed shelves, the base with four center short drawers flanked by two further short drawers above panel doors, raised on stile feet with bracket facings.

80¼in (204cm) high

$2,600-4,000 **L&T**

An 18thC Georgian oak dresser, the molded cornice above two enclosed shelves, the base with three short drawers above a center fixed panel flanked by panel doors, on stile feet.

71in (180cm) high

$1,300-1,800 **L&T**

An 18thC Georgian oak dresser, the upper section with a molded cornice above three plate shelves with an enclosed back, the base with three short drawers with bone escutcheons above an ogee-shaped frieze and undertier, on turned legs with stile feet.

84in (213cm) high

$1,600-2,100 **L&T**

An 18thC George III oak and elm dresser, the molded cornice above a shaped frieze, over three shelves and an enclosed back, the base with a configuration of five short drawers with a shaped apron, on square legs with corner brackets.

80¼in (204cm) high

$1,800-2,400 **L&T**

An 18thC Georgian oak and walnut dresser, the base with four center drawers flanked by short drawers and arch panel cupboard doors, on stile feet.

81¼in (206cm) high

$3,300-4,000 **L&T**

An early-19thC oak potboard dresser, probably South Wales, the raised plate rack with three shelves and applied with iron hooks, the base with three frieze drawers.

71¼in (181cm) high

$2,100-2,600 **WW**

An early-17thC and later oak press cupboard, the carved frieze dated "1614," over a door carved with a deer, flanked by figural pilasters and columns, the lower section with further columns and undertier with a paneled back, on a plinth base and paw feet.

46in (117cm) wide

$1,050-1,200 **L&T**

An early-17thC French Renaissance oak and walnut dressoir, the projecting cornice over a carved panel frieze with masks and brackets, above a pair of doors relief carved with saints, divided by figures in architectural niches, above a pair of short drawers with mask handles, raised on fluted columns on a plinth base with bun feet.

61in (155cm) high

$9,000-10,500 **L&T**

An early-17thC and later carved oak buffet cupboard, with marquetry inlay and carved vine scrollwork, old restored splits in place.

57in (145cm) wide

$1,500-1,800 **SWO**

A Charles I oak standing livery cupboard, with a flower scroll-carved frieze, above a pair of paneled doors, decorated with an urn of flowers and leaves, with an arched center panel, on column supports and an open potboard base, probably Gloucestershire.

48¼in (122.5cm) high

$1,300-1,800 **WW**

A William III oak press cupboard, the cavetto-molded cornice above a painted panel door flanked by a painted panel on each side, the lower section with a pair of painted panel doors, all panels decorated with floral foliage, figures, and animals, on bracket feet, scratches and abrasions, the handles on the lower doors are replacements.

ca. 1700 *77½in (197cm) high*

$4,000-5,300 **DN**

An early-18thC and later Lancashire oak and checker-strung press cupboard, dated and initialed "IB 1709," the cornice above a wheel-carved frieze over doors carved with leaf and flower motifs, the base with four drawers with chamfered panels fronts, above a pair of triple-panel cupboard doors similarly carved, on stile feet.

72in (183cm) high

$2,600-4,000 **L&T**

A mid-18thC George II mahogany hanging corner cupboard, the key molded cornice above a pair of arched triple panel doors, opening to three serpentine shelves and a pair of drawers with iron clasps and locks.

53¼in (135cm) high

$1,100-1,250 **L&T**

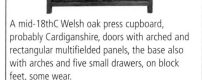

A mid-18thC Welsh oak press cupboard, probably Cardiganshire, doors with arched and rectangular multifielded panels, the base also with arches and five small drawers, on block feet, some wear.

78¾in (200cm) high

$2,200-2,600 **CHEF**

A mid-18thC George II walnut corner cupboard.

90¼in (229cm) high

$1,500-1,800 **L&T**

FURNITURE

A late-18thC Dutch mahogany standing corner cupboard, Neoclassical decoration with egg-and-dart dentils and guilloche moldings, the broken pediment centered with a draped urn above laurel branches.

97½in (247.5cm) high

$1,800-2,400　　**WW**

A late-18thC George III oak, mahogany, and marquetry decorated freestanding corner cupboard, on scrolled bracket feet.

87½in (222cm) high

$550-650　　**TEN**

A late-18thC Dutch yew, walnut, rosewood, and fruitwood inlaid press cupboard, the doors opening to shelves, the base with a pair of cupboard doors enclosing shelves, raised on square tapered legs.

75¼in (191cm) high

$1,300-2,000　　**L&T**

An 18thC Bavarian painted pine cupboard, the frieze painted with names and dated, the center door enclosing fixed shelves, medium rubbing on paint finish.

1755　　57in (145cm) high

$2,600-3,300　　**CHEF**

A George III oak press cupboard, replacement handles, staining on feet, replacement modern hanging rail.

74½in (189cm) high

$650-800　　**CHEF**

An early-19thC large mahogany press cupboard, with fretwork gallery centered by wreath, above paneled doors with reentrant corners and patarae detail, above three long drawers flanked by fluted detail on block feet.

89in (226cm) high

$12,000-15,000　　**L&T**

A mid-19thC Dutch mahogany and marquetry inlaid corner cupboard, the upper section with molded pediment and glazed door, the base with a cupboard door inlaid with an urn, flowers, and birds.

76½in (194cm) high

$400-500　　**TEN**

A 19thC late-Gothic-style carved parchemin panel oak livery cupboard, the cornice over doors, drawers, and panels, carved with tracery, grotesques, scrolling foliage, and fruiting vines with pierced iron-strap hinges and lockplates, on stile feet.

63in (160cm) high

$1,050-1,200　　**L&T**

An early-20thC Georgian-style mahogany housekeeper's cupboard.

72in (183cm) high

$1,600-2,100　　**L&T**

A George II mahogany linen press, in the manner of Giles Grendey, the doors cornered by carved shell and bellflower motifs, opening to three sliding trays, the lower section with two short and two long graduated drawers, on molded and shaped bracket feet, scratches and abrasions, some old repairs.

A George II mahogany linen press, in the manner of Thomas Chippendale, the doors enclosing six oak slides, the base with two frieze drawers, marks, knocks, scratches, abrasions .

ca. 1750   *60¼in (153cm) high*

$6,000-6,600   **DN**

Giles Grendey (1693-1780) was an eminent mid-18thC furniture maker, retailer, and lumber importer. Born in Gloucestershire, apprenticed at 16 to William Sherborne, he started his own business in 1726, and, by ca. 1730, had established a workshop and warehouse in St. John's Square, Clerkenwell, London, which remained his working premises until ca. 1755; appointed Master of the Joiners' Company in 1766, he retired shortly after.

ca. 1760   *75¾in (192.6cm) high*

$7,500-8,500   **DN**

A George III mahogany linen press, flame mahogany doors enclosing a long slide and two short slides, the base with six short drawers and one long drawer, on bracket feet.

ca. 1770   *78½in (199.7cm) high*

$2,100-2,600   **WW**

A Regency mahogany and ebonized-strung linen press, the panel doors, opening to five sliding trays, the lower section with two short and two long graduated drawers, each drawer with lion-mask cast handles, on bracket feet, marks, knocks, and abrasions, small replacement veneer on one door.

ca. 1815   *87¼in (221.5cm) high*

$2,600-4,000   **DN**

CLOSER LOOK—REGENCY LINEN PRESS

A development of the scroll motif employed in Classical Graeco-Roman ornament, the bonnet-top pediment (or "swan-neck" in Great Britain), was a popular form of cresting on Neoclassical furniture.

The door panels are in the form of ogee-type Islamic arches—exotic forms fashionable in around the turn of the 19thC as Western designers became reacquainted with Asian and Egyptian architecture and ornament.

The press is supported on turned and gadrooned feet. Comprising rows of slightly bulbous lobes, gadrooning initialy emerged during the Renaissance as a modification of Classical reeding.

Resembling a spiraled rope, the turned barley-twist forms on the press are thought to have originated in India, and were first introduced to England via Portugal and Holland in the mid-17thC.

An early-19thC late-George III mahogany linen press, with paneled doors, enclosing linen slides, with two short and two long graduated drawers on outsweeping feet.

80¾in (205cm) high

$3,300-4,000   **L&T**

A late-Regency flame mahogany linen press, made in the Channel Islands, the interior (not seen) partly converted with a hanging rail and single remaining slide drawer, the base with four graduated drawers.

97½in (247.5cm) high

$1,200-1,300   **MART**

FURNITURE

A George IV rosewood and brass-inlaid cupboard or dwarf linen press, in the manner of Gillows, on carved lion-paw feet, scratches and abrasions, three later slides in interior, some repairs of veneers and inlays.

ca. 1825   *60¼in (153cm) high*

$5,300-5,900   **DN**

A Victorian oak Gothic Revival linen press, the panel doors with arcading and trefoils enclosing three shelves, above two short and two long drawers and a plinth base, marks, knocks, scratches, the shelves in the interior are later replacement, it was probably originally designed to have linen slides.

ca. 1840   *81¼in (206cm) high*

$2,000-2,600   **DN**

A mahogany linen press, with pierced broken-scroll pediment above two doors with acorn ornament, with two short and two long drawers below, scratches and abrasions, cornice is not securely attached to the press.

ca. 1840 and later   *93¾in (238cm) high*

$4,600-5,300   **DN**

A mid-19thC Victorian mahogany linen press, the twin paneled doors, enclosing four linen slides, the lower part with two drawers, on a plinth base.

69in (175cm) high

$2,400-2,900   **L&T**

A late-19thC amboyna linen press, in George III style, with a hanging rail, the base with two short and two long drawers and bracket feet, scratches and abrasions, one handle loop broken and detached, upper section has been converted from sliding tray to a hanging space.

96½in (245cm) high

$3,300-4,000   **DN**

A George III mahogany clothes press, with a dentil-molded, fluted, and anthemion-molded cornice, the doors, opening to three sliding trays.

ca. 1765   *76in (193cm) high*

$7,500-8,500   **DN**

A George III mahogany clothes press, in the manner of Thomas Chippendale, the pair of panel doors cornered by roundels, opening to five sliding trays, each covered in original marbled paper, the lower section with two short and three long graduated drawers, on bracket feet, with marks, knocks, scratches, and abrasions.

Several of the features demonstrated by this press relate closely to those demonstrated by pieces known to have been produced by the workshop of Thomas Chippendale. This includes the red "wash" applied to the panels on the underside of the press. The paper lining in the interiors of trays is also a feature associated with Chippendale.

ca. 1770   *74in (188cm) high*

$8,500-9,000   **DN**

A George III mahogany clothes press, in the manner of Thomas Chippendale, the dentil cornice above paneled cupboard doors opening to sliding trays, the lower section with two short and two long drawers, on shaped bracket feet.

ca. 1770   72½in (184cm) high
$8,000-9,000   **DN**

A George III mahogany clothes press, in the manner of Thomas Chippendale, the panel doors, opening to five sliding trays, on bracket feet.

ca. 1780   68¼in (173cm) high
$5,300-6,600   **DN**

A George III mahogany clothes press, by Gillows, the paneled doors applied with solid brass molding, opening to an arrangement of slides, the lower section with two short and two long graduated drawers, the underside of one drawer bearing pencil signature, on shaped bracket feet.

The pencil signature on the underside of one drawer of the current linen press is almost certainly the signature of William Bullock, who is recorded as being a cabinetmaker for Gillows in the late-18thC. William Bullock was the brother of renowned furniture designer, maker, and sculptor George Bullock. William Bullock went on to open a museum of curiosities in Birmingham in 1800. Then, in 1801, he moved the museum to Liverpool and his brother George joined him there, where his career began to flourish.

ca. 1790   49¾in (126cm) high
$7,500-8,500   **DN**

A George III satinwood and tulipwood crossbanded clothes press, in the manner of Thomas Sheraton, opening to six sliding trays, the lower section with two short and two long graduated drawers, on bracket feet.

ca. 1800   85½in (217cm) high
$10,000-11,000   **DN**

A George III mahogany clothes press, the paneled doors opening to five sliding trays, the lower section with two short and three longs graduated drawers, on ogee-shaped bracket feet, marks, knocks, scratches, later blocks on the backs of the feet.

ca. 1790   78¼in (199cm) high
$2,000-2,600   **DN**

An early-19thC late-George III mahogany compactum wardrobe, the cornice with urn finials above two short and six long drawers flanked by long cupboards with hanging space and drawers, raised on tapered legs.

89in (226cm) wide
$2,400-2,900   **L&T**

A George IV mahogany clothes press, the paneled doors opening to an adjustable shelf, the lower section with two short and two long graduated drawers, on turned tapering feet.

ca. 1825   63in (160cm) high
$1,600-2,100   **DN**

FURNITURE

An early-19thC William IV breakfront mahogany wardrobe, with two beaded panel cupboards, enclosing shelves, flanking a center paneled cupboard with protruding palmette-carved columns, decorated with patarae, with an egg-and-dart carved plinth on lion-claw feet.

93in (236cm) wide

$4,000-5,300   L&T

A mid-19thC mahogany compactum wardrobe, with two paneled doors, the interior with hanging rail and three coat pegs on left and six slide drawers on right.

85in (215.5cm) high

$1,000-1,100   MART

A 17thC French walnut armoire, of pegged construction, the two cupboard doors with carved rosettes and circular moldings, the base with four geometric panels, the interior with shelves and hanging space.

77½in (197cm) high

$2,200-2,600   TEN

ESSENTIAL REFERENCE—LIMING

Although nowadays limed finishes are perhaps most commonly associated with 18thC and 19thC Scandinavian furniture, their use throughout Europe on furniture, as well as wooden wall paneling and flooring, dates back well over 500 years, and was also often employed in North America from the Colonial period to the late 19thC. Primarily, but not exclusively, used on rustic and provincial furniture and fittings, an important quality of liming was that it provided a degree of protection against damaging insect infestation, such as woodworm, due to the inherently caustic nature of lime. However, applied in paste or wax form, its chief attribute was aesthetic—more specifically, to bleach or lighten the natural color of a wood, and to subtly highlight its natural grain and decorative figuring . This quality made it particularly well suited to open-grained hardwoods, notably oak and ash, and less so to close-grained softwoods, such as pine.

A 18thC French provincial oak marriage armoire, the projecting cornice with egg-and-dart molding, above a frieze carved with scrolling roses and an applied carved flowering urn and pair of doves, over a pair of foliate-carved panel doors with brass mounts, on scrolled feet.

92¼in (234cm) high

$1,700-2,100   L&T

An 18thC French provincial limed oak armoire à deux corps, the pair of molded panel doors opening to shelves, the lower part with further panel doors opening to a fixed shelf, above a shaped apron and raised on scroll-carved legs.

84¾in (215cm) high

$6,000-7,500   L&T

A late-18th/early-19thC Dutch mahogany and marquetry armoire, inlaid with barber's pole stringing, with ribbon-tied baskets of fruit and flowers, the cornice centered with a Rococo cartouche of shells and scrolls, above a pair of shaped paneled doors, with applied portrait rondels and urns, with three shelves and five drawers, the bombé base with three long drawers, the sides inlaid with fan paterae, on carved claw-and-ball front feet.

91½in (232.5cm) high

$4,000-5,300   WW

ESSENTIAL REFERENCE—COFFERS

The English word "coffer," which filtered into common usage during the late Middle Ages, is derived from the Old French word "cofre" or "coffre," itself derived from the Latin "cophinus," and that from the ancient Greek "Kóphinos," meaning "basket." Made of sturdy wooden construction and with hinged, lockable lids, coffers were primarily used for the storage of valuables (hence the phrase "the family coffers"). Traditionally, and in contrast to most standard chests, coffers were fitted with carrying handles, making them and their valuable contents more easily transportable; to that end many, albeit by no means all, coffers were fitted with domed lids that were better able than standard flat-topped chests to throw off potentially content-damaging rain or sea-spray while in transit.

A 16thC pine clamp-end chest, probably North Germany or Sweden, the lid above a carved front panel of geometric motifs.

46in (117cm) wide

$400-500 TEN

A late16th/early-17thC and later oak boarded chest, the hinged lid with a raised panel revealing an interior with a lidded till, the front carved with Gothic arches with tracery, the spandrels carved with oak leaves, roses, shamrocks, grapes, and vine leaves, with stepped cutout ends.

54¼in (139cm) wide

$2,900-3,700 WW

A small late-16th/early-17thC Italian cypress wood pokerwork cassonealto aldige, the paneled front decorated with Renaissance knights in arches, flanking panels of figures with leopards and lions, with penwork decorated sides with scrolling leaves.

23¾in (60.5cm) wide

$650-800 WW

An early-17thC oak board chest, with a board top and cutout end supports.

52¾in (134cm) wide

$400-500 L&T

A Charles II oak coffer, the top above the carved front, incorporating three lozenge carved panels, on stile feet.

ca. 1650   *42¼in (107cm) wide*

$1,600-2,000 DN

A Charles II solid ash coffer, the lid enclosing a compartment with candle box, the panels on the front with vase of flowers decoration, scratches and abrasions, the hinges and lock on the lid are later 18thC examples.

ca. 1680   *48in (122cm) wide*

$2,000-2,600 DN

A late-17thC oak panel chest, the top above a foliate scroll-carved frieze and four-panel front carved with diamond motifs, on stile feet.

62¼in (158cm) wide

$650-800 L&T

FURNITURE

A late-17thC William and Mary brass studded leather chest, attributed to the workshop of Richard Pigg Junior, the top and front covered in brass-stud decoration with flower motifs, scrolls, and fleur de lys, the pierced lockplate and escutcheon in the form of a crown with a rose and thistle.

Richard Pigg Junior worked from the reign of Charles II as "trunk maker to the Great Wardrobe" until his death in 1706, when he was succeeded by William Johnson. A similar chest with crown escutcheon is in the collection of Ightham Mote, Kent. For a discussion of 17thC coffer makers and their products, see Olivia Fryman, "Coffer-Makers to the Late Stuart Court, 1660-1714," Furniture History Society, 2016, pp. 1-16.

A late-17thC oak panel chest, the triple panel top above a scroll and arch-carved triple panel front, raised on stile feet.

50½in (128cm) wide

$1,100-1,250   **L&T**

38½in (98cm) wide

$4,600-5,900   **L&T**

A late-17th/early-18thC carved oak blanket chest, with triple paneled carved front, centered by lozenges, on stile feet.

47¼in (120cm) wide

$1,700-2,100   **L&T**

A George I oak mule chest, the top enclosing a compartment above the base with two short drawers, marks, and abrasions.

ca. 1725   *54in (137cm) wide*

$1,050-1,200   **DN**

An 18thC oak mule chest, the hinged top above three panel front and a pair of drawers raised on later bracket feet.

1763   *48¾in (124cm) wide*

$600-750   **CHEF**

A late-18thC painted pine coffer, the architectural three-paneled front with painted courtyard vistas, some repainting.

59¾in (152cm) wide

$1,250-1,450   **CHEF**

A late-18th/early-19thC George III oak mule chest, with a hinged mahogany crossbanded lid, above six false drawers and three true drawers flanked by fluted quarter columns, on bracket feet.

60¾in (154cm) wide

$4,000-4,600   **L&T**

A 19thC Zanzibar hardwood and mother-of-pearl chest, inlaid with geometric motifs, the lid enclosing two candle boxes, iron carrying handles on the sides, on carved forefeet, some sections of the mother-of-pearl detail have been replaced.

49¼in (125cm) wide

$1,500-1,800   **TEN**

A William & Mary walnut, figured walnut and featherbanded chest-of-drawers, the quarter-veneered top, above two short and three long graduated drawers, on turned bun feet, with marks, knocks, scratches, sections of replacement veneer on top, locks are later replacements, feet are replacements but have age and are in period style.

ca. 1690 *39in (99cm) wide*
$7,500-8,500 **DN**

A William & Mary olivewood, oyster-veneered and holly crossbanded chest-of-drawers, the circular strung top above two short and two long drawers, on turned bun feet, marks, scratches, and abrasions, feet later replaced, later 18thC handles and locks.

ca. 1690 *32¾in (83cm) wide*
$10,500-12,000 **DN**

A William & Mary walnut and parquetry chest-of-drawers, the inlaid top cornered by scroll motifs, above two short and three long graduated drawers, on turned bun feet.

ca. 1690 *34in (86cm) high*
$7,500-8,500 **DN**

A late-17th/early-18thC William & Mary walnut and seaweed marquetry chest-on-stand, the quarter-veneered and crossbanded top inlaid with a center panel and spandrels, with ebonized and fruitwood scrolling leaves, above two short and three long crossbanded drawers with conforming panels, the sides with arched marquetry panels, the stand with a further drawer, on later bun feet.

41in (103.8cm) wide
$5,300-6,600 **WW**

A William & Mary oyster veneered and marquetry chest-on-stand, with holly banding and inlaid all over with scrolling foliage, the top with a center panel and corner spandrels, above two short and two long drawers, the stand with later elements and fitted with a long drawer.

ca. 1690-1700 *39in (99cm) wide*
$4,000-4,600 **WW**

A late-17th/early-18thC William and Mary walnut oyster-veneered and marquetry chest-of-drawers, the quarter-veneered top over two short drawers with floral marquetry, above three crossbanded long drawers, on later bun feet.

40¼in (102cm) high
$3,300-4,000 **L&T**

A Queen Anne walnut and featherbanded chest-of-drawers, the quarter-veneered top, above two short and three long graduated drawers, on turned bun feet, scratches and abrasions, later handles, locks are 18thC.

ca. 1710 *34in (86cm) high*
$8,500-9,000 **DN**

A George I walnut and featherbanded chest-of-drawers, in the manner of Giles Grendy, the caddie top above a brushing slide and four long graduated drawers, on bracket feet.

ca. 1720 *32in (81cm) high*
$15,000-17,000 **DN**

A George II walnut, crossbanded, and pine chest-of-drawers, the caddy top above two short and three graduated drawers, on bracket feet, scratches and abrasions.

ca. 1730 *36¼in (92cm) wide*
$5,300-6,600 **DN**

FURNITURE

A George II walnut chest, the caddy-molded top quarter-veneered with cross-and-feather banding, above a brushing slide and four drawers, on shaped bracket feet, the top three drawers previously with divisions.

ca. 1730-40   *30in (76cm) wide*

$8,500-9,000   **WW**

An early-18thC George I walnut bachelor's chest-of-drawers, the hinged crossbanded top with feather banding, above two short and three long graduated crossbanded drawers, on bracket feet.

34¼in (87cm) wide

$5,300-5,900   **L&T**

A George II walnut and crossbanded chest-of-drawers, the quarter-veneered top above two short and three long graduated drawers, on bracket feet, scratches and abrasions.

ca. 1740   *31½in (80cm) wide*

$4,600-5,300   **DN**

A George II walnut chest-of-drawers, of reverse breakfront outline, the top above four long graduated drawers, on bracket feet, scratches and abrasions, the handles are replacements, the locks are late-18thC.

ca. 1740   *38½in (98cm) wide*

$3,300-4,600   **DN**

A George II walnut and crossbanded chest-of-drawers, with two short and three long drawers, on bracket feet, scratches and abrasions, handles and locks later replacements, section of replacement veneer.

ca. 1740   *35¾in (91cm) wide*

$5,300-6,600   **DN**

A George II walnut chest, the quarter-veneered cross-and feather-banded top with a molded edge, above four drawers, on bracket feet, with oak sides.

29in (74.5cm) wide

$4,000-4,600   **WW**

A mid-18thC George II mahogany bachelor's chest, the hinged fold-over top above a pair of short drawers and three long drawers, on bracket feet.

34in (86cm) wide

$2,600-4,000   **L&T**

A George II mahogany serpentine dressing chest-of-drawers, the drawers interspersed by leaf and ball molding, the top drawer fitted with a baize-inset slide above an arrangement of compartments and lidded compartments around a hinged rectangular mirror, flanked by foliate bellflower-carved canted angles, on blind fretwork bracket feet, scratches and abrasions, locks and escutcheons are replaced.

Many parallels between works by the highly skilled mid-18thC cabinetmaker William Gomm and this chest can be drawn. Based in Clerkenwell Close, London, Gomm's designs were heavily inspired by Thomas Chippendale's Director with combinations of Gothic, Rococo, and Chinoiserie elements included in the furniture. This can be seen in the contrast between the trailing floral carved angles and the blind fretwork feet. This format of chest demonstrates one of Gomm's most prolific designs with at least six "Exceeding fine Serpentine Commode Dressing Tables" supplied to Lord Leigh by William Gomm & Son for Stoneleigh Park in 1763.

ca. 1755   *39½in (100cm) wide*

$26,000-33,000   **DN**

A George III mahogany chest-of-drawers, the brushing slide above two short and thee long drawers, scratches, abrasions, the sides with old splits and cracks, also on the top and some joins opening up.

ca. 1760   *37in (94cm) wide*

$2,600-3,300   **DN**

A George III mahogany serpentine chest-of-drawers, the caddy top above four long graduated drawers, flanked by tablet-molded canted angles, on shaped bracket feet and concealed casters, with original handles, scratches and abrasions.
ca. 1760   *40½in (103cm) wide*
$6,000-6,600   **DN**

A George III mahogany serpentine fronted chest-of-drawers, with ebonized stringing, the shaped top with molded edge, above four graduated drawers, on shaped bracket feet, with marks, scratches, abrasions, the handles are replacements, the gilding refreshed but shows signs of wear and age.
ca. 1765   *44in (112cm) wide*
$8,000-9,000   **DN**

A George III mahogany chest-of-drawers, the top above a blind fretwork-fronted drawer and two short and three long graduated drawers, on ogee shaped bracket feet.
ca. 1770   *37in (94cm) wide*
$5,300-6,600   **DN**

A George III mahogany serpentine dressing chest, in the manner of Gillows, the top with molded edge above a slide flanked by divisions, the slide retracting to reveal an arrangement of lidded divisions, above three further drawers and shaped bracket feet, marks, knocks, scratches, and abrasions, ratchet adjustable mirror in center of fitted drawer no longer present, lock on the fitted drawer is a replacement.

John Frederick Sackville, 3rd Duke and 9th Earl of Dorset ordered one of the illustrated commodes from the firm's Oxford Street premises. The illustrated examples do not have lids or covers to the divisions as the current example, however, a drawn plan clearly including covers for all appropriate divisions and "Boxes" dated 1781 is illustrated.
ca. 1770   *43in (109cm) wide*
$13,000-16,000   **DN**

A George III burl-elm chest-of-drawers, the top above two short and three long drawers, on turned bun feet, with scratches and abrasions, feet are later associated.
ca. 1780   *37in (94cm) wide*
$11,000-13,000   **DN**

A George III mahogany chest-of-drawers, in the manner of Thomas Chippendale, with a brushing slide and four long graduated drawers, on shaped bracket feet, with scratches and abrasions, evidence of old worm on the backboards, feet, and underside.
ca. 1780   *31¼in (79.5cm) wide*
$10,500-12,000   **DN**

A George III mahogany bachelor's chest-of-drawers, the caddy-molded top above a brushing slide and three long graduated drawers, on shaped bracket feet, with knocks and abrasions, split down one side with slender strip of wood added.
ca. 1780   *34in (86.5cm) wide*
$4,000-4,600   **DN**

A George III mahogany chest-of-drawers, with a brushing slide and four drawers, on bracket feet.
ca. 1780   *30¾in (78cm) high*
$2,600-4,000   **DN**

A George III mahogany bachelor's chest-of-drawers, the top, above a brushing slide and four long graduated drawers, on shaped bracket feet.
ca. 1780   *33½in (85cm) high*
$6,500-8,000   **DN**

A George III mahogany serpentine chest-of-drawers, in the manner of Ince and Mayhew, the shaped top above four drawers, the top drawer with a slide and fitted interior with lidded compartments around a center hinged mirror, on bracket feet, scratches and abrasions.

ca. 1780   *39½in (100cm) wide*

$5,300-6,600   **DN**

An 18thC Dutch marquetry chest-of-drawers, the top with center urn motif within flowers, birds, and butterflies, over four drawers with flanking side cupboards on shaped bracket feet, repolished.

                                34¾in (88cm) wide

$3,300-5,300   **CHEF**

A George III mahogany bowfront chest-of-drawers, the top above a brushing slide and three drawers, flanked by reeded columns headed by acanthus-carved terminals, on reeded turned tapering legs, with minor marks, scratches, abrasions, the locks are original but keys are lacking.

ca. 1800   *39¼in (101cm) wide*

$5,300-6,600   **DN**

A George III mahogany and satinwood crossbanded bowfront chest-of-drawers, with four graduated drawers and a shaped and outsweeping apron, on outsweeping bracket feet.

ca. 1800   *40¼in (102cm) wide*

$4,600-5,300   **DN**

A George III serpentine mahogany chest, the crossbanded top over four rosewood crossbanded drawers with original brass ring handles and oak linings, raised on sweeping bracket feet, old scratches and marks.

                                36¼in (92cm) wide

$4,000-4,600   **MART**

A George III mahogany bowfront chest-of-drawers, the top above four long graduated drawers, on shaped bracket feet, scratches and abrasions.

ca. 1800   *36¾in (93cm) wide*

$4,600-5,900   **DN**

A George III mahogany bowfront chest-of-drawers, the shaped top above a brushing slide, three long graduated drawers and a shaped apron, on outsweeping tapering bracket feet, scratches and abrasions, metalware replaced.

ca. 1800   *39½in (100cm) wide*

$4,000-4,600   **DN**

A 19thC mahogany campaign secrétaire chest-of-drawers, in two parts, the upper section with one short and one secrétaire drawer over a long drawer, the lower part with two drawers, with brass recessed handles and corner straps, on turned bun feet.

                                39¾in (101cm) high

$2,600-3,300   **L&T**

A 20thC George III-style mahogany bachelor's chest-of-drawers, the fold-over top above five short over four long graduated drawers, on bracket feet.

                                30¼in (77cm) high

$3,000-3,700   **L&T**

FURNITURE

An 18thC French Régence kingwood and parquetry decorated commode, in the manner of Thomas Hache, the marble top above six drawers with brass floral backplate drop handles flanked by canted corners with reeded brass columns, general scratches.

Thomas Hache (1664–1747) was a French ébéniste.

50¾in (129cm) wide

$2,100-2,600 **TEN**

Derived from the French word meaning "convenient" or "suitable," commodes first appeared in France toward the end of the 17thC, during the reign of Louis XIV. Essentially a replacement for the more rudimentary chest or coffer (see pp. 231-32), their basic form comprised either a low cabinet or chest-of-drawers, raised on legs and used for storing personal items—mostly in boudoirs or bedrooms, but also salons or drawing rooms. Throughout the 18thC and 19thC, numerous variations were conceived, both in terms of the ergonomics of their construction and their decoration—the latter often highly sophisticated in the prevailing styles of the day, most notably earlier Rococo and later Neoclassical. During the 19thC, the word "commode" also acquired a more specific meaning, and was used to describe a bedside cabinet or chair enclosing a chamber pot—and in the United States it became a colloquial synonym for a flush toilet.

A mid-18thC Danish figured walnut and parcel-gilt serpentine commode, the mottled marble top above four long drawers flanked by chamfered angles, above a foliate carved gilded frieze with outsweeping scroll feet.

34¼in (87cm) high

$5,300-6,600 **DN**

A Louis XV rosewood and kingwood petit commode, by Jean-Charles Ellaume, with ormolu mounts, with serpentine marble top above two drawers, stamped "JME J.C. Ellaume."

Jean-Charles Ellaume was made maitre on November 6, 1754. His furniture can be found in the collections of Chateau de Morlanne, Chateau Royal de Wawel in Krakow, and the Musée des Beaux-Arts de Bernay.

ca. 1760 *33in (84.2cm) high*

$2,600-3,300 **WW**

A mid-18thC French fruitwood commode, attributed to Jean-François Hache, scratches, abrasion, signs of old woodworm.

48¾in (124cm) wide

$10,500-12,000 **DN**

A Dutch mahogany and kingwood bombé commode, in the manner of Matthijs Horrix, with ormolu mounts, the serpentine bleu turquin marble top above three drawers and a shaped apron flanked by keeled angles and with quarter-veneered sides, with an old break on the marble.

German-born Matthijs Horrix was the leading cabinetmaker in The Hague in the second half of the 18thC and the preferred purveyor of furniture to the Stadtholder's Court, because he worked "to the most fashionable taste of Paris." He had his workshop at the Spuistraat and specialized in furniture with marquetry decoration in the French style.

ca. 1770 *57¾in (146.8cm) wide*

$3,300-4,600 **WW**

A Continental mahogany commode, possibly Portuguese, with three drawers, cabriole legs, scratches, abrasions.

ca. 1760 *35in (89cm) wide*

$2,000-2,600 **DN**

One of a matched pair of George III sycamore, partridgewood, and tulipwood banded serpentine commodes, gilt metal mounted throughout, above three solid mahogany lined drawers, flanked by gilt-metal mounts with stylized rocaille, foliage, and stylized cabochon motifs, above a shaped apron and shaped bracket feet.

ca. 1770 *46½in (118cm) wide*

$10,500-12,000 the pair **DN**

An 18thC German walnut and inlaid serpentine commode, the quarter-veneered and crossbanded top over three serpentine crossbanded drawers centered by cartouches, on bracket feet.

45¼in (115cm) wide

$1,800-2,100 **L&T**

A late-18thC Continental tulipwood, kingwood, and marquetry commode, the variegated marble top above three graduated drawers, flanked by pilasters, on turned legs.

49¼in (125cm) wide

$2,600-3,300 **DN**

A late-18thC Louis XVI kingwood and floral marquetry breakfront commode, with marble top, above three drawers flanked by canted angles and gilt-metal mounts, on tapering legs with sabots, scratches and abrasions, key present and operates locks.

50½in (128cm) wide

$6,000-7,500 **DN**

A late-18thC French Louis XVI kingwood and fruitwood parquetry commode, the molded marble top above three drawers, flanked by gilt-metal mounts, on tapered legs.

50in (127cm) wide

$5,300-5,900 **L&T**

A French Louis XVI walnut commode, the marble top over a serpentine front, having three short over two long drawers, all with marquetry inlaid fronts, scrolling gilt metal handles and mounts, on short shaped legs, large split on each side, no maker's stamp, mark, or date.

52in (132cm) wide

$2,100-2,600 **SWO**

An 18thC Swedish kingwood bombé commode, with bronze mounts and decorated with parquetry lattice veneers, the alabastro fiorito molded-edge top possibly associated.

36½in (92.5cm) wide

$1,600-2,100 **WW**

An 18thC Continental kingwood and parquetry bombé commode, the bombé body with three drawers with diamond parquetry, over a shaped apron and bracket feet, gilt metal mounts throughout.

39in (99cm) wide

$1,200-1,600 **L&T**

An 18thC and later kingwood and gilt-metal-mounted commode, of bombé outline, the marble top above three short and two long drawers, raised on splayed feet, scratches, abrasions, some replacements of veneers, this is certainly Continental in construction.

49¼in (125cm) wide

$10,000-11,000 **DN**

A late-18thC Directoire mahogany and gilt-metal-mounted commode, with variegated gray marble top, above three short and two long drawers, flanked by fluted three-quarter columns, on turned arrow feet.

51½in (131cm) wide

$1,700-2,100 **DN**

A George III patridgewood and parcel-gilt bowfront commode, the top with line inlaid edge, above three drawers, with reeded tapering columns, on carved lion paw.

ca. 1805   *49¾in (126cm) wide*

$4,600-5,900 **DN**

An early-19thC late-George III satinwood demilune commode, inlaid with ebonized stringing and stars, the top crossbanded in kingwood, above a pair of paneled doors backed with gilt-brass lattice and pleated fabric, enclosing two shelves, on tapering feet.

45¼in (115cm) wide

$3,300-4,000   **WW**

An early-19thC French Empire mahogany and ormolu marble-top commode, by Kolping, with a frieze drawer and three further drawers, all with ormolu mounts, on bracket feet, stamped "KOLPING" on the back.

Othon Kolping (1775-1853) established his workshop in 1804 at no. 3 Cour de la Juiverie, place Saint-Antoine, Paris.

51½in (131cm) wide

$3,300-4,000   **L&T**

An early-19thC mahogany commode, with a variegated marble top above a secrétaire drawer, opening to a leather-lined writing surface and short drawers, three further drawers and a further drawer concealed in the plinth, on scroll feet.

50½in (128cm) wide

$2,400-2,900   **L&T**

A 19thC Continental cherrywood walnut and bird's-eye maple bombé commode, probably North European, inlaid with fruitwood, burl panels, and specimen woods, the top decorated with a pair of birds with leaves and flowers, above three drawers inlaid with flowers.

48¾in (124cm) wide

$1,800-2,100   **WW**

An early-20thC Louis XV-style kingwood and amaranth marble-topped bombé commode, with two drawers with sunburst parquetry and foliate gilt-bronze handles and escutcheons, on tall splay feet with further gilt-bronze mounts.

49¾in (126cm) wide

$4,000-4,600   **L&T**

A 20thC dark green-painted and gilt chinoiserie decorated demilune commode, in George III style, decorated with figures in a fishing village scene, above a center frieze drawer and center cupboard door, lappet-molded turned tapering legs.

50in (127cm) wide

$4,000-4,600   **DN**

ESSENTIAL REFERENCE—KINGWOOD

Introduced to Europe in the late 17thC, and initialy known as "princes" wood," kingwood was one of the most expensive hardwoods used in furniture making. Yielded by the "Dalbergia cearensis" tree, which only grows in a small area of Brazil, it is an extremely dense hardwood and difficult to work with, having a tendency to rapidly blunt bladed tools. However, its brownish-purple color with many fine darker stripes, paler streaks, and occasional irregular swirls made it highly prized on aesthetic grounds, especially for use in parquetry work. Closely related hardwoods also used in furniture making included cocobolo, rosewood, and tulipwood.

An early-19thC Régence kingwood and parquetry commode, with ormolu mounts, with rouge royal marble top, above two short and three long drawers, with figural handles and escutcheons.

52½in (133.3cm) wide

$3,300-4,600   **WW**

A Louis XV-style ormolu-mounted kingwood commode, by Henry Dasson, with two drawers, signed and dated 1884, some veneer missing.

1884   *74in (188cm) wide*

$33,000-40,000   **CHEF**

A 20thC Louis XV-style kingwood parquetry marble-top commode, of double serpentine bombé shape, with pierced foliate gilt-metal handles and escutcheons, on bracket feet with further mounts.

43¾in (111cm) wide

$1,500-2,000   **L&T**

A late-17thC William and Mary oak chest-on-stand, the cornice above a cushion-molded drawer over three long molded panel drawers, the stand with a further drawer, on spiral-turned legs with ball feet and a peripheral stretcher.

50in (127cm) high

$2,000-2,600   **L&T**

A Queen Anne walnut chest-on-stand, the molded cornice over three short and three long drawers, on a base with three drawers over an apron and later scrolled legs, the drawers all with checker stringing and crossbanding and original brass handles within double-D moldings, later escutcheons, legs later.

64¼in (163cm) high

$1,600-2,100   **SWO**

A Queen Anne walnut chest-on-stand, with two short and three long featherbanded drawers, the stand fitted with three frieze drawers and an arc d'arbalete apron, on turned legs united by shaped peripheral stretchers.

ca. 1710   *58¼in (148cm) high*

$10,000-10,500   **WW**

A Queen Anne walnut chest-on-stand, with cross and feather banding, the quarter-veneered top above two short and three long graduated drawers, with lobed burl-veneered panels, the stand with later elements and fitted with a long drawer, on bun feet.

ca. 1710   *47¾in (121cm) high*

$2,600-4,000   **WW**

An early-18thC Queen Anne oak chest-on-stand.

60¾in (154cm) high

$1,000-1,100   **L&T**

An early-18thC Queen Anne walnut seaweed marquetry chest-on-stand.

59¾in (152cm) high

$1,600-2,100   **L&T**

A George I walnut and featherbanded chest-on-stand, the cavetto-molded cornice above three short and three long drawers flanked by canted angles, the stand with four short drawers and a shaped apron, on cabriole legs on molded pad feet, scratches and abrasions, some old veneer repairs.

ca. 1720   *67in (170cm) high*

$10,500-12,000   **DN**

An early-18thC George I walnut chest-on-stand, with three short over three long drawers, the base with three drawers and an arched apron, on square cabriole legs on pointed pad feet.

65¼in (165.5cm) high

$13,000-18,000   **L&T**

An early-18thC George II walnut chest-on-stand, the cornice above three short drawers, three long drawers, flanked by fluted angles, the stand with three drawers and a shaped apron, on cabriole legs on pad feet.

67in (170cm) high

$5,300-6,600 **L&T**

An 18thC George II oak and walnut chest-on-chest, the molded cornice above three short and three long drawers, the lower section with one long and three short drawers above a shaped apron, raised on cabriole legs with pointed pad feet.

64¼in (163cm) high

$1,100-1,250 **L&T**

An early-18thC George II walnut chest-on-chest, the molded cornice above three short and three long cross and featherbanded drawers, the lower part with three further drawers, on later bracket feet.

68½in (174cm) high

$4,600-5,900 **L&T**

A mid-18thC George II figured walnut and featherbanded chest-on-stand, on cabriole legs with pad feet.

64¼in (163cm) high

$1,200-1,600 **TEN**

A George III padouk secrétaire chest-on-stand, in the manner of Thomas Chippendale, inlaid with satinwood and ebony stringing, above two short and four long drawers, with original gilt-brass Rococo handles, originally enclosed by a pair of doors, the secrétaire drawer fitted with pigeonholes, with a center cupboard drawer enclosing three drawers and a later leatherette-lined writing surface.

ca. 1765-70 *67¾in (172cm) high*

$2,600-4,000 **WW**

An 18thC Colonial "red walnut" highboy, with molded frieze drawer over two short and three long drawers, the base section with a single deep drawer, on cabriole legs.

71¼in (181cm) high

$800-900 **CHEF**

A Queen Anne walnut and featherbanded cabinet-on-chest, the cavetto-molded cornice above cushion-molded drawer, the panel doors opening to pigeonholes and short drawers around a center cupboard door, the lower section with a baize-inset slide above two short and two long drawers, on bun feet, scratches and abrasions, some old repairs and replacements, the handles and escutcheons are later replacements, the locks are late-18thC examples.

ca. 1710 *68½in (174cm) high*

$10,500-12,000 **DN**

A Queen Anne walnut chest-on-chest, the quarter-veneered crossbanded top above two short and three long cross and featherbanded drawers, the base with two long drawers, on later bun feet.

ca. 1710 *53in (134.3cm) high*

$8,000-9,000 **WW**

An early-18thC George I burl-walnut and marquetry secrétaire cabinet-on-chest, the molded cornice above a cushion frieze drawer, over a pair of quarter-veneered and featherbanded doors with eight featherbanded drawers, the lower part with a secrétaire drawer fitted with pigeonholes and drawers, over three long drawers, the base drawer with a sunburst concave arch, on bracket feet.

71in (180cm) high

$10,500-12,000 **L&T**

A George II burl-elm and walnut chest-on-chest, with two short and six long cross and featherbanded drawers, flanked by canted angles, on bracket feet.

ca. 1730-40　　　　*66in (167.8cm) high*

$6,000-6,600　　　　**WW**

A George II walnut and crossbanded chest-on-chest, the cavetto-shaped cornice above three short and three long drawers, flanked by reeded canted angles, the lower section with three long graduated drawers, on bracket feet, scratches and abrasions, handles and escutcheons are replaced, various old repairs.

ca. 1740　　　　*74¾in (190cm) high*

$8,500-9,000　　　　**DN**

A George II walnut, burl-walnut and featherbanded secrétaire chest-on-chest, the cavetto-molded cornice above three short and three long drawers, the lower section with a hinged fall front secrétaire drawer opening to pigeonholes and small drawers around a center cupboard door, on two long drawers, on bracket feet.

ca. 1740　　　　*72¾in (185cm) high*

$21,000-26,000　　　　**DN**

A mid-18thC George III mahogany chest-on-chest, the dentil-molded cornice above a lancet frieze, above two short and three long drawers, flanked by fluted corner columns with gilt-metal Corinthian capitals, the base with three drawers, on bracket feet.

70in (178cm) high

$7,500-8,500　　　　**L&T**

A George III solid walnut chest-on-chest, the molded cornice above two short and four long drawers, flanked by fluted quarter columns, the lower section with three long drawers, on ogee bracket feet, scratches and abrasions.

ca. 1770　　　　*69¾in (177cm) high*

$4,600-5,900　　　　**DN**

A George III mahogany chest-on-chest, the molded cornice above a slender fluted frieze, above two short and six long drawers.

ca. 1780　　　　*71in (180cm) high*

$6,500-8,000　　　　**DN**

A George III mahogany chest-on-chest, the dentil cornice above a blind fretwork-decorated frieze and eight drawers with gilt-metal Rococo handles, the lower section surmounted by a slide, on bracket feet, scratches and abrasions, the slide with horizontal split in center section, locks are Victorian.

ca. 1780　　　　*74in (188cm) high*

$3,400-4,000　　　　**DN**

An 18thC George III mahogany chest-on-chest, with three short over three long drawers flanked by fluted angles, the lower part with two short over three long drawers, on bracket feet.

70½in (179cm) high

$3,300-4,000　　　　**L&T**

A George III mahogany chest-on-chest, with center brushing slide.

74in (188cm) high

$1,300-1,700   CHEF

A late-18th/early-19thC George III mahogany chest-on-chest, with dentil-carved pediment and two short over three long drawers, with a slender reeded drawer, all to top, and two drawers in base flanked by fluted quarter columns, on bracket feet.

74¾in (190cm) high

$6,000-7,500   L&T

A George III walnut chest-on-chest, with two short and six long drawers, feet are early-20thC replacements.

72½in (184cm) high

$2,600-3,300   CHEF

An early-19thC late Regency mahogany chest-on-chest, with a molded cornice, two short and six long graduated drawers, flanked by canted angles on reeded feet.

69¼in (176cm) high

$4,000-5,300   L&T

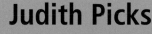

A George I walnut and featherbanded secrétaire cabinet, the doors, opening to two shelves above a center drawer fronted by two false drawer fronts flanked by a drawer on each side, the lower section with a secrétaire fall-fronted drawer, opening to drawers and pigeonholes, above three long drawers, on bracket feet, scratches and abrasions.

ca. 1720   *86¼in (219cm) high*

$7,500-8,500   DN

A George I figured walnut and featherbanded secrétaire cabinet, with molded and mirror inset doors, enclosing 12 drawers, the lower section with a fall-front drawer opening to a tooled leather-inset writing surface and pigeonholes and small drawers, above two short and two long drawers, on bun feet, scratches and abrasions, handles, escutcheons, and feet are replacements.

ca. 1720   *73¾in (187.5cm) high*

$8,000-9,000   DN

An 18thC George III mahogany secrétaire cabinet, the lower section with a gadrooned edge above a secrétaire drawer with a baize skiver, pigeonholes and drawers over a pair of short drawers and three long drawers, on acanthus-carved ogee bracket feet.

65in (165cm) high

$7,500-8,500   L&T

Judith Picks

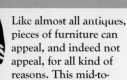

Like almost all antiques, pieces of furniture can appeal, and indeed not appeal, for all kind of reasons. This mid-to-late-19thC French walnut secrétaire, for example, checks a number of boxes for me: I like the bombé shape that's nicely streamlined, not overly bulbous; I like the foliate motif bronze mounts, especially the elegant but sturdy sabots on the shaped feet; I like the fitted interior and the drop-down writing surface that conceals it when closed, which means it doesn't have to sit more obtrusively in a room looking like a desk all the time; I like both the appearance and hard-wearing practicality of its marble top, which, unlike a wooden equivalent, is far less likely to be ring marked or stained by cups or flowerpots that might be left on it from time to time; and, above all, I love the craftsmanship and the visual stimulation of the bold cube parquetry panels and crossbanded borders on the drop-down front and three drawers—oh, and for all of that, I like the price, too!

A 19thC French bombé figured walnut secrétaire.

45¼in (115cm) high

$2,600-3,300   SWO

A George I walnut secrétaire cabinet bookcase, the glazed doors opening to three shelves, flanked by oyster-veneered sides, the lower sections with a drawer incorporating a tooled leather-inset slide, above a pair of feather-banded doors, opening to a shelved interior, on bracket feet.

ca. 1720   73¼in (186cm) high
$1,700-2,100   DN

A mid-18thC George II mahogany lady's secrétaire bookcase, the molded mirrored door flanked by fluted pilasters, opening to adjustable shelves, the lower part with a secrétaire drawer fitted with drawers, pigeonholes, and a leather skiver, over three long drawers, on a plinth base.

Small-scale cabinets with secrétaire drawers are generally considered to have been intended for use in a lady's private dressing room or bedchamber. Their size would be better suited for these personal spaces, designed for intimacy and personal activities, than for the larger public and more formal rooms of the house.

77¼in (196cm) high
$4,600-5,300   L&T

CLOSER LOOK—SECRÉTAIRE BOOKCASE

The top of the bookcase has a broken, stiff arched cornice with a shaped dogtooth and blind fret frieze.

The single door has a shaped mirror within independent, turned and carved columns with blind fret bases and capitals, the door with a dummy escutcheon, opening with one column.

The door opens to reveal adjustable shelves and three drawers, the base with a fitted drawer over three long drawers.

The bookcase has fret cut, shaped bracket feet and four conforming independent carved and brass-mounted columns.

A Chippendale-period mahogany secrétaire bookcase, minor loss in dogtooth frieze, minor veneer loss around secrétaire drawer, one rear foot reattached.

89¾in (228cm) high
$5,300-5,900   SWO

A George III mahogany and inlaid secrétaire bookcase, in the manner of George Hepplewhite, the astragal glazed doors with carved urn terminals, opening to adjustable shelves, the fall-front secrétaire drawer opening to burl-yew veneered and crossbanded drawers and pigeonholes, the pair of cupboard doors beneath opening to a shelved interior, on bracket feet.

ca. 1780   53½in (136cm) high
$4,000-4,600   DN

An 18thC early George III mahogany secrétaire bookcase, with astragal glazed doors enclosing shelves, above a blind-fret carved secrétaire drawer with a fitted interior and four long drawers, flanked by fluted angles, on ogee bracket feet.

83½in (212cm) high
$3,300-4,000   L&T

A late George III mahogany secrétaire bookcase, astragal glazed doors opening to adjustable shelves, the base with a secrétaire drawer with pigeonholes and drawers, above three long drawers, on French bracket feet.

79½in (202cm) high
$1,100-1,250   L&T

An early-19thC Scottish Regency mahogany secrétaire bookcase, astragal glazed doors enclosing shelves, on an associated base with a secrétaire drawer with pigeonholes, drawers, and a leather skiver, over three further long drawers, on later block feet.

87½in (222cm) high
$2,000-2,600   L&T

An early-18thC and later Queen Anne walnut and oak bureau bookcase, the double-arch molded top with turned corner finials, above mirrored doors enclosing drawers and compartments flanked by stop-fluted angles, the associated base opening to pigeonholes, drawers, and compartments, over two short and two long featherbanded drawers, on bracket feet.

85½in (217cm) high

$4,600-5,900　　　　L&T

A Queen Anne walnut and feather-banded bureau bookcase, the doors, opening to a shelved interior, the lower section with a sloped and hinged fall opening to pigeonholes and small drawers centered by a cupboard door, above two short and two long drawers, on bracket feet, the upper and lower sections are associated, scratches and abrasions, locks appear original, all other metalware is replaced.

ca. 1710　　88½in (225cm) high

$2,100-2,600　　　　DN

A George I walnut and feather-banded bureau bookcase, the doors, opening to an adjustable shelf above short drawers and pigeonholes, the lower section with a hinged fall opening to a leather-inset writing surface, a well section with sliding cover and pigeonholes and short drawers, above two short and two long drawers, on bracket feet.

ca. 1720　　82in (208cm) high

$4,000-5,300　　　　DN

A George II walnut and crossbanded bureau bookcase, the doors opening to a shelf above pigeonholes and small drawers, the fall in the lower section opening to baize-inset writing surface, a slide over a well, and pigeonholes and small drawers above two short and three long drawers, on bracket feet, scratches, abrasions.

ca. 1735　　85½in (217cm) high

$3,300-4,600　　　　DN

A George II mahogany bureau bookcase, the door opening to a shelved interior, the lower section with a hinged fall opening to a writing surface, and small drawers and pigeonholes around a center cupboard door, above two short and three long drawers, on bracket feet, scratches and abrasions, leather-inset surface on the fall is later.

ca. 1740　　79½in (202cm) high

$4,000-4,600　　　　DN

A George III mahogany bureau bookcase, the doors, opening to a two shelves, the fall opening to a baize-inset writing surface and an arrangement of pigeonholes and small drawers around a center cupboard doors, above four long graduated drawers, on ogee bracket feet.

ca. 1770　　85in (216cm) high

$6,000-6,600　　　　DN

One of a pair of George III mahogany bureau bookcases, doors opening to a shelved interior and two short drawers, the lower section with a hinged fall opening to pigeonholes and drawers around a parquetry and mirrored recess, the unit making up the mirrored recess removing to reveal three further drawers, above four long drawers, on bracket feet, scratches and abrasions, various old repairs to pierced pediments.

The fretwork friezes of the pediments of these bureau bookcases and waist molding are taken from a design by William Pain illustrated with designs for chimneypieces in "The Builder's Companion and Workman's General Assistant," 1758, pl. 62. Similar rounded cupboard door panels appear on a design for a library bookcase by Thomas Chippendale published in "The Gentleman and Cabinet-Maker's Director," 1st ed., 1754, pl. LXVII. Chippendale also introduced fretwork friezes topped by urns on the flanking elements of a bookcases he designed in 1759, published in the third edition of his Director, 1762. In addition, the fine carving on the edges surrounding the mirror plates are also demonstrated by cabinets and bookcases by Giles Grendey, for an example bearing Grendey's trade label, see Christopher Gilbert, "Marked London Furniture," Furniture History Society, 1996, p. 240, fig. 432.

ca. 1790　　78¼in (199cm) high

$6,500-8,000 the pair　　　　DN

An 18thC Irish George III mahogany bureau bookcase, the molded bonnet-top pediment above a pair of arched molded panel doors opening to shelves and pigeonholes and a center cupboard inlaid with a kilted soldier, above a molded panel slant front enclosing a leather skiver and further pigeonholes, drawers, and secret compartments and another door with a kilted soldier, above four long drawers, on bracket feet.

96in (244cm) high

$8,000-9,000　　　　L&T

FURNITURE

A mid-18thC George III mahogany breakfront bookcase, the astragal glazed doors, enclosing shelves, the lower part with cupboards, on a plinth base.

100¾in (256cm) wide

$8,000-9,000 L&T

A George III mahogany library bookcase, the doors opening to shelves, the lower section with molded panel cupboard doors, each opening to a shelved interior, on a plinth base.

ca. 1780 *103½in (263cm) high*

$4,000-4,600 DN

A George III mahogany breakfront secrétaire library bookcase, in the manner of Thomas Chippendale, the glazed doors opening to shelves, the lower section with a secrétaire drawer flanked by a drawer on each side, above a pair of panel doors and a panel door on each side, opening to a shelved interiors, on a plinth base, with scratches and abrasions.

ca. 1780 *107in (272cm) high*

$6,500-8,000 DN

A George III mahogany breakfront library bookcase, the doors opening to shelves, the lower center section with a pair of field-paneled cupboard doors opening to shelves, flanked by three drawers on each side, on a plinth base, scratches and abrasions.

ca. 1780 *97in (246cm) high*

$4,000-4,600 DN

A George III mahogany breakfront library bookcase, the doors opening to shelves, the base section with four paneled doors opening to fitted drawers, on a plinth base.

For a design of bookcase adopting a similar design of astragal glazing and fitted drawers with circular handles, see Elizabeth White, "Pictorial Dictionary of British 18th Century Furniture Design," Antique Collectors Club, 1990, p. 243, where pl. 45 illustrates a bookcase design from Hepplewhite's "The Cabinet Maker and Upholsterer's Guide." See also Thomas Chippendale," The Gentleman and Cabinet Maker's Director," (Third Edition 1762), Republished John Tiranti Ltd, 1939, pl. LXXXVII, "Two Bookcases" for a bookcase demonstrating the same design of door panel, the molding shaped at the corners to accomadate distinctive, finely carved patera terminals.

ca. 1780 *144in (366cm) wide*

$10,500-12,000 DN

A George III mahogany library breakfront bookcase, the later cornice above geometric glazed doors enclosing shelves, the base with cupboard doors, with outline moldings and turned rondels, enclosing shelves.

ca. 1780 *85½in (217cm) wide*

$7,500-8,500 WW

A mahogany library double breakfront bookcase, the stepped and Greek-key molded cornice above six astragal glazed doors opening to shelves, the lower section with a fluted and roundel molded frieze above molded panel cupboard doors opening to shelves, on a plinth base.

ca. 1790 and later *109in (277cm) high*

$12,000-15,000 DN

A George III mahogany breakfront library bookcase, the doors flanked by a further door on each side, opening to shelves, the lower section with a pair of paneled doors flanked by a further door on each side, opening to a shelved interior, on bracket feet.

ca. 1790 *104¼in (265cm) wide*

$5,300-6,600 DN

A mid-19thC mahogany breakfront library bookcase, in George III style, the doors opening to shelves, the lower section with four roundel molded cupboard doors with trays, on bracket feet, with scratches and abrasions, the interiors of the lower cupboards are all later in date.

97¼in (247cm) high

$6,500-8,000 DN

An 18thC George III stripped-pine breakfront bookcase, the doors enclosing shelves, the lower section with four panel-molded doors enclosing further shelves, on a plinth base.

88½in (225cm) wide

$6,000-6,600 L&T

An early-19thC Regency mahogany and ebonized breakfront bookcase, the doors opening to shelves, the projecting base with three cupboard doors outlined with ebonized molding, opening to shelves, on bracket feet.

90½in (230cm) high

$4,000-4,600 L&T

ESSENTIAL REFERENCE—ST JOHN HORNBY

Provenance: Charles Harold St John Hornby (1867-1946), Chantmarle House, Dorset. St John Hornby, as he was widely known, was both a successful businessman and a private printer. Educated at Harrow and New College, Oxford, Hornby rowed, as stroke, for the university boat in 1890 and the following year traveled the world with his college friend W. F. D. (Freddy) Smith, later Lord Hambledon. Smith asked Hornby to join him on the board of his family firm, W. H. Smith & Son, and the firm remained dominant in their industry and survived World War I under his guidance. Hornby's main passions, outside his work, were the Ashendene Press, his private press, initially based in Hertfordshire but subsequently in Shelley House on the Chelsea Embankment. Hornby had met Emery Walker and Sydney Cockerell (then William Morris's secretary at the Kelmscott Press) in 1900 and they encouraged Hornby to have the typefaces "Subiaco" and "Ptolemy" specifically designed for the press. Ashendene went on to produce many highly regarded and limited books. In 1919, Hornby bought Chantmarle in Dorset, a fine but remodeled house that had started life out as a manor house for the monks of Milton Abbey in the 13thC. It was here that Hornby commissioned the Barnsleys, Powells, and Waals to furnish his new house, and an article in "Country Life" of July 7, 1950, shows a number of pieces of furniture by both Ernest and Sidney Barnsley as well as a set of plates by the Powells illustrating aspects of Hornby's life and interests. The same article also states "The products of the Gimson-Barnsley school are little heard of today, but by breaking with traditional forms and concentrating on simplicity of design, fine finish and beautiful woods, they anticipated in their hand-made pieces several of the ideals of later designers who have accepted the aid of the machine."

A mid-19thC Gothic Revival parcel-gilt oak library bookcase, of inverted breakfront outline, the molded frieze set with carved quatrefoils centered by molded gesso roses, fleur-de-lis, and carnations, above doors enclosing shelves, the lower part with a pair of triple trefoil arch-molded doors flanked by projecting open tiers divided by molded "buttress" pilasters, on a plinth base.

149¾in (380cm) wide

$17,000-21,000 L&T

A Victorian mahogany breakfront library bookcase, the doors opening to shelves, flanked on each side by fluted pilasters surmounted by lappet- and patera-carved capitals, the lower section with four paneled cupboard doors opening to shelves and fitted drawers, on a plinth base.

ca. 1870 *99¾in (253.5cm) high*

$6,500-8,000 DN

A Gothic Revival oak and pollard-oak cabinet breakfront bookcase, with a pair of center lancet-molded and glazed doors, flanked by a molded panel dooron each side, opening to adjustable shelves, on a plinth base.

ca. 1880 *89in (226cm) high*

$13,000-16,000 DN

A walnut breakfront bookcase, by Sidney Barnsley, the center double, glazed doors flanked by single doors, above glazed curtained doors, constructed with dovetail joints, chip-carved ebony banding, on sleigh feet, the shallow overmantel inlaid with ebony diamond band and chip-carved beading, with patinated bronze door furniture.

89½in (227.5cm) high

$33,000-40,000 WW

An early-20thC Edwardian mahogany breakfront library bookcase, with four open sections with adjustable shelves, on a projecting base with four banks of drawers and a plinth base.

134in (340cm) wide

$6,000-6,600 L&T

An 18thC George III mahogany library bookcase, the doors enclosing a shelved interior, the lower section with two doors with X moldings, enclosing shelves, on a plinth base.

93¾in (238cm) high

$5,300-6,600   **L&T**

A late-18th/early-19thC George III mahogany library bookcase, the doors enclosing shelves, the lower part with paneled doors, on a plinth base.

102in (259cm) high

$4,000-5,300   **L&T**

A Victorian mahogany library bookcase, the doors enclosing three sets of shelves, on a base with four cupboard doors, bearing an "Army & Navy Stores" label, general wear.

84¼in (214cm) wide

$3,300-4,000   **SWO**

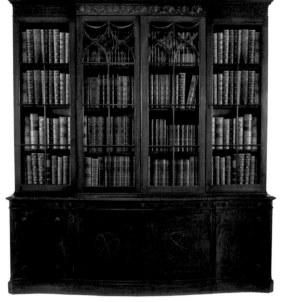

A mid-18thC mahogany bookcase, of Pepysian type, the doors opening to shelves, the pair of lower twin paneled doors opening to a shelved interior, on bracket feet, scratches and abrasions, evidence of old worm.

A late 20thC mahogany library bookcase, in George III style, the doors opening to shelves, the serpentine-front lower section with four slides above four cupboard doors applied with stylized fan and patera terminals, on a plinth base.

86½in (220cm) high

$10,500-12,000   **DN**

A George I walnut cabinet bookcase, the doors opening to adjustable shelves, the doors beneath opening to a shelved interior, on bracket feet, scratches and abrasions.

ca. 1720   *78in (198cm) high*

$4,000-5,300   **DN**

An unusual feature of this bookcase is that the profile of the glazing bars of the upper section has also been used to bisect the panels of the lower section. The profile of the thick glazing bars also suggests dating the bookcase to the second quarter of the 18thC. The same profile of glazing bars is present in the windows of several Spitalfields houses of the period. In addition, the use of mahogany is evident in the construction of the documented staircase at 4-6 Fournier Street, Spitalfields. Mahogany was also known to have been used at Houghton Hall and various churches at this early period. For further discussion and evidence of the early mahogany trade and use of the wood, See Adam Bowett, "The English mahogany trade 1700-1793," thesis, 1996.

91¾in (233cm) high

$4,000-5,300   **DN**

A George III satinwood and tulipwood bookcase, in the manner of Mayhew and Ince, the molded cornice above a fluted inlaid frieze flanked by patera terminals, above a pair of doors opening to three shelves, flanked by tapering pilasters, the lower section with a pair of oval inlaid panel doors opening to a shelved interior, on a plinth base.

ca. 1780   *89in (226cm) high*

$24,000-26,000   **DN**

A late-18thC bookcase, the doors opening to shelves, the lower part with a secrétaire drawer fitted with pigeonholes and drawers and a leather skiver, above three long drawers, raised on French bracket feet.

94½in (240cm) high

$2,600-3,300   **L&T**

An early-19thC Regency mahogany and ebony bookcase, the doors opening to shelves, the projecting base with a frieze drawer over panel doors flanked by reeded columns, opening to shelves and a base drawer, on paw feet.

90½in (230cm) high

$1,100-1,250   **L&T**

A Regency mahogany and brass-mounted cabinet bookcase, the doors opening to two banks of shelves, the lower section with a pair of drawers and a pair of brass-grille paneled doors opening to adjustable doors, on saber-shaped feet.

ca. 1815   *87in (221cm) high*

$6,500-8,000   **DN**

An early-19thC William IV mahogany and gilt-metal mounted bookcase/cabinet, the Gothic doors between columns with Corinthian gilt-metal capitals, the lower section with egg-and-dart molded edge over a frieze drawer and two paneled doors between columns, on a plinth base.

67in (170cm) high

$1,600-2,100   **L&T**

A late-19thC French mahogany and gilt-metal mounted bookcase, the doors enclosing shelves above a brushing slide and pair of further panels doors enclosing slide drawers, on a plinth base and spool feet, knocks, scratches.

101¼in (257cm) high

$2,100-2,600   **DN**

A late-19thC Victorian oak open bookcase, the molded cornice above divided shelves, the lower part with a pair of panel doors, on a plinth base.

100¾in (256cm) high

$800-900   **L&T**

One of a pair of 20thC pine bookcases, in early-18thC style, of Pepysian form, the doors opening to adjustable shelves, the lower sections with acanthus and flower-head carved frieze above a pair of panel doors, on a plinth base.

This form of bookcase was first made by the Master Joiner Thomas Simpson (alias Sympson the Joiner) for the naval administrator and diarist Samuel Pepys to house his vast collection of books at his residence at Seething Lane, London. It is possible that Pepys himself had a hand in the design of the bookcase.

78¼in (199cm) high

$11,000-13,000 the pair   **DN**

FURNITURE

A George III mahogany cartonnier, the top and sides surmounted by a foliate terminal, enclosing three shelves, on foliate carved feet, scratches and abrasions.

In England, this cartonnier type can be traced to a tall medal case pattern that Batty Langley issued in the "City and Country Builders and Workman's Treasury of Designs," dated 1740.

ca. 1780   *36¾in (93cm) wide*

$4,000-5,300   DN

Judith Picks

Combine the never-ending acquisition of an extensive antiques, architectural, and interior design reference library with an undimmed appetite for fiction, and you can understand why, much to my husband's recurring consternation, we're forever running out of shelf space. There's reason alone to covet this pair of turn-of-the-19thC, late-Georgian bookcases! However, there's also the solidity of their solid mahogany construction, the elegant practicality of their graduated shelf "waterfall" design, allowing the accommodation of books of varying size, the usefulness of the under drawers,

their caster-rolling movability and, of course, the impeccable provenance of their manufacturer, Gillows (of Lancaster and London), whose reputation as cabinetmakers during the 18thC and 19thC was such that their furniture received honorable mentions in, a Jane Austen and a Thackeray novel and one of Gilbert and Sullivan's comic operas!

A pair of George III mahogany waterfall bookcases, by Gillows, with brass side-carrying handles, the lower shelf with two drawers, on tapering legs terminating in brass caps and casters, one drawer of each bookcase stamped "GILLOWS, LANCASTER."

ca. 1800   *44in (112cm) high*

$17,000-24,000   DN

A late-18th/early-19thC George III inlaid satinwood and mahogany waterfall bookcase, with a three-quarter brass gallery.

50¾in (129cm) high

$2,400-2,900   L&T

An early-19thC Regency mahogany waterfall bookcase.

56¼in (143cm) high

$2,100-2,600   L&T

A Regency mahogany double-sided open bookcase, in the manner of Gillows, on bulbous turned feet, brass caps and casters, stamped "B. S, & P. Patent."

31¼in (79cm) high

$4,600-5,300   CHEF

An early-19thC Regency mahogany, rosewood, and ebonized small bookcase, the frieze drawer with star and lozenge inlay flanked by carved roundels, above shelves, on a plinth base.

39¾in (101cm) high

$2,400-2,900   L&T

An early-19thC Regency rosewood bookcase.

41in (104cm) wide

$2,100-2,600   L&T

A Regency mahogany double-sided waterfall bookcase, by Mack, Williams & Gibton, the frieze with an unusual lockable compartment, stamped with numbers "9564," scratches and abrasions.

The original partners John Mack and Robert Gibton are listed in the Dublin directories individually from 1784 and 1790, respectively, and appear to have come into partnership from 1803. They were appointed "Upholsterers & Cabinet Makers to his Majesty, His Excellency the Lord Lieutenant and His Majesty's Board of Works" in 1806 and the firm retained this Royal Warranty for many years, supplying and restoring furniture for important public buildings in Ireland, including the Four Courts, the War Office, the Barracks Office, Dublin Castle, and the Treasury and Viceregal Lodge. Some of their more distinguished private commissions include Ballynegall, Co. Westmeath, Oakley Park, Co. Meath, and Strokestown, Co. Roscommon. As demonstrated by the current bookcase, the firm regularly labeled their furniture and used a system of an impressed four-digit number, often together with a letter.

ca. 1815   *55¼in (140cm) high*

$3,300-4,000   DN

One of a pair of George IV mahogany side cabinets, in the manner of Gillows, the gilt metal-grille doors opening to a shelved interior, flanked by tapering reeded uprights incorporating lappet and flower-head carving, on a plinth base.

ca. 1825 — 66¼in (168cm) wide

$15,000-17,000 the pair — **DN**

A George IV mahogany revolving bookcase, in the manner of Morgan and Sanders, the three shelves with faux book divisions and surmounted by a fir-cone finial, the stem, above the triform concave-sided base, on stylized lion-paw feet.

ca. 1825 — 63in (160cm) high

$3,300-4,600 — **DN**

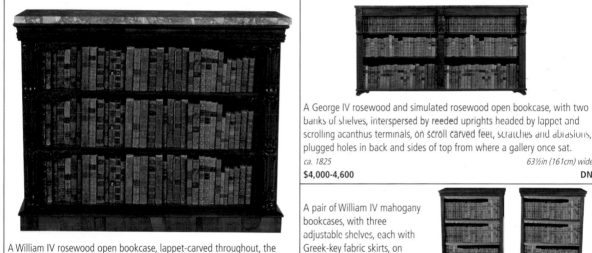

A William IV rosewood open bookcase, lappet-carved throughout, the marble top above three shelves, on a plinth base, scratches and abrasions.

ca. 1835 — 48in (122cm) wide

$2,600-4,000 — **DN**

A George IV rosewood and simulated rosewood open bookcase, with two banks of shelves, interspersed by reeded uprights headed by lappet and scrolling acanthus terminals, on scroll carved feet, scratches and abrasions, plugged holes in back and sides of top from where a gallery once sat.

ca. 1825 — 63½in (161cm) wide

$4,000-4,600 — **DN**

A pair of William IV mahogany bookcases, with three adjustable shelves, each with Greek-key fabric skirts, on molded plinth bases.

ca. 1835 — 45½in (115.5cm) high

$4,000-5,300 — **DN**

A 19thC rosewood double-sided library bookcase, the top inset with gilt tooled leather, with two adjustable shelves on each side, with paneled ends and fluted corners, on brass casters, the iron mount stamped "COPE'S PATENT."

42.5in (108cm) high

$3,300-4,000 — **WW**

One of a pair of Victorian bird's-eye maple and parcel-gilt open bookcases, in the manner of Holland & Sons.

Henry Holland produced designs for similar open bookcases and Holland & Sons are known to have executed various pieces in bird's-eye maple with parcel-gilt highlights.

ca. 1860 — 48in (122cm) high

$7,500-8,000 the pair — **DN**

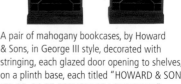

A pair of mahogany bookcases, by Howard & Sons, in George III style, decorated with stringing, each glazed door opening to shelves, on a plinth base, each titled "HOWARD & SONS LTD 25, 26 27 BERNERS ST, LONDON W."

ca. 1890 — 76½in (194.5cm) high

$8,500-9,000 — **DN**

FURNITURE

An olivewood, kingwood, and oyster-veneered cabinet-on-stand, with geometric patterned cupboard doors, the interior with 10 drawers around a center cupboard door, the stand with a long frieze drawer, on spiral-turned supports, right-hand cupboard door split through the center, the spiral-turned legs and stretcher are of later date, stand is Victorian.

ca. 1685   *66¼in (168cm) high*

$16,000-20,000   **TEN**

A William and Mary yew and burl-yew cabinet-on-chest, inlaid with checker and holly banding, doors enclosing 10 drawers around a center cupboard, enclosing four further drawers, the waist molding inset with a brushing slide, above two short and three long drawers, later bracket feet.

ca. 1690-1700   *69½in (176.5cm) high*

$6,500-8,000   **WW**

A late-17thC and later William and Mary walnut oyster-veneered cabinet-on-stand, the doors centered by concentric circles enclosing nine drawers around a center cupboard, the stand with two frieze drawers, on spiral-twist legs.

60¾in (154cm) high

$8,000-9,000   **L&T**

A Queen Anne walnut and featherbanded escritoire, the fall front opening to a baize-inset surface and small drawers and pigeonholes around a center cupboard door, the pigeonhole sections removing to reveal hidden drawers, the lower section with three drawers, on bracket feet, scratches and abrasions.

ca. 1710   *61in (155cm) high*

$3,300-4,000   **DN**

A George II walnut crossbanded mahogany bureau cabinet, with original engraved brass hardware, doors enclosing shelves and three drawers above candle slides, the base with well-fitted interior above four drawers on shaped bracket feet, scratches, abrasions, glazing on the doors later.

ca. 1740   *92in (234cm) high*

$7,500-8,500   **DN**

A George III mahogany cabinet-on-chest.

ca. 1780   *77½in (197cm) high*

$4,000-5,300   **DN**

An 18thC George III mahogany cabinet-on-stand.

68¼in (173cm) high

$850-1,000   **L&T**

A Regency mahogany library cabinet, with a fold-over writing surface, two "silked" and grilled doors below.

52¾in (134cm) high

$850-1,000   **CHEF**

A mid-19thC Dutch Colonial ebony cabinet, the doors with double-turned columns, over an inverted breakfront base.

82¾in (210cm) high

$6,000-6,600 **SWO**

A 19thC Scottish estate-built factor's cabinet.

75½in (192cm) high

$4,000-4,600 **L&T**

A 19thC ebonized boulle marquetry collectors cabinet-on-stand, doors opening to 11 drawers, the stand with a frieze drawer, raised on spiral-turned legs.

54¼in (138cm) high

$1,050-1,300 **L&T**

An early-20thC French walnut and gilt-bronze mounted side cabinet, of reverse breakfront form.

87in (221cm) wide

$1,050-1,300 **DN**

ESSENTIAL REFERENCE—MORISON & CO

Morison & Co. were cabinetmakers and upholsterers established by Mathew Morison in Ayr, Scotland, ca. 1808.

James Morison took over the business from his father. By the time of his death, on June 2, 1862, the cabinetmaker was based in Edinburgh and trading as Morison & Co. William Reid worked for the company and took over the business on James's death. William Reid's eldest son William Robert Reid (1854-1919) was made partner in the business in 1884. The company expanded to become one of the leading cabinetmakers in Scotland and branches were opened in Glasgow and Manchester. The company was one of the first to undertake architectural restoration and the first in Scotland to construct the interiors of trains-de-luxe, for which it became renowned. W. R. Reid ran the company until he sold it in 1902. The company was purchased by W Turner Lord and Co of London, which continued to use the Morison and Co. name.

A French kingwood, Sèvres-style porcelain and gilt-metal mounted vitrine.

ca. 1870 *91¾in (233cm) high*

$5,300-5,900 **DN**

A French rosewood Vernis Martin vitrine, in Louis XV style, with ormolu mounts with espagnolettes, Rococo scrolls, leaves, and rocaille, of bombé form, the base with five painted panels of landscapes, cherubs, and an amorous couple.

ca. 1880 *81in (205.5cm) high*

$6,500-8,000 **WW**

An early-20thC Edwardian mahogany folio cabinet, by Morison & Co. Edinburgh, the door opening to shallow compartments, above open shelves and vertical compartments, the back stamped "MORISON & CO." and "A4954."

62¼in (158cm) high

$2,000-2,600 **L&T**

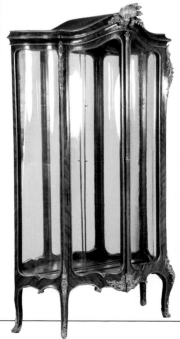

A French kingwood and gilt-metal mounted vitrine, of serpentine outline, the glazed shelves enclosed by a pair of glazed doors, with mirrored back, scratches and abrasions.

ca. 1880 *83in (211cm) high*

$33,000-40,000 **DN**

A late-19thC Dutch mahogany and marquetry inlaid display cabinet.

86¼in (219.5cm) high

$3,300-4,000 **DN**

A late-19thC French mahogany Vernis Martin and gilt-bronze mounted display cabinet, on cabriole legs.

78in (198cm) high

$3,300-4,000 **L&T**

A late-19thC Victorian oak display cabinet-on-stand, in the manner of Robert Lorimer.

66½in (169cm) high

$6,000-6,600 **L&T**

A French mahogany and Vernis Martin vitrine, in Louis XV style, with ormolu mounts, the marble top above a glazed door, flanked by glazed concave panels, the base with three painted panels depicting a lady and a gentleman in landscapes.

ca. 1890-1900 *63¼in (160.6cm) high*

$1,200-1,600 **WW**

A Queen Anne figured-walnut collector's cabinet, with a quarter-veneered door, opening to pigeonholes above short drawers, scratches and abrasions, hinges have been replaced, feet are later associated.

ca. 1710 *21in (53cm) high*

$2,600-3,300 **DN**

A George III rosewood and satinwood crossbanded side cabinet, in the manner of Thomas Sheraton, the grille doors opening to a shelved interior, flanked by a concave false grille door on each side, scratches and abrasions.

ca. 1790 *38½in (98cm) high*

$7,500-8,000 **DN**

A late-18thC George III satinwood inlaid secrétaire cabinet, with a secrétaire drawer with oval inlay, fitted with pigeonholes, drawers, and a leather skiver, over a fall front enclosing three drawers, on square tapered legs.

39in (99cm) high

$3,300-4,000 **L&T**

An 18thC Continental scarlet tortoiseshell, rosewood, ebonized, and gilt-metal mounted cabinet, the cavetto-molded top with a long drawer, above 10 drawers around a pair of doors, the doors opening to a mirrored interior incorporating columns and carved figures, the base with two frieze drawers, on egg-and-dart feet.

51½in (131cm) wide

$8,000-9,000 **DN**

A pair of early-19thC Regency rosewood brass inlaid side cabinets, the tops outlined with key and sawtooth brass banding, above pairs of doors with brass grilles.

51½in (131cm) wide

$26,000-33,000 **L&T**

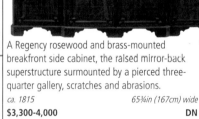

One of a pair of George III figured mahogany side cabinets or serving tables, in the manner of Thomas Sheraton, with a center frieze drawer flanked by a false drawer front on each side, with scratches and abrasions.

ca. 1810 *50¾in (129cm) wide*

$11,000-13,000 the pair **DN**

A Regency fiddleback mahogany and brass mounted breakfront side cabinet, in the French manner, with three frieze drawers and four brass grille cupboard doors.

78in (198cm) wide

$10,500-12,000 **WW**

One of a matched pair of rosewood and gilt-metal mounted side cabinets, one cabinet opening to eight drawers, the other opening to a shelved interior.

ca. 1815 and later *42¼in (107cm) wide*

$7,500-8,500 the pair **DN**

A Regency rosewood and brass-mounted breakfront side cabinet, the raised mirror-back superstructure surmounted by a pierced three-quarter gallery, scratches and abrasions.

ca. 1815 *65¾in (167cm) wide*

$3,300-4,000 **DN**

An early-19thC Regency rosewood, gilt, and brass inlaid side cabinet.

43¼in (110cm) wide

$850-1,000 **L&T**

An early-19thC Regency rosewood marble-topped breakfront side cabinet.

72½in (184cm) wide

$2,600-3,300 **L&T**

An early-19thC Regency rosewood side cabinet.

41¼in (105cm) wide

$1,100-1,250 **L&T**

An early-19thC Regency Tunbridge-ware harewood and Goncalo alves collector's table cabinet, by Robinson's Manufactory, inlaid with stringing and with five parquetry panels of specimen woods, the doors revealing two short and four long cedar drawers with silver-plated handles, the top right drawer with a printed paper label "From Robinson's Manufactory No.53 Piccadilly and Tunbridge Wells."

11¾in (30cm) high

$2,000-2,600   **WW**

A Regency rosewood breakfront side cabinet, with parcel-gilt decoration and egg-and-dart and nulled moldings, with a pair of brass-grille and pleated-silk doors enclosing shelves, flanked by fluted pilasters, with applied corbels and two further conforming cupboards, on bun feet.

ca. 1815-20   *72in (183cm) wide*

$12,000-15,000   **WW**

An English black-lacquer and gilt chinoiserie decorated cabinet-on-stand, the doors each decorated with perching ho-ho birds, opening to small drawers and pigeonholes around a removable slide fronted drawer concealing hidden drawers.

ca. 1815-25   *52¾in (134cm) high*

$5,300-6,600   **DN**

An early-19thC George IV marble-topped amboyna, partridge wood, and ebonized side cabinet, flanked by protruding sphinxes raised on a plinth.

35in (89cm) wide

$3,300-4,600   **L&T**

A George IV mahogany side cabinet, in the manner of Gillows.

ca. 1825   *72in (182.5cm) wide*

$1,700-2,100   **DN**

A George IV mahogany side cabinet, the frieze centered by a lappet and foliate mount and flanked by roundels, above a pair of brass grille doors, opening to a shelved interior, scratches and abrasions.

ca. 1825   *43¼in (110cm) wide*

$4,000-4,600   **DN**

A William IV rosewood side cabinet, by Holland & Sons, the top of one door stamped "HOLLAND & SONS, 50904," the inside of the same door stamped "FROM TAPRELL, HOLLAND & SON, Upholsterers & c, 19 Marylebone St , ST. James S, LONDON," scratches and abrasions, some old splits and chips.

ca. 1835   *72½in (184cm) wide*

$6,500-8,000   **DN**

A mid-19thC Victorian burl-walnut, walnut, ebonized and marquetry side cabinet, of breakfront outline, the door with an oval reserve with a musical trophy, opening to shelves, flanked and divided by ebonized columns and further panels with torches, with gilt metal mounts.

53½in (136cm) wide

$3,300-4,000   **L&T**

A Victorian burl-walnut and eboniszd display cabinet, in the manner of Holland and Sons, with gilt-brass mounts and inlaid with stringing, crossbanded in harewood and purpleheart.

49½in (125.5cm) wide

$1,500-1,800 WW

A Napoleon III ebony and boulle marquetry side cabinet, attributed to Mathieu Befort Dit Befort Jeune, with gilt-bronze mounts, the doors decorated with two of the four seasons, Ceres and Saturn, the sides with Hercules masks, the underside of the top with a label, "Lady Vernet," dated "Aug. 6 1875."

Provenance: Lady Alice Emily Verner (1853-1908), who married Christopher Neville Bagot (1827-77) in 1875. This meuble d'appui can be firmly attributed to the cabinetmaker Matthieu Befort called Befort Jeune who was recorded at Neuves-Saint-Gilles from 1844 until 1880. He specialized in furniture in the Louis XIV and Régence style and copied a number of pieces from those periods. One of his most famous works was a copy of André-Charles Boulle's armoire à medaille.

ca. 1875 *49¾in (126.5cm) wide*

$8,500-9,000 WW

A 19thC Victorian walnut, ebonized, and inlay gilt-metal mounted side cabinet, the center door inlaid wtih a musical trophy, foliate scrolls, and line inlay, flanked by curved glazed doors enclosing shelves.

60¼in (153cm) wide

$1,500-2,000 L&T

A late-19thC Napoleon III brass, tortoiseshell, and ebonized boulle marquetry side cabinet, of arc en arbelette form.

50½in (128cm) wide

$6,500-8,000 L&T

A pair of 19thC Scandinavian purpleheart and burl-ash marble-topped ecoigneurs.

31½in (80cm) high

$850-1,000 L&T

A Victorian satinwood, tulipwood, and polychrome-painted side cabinet, in Sheraton Revival taste, the top with floral swags and Classical maidens, above a center pair of doors, each decorated with a flowering basket, flanked by doors with a Classical maiden.

ca. 1890 *60¼in (153cm) wide*

$2,600-3,300 DN

A French kingwood and Vernis Martin bijouterie cabinet, of bombé outline, the door painted with lovers in a landscape, the glass with scratches and marks; the front piece is plastic and not glass, this is a replacement, the other panels are glass.

ca. 1900 *47¼in (120cm) high*

$4,600-5,300 DN

FURNITURE

A pair of late-18thC Italian walnut bedside cabinets.

24¾in (63cm) high

$4,000-4,600   **DN**

A George III mahogany bedside cabinet, the top with shaped three-quarter gallery with carrying handles, above the hinged fall door and shaped apron, scratches and abrasions, handle is a period replacement.

ca. 1780   *45¼in (115cm) high*

$5,300-6,600   **DN**

A pair of mid-19thC William IV bird's-eye maple marble-topped bedside cupboards.

34¼in (87cm) high

$3,300-4,000   **L&T**

A matched pair of Victorian mahogany bedside cabinets, by Holland & Sons, each with a panel door opening to a shelved interior, each door stamped "HOLLAND & SONS."

ca. 1850   *32¾in (83cm) high*

$2,600-3,300   **DN**

An early-20thC Whytock and Reid mahogany bedside cabinet.

32in (81cm) high

$1,600-2,100   **L&T**

A George III mahogany night commode, the galleried top with pierced handles, the pair of doors above a further drawer with a shaped apron, on square-section legs.

ca. 1780   *31¼in (79cm) high*

$1,800-2,400   **DN**

A George III mahogany night commode, with shaped gallery with pierced side-carrying handles, above a pair of cupboard doors and a lower drawer, scratches and abrasions, seat panel from commode drawer has been removed.

ca. 1780   *29½in (75cm) high*

$2,000-2,600   **DN**

A matched pair of George III mahogany bedside commodes, in the manner of Thomas Chippendale, each top with pierced and shaped galley with carrying handles, above a drawer and a pair of cupboard doors, the lower drawer with a shaped apron.

ca. 1780   *31¼in (79cm) high*

$4,000-5,300   **DN**

A pair of mid-20thC burl-walnut, mahogany, and gilt-metal mounted petit commodes or bedside chests, in Louis Phillipe style.

32in (81cm) high

$4,600-5,300   **DN**

A 17thC Italian Baroque walnut credenza, Tuscany, the top above a pair of lozenge paneled drawers, above a pair of conforming doors enclosing a shelf.

51¼in (130cm) wide

$5,300-6,600   **WW**

A 19thC Napoleon III ebonized, brass and red tortoiseshell boulle credenza and mirror, the mirror in a première and contre partie boulle marquetry and ebonized frame with gilt-metal ribbon-tied mount.

96in (244cm) high

$3,300-4,000   **L&T**

A 19thC Victorian walnut credenza, the doors with foliate scroll inlay, flanked by curved glazed doors enclosing shelves, flanked by tapered columns with brass foliate mounts.

72in (183cm) wide

$2,400-2,900   **L&T**

A late-19thC Victorian gilt-bronze mounted walnut, amboyna, and mahogany credenza, the door centered by a Sèvres-style porcelain plaque and foliate line inlay, opening to shelved interior, flanked by mirrored open quarter-round shelves.

54in (137cm) wide

$3,300-4,000   **L&T**

An early-19thC Regency rosewood secrétaire chiffonier, with two tiers and pierced gallery with brass trellis supports, mirror back, above secrétaire drawer with baize writing surface, center cupboard flanked by pigeonholes, above a pair of doors with brass grille inserts, claw-and-ball gilt feet.

55¼in (140cm) high

$2,400-2,900   **L&T**

An early-19thC Regency mahogany and ebony chiffonier, the waterfall top with two shelves and a pierced brass gallery, above a base with a pair of frieze drawers over panel doors enclosing a shelf.

48in (122cm) high

$1,000-1,100   **L&T**

A Regency rosewood chiffonier, the frieze decorated with a gilt gesso rope-twist molding above two pairs of cupboard doors, the top with infilled holes where a raised back would be.

74½in (189cm) wide

$1,800-2,400   **CHEF**

A 19thC William IV Goncalo alves chiffonier, attributed to Gillows.

53½in (136cm) high

$1,600-2,100   **L&T**

FURNITURE

A late George III mahogany sideboard, the crossbanded bowfront top over a center drawer and arch recess flanked by a deep drawer and a cupboard, on tapered legs with spade feet and brass caps and casters.

51½in (131cm) wide

$1,600-2,100   **L&T**

An 18thC late George III mahogany serpentine sideboard, the stage back above a serpentine base with three frieze drawers flanked by deep drawers, on square tapered legs outlined with stringing.

85½in (217cm) wide

$4,000-4,600   **L&T**

A George III mahogany breakfront sideboard, the brass rear gallery above the center drawer section, flanked by a drawer and a cupboard door on one side, and a deep cellaret drawer on the other, on fluted tapering legs.

ca. 1800   *83in (211cm) wide*

$1,700-2,400   **DN**

An early-19thC mahogany serpentine sideboard, the fitted center drawer, flanked by cellaret drawer and single drawers, on square tapered legs on casters.

72½in (184cm) wide

$8,000-9,000   **L&T**

An early-19thC Scottish George III mahogany and inlaid sideboard, the top above a center drawer and arched recess, flanked by banks of short drawers and a deep drawer, separated by fan medallions.

71¾in (182cm) wide

$2,100-2,600   **L&T**

CLOSER LOOK—REGENCY SIDEBOARD

Based on ornate dishes known in Latin as "pateras," and originally used in religious ceremonies, the patera became a much-employed decorative motif in the Neoclassical vocabulary of ornament during the late 18thC and early 19thC.

As with many other late-18thC and early-19thC fine-quality buffet-style sideboards, this one includes a pair of cellarets.

While the four cupboard door pulls on the stage back above are in the form of brass rosettes, the six ring pulls on the drawers below are brass wreaths.

The sideboard's six tapering, ring-turned legs, like the pilasters directly above them and on the stage back, feature sections of fluting.

An early-19thC Scottish Regency mahogany and inlaid sideboard with a four-cupboard stage back, with a pair of frieze drawers flanked by a pair of deep drawers above a pair of cellarettes.

65¾in (167cm) wide

$1,600-2,000   **L&T**

A George IV mahogany and brass inlaid sideboard, of bowed breakfront outline, with three frieze drawers flanked by a cupboard and deep drawer, above spiral-twist legs and hairy paw feet, marks, knocks, the handles are replacements.

ca. 1825   *97¼in (247cm) wide*

$8,500-9,000   **DN**

An early-19thC breakfront mahogany sideboard, with brass rail gallery, over a center drawer and arched kneehole, with two drawers on the left and a cupboard on the right with faux-drawer front door.

72in (183cm) wide

$900-1,050   **MART**

A William and Mary walnut and featherbanded kneehole desk, the quarter veneered top, above one long and three short frieze drawers, above the center recessed cupboard door, flanked by a bank of three drawers on each side, on bun feet, scratches and abrasions, sections of replacement veneer, the feet are replacements.

ca. 1690   *37in (94cm) wide*

$5,300-6,600   **DN**

A Queen Anne burl-elm kneehole desk, fitted with one long and six small drawers to a center cupboard, with later brass handles and bracket feet.

32¼in (82cm) wide

$3,300-4,000   **SWO**

A Queen Anne walnut and crossbanded kneehole desk, the top above a frieze drawer, the recessed cupboard door flanked by three drawers on each side, on bracket feet, scratches and abrasions, old veneer repairs, feet are later.

ca. 1710   *27½in (70cm) high*

$2,600-4,000   **DN**

ESSENTIAL REFERENCE – DESKS

In English, the word "desk" emerged around the middle of the 14thC and was an adaptation of the medieval Latin word "desca," meaning a table to write on, and that itself from the Latin word "discus," meaning platter and, similarly, the Greek "diskos." However, while sturdy desklike tables with slots and hooks for bookmarks and writing implements were in evidence during the Middle Ages, and while more refined examples with divided drawers (for inkpots, blotters, powder trays, and pens) were developed during the Renaissance, it wasn't until the 17thC and 18thC that cabinetmaking skills and techniques became much more sophisticated, when the desk forms we know today began to appear. Ranging from bonheurs-du-jours and Davenports, to fall fronts and kneeholes, to partners and pedestals and rolltops, to name but a few, they are as numerous and diverse in terms of their ergonomics as they are in style.

A George II figured walnut and crossbanded kneehole desk, the top above a frieze draw, the center recessed cupboard door flanked by two banks of three drawers on each side, on bracket feet.

ca. 1740   *33in (84cm) wide*

$6,000-6,600   **DN**

A George II walnut and burl-walnut secrétaire kneehole desk, the quarter-veneered top above a secrétaire drawer with pigeonholes and three drawers, above a slim drawer and six further drawers flanking a kneehole with a cupboard enclosing a shelf, on bracket feet.

27in (69cm) wide

$10,500-12,000   **WW**

A George II mahogany serpentine kneehole desk, in the manner of Paul Saunders, the top above nine short drawers around a center recessed cupboard door, flanked by trailing foliate carved canted angles headed by scrolling terminals, some old veneer repairs.

Born in 1722, Paul Saunders was a very successful and well-connected cabinetmaker, upholsterer, and gilder who at various times, prior to his death in 1771, had workshops in St Martin-in-the-Fields, Soho, and Lincoln's Inn Fields, in London. His clients for tapestries and for furniture, essentially "Chippendale" or "French" in style, included, to name but a few, King George II, the Earl of Leicester, and the Dukes of Cumberland, Norfolk, and Northumberland.

ca. 1755   *51¼in (130cm) wide*

$5,300-5,900   **DN**

A George III mahogany partners' pedestal desk, the top with tooled leather-inset writing surface, both sides with three frieze drawers and two banks of three drawers each side of the center kneehole, flanked by brass side-carrying handles, on bracket feet.

ca. 1780   *58¼in (148cm) wide*

$9,000-10,500   **DN**

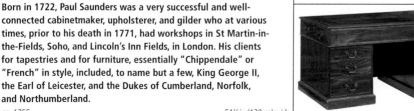

A late-18thC George III mahogany pedestal desk, the top with a leather skiver above frieze drawers on each end, on pedestals with banks of three drawers and cupboards opposing.

54in (137cm) wide

$2,600-3,300   **L&T**

A George III mahogany desk or "writing table," attributed to Gillows, the top lifting on a double ratchet mechanism and with hinged rear edge doubling as a candle stand, above a long drawer fitted with a leather-inset slide above 12 lidded

compartments, each marked alphabetically, the recessed kneehole cupboard door flanked on each side by a bank of three drawers, the rear of the desk with three center drawers flanked by a cupboard door on each side, scratches and abrasions.

ca. 1790   *52in (132cm) wide*
$10,000-11,000   **DN**

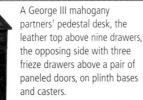

A George III mahogany partners' pedestal desk, the leather top above nine drawers, the opposing side with three frieze drawers above a pair of paneled doors, on plinth bases and casters.

ca. 1800   *52in (132cm) wide*
$1,600-2,100   **DN**

A late-18th/early-19thC George III mahogany twin pedestal desk, with a center drawer with three short drawers, on bracket feet.

      70in (178cm) wide
$15,000-20,000   **L&T**

A late George III mahogany partners' desk, the top with a leather skiver above three drawers with brass lion-mask handles, the same opposing, on twin pedestals with cupboards, outlined with stringing, on bracket feet.

      52½in (133cm) wide
$1,200-1,600   **L&T**

A William IV mahogany partners' pedestal desk, by Gillows, with leather-inset top, above nine drawers around the kneehole on one side and two cupboard doors on the other, stamped "GILLOWS LANCASTER."

ca. 1835   *54in (137cm) wide*
$3,300-4,000   **DN**

ESSENTIAL REFERENCE—JOHN COBB

Born ca. 1710, apprenticed in 1729, married to Giles Grendey's daughter in 1755, and partnered with William Vile from 1750 to 1765, upholster and cabinetmaker John Cobb was, according to contemporaries, of "singularly haughty character." It may have been a trait that did not always endear him to his customers, but they did include George III and Queen Charlotte, the 1st Earl of Leicester (at Holkham Hall), the 4th Duke of Devonshire (at Chatsworth House), and the 4th Duke of Bedford (at Woburn Abbey). Indeed, some of Cobb's work is today in the Royal Collection at Buckingham Palace. Most of the pieces when working with Vile were in an Anglicized Rococo style, but after Vile's retirement in the mid-1760s, Cobb embraced the Neoclassical style (for which he is best known), and earned a reputation for exceptionally elegant work, executed to the highest standard, with many pieces featuring exquisite marquetry and other exotic inlay work. Cobb died in 1778.

A George III mahogany and bronze-mounted tambour-top writing desk, attributed to John Cobb, the top released with a concealed catch to reveal a tooled leather-inset writing surface and four pigeonholes, above five frieze drawers around a center kneehole, with an opposing arrangement of false drawer fronts, on tapering legs, with brass caps and casters, scratches and abrasions.

ca. 1790   *46½in (118cm) wide*
$16,000-18,000   **DN**

An early-19thC mahogany pedestal desk, the top with leather skiver, over a long frieze drawer flanked by short drawers, on banks of three drawers, with cupboards on the reverse.

      60¾in (154cm) wide
$2,100-2,600   **L&T**

A 19thC French "plum pudding" mahogany and gilt-metal-mounted pedestal desk, in Empire style, the mounts with Neoclassical motifs including anthemion and capital terminals, the gilt-tooled leather inset writing surface above nine drawers, the side panels surmounted by slides, the opposite side with nine false drawers.

      63½in (161cm) wide
$4,000-4,600   **DN**

A late-19thC oak writing desk, by Howard and Sons, the top with a leather surface and three-quarter pierced brass gallery, over a frieze drawer flanked by banks of one short and one deep drawer with a bracketed shelf on each side, on outsweeping legs with undertiers, stamped "HOWARD AND SONS" on the drawer.

42¼in (107cm) wide

$1,600-2,100 **L&T**

ESSENTIAL REFERENCE—WHYTOCK & REID

Although Edinburgh-based Whytock and Reid were formed in 1876, following the merger of two companies, one owned by Richard Whytock, the other by John Reid, the roots of the company date back to the one founded ca. 1807 by the Whytock family. They ceased trading in 2004, but nowadays they are best remembered for their high-quality furniture; they weren't just cabinetmakers but also upholsters, gilders, French polishers, tapestry and carpet makers, and interior decorators. Indeed, during their 19thC and early-20thC heyday they, often in partnership with architect Robert Lorimer, remodeled and furnished not only many of the great houses and castles of Scotland—including Balmoral, Holyrood, Skibo, and Culzean—but also prestigious modes of transportation, such as luxury steam yachts and Pullman-type train carriages.

A 20thC Whytock and Reid, Queen Anne-style mahogany desk, the crossbanded rounded top with a leather skiver, above a frieze drawer and shaped kneehole arch flanked by banks of two short drawers, on cabriole legs, maker's stamps in the drawers.

66¼in (168cm) wide

$12,000-15,000 **L&T**

CLOSER LOOK—ITALIAN DESK

This Italian walnut and ivory-inlaid twin pedestal desk was probably made in Lombardy.

The top is inlaid with a center Classical scene of centurions with chariots, flanked by mythical female term figures with wings and horse's legs, holding urns with scrolling leaves.

Each twin pedestal has a hinged cupboard door decorated with a figure of a saint, and enclosing a shelf.

The sides and back with ebonized outline moldings and inlaid with further Classical figures and grotesques.

A 19thC Italian desk, with three frieze drawers.

46½in (118cm) wide

$26,000-33,000 **WW**

An Edwardian oak cartographer's desk, with leather top, above twelve drawers to one side, and nine drawers around a kneehole recess on the other.

67¾in (172cm) wide

$2,600-4,000 **L&T**

A George III satinwood and purpleheart bonheur du jour, attributed to Gillows, with kingwood banding, the raised lift-off back with a pair of cupboard doors, flanking a shelf, above a hinged front inset with a writing surface, above a frieze drawer, the right side with a pull-out drawer for pen and ink.

ca. 1790-1800 *45¼in (114.8cm) high*

$2,100-2,600 **WW**

A late George III mahogany and satinwood bonheur du jour, with two short and two long drawers outlined with stringing and ivory pulls, the base with a long frieze drawer fitted for writing over a sliding work bag, on tapered legs with brass caps and casters.

41in (104cm) high

$1,500-1,800 **L&T**

An Edwardian mahogany, satinwood crossbanded, and inlaid bonheur du jour, in George III style, stamped "H. Mawer & Stephenson."

H. Mawer & Stephenson are listed in "The Dictionary of English Furniture Makers," FHS and Maney, 1986, although no address is recorded. It is probable that the company were furniture brokers and depositories rather than makers.

ca. 1905 *46½in (118cm) high*

$2,600-3,300 **DN**

FURNITURE

A William and Mary walnut and ash featherbanded bureau, the sloped and hinged top opening to a leather-inset writing surface and pigeonholes and small drawers, above two short and one long drawer and an arched apron, on turned legs, joined by an X-shaped stretcher, scratches and abrasions, handles and escutcheon are associated.

ca. 1690   *39½in (100cm) high*

$5,300-5,900   **DN**

A George I walnut bureau, with cross and featherbanding, the interior with pigeonholes, drawers, and a center cupboard door flanked by a pair of secret pilaster compartments, with a sliding well cover and a writing surface, above two short and two long drawers, bracket feet.

ca. 1715   *38¼in (96.8cm) high*

$1,800-2,400   **WW**

An 18thC George I walnut bureau, the cross and chevron-banded front opening to pigeonholes, drawers, and a covered well, over two short and two long drawers, on bracket feet.

44in (112cm) wide

$1,600-2,100   **L&T**

An early-18thC George II walnut bureau, the slant front opening to drawers and pigeonholes, over two short and three long drawers, on ogee bracket feet.

41¼in (105cm) high

$2,600-3,300   **L&T**

A George II walnut and featherbanded bureau, the fall opening to pigeonholes and drawers, with a cupboard door on each side, above a frieze drawer and three long concave-shaped drawers, scratches, abrasions, the handles on the frieze drawer are later.

The design of this bureau is unusual, and although all features would support it being English, it is perhaps by a Huguenot cabinetmaker of Dutch or German origin working in England.

ca. 1740   *47¾in (121cm) high*

$1,700-2,100   **DN**

A mid-18thC George II walnut, burl-walnut, and featherbanded bureau, with a fall front with eight pigeonholes above five small drawers, the base with four drawers with engraved brass solid backplate handles and escutcheons, on bracket feet.

40¼in (102cm) high

$2,400-2,900   **TEN**

An 18thC Italian walnut bureau, probably Lombardy, inlaid with fruitwood leaf scrolls, the hinged fall revealing six drawers, above three serpentine-front drawers.

ca. 1760   *47¾in (121.5cm) wide*

$2,600-4,000   **WW**

A late George II bureau, in the manner of Thomas Chippendale, in two sections, veneered in flame-figured mahogany, with a brass escutcheon with a push-button mechanism to lift the keyhole cover, the escutcheon plate engraved with a lion and coronet crest above a coat of arms and the motto "Virtute Non Vi" for the Newdich (Newdick) family of Worcestershire (arms granted in 1580), the fall revealing a fitted interior inlaid with parquetry banding, with drawers and pigeonholes, one drawer fitted for pens and ink with a secret drawer behind, the fall with a baize-lined writing surface, above a baize-lined brushing slide and three banks of four drawers that pull out as one, possibly for traveling, each side with two bronze handles for carrying, on later wooden casters.

ca. 1760   *45½in (115.3cm) wide*

$16,000-21,000   **WW**

An 18thC George III mahogany bureau, the interior with pigeonholes, drawers, and a leather skiver, above four drawers, on bracket feet.

47¼in (120cm) wide

$1,500-2,000　　　　　L&T

An early-19thC French Empire mahogany bureau à cylindre, the marble top above three short drawers, the cylinder front opening to a leather writing surface and pigeonholes and drawers, five further drawers on winged sphinx legs, applied with Neoclassical gilt-metal mounts.

49¾in (126cm) wide

$8,000-9,000　　　　　L&T

A late-19thC French kingwood and marquetry bureau à cylindre, the marble top with a brass gallery above a cylinder front inlaid with a musical trophy, with a fitted interior and slide-out writing surface, above three short and one long frieze drawer, on cabriole legs with gilt metal mounts.

42½in (108cm) high

$2,000-2,600　　　　　L&T

A late-19thC Napoleon III ebonized bureau, the superstructure with twin cupboards with pierced brass galleries, flanking drawers and a recessed mirror, the base with a leather insert above a frieze drawer, on cabriole legs, with Sèvres-style porcelain plaques and gilt-metal mounts.

47¼in (120cm) high

$3,300-4,000　　　　　L&T

A late-19th/early-20thC French mahogany brass-mounted bureau, in the Louis XVI style, the top with a leather writing surface, with two slide extensions on both ends, above a frieze drawer, flanked by a deep drawer and two short drawers.

58in (147cm) wide

$4,600-5,300　　　　　L&T

A Louis XV kingwood, tulipwood, and gilt metal-mounted bureau plat, the top with tooled leather-inset surface, above three frieze drawers, on cabriole legs terminating in sabots.

ca. 1770　　　　*70in (178cm) wide*

$21,000-26,000　　　　　DN

An early-19thC rosewood and marquetry table à écrire in Louis XVI style, retailed by Edward Holmes Baldock, with gilt bronze mounts, the maple top inlaid with a panel with a shepherd and flock within a floral ribbon-tied rondel, the frieze drawer fitted with a leather-lined slide and with a gilt metal inkwell and sander, underside with initial "E H B."

Edward Holmes Baldock (1777-1844) was a prominent London furniture dealer who numbered King George IV, William Beckford, and the 5th Duke of Buccleuch as clients. He worked with cabinetmakers, such as George Trollope and Blake, to provide Louis XV and XVI-style pieces for his clients.

28in (71.2cm) high

$3,300-4,000　　　　　WW

An early-Victorian bird's-eye maple and parcel-ebonized writing table, in the manner of Holland & Sons, the leather-inset top above a pair of blind frieze drawers, lobed finials, architectural carved ends with lappet-carved vase, bipedal outsweeping feet, scratches, abrasions, one section of ebonized molding is detached.

ca. 1850　　　　*42¼in (107cm) wide*

$1,800-2,400　　　　　DN

A mid-19thC early-Victorian walnut kidney-shaped writing table, the top with a pierced brass gallery, on foliate-carved end supports on cabriole legs with scrolled feet and ceramic casters.

47¼in (120cm) wide

$2,400-2,900 **L&T**

A Victorian bird's-eye maple and tulipwood crossbanded and specimen marquetry bureau plat, decorated with floral marquetry, the top above a frieze drawer at each end, on cabriole legs headed with "Green man"-mask cast mounts and with sabots.

This wood is called "bird's-eye" maple because the tiny knots in the grain resemble small bird's eyes. The figure is mainly caused by unfavorable growing conditions for the tree. The tree attempts to start new buds, but, with poor conditions, the new shoots are terminated and tiny knots remain.

ca. 1870　　　　　*55¼in (140cm) wide*

$3,300-4,000 **DN**

A Victorian kingwood and rosewood bureau plat, in Louis XV style, with ormolu mounts, the top with a suede writing surface, above three frieze drawers with false fronts on the reverse, on cabriole legs.

89in (175cm) wide

$4,600-5,300 **WW**

A Victorian satinwood writing table, in George III style, after a design by Thomas Sheraton, inlaid with boxwood and ebonized lines, the top with leather and stepped three-quarter gallery concealing a rising screen and two sprung stationery compartments operating with button release, above a frieze drawer, scratches, abrasions.

Thomas Sheraton illustrated a 1792 pattern for this "Lady's Writing-Table," with candle branches fitted on the top at each side, in his "The Cabinet-Maker and Upholsterer's Drawing Book," 1793 (part III, pl. 37).

ca. 1890　　　　　*36in (91.5cm) high*

$5,300-6,600 **DN**

A Victorian walnut and marquetry bureau plat, in Louis XV style, with gilt-brass mounts, the top inset with a leather writing surface, above a pair of frieze drawers, on cabriole legs.

ca. 1870　　　　　*48½in (123cm) wide*

$3,300-4,000 **WW**

A late-19th/early-20thC French mahogany and ormolu-mounted bureau plat, in Louis XVI style, the stepped frieze fitted with three drawers centered by a cartouche supported by cherubs, on fluted legs with stiff-leaf sabots.

62in (157.5cm) wide

$2,600-4,000 **DN**

A late-19th/early-20thC French rosewood, amboyna, and box-strung lady's writing table, with floral marquetry panels, the superstructure with drawers and shelves, the slide above three frieze drawers on gilt-metal mounted cabriole legs, old chips and splits, some lifting of veneers.

36¾in (93cm) high

$1,300-1,800 **DN**

A late-19th/early-20thC, Louis XV-style kingwood, amboyna, and mahogany bureau plat, in the manner of Charles Cressent, the top with a leather insert, above a frieze with three short frieze drawers with dummy drawers opposing, on cabriole legs, with gilt bronze mounts.

67in (170cm) wide

$5,300-6,600 **L&T**

A mid-20thC, Louis XV-style kingwood, parquetry, and gilt-bronze bureau plat, the top with a leather insert above three frieze drawers with dummy drawers opposing, the sides with gilt-bronze mounts depicting the centaur Nessus with Deianira.

80¾in (205cm) wide

$6,500-8,000 **L&T**

ESSENTIAL REFERENCE—DAVENPORTS

An entry made in the 1790s in the record books of the prestigious cabinetmakers Gillows of Lancaster states: "Captain Davenport, a desk," and it's this that is thought to be the first recorded example of the small writing cabinets that came to be named after the captain. Popular until around the end of the 19thC, davenports had a basic form that changed little, comprising a small chest-of-drawers with a desk compartment above. Pull-out drawers on one side, with dummy drawers opposite, were a common feature, as were feet with casters for ease of movement. However, there were numerous variations: the most fundamental being the earlier examples had a top section with a writing slope that slid forward when in use to accommodate the writer's legs, whereas from the mid-1840s most had the desk section fixed in the writing position, supported on brackets, thereby allowing a permanently recessed space for legs. Other variants included concealed drawers, real or dummy cupboard doors, wooden or brass galleries, pull-out candle sconces (rare). Decorative embellishments, such as elaboration of carving or inlay work, also varied considerably—generally, earlier examples are understated, while late-Victorian ones are often overornamented. Also, being small—usually no more than 18in (46cm) wide and deep prior to the 1830s, albeit broadening to around 24in (60cm) thereafter—davenports were primarily used by women.

An early-19thC Regency rosewood davenport, in the manner of Gillows, opening to an interior with small drawers, one side with an ink drawer and four graduated drawers, with a slide on the other, raised on lobed feet with brass casters.

30in (76cm) high

$1,600-2,100   **L&T**

A George IV mahogany davenport, attributed to Gillows, the swivel top with a pierced brass gallery centered with a handle, above a writing slope, a vacant interior with two drawers, the left side with four drawers, the right with a small drawer for pens and ink, and a pull-out candleslide above four false fronts, on brass caps and casters.

ca. 1820-25   *32in (81.5cm) high*

$2,600-3,300   **WW**

A mid-19thC George IV rosewood davenport, with two dummy and three short drawers, the frieze with a stationery drawer and slides on column supports, the hinged panel side enclosing three further drawers, on squat bun feet with sunken brass casters.

41¼in (105cm) high

$900-12,000   **L&T**

A mid-19thC Victorian walnut, maple, and marquetry davenport, sides inlaid with foliate motifs, the side with a door enclosing four drawers, on disk feet with casters.

35¾in (91cm) high

$800-900   **L&T**

A Victorian figured-walnut davenport, with cushion-shaped stationery drawer and hinged writing surface, on turned pilaster supports.

$350-400   **WHP**

A Victorian burl-walnut, strung, and marquetry davenport, the inkwell over a rolltop and fitted interior with four drawers on the side, scrolled foliate supports and casters.

22¾in (58cm) wide

$900-1,050   **WHP**

A Victorian walnut davenport, the burl-walnut top with pen and stationery box, the interior in satin birch with a single drawer, over a base with four side drawers and four faux drawers.

32in (81.25cm) high

$450-600   **MART**

A late-17thC Charles II carved giltwood mirror, the pierced frame decorated with carved putti and foliate decoration.

39in (98cm) wide

$18,000-24,000   **ROS**

A William and Mary olivewood oyster-veneered cushion-framed wall mirror, small old losses, some old repairs.

ca. 1690   *30in (76cm) high*

$4,000-4,600   **DN**

A George I carved giltwood wall mirror, in the manner of John Belchier or James Moore, the beveled mirror plate within a foliate and egg-and-dart molded frame, surmounted by a scrolling foliage molded architectural cresting centered by a plume of feathers and putto mask above a lambrequin, mirror plate and backboard 19thC replacements.

Remarkably similar wall mirrors by John Belchier are in the collection at Erddig, Clwyd, North Wales (NT 1146961), see Adam Bowett, "Early Georgian Furniture 1715-1740," Antique Collectors Club, 2009, p. 292, pl. 6:50 and 6:51. The renowned Huguenot immigrant cabinetmaker John Belchier supplied furniture and mirrors to John Meller at Erddig during the 1720s (during this period he also received orders for mirrors for St. Pauls Cathedral). Many parallels can be drawn between this mirror and know examples by Belchier.

ca. 1720   *71in (180cm) high*

$13,000-18,000   **DN**

A George II walnut and parcel-gilt mirror, the egg-and-dart molded frame with shaped apron, flanked by trailing vines, surmounted by a scrolling pediment centered by a ho-ho bird.

ca. 1740   *52in (132cm) high*

$6,000-6,600   **DN**

A mid-18thC George II walnut parcel-gilt mirror, with a scrolled frame with a bonnet-top pediment centered by a fruit and flower-filled basket.

53¼in (135cm) high

$2,400-2,900   **L&T**

A George II carved giltwood wall mirror, with a carved frame with stylized foliate motifs, old splits and cracks to the frame.

ca. 1750   *48in (122cm) high*

$4,000-5,300   **DN**

A George III giltwood wall mirror, in the manner of John Linnell, with two shaped plates divided by a band of rockwork, the lower flanked by columns, within a rocaille, leaf, and scroll-carved frame, with a basket of flowers surmount, regilt.

35in (89cm) wide

$10,500-12,000   **WW**

A late-18thC Continental silvered wall mirror, the plate within a foliate-carved frame, old splits and chips, mirror plate has age but is later.

It is probable that this was once a picture frame.

48¾in (124cm) high

$2,600-3,300   **DN**

An 18thC George III giltwood, gesso, and painted trumeau mirror, with a panel painted with a bridge in a landscape.

36¼in (92cm) high

$1,000-1,100 **L&T**

An early-19thC Regency giltwood and ebonized convex wall mirror, surmounted by an eagle, restored.

35½in (90cm) high

$4,600-5,300 **L&T**

A late George III giltwood and parcel-ebonized pier mirror, with trophy motif on the tablet flanked by an acanthus cornice above the frieze and split marginal plates, flanked by fluted pilasters.

ca. 1815 *66½in (169cm) high*

$4,600-5,300 **DN**

An early-19thC Swedish Neoclassical gilt and painted wood pier mirror, with a ribbon cresting above frieze carved with a center urn, with trailing vine leaves below.

39½in (100cm) high

$2,000-2,600 **L&T**

An early-19thC George II style giltwood mirror, in a Rococo style frame with "C" and foliate scrolls and rocaille motifs with a large foliate cresting.

45¼in (115cm) high

$2,600-3,300 **L&T**

ESSENTIAL REFERENCE—GIRONDOLES

Named for their flickering, light-giving properties after the Franco-Italian word for a rotating or swirling firework, girondoles first appeared in the second half of the 17thC, initially as ornamental branched candle holders, commonly made and used in pairs, and either in stand form on a table, or bracketed on and projecting from a wall. During the course of the 18thC and 19thC, it became increasingly popular to integrate the wall-hung versions into ornate mirror frames, especially examples with round and often convex mirror glass, such as the two pairs of early-19thC gilt-framed girondoles shown here. Decorative appeal aside, on a purely functional level, siting a mirror, especially a convex one, behind burning candles illuminated, via reflection, an interior considerably more than candles could alone—a desirable asset prior to the late-19thC/early-20thC introduction of electric light.

A George IV carved-giltwood wall mirror, the frame carved with scrolling acanthus and trailing floral branches.

ca. 1825 58in (147cm) high

$1,800-2,400 **DN**

A pair of early-19thC William IV giltwood girondoles, in the Rococo Revival style, with pierced and carved frames with rocaille, C scrolls, flowers, and issuing twin scrolling candle arms.

45in (114cm) high

$2,000-2,600 **L&T**

A pair of 19thC George III-style giltwood girandole mirrors, with pierced foliate-carved frames with ribbon-tied cresting and issuing twin foliate-carved candle arms.

40¼in (102cm) high

$4,000-4,600 **L&T**

A gilt and gesso Rococo-style mirror, the mirror plate within an acanthus-decorated frame with four small platform shelves, two supporting dragons, the scrolled plume surmounted by a pierced foliate pediment.

ca. 1870   *59in (150cm) wide*

$2,600-4,000   **TEN**

A 19thC carved mahogany wall mirror, in mid-18thC style, with an egg-and-dart carved border, flanked by stylized dolphins and trailing bell flowers.

54in (137cm) high

$3,300-4,000   **DN**

A 19thC Venetian cut and enameled glass wall mirror, the acanthus cartouche crest above a slip frame, with enamel border, enclosing a beveled pane.

52in (132cm) high

$2,600-3,300   **L&T**

A 19thC French carved giltwood and composition wall mirror, with a C-scroll crested cartouche, centered with a rose and flanked by scrolling acanthus, crest broken and restored, general wear.

61in (155cm) high

$3,300-4,000   **SWO**

A 19thC Chippendale-style giltwood mirror, with a pheonix on the cresting above a floral-carved asymetric frame, the right-hand side carved with a squirrel.

77½in (197cm) high

$6,000-7,500   **L&T**

A 19thC Continental gilt-framed mirror with floral and shell-molded arch top marginal frame.

39in (98cm) wide

$2,100-2,600   **BELL**

A late-19thC Gothic Revival wall mirror, frame with gilt and enamel decoration, with minor wear.

47¼in (120cm) high

$4,000-4,600   **SWO**

A late-19thC/early-20thC black-japanned pier mirror, in Queen Anne style, decorated in gilt with chinoiserie with birds, buildings, flowers, and foliage.

30in (77.5cm) wide

$1,500-1,800   **WW**

A late-19thC/early-20thC French giltwood wall mirror, in Louis XV style, with a scroll, rocaille, leaf, and flower-carved frame.

67¾in (172cm) high

$800-1,050   **WW**

A large 18thC Venetian carved giltwood overmantel mirror, the scrolling-foliate frame set with stylized masks, with losses and repairs, crest has been broken off and repaired.

59in (150cm) wide

$2,600-4,000 SWO

An early-19thC Regency gilt and ebonized overmantel mirror, the dentil-molded pediment painted with a cartouche, the plate flanked by pilasters.

55¼in (140cm) high

$4,000-4,600 L&T

A carved giltwood overmantel mirror, in a Rococo-style surround decorated with pierced foliate and scroll decoration, wear and rubbing, one front frond of the carved frame is missing.

ca. 1830 *78¾in (200cm) high*

$2,600-4,000 DN

Judith Picks

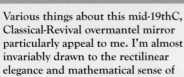

Various things about this mid-19thC, Classical-Revival overmantel mirror particularly appeal to me. I'm almost invariably drawn to the rectilinear elegance and mathematical sense of proportion that underpins Classically inspired forms. I like the simplicity and geometric purity of the recurring ball-motif decoration (above the frieze). I've long preferred the Corinthian columns from the Classical Orders of architecture, especially because of their scrolling acanthus-leaf capitals, and the gilded finish lends the overall composition a pleasing sense of opulence. Above all, however, I love the carved tableau on the frieze, which depicts Aurora, Greek goddess of the dawn, leading toward a sitting and standing couple the Greek sun god Apollo, in

his chariot and accompanied by attendants and winged messengers. I like to think it heralds not only a new dawn and a bright future for the couple, but also for whoever's lucky enough to have it above their fireplace, too.

A mid-19thC Victorian giltwood and gesso overmantel mirror, with three rectangular beveled plates flanked by Corinthian cluster columns, the frieze decorated with Aurora leading Apollo's chariot, with a ball-decorated frieze.

55¾in (141.5cm) wide

$1,300-1,800 WW

A French giltwood and composition overmantel mirror, with scroll surmount above the arched plate and surround with oak and laurel fruiting foliage decoration, chips and losses on areas of the gilding.

ca. 1860 *76¾in (195cm) high*

$4,600-5,300 DN

An early-Victorian giltwood overmantel mirror, the frame with C and foliate scrolls, rocaille, and flower tendrils.

67¾in (172cm) wide

$2,000-2,600 L&T

A 19thC Victorian giltwood and gesso overmantel mirror, the center mirror plate flanked by smaller mirror plates within a scrolled foliate frame.

59½in (151cm) wide

$1,600-2,100 L&T

FURNITURE

A late-19thC carved giltwood and composition overmantel mirror, the frame with foliage and flower heads.

84¾in (215cm) high

$2,600-3,300   **DN**

A late-Victorian carved giltwood and composition overmantel mirror, with cherub scroll fretwork and foliate cresting above a rope-twist surround and stepped scrolling base, old splits and cracks, the surface appears refreshed overall and is almost certainly not original.

ca. 1890   *71in (180cm) wide*

$1,200-1,600   **DN**

A large 19thC French Régence-style giltwood overmantel mirror, in an openwork giltwood frame with foliate scrolls, trailing flowers, and flower heads.

71in (180cm) high

$4,000-4,600   **L&T**

A late-19thC Continental silvered-brass Neoclassical-style pier mirror, with scrolling foliate cresting centered by a rosette, within a bead molded frame.

53½in (136cm) high

$3,300-4,000   **L&T**

CLOSER LOOK—ITALIAN MIRROR

This mirror is North Italian, almost certainly Venetian, ca. 1880. The lacquer and parcel-gilt decoration are used to create the chinoiserie effect.

The arched pediment centered by a jutting Manchu gentleman's head. The Manchu formed the last Imperial Dynasty of China, 1644-1912.

The arched pediment is flanked by scroll-bodied moustachioed dragons.

The decoration is further enhanced with peonies and figurative panels over the rectangular mirror plate.

A late-19thC mirror, with small losses, one angle mount missing.

ca. 1880   *70½in (179cm) high*

$4,000-5,300   **CHEF**

A late-19thththC/early-20thC giltwood Florentine overmantel mirror, the plate within stiff leaf carved slip, and a pierced scrolling thick leaf frame, old repairs on frame.

105½in (268cm) high

$4,600-5,300   **DN**

A 19thC Louis XVI-style white-painted and giltwood overmantel mirror, with egg-and-dart cornice above ribbon cresting and twin swags of foliage on the frieze.

79½in (202cm) high

$1,200-1,600   **L&T**

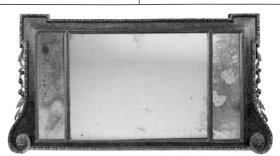

An early-20thC George II-style walnut and giltwood triple overmantel mirror, in a gilt-molded and walnut frame with an egg-and-dart molded edge and fruiting trails.

51¼in (130cm) wide

$1,700-2,100   **L&T**

An early-19thC late Regency mahogany cheval mirror, in the manner of George Smith, the mirror plate between lotus-carved pierced uprights on trestle bases with brass casters.

62¼in (158cm) high

$800-1,050   L&T

A Victorian walnut and burl-walnut double-sided cheval mirror, the mirror plate with carved and pierced foliate surmount, between fluted supports headed foliate carved terminals.

ca. 1870   56in (142cm) high

$1,600-2,100   DN

A Victorian mahogany cheval mirror, the plate flanked by carved heron supports, above a shaped base on outsweeping legs, brass casters, some old splits and chips.

ca. 1870   74in (188cm) high

$4,000-4,600   DN

A George II walnut and feather-banded dressing mirror, the base with three frieze drawers, on bracket feet.

ca. 1735   26½in (67cm) high

$1,000-1,100   DN

A Regency lacquered dressing table mirror, the box base with a fall-front over three drawers, decorated in chinoiserie with pagodas, bridges, and butterflies among foliage, finials damaged and repaired.

15in (38cm) wide

$800-900   SWO

A mid-19thC Scottish Victorian carved parrot coal dressing mirror.

Parrot coal, also known as cannel coal appears to get its name from the sound it makes when burning, a crackling similar to that of a parrot's beak clicking. It was used during the 19thC to make furniture and works of art, due to its similar characteristics to marble. Unlike household coal, it can be carved. Thomas Williamson, a stonemason from West Wemyss, Fife, is known for the parrot coal pieces he created during the mid-1800s, now in the collection at Kirkcaldy Galleries. A garden seat by Williamson was acquired by Prince Albert, and exhibited at the Great Exhibition in 1851, which is now at Osborne House.

29¼in (74cm) high

$1,600-2,100   L&T

A 19thC Chinese black-lacquer chinoiserie-decorated toilet mirror, the base with four drawers, with lifting and some discoloration to lacquer.

36¼in (92cm) high

$1,100-1,250   CHEF

A 19thC French Empire rosewood, satinwood, and porcelain-mounted dressing mirror, the column supports surmounted by gilt-metal swans, the base with three drawers with floral-painted porcelain panels.

21¾in (55cm) high

$1,600-2,100   L&T

A George III mahogany cellaret, in the manner of Thomas Chippendale, with a lead-lined interior with nine divisions, the body with outlined moldings and fluted canted angles, the front with a tap, the sides with brass carrying handles, the chamfered legs with applied brackets and brass roller casters.

ca. 1770   *27½in (70.2cm) high*

$5,300-5,900   **WW**

A George III mahogany wine cooler, by Thomas and George Seddon, the top centered by a reed- and lappet-carved finial, with a lead-lined interior, above the panel-molded front, the top of the panel stamped "T & G SEDDON."

ca. 1800-1804   *38¼in (97cm) wide*

$2,000-2,600   **DN**

A large mahogany and brass-bound wine cooler, in the Irish Regency style, the rim decorated with shells, with a lead lining, the ribbed body with lion-mask and ring handles, on paw feet and casters.

42½in (108cm) wide

$11,000-13,000   **WW**

An early-19thC Regency mahogany wine cooler, with parcel-gilt decoration, with a lead-lined interior, the body with rosette panels, on lobed feet and a stepped plinth.

32in (81.5cm) wide

$2,100-2,600   **WW**

An early-19thC Regency mahogany and ebony wine cooler, in the manner of Thomas Hope, of sarcaphogus form, the cover opening to a lined and compartmented interior, panels with carved palmette moldings, with brass lion-mask handles, on paw feet with recessed brass casters.

26in (66cm) wide

$4,000-4,600   **L&T**

A George IV oak and pollard oak wine cooler, of sarcophagus form, with a lined interior, with flanking handles and on plinth feet, with some damage, the interior with old oxidation.

ca. 1830   *51¼in (130cm) wide*

$1,600-2,100   **DN**

A 19thC Irish mahogany oval wine cistern, in George II style, with metal liner in the interior, with carved frieze with scrolling foliage centered by palmettes, each leg surmounted by a carved male mask.

32¾in (83cm) wide

$2,600-4,000   **DN**

Judith Picks

Since producing the first Miller's Antiques Price Guide over 40 years ago, I have seen numerous wine coolers, both in pictures and in the flesh, and I have to say that this one is my favorite of the lot by far. First and foremost, it brilliantly accommodates so many of the diverse stylistic elements championed around the turn of the 19thC by George the Prince Regent before he became King George IV, and which became collectively known as Regency style. Here, two lion monopedia and four corner vases of Classical Graeco-Roman inspiration are matched with a center lotus leaf-embellished column of ancient Egyptian form, while the red lacquered and gilt finish, and the painted and gilded chinoiserie scenes around the perimeter of the lead-lined cooler box, are from the Asian vocabulary of ornament. All in all, I simply can't think of a more opulent and dramatic-looking cooler in which to put champagne on ice—or a nice white Burgundy for that matter!

A 19thC Regency Revival gilt and red-lacquered wine cooler, the lead-lined cooler within a carved foliate and gilt border, supported by carved and gilded lion monopedia and a center column on a shaped platform base, probably regilded.

28¼in (72cm) wide

$7,500-8,500   **SWO**

ESSENTIAL REFERENCE—CANTERBURYS

Purportedly named after an Archbishop of Canterbury for whom the first one was made, canterburys were introduced in the 1780s and are referred to in Thomas Sheraton's influential "The Cabinet Dictionary" of 1803 as being of two basic types. The first, being by far the most common and best known, was an open-topped wooden stand or rack with slatted partitions originally intended for storing bound or loose sheets of music, and generally raised on four short legs with casters, enabling it to be both inconspicuously stored under a piano, and easily pushed or kicked aside as required; subsequently, it was also often used for storing magazines. The second type Sheraton referred to is far less commonly found: taller, also fitted with casters, and designed to hold plates, cutlery, and other dining paraphernalia, it stood next to, and could be easily moved around a dining table at informal meals, and was thus essentially a form of dumbwaiter.

A George III mahogany canterbury, of "country house" proportions, slatted divisions with shaped supports, above a drawer, flanked by reeded pilasters, on casters.

ca. 1810   *24in (61cm) wide*

$1,300-2,000   **DN**

An early-19thC Regency rosewood canterbury, with three divisions and a drawer in the base, on turned tapering legs, caps and casters.

22in (56cm) high

$1,200-1,300   **L&T**

A Regency mahogany canterbury, the slatted top with four divisions, above a frieze drawer, on tapering legs, with brass caps and casters, the drawer with plaque for "ANTIQUE FURNITURE from NORMAN ADAMS LTD, 8-10, HANS ROAD, LONDON. S. W. 3."

ca. 1815   *18¼in (46cm) high*

$2,600-3,300   **DN**

A Regency mahogany canterbury, with four divisions, above a drawer, on brass caps and casters.

ca. 1810   *20in (50.5cm) high*

$1,500-1,800   **WW**

An early-19thC Regency mahogany canterbury, on turned supports over a base drawer and tapered feet.

19¼in (49cm) high

$800-900   **L&T**

A William IV ash and tulipwood banded canterbury, to a design of J. C. Loudon, the three divisions fronted by a lappet-carved wreath and pierced S scroll-carved frieze, above a mahogany and cedar-lined drawer, faceted legs with brass caps and casters.

This model of canterbury is illustrated in the "Pictorial Dictionary of British 19th Century Furniture Design," p. 422, with an illustration taken from Loudon, dated 1833.

ca. 1835   *21¾in (55cm) high*

$1,600-2,000   **DN**

A Victorian mahogany canterbury, the carved scroll dividers above a frieze drawer and bulbous legs with brass caps and casters.

ca. 1880   *20in (51cm) high*

$550-650   **DN**

An early-20thC giltwood and painted canterbury, with carved decoration, two inset Jasperware plaques and molded saber legs, some paint loss.

28in (71cm) high

$400-500   **SWO**

FURNITURE

An early-19thC Regency mahogany whatnot, attributed to Gillows, the ratchet-adjustable hinged top with a removable bookrest, over two tiers divided by turned supports, the base with a drawer, on lobed feet.

42in (106.5cm) high

$2,600-3,300   **L&T**

An early-19thC Regency mahogany whatnot, with four tiers raised by baluster supports with urn finials, the base with a drawer, on tapered legs with brass caps and casters.

50½in (128cm) high

$800-900   **L&T**

A 19thC William IV walnut whatnot, with three tiers, with scrolled and pierced galleries, raised on spiral turned legs, the lower tier with a shaped apron and turned feet with brass casters.

41in (104cm) high

$750-850   **L&T**

A mid-19thC early-Victorian walnut whatnot, with three tiers raised by bobbin-turned supports, the base fitted with a drawer, the legs with brass caps and casters.

41¼in (105cm) high

$800-900   **L&T**

A Regency mahogany two-tier dumbwaiter, in the manner of Gillows, the top tier with gilt-brass gallery with Greek keys above the baluster supports and conforming undertier and outsweeping legs, some small losses.

ca. 1815   *42½in (108cm) high*

$3,300-4,000   **DN**

A Regency mahogany two-tier dumbwaiter, attributed to Gillows, each tier joined by columnar brass supports and with pierced brass galleries, on three outsweeping tapering legs, with brass caps and casters.

ca. 1815   *37in (94cm) high*

$7,500-8,500   **DN**

A Regency oak three-tier étagère, with a pierced trellis three-quarter gallery, the legs on brass caps and casters, old splits and chips, casters stamped "COPE'S PATENT."

ca. 1815   *35in (89cm) high*

$3,300-4,000   **DN**

A 19thC French Louis XVI-style mahogany and marble étagère, the marble top with a brass gallery over a foliate metal-mounted frieze with a larger tier below, the fluted legs on tapered feet.

34¼in (87cm) high

$1,500-1,800   **L&T**

A pair of kingwood and marquetry étagère in Louis XVI style, with gilt-brass mounts and pierced galleries, the tiers quarter veneered and crossbanded, with leaf and flower inlay, on leaf scroll sabot.

ca. 1880   *23½in (59.2cm) high*

$4,000-4,600   **WW**

A Regency rosewood and gilt metal-mounted jardinière stand or torchère, with gilt-brass ball feet.

ca. 1820   *34¾in (88cm) high*

$4,600-5,300   **DN**

A near pair of Louis Philippe palisander and kingwood jardinières, the frieze with Sèvres-style porcelain mounts.

ca. 1840   *31¼in (79cm) high*

$3,300-4,000   **DN**

One of a pair of mid-19thC rosewood oval jardinières or planters.

26½in (67cm) high

$5,300-5,900 the pair   **DN**

A 19thC French amboyna, mahogany, kingwood, marquetry, and gilt metal-mounted jardinière, by Tahan, Paris.

31½in (80cm) high

$1,100-1,250   **L&T**

ESSENTIAL REFERENCE—THE NUBIAN GIRAFFE

The giraffe depicted on this tray, a gift to George IV from the Pasha of Egypt and the first of the species to be seen in England, arrived at Windsor in 1827, where it was housed in the menagerie at Sandpit Gate on the edge of the Great Park. Jacques-Laurent Agasse was commissioned to paint the giraffe with her two Arab keepers, the cows maintained to provide milk, and Edward Cross, the owner of the Exeter Change menagerie. The giraffe's arrival prompted a brief period of so-called "giraffamania," during which the decorative arts and fashion were inspired by the striking patterns and height of the animal. At the same time, a raft of satirical prints poked fun at the monarch and his new pet. It is probable that this tray was made during this period. The giraffe, never especially healthy, died after only two years.

A mahogany and brass-mounted butler's tray on folding stand.

ca. 1830   *tray 31in (79cm) wide*

$1,700-2,100   **DN**

A rare William IV figural papier-mâché tray by Jennens & Bettridge, painted with an adaptation of the "Nubian Giraffe" after Jacques-Laurent Agasse (1767-1849), within a border gold painted with foliage and cartouches, stamped "JENNENS & BETTRIDGE 2ND" on the rear.

ca. 1835   *30in (76cm) wide*

$10,500-12,000   **DN**

A black-lacquered papier-mâché tray on faux bamboo stand.

29¾in (75.5cm) wide

                          CHOR

$800-900

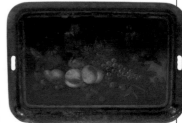

A 19thC toleware painted galleried tray, decorated with a still-life study of fruit.

30¼in (77cm) wide

$260-400   **SWO**

A pair of George III mahogany dining room urns and pedestals, in the manner of Gillows.

ca. 1775-80   *71¾in (182cm) high*

$26,000-33,000   **WW**

A 19thC Louis XV-style walnut and kingwood porcelain-mounted tea poy, with a Sèvres-style porcelain plaque.

29¼in (74cm) high

$2,600-3,300   **L&T**

A French kingwood jewel casket in Louis XV style, with ormolu mounts and Sèvres-style plaques.

ca. 1875   *42¼in (107.5cm) high*

$6,500-8,000   **WW**

A pair of 19thC Regency rosewood reading stands.

44in (112cm) high

$3,300-4,000   **L&T**

A George III mahogany candle stand, stem with a carved acanthus terminal, on cabriole legs, with acanthus-carved knees and scroll feet.

ca. 1760   *22in (56cm) high*

$6,500-8,000   **DN**

A George II carved mahogany candle stand, stem with acanthus-carved terminals, on shell and bellflower cabriole legs.

ca. 1750   *22in (56cm) high*

$6,000-6,600   **DN**

A Regency satinwood and rosewood inlaid music stand, the angle adjustable rest above a brass height-adjustable stem.

ca. 1820   *59in (150cm) high*

$2,100-2,600   **DN**

A George IV mahogany folio stand, attributed to Gillows, the hinged slatted uprights on ratcheted adjustable stands.

ca. 1825   *40½in (103cm) high*

$5,300-6,600   **DN**

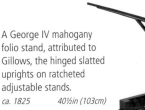

A flight of Gothic Revival mahogany library steps.

ca. 1870   *37¾in (96cm) high*

$2,600-3,300   **DN**

A George III mahogany four-poster bed, in the manner of Thomas Chippendale.

Four-poster beds with related turnings to these posts are in Dumfries House, Ayrshire, Scotland. Dumfries House is known to retain much of the furniture commissioned from Thomas Chippendale

ca. 1760   *90½in (230cm) high*
$6,500-8,000   **DN**

A late-18thC George III mahogany four-poster bed.

80¾in (205cm) high
$4,600-5,300   **L&T**

A French Directoire mahogany and gilt brass-mounted bed frame, decorated with patera cast mounts, with fluted pilasters, with pineapple finials, on toupie feet.

ca. 1800   *87½in (222cm) long*
$4,600-5,300   **DN**

A George IV mahogany and pine four-poster bed frame, in the manner of Gillows.

ca. 1825   *104¾in (266cm) high*
$10,500-12,000   **DN**

A Gothic Revival painted four-poster bed, with a fret-carved palmette frieze, quatrefoil and arch decorated headboard with cluster column posts.

92½in (235cm) high
$10,000-11,000   **SWO**

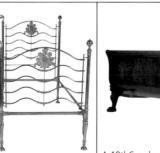

A Victorian gilt-brass double bed frame, constructed as a pair of single beds that are joined by the cast "tied knot" terminals.

ca. 1880   *82in (208cm) long*
$13,000-16,000   **DN**

A 19thC mahogany and gilt metal-mounted double bed frame, in Empire style, decorated with Neoclassical motifs, the headboard with mounts with masks of mythical creatures.

84¾in (215cm) long
$3,300-4,000   **DN**

A 19thC Scottish mahogany double tester-bedstead, with two carved parcel-gilt front posts, footboard with unicorn armorial device, stamped "Wylie and Lochhead Glasgow, 2596."

97¼in (247cm) high
$6,500-8,000   **CHEF**

A mid-18thC German brass-bound tulipwood sarcophagus tea caddy, attributed to Abraham Roentgen, with triple canister interior and side-sprung spoon drawer on brass ogee bracket feet.

Born in Mülheim am Rhein, the German ébéniste Abraham Roentgen (1711-93) initially learned cabinetmaking from his father, and subsequently furthered his career at established workshops in The Hague, Rotterdam, Amsterdam, and then London, becoming best known for his expertise in marquetry work, especially metal inlay. In 1738 he joined the Moravian Church, returned to Germany, and in 1750 moved to a Moravian settlement at Neuwied, near Coblenz, where he established a furniture manufactory, from which his pieces gradually becoming more mechanically complex and luxuriously decorated. On his retirement in 1772, his son, David Roentgen, took over the business and established his own reputation.

9in (22cm) wide

$3,300-4,000   **BELL**

A George II mahogany tea caddy, the hinged top revealing an interior with three divisions.

ca. 1750-60   *10in (25.3cm) wide*

$400-450   **WW**

A late-18thC kingwood and sycamore tea chest, in the manner of Abraham Roentgen, inlaid with tulipwood banding, barber-pole, and parquetry stringing, with marquetry fan paterae, the hinged lid revealing a chevron veneered interior with three pull-out canisters with fan inlaid lids, one canister slightly smaller to accomodate a sliding cover to reveal a secret compartment, with an ebony base molding.

9½in (24.2cm) wide

$6,000-6,600   **WW**

CLOSER LOOK—GEORGE III TEA CADDY

The satinwood frame is augmented with ebony banding—a decorative color contrast that also serves to further define the distinctive hexagonal form of the caddy.

The panels around the perimeter of the lid are embellished with highly stylized floral forms, created from thin strips of rolled and gilded paper. This decorative technique, known as "quilling" or paper filigree work, dates back to at least the 15thC.

Paper filigree work ("quilling"), is also employed on five of the side panels and the top of the lid to create naturalistic floral and foliate imagery; it is enhanced, especially on the lid, with selective polychrome painting.

The side panel accommodating the locking mechanism features a painted silk panel of a young girl and is surrounded by serpentine-like forms in gilt-paper filigree set against a contrasting mat green ground.

A late-18thC George III satinwood tea caddy with painted silk and scrollwork decoration.

7in (17.5cm) wide

$6,500-8,000   **WW**

A George III rolled paper tea caddy, with gilt highlights and decorated with leaves and flowers, the lid revealing a lidded compartment, the front with initials "M B" and with a miniature watercolor rondel.

6in (15.7cm) wide

$750-850   **WW**

A George III mahogany and marquetry tea caddy, inlaid with urns and flowers, the lid revealing a lidded interior.

5.6in (14.2cm) wide

$650-800   **WW**

A George III mahogany and marquetry tea chest, with ebony banding, barber-pole stringing, and satinwood panels, the hinged lid with a bone handle revealing three lift-out lidded canisters.

9in (23.2cm) wide

$600-750   **WW**

A late-18thC/early-19thC treen fruitwood pear tea caddy, with a stem finial, the lid revealing an interior with traces of foil lining, with a steel escutcheon.

5½in (14cm) high

$2,600-3,300   **WW**

A late-18th/early-19thC George III tortoiseshell dodecagonal tea caddy, with ivory banding, with silver-colored metal handle, escutcheon and shield-shaped plaque, inscribed "MA to L," the hinged tent top revealing a foil-lined interior.

4¼in (11.2cm) high

$1,600-2,100   **WW**

A George III blonde tortoiseshell tea caddy, inlaid with ivory stringing, the hinged cover revealing a foil-lined lidded interior.

ca. 1800   *4½in (11.3cm) wide*

$850-1,000   **WW**

A George III silver and ivory strung tortoiseshell tea caddy, with twin lidded interior.

7½in (19cm) wide

$600-650   **BELL**

A Regency blonde tortoiseshell tea caddy, inlaid with pewter stringing and with silver-colored metal finial and escutcheon, the cover revealing a twin-lidded interior, on ball feet.

ca. 1815-20   *5¾in (14.7cm) high*

$800-900   **WW**

An early-19thC Regency pressed tortoiseshell tea caddy, the sides depicting Palladian facades, the void interior with traces of original lining.

4in (10cm) high

$1,500-2,000   **L&T**

A Regency mother-of-pearl inlaid tortoiseshell tea caddy, with swept top and bow front, enclosing a twin lidded interior.

8¼in (21cm) wide

$550-600   **BELL**

An early-19thC "Belgian Spa" painted tea caddy, decorated with landscape scenes titled "La Sauveniere," "Cascade de Coo," with a vacant interior.

The mineral water springs at the town of Spa, in modern-day Belgium, were among the first to attract substantial numbers of visitors, initially for the health-giving properties of the waters, but later also as tourists. Subsequently, Spa not only gave it's name to all other resorts with mineral springs—"spa towns" (such as, in England, Bath and Tunbridge Wells)—but also became a collective term for many of the souvenirs, such as tea caddies and other boxes, sold to the visiting tourists. This particular Belgian Spa caddy is painted with local scenes of "La Sauvenière" and "Cascade de Coo."

6.5in (16.3cm) wide.

$750-800   **WW**

An early-19thC ivory and white metal mounted tortoiseshell tea caddy, with two lidded compartments.

7in (18cm) wide

$750-850   **TEN**

CLOSER LOOK— REGENCY TEA CADDY

European "chinoiserie" imagery was often not exclusively Chinese but instead a more eclectic fusion of Asian imagery, such as, as here, Chinese figures, pagodas, and junks with an Indian elephant.

The lock features a distinctive kite- or shield-shaped escutcheon fashioned from bleached bone, in marked color contrast to the gold-on-black lacquerware decoration.

A Regency sarcophagus-shaped tea caddy with gold-on-black penwork chinoiserie scenes, the lid concealing a twin-compartment interior.

Funeral receptacles for interring corpses above ground, sarcophagi—the word derives from the Greek for "flesh-eating stone"—date back to the ancient Egyptian pharaohs. Following archaeological excavations in Egypt, their distinctive, decorative shape became popular for other less morbid boxes, notably tea caddies, in the early 19thC.

9in (22.2cm) wide

$750-850   **WW**

A George IV tortoiseshell tea caddy, the hinged domed lid inlaid with pewter stringing, with a silver-colored metal acorn finial, the body applied with pressed tortoiseshell Gothic panels, the interior with a single lid, on brass ball feet.

ca. 1820-25   *6in (15.3cm) high*

$2,600-4,000   **WW**

A Regency amboyna tea chest, inlaid with kingwood banding and boxwood stringing, the interior with part-hinged twin-lidded pull-out canisters flanking a cut-glass sugar bowl.

ca. 1815-20   *12¼in (31cm) wide*

$750-850   **WW**

An early-19thC fruitwood tea caddy, possibly German or French, the hinged lid decorated with a panel of fabric and cut-paper flowers under glass, the body with stencil-printed landscape scenes.

4¾in (12cm) diam

$850-1,000   **WW**

An early-19thC mahogany and specimen wood tea caddy, inlaid with barber-pole stringing, with a hinged lid and a twin lidded interior.

6in (16cm) wide

$550-600   **WW**

An early-19thC satinwood and ebonized single tea caddy, the lid painted with leaves and flowers.

4in (10.4cm) diam

$450-550   **WW**

An unusual 19thC rosewood and shell-encrusted tea caddy, the interior with a pair of mahogany lidded compartments, on flattened bun feet.

ca. 1820-40   *8¾in (22cm) wide*

$2,600-3,300   **WW**

A William IV rosewood and cut-brass marquetry tea chest, with scrolling leaves and palmettes, the underside of the lid inlaid with an urn, the interior fitted with a pair of pull-out lidded canisters flanking a sugar bowl aperture.

ca. 1830   *12½in (32cm) wide*

$600-650   **WW**

A William IV oak tea chest, carved with scrolling leaves, the hinged top revealing a handwritten label, indistinctly inscribed "This box made out of a beam of oak Windsor Castle. Given to Jessie Forbes by Edward Lloyd Gatacre on the occasion of their marriage 1838.," above a pair of part-hinged lidded lift-out canisters, flanking a sugar bowl aperture.

The Gatacres were an old Shropshire family. Jessie Forbes was the daughter of Sir William Forbes of Callendar, near Stirling, who made his fortune cladding the hulls of the ships of the Royal Navy in copper to prevent termite attacks. Their youngest son was General Sir William Forbes Gatacre of Boer War fame.

ca. 1830   *14¾in (37.4cm) wide*

$260-330   **WW**

A 19C early-Victorian mother-of-pearl pagoda-shaped tea caddy, the hinged lid revealing ivory edging and twin divisions with tent-top lids, with flower-head handles and on disk feet.

7in (17.8cm) wide

$650-800   **WW**

A 19thC mahogany tea caddy, in Sheraton Revival style, painted with ribbons, flowers, and laurel leaves, with a twin-lidded interior, on bone feet.

11in (28.2cm) wide

$550-650 WW

A 19thC early-Victorian tortoiseshell and mother-of-pearl tea caddy, the hinged lid revealing a twin-lidded interior with ivory edging, on vegetable ivory feet.

7in (17.7cm) wide

$600-750 WW

A 19C Victorian Tunbridge ware and rosewood tea caddy, decorated with mosaic bands of geometric parquetry and roses, the hinged cover inlaid with a view of Tonbridge Castle, with a twin-lidded interior, on disk feet.

ca. 1850 *10½in (26.7cm) wide*

$600-750 WW

A 19thC penwork-style tea chest, decorated with printed landscape scenes, with urns of fruit and flowers, with butterflies, a grapevine, and classical lyres, the interior with a pair of lidded compartments flanking a glass sugar bowl.

12in (30.5cm) wide

$550-650 WW

A 19thC early-Victorian Tunbridge ware and rosewood tea caddy, decorated with specimen wood parquetry panels and bands of lozenges, the hinged lid revealing a twin lidded interior.

8in (20.6cm) wide

$600-750 WW

A Victorian coromandel tea chest, with brass mounts, the hinged lid revealing an interior fitted with a pair of dome-lidded lift-out canisters, with an associated glass sugar bowl, with a Brahma lock with key.

ca. 1860 *13½in (34cm) wide*

$1,100-1,250 WW

A 19thC papier-mâché tea caddy, by Jennens & Bettridge, Makers to The Queen, of bombé slipper form, the painted top enclosing a twin-lidded interior.

9in (23cm) wide

$350-400 BELL

A Victorian Welsh painted slate tea caddy, or tobacco box, with marbled decoration, painted with lakeland scenes, the lid revealing an interior with twin divisions, on brass ball feet.

10in (25.5cm) wide

$750-850 WW

A Victorian coromandel tea caddy, with brass strapwork mounts, the interior with a pair of dome-lidded compartments.

ca. 1860-70 *9in (22.8cm) wide*

$180-260 WW

An early-19thC tortoiseshell traveling case, the interior fitted with an ivory-mounted manicure set, etc., with drawer on the side and writing slope.

15½in (39cm) wide

$650-800   **CHOR**

A William IV silver-mounted gentleman's traveling dressing table set, by Archibald Douglas, London, retailed by Briggs, Piccadilly, London, with a pair of cologne bottles, seven toilet boxes, four ivory razors, the pull-out tray reveals other implements, with a pair of boot hooks, a pen, a pair of ivory military brushes, the interior of the cover with a mirror and stationary case, in a fitted brass-bound rosewood case, the cover with a crest.

1830   13in (32cm) wide 7.5oz

$1,700-2,100   **WW**

A Victorian silver-mounted traveling dressing table set, by Thomas Whitehouse, London, retailed by Pearce, 77 Cornhill London, with three scent bottles, four toilet jars, and three toilet boxes, with a pull-out tray, four ivory manicure items, and a pair of scissors, with a push-button secret jewelry drawer, the inside of the cover with a stationary wallet and mirror, in a fitted coromandel case with brass banding.

1862   6.5oz.

$1,200-1,700   **WW**

A Victorian ebony and brass dressing case, by Leuchars & Son, London, the interior fitted with trays, a mirror, writing and toilet accessories, and cut-glass bottles and boxes with silver-gilt lids, the silver with marks for Thomas Johnson, London, name engraved locks and plaque "LEUCHARS & SON/38 & 39 Piccadilly London W."

1869   13½in (34cm) wide

$2,000-2,600   **L&T**

A Victorian coromandel, brass-bound, silver, and mother-of-pearl mounted dressing case, the casket with hidden side drawer and frieze drawer, interior fitted with implements and vessels, the silver covers and lock plate stamped for Betjemann, with retailers label "HOWELL. JAMES & CO REGENT STREET.LONDO."

Founded by cabinetmaker John Betjemann in the late 1840s, the firm of Betjemann and Sons were well known for their automated mechanisms, of which the cleverly hidden side drawer in the present casket is an example. Their work was featured in the 1852 and 1867 International Exhibitions in London and Paris. The poet Sir John Betjemann was a descendant of the founders. Howell, James & Co were renowned silversmiths and jewelers whose work also regularly appeared at exhibitions.

ca. 1871   11¾in (30cm) wide

$2,000-2,600   **DN**

An Edwardian 9ct gold mounted lady's traveling toilet set, with a pig skin case, with eight glass toilet bottles and jars, two tortoiseshell hairbrushes, a tortoiseshell jar, two tortoiseshell clothes brushes, a tortoiseshell hand mirror, and four cork-lined bottle and jar tops, excluding the liquor flask, with beaker base, London.

1905   9ct gold 144gm

$4,000-4,600   **BELL**

An early-19thC Regency penwork wood jewelry box, with domed top opening to red silk-lined interior, over two doors opening to an interior fitted with drawers and ivory handles, decorated all over with Asian scenes.

11¾in (30cm) high

$1,600-2,400   **L&T**

An early-19thC Napoleonic prisoner-of-war straw-work jewelry box, the lid with ship sailing off a French townscape, lid with inset mirror and lidded compartment.

8¾in (22cm) wide

$550-650   **CM**

A late-18thC prisoner-of-war straw workbox, the top revealing a twin compartment interior, decorated with town scenes and fauna.

10in (26cm) wide

$200-260   BELL

A Regency simulated rosewood workbox, the lid with a printed view of Brighton Pavilion, titled "VIEW of the WEST FRONT of the PAVILION," the front with two views of Brighton, the lid with a colored print, titled "THE CHAIN PIER & MARINE PARADE BRIGHTON."

10.5in (27cm) wide

$450-550   WW

An early-19thC brass-bound rosewood artist's paint box, by Reeves & Sons, the cover enclosing an interior with box of paints, marble mixing palette and water pot over a drawer with creamware mixing dishes and an ivory palette, printed "W.R.REEVES & SON, 80 HOLBORN BRIDGE, LONDON" and "THE SOCIETY FOR THE ENCOURAGEMENT OF ARTS MANUFACTURERS AND COMMERCE ADELPHI MAY 17 1781," cover repaired, two mixing bowls cracked and repaired, leather inset with wear.

12¼in (31cm) wide

$2,600-3,300   TEN

A Regency painted sycamore cottage sewing box, possibly Tunbridge ware, naively painted with windows and doors, the roof revealing a lift-out tray, originally with divisions, with a bone tape measure and a thimble, above a compartment, the base with a drawer with six divisions for spools.

Possibly given by the Music Hall star Marie Lloyd to her seamstress for her 21st birthday.

ca. 1800-15   *6in (15cm) wide*

$1,000-1,100   WW

A marquetry workbox, the lid inlaid with an early twin-funnel paddle steamer within a Tunbridgeware border, compartmented tray inside.

ca. 1850   *12¼in (31cm) wide*

$180-240   CM

An artist's mahogany box, by Ackermann and Co., the interior with paint blocks, watercolor powder bottles, palettes, etc., a drawer with palettes beneath and apothecary's brass scales, in a mahogany case.

12¼in (31cm) wide

$1,600-2,000   CHOR

A Regency penwork decorated workbox, decorated with scenes of figures in the chinoiserie taste, in traditional dress, the lid opening to a removable divided tray incorporating lidded sections, and a compartment beneath, on brass lion paw feet.

The decoration, including a Chinese landscape vignette in India-fashion penwork, relates to examples illustrated in A. Clarke & J. O'Kelly, "Antique Boxes," 2003.

ca. 1815   *10in (25cm) wide*

$1,300-1,800   DN

A William & Mary walnut oyster-veneered and marquetry-inlaid lace box, in the manner of Thomas Pistor.

This box bears the influence of Dutch and French cabinetmakers working in the last quarter of the 17thC, such as Gerrit Jensen, Jan van Meekeren, and Pierre Golle. Golle, a Dutchman who moved to Paris to work for the court, was the spearhead of this art of richly inlaid designs of floral motifs and also creator of the brass and tortoiseshell technique made famous by his son-in-law André-Charles Boulle. Golle's son, Cornelius, as many Protestant craftsmen in France, was obliged to move to England and worked in London with Jensen, establishing the interest for floral wood marquetry in this country. Recent research has revealed another prominent cabinetmaker working in this technique at the turn of the century, Thomas Pistor. Pistor is documented as working for James Grahme, Keeper of the Privy Purse and Master of the Buckhounds to James II. A center table and a cushion-framed mirror, commissioned for Bagshot Lodge and later in Levens Hall, relate to this box, because they share similarities in the handling of the inlaid decoration and its designs. Through the inventories from Bagshot and Levens Hall between 1686 and 1697, we know that Grahme also patronized the royal cabinetmakers John Gumley and Gerrit Jensen. Thomas Pistor Senior was a London cabinetmaker recorded in Moorfields in 1678. He was also living in Bell Court by 1693 where he probably had his workshop.

ca. 1690   *21in (53.5cm) wide*

$6,000-6,600   DN

An early-18thC Queen Anne black-lacquered and gilt-chinoiserie writing box, the cover with a figural scene of men in traditional costume in a garden, above an elaborately engraved lock plate, opening to a speckled ground interior, knocks and scuffs, and the gilt has rubbed down to an underlying layer of green.

11¾in (30cm) wide

$350-450   **DN**

A George IV rosewood brass-bound writing slope, the lid revealing an interior with a later baize-lined slope, compartments for pen and ink and with two secret drawers.

ca. 1820   *16in (40.6cm) wide*

$260-400   **WW**

A George IV rosewood and brass-inlaid campaign writing slope, with candle sconces, inkwells, and lockable interior with lift-out tray, paper trade label for T. Randford, lock marked "Tompson."

18in (45.5cm) long

$750-850   **CHOR**

A 19thC Anglo-Indian brass-bound amboyna writing slope, with fitted interior.

19¾in (50cm) wide

$240-290   **BELL**

A 19thC ebony and brass boulle marquetry inkstand, with a pair of cut glass inkwells flanking a handle and a lidded compartment, with two dished pen trays above a drawer, on cast ormolu scroll and shell feet.

ca. 1840   *15¾in (39.8cm) wide*

$1,500-2,000   **WW**

A late-19th/early-20thC Damascus inlaid stationery box.

8¾in (22cm) wide

$400-450   **CHEF**

A George II shagreen perfume box, with engraved brass mounts and side carrying handles, lid opening to reveal original cut glass perfume decanters, there are damages to the shagreen, two of the bottles have chips on the rims.

ca. 1740   *11¾in (30cm) wide*

$800-900   **DN**

A 19thC inlaid tabletop liquor cabinet with key, the cover opening to reveal four gilt-decorated decanters and ten glasses, two decanters with damages, all four stoppers chipped.

12½in (32cm) wide

$550-650   **CHEF**

A Victorian brass-bound coromandel decanter box, the cover opening to reveal four cut glass decanters and stoppers.

11¾in (29.5cm) high

$850-1,000   **CHEF**

A mid-18thC George II miniature shagreen-covered and metal-mounted knife box, the interior with four knives cast with beaded-and-faceted "barrel-end" grips, and four conforming forks, key present.

8in (20cm) high

$900-1,200 DN

A mid-18thC George II shagreen-covered and silvered metal-mounted knife box.

11in (28cm) high

$650-800 DN

ESSENTIAL REFERENCE—KNIFE BOXES

Although knife boxes first appeared in the 17thC—King Charles II of England is on record as gifting one to one of his mistresses—they didn't really come into fashion until the second quarter of the 18thC and the reign of George II, when the convention of a dinner host providing his or her guests with cutlery, instead of them bringing their own, became firmly established among the wealthier classes. Often supplied in pairs as ornamental containers for expensive silver cutlery (initially just knives, but eventually forks and spoons, too), their basic, serpentine-front form remained mostly unchanged until the 1780s, with early decorative differences primarily residing in their finish: either wood veneered or covered in silk velvet or shagreen.

However, stylistic variations did emerge, notably, in the 1760s, with bow-front mahogany boxes with hinged slopes and drop handles, and shaped bracket or ball-and-claw feet. From the 1770s, increasingly lavish embellishments, such as crossbanding, feather banding, and parquetry work also became more prevalent, while in the 1780s the Neoclassical vase-form knife box, or cutlery urn, emerged, designed to stand on pedestals or at each end of a sideboard. However, during the early 19thC, knife boxes and cutlery urns were rendered increasingly redundant by sideboards with drawers fitted for storage.

A late-18thC George III mahogany and paktong mounted knife box, fitted for cutlery.

This box is nearly identical to the knife box illustrated in "Paktong, The Chinese Alloy in Europe 1680-1820," by Keith Pinn, published by the Antique Collectors' Club, 1999. It is illustrated in color on the dust jacket and in black and white on p. 121, pl. 98 and 98A.

13¾in (35cm) high

$1,050-1,200 L&T

A George III mahogany knife box, with white metal mounts, indistinctly marked.

14¼in (36cm) high

$1,050-1,200 CHEF

A George II mulberry and line inlaid knife box, the top centered by an inlaid silver scrolling crest, scratches and abrasions, the key escutcheon is probably a replacement, the engraved metal inset crest should be referred to as silver-colored metal.

ca. 1750 *14¼in (36cm) high*

$1,250-1,450 DN

A 19thC early-Victorian oak tobacco box, presumably made from the remains of York Minster after the fire of 1840, with a silver plaque engraved with a view of the burning York Minster and dated "May 20th 1840."

The fire at York Minster on the May 20, 1840, was the second great fire at the Minster; the first was in 1829.

1840 *6in (15.3cm) wide*

$400-450 WW

A French silver-plated mounted ebonized fruitwood cigar box, with twin compartment interior.

9in (23cm) wide

$350-400 BELL

An early-20thC Victorian novelty humidor in the form a barge, the tambour top opening to reveal a compartmented interior and lift-out tray, the deck and cabin exterior with brass fittings, stamped "Rd 137636."

16¼in (41cm) long

$900-1,050 L&T

An 18thC inlaid Indo-Portuguese box, the top above a fall front with three drawers, inlaid with scrolling symmetrical designs in pale wood and ivory.

18¼in (46cm) wide

$4,000-5,300   CHEF

An early-19thC Scottish penwork games box, decorated with scenes after David Wilkie, the cavetto-molded hinged lid depicting a domestic scene probably involving payment of rent, the front, back and sides illustrating fox hunting scenes, the interior with a removable divided tray and four boxes, each lid with scenes of everyday life, with paper label, "Smith and Co. Carvers and Gilder's, 78 Union Street, Aberdeen."

The penwork scene decorating the lid of this fine box is adapted from Sir David Wilkie's 1807 painting "The Rent Day." One of interior boxes in the interior also features a detail of this picture, as well as three other genre scenes presumably after Wilkie. Literature: Tromans, Nichols "David Wilkie. The People's Painter," published Edinburgh 2007, plate 2.

$2,600-4,000

11¼in (28.5cm) wide

L&T

An early-19thC portable pressure copying press, probably by James Watt, the mahogany case with brass edges, with a base drawer, the fitted interior with two brass sconces, a tin-cased ink bottle, ivory brush, and lift-out section.

21¼in (54cm) wide

$4,600-5,300   SWO

A 19thC early Victorian tortoiseshell box, the lid inset with a mother-of-pearl parquetry panel.

ca. 1840   *4½in (11.5cm) wide*

$350-400   WW

A 19thC Italian pietra dura and ebony box, the cover with a pietra dura panel with two birds on a branch with flowers.

7½in (19cm) wide

$650-800   L&T

A late-19thC oak mailbox in the form of a sentry box, the front with a brass mail slot labeled "LETTERS" with a gouache painted figure of a Grenadier Guard, signed "CL Buck 1880" and bearing a silvered presentation panel inscribed "From Married Women/2nd Bn Gren. Gds/TO/COLONEL H. TROTTER/29th April 1889."

Major General Sir Henry Trotter GCVO, DL was a senior British Army officer. Born in 1844 and commissioned into the Grenadier Guards in 1862, he commanded the regiment from 1889 to 1894 and was promoted to Major General in 1895, appointed Major General commanding the Brigade of Guards and General Officer Commanding the Home District in 1897, serving until 1903. During preparations for the coronation of King Edward VII in 1902, Trotter acted as Chief Staff Officer to the Duke of Connaught, who was in supreme command of the troops taking part in all military ceremonies connected with the coronation. He resided at Mortonhall, a Georgian country house on the southern edge of Edinburgh. The Trotter family acquired the estate in 1635 and the house was built in 1769. Trotter and his wife had four sons and a daughter, the sons all had military careers although two were killed in action during World War. I

17¾in (45cm) high

$7,500-8,000   L&T

A late-19thC French kingwood, ivory, ebonized, parquetry box, on brass feet.

11½in (29cm) wide

$550-650   L&T

An early-20thC Edwardian mahogany ballot box.

16½in (42cm) high

$180-240   CHEF

A George III mahogany cheese coaster, with arc d'arbalète sides and twin baluster lifts, on brass and leather roller casters.

The arc d'arbalète sides of the cheese coaster refers to their distinctive profile, the double-S scrolling form of which is based on that of the bow component of a traditional European crossbow. Etymologically, the modern French word "arbalète" is derived from the old French "arabalèste," and that, in turn, from the Latin "arcuballista," meaning a "bow ballista."

ca. 1800   16½in (42.2cm) wide

$1,050-1,200   **WW**

A Regency mahogany cheese coaster.

16in (39.6cm) wide

$600-650   **WW**

An early-19thC Regency mahogany cheese coaster, with twin-split baluster lifts and two divisions, on leather roller casters.

17¼in (43.5cm) wide

$350-400   **WW**

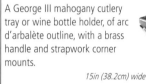

A George III mahogany cutlery tray or wine bottle holder, of arc d'arbalète outline, with a brass handle and strapwork corner mounts.

15in (38.2cm) wide

$260-400   **WW**

A 19thC mahogany cutlery tray, with three divisions and a brass handle.

16in (40cm) wide

$260-330   **WW**

A late Regency rosewood book carrier, in the manner of Gillows, double-sided, with twin baluster handles and turned spindle supports, on lobed bun feet.

ca. 1820   16¾in (42.5cm) wide

$1,600-2,100   **WW**

A George IV rosewood and brass-mounted book carrier, with a pierced arcaded gallery and a pair of leaf scroll handles.

ca. 1825   22in (56cm) wide

$850-1,000   **WW**

A George III mahogany serpentine tray, with spindle gallery, scratches and abrasions.

ca. 1780   24in (61cm) wide

$1,700-2,400   **DN**

A George III mahogany dodecagonal tray, brass bound, with two pierced handgrips.

ca. 1800   15in (38cm) wide

$1,800-2,400   **WW**

A 19thC toleware coffeepot, with gooseneck spout, minor wear.

10½in (26.5cm) high

$1,100-1,250 POOK

A black toleware coffeepot, with a gooseneck spout.

ca. 1900 *10½in (26.5cm) high*

$4,000-4,600 POOK

A large 19thC black toleware tray.

17¼in (44cm) wide

$550-650 POOK

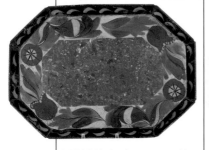

A 19thC black toleware tray, with asphaltum center, minor wear.

12½in (32cm) wide

$2,000-2,600 POOK

A 19thC black toleware tea caddy.

7¾in (19.5cm) high

$550-650 POOK

An early-19thC Tunbridgeware white wood watch stand, in the form of a castle entrance guarded by two cylindrical crenellated towers.

Unique to South East England, and particularly Tunbridge Wells, is the manufacture of painted, sycamore and birch architectural models, concealing various functions, usually for the ladies of Regency England. This rare form appears as a watch tower, where a pocket watch is placed in the holder overnight.

8in (20.5cm) wide

$2,000-2,600 SWO

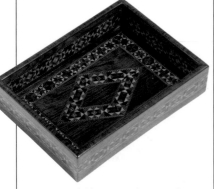

A Victorian Tunbridgeware and rosewood tray, in the manner of Thomas Barton, inlaid with parquetry bands.

ca. 1850 *7¾in (19.7cm) wide*

$260-330 WW

A 19thC Victorian Tunbridgeware and ebony sewing box, in the manner of Thomas Barton, the lid decorated with a view of Bayham Abbey, East Sussex.

10½in (26.5cm) wide

$260-400 CHEF

A 19thC Tunbridgeware and walnut workbox, with marquetry inlaid panels depicting yachts, sailing ships, and a steamboat, the interior originally with a tray.

12¼in (31.2cm) wide

$1,100-1,250 WW

A mid-18thC George II walnut miniature chest, possibly an apprentice piece, inlaid with checker banding, the top inset with an ebony-and-bone parquetry square, above four drawers.

9in (22.7cm) high

$6,000-6,600   **WW**

An early-19thC mahogany miniature chest, possibly an apprentice piece, inlaid with stringing and satinwood banding, with two short and three long drawers, on bun feet.

6½in (16.3cm) high

$450-600   **WW**

An early-19thC French miniature bombé commode, with three drawers, the top inlaid with musical trophies, on splayed legs and ball feet, one rear foot has been detached.

18½in (47cm) wide

$1,050-1,200   **SWO**

A 19thC miniature oak bureau, the fall flap enclosing a fitted interior, over four drawers, on bracket feet.

10in (25.5cm) high

$550-650   **L&T**

A 19thC Victorian miniature apprentice-piece pitch pine kitchen dresser.

33½in (84.75cm) high

$350-400   **MART**

An early-20thC walnut miniature chest-on-stand, in William and Mary style.

16in (40.5cm) high

$400-450   **WW**

An early-19thC mahogany miniature faux bamboo open armchair, possibly an apprentice piece, with a rush seat.

11¼in (28.5cm) high

$1,000-1,100   **WW**

A mid-19thC Victorian cast-iron miniature fireplace, possibly a traveling salesman's sample, the top with the Royal Coat of Arms flanked by a lion and unicorn and with a pair of chinoiserie figures, the sides with pairs of cherub heads, with a brass miniature grate and fire tongs.

17¼in (43.8cm) high

$1,000-1,100   **WW**

An early-18thC Queen Anne tortoiseshell and silver-mounted snuff box, the hinged lid with a band of pique decoration and with a plaque engraved with initials "W*W."

3¾in (9.5cm) wide

$260-400 WW

An early-18thC treen burr oak, folk art snuff box, the lid carved with Eve with animals beside the tree of the knowledge of good and evil, above a Latin motto "Totus Mundus In Maligno Mali Positus," with a brass band and a leaf border, the base carved with a figure and an indistinct motto "...Here Redde Diem."

4¼in (10.7cm) wide

$1,000-1,100 WW

Judith Picks

I've never taken snuff, and I've never collected snuff boxes, but I'd really like this particular snuff mull—partly because I'm a Scot, and partly because of its remarkable, albeit somewhat macabre and most certainly poignant provenance.

The mull was originally the possession of Arthur Elphinstone, 6th Lord of Balmerino (1688-1746), one of the most fervent and high-profile leaders of the Jacobite Rising of 1745. Earlier, on the accession to the throne of the Hanoverian King George 1 in 1714, Arthur had immediately resigned his commission in the army and taken part in the Jacobite Rising of the "Old Pretender," in 1715.

After that had been put down, he made his escape to France and joined the army there, not returning to Scotland until 1744 to join forces with Prince Charles Edward Stuart, the "Young Pretender." Captured at the infamous Battle of Culloden, Arthur was taken with two other Scottish noblemen for trial by his peers in Westminster and found guilty. On the day of his execution, immediately before he was beheaded on Tower Hill, he presented his snuff mull—a most quintessentially Scottish personal possession at that time—to the Captain of the Guard and delivered a resounding, unrepentant cri de Coeur "If I had a thousand lives, I would lay them all down in the same cause!"

A Scottish silver-mounted snuff mull, the lid engraved with crest, helm, and shield of arms, motto "FOLLOW ME," and "Colin Campbell," the underside inscribed "The Mull Used by LORD BALMERINO (Beheaded on Tower Hill in 1746) Given by him on the scaffold to the officer on guard/If Lost to be Returned to Mr Josh. Knowles No 2 New Inn London," and warrant of William Henry Cavendish Bentinck Scott Marquis of Titchfield, partly printed, appointing Joseph Knowles to be Adjutant Captain of the Corps of St Andrew & St George the Martyr Volunteers, signed, sealed, and delivered, January 28, 1803.

ca. 1740

3¾in (9.5cm) high

$6,000-6,600 M&K

An 18thC carved, coquilla-nut snuff box, commemorating the Franco-Ottoman alliance, carved with profile portraits of a French officer and Ottoman ruler.

2¾in (7cm) long

$3,300-4,600 L&T

A George III, Welsh horn, primitive snuff box, the lid inscribed "John Thomas Brunaura Clynnog 1791," the base inscribed "Jn Thom. Brynayra. yw gwir Berehen og y Blwch yma a Phwy bynag a ddygo hwn oddiarno fo geiff yscras byth oddiwrtho," which translates as "John Thomas of Brunaura is the true proprietor of this box and whoever steals this from him will receive disgrace for ever from it."

3¼in (8.5cm) high

$2,600-3,300 WW

An early-19thC Scottish horn, elephant snuff mill, with bone eyes and tusks, with silver mounts, unmarked, the hinged cover with a plaque, inscribed "G. Phillips."

3¼in (8cm) high

$1,100-1,250 WW

An early-19thC treen horse's-head snuff box, with brass tack decoration and inlaid with a bone rondel, the underside with a hinged cover.

3in (7.5cm) long

$1,600-2,000 WW

An early-19thC treen, folk art frog snuff box, with a hinged compartment.

4in (10cm) long

$1,600-2,100 WW

ESSENTIAL REFERENCE—MAUCHLINEWARE

Highly collectible Mauchline wares had their origins in the fine-quality wooden snuff boxes and tea caddies initially made in the late-18thC and early-19thC by Charles Stiven of Laurencekirk, Kincardinshire. Exquisitely decorated with hand-painted or pen-worked portraits, landscapes, or flora and fauna, they proved so popular other Scottish craftsmen— notably in the towns of Cumnock and Mauchline—also began to make them.

Although a decline in taking snuff forced many snuff box makers out of business by the 1840s, a surge of interest in Scottish culture, and an attendant increase in tourism north of the border in the mid-19thC, afforded commercial opportunities that were seized upon by William and Andrew Smith of Mauchline, who rapidly diversified their output to produce a vast range of decorative but useful wooden objects as souvenirs for the tourists. From ca. 1850, they also substantially increased their output by using not only pen- and brushwork for decoration, but also transfer-printing and, from ca. 1860, photographic images. Further growth then ensued by making these souvenirs for numerous other cities, towns, spas, and resorts throughout Great Britain, much of Europe, and the United States.

In an industry that boomed well into the 1930s, the success of W & A Smith of Mauchline was such that even as other manufacturers sprang up around the country—most notably The Caledonian Box Works in Lanark—all such souvenirs, regardless of date or place of manufacture, or the geographic location of their decorative imagery, became collectively known as Mauchlineware.

An early-19thC Scottish sycamore Mauchline ware and penwork snuff box, decorated with a stylized seaweed design, the hinged lid with a lurcher chasing a hare in a landscape setting, with a foil-lined interior.

4¼in (11.2cm) wide

$350-400 WW

An early-19thC Scottish Mauchline ware penwork snuff box, decorated with thistles, flowers, and leaves.

3¾in (9.4cm) wide

$260-400 WW

A Scottish William IV Mauchline tartan ware snuff box, by W & A Smith, the "hidden-hinged" lid with a gold Rococo thumbpiece, the foil-lined interior stamped with the Royal Coat of Arms and "Smith Mauchline Manufacturers to His Majesty" and "Warranted Made from the Solid."

ca. 1835-40 *3¼in (8.5cm) wide*

$260-400 WW

A William IV oak "Houses of Parliament" snuff box, the lid with a silver plaque, unmarked, inscribed "Made From Wood found in the Ruins of the Houses of Parliament destroyed by Fire 16th Octr 1834."

The Palace of Westminster, the medieval Royal palace used as the home of the British parliament, was largely destroyed by fire on the 16th October 1834. The blaze was caused by the burning of small wooden tally sticks which had been used as part of the accounting procedures of the Exchequer.

1834 *4in (10.3cm) diam*

$1,050-1,200 WW

A Scottish ram's-horn snuff mull, the cover with white metal thistle decoration, the collar engraved "Peter Turner 1835."

3½in (9cm) long

$240-290 CHOR

A treen horse's-head snuff box, naively carved with bone inset eyes, the underside with a sliding cover with stop.

ca. 1840 *3¼in (8.5cm) long*

$1,600-2,000 WW

An early/mid-19thC German lacquered papier-mâché faux wood snuff box, in the manner of Stobwasser, painted to depict a section of timber with a textured bark-style rim.

3½in (9cm) diam

$750-850 WW

A mid-19thC Scandinavian treen, birch dog snuff box, probably Swedish, the underside with a hinged cover, the interior with traces of original lining.

5½in (14cm) long

$1,600-2,000 WW

A 19thC treen mahogany snuff shoe, with brass tack inlay of swags and flowers, with a sliding cover.

6¾in (17cm) long

$550-650　　　　　　　　　**WW**

A mid-19thC treen rosewood table snuff shoe, inlaid with ivory buttons and a vacant plaque, with brass tack decoration and a hinged lid.

9in (23cm) long

$1,300-1,700　　　　　　**WW**

A mid-19thC treen frog snuff box, with glass eyes, the underside with a sliding cover.

2¾in (7cm) long

$550-650　　　　　　　　**WW**

A treen frog snuff box, with ebonized eyes, the underside with a hinged cover.

ca. 1860　　　　　*2¼in (5.7cm) long*

$1,700-2,100　　　　　　**WW**

A 19thC treen frog snuff box, with a painted finish and brass eyes, the underside with a sliding cover.

3¼in (8cm) long

$1,250-1,450　　　　　　**WW**

A 19thC treen horse's-head snuff box, with brass tack inlay and ebonized eyes, his forehead with an ivory dot, the hinged lid with initials "J. B."

3½in (9cm) long

$1,000-1,100　　　　　　**WW**

A late-19thC Scandinavian treen birch dog snuff box, probably Swedish, the underside with a hinged cover.

4¾in (12cm) long

$750-850　　　　　　　　**WW**

A late-19thC treen "pinch of snuff" snuff box, carved in the form of a hand sporting a brass ring, the base with a hinged cover.

2¾in (7cm) high

$600-750　　　　　　　　**WW**

A late-19thC treen "pinch of snuff" snuff box, the base with a pull-off cover.

4¼in (11cm) high

$400-450　　　　　　　　**WW**

A 19thC Scandinavian treen birch dog snuff box, probably Swedish, the underside with a hinged cover, the interior with traces of foil.

5in (12.5cm) long

$550-650　　　　　　　　**WW**

ESSENTIAL REFERENCE—NUTCRACKERS

Nuts have been a significant source of nutrition since the beginning of time, and over the centuries humankind has, beyond primitive efforts with rocks or stones, created many ingenious devices for cracking open their hard shells. While metal nutcrackers— in use for nigh on 2,500 years—have been both effective and popular, it has generally been those carved from wood that have proved among the most decoratively appealing and, indeed, collectible nowadays.

Different forms of cracking mechanism are the primary focus for some collectors, notably those variations on exerting pressure on the shell via a screwing mechanism—generally available by the 17thC, and experimented with earlier by no less than Leonardo da Vinci! It is, however, the carved figural nutcrackers, mostly produced from the 15thC onward, that command the attention of most collectors. Whether anthropomorphic or zoomorphic, stylized, or, more usually, naturalistic, their often intricately carved forms are as much small, exquisite works of sculpture as functional dining paraphernalia!

An early-18thC treen lever-action nutcracker, with a snake-head terminal and zigzag decoration.

6¼in (16cm) long

$1,250-1,450   WW

A mid-18thC treen primitive lever-action nutcracker, in the form of a man wearing a hat and with a flat face, inscribed with two dates "1758" and "1773."

5½in (14cm) long

$1,800-2,400   WW

A late-17thC/early-18thC primitive treen carved oak lever-action nutcracker, in the form of a man with a flat face.

11½in (29cm) long

$4,000-4,600   WW

A primitive treen lever-action figural nutcracker, in 17thC style but probably 19thC, carved in the form of a man with a flat face.

8in (20.2cm) long

$2,000-2,600   WW

An early-19thC carved coquilla-nut nutmeg grater, the screw-off cover revealing a steel grater.

3in (7.5cm) high

$50-80   WW

An early-19thC treen boxwood screw-action nutcracker.

2½in (6.5cm) high

$350-400   WW

A 19thC carved treen fruitwood ladle, of King's pattern, pierced for suspension.

11¾in (29.5cm) long

$200-260   WW

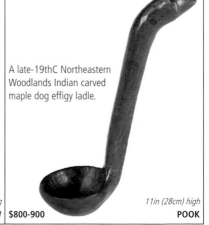

A late-19thC Northeastern Woodlands Indian carved maple dog effigy ladle.

11in (28cm) high

$800-900   POOK

A Charles II lignum vitae dated wassail bowl, engraved with an inscription in Latin "Implentur veteris bachi pinginsg Ferince=Tendinus in Latinum Anno domini 1681 Ex dono Jacobi Smith Exons," which translates as "Fill up with old wine that is really juicy. Tried in Latin in the year 1681. The gift of Jacob Smith Esq.," above a coat of arms on each side, one with three roses between "fess dancetty" for the Smith family and the other shield with a leopard's face on a canton for the Isaac family.

The word "wassail" means "Good health" and is an expression of well wishing equivalent to the word "cheers," offered in the context of convivial drinking. This is apt in the context of the present example, which was probably presented as a gift and used at a wedding between the Isaac and Smith families in 1681. It is fairly rare to find a wassail bowl with a date and an inscription.

11½in (29.5cm) diam

$11,000-13,000   WW

A possibly 19thC lignum vitae wassail bowl, in the 18thC style, the bowl on turned stem and spreading circular foot.

7in (18cm) diam

$4,000-4,600   CHEF

A 19thC turned treen dairy bowl, with reeded bands on the exterior.

18¼in (46cm) diam

$550-600   CHEF

A 19thC American New England burlwood bowl.

15½in (39.5cm) diam

$1,050-1,200   POOK

A large late-19thC sycamore dairy bowl, with turned bands.

15½in (39cm) diam

$750-850   SWO

A 19thC treen stained-sycamore dairy bowl, the exterior with molded and incised bands.

11¼in (28.3cm) diam

$400-450   WW

A late-19th/early-20thC North European treen burr-birch urn, on an ebonized plinth base.

9¾in (24.5cm) diam

$550-650   WW

A turned and carved 19thC painted tobacco canister, probably central Pennsylvania, retaining its original salmon and yellow surface, repaired age crack on lid.

8in (20.5cm) high

$2,600-4,000   POOK

A late-19thC Norwegian folk art, carved and stained pine box, of staved construction and with bentwood straps, all over carved with scrolling leaves, with a paper label, inscribed "Molde, Norway."

11¾in (29.5cm) wide

$600-650   WW

A George IV Scottish mahogany wine decanter coaster, attributed to James Mein of Kelso, on three leather and brass roller casters.

9½in (24cm) diam

$1,250-1,450 WW

An early-19thC Regency Welsh or sailor's treen love token, with chip carved-style decoration, pierced and containing one ball, dated "1814" with initials "M H," the end hung with a bank token dated "1813."

3¾in (9.7cm) long

$180-210 WW

A William IV wooden, turned and painted tipstaff, decorated with Royal Arms of the Order of the Garter, flanked by Lion & Unicorn.

ca. 1830 *11½in (29cm) long*

$150-200 MART

A Victorian treen, folk art staff "hunt tally," carved with a hunt scene, with horses and huntsmen chasing a fox, dated "1871," with a brass suspension ring.

ca. 1871 *8¾in (22.2cm) long*

$550-650 WW

A George II treen, lignum vitae coffee grinder or mill, with a screw-off stylized acorn finial, the body in three sections, with a folding iron handle.

9¾in (24.5cm) high

$2,400-2,900 WW

A pair of George IV mahogany salver stands, by Gillows, each weighted base with molded upright and turned rests, the backs stamped "GILLOWS."

ca. 1825 *16½in (42.2cm) high*

$4,000-5,300 DN

A pair of mid-18thC treen novelty boots pin cushions.

3in (7.8cm) high

$650-800 WW

A mahogany cigarette dispenser, in the form of a motor torpedo boat, the mechanism hinging on a Union Jack flag, with a gathering platform in the form of a step, some damage.

ca. 1930 *20½in (52cm) wide*

$800-900 SWO

A late-19thC/early-20thC novelty treen monkey inkwell, with glass eyes, the head opening to a ceramic inkwell.

2¾in (7.4cm) high

$130-200 MART

ESSENTIAL REFERENCE—BLACK FOREST CARVINGS

Primarily drawing for inspiration and subject matter on the flora and fauna of the forest, the woodcarvings that originated in the 1800s in and around the Swiss town of Brienz are collectively known as Black Forest carvings (and occasionally referred to as "Brienzerware").

- Typical subjects include bears, dogs, foxes, stags, boars, birds (from eagles to cockerels), as well as trees and branches.
- Types of object range from stand-alone sculptures to diverse items of furniture and other domestic artifacts, such as hall stands, clock cases, table centerpieces, tobacco jars, and inkwells.
- During the second half of the 19thC, and the early years of the 20th, the industry flourished, promoted in no small part internationally by displays of Black Forest carvings at the Great Exhibition in London (1851), the World's Fairs in Philadelphia (1876) and Chicago (1893), and the Exposition Universelle in Paris (1900).
- The industry also benefited considerably from a significant rise in tourism during the 19th and early 20th centuries, with many wealthy travelers eager to bring back Black Forest carvings as souvenirs of their overseas trips.
- By ca. 1910, there were some 1,300 individual carvers plying their trade in and around Brienz, and inevitably with so many sources quality can vary—from work of art to kitsch souvenir. In terms of the former, pieces signed by woodcarvers from the Huggle family are particularly sought after.

A late-19thC carved-oak bear figure, realistically modeled holding a fish and a molded tree branch.

31½in (80cm) high

$1,300-1,600 TEN

A late-19thC Black Forest carved-linden wood model of a prowling bear, with glass eyes.

10¾in (27.5cm) long

$850-1,000 WW

A Black Forest bear, with glass eyes and a painted snout and mouth, repolished and finished, knocks and scratches.

ca. 1900   *19¾in (50cm) high*

$3,300-4,000 SWO

An early-20thC Black Forest bear, with painted eyes, snout and mouth.

13in (33cm) high

$800-900 SWO

A late-19th/early-20thC Black Forest carved-wood bear tobacco jar, with glass eyes, with a hinged lid, and a brass bowl.

9in (23.3cm) high

$850-1,000 WW

A late-19th/early-20thC Black Forest carved-wood smoker's table, the top with a pair of lidded compartments, each surmounted by a bear and with a pair of brass lift-out bowls, supported by a bear holding a tree trunk and leaning on a pipe.

33in (83.5cm) high

$4,600-5,900 WW

A Black Forest hall stand, carved as a bear on skis clutching a tree with a cub climbing aloft, complete with mirror, skis possibly later additions, cracking to feet.

76¾in (195cm) high

$2,100-2,600 CHEF

A late-19th/early-20thC Black Forest carved-wood smoker's table, the table with three sitting bears, with two hinged compartments, one when open activates a Swiss musical box, flanking a brass bowl, with a bear clambering up the tree trunk, with a hinged lid and glass eyes.

35in (87.8cm) high

$3,300-4,000 WW

A late-19thC Black Forest carved-wood head of a bloodhound, on a walnut plinth.

8in (20.7cm) high

$1,800-2,400   **WW**

A late-19th/early-20thC Black Forest carved-lindenwood model of a Saint Bernard, glass eyes.

7½in (19cm) wide

$850-1,000   **WW**

A late-19th/early-20thC Black Forest carved-lindenwood model of a retriever, with glass eyes.

7in (17.5cm) high

$850-1,000   **WW**

A pair of late-19th/early-20thC Black Forest carved-wood dog door porters, each in the form of a begging spaniel, with glass eyes, standing on a cushion.

30in (74.9cm) high

$8,500-9,000   **WW**

A Black Forest carved-wood cat tazza, supporting a turned wood bowl on three paws, some chipping on ears, the bowl and tail with repairs.

11in (28cm) high

$750-850   **CHEF**

A late-19thC Black Forest carved box, with two hens with three chicks on a wheat sheaf.

11½in (29cm) wide

$1,800-2,400   **L&T**

A Black Forest owl tobacco box, hinged at the neck, carved beside a stump match holder, some old signs of woodworm.

10in (25cm) high

$650-800   **CHEF**

A mid-20thC Black Forest carved-wood stag's head, with mounted antlers, minor rubbing.

47¼in (120cm) high

$1,100-1,250   **SWO**

A late-19thC Black Forest carved-wood oval box, the hinged lid carved with game birds, the body relief-decorated with leaves and flowers, on scroll feet.

14in (34.5cm) wide

$850-1,000   **WW**

A pair of limewood figural candlesticks, by the circle of Tilman Riemenschneider, modeled as kneeling attendants holding candlesticks, both restored, one with iron pricket missing.

ca. 1460-1531   *15½in (39.5cm) high*

$3,300-4,600   **TEN**

A 17thC Spanish carved-wood figure of Saint Michael, supporting a cross, with traces of old paint, on an associated reliquary base.

19in (48cm) high

$800-900   **CHEF**

A pair of possibly early-18thC carved kneeling female figures, possibly limewood, on "cloud" bases.

42¼in (107cm) and 40½in (103cm) high

$3,300-4,000   **CHEF**

A 17thC carved-limewood saint.

26¾in (68cm) high

$400-550   **CHEF**

A 17thC carved-limewood torso of a young man, possibly the Christ Child, with traces of polychrome paint decoration.

19in (48cm) high

$850-1,000   **CHEF**

A 19thC carved, painted-wood cherub, with inset glass eyes, later hoof suspension.

29¼in (74cm) high

$650-800   **CHEF**

A pair of late-16th/early-17thC carved gryphon-type mounts, with wings and scrolling tails.

19¾in (50cm) high

$6,500-8,000   **CHEF**

A late-17th/early-18thC Italian carved-wood wall sconce, carved as a mask with an arm extending from the mouth.

16½in (42cm) deep

$650-800   **L&T**

A carved and painted eaglet on nest, by Wilhelm Schimmel (Cumberland Valley, Pennsylvania 1817-90), with original polychrome surface, chip on beak, lacking one leaf.

This is a rare form for Schimmel, with only a few known.

7in (18cm) high

$33,000-40,000   POOK

A carved and painted eagle, by Wilhelm Schimmel (Cumberland Valley, Pennsylvania 1817-1890), with original polychrome surface with an old darkened varnish over top, chips wings and talons.

17½in (44.5cm) wide

$15,000-20,000   POOK

A 19thC carved and painted pine bird on perch, with vibrant red surface, loss from rear of one foot, small chip on beak and tip of one wing.

11¼in (28.5cm) high

$2,200-2,600   POOK

An American carved and painted counter top cigar store "Indian Maiden," attributed to Samuel Robb (1851-1928), New York, with old layered-paint history, a couple of old repaired breaks to headdress, old repair to nose and base.

ca. 1900   38½in (98cm) high

$16,000-21,000   POOK

A 20thC folk art, carved and painted pig pull toy, with leather ears and tail, glass eyes, some paint loss.

13½in (34.5cm) long

$1,600 2,100   POOK

A 19thC Pennsylvania painted poplar dresser box, the lid decorated with a house in a landscape, the front and sides with American eagle and flowers, inscribed on underside of lid "William Platner Delaware County."

10¾in (27.5cm) wide

$6,000-6,600   POOK

A 19thC Pennsylvania, painted poplar bentwood sewing box.

5¼in (13.5cm) diam

$1,000-1,100   POOK

A 19thC wallpaper covered bentwood box, depicting the Deaf and Dumb Asylum, New York, wear on edge of lid.

18in (45.5cm) wide

$2,200-2,600   POOK

A New Hampshire, painted pine hanging wall box, with original floral and bird decoration, with black and yellow striping, the back dated and initialed "BW," chip on corner of drawer.

1830   21in (53.5cm) high

$12,000-15,000   POOK

An important Charles II/James II ebonized eight-day longcase clock, by Edward East, London, the six-finned and latched-pillar movement with plates measuring 7 x 5in (18 x 12.5cm) enclosing fine delicate wheelwork, the going train with bolt-and-shutter maintaining power and anchor escapement regulated by seconds pendulum and the strike train with internal locking integral with the rim of the great wheel and striking a domed bell mounted above the plates, the dial-engraved signature "Edwardus East Londini," the ebonized case with projecting ogee cornice and foliate scroll-pierced frieze, the trunk with panels each bordered with fine architectural moldings within a half-round molded surround.

ca. 1685   *75¼in (191cm) high*

$90,000-100,000   **DN**

A William and Mary walnut and floral marquetry longcase clock, of one month duration, the four-finned pillar bell striking movement with plates, high position external countwheel, and separately cocked pallet arbor for the anchor escapement regulated by seconds period pendulum, the dial signed "John Wise, London," the lower half of the base has been restored with replacement marquetry, clock has pendulum, two brass-cased weights, a winder, and a case key.

John Wise senior is recorded in Brian Loomes' "Clockmakers of Britain 1286-1700" as born in Banbury, Oxfordshire, in 1624 and apprenticed to Peter Closon through Thomas Dawson in 1638, gaining his Freedom in October 1646. He apparently lived in Warwick 1653-68, where he repaired the clocks at St. Nicholas's and St. Mary's churches, the latter providing the venue for the baptism of three of his children. He moved back to London in 1669 where he was readmitted to the Clockmakers' Company by redemption. He took many apprentices, including no less than six of his sons; Richard (Free 1679), John (Free 1683), Thomas (Free 1686), Joseph (Free 1687), Peter (Free 1693), and Luke (Free 1694). He worked from "neer the Popeshead in Moorfields" and was recorded as a recusant in 1682/3. John Wise senior died in 1690 and was buried at St. Andrew's, Holborn.

ca. 1690   *80in (203cm) high*

$8,500-10,000   **DN**

A Philadelphia William and Mary walnut tall-case clock, by Peter Stretch, Philadelphia (1670-1746), with a sarcophagus bonnet enclosing a 30-hour works, with brass face, finials, and feet replaced, sarcophagus reglued to bonnet.

The engraving on the dial and the single-hand movement determines this clock to be one of his earliest, probably 1703-20.

98½in (250cm) high

$26,000-33,000   **POOK**

An early-18thC George I mahogany chiming longcase clock, by Joshua Wilson, London, with pagoda top, brass ball finials, signed, stop-fluted pilasters, brass inlay, molded arched trunk door, brass stop-fluted quarter columns, chimes on four bells.

96½in (245cm) high

$6,500-8,000   **L&T**

A George I walnut eight-day longcase clock, by James Leicester, London, the five-finned pillar rack-and-bell striking movement with anchor escapement for regulation by seconds pendulum, the brass break-arch dial signed "James Leicester, ye Strand, London."

James Leicester is recorded in Baillie, G. H. "Watchmakers & Clockmakers of the World" as working from ca. 1710-29, when he was declared bankrupt.

ca. 1725   *95in (241cm) high*

$2,600-3,300   **DN**

A George I/II green japanned eight-day longcase clock, the five-finned pillar rack and bell striking movement with anchor escapement regulated by seconds pendulum, the dial inscribed "Charles Clay, Inventor of the, Machine Watches, London," in a case decorated with figural chinoiserie scenes, clock has pendulum, weights, case key, and winder.

Charles Clay was a fine and inventive clockmaker who originated from near Huddersfield and gained his freedom of the Clockmakers' Company prior to 1716. In 1723, he was appointed Clockmaker in His Majesty's Board of Works. He is best known for his organ clocks, one of which now resides at Windsor Castle, which was acquired from his widow three years after his death in 1743.

ca. 1725-30   *92¼in (234cm) high*

$4,000-4,600   **DN**

A George II mahogany month-going longcase clock, by Daniel or Nathaniel Delander, London, the month-going movement with duplex escapement with bolt-and-shutter retaining power, the engraved silvered brass dial with a Duplex escapement, signed "Delander/London," the hood with a shaped and molded cornice with reeded block finials and scroll brackets, and flanked by canted angles with brass-lined stop fluting.

The Delander family of clockmakers spanned several generations from the 17thC into the latter 18thC, and produced superbly crafted and innovative clocks and timepieces. Arguably the most famous of the Delanders was Daniel, who was apprenticed in 1692 to Charles Halstead and, later, to Thomas Tompion and became a member of the Clockmakers' Company in 1699. Among his innovations were a patented watchcase spring-closing mechanism and a year-going equation. He is credited with improving the duplex escapement so that it could be used in longcase clocks. He died in 1733.

ca. 1730s *81½in (207cm) high*
$17,000-21,000 **L&T**

A George II burr walnut quarter-chiming eight-day longcase clock, by Samuel Thorne, London, the triple-train five-pillar movement with anchor escapement regulated by seconds pendulum chiming the quarters on a graduated nest of eight bells and sounding the hour on a further larger bell, the gilt-brass, break-arch dial with nameplate engraved Samuel Thorne, London, the case with break-arch cavetto cornice with fluted canted angles, the trunk with canted angles flanking a book-matched burr-veneered herringbone-banded shaped-top trunk door, clock has three brass-cased weights, pendulum, and two case keys.

ca. 1740 *91¼in (232cm) high*
$15,000-18,000 **DN**

A George II green japanned eight-day longcase clock, with automaton, by Stephen Rimbault, London, the five-pillar rack-and-bell striking movement with anchor escapement regulated by seconds pendulum, the dial with nameplate engraved "Step'n Rimbault, London," with pierced steel hands and applied twin bird-and-urn cast spandrels to angles beneath arch centered with a silvered disk engraved with a disgruntled face incorporating "rocking eye" automaton and flanked by dolphin cast mounts, cluck with pendulum, two weights, winder, and case key.

ca. 1750 *90in (229cm) high*
$11,000-13,000 **DN**

A New Jersey Queen Anne gumwood tall-case clock, the sarcophagus bonnet enclosing an eight-day works with brass face, inscribed "Aaron Miller," sarcophagus top rebuilt, feet replaced.

ca. 1760 *96¾in (245.5cm) high*
$9,000-10,500 **POOK**

A William III walnut and floral marquetry eight-day longcase clock, by John Clowes, London, the five-finned pillar outside countwheel bell striking movement and anchor escapement regulated by seconds pendulum, the brass dial signed "John Clowes, London" the case has minor bumps, scuffs, shrinkage, the clock has pendulum, weights, two case keys, and a winder.

ca. 1700 *77¼in (196cm) high*
$8,500-10,000 **DN**

A Chippendale walnut tall-case clock, Philadelphia, the broken-arch bonnet with a carved centered finial, enclosing an eight-day works with brass face, inscribed "E. Duffield Philada.," rosettes replaced, the name boss, inscribed "E. Duffield Philad" is probably not original.

ca. 1770 *99in (251.5cm) high*
$13,000-18,000 **POOK**

A George III mahogany eight-day longcase clock, by Thomas Field, Bath, the four-pillar rack-and-bell striking movement with anchor escapement regulated by seconds pendulum, the brass break-arch dial signed "Thomas Field, BATH," the case with swan-neck pediment over dentil-molded, break-arch frieze and fluted Corinthian columns, clock has pendulum, two weights, and a winder but no case key.

ca. 1770 *94in (239cm) high*
$1,600-2,100 **DN**

CLOSER LOOK—JOHN MURDOCH

Classicism is at the forefront of the clock case's pediment, in which a pair of "swan's necks" (inspired by Classical S scrolls) surmount a Roman arch, flank a Roman urn brass finial, and each terminate in patera-like brass rosettes.

Reference to the Classical Roman vocabulary of ornament is also evident in the choice of Roman, instead of Arabic, numerals on the clock's brass dial.

The Classical Orders of architecture are also referenced in not only the brass-mounted fluted columns flanking the clock face, but also in the longer, fluted quarter columns flanking the finely figured mahogany pendulum door.

The essentially Classical columnar form of the longcase clock extends to the base, which is of plinthlike form and raised on ogee-bracket feet.

An 18thC Scottish George III mahogany longcase clock, by John Murdoch, Edinburgh, the eight-day movement striking a bell.

The Edinburgh clockmaker John Murdoch was active from 1752-75, having been apprenticed to Andrew Dickie. His son, also John, worked as his father's apprentice from 1767.

89in (226cm) high

$1,600-2,100   L&T

A George III mahogany eight-day longcase clock with rolling moonphase incorporating tidal indication, by John Baker, Hull, the four-pillar rack-and-bell striking movement with anchor escapement regulated by seconds pendulum, the dial signed "IOHN BAKER HULL" and calibrated for age of the moon and high-water times to the circumference of the lunar disk over lunettes engraved with globe delineations, the case with gilt ho-ho bird centered oval fretwork panel on the pagoda upstand, clock is complete with pendulum, weights, case key, and winder.

John Baker is recorded in Brian Loomes's "Watchmakers & Clockmakers of the World, Volume 2" as believed working in Hull during the late 18thC. The current clock is perhaps a little unusual in having two steel pointers within the moonphase; the first is intended for the age of the moon while the other can be adjusted to provide the times of high water for a given port to be read from the scale engraved on the edge of the disk.

ca. 1780   *89¾in (228cm) high*

$4,000-5,300   DN

A late-18thC Scottish George III mahogany longcase clock, by William Philip, Edinburgh, the eight-day movement striking a gong, the swan-neck pediment with brass roundels and an orb and eagle finial, dial with a boss engraved "Wm Philip/ Edinburgh."

88½in (225cm) high

$6,500-8,000   L&T

A late-18thC George III mahogany longcase moonphase clock, by John Brownbill, Liverpool, the eight-day movement striking a bell.

92¼in (234cm) high

$2,400-2,900   L&T

An 18thC George III black lacquered longcase clock, by Robert Clidsdale, Edinburgh, the eight-day twin-train movement striking a bell, the nameplate signed "Robt Clidsdale/ Edinburgh," with an arch-molded trunk door with prints of George III and Queen Charlotte, the base decorated with chinoiserie.

87½in (222cm) high

$2,600-3,300   L&T

A Federal walnut tall case clock, Reading, Pennsylvania, with an eight-day works, the case with eagle-inlaid door and base, finials replaced.

ca. 1795   *92½in (235cm) high*

$5,300-6,600   POOK

An 18thC or later 30-hour single-handed longcase clock, signed "Jno Ogden, Darlington," four-pillar movement with an anchor escapement and outside countwheel striking on a bell, case has been repainted.

87in (221cm) high

$1,050-1,200   TEN

A George III mahogany longcase clock, with four-pillar eight-day movement, dial signed "Isaac Sharatt, Burslem," the hood with swan-neck pediment, quarter pilasters upon paneled plinth base with faux brick corners, some restoration and cleaning to movement, some damage to blind fretwork on hood.
ca. 1800   *96½in (245cm) high*
$2,000-2,600   **CHEF**

A George III oak longcase clock, by William Coe, Cambridge, with five-pillar eight-day movement.
94½in (240cm) high
$800-900   **CHEF**

A George III mahogany longcase clock, with five-pillar movement, the one-piece silvered dial signed "John Rowning Newmarket," the pagoda hood with fretwork panels and shaped cresting, three brass ball finials, some damage to fretwork, movement cleaned, front movement plate has a few unused holes—therefore a possible replacement movement.
96in (244cm) high
$2,200-2,600   **CHEF**

An early-19thC late-George III mahogany longcase clock, the eight-day twin-train movement striking a bell, the dial signed "James McCabe/ Royal Exchange/ LONDON," in a molded arch case with brass finial and canted stop-fluted angles with brass insert, above an arched-molded door flanked by stop-fluted angles with further brass inserts.
91¼in (232cm) high
$5,300-6,600   **L&T**

A Regency domestic longcase regulator, by Chater and Son, London, the five-pillar movement with deadbeat escapement.
74¾in (190cm) high
$1,600-2,100   **CHEF**

An early-19thC Scottish late-Regency mahogany clock, by Thomas Mcgregor, Ayton, the eight-day twin-train movement striking a bell, in an arch-molded case with brass finial, above an arched crossbanded trunk door flanked by reeded quarter columns.
87¾in (223cm) high
$1,500-1,800   **L&T**

An early-19thC George III mahogany longcase clock, the twin-train movement striking a bell, signed "JOSEPH HERRING, LONDON," enclosed by a pagoda hood with fretwork panel.
93¾in (238cm) high
$1,600-2,100   **L&T**

An early-19thC Scottish mahogany longcase clock, by George Innes of Glasgow, the eight-day brass movement with an anchor escapement striking on a bell, the silver dial, signed "Geo. Innes Glasgow," the architectural flame-veneered case with ebonized edging.

77½in (197cm) high

$1,300-1,800   **WW**

An early-19thC Scottish George III mahogany longcase clock, the twin-train eight-day movement striking a bell, inscribed in the arch "JAMES SMITH EDINBURGH," the hood with swan-neck pediment and fret carving.

89¾in (228cm) high

$3,300-4,000   **L&T**

A three-train musical longcase clock, Whitehurst, Derby, the movement chiming on eight bells via a pin barrel, and striking a further bell, in a later carved oak case, dial with two blanked off winding holes from the rear of the dial for an eight-day movement.

83in (211cm) high

$1,600-2,100   **CHEF**

An early-Victorian specimen wood longcase clock, the eight-day movement striking a bell, the painted arch dial painted with a village scene in a case with swan-neck pediment and feather finial.

88½in (225cm) high

$600-750   **L&T**

Judith Picks

One often-present element of 19thC Biedermeir-style furniture that particularly appeals to me is, as in this Swedish longcase clock, the cabinetmakers' exploitation of the inherent figuring and grain of the wood employed—in this case birchwood—thereby making it the primary form of decoration, over and above any applied decorative elements. One consequence of this is it almost invariably serves to emphasize rather than obfuscate the overall simplicity of line and form also characteristic of the Biedermeier style, and clearly evident here. It strikes me that this clarity of line, understated decoration, and sense of functionality that underpins the Biedermeir style—which emerged in Austria and Germany ca. 1818, and was popular there and elsewhere in Europe until ca. 1860—was impressively prescient of the "form follows function" tenets of 20thC Modernism.

A mid-19thC Swedish Biedermeier satin birch longcase clock, by Johan Langstrom, Skelleftea, the dial with two winding holes and signed "Joh. Langstrom/ Skelleftea 1854."

94in (239cm) high

$1,050-1,200   **L&T**

A Regency-style eight-day longcase clock, four-pillar movement with an anchor escapement and rack striking on a bell, dial engraved with a masonic scene, with pendulum and two weights.

ca. 1890   *78¾in (200cm) high*

$900-1,050   **TEN**

A late-19thC mahogany chiming longcase clock, triple-weight driven movement with an anchor escapement, chiming on eight bells and striking the hours on a gong, with chapter ring inscribed Thos Williams Axbridge, arch with moonphase aperture, later case, with three weights and a pendulum.

91¾in (233cm) high

$1,700-2,100   **TEN**

An early-18thC French Louis XIV gilt-brass-mounted Boulle bracket clock, by Etienne Le Noir, Paris, the five-baluster pillar movement pinned at the rear, with large spring barrels and verge escapement regulated by half-seconds disk-bob pendulum with silk suspension.

32in (81cm) high

$3,300-4,000 DN

A Louis XV ormolu-mounted, tortoiseshell, and brass-inlaid Boulle bracket timepiece, by Jean-Claude, Fieffe, Paris, with quarter-pull repeat, the single-barrel movement with later escapement and with quarter-pull repeat striking the quarters on two bells.

25½in (65cm) high

$2,000-2,600 CHOR

A George III mahogany eight-day bracket clock, by Daniel Vauguion, the twin-fusee movement with a verge escapement, hour bell strike with repeat.

ca. 1770 *13¾in (35cm) high*

$10,000-11,000 SWO

A mid-18thC ebonized bracket clock, by William Smith of London, fitted with a twin-fusee movement, the dial with mock pendulum and date aperture.

William Smith is recorded as working as a clockmaker in Cheapside, London, from 1750-80.

20in (51cm) high

$2,600-3,300 CHOR

An 18thC George III mahogany bracket clock, by William Liptrot, London, the case after a design by Thomas Chippendale, the eight-day movement with verge escapement striking a bell and chiming on six bells, the backplate signed "Wm. Liptrot/ London," with a bob pendulum.

27in (68.5cm) high

$12,000-15,000 L&T

A George III mahogany bracket clock, the eight-day brass repeating movement with a verge escapement striking on a bell, inscribed "JAMES MUCKARSIE HOLBORN," the arch with a strike/silent dial and with gilt Rococo spandrels.

23¼in (59cm) high

$4,600-5,900 WW

A George III mahogany bracket clock, by Samuel Honychurch, London, the brass eight-day movement with four-turned pillars and a later anchor escapement striking on a bell, with pull repeat, with pendulum, a case key, and winding key.

ca. 1770 *52.1cm high*

$2,600-4,000 WW

A late-18thC George III mahogany and brass repeating bracket clock, with a twin-train movement with verge escapement and bell strike.

23¼in (59cm) high

$3,300-4,600 L&T

A George III ebonized bracket clock, the eight-day brass repeating movement with a verge escapement striking on a bell, plaque inscribed "Stepn Rimbault LONDON."

18¾in (47.5cm) high

$4,600-5,300   **WW**

A mahogany musical bracket clock, signed "Geo Clarke, London," the repeating movement striking on seven bells, the gilt-metal mounted case later.

19¾in (50cm) high

$4,600-5,300   **SWO**

An early-19thC ebonised bracket clock, by French, Royal Exchange, London, with a twin-fusee movement striking on a bell, the case with perhaps added domed top and globe finials.

24in (61cm) high

$4,600-5,900   **CHOR**

A Regency brass-inlaid, mahogany quarter-chiming bracket clock, by F. B. Adams, London, the substantial six-pillar triple-chain fusee movement with anchor escapement regulated by lenticular bob half-seconds pendulum.

Francis Bryant Adams is recorded in Brian Loomes's "Watchmakers & Clockmakers of the World, Volume 2" as apprenticed in 1821 and working in London from 1828. In 1832, he went into partnership with his sons and served as Master of the Clockmaker's Company 1848-49. The business is thought to have continued with his sons until ca. 1875.

ca. 1825   *30in (76cm) high*

$8,000-9,000   **DN**

A Regency brass-inlaid, rosewood bracket clock, with trip-hour repeat and fired enamel dial, by John Peterkin, London, the five-pillar twin-fusee bell striking movement with anchor escapement regulated by lenticular bob pendulum.

John Peterkin is recorded in G. H. Baillie's "Watchmakers & Clockmakers of the World" as working in London ca. 1811-40. From his surviving work, it would appear that John Peterkin was primarily a watchmaker, with many of his watches signed along with the address "25 Cleveland Street, London."

ca. 1825   *15¾in (40cm) high*

$6,500-8,000   **DN**

A George IV mahogany and parquetry triple-fusee musical bracket clock, by William Jordan of Rickmansworth, movement striking the hours on a nested set of 11 bells playing 6 airs and chiming on a 12 bell.

18½in (47cm) high

$4,600-5,300   **MART**

A George IV rosewood bracket clock, by Cummins, London, the brass eight-day movement with four turned pillars and an anchor escapement striking on a bell, with pendulum, winding key, and case key.

ca. 1825-30   *16½in (42.2cm) high*

$4,000-4,600   **WW**

A burr oak Gothic Revival bracket clock, by Barnard of London, the brass three-train movement with turned pillars and an anchor escapement chiming on eight bells and striking the hours on a gong, with pull repeat, signed, with an associated walnut and oak bracket.

ca. 1825-30   *26¾in (68cm) high*

$2,600-4,000   **WW**

A William IV rosewood and patinated bronze bracket clock, the brass eight-day movement striking on a bell, signed "Frodsham & Baker Gracechurch St. London," the front decorated with a lion and foliage, with a fan pagoda top with a retractable handle, with pendulum, winding key, and case key.

ca. 1830-35   *11¼in (28.5cm) high*

$5,300-6,600   **WW**

A Victorian mahogany quarter-chiming bracket clock, by Robert Hay, London, the six-pillar triple-chain fusee movement with thick plates and half-deadbeat escapement regulated by long lenticular bob pendulum.

Robert Hay, London, does not appear to be recorded in the usual sources. From this, it is perhaps appropriate to speculate that he was either a retailer or a journeyman who spent his career exclusively working for others instead of setting up on his own.

ca. 1850   *23¾in (60cm) high*
$1,300-1,800   DN

A Victorian ebonized and gilt-brass mounted quarter-striking bracket clock, by Winterhalder & Hofmeier, the eight-day twin-train movement striking two coils and signed "D.R. Patent W. & H. Sch."

17in (43cm) high
$1,050-1,200   MART

A 19thC rosewood-cased bracket clock, the double-fusee eight-day movement striking the half hours on a bell, the dial inscribed "W P Fromol, Liverpool," two urn finial replaced, pendulum retaining knob missing, sides with splits.

17¾in (45cm) high
$1,050-1,200   SWO

A late-19thC French Boulle inlaid striking bracket clock, by Hatton of Paris, Japy Frères twin-barrel movement with outside countwheel strike on the hour and half hour on a bell, no. 1400.

12in (30.5cm) high
$550-650   MART

Judith Picks

This French bracket clock was made in the late 19thC in a revival of an early-18thC style known as Régence, which dominated French taste from ca. 1710-30 and was named after the period 1715-23, when the Duc d'Orléans was Regent to Louis XV upon the death of his father, Louis XIV, and until he came of age. The style is characterized by a move away from the heavy, academically correct Classicism that characterized the court style of Louis XIV toward a lighter, less austere, and more curvaceous approach to form and decoration—one which was to gradually evolve into the even more flamboyant and sinuous Rococo style.

To me, part of the appeal of the clock lies in the fact that its Régence style, while transitional, also manages to be distinctive in its own right—to the extent of being considered well worth reviving some 150 years later! The quality that really attracts me, however, is the fact that although its Greco-Roman imagery—from the Roman goddess Minerva surmount to the four pairs of flanking female therms and the pair of ram's heads—was employed in decorative Classicism throughout Europe, and although crafting that imagery in the form of gilt-brass mounts and contrasting it with exotic veneers (here, red tortoiseshell) was also far from exclusive to France, there is no way this splendid clock can be anything other than French.

A late-19thC Régence-style gilt-brass mounted tortoiseshell bracket clock, the two-train eight-day ting-tang gong quarter striking movement with Vincenti et Cie stamped roundel on backplate, the case with Minerva surmount on the superstructure.

69¼in (176cm) high
$10,000-11,000   DN

An Edwardian ebonized and gilt-metal-mounted quarter-chiming bracket clock, the eight-day quarter-striking triple-fusee movement chiming on either 10 bells or 4 coiled gongs, the dial inscribed "A HAMILTON, CRIGHTON & CO., 41 GEORGE ST. EDINBURGH," has pendulum, winding key, and case key.

ca. 1900   *26in (66cm) high*
$6,500-8,000   DN

A late-19th/early-20thC Louis XV-style red boulle and gilt-brass bracket clock, the drum movement striking on a single bell, the dial with porcelain numerals.

16½in (42cm) high
$1,000-1,100   SWO

An early-20thC Edwardian mahogany chiming bracket clock, the eight-day movement striking a gong and chiming on eight bells, the backplate stamped "2923."

28in (71cm) high
$3,300-4,000   L&T

A late-16thC Danish Renaissance gilt-brass steel-framed table clock, by Daniel Kersten, Odense, the posted movement now with back-wound fusee, flanged spring barrel, and verge escapement regulated by sprung three-arm brass balance to the going train, lower section with winding hole labeled "GA WERK" over signature "DANEL KERSTEN y ODENSE."

8½in (21.5cm) high.

$8,000-9,000 DN

A William III ebony table timepiece, with silent pull-quarter repeat, by Samuel Watson, London, the five-finned pillar single-fusee movement with verge escapement regulated by short-bob pendulum and silent pull-quarter repeat on two bells, backplate signed "Samuel Watson, LONDON."

ca. 1695 *11in (28cm) high*

$26,000-33,000 DN

A William III ebonized table timepiece with alarm, by John Bushman, London, the five-finned baluster pillar single-fusee movement with verge escapement regulated by disk-bob pendulum and pull-wind alarm mechanism.

John Bushman (Buschmann) is recorded in Brian Loomes's "Clockmakers of Britain 1286-1700" as a "High German" watchmaker born in Hagen (Augsburg) ca. 1661 and was made brother of the Clockmakers" Company in September 1692.

ca. 1695 *13¾in (35cm) high*

$11,000-13,000 DN

A George I brass mounted ebony table clock, with pull-quarter repeat on six bells, by Robert Markham, London, the five-finned pillar twin-fusee bell striking movement with verge escapement regulated by short-bob pendulum and pull-quarter repeat on a nest of six graduated bells.

ca. 1720 *19¾in (50cm) high excluding handle*

$4,000-5,300 DN

A mid-18thC George II miniature ebony table clock, by Henry Fish, London, the six-pillar twin-chain fusee bell-striking movement now with anchor escapement regulated by disk-bob pendulum the silvered plate signed "Henry Fish, LONDON," the movement has been converted from verge escapement to anchor escapement, clock has pendulum, case key, and winder.

Miniature table clocks are particularly scarce and are generally defined as being less than 12in (30cm) in height for a break-arch dial example.

9in (23cm) high

$22,000-26,000 DN

A George III green japanned table clock, with pull-quarter repeat on six bells, by Marmaduke Storr, London, the six-pillar twin-fusee movement with verge escapement, backplate signed "Marm: Storr, London."

Marmaduke Storr is recorded as working in London 1724-75. The current clock is a rare survivor retaining its original decoration untouched and with the movement and dial reflecting the case's originality.

ca. 1760 *20½in (52cm) high excluding handle*

$13,000-16,000 DN

A George III striking table clock, signed "NathL Style, London," twin-fusee movement with a verge escapement and rack striking on a bell, veneers with small cracks.

ca. 1760 *21¼in (54cm) high over handle*

$2,600-4,000 TEN

A George III ormolu mounted ebonized quarter-chiming table clock, with pull-trip repeat, by Ellicott, London, the substantial six-pillar triple-chain fusee movement chiming the quarters on a graduated nest of six bells and sounding the hours on a further larger bell.

John Ellicott is particularly noted for the development of the cylinder escapement and a form of compensated pendulum.

ca. 1765 *25½in (65cm) high*

$10,500-12,000 DN

An alarm table timepiece, signed "Geo Lindsay, London," single-fusee movement with a verge escapement, alarm striking on a bell, movement backplate signed "Geo Lindsay Serv to His Majesty."

ca. 1770 *14½in (37cm) high*

$6,500-8,000 TEN

TABLE 311

CLOCKS

A George III mahogany table clock, by Robert Ward, London, the five-pillar twin-fusee movement with verge escapement regulated by short-bob pendulum, nameplate signed "Rob't Ward, London."

Robert Ward is noted as specializing in supplying musical clocks for the Middle Eastern market.

ca. 1770   22in (56cm) high
$4,000-5,300   DN

A George III brass-mounted mahogany quarter-chiming table clock, with concentric calendar, the dial signed for "James Tregent, London," the six-pillar triple-fusee movement with verge escapement regulated by short bob pendulum, clock is complete with winder and case key.

ca. 1775   20in (51cm) high
$6,500-8,000   DN

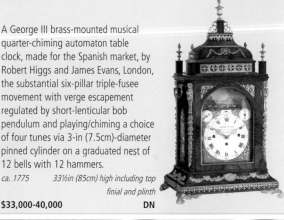

A George III brass-mounted musical quarter-chiming automaton table clock, made for the Spanish market, by Robert Higgs and James Evans, London, the substantial six-pillar triple-fusee movement with verge escapement regulated by short-lenticular bob pendulum and playing/chiming a choice of four tunes via 3-in (7.5cm)-diameter pinned cylinder on a graduated nest of 12 bells with 12 hammers.

ca. 1775   33½in (85cm) high including top
                          finial and plinth
$33,000-40,000   DN

A rare George IV brass-mounted mahogany table regulator, by Barwise, London, the four swollen columnar-pillar single-chain fusee movement with inverted pear-shaped plates, Harrison's maintaining power and delicate pin-wheel escapement incorporating adjustable pallets regulated by heavy disk-bob half-seconds pendulum with fine beat adjustment on crutch and suspension bar.

ca. 1825   16¼in (41cm) high
$40,000-46,000   DN

A late-18thC Austrian ebonized quarter-striking table clock, by Jacob Tenzel, Vienna, the four-pillar triple-standing barrel movement with four-wheel trains, verge escapement regulated by short-bob pendulum.

16in (41cm)
$1,300-1,800   DN

A mahogany chiming table clock, retailed by Webber, Liverpool, triple-fusee movement with an anchor escapement chiming on a nest of eight bells and striking the hours on a gong, movement backplate numbered "4178," with pendulum.

ca. 1890   30in (76cm) high
$3,300-4,600   TEN

An early-20thC French Boulle striking table clock, twin-barrel movement striking on a gong.

19½in (49.5cm) high
$650-800   TEN

A French Louis XV boulle marquetry mantel clock, the eight-day brass movement with an outside countwheel and striking on a bell, the backplate signed "Charles Voilin Paris," signed "CHLES BEAUVILLAIN A PARIS."

30½in (77.5cm) high

$2,600-3,300 WW

A mid-18thC and later ormolu- and porcelain-mounted mantel clock, the eight-day watch movement with a pierced and engraved clock and signed "J. Jolly a Paris," the case decorated with mid-18thC Meissen porcelain figures, with a fruit seller modeled by J. F. Eberlein.

12½in (31.8cm) high

$8,000-9,000 WW

A late-18thC French Louis XVI patinated bronze, ormolu, and white marble figural mantel clock, by Jaques Gudin, Paris, the circular two-train countwheel bell striking movement with anchor escapement and silk pendulum suspension.

Jacques Jerome Gudon is recorded in G. H. Baillie's "Watchmakers & Clockmakers of the World" as becoming a Master of his trade in 1769 and dying in 1789.

21½in (55cm) high

$2,600-4,000 DN

An early-19thC French Empire ormolu and patinated bronze mantel clock in the form of a teapot, Fournier horloger, Grenoble, the case by Claude Galle, Paris, the circular eight-day two-train countwheel bell striking movement with anchor escapement regulated by disk-bob pendulum incorporating silk suspension, with pendulum and winding key.

The Fournier family of clockmakers can be traced back to the 1740s, with Louis Fournier as a second generation Parisian clockmaker appointed a Master of his trade in 1748. Subsequent generations worked in Paris throughout the 18thC and early 19thC, including a C. L. Fournier during the Empire period.

10in (25.5cm) high

$11,000-13,000 DN

An early-19thC French Florentine marble and pietra dura mantel clock, by Hunziker, Paris, with a twin-train eight-day movement, the lapis lazuli dial with Roman number chapters, signed with engraved script on the backplate "HUNZIKER."

21¾in (55cm) high

$24,000-26,000 L&T

An early-19thC late Regency mahogany, ebony, and brass inlaid mantel clock, by Molyneux, London, the twin-train eight-day movement striking a bell, the backplate signed "MOLYNEUX/ LONDON."

14¼in (36cm) high

$1,600-2,100 L&T

An early-19thC mantel clock, by French, Royal Exchange, London, the twin-fusee movement with pull repeat and striking on a bell.

17½in (44.5cm) high

$1,050-13,000 CHOR

An early-19thC French Empire sculptural gilt-bronze mantel clock, the silk-thread movement striking a bell, signed "Ch.s Oudin El. de Breguet," case mounted with a scene of Cerberus and Orpheus.

18in (45.5cm) high

$1,300-1,800 L&T

An early-19thC French Empire gilt and patinated bronze mantel clock, the eight-day movement with silk suspension and bell strike, mounted with a bronze figure of Urania.

15½in (39cm) high

$2,900-3,700 L&T

An early-19thC French Empire ormolu mantel clock, the eight-day countwheel bell striking movement with silk pendulum suspension, the case with surmount cast as Amor, clock with pendulum and winding key.

18¼in (46cm) high

$2,600-4,000 **DN**

A Regency ormolu and patinated bronze figural mantel timepiece, unsigned but probably by Baetens, London, the four columnar-pillar eight-day single-chain fusee movement with anchor escapement regulated by a lenticular bob pendulum, timepiece has a pendulum and winding key.

Several models of this timepiece share the same castings, form and specification are known, signed by Joseph van Baetens, F. Baetens, or just Beatens, who were a family firm of bronziers that also produced timepieces. Working in a similar vain to the Vulliamy family, they were based at 23 Gerard Street, Soho, and according to G. H. Baillie (in "Watchmakers & Clockmakers of the World") were active around 1832.

ca. 1825   *12½in (32cm) high*

$4,000-4,600 **DN**

A Victorian gilt-brass-mounted mahogany quarter-striking mantel clock, the five-tapered baluster pillar twin-chain fusee "three-in-two" movement ting-tang striking the quarters on a graduated pair of gongs and sounding the hour on the larger of the two, with half-deadbeat escapement regulated by disk-bob pendulum, dial signed "MARTIN, BASKETT & MARTIN, CHELTENHAM," clock with pendulum, case key, and winder.

ca. 1845   *10¼in (26cm) high*

$6,000-7,500 **DN**

A mid-19thC mahogany and inlaid mantel clock, with a two-train movement engraved "GEO GROVE LONDON," with hammer striking a coiled gong.

16¼in (41cm) high

$550-650 **BELL**

A mid-19thC rosewood, ormolu, and marquetry portico clock, by Leroy of Paris, the signed movement no. 515, with bell strike on the hour and half hour and outside countwheel strike.

20¼in (51.5cm) high

$800-900 **MART**

A Gothic Revival Hart, Son, Peard and Co. brass mantel clock, by Bruce James Talbert (1838-81), the twin-train movement striking a bell inscribed "GV/ 1507," the case mounted with an agate set finial.

ca. 1870   *10¾in (27.5cm) high*

$5,300-6,600 **L&T**

A Reformed Gothic brass mantel clock, designed by Bruce Talbert, probably manufactured by Cox & Co. or Hart, Son, Peard & Co.,the pinnacle set with quartz stone flower finial.

15½in (39.5cm) high

$11,000-13,000 **WW**

An Empire ormolu and bronze mantel clock, of Cupid and Psyche, with twin-train drum-shaped movement with countwheel strike on a bell, one pendulum and one key.

22in (56cm) high

$4,000-4,600 **BELL**

A 19thC French porcelain and ormolu-mounted vase-shaped clock and cover, probably Sèvres, with eight-day movement, the dial inscribed "Monbro Fils Aine," case painted with an 18thC scene depicting a party being greeted ashore.

25¼in (64cm) high

$5,300-6,600 **CHEF**

A 19thC "Gothic" case lacquered brass mantle timepiece, with single-fusee movement, marked "W.H.Young, Swaffham."

15in (38cm) high

$650-800   **CHEF**

A Napoleon III French figural ormolu mantel clock, by Lerolle Frères, the eight-day two-train bell striking movement stamped "LEROLLE F..., PARIS, 138, AH" on backplate, the case depicting Minerva standing, supporting a shield surmounted by her attendant owl, the shield incorporating the clock dial, the base with Ceres or Fortuna, clock with pendulum and winding key.

The important firm of bronziers and sculptors Lerolle Frères was founded in 1836, when Louis Lerolle passed on the business to his two sons. They exhibited ornamental clocks, garnitures, chandeliers, and candelabras, predominantly gilt bronze or silvered, at most of the international exhibitions held during the second half of the 19thC.

ca. 1875   *27¾in (70.5cm) high*

$16,000-21,000   **DN**

A late-19thC French ormolu figural chariot mantel clock, after the model by Frédéric-Eugène Piat, the eight-day countwheel bell striking movement stamped indistinctly "*R *501," the case "Chérubins assis dans un char tiré par un tigre," modeled as a Bacchic scene with sitting satyr in leopard-drawn chariot, attended by three putti, base signed "E Piat," the case with Arrow foundry mark on underside of satyr's foot, the clock with a pendulum and winding key.

Frédéric-Eugène Piat (1827-1903) was artistic director of the Maison Marchand producing designs primarily in bronze for clocks, fireplace furniture, sculpture, and fountains. Perhaps his most famous creation, in association with Maison Millet Paris, was the "Grande Horloge," a monumental clock in ormolu, bronze, and Carrara marble standing 106in (270cm) high. The Saint-Loup Museum of Fine Arts in Troyes, Champagne-Ardenne, holds the largest collection of his artwork and designs.

31in (78.5cm) wide

$13,000-18,000   **DN**

A late-19thC French ormolu and white marble figural mantel clock, in Louis XVI style, by Grohé Frères, Paris, with eight-day bell striking movement with outside countwheel stamped with "Japy Frères."

Guillaume & Jean-Michel Grohé went into partnership in 1829 and formed the atelier "Grohé Frères" in 1847. They went on to supply the highest quality furniture, furnishings, clocks, and bronzes to European royalty, including Prince Albert at the Paris Exhibition of 1855.

17½in (44.5cm) high

$6,000-7,500   **DN**

A late-19thC French gilt-bronze four glass mantel clock, the dial signed "W. Gibson & Co, Paris" and lower panel both painted with scenes of hawking.

17¼in (44cm) high

$800-900   **CHEF**

A late-19thC French ormolu clock, twin-train eight-day movement striking on a bell, the dial signed "Graux Marly Ft De Bronzes A Paris," the case decorated with female figures symbolic of fertility and twin cherub surmount, with pendulum and winding key.

Graux-Marly Frères exhibited at the 1878 Paris Exhibition and was known for its figurative sculptures as well as decorative ornaments. Work by Graux-Marly is relatively uncommon.

19¾in (50cm) high

$4,000-5,300   **DN**

A late-19thC French parcel-gilt and patinated bronze-mounted and rouge griotte mantel clock, with two-train eight-day striking movement, with a figural group after François Rude (French, 1784-1855), of the Education of Achilles.

20½in (52cm) high

$1,800-2,400   **DN**

A late-19thC large Black Forest carved mantel clock, depicting a pair of St. Bernards, dial signed "CAMERER KUSS & CO./186 UXBRIDGE ROAD LONDON W."

25¼in (64cm) high

$4,000-4,600   **L&T**

A French Sèvres-style porcelain and gilt metal-mounted mantel clock, the eight-day two-train bell striking, movement stamped for "Japy Frères" and mark for "Villard," the dial bearing inscription for "Leroy A Paris," the arched case surmounted by an urn with swags of fruit, the inset panels decorated with a child holding a bird, and with further birds and flowers, Sèvres-style mark within, clock with a winding key and pendulum.

19in (48cm) high

$3,300-4,000   **DN**

A late-19thC French ormolu figural mantel clock, by Deniere Paris, the twin-train, eight-day bell striking movement stamped "DENIERE A PARIS," numbered "594," the case modeled as a cherub sitting on top of a column pedestal holding aloft the clock, on molded red marble base with gilt feet.

24in (61cm) high

$10,000-11,000   **DN**

A late-19thC French white marble, ormolu- and bronze-mounted mantel clock, by Raingo Frères, with eight-day bell striking movement with outside countwheel.

16½in (42cm) high

$1,800-2,400   **DN**

A late-19thC French ormolu and patinated-bronze clock, in the Louis XV style, by Raingo Frères and Defreville, twin-train movement striking on a bell, movement with Raingo stamp, the case with Bacchic cherubs, case, movement and pendulum numbered "1175," inscribed "Defreville" on the underside, with pendulum and winding key.

Although apparently unsigned, the design of the clock is in the manner of one of Defreville's leading designers and bronze fondeurs Henri Picard (fl. 1831-1864).

29½in (75cm) wide

$8,000-9,000   **DN**

A 19thC French ormolu mantel clock, with bell striking drum movement.

15½in (39.5cm) high

$650-800   **CHEF**

An Empire-style ebonized mantel clock, with twin gilt-metal lion surmount and enamel dial detailed "Peter Pan in Wein."

9¾in (24.5cm) high

$1,000-1,100   **BELL**

A turquoise cartouche-shaped mantel clock and stand, by Jacob Petit.

21in (53.5cm) high

$800-900   **CHEF**

A Meissen figural clock, the movement striking on a bell and inscribed "J.D. Brevete SGDG," with retailers inscription "Exam.d by Lund & Blockley."

13½in (34cm) high

$4,000-4,600   **WHP**

A 20thC Jaeger Le Coultre Embassy green "Atmos" clock, the brass case with faux green marble front and side panels, in its original fitted case, with instruction booklet.

8¾in (22cm) high

$1,500-1,800   **L&T**

CLOCKS

A late-18thC Swiss Louis XVI grande-sonnerie striking "Pendule d'Officier," with pull trip-repeat and alarm, by Robert & Courvoisier, La Chaux-de-Fonds, the four-pillar movement with chain-fusee and verge escapement regulated by sprung three-arm monometallic balance with rack-and-pinion regulation on the going train, with winding key.

The partnership between Louis Courvoisier (1758-1832) and his father-in-law Captain Louis-Benjamin Robert was established in 1781. In 1787 Robert died. In 1811, Louis Courvoisier took his son, Frederic Alexander, to form "Courvoisier et Cie." This clock is an early design of pendule portative termed "Pendule d'Officier." Although this form of portable timepiece originated during the 1780s, they became popular during the Napoleonic wars, particularly among the officer class, hence the term "Pendule d'Officier." The firm of Robert and Courvoisier were the leading makers of this type of portable timepiece during this period.

7½in (19cm) high excluding handle

$4,600-5,300 DN

An early-Victorian gilt-brass chronometer carriage timepiece, by James McCabe, the eight-day brass single-chain fusee movement with maintaining power, the backplate signed "James McCabe London 2903," with a probably original leather traveling case.

English chronometer carriage timepieces are relatively rare, especially by James McCabe.

ca. 1856 *6¾in (17cm) high*

$26,000-33,000 WW

A French malachite cabochon-mounted, engraved gilt-brass carriage clock, by Roblin and Fils Frères, Paris, the eight-day two-train bell striking movement with silvered platform cylinder escapement and stamped with oval trademark "ROBLIN, FILS & FRERES, A PARIS" over serial number "20255."

ca. 1860 *5¼in (13.5cm) high*

$3,300-4,000 DN

A French gilt-brass singing bird automaton carriage clock, by Japy Frères for Henry Marc, Paris, the eight-day twin-train bell striking movement with platform lever escapement and stamped with oval trademark "JAPY FRERES ET CIE, EXPOSITION, 1855 GRANDE,MED., D'HONNEUR" over another "H'Y MARC, PARIS," the underdial motionwork with counterweighted detent for the hourly release of the going barrel-driven musical mechanism for sounding a two-note bird call, the one-piece caddy molded upper section enclosing an automaton of a bird that moves from side to side and bobs up and down while the musical mechanism in the base is running.

The firm of Japy Frères et Cie was founded by Frederick Japy in 1774 who set up a modest workshop in Montbeliard as a watch and machine toolmaker. Japy expanded his business rapidly and, by 1804, the year he was awarded the Legion d' Honneur by Napoleon (in recognition for his Brevets in horological machinery), he employed 300 people. From 1806, he took five of his sons into partnership and the firm expanded to become one of the largest makers of clocks in Europe.

ca. 1860 *11¼in (28.5cm) high*

$13,000-18,000 DN

A Limoges enamel-paneled gilt brass-cased carriage clock, probably by A. Dumas, Paris, the eight-day two-train movement with silvered platform lever escapement, striking the hour on a gong and with alarm sounding on the same gong.

The exquisite dial and side panels of this clock are textbook examples of the finest enamel-work produced in the Limoges workshops during the second half of the 19thC.

ca. 1878 *7in (18cm) high*

$10,500-12,000 DN

A late-19thC gilt-brass petite sonnerie carriage clock, the eight-day movement with a platform lever escapement, with a repeat and striking on two bells, the backplate stamped "J. KLAFTENBERGER 157 REGENT STREET."

4½in (11.5cm) high

$4,600-5,300 WW

A late-19thC French gilt-brass carriage clock with Aesthetic-style porcelain panels and push-button repeat, Paris, the eight-day gong two-train gong striking movement with silvered platform lever escapement, the dial panel painted in polychrome and gilt with asymmetric panels incorporating coastal landscape scene.

6¾in (17cm) high

$7,500-8,000 DN

A late-19thC French frosted gilt-brass carriage clock, the eight-day two-train gong striking movement with silvered platform lever escapement and alarm sounding on the same gong.

7in (18cm) high

$7,500-8,000 DN

A multicolor grande-sonnerie striking and repeating moonphase calendar alarm carriage clock, the eight-day two-train movement ting-tang striking the quarters on a graduated pair of gongs and then sounding the hour every quarter hour on the larger of the two, with silvered platform lever escapement, the underside with three-position strike selection lever labeled "G'de Campanco/P'te Campanco/Silencio," unsigned.

The decorative panels of this clock employs differing techniques to gild, silver, copper, and chemically patinate the cast and engraved scenes. The high number of complications in the movement and dial would place this clock as one of the finest available at the time.

ca. 1880 *6¾in (17cm) high*

$22,000-26,000 DN

A late-19thC French gilt-brass bamboo-cased carriage clock, with relief-enameled panels and push-button repeat, probably by Jules Brunelot, Paris, the eight-day gong striking movement with platform lever escapement and stamped with trademark B within a circle.

The trademark stamped on the lower left-hand corner of the backplate of this clock, (letter B within a circle) is possibly for Jules Brunelot.

The enamel panels of this clock are unusual in that details, such as the cranes, insects, and larger floral blooms, are picked out in relief, giving the scene a three-dimensional appearance. Traditionally, cranes in Chinese art represent peace and longevity.

6½in (16.5cm) high

$4,600-5,300 DN

A French engraved-brass carriage clock, quarter repeating, striking, plus alarm, day and date features, and subsidiary dials.

7¾in (19.5cm) high

$4,000-4,600 PSA

A fine late-19thC engraved, gilt-brass oval grande-sonnerie striking calendar carriage clock, with push-button repeat and alarm, by Drocourt, Paris, for retail by Tiffany and Company, the eight-day two-train movement ting-tang striking the quarters on a graduated pair of gongs and sounding the hour every quarter hour on the larger of the two, with silvered platform lever escapement, alarm sounding on the smaller gong.

This clock is a good example of Drocourt's work, having both grande-sonnerie striking and calendar work.

6in (15cm) high excluding handle

$14,000-16,000 DN

A late-19thC French gilt-brass carriage clock, with multicolor relief-cast chinoiserie panels and push-button repeat Gay, Lamaille and Company, Paris, the eight-day two-train gong striking movement with silvered platform lever escapement and stamped with oval "PATENT SURETY ROLLER."

The firm of Gay, Lamaille and Company and their patent for the "surety roller," a mechanism that prevents the strike star wheel from accidentally jumping out of sync while the clock is being transported, was invented by Moritz Immisch. The patent was subsequently secured by Messrs Gay, Lamaille and Company of Paris and London.

6¾in (17cm) high

$8,500-10,000 DN

A late-19thC French porcelain-panel inset, silvered, and gilt-brass grande-sonnerie striking carriage clock, with push-button repeat and alarm, retailed by Tiffany and Company, with panels by Lucien Simonnet, Paris, the eight-day two-train movement ting-tang striking the quarters.

Lucien Simonnet (1849-1926) was a Sèvres-trained painter of porcelain who specialized in panels often based on works by well-known artists of the period. This clock draws inspiration from the European Renaissance, again romanticized. The fact that this clock is signed Tiffany would suggest that the prestigious firm of New York retailers were one of the primary stockers of such clocks.

7¼in (18.5cm) high

$8,000-9,000 DN

A late-19thC gilt-brass carriage clock, with push-button repeat, alarm, and musical movement in base, the eight-day gong striking movement with silvered platform lever escapement, unsigned.

The provision of a musical movement in the base of this clock is a rare detail.

7¼in (18.5cm) high

$8,500-9,000 DN

A brass striking and repeating alarm carriage clock, retailed by E W Streeter, London, twin-barrel movement with a silvered platform lever escapement stamped "JS" for (Joseph Soldano).

ca. 1890 *6½in (16.5cm) high*

$1,300-1,800 TEN

A French petit-sonnerie striking carriage clock, with push-button repeat and alarm, the eight-day two-train movement ting-tang striking the quarters on gongs and sounding the hour every quarter hour, chapter ring inscribed "LE ROY & FIS, 52 NEW BOND STREET, MADE IN FRANCE, PALAIS ROYAL, PARIS."

ca. 1900 *7in (18cm) high*

$4,000-5,300 DN

A 19thC repeater carriage clock, the movement striking on a gong.

6in (15cm) high

$400-450 WHP

CLOCKS

A 17thC brass striking lantern clock with unusual early conversions to a side-fitted pendulum and half-hour passing strike, two-train 30-hour weight-driven movement with outside countwheel striking on a top-mounted bell and an early conversion second hammer passing strike on the half hour, with two weights.

The manner of the conversion, as well as the addition of a second hammer to strike half-hours, very much a feature of French clocks, strongly suggests the clock was converted to pendulum in France.

ca. 1660   *14½in (37cm) high*
$8,500-10,000   **TEN**

A late-17thC brass striking lantern clock, signed William Hulbert, Bristol, two-train 30-hour single-weight driven movement, converted to an anchor escapement, outside countwheel striking on a top-mounted bell.

ca. 1695   *15½in (39cm) high*
$4,000-5,300   **TEN**

A late-17thC brass striking lantern clock, signed William Jackson, Loughborough, two-train 30-hour weight-driven movement with a verge escapement and outside countwheel striking on a top-mounted bell, pendulum rod and bob have been replaced, with one weight.

ca. 1695   *15in (38cm) high*
$5,300-6,600   **TEN**

A late-17thC brass lantern clock, anchor escapement with outside countwheel, signed "John Spershott Tetchfield," lacking long pendulum and weight.

14¼in (36cm) high
$2,100-2,600   **CHEF**

An early-18thC brass striking lantern clock, signed John Lee, Loughborough, two-train 30-hour single-weight driven movement, repair to top bell, pendulum rod and bob are later.

ca. 1720   *14¼in (36cm) high*
$2,600-3,300   **TEN**

An early-18thC brass lantern clock, by John Buffett of Colchester, the 30-hour birdcage movement striking on a bell, signed "John Buffett in Colchester fecit," later mounted on a walnut bracket.

14¼in (36cm) high
$2,600-3,300   **WW**

A mid-18thC Victorian lacquered brass "Litchfield Cathedral"-hour striking skeleton clock, attributed to John Smith and Sons, London, for Hirst, Leeds, the twin-chain fusee gong striking movement with anchor escapement and five-spoke wheel crossings set between characteristic pierced plates united by six turned pillars.

19in (48.5cm) high
$2,400-2,900   **DN**

A brass skeleton mantel clock with passing hour strike, single-fusee movement with an anchor escapement, and passing hour strike on a top mounted bell, six-spoke wheels, with pendulum.

ca. 1870   *23¾in (60cm) high*
$1,700-2,400   **TEN**

A 19thC brass skeleton clock and dome, with a bell strike with single-fusee movement with anchor escapement. clock

11½in (29cm) high
$450-550   **L&T**

A Charles II walnut hooded wall clock, by Nathaniel Barrow, London, the five-finned and latched-pillar movement of about three-and-a-half-day duration, anchor escapement regulated by seconds pendulum and outside countwheel for striking the hours on a bell mounted above the plates.
ca. 1675-80   *24in (61cm) high*
$20,000-26,000   **DN**

An 18thC hook and spike lantern-form wall clock, signed "Geo Clarke, Leaden Hall Street, London," two-train 30-hour weight-driven movement with a verge escapement and outside countwheel striking on a top-mounted bell.
ca. 1780   *13¾in (35cm) high*
$2,000-2,600   **TEN**

A George III giltwood cartel wall timepiece, by William Gibbs, London, the four-pillar single-fusee movement with verge escapement regulated by short-bob pendulum.
ca. 1760   *28¾in (73cm) high*
$4,600-5,900   **DN**

A late-18thC George III giltwood cartel timepiece, by Thomas Law, Southwark, the four-pillar single-fusee movement with verge escapement regulated by short-bob pendulum and with asymmetric plates to allow for offset mainspring barrel, with a winding key.
35½in (90cm) high
$4,000-4,600   **DN**

John Knibb was born in 1650 and was apprenticed to his older brother Joseph in around 1664. When Joseph moved to London in 1670 to set up business, John took on the Oxford workshop. John Knibb became a high-profile figure within the city of Oxford. Twice becoming mayor, he continued in business until his death in 1722. Due to the comparative rarity of clocks signed by John Knibb, it has been suggested that his workshop may have generally served to supply Joseph's larger concern in London. The strong similarities between John's best work and those signed by Joseph would certainly support this view. However, it is also clear that John was a high profile tradesman in the city of Oxford who trained no less than 10 apprentices, therefore it is perhaps more probable that, although the two workshops were closely connected, they generally worked separately to supply clocks to differing groups of clients. The current clock belongs to a rare group of probably less than 10 surviving examples of small hooded wall clocks from workshops of both John and Joseph Knibb. Although these clocks were generally made for a common purpose, it seems that they do vary in detail and specification to the extent that no two are exactly the same. The majority of the other surviving examples appear to have posted movements based on miniature lantern clocks with standard "Knibb" castings.

A Charles II walnut 30-hour striking small hooded wall clock with alarm, by John Knibb, Oxford, the four-finned pillar outside countwheel bell striking movement with plates measuring 6 x 3½in (15 x 9cm) and verge escapement regulated by short bob pendulum.
ca. 1685   *13¾in (35cm) high*
$33,000-40,000   **DN**

A late-18thC George III black-japanned tavern clock, by Haley, London, the single-train eight-day movement, the trunk decorated with a chinoiserie scene of two figures by a pagoda, inscribed "HALEY, LONDON."
44in (112cm) high
$10,500-12,000   **L&T**

An 18thC Swiss/Bavarian polychrome-painted wooden striking alarm wall clock, foliot escapement and striking on a top-mounted bell, wooden case with polychrome painted side-latched panels and depicting buildings scenes.
14¼in (36cm) high
$4,600-5,300   **TEN**

A late-18thC and later mahogany fusee dial wall timepiece, signed for Benjamin Ward, four-pillar single-fusee movement now with anchor escapement regulated by lenticular bob pendulum and tapered plates, case probably of 20thC construction.
15¼in (39cm) high
$1,800-2,400   **DN**

An early-19thC mahogany drop dial striking wall clock, twin-fusee movement with an anchor escapement and rack striking on a bell.
29½in (75cm) high
$850-1,000   **TEN**

CLOCKS

An early-19thC Elnathan Taber Massachusetts, Federal mahogany banjo clock, the face inscribed "E. Taber Roxbury."

32½in (82.5cm) high

$4,600-5,300   POOK

A late-19thC French Boulle wall clock, in the Régence taste, the eight-day two-train gong striking movement with decorative sunburst bob pendulum, with pendulum and winding key.

53¼in (135cm) high

$7,500-8,500   DN

A 19thC French gilt-wood cartel wall clock.

33½in (85cm) high

$3,300-4,000   L&T

A late-19thC Louis XVI style gilt-brass cartel clock, retailed by E. White, London, after a design by Jean-Charles Delafosse, the eight-day two-train bell striking movement with Brocot-type pendulum regulation and stamped "W. WHITE, 20 COCKSPUR STREET" on backplate.

31½in (80cm) high

$1,300-1,800   DN

A 19thC fusee wall clock, the circular concave face with black enameled Roman numerals, within a mahogany case.

22in (56cm) high

$650-800   WHP

A 19thC walnut eight-day kitchen dial, fitted with a single-fusee movement.

$350-400   CHOR

A Louis XV-style gilt-brass cartel clock, the eight-day two-train gong striking movement with Brocot-type pendulum regulation.

ca. 1900   *36¾in (93cm) high*

$1,700-2,400   DN

A tavern clock, the brass movement within an ebonized case decorated in the chinoiserie manner and inscribed "Jo.N (John) Hawling Oxford," the dial with Roman and Arabic numerals.

58in (147cm) high

$5,300-6,600   WHP

A Louis XVI-style gilt and patinated bronze cartel clock, the movement by Samuel Marti et Cie, Paris, the eight-day two-train bell striking movement with vertically planted platform cylinder escapement and stamped with "S. Marti et Cie MEDAILLE D'ARGENT, 1889."

ca. 1900   *28in (71cm) high*

$4,600-5,300   DN

ESSENTIAL REFERENCE—GARNITURES

Derived from the Old French verb "garnir," which meant "to equip, trim, or decorate," the word garniture in the context of antiques is primarily used to describe a number or collection of matching, albeit rarely identical, decorative objects intended to be displayed together in close proximity. Initially popular during the second half of the 17thC, and remaining widely in vogue until the early 20thC, garnitures were often displayed on tables, in niches around the walls of a room, or on ledges above a door, but the most popular location was on the shelf of a mantelpiece above a fireplace.

Many garnitures were in the form of decorative ceramics, sometimes figurines, but more usually vases—Madame de Pompadour, mistress of Louis XV, for example, ordered a garniture from Sèvres in the form of a porcelain pot-pourri vase in the shape of a ship with two flanking pairs of vases en suite. However, almost the most popular form of garniture, especially during the late 18thC and the 19thC, comprised a centered mantel clock with flanking candelabra (like the examples on these pages)—a combination that, especially when placed in front of an overmantel mirror, illuminated not only the time but also the room.

A 19thC French Louis XV-style gilt-bronze three-piece clock garniture, the eight-day silk-cord movement with a bell strike and signed "J. CONTOUR/ A PARIS" and stamped "778," the associated candelabra with a centered stiff and four scrolled candle branches.

Clock 14½in (37cm) high

$2,400-2,900   **L&T**

A gilt-brass and Wedgwood pottery-mounted clock garniture, the French brass drum eight-day movement striking on a gong, the dial signed "J. W. Benson, 25 Old Bond Street, London," case applied with Neoclassical green jasper plaques and leaf-wrapped columns, with a pair of three-light candelabra and a pair of vases with lids, with pendulum and winding key.

ca. 1870-80   *17¼in (44cm) high*

$4,000-4,600   **WW**

A 19thC French gilt and patinated-bronze and marble mantle clock garniture, after Clodion, the eight-day movement striking a bell and stamped "146/416," in a waisted white marble case surmounted by a pair of putti emblematic of Fall, with a pair of four-light figural candelabra, each with a putto holding a cornucopia issuing floral candle arms.

Clock 23¼in (59cm) wide

$4,000-4,600   **L&T**

A late-19thC French Sèvres-style porcelain and gilt-metal mounted clock garniture, by Japy Frères, the eight-day bell striking movement with roundel and serial number 229 on backplate, the case surmounted by cherubs, the garniture of twin-light candelabra.

Clock 14¼in (36cm) high

$2,200-2,600   **DN**

A 19thC Louis XVI-style green marble and gilt-metal clock garniture, the eight-day movement striking a bell and stamped "MADE IN FRANCE," with a pair of figural four-light candelabra with putti holding urns issuing four scrolling candle arms with flower sconces.

Clock 17¼in (44cm) high

$1,200-1,450   **L&T**

A 19thC French clock set, the eight-day clock in a gilt-brass case with galleried top and pierced fretwork panel decorated acanthus scrolls etc., with fluted columns on the sides, and a pair of matching vases.

13in (33cm) high, vases 24in (61cm) high

$800-900   **CHOR**

A late-19thC French marble and gilt-bronze three-piece clock garniture, the eight-day movement striking a bell, the candelabra with twin scrolling candle arms and centered flaming urn.

Clock 20in (51cm) high

$650-800   **L&T**

A French porcelain inset ormolu "Japonaise" mantel clock garniture, the porcelain front panel signed for C. Kiffert, the circular eight-day gong striking movement with recoil escapement for regulation by disk-bob pendulum incorporating Brocot-type rate adjustment to the suspension, the blue ground simulated cloisonné porcelain dial panel painted with bird and butterfly among chrysanthemum blooms in center within pseudo-Japanese character gilt cartouche numeral chapter ring.

The full identity of the painter of the porcelain panels of this clock, C. Kiffert, appears not to be recorded. However, this signature is sometimes seen on large impressive porcelain vases often executed in the style of Sèvres. The painted porcelain surmount adorning the present clock is unusually modeled as a carp with a dragon's head. This form comes from the legend of Koi-no-Takinobori, which has its roots in ancient China wherein carp swim, against all odds, up a waterfall known as the "Dragon Gate" at the headwaters of China's Yellow River. The gods are impressed by the feat and reward the few successful carp by turning them into powerful dragons. The story symbolizes the virtues of courage, effort, and perseverance, which correspond to the nearly impossible struggle of humans to attain Buddhist enlightenment.

ca. 1880   Clock 20in (51cm) high
$12,000-15,000   DN

A French gilt-brass mantel clock garniture, in the Chinese taste, by Achille Brocot, Paris, the circular two-train eight-day gong striking movement with anchor escapement regulated by disk-bob pendulum incorporating Brocot-type regulation to suspension.

Achille Brocot was born in 1817 and died in 1878. Achille patented several improvements in clock mechanism escapements, and invented the "Brocot suspension," an adjustable pendulum spring that enabled time keeping to be regulated by altering the length of the pendulum suspension spring by a key turned in the dial. He also introduced a jeweled deadbeat escapement.

ca. 1880   clock 15½in (39cm) high
$1,800-2,400   DN

A 19thC French champlevé enamel and gilt-brass three-piece clock garniture, in the Islamic taste, the eight-day movement stamped "Vincenti & Cie Medaille d'argent 1855," the case with dome top and corner finials, the candlesticks on stepped bases.

clock 11½in (29cm) high
$1,200-1,450   L&T

A late-19thC French Louis XVI-style ormolu and white marble mantel clock garniture, the movement by Samuel Marti, Paris, the circular eight-day two-train bell striking movement with anchor escapement regulated by short disk-bob pendulum incorporating Brocot-type regulation to suspension and stamped with "Samuel Marti, MEDAILLE D'OR" roundel, the five-light candelabra side pieces with branches cast as rose stems and blooms forming the sconces, over single putto uprights and floral swag decorated stands.

Clock 19½in (49.5cm) high
$2,100-2,600   DN

A French gilt-brass and painted porcelain mantel clock garniture, by Vincenti et Cie, Paris, the circular two-train eight-day gong striking movement with anchor escapement regulated by disk-bob pendulum incorporating Brocot-type regulation to suspension, the backplate stamped with "VINCENTI & CIE, MEDAILLE D'ARGENT, 1855."

ca. 1875   Clock 15½in (39cm) high vases 12½in (32cm) high
$550-650   DN

A 19thC French gilt-bronze and blue turquin marble clock garniture, the eight-day movement signed "J DENIERE A PARIS 2766" and striking a bell, with cornucopia mounts and surmounted by a ribbon-tied quiver, arrow, and floral wreath, with matching candelabra.

clock 13in (33cm) high
$1,600-2,400   L&T

A 19thC French marble, gilt and patinated-bronze three-piece clock garniture, the eight-day movement striking a bell, the case surmounted with a pair of putti and a centered flame finial, with associated figural candelabra.

clock 17in (43cm) wide
$2,000-2,600   L&T

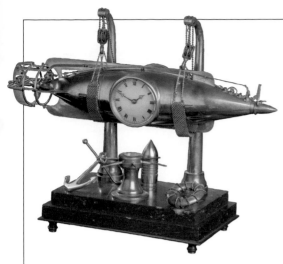

A rare late-19th/early-20thC French brass and silvered torpedo industrial timepiece, with an automaton propeller, the eight-day brass drum movement with a lever escapement, stamped "4624" and "93," the case in the form of a torpedo hung on chains with pulleys, the base with nautical-themed decoration, the center inset with a compass, signed "Radiguet Paris," on a rosso antico marble base.

This model was probably based on the Whitehead torpedo, the world's first self-propelled torpedo.

18¼in (46.2cm) wide

$53,000-63,000   WW

A late-19thC French chrome and brass diver's-helmet industrial timepiece, the clock flanked by a thermometer and aneroid barometer dials, the top with a compass, the back of the helmet inscribed "Morton Eden 25th June 1880 from H. E. Surtees," on a rosso antico marble plinth.

8in (20.7cm) high

$12,000-15,000   WW

A Black Forest-type cuckoo clock, the movement striking on a gong, within an oak case of chalet form.

17¼in (44cm) high

$260-400   WHP

A 19thC gilt-metal and marble "water well" timepiece, with an eight-day movement, dial inscribed Burt & Escare London, the movement above a marble wishing well.

17¼in (44cm) high

$1,000-1,100   DN

A late-19thC French gilt and patinated metal automaton quarter-deck clock, by Guilmet, Paris, the eight-day movement striking a gong, the case in the form of a ship's stern, the upper poop deck with a figure of a helmsman, the lower deck centered by a gilt Roman numeral dial with twin winding holes, a ladder on the left and the figure of a sailor coiling rope on the right, the backplate stamped "MEDAILLE D'OR/ GLT/ SGDG PARIS" and "2385," and "MEDAILLE BRONZF/ St. Marti et Cie."

10¼in (26cm) high

$15,000-18,000   L&T

A late-19thC French industrial lighthouse clock, attributed to Guilmet, the rotating top with clock, barometer, and two thermometer scales, in a brass and copper case in the form of a lighthouse.

The French firm founded by André Romain Guilmet made a series of clocks with industrial and maritime themes between ca. 1875 and the 1910s.

18¼in (46cm) high

$9,000-10,500   L&T

A late-19thC French industrial automaton windmill clock, by Guilmet, with a barometer dial and twin-thermometer scales, the silvered-brass and brass case in the form of a windmill with automata action of the sails and weathervane.

17¾in (45cm) high

$5,300-6,600   L&T

A Victorian cast iron and brass hour-striking turret clock movement, by W. J. Thompson, Ashford, internal rack striking mechanism now sounding on a small bell set above the train, maintaining power, and deadbeat escapement with adjustable pallets and fine-beat crutch adjustment for regulation by long pendulum, and mounted on a later wood display stand.

ca. 1870   *80¼in (204cm) high*

$4,000-5,300   DN

A 22ct-gold open-face pair case pocket watch, by Justin Vulliamy, hallmarked London, cylinder fusee repeater movement, diamond end stone, the back cover engraved with a coronet above "SX."

1786 *2¼in (5.4cm) diam 5.6oz*

$4,600-5,300 DN

A George III silver-cased key wind open-face gentleman's pocket watch, the gilt fusee movement with a verge escapement, detailed on the backplate "Jno Williams, London No 714, London 1787."

$200-260 BELL

A gold and enamel open-face pocket watch, aperture and 12 o'clock for "Jump Hour" display, the back case with enamel butterfly, with box.

ca. 1830 *1½in (4.2cm) wide*

$3,300-4,000 WW

An 18ct cased half-hunter pocket watch, by Waltham.

ca. 1892/3 *4.15oz*

$2,600-3,300 LOCK

A 18ct Waltham gold half-hunter pocket watch, with top winder.

4oz

$2,400-2,900 PSA

A gentleman's 18ct cased full-hunter pocket watch, the signed white dial by "Russells Ltd. of Liverpool," movement signed "Russells Ltd - makers to the late Queen - 18 Church Street, Liverpool-No. 88302," hallmarked Chester.

1901 *2¼in (5.5cm) diam 4.8oz*

$2,600-3,300 LOCK

An 18ct-gold half-hunter side-wide mechanical pocket watch, movement signed "J.W. Benson, 62 and 64 Ludgate Hill, London," hallmarked 18ct gold.

1902 *1¾in (4.8cm) wide 3oz*

$1,800-2,400 SWO

An 18ct-yellow gold full hunter dress watch, by Waltham, retailed by Hopkns & Hopkins, Dublin.

1¾in (4.5cm) diam 2.7oz

$1,300-2,000 WHP

An 18ct-gold open-face dress watch, by Vertex.

1¾in (4.6cm) diam overall 2oz

$850-1,000 WHP

A Waltham 18ct-gold pocket watch, with top winder.

3.5oz

$2,000-2,600 PSA

A 9ct Bravingtons gold full-hunter pocket watch, with top winder.

3.3oz

$900-1,050 PSA

A gentleman's 18ct-gold open-face pocket watch, by James Brock, George Street, Portman Square, London, crest and motto of Trotter.

1942

$2,000-2,600 CHOR

A gentlemen's 18ct gold Audemars Piguet automatic bracelet watch, bark-textured case with integral Milanese tapered bracelet, marked "750 K18," case no. "65295."

6½in (16.5cm) long 2.9oz

$4,600-5,300   SWO

A lady's 18-carat gold and diamond wristwatch, by Breguet, "Classique" ref. 8068, no. 4895 AN, automatic movement, 20 jewels, cal. 537/1, adjusted to five positions, with a Breguet guarantee, precious stones certificate, and instruction booklet.

ca. 2011   *1¼in (3cm) diam*

$6,000-7,500   DN

ESSENTIAL REFERENCE—CARTIER TANK

Louis Cartier created the first Cartier "Tank" watch in 1917. It's design was specifically inspired by the overhead silhouette of the new Renault battle tank, first used on the Western Front toward the end of World War I. However, the origins of its overtly machinelike form must also been seen in the context of the aesthetics championed at that time by the Bauhaus movement in Germany.

After the prototype had been presented by Cartier to General John Pershing of the American Expeditionary Force, the "Tank" went into production in 1919, and although many variations on the original design—including the "Louis," the "Cintrée," the "LC," the "MC," the "Chinoise," the "Americaine," the "Francaise," and the "Solo"—have been introduced since then, its core features have remained essentially untouched. Comprising a square or rectangular face, a strap seamlessly integrated into vertical sidebars known as "brancards," a bold Roman numeral dial with a "chemin de fer" chapter ring, sword-shaped, blued-steel hands, and a sapphire cabochon-surmounted crown, they're at the heart of the appeal of an iconic timepiece that is timeless.

A ladies 18ct-yellow gold and stainless steel wristwatch, by Bulgari, the circular black dial with gold-color Arabic and baton numerals and date aperture on an articulated bracelet strap, with box and guarantee.

1¼in (3.3cm) diam

$1,800-2,400   WHP

A gentleman's stainless steel cased Cartier "Pasha" automatic chronograph wristwatch.

$1,600-2,100   LOCK

A Cartier stainless steel wristwatch, Tank Solo model, ref: WSTA0028, quartz movement, case back signed and with serial number "3169 584513ZX," Cartier strap, and Cartier stainless steel deployant clasp, signed Cartier, with Cartier box, International Warranty card, instruction booklet.

ca. 2018   *1½in (3.4cm) wide*

$3,300-4,000   TEN

A gentleman's Girard-Perregaux 18ct cased wristwatch.

1945

$3,300-4,000   LOCK

A gentleman's gold-plated Heuer twin-dial chronograph wristwatch, the silvered dial with two further dials at 9 and 3 o'clock, on a modern leather strap.

$2,600-3,300   LOCK

A midsize 18ct cased Jaeger-LeCoultre "Fabrique En Suisse" wristwatch, on an 18ct-gold bracelet.

ca. 1950   *2.2oz*

$2,600-4,000   LOCK

WATCHES

A Lemania WWII military WW2 RAF wristwatch, with stainless steel case.

$2,600-3,300   **PSA**

A gentleman's 9ct -ellow gold automatic wristwatch, by Longines.

1¼in (3.4cm) diam 1.9oz

$1,050-1,200   **WHP**

A stainless steel "Seamaster Professional" 300m/1,000ft calendar, center seconds wristwatch, caliber 1538 quartz movement, screw back with "Omega Seamaster" emblem, case serial number 55554709, Omega stainless steel bracelet with a deployant clasp, with Omega boxes.

ca. 1995   1½in (3.8cm) wide

$2,600-3,300   **TEN**

A stainless steel Omega "Seamaster Professional" gentleman's calendar, center seconds wristwatch, ref: 196.1502, Cal. 1538 quartz movement, signed "Omega Seamaster Professional 300m/1000ft Swiss Made."

ca. 1995

$1,300-2,000   **MART**

A stainless steel coaxial "James Bond 007" limited-edition automatic calendar, center seconds wristwatch, "Seamaster Co-Axial Professional Chronometer" model, 300m/1000ft, ref: 22268000, limited number 08934 of 10007, calibre 2500 co-axial movement, Omega stainless steel bracelet with a deployant clasp, signed "Omega," with Omega boxes.

ca. 2007   1¾in (4.3cm) wide

$5,300-6,600   **TEN**

A stainless steel coaxial automatic calendar, center seconds wristwatch, "Seamaster Professional Co-Axial Chronometer," "Planet Ocean" model, ref: 22005000, caliber 2500 coaxial movement, Omega stainless steel bracelet, signed "Omega," with Omega boxes.

ca. 2012   1¾in (4.5cm) wide

$4,600-5,300   **TEN**

A stainless steel wristwatch, by Patek Philippe, ref. 1461, no. 626517 910864, manual wind movement, 18 jewels, adjusted to five positions, three heat, cold, isochronism, silvered dial, engraved "Dr Lewis H, Weed. Baltimore, MD."

Lewis Hill Weed (1886-1952) was born in Cleveland, Ohio. He received his B.A. in 1908 and his M.A. in 1909, both from Yale University, and his M.D. in 1912 from the Johns Hopkins University School of Medicine. After his graduation from medical school, Weed served two years as Arthur Tracy Cabot Fellow in charge of surgical research at Harvard University. In 1914, he returned to Johns Hopkins as instructor of anatomy in the school of medicine; in 1919, he was named head of the department. Weed served as Dean of the School of Medicine from 1923-29, and as director of the medical school until 1946. In 1939, Weed was appointed chairman of the Division of Medical Sciences of the National Research Council. In 1947, he resigned his Johns Hopkins posts in order to devote more attention to this position, at this time he was also appointed as a consultant to the U.S. Army Medical Department. He discovered the origin of the cerebrospinal fluid and mapped out its circulation, an accomplishment which led to a number of important clinical developments.

ca. 1940   1¼in (3.1cm) diam

$7,500-8,500   **DN**

A "Calatrava" gentleman's 18ct-gold wristwatch, by Patek Philippe, ref. 5022R-001, manual wind Cal. 215 18 jewel movement, signed "Patek Philippe Geneve Swiss," case hallmarked and signed "PPCo." original black crocodile strap.

ca. 1999   1¼in (3.3cm) diam case

$10,500-12,000   **MART**

A gold-color wristwatch, by Patek Philippe, "Calatrava," ref. 3445, no. 324619, automatic movement, 37 jewels, cal. 27-460M, adjusted to heat, cold, isochronism and five positions.

ca. 1970   1¼in (3.5cm) diam bracelet
6¾in (17cm) long 1.8oz

$17,000-20,000   **DN**

A lady's steel and gold diamond-set automatic calendar, center seconds wristwatch, ref: 69173, "Datejust" model, caliber 2135 lever movement signed, adjusted to five positions and temperature, Rolex steel and gold jubilee bracelet with a deployant clasp, signed "Rolex, Oyster Perpetual Superlative Chronometer Officially Certified," with Rolex boxes.
ca. 1989   *1in (2.6cm) wide*
$8,500-10,000   **TEN**

A Rolex Oyster "Perpetual Air-King" precision gentlemans wristwatch, stainless steel with silver dial and steel bracelet, with leather wallet, guarantee, and paperwork.
1990
$3,300-4,000   **PSA**

A lady's stainless steel automatic calendar, center seconds wristwatch, ref: 69240, Date model, caliber 2135 lever movement signed and numbered 3282568, adjusted to five positions and temperature, signed "Rolex, Oyster Perpetual, Superlative Chronometer Officially Certified," with Rolex boxes, booklet.
ca. 1994
$3,300-4,000   **TEN**

A Rolex Oyster "Perpetual Datejust" gentleman's wristwatch, stainless steel and 18ct gold, with original box, guarantee, and paperwork.
$5,300-6,600   **PSA**

A ladies Rolex oyster "Perpetual Date" wristwatch, in its original Rolex box with tag and paperwork.
ca. 2001
$4,000-4,600   **LOCK**

A boxed gentleman's 18ct cased Rolex Precision wristwatch, the white dial with gilt markers, on an 18ct Rolex bracelet.
$7,500-8,500   **LOCK**

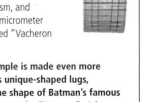

An 18ct gold automatic calendar, center seconds wristwatch, with unusual shaped "Batman" cowl shaped lugs, "Chronometre Royal" model, ref: 6694, calibre K1072 lever movement signed and numbered 570887, stamped twice with a Geneva seal mark, adjusted to heat, cold, isochronism, and five positions, micrometer regulator, signed "Vacheron Constantin."

This rare example is made even more unusual by its unique-shaped lugs, resembling the shape of Batman's famous cowl, hence its catchy "Batman" nickname by collectors.
ca. 1965   *1½in (3.5cm) wide 3.8oz*
$10,500-12,000   **TEN**

A gentleman's Tag Heuer Carrera twin-time automatic stainless steel cased wristwatch, boxed.
$1,000-1,100   **LOCK**

A Timor WWII military wristwatch, stainless steel case with the backplate marked with broad arrow and "K5302 35202."
$1,700-2,100   **PSA**

A late-18thC George III mahogany stick barometer, by P. Donagan & Co., London, with a mercury thermometer.

37in (94cm) high

$1,050-13,000   L&T

A George III mahogany stick barometer, visible mercury tube with a single vernier silvered dial signed "J.Hillum, 109 Bishopsgate St Within London."

ca. 1800   36¼in (92cm) high

$550-650   TEN

An early-19thC Regency mahogany bowfronted cistern tube mercury stick barometer, by Dollond, London, with silvered vernier scale calibrated in barometric inches.

Peter Dollond is recorded in Edwin Banfield's "BAROMETER MAKERS AND RETAILERS 1680-1860" as b. 1730 and d. 1820. He was the son of John Dollond, a Huguenot silk weaver and started business as an optician in 1750. He was joined by his father in 1752 until his death in 1761, and then by his brother, John, until his death in 1804. The family businesss was continued by Peter Dollond's nephew, George Huggins, who changed his surname to Dollond. George Dollond became instrument maker to William IV and Queen Victoria, exhibited at the Great Exhibition in 1851 and died 1856.

39½in (100cm) high

$4,000-5,300   DN

A late-Regency mahogany wheel barometer, by F. Amadio & Son of London, with a silvered hygrometer, aneroid thermometer, signed.

42¾in (108.5cm) high

$800-850   MART

An early-19thC mahogany marine stick barometer, brass mounted, signed "G. Stebbing Portsmouth," with an adjustable vernier scale, the inside of the door a thermometer.

38in (96.5cm) high

$850-1,000   WW

A Regency mahogany bowfronted "flat to the wall" mercury stick barometer, by Bate, London, with silvered Vernier scale calibrated in barometric inches and annotated "Very Dry, Set Fair, FAIR, Change, RAIN, M'ch Rain, Stormy."

This barometer is almost certainly by Robert Brettell Bate, who is recorded in Gloria Clifton's "Directory of British Scientific Instrument Makers 1550-1851" as working from Poultry, London, 1808-42 and then 33 Royal Exchange 1846-47. Bate was known as a maker of all types of instruments, but was celebrated for his nautical instruments, including marine barometers, and latterly was appointed Instrument maker to Her Majesty's Honourable Boards of Excise and Customs.

ca. 1825   39½in (100.5cm) high.

$3,300-4,600   DN

An Irish mahogany ship's stick barometer, signed "Hunt, Cork," concealed mercury tube with a single ivory scale signed, thermometer box with dial signed, turned metal cistern.

ca. 1850   7¾in (96cm) high

$2,200-2,600   TEN

A 19thC French Louis Phillipe giltwood barometer/thermometer, by Selon Toricelli, signed on the dial.

35½in (90cm) high

$550-650   L&T

A Victorian giltwood "Wellington" barometer, by Roe of Salisbury, case commemorating the life of the Duke of Wellington, decorated with a ducal coronet above tassels, a spear and his sword, the base with a portrait relief medallion, inscribed with "Waterloo," "Badaioz," "Assaye," and "Vittoria."

47½in (120.8cm) high

$2,600-3,300   WW

A Victorian oxidized brass "Fortin"-type mercury forecasting barometer, by George S. Wood, Liverpool, with adjusted Vernier slide on right-hand side, opposing an arrangement of three plates engraved with detailed forecasting predictions.

George S. Wood is recorded in Edwin Banfield's "BAROMETER MAKERS AND RETAILERS 1660-1900" as taking over the business of Abraham Abraham and Company located at 20 Lord Street, Liverpool, in 1875 and working until 1894. This barometer is made to the principles laid down by Nicholas Fortin (1750-1831) and incorporates a glazed cistern so that the level can be calibrated via the adjustment screw on the base against an inverted conical ivory cone in the cistern to obtain consistency in the readings. This particular type of barometer provides an accurate reading hence was generally adopted for laboratory use throughout the 19th and early 20thC. The combination of comprehensive scales complete with detailed observations to assist in forecasting (based on those laid out by Admiral Fitzroy in the 1850s) and fine bowfronted case suggests that the current lot was either made to be exhibited by the maker or for a wealthy client or institution.

A Victorian carved oak stick barometer, the ivory dials for yesterday and today with twin adjustable vernier scales, signed "Carpenter & Westley 24 Regent Strt. London," in a Jacobean revival case.

40in (102cm) high

$1,300-1,600   **WW**

A Victorian mahogany marine stick barometer, the ivory dials for yesterday and today with twin adjustable vernier scales, signed "LILLEY & SON LONDON," the trunk with a sympiesometer and a thermometer.

36in 5in (92.7cm) high

$1,500-1,800   **WW**

ca. 1880

$5,300-6,600   **DN**

A 19thC mahogany stick barometer, by Bate, London.

35½in (90cm) high

$1,000-1,100   **CHEF**

51in (130cm) high

A 19thC marine stick barometer, by Newcomb & Mansell, Waffing, Liverpool, with signed ivorine dials, with thermometer, brass mount on the foot marked "D. F. Brocklebank 1864 Harrington."

39½in (100cm) high

$1,300-1,600   **CHEF**

A Victorian mahogany carved wheel barometer, thermometer tube box, dial signed, signed "T.Pritchard, London."

ca. 1850   *39¾in (101cm) high*

$450-600   **TEN**

An Edwardian walnut and marquetry aneroid wheel barometer, with silvered dial and mercury thermometer.

35in (89cm) high

$120-150   **MART**

A Fortin-style barometer, by Philip Harris.

ca. 1950

$200-260   **WHP**

A George IV 15in (38cm) terrestrial library globe, of 12 hand-colored and engraved gores, inscribed "NEWTON'S New and Improved TERRESTRIAL GLOBE, acurately delineated from the observations of the most esteemed Navigators and Travellers To the Present Time, MANUFACTURED BY J. & W. Newton, No. 66. Chancery Lane, London Published 1818 with additions to 1823."

40in (102cm) high

$5,300-6,600   **WW**

A pair of 15in (38cm) English library globes, by G A & J Cary, the stands possibly by Gillow, comprising of Cary's "New Celestial Globe on which carefully laid down the whole of the stars and Nebulae contained in the catalogues of Wollaston Herschel Bode Piazzi, Zach and C, calculated to the year 1820," made and sold by J. W. Cary, No.181 Strand, London 1818. The terrestrial globe is drawn from the most recent geographical works showing the whole of the new discoveries with the tracts of the principal navigators and every improvement in geography to the present time. The celestial globe in poor condition, numerous scratches and repairs throughout, the stand is in good condition, however, one of the molded feet is damaged and the compass has no pointers. The terrestrial globe has some old scratches.

1820 and 1842   *41¼in (105cm) high*

$13,000-20,000   **TEN**

A Smith's 12in (30cm) terrestrial library globe, with hand-colored engraved gores, graduated brass meridian ring and horizon ring with signs of the Zodiac and calendar, on a mahogany stand, inscribed "Smith's TERRESTRIAL GLOBE Containing the whole of THE LATEST DISCOVERIES and Geographical Improvements also the TRACKS of THE MOST CELEBRATED CIRCUMNAVIGATORS LONDON C SMITH & SON 172 STRAND 1846," in restored condition.

ca. 1846   *36¼in (92cm) high*

$2,400-2,900   **TEN**

An early-Victorian plaster tabletop celestial globe, by Loring's, on a fruitwood stand, with a horizon ring and maker's marks.

1841   *17¾in (45cm) high*

$3,300-4,000   **L&T**

A 12in (30cm) terrestrial globe, on three melon-fluted legs, inscribed "CRUTCHLEY'S NEW TERRESTRIAL GLOBE From the most recent authorities EXHIBITING THE LATEST DISCOVERIES IN CENTRAL AFRICA And the new SETTLEMENTS & Divisions of AUSTRALIA, NEW ZEALAND, CALIFORNIA, TEXAS & SEA G F CRUTCHLEY MAP SELLER, GLOBE MAKER & PUBLISHER 81 FLEET STREET Natural Scale 1: 41, 817, 600_666m21in 1865," in restored condition.

ca. 1865   *19in (48cm) high*

$1,100-13,000   **TEN**

A pair of mid-19thC Victorian 12in (30cm) library table globes, the terrestrial sphere applied with 12 colored printed gores incorporating panel inscribed "NEWTON'S, New & Improved, TERRESTRIAL GLOBE, Embracing every recent, DISCOVERY, to the Present Time, MANUFACTURED BY NEWTON & SON, 66 Chancery Lane & 3 Fleet Str't Temple Bar, London, Published Jan 1st. 1862" on North Pacific. Extensively annotated with principal cities, towns, rivers, lakes, mountains, and other significant topographical features, the oceans with all significant islands labeled, the West Pacific with "AN IMPROVED ANALEMMA..." of the equation of time, and the equator and elliptic lines graduated in minutes.

24½in (62cm) high

$13,000-18,000   **DN**

A late-19thC Ernst Schotte & Co. 15in (38cm) terrestrial table globe, with maker's label, on a turned ebonised stand.

23¾in (60cm) high

$1,050-1,200   **L&T**

A late-Victorian 30in (76cm) terrestrial library globe, the sphere applied with 36 pairs of gores engraved and color tinted with extensive annotations for cities, countries, significant topographical features, oceans, including shipping routes, islands, and other features, the North Pacific with applied label "30 INCH, TERRESTRIAL GLOBE, BY, W. & A.K. JOHNSTON. LIMITED, Geographers, Engravers & Printers, EDINBURGH & LONDON.," and the South Pacific with an "ANALEMMA, OR TABLE OF, EQUATION OF TIME, and Sun's declination, for every day, in the Year," on four turned supports with conforming baluster stretcher to carry the meridian ring at the base.

ca. 1890   *45¾in (116cm) high*

$33,000-40,000   **DN**

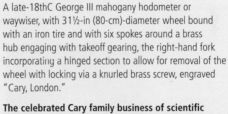

A compound monocular microscope, the 8½in (21cm) main tube with swiveling nose pieces, adjustable platform, plano-convex mirror, signed "Newton & Co. Fleet Street, Temple Bar, London," with fitted box slides, bull's-eye lens, alternate eyepieces, etc.

ca. 1865   *box 19in (48cm) high*

$1,050-1,200   **CM**

A Victorian lacquered brass monocular compound microscope, the tube with rack-and-pinion course focus adjustment above fine screw on the single objective end, the stage fitted with slide clips and the underside with pivoted double-sided plano-concave mirror, engraved "J. WHITE, GLASGOW," in original mahogany box with two objective lenses, two eyepieces, a condenser lens etc.

ca. 1870   *the box 15¼in (39cm) high*

$550-650   **DN**

An early-20thC brass telescope and stand, on tripod stand, inscribed "Watson & Sons, 313 High Holburn, London, no.806.

39½in (100cm) long

$600-750   **L&T**

A pair of German naval binoculars, by Emil Busch A-G, of chrome-plated metal, rubber, and brass, mark on binoculars "+ D.F. 10 x 80 Busch Rathenow 6575 F," tripod signed "Chicago Steel Tape Co. Made in USA."

ca. 1935   *80½in (204.5cm) high*

$4,000-5,300   **DRA**

A late-18thC George III mahogany hodometer or waywiser, with 31½-in (80-cm)-diameter wheel bound with an iron tire and with six spokes around a brass hub engaging with takeoff gearing, the right-hand fork incorporating a hinged section to allow for removal of the wheel with locking via a knurled brass screw, engraved "Cary, London."

The celebrated Cary family business of scientific instrument and globe makers was established by John Cary in London in 1782. He was primarily an engraver of maps, charts, and globes. By 1791, he had entered into partnership with his brother, William; this partnership lasted until ca. 1816. The following year John Cary was succeeded by his sons John (II) and George Cary, who continued until 1851/2, when the business was acquired by Henry Gould. This waywiser would have been a particularly valuable instrument for surveyors charged with creating maps and plans during the latter years of the 18thC. The importance of the instrument's role is reflected in the quality of its construction with the dial, in particular, being finely engraved and finished.

54in (137cm) high

$4,000-4,600   **DN**

A copy of antique barograph by Comitti, mahogany-cased example with beveled glass, and drawer below.

14¼in (36cm) wide

$450-550   **PSA**

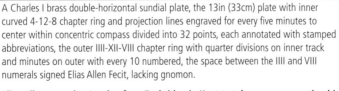

A Charles I brass double-horizontal sundial plate, the 13in (33cm) plate with inner curved 4-12-8 chapter ring and projection lines engraved for every five minutes to center within concentric compass divided into 32 points, each annotated with stamped abbreviations, the outer IIII-XII-VIII chapter ring with quarter divisions on inner track and minutes on outer with every 10 numbered, the space between the IIII and VIII numerals signed Elias Allen Fecit, lacking gnomon.

Elias Allen moved to London from Tonbridge in Kent to take up an apprenticeship with the instrument maker Charles Whitwell in around 1602. He set up business at Blackhorse Alley, Fleet St., in 1606 and succeeded his former master in 1611. He gained his freedom of the Goldsmith's Company in 1612 and the Clockmaker's Company in 1633. He continued working until his death in 1653. The double-horizontal dial was designed by the 17thC English mathematician William Oughtred. Elias Allen was a friend of Oughtred and he produced several double-horizontal dials. They were useful not only for telling the time but also for demonstrating the motion of the sun through the day and also through the year. A number of double-horizontal dials survive from the 17thC, but it appears that they were not produced much after 1700.

An American Tellurian Vetter Co. "Planetarium Ideal," signed on the base "The Vetter Co Buffalo N.Y," with instructions and case.

ca. 1930   *22½in (57cm) wide*

$600-650   **BELL**

ca. 1630-40   *14in (36cm) wide*

$3,300-4,600   **DN**

A Regency eight-day marine chronometer, the four-pillar single-chain reverse fusee movement with stepped bridge for the mainspring barrel, Harrison's maintaining power, Earnshaw-type spring detent escapement regulated by Pennington "double-L"-type split bimetallic balance with helical balance spring and faceted diamond endstone set within separate subplate assembly, the backplate signed "Barrauds Cornhill, LONDON 750," key escutcheon, bowl, gimbals, and box probably mid-19thC replacements.

Paul Phillip Barraud (b. 1752) worked with his father at first until his death in 1795, after which Barraud turned his attention more toward chronometers. Using the valuable experience gained while working on Mudge's timekeepers with W. Howells and G. Jamieson to good effect, he became very successful. After his death in 1820, the business was continued by his sons, who took John Richard Lund, a former apprentice of John Pennington (who developed the auxiliary compensation balance weight to correct for middle temperature changes), into partnership in 1838.

ca. 1815   6in (15cm) wide
$8,500-10,000   DN

A Victorian small two-day marine chronometer, by Charles Frodsham, London, the four-pillar full-plate single-chain fusee movement with Harrison's maintaining power, split bimetallic balance with keystone-shaped compensation weights, helical balance spring, and faceted diamond endstone.

Charles Frodsham was born in 1810 into a family of clockmakers that included William, his grandfather, who had moved to London prior to 1781, where he was admitted to the Clockmakers Company. Charles subsequently set up on his own in Islington in 1834. He was admitted to the Clockmakers Company in 1845 and went on to serve as master twice in 1855 and 1862; he was also a founder member of the British horological Institute in 1858 and became one of the most eminent chronometer makers of his generation. Charles Frodsham died in January 1871 and was succeeded by his son, Harrison Mill Frodsham. The firm is still trading today as specializers in chronometer, watch, and clock makers.

ca. 1845   the box 6in (15cm) wide
$12,000-15,000   DN

A two-day marine chronometer, the fusee movement mounted between plain plates with Earnshaw escapement bimetallic standard balance with blued helical spring and jeweled detent, the silvered dial signed "Dent, London" and numbered "2318" and inscribed "A.158," within later box.

ca. 1850   7½in (19cm) wide
$2,600-4,000   CM

A rosewood two-day marine chronometer, single-fusee movement with a detent escapement, maintaining power, free-sprung blue helical hairspring, bimetallic balance with timing screws and weights, diamond endstone, signed "T.J.Williams, 2 Bute Docks, Cardiff, No.1765."

ca. 1860   7½in (19cm) high
$3,300-4,000   TEN

A Victorian brass-inlaid rosewood two-day marine chronometer, by Hennessy, Swansea, the four-pillar full-plate single-chain fusee movement with spotted plates, Harrison's maintaining power and Earnshaw-type spring detent escapement regulated by split bimetallic balance.

ca. 1875   7in (18cm) wide
$3,300-4,000   DN

A Victorian brass-bound rosewood two-day marine chronometer, the four-pillar full-plate single-chain fusee movement with spotted plates, Harrison's maintaining power and Earnshaw-type spring detent escapement regulated by split bimetallic balance with circular timing weights and helical balance spring with faceted diamond endstone, the dial inscribed "PARKINSON & FRODSHAM, ROYAL EXCHANGE, LONDON."

William Parkinson and William James Frodsham founded the highly regarded firm of Parkinson & Frodsham in 1801 in London. William Parkinson died in 1842 and William Frodsham in 1850. Initially, the firm specialized in marine and pocket chronometers. It had an extensive export business, and supplied the Admiralty and numerous shipping companies.

ca. 1880   7¼in (18.5cm) wide
$3,300-4,000   DN

A Victorian two-day marine chronometer, the four-pillar full-plate single-chain fusee movement with spotted plates, Harrison's maintaining power and Earnshaw-type spring detent escapement regulated by split bimetallic balance with circular timing weights, inscribed "THO'S S. COGDON, Dalston, London, No., 5146," set in a lacquered brass bowl with screw-down bezel mounted within pivoted gimbals with locking screw, in a later mahogany two-tier box.

ca. 1880 and later   7¼in (18cm) wide
$800-850   DN

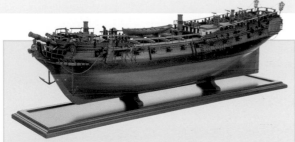

A 1:36 scale Admiralty board-style model, for the sixth rate 28-gun ship "Enterprise," 1774, modeled in alder wood, fruitwood, and ebony, mounted on ebonized cradle stand on wooden display base.

Ordered in 1771 and completed in 1775 by Adam Hayes of Deptford Dockyard to designs by John Williams for a total (fitted) cost of £14,715.08 (about $20,000), Enterprise was the name-ship for a class of five built in response to the Falkland Islands emergency. Displacing 593 tons, she was 120ft long with a 33ft beam and draft of 11ft. Commissioned in 1775 under Capt Sir Thomas Rich, she served initially in the Mediterranean and at the Siege of Gibraltar where her crew bravely saw off a concerted fireship attack by the Spanish. In 1781, she was refitted and coppered at Woolwich for a further £5,185.19.2d (about $6,500). Sailing to the Leeward Islands, she took the 22-gun U.S. privateer Mohawk later in 1782, which entered the RN in her own name. Latterly, she was moored by the Tower of London and used to receive impressed men before being paid off, and was broken at Deptford in 1807.

48in (122cm) long

$26,000-33,000   **CM**

A fine French Napoleonic prisoner-of-war bone model for H.M.S. "Caledonia," the 10in (25cm) hull planked and pinned with bone, baleen main and secondary wales, polished brass guns with Venetian red gun ports, finely carved figurehead, stern, and quarter lights, brass anchors with bound bone stocks, planked and pinned deck with fittings, including capstan, gratings, belfry with bell, water casks, companionway, binnacle compass, deck lights, chicken coop, and other details, bound masts with yards, stuns'l boons, standing and running rigging with bone blocks with two ship's boats slung out between main- and foremast, mounted to inlaid wooden display base with bone finials and contained within an ebonized, glazed display case.

22¼in (56.5cm) long

$33,000-40,000   **CM**

A Napoleonic French prisoner-of-war bone model for the 74-gun 3rd rate "Illustrious," the planked and pinned hull with polychrome warrior figurehead, with glass dome cover, restored by the Parker Gallery with replaced rigging and some components, such as flags and fighting tops refreshed.

ca. 1810   *12in (30.5cm) long with glass dome*

$11,000-13,000   **CM**

An historically interesting model of the Ramsgate Hovellers' Lugger "Prince of Wales," built by H. Twyman and displayed at the Great Exhibition, London, 1851, within original morocco case.

36in (91.5cm) long

$20,000-26,000   **CM**

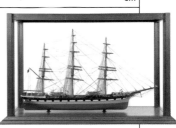

A exceptional 1:64 scale static display model of the clipper "Loch Etive," built at Glasgow, 1877, modeled by Captain D. Fraser, with carved and painted 34in (86cm) hull, scored lacquered decks complete with fittings, including deck rails, boomkins, catheads with wooden anchors, davits, capstan with silver chain.

ca. 1910   *63in (160cm) long*

$10,000-10,500   **CM**

A builder's model of the S.S. "South Pacific," by Joseph L. Thompson & Sons, Sunderland for Pacific Shipping Ltd, within original wooden case with later brass plates, name reapplied, replacement brass plates, rigging restored.

1913   *69in (175cm) long*

$20,000-26,000   **CM**

A boardroom model for the "M.V. Trewidden," built by Readhead & Sons, South Shields for Hain Steamship Company, modeled by the Sunderland Model Co. Ltd, mounted in glazed brass bound case, with maker's and specification plates.

1960   *67½in (171.5cm) long*

$16,000-21,000   **CM**

An early-20thC ship model diorama of the paddle steamer "Britannia," full hull model in a painted shadowbox frame.

33in (84cm) wide

$600-750

L&T

A 19thC Victorian spun-glass cased ship model, modeled as a three-masted ship and smaller ship in a rolling sea, in white, red and blue glass, on a plinth base in a glass dome.

17¾in (45cm) high

$400-550

L&T

A full-scale bell metal replica of the Lutine Bell, probably 19thC, after the original of 1779 recovered in 1858 and now hanging in Lloyd's of London, with original French inscription reading "Saint Jean 1779," with crucifix and fleur-de-lys device.

Built at Toulon in 1779, "La Lutine" was a 36-gun frigate of 950 tons and was one of a number surrendered to Admiral Lord Hood in 1793 by French Royalists eager not to let them fall into the hands of the revolutionaries. After a refit in Gibraltar, she returned to England under the command of William Haggit and entered the Navy List as the 5th Rate H.M.S. "Lutine." Four years later, under the command of Captain Lancelot Skynner, she sailed from the Yarmouth Roads laden with merchant's gold and coin for payment of British troops in Holland. Setting sail from Woolwich on October 8, 1799, a strong gale whipped up after midnight and she struck a sandbank between Terschelling and Vlieland, sinking immediately. Salvage attempts recovered her bell on July, 17, 1858. It was donated to the insurance underwriters Lloyd's of London and hangs in the underwriters' room to this day. Traditionally, the bell was sounded to ensure that all were aware of news simultaneously: once for the loss of a ship, and twice for her return.

51in (129.5cm) high

$5,300-6,600

CM

The main ship's bell from the S.Y "Iolanda," designed by Cox & King for Morton Plant N.Y.Y.C, built by Ramage & Ferguson in Leith, cast in brass with molded shoulder and rim, painted red internally with iron clapper, inset with name and date and a decorative device between.

One of the most distinctive yachts of her time, after World War I she was managed by Camper & Nicholson for chartering before being sold to the U.S. banker Moses Taylor. During World War II, she served as a survey ship and renamed "White Bear" for the duration. Sold into commercial service in 1947, she disappears from Lloyd's Register by 1953. Morton Plant owned several shipping lines and "Iolanda" was one of four steam yachts and two large racing yachts he maintained. He seems to have had connections with the Italian royal family, because one of his racing yachts was named "Elena" after the queen, and "Iolanda" was the Italian Princess Royal.

1908   *15in (38cm) high*

$1,600-2,100

CM

A ship's brass bell from the Algerine class minesweeper, by Harland & Wolff, lacking clapper, black-filled lettering inscribed "PINCHER" and dated.

Essentially an enlarged "Bangor" Class vessel, ultimately 110 of these 950 ton ships were built by yards in the UK and Canada 1941-45. Originally intended to be turbine powered, supply issues meant that only 27 were thus built, including "Pincher," the rest were VTE (vertical triple expansion) engined, however both types were capable of developing 16.5 knots. Armed with a single 4in. quick-firing gun and four 40mm Bofors, they needed up to 138 crew to man them. Only half a dozen were lost on active service, including the name-ship of the Class to an Italian submarine, and most were used as antisubmarine escorts. Most of the surviving ships were sold for breaking in the 1960s, with "Pincher" broken at Dunston in March 1962.

1943   *18in (46cm) high*

$1,050-1,200

CM

A pair of 7x50 naval binoculars, formerly owned by Admiral Sir Cecil Harcourt, signed in the backplate "Barr & Stroud 7x C.F.30, Glasgow and London/ C.H.J.Harcourt," in original leather case.

Admiral Sir Cecil Halliday Jepson Harcourt GBE KCB (1892-1959) saw action in both world wars and, from September 1945 to June 1946, was the de facto governor of Hong Kong. He was appointed Director of the Admiralty Operations division in 1939; in 1941 was Flag Captain of the Home Fleet aboard the Duke of York; and in 1942–44 was involved in the North Africa Campaign culminating in the landings at Salerno. However, his fame was secured when he took the surrender of the Japanese forces in Hong Kong. He was knighted in 1945 (KCB), promoted vice admiral in 1946, and awarded the grand cordon of the Chinese order of the Cloud and Banner. He retired in 1952.

10.5in (27cm) high

$4,600-5,900

CM

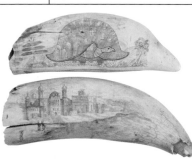

Top: A 19thC scrimshaw-decorated whale's tooth, incised with natural history scenes comprising a giant Galapagos tortoise, a full profile of an Orca and a serpent.

8in (20.5cm) 615g 21.7oz

$1,300-1,800

CM

Bottom: A 19thC scrimshaw decorated whale's tooth, incised with a Byzantium townscape.

8.5in (21.5cm) long

$1,800-2,400

CM

A silver vesta case, a memento of the Great War's first hospital ship, hallmarked Birmingham, 1912-13, the front bearing crossed enameled flags of Saint George and the Royal Fleet Auxiliary, and engraved "J.G. from G.H.H., 1914-15, H.M.H.S. Oxfordshire."

This is one of a small number commissioned by Captain G.H. Harris, the Master of H.M.A.S. "Oxfordshire" and who presented them to his officers to commemorate their time together. "Oxfordshire" was built in 1912 for the Bibby Line's Rangoon Service by Harland & Wolff. In World War I, she enjoyed the distinction of being the first British merchant ship to be requisitioned. On passage from Liverpool to London on August 2, 1914, she was off the Isle of Wight when she received orders to proceed to Tilbury, where she was rapidly converted into Naval Hospital Ship No. 1 and commissioned a mere nine days later. Surviving the war, she was released back to her owners and refitted for peacetime. In all, she made 235 voyages and carried some 50,000 wounded (the highest of any hospital ship in the Great War), and steamed a total of 172,000 miles without a single mechanical problem. History repeated itself 20 years later when, on September 3, 1939, she was again taken up for War Service and refitted this time as Hospital Ship No. 6. Used for trooping and refugee duties, her role extended long past the war's end. She was finally broken up at Karachi in 1958 after what one source describes as "46 years of impeccable service."

2¼in (5.5cm) wide 2.3oz

$850-1,000   CM

A New Zealand kauri wood ditty box, from the Shaw, Savill & Co. New Zealand immigrant ship S.V. "Lady Jocelyn," carved in the round with local flora and fauna and geometric shapes, inscribed on one side "Lady Jocelyn 1878," with sliding lid.

1878   12in (30.5cm) wide

$1,200-1,450   CM

A Sunderland glass rummer, etched with a brig sailing under the iron bridge inscribed "Sunderland Bridge over the river Wear," the reverse with "J/HN" flanked by wheat and hops.

ca. 1800   6in (15cm) high

$450-600   CM

A large and exceptionally fine sailor's woolwork picture, depicting a fully rigged ship passing a signal station, each displaying a hoist of Marryat signal flags, with pilot cutters approaching, framed and glazed.

ca. 1880   41in (104cm) wide

$8,000-9,000   CM

A sailor's woolwork picture, depicting an Admiral of the Red aboard either H.M.S "Black Prince" or "Warrior."

ca. 1860   18in (46cm) wide

$1,500-1,800   CM

A sailor's woolwork picture, depicting a three deck first-rate of the Royal Navy at anchor, within original maple frame.

ca. 1860   30in (76cm) wide

$4,600-5,900   CM

A figurehead maquette, for the clipper ship "Abergeldie," built by John Duthie, Sons & Co., Aberdeen, in the form of a 34in (86cm) high full-length highland clansman, paintwork sympathetically restored.

1869   53in (134.5cm) high

$10,500-12,000   CM

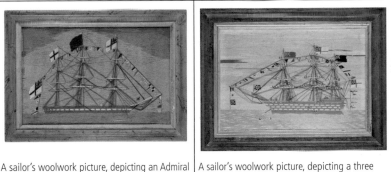

A 19thC sawfish rostrum, decorated on one side in polychrome depicting yachts at anchor off a waterfront, possibly Venice, with paint shrinkage and embedded dirt.

41in (104cm) long

$2,100-2,600   CM

A 19thC Swiss interchangeable cylinder musical box, the six cylinders playing six airs each, the case walnut with kingwood crossbanding and ebonized borders.

42¼in (107cm) wide

$6,500-8,000   SWO

A Swiss rosewood musical box playing six airs, strung inlaid case, in restored and working order.

15¾in (40cm) wide

$350-400   PSA

A late-19thC Swiss 10 airs, three-bell music box with butterfly hammers, label in inside of lid (no. 5847), key for lock present and working.

19¼in (49cm) wide

$600-750   LOCK

A 19thC Swiss music box, inlaid with walnut, label in inside of lid, all teeth intact, case lock damaged.

21¾in (55cm) wide

$400-450   LOCK

A 19thC Swiss musical box with drum and four bells, struck by a pair of polychrome Mandarin automata playing 10 airs on 15in (38cm) cylinders and 86 tooth triple comb no. 38001, in an inlaid rosewood case.

25¾in (65.5cm) wide

$1,300-2,000   CHOR

An early-20thC German gilt-metal singing bird music box automaton, attributed to Karl Griesbaum, decorated with Greek key and Rococo-style decoration, the top centered by a hinged cover opening to reveal a bird with bright plumage, moving and singing, rising from an ornate foliate pierced grill.

4¼in (11cm) wide

$2,400-2,900   MART

A Bontems-type singing bird automaton, with black and white plumage and moving head, under a domed brass cage on a giltwood base.

22in (56cm) high

$1,000-1,100   CHEF

A 19thC French musical picture clock, the twin-train clock movement striking the hour and half hour on a gong, the box frame with additional musical movement playing three airs, the oil-on-canvas painting depicting a village with clock tower and bridge over a river, within a swept gilt box frame.

39in (99cm) wide

$1,050-1,200   MART

ESSENTIAL REFERENCE—18THC SILVER CANDLESTICKS

A real shortage of silver occurred when Oliver Cromwell was Lord Protector of England, Scotland, and Ireland (1653-58), when quantities of silver were melted down for coinage. Supplies of silver began to gradually increase again with the Restoration of the Monarchy in 1660, so that by the first decades of the 18thC, silversmiths again had enough material to make more than just small items. Once again, people were able to commission and buy large pieces and items for the dining room, and they became highly sought after.

- In an age with no electricity and before the advent of the oil and gas lighting of the 19thC, candlelight illuminated every activity after dusk. Imagine an 18thC dining room with its highly polished mahogany furniture, table set with beautiful porcelain (itself a new discovery) with its glossy glaze and lit by candles in polished silver holders. Everything was designed to reflect and magnify light.
- Silversmiths in the 18thC tended to specialize. Small workers fashioned buttons, buckles, and other little accessories and decorative objects. Large workers focused on platters, serving dishes, plates, and centerpieces. Some makers made only flatware, others only coffeepots and milk pitchers, and still others who specialized in candlesticks.
- The 18thC saw the emergence of some of the most important silversmiths of all time. These included Paul de Lamerie, the Garrards silversmiths; the Bateman Family; Paul Storr, and Paul Revere. Paul Storr (1771-1844) worked in the fashionable Neoclassical style, crafting grand pieces of tableware for the English nobility and King George IV.
- This movement away from the Rococo to the Neoclassical is further illustrated in the work of the American patriot silversmith Paul Revere (1734-1818). Before the Revolutionary War, Revere generally worked in the Rococo style.

A pair of Queen Anne silver taper candlesticks, by Jacob Margas, London, octagonal baluster form, spool-shaped capitals, on raised circular bases.

1708   *4in (10cm) high 7oz*

$8,500-10,000   **WW**

A group of four George II silver candlesticks, three by John Quantock, London, one 1751 and two 1753, and one by Thomas Heming, London, 1750, the base engraved with a coat of arms, the base and sockets further later engraved with a crest, numbered and engraved with scratch weights of "No 1 19"0"; "No 2 19"13"; "No 3 19=9"; and "No 4 19=15," surface scratching and wear.

The arms and crest are those of Powlett. The seeming absence of an engraved duke's coronet suggests that instead of being made for Charles, 3rd Duke of Bolton (1685-1754,) they may instead have been made for his brother Harry, 4th Duke of Bolton (1691-1759) or his nephew Charles, 5th Duke of Bolton (ca. 1718-65).

9in (23cm) high, 72oz

$6,000-6,600   **TEN**

A matched pair of George II Irish cast-silver candlesticks, possibly by Phillip Kinnersly or Peter Racine, Dublin, knopped baluster form, spool-shaped capitals, scratch weights on underside "14"8" and "14"3," one lacking date letter.

1728   *6¾in (17.3cm) high 28.8oz*

$4,600-5,900   **WW**

A pair of George II cast-silver candlesticks, by John Jacob, London, engraved with an "R" cypher beneath a baron's coronet, overall surface wear with minor scuffs, the sconces later, with rubbed Victorian duty mark and only standard mark.

1734   *9¼in (23.5cm) high 61.3oz*

$8,500-10,000   **DN**

A George II silver taperstick, maker's mark "I?," knopped stem, spool-shaped capital, London.

1736   *4in (10cm) high 3.3oz*

$600-750   **WW**

A set of four George II cast-silver candlesticks, by William Gould, London, detachable unmarked drip pans, on spread bases with foliate and shell decoration, engraved with a crest and armorial.

1749   *9½in (24.2cm) high 108oz*

$8,000-9,000   **WW**

A pair of late George II cast-silver candlesticks, by John Perry, London, the molded bases engraved with a crest, the bases have rubbed stippled remains of an engraving.

The crest for TARLETON.

1755   *8in (20cm) high 31.7oz*

$3,300-4,000   **DN**

A pair of George III silver candlesticks, by Ebenezer Coker, London, of fluted-column form, Ionic capitals, detachable drip pans, gadroon borders, on stepped square bases with gadroon borders, engraved with crests, wooden undersides.

1765   *11¾in (30cm) high*

$2,000-2,600   **WW**

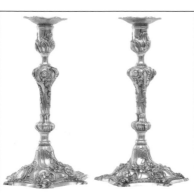

A pair of George III sterling silver candlesticks, by William Cafe, engraved with a coat of arms and crest, marked on underside and wax pan of each and on one socket.

1768   *11½in (29cm) high 43.5 oz*

$4,000-5,300   **DRA**

A pair of George III silver candlesticks, probably by John Carter, London, shaped baluster stems, gadroon borders, spool-shaped capitals, detachable drip pans, part-fluted decoration, on raised shaped square bases, the bases also marked "RD" four times, once on each side of the base.

1770   *11in (27.8cm) high 46oz*

$3,300-4,000   **WW**

A pair of George III silver candlesticks, by Matthew Boulton, Birmingham, with gadroon, shell, and leaf borders.

1821   *9½in (24cm) high*

$900-1,050   **DAWS**

A pair of George IV cast-silver-gilt candlesticks, by Sebastian Crespell II, London, the columns modeled as Neptune holding coral-mounted urn capitals, removable shell drip pans, on raised shaped bases with foliate scroll decoration, engraved with a crest and monogram, the underside of the base with a later presentation inscription "The Gift of Mrs Elilz. Drew to Col C.K.K. Tynte Jan 3 Obt. 5 1856."

1824   *7¼in (18.5cm) high 27oz*

$6,000-7,500   **WW**

A pair of Victorian silver three-light candelabra, by Robert Garrard II, London, with detachable foliate sconces, leaf- and scroll-chased baluster capitals, foliate scroll curved branches, the asymmetric reserves engraved with a crest, the bases with rocaillework and scrollwork, light scratches.

1848   *20in (50.5cm) high 146.3oz*

$16,000-18,000   **DN**

A set of four Victorian silver candlesticks, by Elkington & Co., weighted, marked on foot rim and wax pan of each.

1898   *8¾in (22cm) high*

$2,600-3,300   **DRA**

A pair of Queen Anne style silver tapersticks, by George Unite, Birmingham.

1904   *4¼in (10.5cm) high*

$400-550   **CHOR**

A pair of silver three-light candelabra, by A. Crichton, London, the center light with a detachable urn finial, on raised shaped oval bases, with reeded borders.

1919   *18¼in (46.5cm) high weight of arms 44oz*

$4,000-4,600   **WW**

A pair of Elizabeth II silver two-light candelabra, by C. J. Vander, London, in the early-18thC style, the detachable branches with two arms, each terminating in spool-shaped sockets with plain wax pans, with a center baluster finial, with some tarnish.

1964   *8in (20.5cm) high 31oz*

$800-900   **TEN**

A pair of Austrian silver candelabra, signed with unidentified impressed maker's mark "CW" and Austrian hallmark.

ca. 1900   *22½in (57cm) high 74.1 ozt*

$4,600-5,300   **DRA**

A pair of 20thC French silver five-light candelabra, by Tétard Frères, marked on foot rim of each example and engraved "Tetard Paris."

9¼in (23cm) high 122.2 oz

$6,000-6,600   **DRA**

A pair of silver three-branch candelabra, loaded, maker DMS, London.

1977   *11in (28cm) high*

$400-550   **WHP**

A Victorian silver centerpiece, by Horace Woodward, Birmingham, tapering fluted column, with three pierced arms with Classical decoration and ram's heads, each supporting a circular bowl holder, beaded borders, on a shaped triangular base set with three Pegasus horses, with four later glass bowls.

1874   *24¾in (62.8cm) 148oz*

$4,000-5,300   **WW**

A 19thC Italian silver-gilt chamber stick, probably by Castellani, Rome, modeled as a sitting devil with arms out to hold a candlestick, his tail forming the ring handle, the shaped base with flame decoration, the front with a grotesque mask, unmarked.

The design for this chamber stick is by Michaelangelo Caetani, who was Castellani's principle patron. A number of candlesticks designed as demons are noted in Castellani's stock registers up to 1899.

ca. 1880-1890   *4¼in (11cm) long 8.7oz*

$6,000-6,600   **WW**

An Elizabeth I silver chalice, by Robert Durrant, London, with engraved foliate decoration, on a knopped stem on a raised circular foot, with an engraved border.

1565   *7in (18cm) high 8.1oz*

$16,000-20,000   **WW**

A Charles II/William & Mary silver communion cup, attributed to Thomas Cooper, London (maker's mark struck only twice), with old solder repair in bottom of bowl and two on angles, the flat bottom of bowl has the stem pushed into it.

6in (15cm) high 9.2oz

$6,000-6,600   **DN**

A rare Charles II West Country porringer, by John Peard, Barnstable, scroll handles, the front prick-dot initialed "Prudence Hobson, April 17 1674."

ca. 1674   *3¼in (8cm) high 7oz*

$6,500-8,000   **WW**

A Charles II provincial silver mug, by Marmaduke Best, York, the scroll handle scratch initialed "FL" over "WM."

1680   *4½in (11.5cm) high 12.8oz*

$5,300-5,900   **WW**

A William III West Country silver mug, by John Murch, Plymouth, part-fluted decoration, rope-work girdle, with punched decoration, reeded scroll handle, scratch initialed "S" over "IM."

ca. 1695 3¾in (9.5cm) high 4.5oz

$4,000-4,600 WW

A William III Scottish silver mug, by John Seatoune, Edinburgh, thistle form, with applied cut-card decoration, inscribed "B."

1701 3¾in (9.5cm) high 6oz

$6,000-7,500 WW

A Queen Anne silver mug, by Paul de Lamerie, London, engraved with an armorial and motto within foliate-scroll mantling.

The arms are those of Orfeur of High Close and Plumbland Hall, Co.Cumberland, for Charles Orfeur, who died in 1725.

1713 4¼in (10.8cm) high 13.85oz

$20,000-24,000 WW

A George I silver mug, by Timothy Lee, London, with inscription "The Gift of James Jennings Esq. to the Company of Skiners [sic] in Abingdon in the year 1714, Humphry Williams Master."

1714 4¼in (11cm) high 8.3oz

$3,300-4,600 WW

A George I silver "College" or "Ox-eye" cup, by George Gillingham, London, with a monogram "SJW," the reverse "Felices ter & amplius Quos irrupta tenet copula, nec. malis Divulsus querimomis Suprema citius solvit amor die."

The inscription translates as "Three times happy are they and more, who are held by unbreakable bonds and whose love, undivided by evil quarrels will be dissolved on the final day."

1720 4in (10.3cm) high 9.5oz

$17,000-21,000 WW

A George I silver loving cup, Hugh Arnett & Edward Pockock, London, with later inscription to "Francis Barlow Robinson Esq by Mrs Belt in grateful remembrance of his kindness to her and the Children of his esteemed friend Rob't Belt Esq, 1842."

1723 22.3oz

$1,050-1,200 CHOR

A George IV silver mug, by Paul Storr, decorated with fruiting vine and with a rustic handle, on a decorated circular foot, London.

1825 3in (7.5cm) high 179 gm

$1,800-2,400 BELL

A parcel-gilt silver cup, Hunt and Roskell, late Storr and Mortimer London, featuring winged cherubs and scrolling foliage, presentation inscription on base "Kenneth Murray Kennedy from his Grandmother Emily Kennedy Oct 1895."

1892 4in (10cm) high 12.2 oz

$4,000-4,600 DRA

A Charles II silver tankard, possibly by Phillip Price, London, the cover with an armorial within ribbon-tied foliate mantling and with a scroll thumbpiece, the front of the tankard initialed "T*K" over "A*H" with plume mantling, dated "1672."

The arms are those of Kennedy quartering those of France. The initials are for Sir Thomas Kennedy who married Agnes Haldane on November 1, 1670. Sir Thomas was Lord Provost of Edinburgh in 1685 and died in 1715.

1663   *6¾in (17cm) high 28oz*
$17,000-21,000   **WW**

A Charles II silver tankard, probably by Thomas Manwaring, London, the scroll handle scratch initialed "M.D" over "P."

1675   *6¾in (16.8cm) high 26.5oz*
$9,000-10,500   **WW**

A rare William III silver bougie box, by Daniel Garnier, London, cylindrical form, reeded scroll handle, the hinged cover with a sliding wick holder and cutter, the front with a monogram below a Barons coronet, the underside with a scratch weight.

The bougie box, or taper box, was a cylindrical container to hold a wax taper coil when not in use. The cover was originally flat and a tube at the top of the cover permitted the coiled taper to emerge. Some had a chain-attached candle estinguisher.

1697   *2½in (6.5cm) high 4oz*
$6,000-7,500   **WW**

A William III Britannia standard silver tankard, by John Porter, with an engraved crest, engraved on underside "A.D. 1704 T.M.S. A.D. 1899" with scratch weight "24 = 16," fully marked.

1704   *7in (18cm) high 24.4 oz*
$3,400-4,200   **DRA**

A Queen Anne silver tankard, by Humphrey Payne, London, scroll handle with a later crest, the cover embossed with grapes and a mask, later embossed with playful Bacchanalian cherubs.

1704   *7¼in (18.5cm) high 25.9oz*
$3,300-4,000   **WW**

A George I silver tankard, by Joseph Clare, London, engraved with an armorial within foliate scroll mantling, the scroll handle engraved with a bird and inscribed "Beak Galley In Norris."

The armorial Is that of Norreys/Norris.

1716   *7¼in (18.7cm) high 23.9oz*
$10,000-10,500   **WW**

An 18thC Scandinavian silver peg tankard, probably Danish, and possibly by Asmus Fridrich Holling, the hinged cover set with an Austrian silver Thaler of 1623, and with a rampant lion-and-ball thumbpiece, the underside of the base inscribed.

ca. 1730   *7.5in (19.5cm) high 23.2oz*
$3,300-4,000   **WW**

A silver tankard, by Jonathan Clarke, the handle with scroll thumbpiece and William III coin terminal, marked on underside.

ca. 1740   *8¼in (21cm) high 26.5 oz*
$17,000-21,000   **DRA**

A George III provincial silver tankard, by John Langlands, Newcastle, the scroll handle scratch initialed "S" over "TA" and terminating in a heart motif.

1769   *6½in (16.5cm) high 21.6oz*
$3,300-4,000   **WW**

A George III provincial silver tankard, by John Langlands, Newcastle, of tapering circular form, the domed hinged cover with a pierced thumbpiece, the scroll handle scratch initialed "M" over "WN," terminating in a heart motif.

1773   *6¾in (17.2cm) high 21.6oz*

$3,300-4,000   **WW**

A sterling silver marine-themed tankard, by Tiffany & Co., chased with sea nymph, dolphin, seaweed, and shell decoration, marked on underside "8838 5920."

1873-91   *8¾in (22cm) high 46.2 ozt*

$13,000-16,000   **DRA**

An Edwardian silver half-pint tankard, by Wakely & Wheeler, London, based on the 17thC Balliol College tankard with thumbpiece in the form of a hedgehog.

1907   *5½in (14cm) high 16oz*

$550-650   **WHP**

ESSENTIAL REFERENCE—NO TEA PARTY!

Antique tea caddies, teapots, and all the other paraphernalia essential to tea drinking are especially collectible, but what of tea itself? Well, the fact that over hundreds of years tea has fueled trade on a global scale, been subject to punitive taxation, and triggered wars between nations, clearly elevates it beyond the status of just a refreshing libation!

- While tea drinking began in China some 5,000 years ago, and had been introduced to Japan and China in the 3rdC by Buddhist monks, it wasn't until the early 17thC that tea was exported in any quantity to Europe, initially under sail to the Netherlands by the Dutch East India Company. However, tea drinking in Britain didn't begin until the mid-17thC, when Catherine of Braganza, who had acquired the taste in her native Portugal, married King Charles II and introduced it to the English aristocracy. It's subsequent popularity, and the British East India Company entering the increasingly profitable tea-trading market, was to have profound political consequences.

- Chief among these was the infamous "Boston Tea Party" of 1773, in which North American colonists threw chests of East India Company tea into Boston's harbor in protest against the "Tea Act" of 1773, which allowed the Company, unlike the colonists, to sell tea from China without paying the high tax on it—an event that triggered the American War of Independence, the subsequent loss of Britain's colony, and, ultimately, the foundation of the United States!

A George II Scottish silver bullet teapot, by James Kerr, Edinburgh, chased with foliate scroll decoration, the leaf-capped scroll handles with wooden insulators, the underside of the foot initialed "JC," assay master's mark lost.

1737   *9¾in (24.5cm) long 22oz*

$1,050-1,200   **WW**

A George II Scottish silver teapot, by Edward Lothian, assay master Hugh Gordon, Edinburgh, with leaf-capped scroll handle set with stained ivory insulators, flush-hinged domed cover with a cone finial, engraved with a crest.

1749   *10¾in (27cm) long 22oz*

$1,050-1,200   **WW**

A George I silver teapot, maker's mark worn, London, with traces of other marks, square pear form with canted corners, the raised hinged cover with a knop finial, scroll handle, engraved with an armorial within foliate scroll mantling.

1718   *6¼in (16cm) high 17oz*

$8,000-9,000   **WW**

An 18thC Dutch silver teapot, by Matthijis Crayenschot, Amsterdam, with a worn armorial.

1762   *8¼in (21cm) long 13oz*

$2,200-2,600   **WW**

A George III silver teapot and stand, by Peter, Ann, and William Bateman, bright-cut decoration, London.

1800   *11in (27.4cm) wide 19.5oz*

$750-850   **WW**

A sterling silver teapot, by Peter, Ann, and William Bateman, with repeating patterns and a sunburst medallion with monogram, marked to underside and cover.

1800   *6¾in (17cm) high 17 oz*

$450-600   **DRA**

A George III provincial silver teapot, by Barber and Whitwell, York, the flush-hinged cover with an ivory finial.

1815   *10in (25cm) long 20.9oz*

$750-850   **WW**

A George III silver teapot, by Crispin Fuller, London, with embossed foliate decoration, leaf-capped spout with ivory insulators.

1817   *11½in (29.3cm) long 24.2oz*

$450-550   **WW**

An early-19thC teapot, possibly Colonial, leaf-capped handle with ivory insulators, the hinged cover with a knop finial, the spout with chased foliate decoration, engraved with a crest, marked "AS" twice and "AG" below a sailing boat twice, marks unidentified.

ca. 1820   *10in (25.5cm) long 24.8oz*

$1,800-2,400   **WW**

A William IV silver teapot, by Paul Storr, London, leaf-capped scroll handle with wooden insulators, shaped foliate-hinged cover with a foliate finial, the spout of simulated bark form with leaf mounts, stamped "STORR & MORTIMER."

1831   *9¼in (23.4cm) long 18.2oz*

$2,600-3,300   **WW**

A William IV silver teapot, by Richard Atkins & William Somersall, embossed and chased with rose decoration, engraved with an armorial, the leaf-capped scroll handle with ivory insulators, the hinged cover with a rose finial, London.

1832   *11in (27.5cm) wide 29oz*

$1,000-1,100   **WW**

A William IV Irish silver teapot, by James Fray, Dublin, scroll handle with ivory insulators.

1837   *12¼in (31cm) long 25.3oz*

$1,000-1,100   **WW**

A Victorian silver teapot, by Messrs. Lias, London, with embossed foliate decoration, scroll handle with ivory insulators.

1872   *9¼in (23.5cm) high 22oz*

$600-750   **WW**

A Victorian silver teapot of Neoclassical design, by Walker & Hall, Sheffield.

1897   *22oz*

$350-400   **WHP**

A silver teapot, by Walker and Hall, Sheffield, heavy gadroon and shell border, ivory scroll handle issuing from snake sockets, domed cover with an ivory finial.

1932   *11¾in (29.5cm) long 33.9oz*

$800-900   **WW**

A George II silver coffeepot, illegible maker's mark on underside.

1734   *8in (20cm) high 25oz*

$1,000-1,100   DRA

A George II silver coffeepot, by John Kincaid, with chased foliate-scroll decoration, acorn finial, hallmarked London.

1743   *9½in (24cm) high 25.6oz*

$1,050-1,200   LOCK

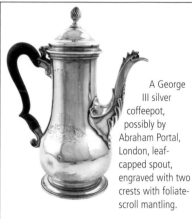

A George III silver coffeepot, possibly by Abraham Portal, London, leaf-capped spout, engraved with two crests with foliate-scroll mantling.

The crest is that of Cresswell (London and Northumberland).

1765   *10¼in (26cm) high 25oz*

$900-1,050   WW

A George III Irish provincial silver coffeepot, by Carden Terry, Cork, the spout with a replacement mythical bird's-head end, engraved with an armorial.

The armorial is that of Warren impaling another.

ca. 1785   *9¾in (24.5cm) high 27.8oz*

$6,500-8,000   WW

A George III silver hot water ewer/ coffee pitcher, by Smith and Sharp, engraved foliate decoration above part-fluted decoration, gadroon borders, the hinged cover with a cone finial, London.

1788   *11.6in (29.5cm) high 27.5oz*

$1,250-1,450   WW

A George III silver coffee pitcher-on-stand with a burner, by John Emes, London, the hinged cover with a fluted ball finial, the body with a fluted border, engraved with an armorial, the stand on three scroll legs with drop rings and with paw feet.

1807   *47.8oz*

$1,800-2,400   WW

A William IV silver coffee pitcher-on-stand, by Benjamin Preston, London, the flush-hinged cover with a flower finial, the stand on three leaf-capped scroll feet, with a burner, the body with traces of a crest.

1831   *12¾in (32.5cm) high 41oz*

$1,050-1,200   WW

A William IV silver coffeepot, by The Barnards, London, part-fluted decoration, scroll handle, domed hinged cover with a fluted finial, on a raised circular foot with fluted decoration.

1834   *9in (23cm) high 22oz*

$550-650   WW

CLOSER LOOK—SILVER COFFEEPOT

Bird heads with open beaks were particularly well-suited functional and decorative forms for coffee- and teapot spouts.

The scrolling handle opposite, as here, was often configured to represent the bird's tail.

The flora and fauna imagery on the body, spout, and handle is extended to the hinged lid with finial, in the form of a peasant carousing while astride a large tortoise on a leaf.

The main body of the pot is decorated in a style popularized by the Flemish painter David Teniers the Younger in the 17thC, which depicted peasants making merry in rural landscapes—a pastoral idyll that enjoyed a resurgence of popularity in the late-18thC and 19thC, in no small part as a reaction to ever-increasing industrialization and urbanization.

Raised on four figural feet, the body of the pot is of bulbous baluster shape—a form developed during the Renaissance, and essentially derived from vases from Greco-Roman antiquity.

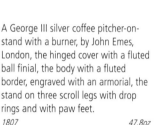

A Victorian silver coffeepot, maker probably Edward Farrell, London.

1845   *43oz*

$4,000-5,300   BELL

A Victorian silver kettle on stand, by Benjamin Smith III, London, engraved for Smith as retailer, engraved with flowers, the base with a burner, flower-and-scroll foliate engraved, on four openwork rocaille feet, light scratches.

1847   *14¼in (36cm) high 98.2oz*

$4,600-5,300   DN

A Victorian silver kettle-on-stand, by Martin, Hall & Co., Sheffield, a cast bird's head and bearded masks spout issuing from rocaillework, foliage, stand with a burner, the S-scroll supports terminating in dolphin heads, maker's mark on body obscured, light scratches and wear.

1855   *15½in (39.5cm) high 67.5oz*

$3,300-4,000   DN

A Victorian silver ovoid kettle on stand, by John Samuel Hunt, London, stamped "Hunt & Roskell late Storr & Mortimer 467," embossed and engraved with flower groups, rocaille, and trellis panels, engraved with arms, with a burner, light scratches and wear.

The arms of PRAED quartering MACKWORTH with EUAN in pretence.

1860   *16in (41cm) high 78.8oz*

$3,300-4,000   DN

A Victorian silver kettle-on-stand, by John Samuel Hunt, London, chased with foliate decoration, a cradle stand with a burner, light scratches and wear.

1846   *17in (43cm) high 109.1oz*

$6,000-6,600   DN

A Victorian silver kettle-on-stand, by Henry William Curry, London, in early-18thC style, the stand with twin lion mask bale handles, the burner elaborately chased, the three bold scroll supports issuing from lion masks, the paw feet on lobed balls, light scratches and wear.

1873   *18in (45.5cm) high 231.2oz*

$9,000-10,500   DN

An Edwardian silver kettle on a matched stand, by Heath and Middleton, Birmingham, the stand London 1904.

1907   *11¾in (29.5cm) 40oz*

$1,050-1,200   WW

An American silver kettle-on-stand, by Redlich and Company, New York, chased foliate decoration, the stand with leaf-capped supports and with a burner.

ca. 1920   *15¼in (38.5cm) high 65oz*

$1,500-1,800   WW

A George III silver Argyle, by Aldridge and Green, London, later embossed foliate decoration, the hinged cover with an urn finial, the interior with a covered compartment and with a metal heating rod.

1779   *5¼in (13cm) high 10.5oz*

$850-1,000   WW

A George III silver milk pot, by Paul Storr, London, in the French manner, engraved with a crest.

The crest is probably that of Bull.

1793   *3¾in (9.5cm) high 6oz*

$6,500-8,000   WW

A William IV silver "argyle," by Robert Hennell, London, of baluster form, leather-bound scroll handle, the hinged cover with a knop finial, the hinged cover opens to reveal a pull-out heating section with a cover and a metal rod.

1832   *4¼in (11cm) high 8oz*

$1,600-2,100   WW

A George IV three-piece silver tea service, by Edward Farrell, with decoration after David Teniers, with silver-gilt interiors on sugar bowl and cream pitcher.

1822-23   *7½in (19cm) high 81.68oz*
$11,000-13,000   **DRA**

A silver seven-piece tea and coffee service, by Samuel Kirk & Son, with floral repoussé decoration with heron, dragonfly, and fish, and Chinese figural finials, marked on underside of each "S. Kirk & Son 11 oz," engraved inscription on underside of each "Elizabeth J. Smith December 25, 1892."

1892   *14¼in (36cm) high 348oz*
$26,000-33,000   **DRA**

A French silver kettle, teapot, and coffeepot by Maison Odiot, Paris 1838-1972, 1st standard, the handles with ivory spacers, with light scratches and wear.

ca. 1895   *coffeepot 11¼in (28.5cm) high 167.4oz*
$4,000-5,300   **DN**

A four-piece Victorian silver tea and coffee set, by George Angell, London, engraved foliate decoration, scroll handles with ivory insulators, domed hinged covers with crown finials, engraved with a crest.

1850   *11in (28cm) 61oz*
$3,300-4,000   **WW**

A silver four-piece tea and coffee service, by William Aitken, Birmingham, the tea- and coffeepots with bird finials on the covers, the leafy S-scroll handles with ivory spacers, with vacant reserves, trellis panels, flowers, and foliage.

1911   *11in (28cm) high 102.5oz*
$2,600-4,000   **DN**

A 20thC silver six-piece "Baltimore Rose" coffee and tea service with tray, by Schofield Co., marked "Sterling 1915," with Schofield manufacturer's mark and pattern number "3500" on underside of kettle-on-stand and waste bowl.

tray 30½in (77.5cm) wide 330.9 oz
$13,000-15,000   **DRA**

A three-piece silver tea set, Birmingham.

1934   *42.6oz*
$850-1,000   **CHOR**

A pair of George I silver tea caddies, by John Farnell, London, later chased foliate-scroll decoration, slide-off bases, pull-off covers, removable tin liners, with a later monogram.

1721   *5½in (14cm) high 16.9oz*
$2,600-4,000   WW

A George II silver tea caddy, by Edward Wakelin, London, engraved with foliate diaperwork enclosing roses and forget-me-nots in the manner of a textile pattern, engraved with crest.

1754   *4½in (11.5cm) high 14.6oz*
$5,300-5,900   WW

A suite of two George III silver tea caddies and a sugar box, by Pierre Gillois, London, the tea caddies with a bird-and-foliate finial, the sugar box with a flower finial, on four shell feet, engraved with a later crest, in a later silver-mounted shagreen case.

1755 case ca. 1784   *10.5in (26.8cm) wide 23.5oz*
$8,000-9,000   WW

A George III silver double-tea caddy, by John Swift, London, with two hinged compartments, both crested, the front and back with an armorial within foliate scroll mantling.

The arms are those of John Butler, Bishop of Oxford (1777) and Hereford (1788-92).

1769   *5in (12.3cm) wide 21.7oz*
$7,500-8,000   WW

A George III silver tea caddy, by Aaron Lestourgeon, London, engraved foliate decoration, the flush-hinged cover with a later finial, with a lock and key.

1772   *4¼in (11cm) wide 8.9oz*
$1,500-1,800   WW

A pair of William IV silver chinoiserie tea caddies, by Michael Starkey, London, in the Rococo manner, after Paul De Lamerie, embossed and chased with figures picking tea leaves, and with lion masks, buildings, foliate scroll, and shell decoration.

1831   *6in (15.4cm) high 23oz*
$8,500-9,000   WW

A William IV Scottish silver tea caddy, possibly by John McKell, Glasgow, embossed with pagodas and foliate and shell decoration, the hinged cover with a finial modeled as a sitting Chinaman, engraved with a crest, the interior of the base with a fitting to hold a divider.

The crest is that of Colley (Ireland).

1834   *½in (19cm) high 29.3oz*
$4,600-5,900   WW

A Victorian silver tea caddy and caddy spoon, by Samuel Walton Smith, London, the caddy spoon by Francis Higgins, engraved ribbon-tied decoration and borders, the caddy spoon with a shell bowl, in a fitted case.

1886   *3¼in (8.3cm) wide 8.4oz*
$850-1,000   WW

A late Victorian silver tea caddy and stand, by the Goldsmiths and Silversmiths Company, London, decorated in the chinoiserie manner with a figure and dragon within foliate settings.

1900   *7¼in (18.5cm) high 15oz*
$2,200-2,600   WW

An Elizabeth I silver apostle spoon, possibly Saint James the Greater or Saint Thomas, maker's mark "T" over a crescent, London, fig-shaped bowl, faceted tapering stem, gilded finial, with Holy Dove nimbus.

1594 *(18.1cm) long 1.9oz*

$5,300-5,900 **WW**

An Elizabethan sterling silver seal-top spoon, by William Cawdell, final prick-engraved "E*D," marked to bowl and stem.

Charles Oman (1901-82) was Keeper of Metalwork at the Victoria and Albert Museum from 1945 until 1966. Oman wrote the following note regarding the spoon: "After the 1951 exhibition at Goldsmiths' Hall the Wardens voted me £100 [$130] to buy a piece of silver. I had enough silver and had no ambition to become a collector, so I bought these seal-tops. On later occasions I always arranged that I should be rewarded with a travel grant." The 1951 Goldsmiths' Hall exhibition to which Charles Oman refers was "The Historic Plate of The City of London," for which he wrote the catalogue introduction.

1597 *6¾in (17cm) high 1.8 oz*

$4,000-4,600 **DRA**

A James I West Country silver-gilt decorated seal-top spoon, by John Quick, Barnstaple, engraved decoration, the faceted tapering stem with engraved decoration and engraved "Honour God," the seal-top prick-dot initialed "C.H."

1620 *7in (17.5cm) long 1.9oz*

$13,000-18,000 **WW**

A Charles I provincial silver Apostle spoon, the reverse of bowl prick-engraved "S/ EM 1652," marked "D.C," possibly for David Claydon, on bowl and on back of stem three times.

ca. 1630 *7½in (19cm) high 1.9 oz*

$4,000-4,600 **DRA**

An early-17thC Norwegian silver cherub-knop spoon, probably Bergen, the fig-shaped bowl with engraved decoration, the tapering stem with a cherub-head final, with traces of gilding, maker's mark "A?" conjoined.

ca. 1610 *6in (15.4cm) long 1.3oz*

$750-850 **WW**

A rare Charles I East Anglian silver "Lion Sejant" spoon, Norwich, SI or IS with a pellet below or above, fig-shaped bowl, faceted tapering stem, the "Lion Sejant" finial with traces of gilding, the reverse with an old collection label that reads "1636 Norwich by John Stone."

A "Lion Sejant" is sitting on his haunches, with both forepaws on the ground. This most important spoon is, at present, the only known "Lion Sejant" that can definitely be ascribed to Norwich.

Illustrated in How, G., in collaboration with J. How's "English and Scottish Silver Spoons, Volume One," Chapter II, Section VII, pages 264-66, plate 5, right-hand spoon.

1636 *6¾in (17cm) long 1.4oz*

$33,000-40,000 **WW**

A Charles I provincial silver spoon, by Richard Chandler, with tapering faceted stem and a gilded Buddha knop, stem engraved with a fleur-de-lys, the back of bowl prick-engraved "1640/WK/G*M."

ca. 1640 *7½in (19cm) long 1.3 oz*

$3,300-4,000 **DRA**

A Charles I silver seal-top spoon, by Steven Venables, London, fig-shaped bowl, tapering faceted stem, the seal-top finial scratch initialed "B" over "IA."

1647 *(16.8cm) long 1.4oz*

$1,600-2,000 **WW**

A Charles II West Country silver Apostle spoon, Salisbury, with an Apostle finial of Saint Thomas with traces of gilding and a large nimbus, marked with an anchor with two pellets in a circle, prick dot initialed "T.M" over T.W" and the date "1662."

ca. 1650 *7in (18.2cm) long 1.8oz*

$2,100-2,600 **WW**

A Charles II Puritan sterling silver spoon, by Jeremy Johnson, marked on bowl and reverse of stem, obverse of stem engraved "William Taunton Borne good friday the 13th April 1655 Baptised the 24th of the same month 1655," the reverse engraved "S/AD 1708."

1662 *7½in (19cm) high 1.8 oz*

$6,000-6,600 **DRA**

A Charles II West Country silver Apostle spoon, by Thomas Dare I, Taunton, stem with a gilded Apostle finial of Saint Matthew with a large plain nimbus, with traces of prick-dot initials.

ca. 1670   *7½in (18.8cm) long 1.7oz*

$3,300-4,000   **WW**

A Charles II silver seal-top spoon, by Robert King, London, fig-shaped bowl, faceted thick tapering stem, the finial scratch initialed "S" over "R.M."

1671   *6¼in (16cm) long 1.7oz*

$2,600-3,300   **WW**

A Charles II West Country silver-gilt Apostle spoon, by Thomas Dare I, overstamping another mark, Taunton, stem with a gilded Apostle finial of Saint Matthew, with a large plain nimbus, with prick dot initials "I.P over T.W" "1673."

1673   *7¼in (18.5cm) long 1.6oz*

$2,400-2,900   **WW**

A William and Mary East Anglian silver Trefid spoon, by Thomas Havers, Norwich, the bowl later gilded, with a raised rattail, the reverse of the terminal with prick dot initials "G" over "I.M."

1691   *6¾in (17cm) long 1.1oz*

$2,400-2,900   **WW**

An early-18thC American silver "dog-nose" spoon, by John Coney, Boston, the bowl with a raised rattail, the reverse of the terminal later scratch initialed "M.C" over "T.A" over "1728."

ca. 1720   *8in (19.5cm) long 0.9oz*

$750-850   **WW**

An early-18thC Dutch silver combination folding fork and spoon, maker's mark "HG" over "A," unidentified, Amsterdam, the baluster terminal screws off to reveal a spike, the tapering stem inscribed.

6in (15.3cm) long 1.6oz

$1,700-2,100   **WW**

A George I silver marrow scoop, by William Scarlett, London, some surface scratching and wear.

1719   *8¼in (21.2cm) long 1oz*

$350-450   **TEN**

A George III Irish provincial silver marrow scoop, of plain form, the reverse with initials, with maker's mark twice "PC" in an oval punch, probably for Patrick Connell, Limerick.

ca. 1790   *9in (22.8cm) long 1.3oz*

$1,600-2,100   **WW**

A George III Irish provincial silver meat skewer, by William Ward, Limerick, with bright-cut decoration.

ca. 1800   *10in (25.7cm) long 1.4oz*

$1,700-2,100   **WW**

ESSENTIAL REFERENCE—THE CADDY SPOON

Tea was introduced to Great Britain in the early 1660s. It was shipped in wooden containers, packed around pieces of porcelain that silversmiths imitated the shapes of in their crafting of tea caddies.

- Around the 1760s, caddies became box shaped, with flat or slightly domed lids. The newer versions were too large for measuring tea. Therefore separate spoons were created to measure out the tea.

- Early caddy spoons generally had shell-shaped bowls. This probably stems from tea merchants using sea shells to let customers sample the tea by smell and taste before making a purchase. They were even called "Caddy Shells" until the 1840s. Many of these spoons had deeply curved terminals so that the spoon could be hooked over the rim of the tea caddy itself while not in use. Typically, they also had deeply molded bowls.

- Examples from before the mid-19thC were usually made of thin sheet silver. Silver was the preferred material when it came to caddy spoons, because tea was a luxury, and using silver utensils would enhance the taste and flavors, where other materials may be detrimental to the experience.

- From about the second decade of the 19thC ,ornate examples were cast. A popular shape was that of the jockey cap, the inside of the cap being the ladle and the visor the handle. Others have the bowl in the shape of a leaf, bird's wing, salmon, a shell, or a shovel. At the beginning pf the 19thC, war trophies were fashionable, including cannon, drum, and sword. The bowl of the spoon would be embossed with one of these and sometimes the handle would also bear the name of a victory.

A George III novelty silver filigree jockey cap caddy spoon, with basket-weave decoration, filigree brim, unmarked.

ca. 1800   *2in (5cm) wide 0.3oz*

$450-600   **WW**

A George III silver-mounted shell caddy spoon, Matthew Linwood, Birmingham, the shell with plain silver mounts, with a bifurcated "Fiddle and Thread" handle.

ca. 1800   *2¾in (7.2cm) long*

$750-800   **WW**

A George III novelty silver jockey cap caddy spoon, with a filigree brim and applied decoration, with initials, unmarked.

2¼in (5.8cm) wide 0.4oz

$550-600   **WW**

A George III silver eagle's wing caddy spoon, by Joseph Willmore, Birmingham, the handle modeled as the eagle's head, textured feather decoration.

1814   *3in (7.6cm) long 0.3oz*

$8,500-9,000   **WW**

A George III novelty silver jockey cap caddy spoon, by Joseph Taylor, Birmingham, with bright-cut decoration.

1798   *2in (4.8cm) wide 0.2oz*

$600-750   **WW**

A George III novelty silver jockey cap caddy spoon, London, with bright-cut decoration, with a shield cartouche, maker's mark "?N."

1817   *3¼in (8cm) wide 0.6oz*

$550-650   **WW**

An early-19thC silver caddy spoon, by Cocks and Bettridge, Birmingham, pierced to simulate filigree decoration, with two doves supporting an olive branch with the Prince of Wales Feathers and the Royal Crown, beaded borders, the handle with a pierced rosette.

ca. 1820   *3in (7.6cm) long 0.3oz*

$6,000-6,600   **WW**

A rare George IV silver caddy spoon, by Robert Mitchell, Birmingham, of shovel form, the bowl embossed with a panel depicting The Brighton Pavilion, foliate tapering handle.

1825   *2½in (6cm) long 0.2oz*

$4,000-4,600   **WW**

A George IV cast-silver caddy spoon, by Reily and Storer, London, leaf-shaped bowl, the handle with grapes and pierced vine decoration.

1828   *4¼in (11cm) long 1oz*
$1,000-1,050   **WW**

A matched pair of William IV cast-silver-gilt caddy spoons, by Paul Storr, London, one with an Austrian import mark, shell bowls, long foliate scroll handles with shell motifs, one bowl with a crest and motto.

The crest is that of Ferguson.

1832   *5¼in (13cm) long 3.8oz*
$6,000-6,600   **WW**

A William IV silver caddy spoon, with shell bowl, maker's mark "IB," Birmingham.

1832   *3½in (9cm) long*
$70-80   **WHP**

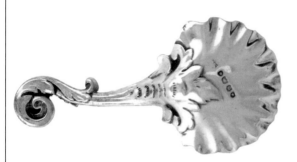

A William IV cast-silver-gilt caddy spoon, by Paul Storr, London, shell bowl, foliate-scroll handle with a shell motif.

1834   *3¾in (9.7cm) long 1.3oz*
$2,600-4,000   **WW**

A Victorian cast-silver caddy spoon, by Francis Higgins, London, the bowl cast as a limpet shell, the handle with pierced and foliate-scroll decoration.

1843   *4¼in (10.8cm) long 1.3oz*
$4,600-5,300   **WW**

A Victorian cast-silver flower caddy spoon, by Francis Higgins, London, the handle modeled as the stem with leaves.

1843   *4in (9.8cm) long 1.3oz*
$4,000-4,600   **WW**

A Victorian parcel-gilt cast-silver caddy spoon, by Francis Higgins, London, shell bowl, with a lily-pad handle with gilded leaves.

1852   *3½in (8.8cm) long 1oz*
$3,300-4,000   **WW**

A Victorian cast-silver caddy spoon, by Charles and George Fox, London, shell bowl, the interior gilded, the heavy scroll handle with foliate decoration and with a head finial.

1860   *4¼in (11cm) long 2.5oz*
$1,500-1,800   **WW**

Two George II silver cream boats, one by Edward Wakelin, London, 1758, the other by John Parker and Edward Wakelin, engraved with a crest within the Garter of the Order of the Bath and below a duke's coronet, surface scratching and wear,

The crest is that of Powlett, for Charles Powlett, 5th Duke of Bolton (ca. 1718-65). Presumably commissioned by Charles, 5th Duke of Bolton, on succeeding his father as Duke of Bolton in October 1759. While the title passed to Charles's brother in 1765, the 5th Duke left his fortune, and presumably the present sauceboats, to his illegitimate daughter Jean Mary Browne-Powlett, who married Thomas Orde. Orde was later to assume, by Royal license, the surname Powlett. When Charles's brother died in 1794 without male issue, the Dukedom of Bolton became extinct and Orde was created Baron Bolton.

ca. 1758   *5¾in (14.5cm) wide 16oz*
$4,600-5,300   **TEN**

A George III silver cream pitcher, with leaf capped C-scroll handle, London.

1778   *3¾in (9.5cm) high 2oz*
$200-260   **WHP**

A George IV silver beer pitcher, by William Eley II, London, embossed with a stag and deer, leaf-capped scroll handle, gilded interior, initialed.

1824   *12½in (32cm) high 52oz*
$4,000-4,600   **WW**

A Queen Anne silver sugar caster, by Thomas Farren, London.

The crest is that of Littleton of Shropshire.

1710   *8in (20cm) high 10oz*
$1,600-2,100   **WW**

An American silver water pitcher by the Bailey, Banks & Biddle Company, Philadelphia, PA., light scratches and wear.

ca. 1900   *8½in (21.5cm) high 25.2oz*
$600-750   **DN**

An American silver pitcher, by A. T. Gunner and Co, with leaf-capped scroll handle and foliate scroll border.

6¼in (16cm) high 12oz
$260-400   **WW**

A George II silver sugar caster, by Samuel Wood, London.

1735   *7.5in (19cm) high 12oz*
$600-750   **WW**

A late-Victorian novelty silver sea lion pepper pot, overstamped with maker's mark of Charles and Charles (Junior) Asprey, London, the pull-off head set with red eyes.

1882   *4in (9.5cm) long 2.3oz*
$1,300-1,800   **WW**

A pair of Victorian novelty Eddystone Lighthouse pepper pots, by Deakin and Francis, Birmingham, engraved with windows, ladders and "1759," the undersides inscribed "Smeaton's Edystone [sic] Lighthouse."

The Eddystone lighthouse is located approximately 12 miles SSW of Plymouth Sound. The first lighthouse on the site was a wooden structure constructed in 1698 by Henry Winstanley. The Smeaton lighthouse was the third lighthouse, made of granite and Portland stone. The light was first lit on October 16, 1759. Smeaton's lighthouse was 59 feet (18m) high and had a diameter at the base of 26 feet (8m). It was lit by a chandelier of 24 large tallow candles.

1895   *4¾in (12cm) high 5.8oz*
$1,100-1,250   **WW**

A Britannia standard silver salver, possibly James Morrison, London, with piecrust shell border and later inscription on the marriage of Miss Bailey 1888.

1750   *11½in (29cm) diam 37.7oz*

$2,000-2,600   **CHOR**

A George II silver second course plate, by Edward Wakelin, London, engraved with an armorial, the underside scratch initialed "No. 14 31=0."

The arms are that of Crompton impaling Rookes quartering Stansfield: William Rookes Crompton Stansfield (1790-1871).

1754   *11¾in (30cm) diam 29.3oz*

$1,050-1,200   **WW**

A George III silver plate, by Charles Wright, London, with gadrooned rim, crested.

1774   *9¾in (24.5cm) diam 19.4oz*

$850-1,000   **CHOR**

A George II silver plate, by George Wickes, London, of wavy outline with gadrooned rim, bears armorial.

Note: The arms are those of Walker impaling Cope, presumably for the marriage on October 15, 1763, of John Walker of Compton Basset and Arabella Cope, daughter of Jonathan Cope and Lady Arabella Howard, eldest daughter of the 4th Earl of Carlisle. Jonathan Cope was son and heir to Sir Jonathan Cope of Brewerne, created Baronet in 1713, but predeceased his father, dying just two weeks after the above marriage, and was succeeded by his son Charles, brother of Arabella, as 2nd Baronet. John Walker, who later represented Cricklade in parliament for nine years, assumed by Royal Licence in 1777 the additional surname and arms of Heneage to inherit the significant estates of his cousin Elizabeth Heneage. Dying without issue in 1806, these estates were passed by the will of his widow, Arabella Walker-Heneage, in entail to his great-nephew George Heneage Wyld, who also assumed the name of Walker-Heneage by Royal Licence. The family had also held the hereditary office of Chief Usher to the Exchequer since 1603.

1758   *9¾in (24.5cm) wide 15.2oz*

$1,000-1,100   **CHOR**

A George III silver meat platter, by Paul Storr, London, gadroon and foliate shell border, engraved with an armorial.

1808   *17in (43cm) wide 57.7oz*

$4,600-5,300   **WW**

A George III silver meat dish, by John Houle, London, with a raised gadrooned rim.

1813   *22¼in (56.5cm) wide 86.9oz*

$1,700-2,100   **DN**

A set of 12 late George III silver hexafoil soup plates, by Paul Storr, London, numbered "982," the gadrooned rim with foliage at intervals, light scratches.

The crest is that used by the BISS family. The full arms were granted in 1637 in Ireland, although the family probably settled there from England. Blazon for crest: an eagle preying on a partridge all proper.

1813   *10in (25.5cm) diam 8180g 288.5oz*

$29,000-37,000   **DN**

A George IV silver salver, by William Bateman, London, with shell- and scroll-cast border, engraved with initials, some minor overall surface scratching and wear, the engraved initials are crisp and are possibly later.

1825   *9¼in (23.5cm) diam 16oz*

$550-650   **TEN**

A George III silver tray, overstruck with maker's mark by Crouch and Hannam, London, reeded border and foliate-capped handles, engraved with roundels and foliate decoration, the center with an armorial, on four bracket feet.

The arms are those of those of Grosvenor impaling Leveson-Gower. Hugh Lupus Grosvenor (1825-1899), Baronet of Eaton Hall in Cheshire, Earl Grosvenor, English landowner, politician, and racehorse owner. He married Lady Constance Sutherland-Leveson-Gowe, daughter of the Duke of Sutherland and became first Duke of Westminster in 1874.

1793   *24¾in (63cm) wide 93.5oz*

$6,000-6,600   **WW**

A late Victorian silver tray, by Harry Brasted, London, with a Vitruvian scroll rim to the bar-pierced gallery with oval panels of Classical busts and laurel swags, with a vacant, shaped oval reserve and embossed floral swags suspended from masks and from foliage, some scratches.

1896   *29½in (75cm) long 166.5oz*

$6,000-6,600   **DN**

A silver tray, by Thomas Bradbury & Sons Ltd, London (jubilee mark), engraved for Asprey, London as retailers, with incurved angles, molded rim and handles, engraved with an office building and a presentation reading "Presented to The Hon. Sir Roy Welensky KCMG, MP Prime Minister of the Federation of Rhodesia and Nyasaland by The Chairman and Directors of Pearl Assurance Company Limited on the occasion of the opening of Pearl Assurance House, Salisbury, Southern Rhodesia. 6th March 1959."

Sir Roland "Roy" Welensky, KCMG PC (né Raphael Welensky, 1907-91) was a Northern Rhodesian politician and the second and last Prime Minister of the Federation of Rhodesia and Nyasaland.

1934   *26½in (67cm) long 130.6oz*

$4,000-5,300   **DN**

A Victorian silver tray, by Charles Boyton, London, beaded and fluted border and scroll handles, with engraved foliate-scroll decoration, on four scroll bracket feet.

1886   *23¾in (60.5cm) wide 43oz*

$1,500-2,000   **WW**

A Victorian silver two-handled tray, by Gibson and Langman, London, with engraved foliate decoration, beaded and foliate shell border and handles, the center with engraved foliate decoration over initials, on four bun feet.

1898   *30in (75.5cm) long 124oz*

$2,600-3,300   **WW**

An Edwardian silver dressing table tray, Birmingham, embossed foliate-scroll decoration on a matted background, with a centered vacant cartouche.

1901   *11¾in (30cm) wide 8.3oz*

$200-260   **WW**

A silver tray, by the Goldsmiths and Silversmiths Company, London, ribbon and reed border and handles.

1910   *25in (63.5cm) wide 76.8oz*

$2,600-3,300   **WW**

A pair of 17thC silver-gilt German tazza tops with Victorian silver-gilt bases, bases by Robert Hennell, London 1841, the tops Nürnberg, possibly by Johann Eißler, ca. 1680, one embossed with Classical figures, and ribbon-tied garlands of flowers, with 19thC initials, the other embossed with birds, war trophies, sheep, and fish, with an armorial and date.

1681   *10in (25.5cm) diam 41oz*

$4,000-5,300   **WW**

A George III silver entrée dish and cover, by Paul Storr, London.

1817   *12¼in (31cm) long 63.5oz*
$3,300-4,000   **WW**

A pair of George III silver entreé dishes and covers, by Benjamin Smith, London.

The crest is that of Smith.

1819   *7¾in (19.7cm) wide 115oz*
$3,300-4,000   **WW**

A pair of George IV silver entrée dishes and covers, by Joseph Craddock and William Reid, London.

1821   *11¾in (30.1cm) long 125oz*
$3,300-4,000   **WW**

A late George III silver soup tureen and cover, by Robert Garrard I, London, with a leaf-capped and gadrooned scrolling handle on the ogee-domed cover, date letter to body partially obscured, rest clear.

1815   *9½in (24cm) diam 113.7oz*
$8,500-10,000   **DN**

A pair of William IV silver entrée dishes and covers, by Samuel Keeley, Birmingham.

1836   *13¾in (35.2cm) long 122oz*
$6,000-7,500   **WW**

A pair of early Victorian silver entrée dishes and covers, by Benjamin Smith, London.

1843   *11¾in (29.8cm) long*
                                    100oz
$2,600-3,300   **WW**

A pair of Victorian silver tureens and covers, possibly for caviar, by Richard Harper, London, with four ram's heads and acanthus supports, the finials modeled as a warrior's head and helmet, on raised foliate bases.

1868   *7½in (19cm) high 58oz*
$3,300-4,000   **WW**

A pair of Victorian silver soup tureens and covers, by the Barnards, London, retailed by C. Taylor and Son, Bristol, leaf-capped and fluted side handles, gadroon and shell borders, engraved with an armorial, the covers with a finial of a lion holding an ax.

1854   *14½in (37cm) wide 187oz*
$11,000-13,000   **WW**

A French silver tureen and cover, by A. Risler and Carre, Paris, foliate-capped and fluted side handles, the pull-off cover with engraved foliate decoration, bead and swag borders, and with a large foliate cone finial.

ca. 1900-20   *13in (33cm) wide*
                                    88oz
$1,700-2,400   **WW**

SILVER & METALWARE

A George III silver meat dish cover, by Paul Storr, part-marked for London, engraved with two armorials, the handle modeled as a crown, beaded border.

The arms are those of Baron Foley, Witley Court, Worcestershire.

1806   *14¼in (36cm) long 52oz*

$6,500-8,000   **WW**

A 19thC French silver-gilt sugar bowl and cover, leaf-capped side handles, stiff leaf borders, in a fitted case, maker's mark of C. P.V. Vahland, Paris.

ca. 1819-1838   *7in (18cm) wide 30oz*

$6,000-6,600   **WW**

A mid-19thC Indian Colonial silver tureen and cover, by George Gordon & Co., Madras, the finial modeled as a family crest to the shallow domed cover, twin lion-mask ring handles, slight surface scuffs and scratches.

The crest finial for Cockes, Cokes, Maynor, Minors, Mynors, Rowed, Shattock, and Tawke. George Gordon & Co. traded from 18 Popham's Broadway from 1821-45.

7¾in (19.5cm) diam 35.3oz

$4,600-5,300   **DN**

A 19thC Indian silver box, of circular form, raised cover with a pointed finial, the front inscribed "KAISER BAGH, Lucknow March 14th 1858, R.O.S from F.A.W," unmarked.

Built by Nawab Wajid Ali Shah between 1848 and 1850, in the city of Lucknow, Kaiser Bagh (or Qaisarbagh) was one of the most remarkable palace-garden complexes ever made, consisting of huge courtyards with fantastic buildings on all sides. It is located from the eastern end of the Chattar Manzil to the Tarawali Kothi. Pathways through the various courtyards of the garden were intended to be indirect to confuse visitors. The palace complex itself was an exotic blend of styles with Ionic columns, Moorish minarets, and Hindu arches and pediments.The Kaiser Bagh, with its many enclosures, courtyards, and pathways, was the scene of fierce fighting during the Indian Mutiny and proved difficult to capture during Sir Colin Campbell's final assault on Lucknow in March 1858. Once it was secured, the British ransacked and looted the complex.

6½in (16.8cm) diam 13.5oz.

$4,000-5,300   **WW**

A George V silver covered cup, by Harman & Co., in the Regency style, marked on body, cover, and finial "Barnard Bros.," and impressed on underside "Harman 177 New Bond St. London."

1911   *16¼in (41cm) 122 oz*

$6,000-6,600   **DRA**

A Charles II silver porringer, maker's mark attributed to John Burges, London, caryatid scroll handles, embossed with a unicorn and lion within foliate decoration, the underside inscribed "ATWILL-LAKE" and with a scratch weight "27=5=oz," with traces of gilding.

ca. 1662   *9¾in (24.5cm) wide 26oz*

$6,500-8,000   **WW**

A Charles II silver porringer and cover, by Benjamin Pyne, London, engraved with birds and foliate decoration in the chinoiserie taste.

1683   *7¾in (19.5cm) high 28.5oz*

$46,000-53,000   **WW**

An 18thC Dutch silver tobacco jar and cover, by Wijnand Warneke, Amsterdam, embossed foliate decoration.

1775   *7in (17.5cm) high 21oz*

$3,300-4,000   **WW**

A silver cup and cover, by Ramsden & Roed, London, for The Worshipful Company of Mercers, modeled as the head and upper torso of the Maiden of the Mercer's Company.

1936   *11in (28cm) high 85oz*

$4,600-5,900   **WW**

A Victorian silver centerpiece bowl, by Henry Curry, London, embossed with panels of Neptune and Classical figures, bifurcated caryatid-scroll handles, on four recumbent dragon feet.

1879   *13in (33cm) long 39oz*
$2,100-2,600   **WW**

A Queen Anne silver bowl, by Robert Timbrell, London, mask-capped drop-ring handles, embossed and chased foliate-scroll decoration, with a worn armorial.

1702   *10in (25.5cm) diam 39oz*
$6,500-8,000   **WW**

A late Victorian silver rose bowl, by Martin, Hall and Company, Sheffield, embossed fluted decoration, gadroon and shell borders.

1896   *12in (30.5cm) diam 48oz*
$1,700-2,400   **WW**

An Indian silver bowl, by Dass and Dutt, Bhowanipore, Calcutta, embossed and chased with elephants, village scenes, and animals.

ca. 1900   *10½in (26.7cm) diam 28.5oz.*
$800-900   **WW**

A George III silver sugar basket, by Peter and Jonathan Bateman, London, bright-cut decoration, replacement unmarked handle.

1790   *7in (16.8cm) 9oz*
$2,100-2,600   **WW**

A George III silver sugar basket, by Peter and Ann Bateman, London, bright-cut decoration, reeded borders and swing handle, engraved with a crest and initials.

The crest is that of Patton, Pawson, Pemberton, and Phetoplace.

1797   *6¼in (16.2cm) high 6.9oz*
$260-400   **WW**

A pair of George III silver salt cellars, by David and Robert Hennell, London, engraved with a crest and initials, with later blue glass liners, some overall scratching and wear.

1766   *3¾in (9.5cm) wide, 6oz*
$400-550   **TEN**

Two George III silver salt cellars, by David and Robert Hennell, London, with blue glass liners, surface scratching.

1770 and 1771   *3¼in (8.3cm) wide 3oz*
$220-260   **TEN**

A pair of Victorian silver salt cellars, by Nathan and Hayes, Chester, in the form of an Irish dish ring, pierced with foliage scrolls with animals, with clear glass liners.

1898   *3½in (9cm) diam 4oz*
$260-330   **TEN**

A George III silver basket, by William Plummer, London, engraved with a coat of arms, on four foliate scroll bracket feet.

1765   *15in (38cm) wide 55.2oz*
$2,100-2,600   **DN**

A late George III silver-gilt bread basket, by J. E. Terrey & Co., London, the handle cast and chased with flowers, foliage, and scrolls and with dolphin terminals, the broad rim cast and chased with masks of Ceres or Demeter within wheat sprays, dragons, flowers, leaves, scrolls, and agricultural tools, the sides pierced with scrolls and trellis, on four cast and chased supports of scroll and foliate form with animal heads at the feet.

1819   *15½in (39cm) wide 91.2oz*
$8,000-9,000   **DN**

A George I silver wax jack, maker's mark only, that of Abraham Buteux, London, sprung wax-holding grips and cutter on a pierced circular foot.

A wax jack is a device used to hold a taper of sealing wax intended to create sealings on documents. It comprised a vertical or horizontal shaft around which a thin beeswax taper was coiled. The top end protruded through a hole in a pan that had a pincer to hold the taper in place. This allowed for the taper to be lit and the resulting puddle of wax to be easily controlled. They were often used when traveling.

ca. 1725   *5¾in (14.5cm) high 9oz*
$1,600-2,100   **WW**

A George II silver wax jack, possibly by John Lampfert, London, sprung-action wax holder and cutter with a circular drip pan.

1741   *5¾in (14.5cm) high 12oz*
$1,250-1,600   **WW**

A George IV silver wax jack, by Aldridge and Green, London, the sprung-hinged wax holders with pierced handles and with a baluster finial, with a shield cartouche and crest.

The crest is that of Edwards or Pennant.

1777   *7in (18cm) high 8oz*
$3,300-4,000   **WW**

An early-18thC French provincial silver snuffers stand and associated snuffers, possibly by Jacques Dubaine or Etienne Desbarbes, Bayonne, the snuffers maker's mark "?D" over "P, Bayonne," engraved with an armorial, the snuffers with ring handles.

ca. 1710-15   *8¾in (21.8cm) long 11.8oz*
$2,400-2,900   **WW**

ESSENTIAL REFERENCE—POMANDER

A pomander, from French "pomme d'ambre," roughly translated as "apple of ambergris" or "apple of perfume," and is a ball made for perfumes. It was popularized in Europe around the late Middle Ages. At this time, pomanders were used for protection against infection, pestilence, and disease, or simply bad smells. All of which were far too common at the time due to poverty— sanitation during the era was lamentably lacking. The streets and even some homes were strewn with filth. People thought that the cause of their problems lay in the resulting stench lingering about the city—the belief went that the pleasant scent of a pomander could repel the disease in the air. Several recipes for pomanders survive from the era. To a base of ambergris, musk, civet, or rose water, other perfumes and spices were added. The pomander was worn or carried in a vase, also known by the same name. The globular cases that contained the pomanders were hung from a neck chain or belt, or attached to the girdle, and were usually perforated in a variety of openwork techniques, and made of gold or silver. Sometimes they contained several partitions, as in the example here, in each of which was placed a different perfume.

● **The term "pomander" can refer to the scented material itself or to the container that contains such material. The container was usually made of gold or silver Smaller versions were made to be attached by a chain to a finger ring and held in the hand.**

An Elizabeth I silver pomander, unmarked, with six hinged sections engraved with royal portraits, the screw-up finial opens the six segments. each with engraved decoration and open compartments, and with a centered hexagonal column with engraved decoration, on a circular foot with rope-work borders.

ca. 1600   *3¼in (8cm) high 4oz*
$18,000-24,000   **WW**

A George I silver sugar box, by Matthew Cooper, overstriking other marks, London, cover with a crest, the front with an armorial within foliate mantling.

The crest is probably that of Frowicke and other families.

1717   *5¼in (13cm) wide 15oz*
$9,000-10,500   **WW**

A Victorian silver cup and cover, by Frederick Courthope, London, embossed foliate-scroll decoration, the side handles modeled as two naked maidens, their hands bound with snakes, the pull-off cover with a cast statue of Saint George killing the dragon, the foot applied with four masks, gilded interior.

1886   *19¾in (50cm) high 178oz*

$15,000-20,000   **WW**

A silver-gilt cup and cover, of Classical urn form, with ribbon-tied drapes and medallions, on a swirl-fluted foot on a square base, applied with a plaque inscribed "The Golden Cup, A Symbol of Charity and Generosity The Butchers Charitable Institution," and set with a George III Guinea, underneath inscribed "1773," with canceled marks and London Assay Office marks for 2020.

24in (61cm) high 116oz

$4,000-5,300   **WW**

An American silver trophy, decorated with foliage and chestnuts, stamped "Sterling" on base, embossed on side "Directors Cup, Burroughs Adding Machine Company, Detroit, Michigan U.S.A," reverse engraved with previous winners.

ca. 1910-24   *19in (48cm) high 106oz*

$2,600-3,300   **LOCK**

A 19thC Danish silver cornucopia, mark of Assay Master Simon Groth, engraved with Celtic decoration and two cartouches with warrior's heads, the cover with two bands of symmetrical decoration and topped with a drinking-warrior finial.

ca. 1883   *10in (25cm) high*

$550-650   **CHEF**

A pair of 19thC French Parisian silver canisters or toilet jars and covers, with applied swags and ribbon-tied garlands of flowers, chased decoration, applied with armorials, with silver-gilt liners, post 1838 mark, the inside of the covers inscribed "DONNÉ A MA CHERE FILLE MARIE" and also the initials "B.C.P" and earlier date "1826."

5½in (14cm) high 32oz

$2,200-2,600   **WW**

A Victorian novelty silver owl sugar vase and cover, by Charles and George Fox, London, cover set with red glass eyes and with gilded eye sockets, the body with textured feather decoration, base, with gilded talons and feet, the interior rim inscribed "Mary Ann 28 July 1849."

1847   *8¾in (22.5cm) high 19.4oz*

$12,000-15,000   **WW**

A Victorian suite of four silver centerpieces, by John, Edward, Walter & John Barnard (Barnard & Sons Ltd), London, with three cut-glass bowls resting on fruiting vines, with figures of children with farm animals to the grass-topped triform bases, presentation engraved to Sir Peter Spokes, one time Mayor of Reading, three of the four bowls are all that is present.

The inscription reading "Presented To Sir Peter Spokes, Kt. Mayor of Reading, November 9th 1871. by his fellow townsmen, as a token of their respect, and of their cordial approval of the efficient manner in which he has discharged the duties of the Mayorality during two successful years. 1869-70. 1870-71." Sir Peter Sopkes (1830-1910) was a banker as well as a past mayor.

1871   *one 20½in (52cm) high, the others 13½in (34cm) high 228.7oz*

$16,000-20,000   **DN**

A George III silver cruet stand, possibly by Robert, David & Samuel Hennell, London, with eight silver-mounted jars and bottles all Hennell 1800-02, lids of two jars matched.

ca. 1802   *9in (23cm) high*

$550-650   **CHOR**

A George III silver cruet stand, by John Edward Terrey, London, with fitted two silver-mounted cut-glass jars and six cut-glass bottles and stoppers.

1818   *8¼in (21cm) high*

$400-550   **CHOR**

A Charles II silver tobacco box, London, maker's mark "BB," a crescent and two pellets below, the cover engraved with an armorial and crest, the underside engraved "R.C" and an earlier date "1663."

The arms are those of Cann of Compton Greenfield, Gloucestershire, baronets, for Sir John Cann, 1st Bt. He was a leading merchant of Bristol, who also owned property in Jamaica. He was twice mayor of Bristol, 1662-63 and 1675-76. He went on to be an MP for the city.

1673   3½in (8.9cm) high 3.4oz
$6,000-6,600   WW

A rare William and Mary silver counter box, maker's mark "TS," attributed to Thomas Steed, London, the cover with an armorial, the base with a monogram.

The arms are those of an unknown family impaling Campbell quartering Lorn for the Dukes of Argyll.

1690   2in (4.8cm) wide 1.7oz
$7,500-8,000   WW

A George I silver tobacco box, by Edward Cornock, London, with an armorial and crest, the base engraved "Henry Weekley Tuthill [sic] Street Westminster," and with three armorials and a vignette of Saint George on horseback slaying the dragon, and later dated "1735."

Henry Weekley is recorded as a cloth worker in Tothill Street, Westminster. The arms on the cover are unrecorded, the arms on the base are for The Worshipful Company of Grocers, The City of London, and The Worshipful Company of Clothworkers.

1723   3¾in (9.7cm) long 4.1oz
$3,300-4,000   WW

A George III silver seal or skippet box, by William and Aaron Lestourgeon, London, the cover engraved with the arms of Oxford University with foliate and Rococo mantling, molded border.

1770   3½in (9cm) high 2.4oz
$2,600-3,300   WW

A rare 17thC silver Dunbar medal, in an early-18thC locket, the front with scroll and shell decoration and mounted with the Dunbar medal (type F), the interior with a portrait of Sir Thomas Fairfax, gold surround, the reverse with a scene of Saint George slaying the dragon.

The Dunbar Locket: The medal has the portrait bust of Oliver Cromwell and the signature of "T.Simon. FE." It was intended as a reward for those on the winning Parliamentarian side who took part in the Battle of Dunbar on September 3, 1650. Cromwell's army defeated a Scottish force commanded by David Leslie, which was loyal to King Charles II of England, who had been proclaimed King in Scotland on February 5, 1649.

2½in (6cm) high 1.3oz
$4,000-5,300   WW

A Victorian engraved silver aide-mémoire, by Wheeler and Cronin, Birmingham, engraved with Crystal Palace, the underside with scroll decoration and a vacant cartouche, silk-lined interior with ivory leaves and a pencil.

1850   3¼in (8.2cm) wide
$550-650   WW

An American silver luggage label, by Whiting Manufacturing Company, Providence, Rhode Island, in the form of a traveling bag with an umbrella attached, engraved "M.K.INCHES ST JOHN N.B.."

ca. 1900   2in (5cm) wide
$200-260   TEN

A silver model of a pheasant, by Neresheimer of Hanau, textured feathers, detachable head, with London import marks for 1930, importer's mark of Berthold Muller.

7½in (19cm) high 14.5oz
$3,300-4,000   WW

An 18thC Dutch silver table bell, by Benjamin D'Hoy, Middelburg, also marked with a later tax mark, with chased foliate decoration, the handle with a centered stem and with two flowers.

1786   6in (15.5cm) high 9.6oz
$7,500-8,500   WW

Essential reading for every collector

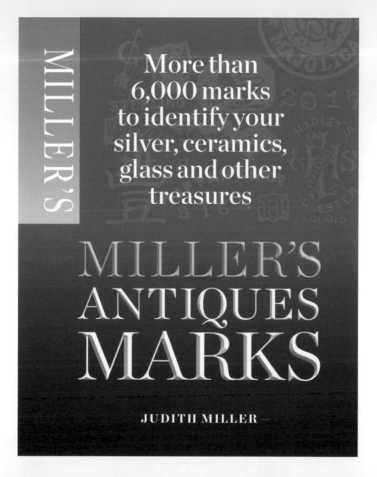

More than 6,000 marks to identify your silver, ceramics, glass and other treasures

MILLER'S

MILLER'S ANTIQUES MARKS

— JUDITH MILLER —

Identify and date your treasures in this handy pocket guide.

Featuring full-colour photographs to help you decipher the marks on your silver, ceramics and glass.

A William IV silver-gilt-mounted hardstone inkwell, by Paul Storr, London, the hardstone body carved in the form of a horse's hoof, the silver-gilt mounts cast and chased with hair, opening to reveal the silver-gilt-mounted conforming glass bottle, with an associated gilt-metal pen, fully marked, some surface scratching and wear.

1832   *5in (12.5cm) wide*
$7,500-8,000   **TEN**

An Edwardian silver inkstand, by Sebastian Garrard, London, cover mounted with a sphinx, the two inkwells with palm decoration, the hinged covers with crown finials, the borders with Egyptian motifs and with masks, with two pen wells, also stamped "Garrard and Co., Haymarket, London."

1908   *19in (48cm) long 110oz*
$8,500-10,000   **WW**

A Victorian silver inkstand, by John and Henry Lias, London, applied with cast convolvulus-form mounts, with branch-form handle and silver-mounted glass bottle, some elements lacking.

1843   *6¾in (17cm) wide 8oz*
$350-450   **TEN**

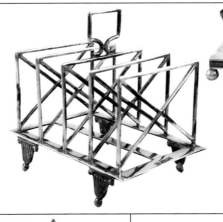

A late-Victorian silver toast rack, by William Hutton and Sons, Sheffield.

1900   *5in (12.8cm) long 7.8oz*
$450-600   **WW**

A pair of early-19thC French silver oil and vinegar stands, by Jean Baptist Claude Odiot, Paris, the grip formed by two dolphins, engraved with an armorial.

ca. 1820   *6¾in (17cm) high 10.3oz*
$1,600-2,400   **WW**

A George III silver sifter, repoussé decorated with stylized flowers, London.

1787   *6in (15cm) high 2.5oz*
$130-180   **WHP**

A late Victorian silver sifter, by Charles Stuart Harris, London, decorated in the Neoclassical manner and with bayonet fixing.

1898   *6¼in (16cm) high 6.5oz*
$130-180   **WHP**

A silver sardine server, by James Dixon and Sons, Sheffield, fluted terminal, pierced serving blade.

1897   *6in (14.8cm) long 1oz*
$180-240   **WW**

A Charles II silver-mounted velvet-covered book stand, mounted on the red velvet with embossed foliate-scroll panels, the front with an armorial, with silver thread borders, unmarked.

ca. 1680   *16¾in (42.3cm) wide*
$2,200-2,600   **WW**

A 17thC Dutch silver-mounted green glass shaft-and-globe bottle, possibly by Hans C. Brechtel, The Hague, the mounts with pierced and embossed foliate and flower decoration, the cover with a silver-mounted cork stopper, embossed with a reclining cherub, with damage.

1664   *11¾in (29.5cm) high*
$60,000-70,000   **WW**

A William IV silver claret pitcher, by Edward, Edward Junior, John & William Barnard, London, with a high fruiting vine stock handle, marks are slightly rubbed, light scratches.

1831   *12in (30.5cm) high 1045g 36.8oz*
$1,600-2,100   **DN**

A William IV silver twin-bottle decanter frame, by Robert Garrard II, London, the bottle frames with four-leaf flowers and strapwork, an asymmetric shield engraved with a crest and issuing grasses and a branch with a shell at the base, anthemion lyre supports, the base with scrolls and shells.

The crest of JORDAN of Surrey.

1835   *11in (28cm) high 32.1oz*
$2,000-2,600   **DN**

A Victorian silver-mounted claret pitcher, by Fenton Bros., Sheffield.

1876   *12½in (32cm) high*
$400-450   **CHOR**

A late Victorian silver "Armada" pattern claret pitcher, by Sibray, Hall & Co. Ltd., London, with an open scrollwork finial on the cover, the body with a leopard head in relief, winged figures in semirelief.

1899   *18½in (47cm) high 69.6oz*
$6,000-6,600   **DN**

An Edwardian silver-mounted glass decanter, by William Comyns, London, etched with trailing flowers, the mount with a scroll handle, pierced foliate decoration, the cover with a cone finial.

1904   *10¾in (27cm) high*
$1,250-1,600   **WW**

A late George III silver wine cooler, liner, and collar, by Henry Cornman, London, the collar cast and chased with shells, flowers, foliage, and C scrolls, the handles modeled as eagles, the front and rear with engraved shields of arms, chased with asymmetric cartouches with panels of massed flowers on matted grounds, the flared pedestal with shells, flowers, foliage, and two "Green Man" masks and framed by scrolls, light scratches and wear.

The arms for Colonel John Bolton (1756-1837) of Duke Street, Liverpool, who in 1797 married Elizabeth Littledale (1768-1848)
daughter of Henry Littledale of Whitehaven, at St George Hanover Square, Westminster. John Bolton was the youngest son of Abraham Bolton (originally Boulton; 1714-64) apothecary of Kings Street, Liverpool by Ann Philipson. He was first apprenticed as a Liverpool–West Indian Merchant and later assumed a prominent role in local Tory politics. In 1803, he raised and equipped 800 men, who became the 1st Battalion of Liverpool Volunteers (Bolton's Invincibles). He took part in a fateful duel in 1805, when a Major Edward Brooks was killed by Bolton, but he avoided conviction for murder. He later (before 1808) purchased Storrs Hall on Lake Windermere, a building that exists today as a hotel.

1818   *10in (25.5cm) high 146.8oz*
$6,000-6,600   **DN**

A George IV silver brandy pan and stand, with an associated George III cover, by John Wakefield, London, the cover possibly by Hester Bateman, London 1783, side handle initialed "B."

1823   *10in (25.2cm) long 19.5oz*
$850-1,000   **WW**

A George III silver wine funnel and stand, the stand Peter & William Bateman, London.

1805 the funnel ca. 1810   *4in (10cm) diam 4.3oz*
$550-650   **CHOR**

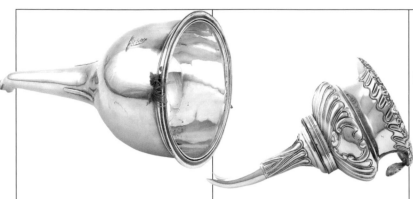

A George III silver wine funnel, by William Fell, London, reeded border with a shell side clip, London.

1818   *5in (13.8cm) long 4oz*
$600-750   **WW**

A George IV silver wine funnel, probably by Joseph Biggs, London, part-fluted decoration, foliate border with a shell side clip, vacant cartouche.

1820   *6½in (16.7cm) long 5.9oz*
$1,250-1,450   **WW**

An early-19thC Colonial silver wine funnel, the plain pull-out straining section with a shell side clip, marked "A.K." with a sailing boat between, and twice with maker's mark, unidentified.

ca. 1830   *6½in (16.5cm) high 6.7oz*
$750-850   **WW**

A late-18thC French silver wine taster, marks worn, also with a later mark, fluted decoration, fluted ring handle, inscribed "J.P DELAYE."

4in (9.4cm) long 3.8oz
$260-330   **WW**

An early-18thC Dutch silver brandy bowl, Zierikzee, date letter "B," maker's mark partially worn, pierced foliate-and-scroll handle, the center embossed with fruit and leaves, the underside of one of the handles scratch initialed "KCB."

8in (20.5cm) long 4.7oz
$1,500-2,000   **WW**

A George III silver stirrup cup, by Henry Tudor and Thomas Leader, Sheffield, modeled as a snarling fox head, scratching and wear.

1777   *4¾in (12cm) long 5oz*
$10,000-11,000   **TEN**

A pair of George III silver coasters, by Thomas Nash II, London, pierced sides with the reserves engraved with a crest, both slightly wobble, light scratches and wear.

ca. 1771   *4¾in (12cm) diam*
$1,700-2,100   **DN**

A pair of 18thC silver wine coasters, possibly Irish, pierced and embossed with figures, birds, and foliate-scroll decoration, rope-work borders, wooden bases, engraved with a crest of Newcome, unmarked.

1780   *5¾in (14.5cm) diam*
$2,600-3,300   **WW**

A pair of George IV silver wine coasters, by John & Thomas Settle, Sheffield, chased with trailing grapevines, gadroon borders, wooden bases set with centered buttons.

1825   *6in (14.8cm) diam*
$2,100-2,600   **WW**

A George IV silver wine coaster, by Benjamin Smith, London, pierced and chased with foliate lattice decoration, the silver base engraved with a crest, motto, and inscription, wooden underside.

1826   *5¾in (14.5cm) diam*

$850-1,000   **WW**

A George II silver wine label, by Sandilands Drinkwater, London, with chased vine decoration and incised "PORT."

ca. 1745   *2¼in (5.3cm) wide 0.3oz*

$350-400   **WW**

A pair of George III provincial silver wine labels, by John Hampston & John Prince, York, for White Wine and Red Port.

ca. 1790   *1¾in (4.5cm) wide*

$2,000-2,600   **CHOR**

A George IV Scottish silver "cut-out" label, by George McHattie, Edinburgh.

ca. 1820   *2in (5cm) long 0.5oz*

$260-400   **WW**

A set of six Victorian cast-silver wine labels, by William Eaton, London, of vine leaf form with a bunch of grapes, pierced "MADEIRA," "RUM," "PORT," "HOLLANDS," "SHERRY," and "WHISKEY."

1839   *3.4oz*

$350-400   **WW**

A pair of early-Victorian silver vine-leaf wine labels, by Joseph Willmore, Birmingham, incised "MADEIRA" and "MARSALA."

1839-40   *2¾in (7.2cm) wide 0.7oz*

$130-170   **WW**

An 18thC Dutch silver pocket corkscrew, by Hermanus Van den Kierboom, Dordrecht, the handle with a lion.

1759   *4in (9.8cm) high 1.8oz*

$2,000-2,600   **WW**

An 18thC Dutch silver pocket corkscrew, by Jan Reghter, Delft, the screw-off sheath with chased shell-and-scroll decoration, the handle with a cherub sitting on a foliate scroll motif.

1777   *4in (10cm) high 1.8oz*

$2,600-3,300   **WW**

A Victorian silver open-frame triple-nut fly corkscrew, by William Summers, London.

1888   *5.5in (14.2cm) long*

$2,600-3,300   **WW**

An American sterling silver punch ladle, by Gorham Manufacturing Company, with bacchic and grapevine decoration, with silver-gilt bowl, engraved monogram on verso "LM" and marked "707."

1895   *18in (46cm) high 23.5 oz*

$6,000-6,600   **DRA**

A pair of early-19thC Old Sheffield-plate three-light candelabra, with tapering, lobed circular columns, leaf-capped scroll arms, campana-shaped capitals with detachable foliate-scroll drip pans, and with centered detachable flame finials, on raised lobed circular bases with foliate borders, unmarked.

ca. 1830   *24¾in (62.5cm) high*

$600-650   **WW**

A Victorian electroplated three-light candelabrum, by H and L, of Corinthian column form, beaded borders, pierced capitals, leaf-capped scroll arms, on a raised stepped square base, one arm solder repaired.

21½in (54.5cm) high

$130-200   **WW**

A pair of George III Old Sheffield-plated sauce tureens and covers, the pull-off covers with fluted decoration and fluted finials, lion-mask drop-ring handles, on four paw feet.

ca. 1810   *6¾in (17cm) long*

$750-850   **WW**

A Victorian electroplated kettle-on-stand, by Elkington and Co., embossed foliate-scroll decoration, the hinged center handle with ivory insulators, the hinged cover with a flower finial, lacking burner.

1853   *17¼in (44cm) high*

$400-450   **WW**

An early-19thC Old Sheffield-plated wine cooler, embossed foliate-scroll decoration, leaf-capped side handles, foliate-scroll borders, with a liner.

ca. 1830   *9½in (24cm) high*

$260-330   **WW**

An electro-gilded tea caddy, with Rococo figures and foliate-scroll decoration on a matted background, with a crest, the pull-off cover with a figural finial, on four scroll feet.

ca. 1900   *5¼in (13cm) high*

$180-240   **WW**

A novelty electroplated table vesta holder, modeled as an early vintage car with a compartment for vestas and a striker, later lacquered, unmarked.

3in (7.5cm) long

$200-260   **WW**

A Victorian electroplated lemon squeezer, by Hukin and Heath, with a hinged cover and turning screw, on three wirework legs with a wirework frame, marked with a registration number.

12¼in (31cm) high

$750-850   **WW**

A French novelty electroplated Champagne bottle, the bottle opens in three places to reveal a compartment, a slide drawer probably for vestas, and the cork comes off to reveal a table cigar lighter or bitters bottle, the label reads "Louis Roederer, Reims."

8in (20cm) high

$260-330   **WW**

A late-17thC English repoussé brass candlestick, the underside with initials "S W M," candlestick bears the usual minor marks, consistent with age and use.

17¾in (45cm) high

$3,300-4,600   **DN**

A late-17thC Dutch brass Heemskerk candlestick, with a pierced socket, on a turned stem and a dished drip pan, on a domed foot.

8in (20cm) high

$350-400   **WW**

A late-17th/early-18thC Dutch brass Heemskerk candlestick, the gun-barrel-pierced socket above a baluster-turned stem and a dished drip pan.

9in (22.7cm) high

$180-260   **WW**

An early-18thC pair of Queen Anne brass candlesticks.

This form of candlestick incorporating a stylized "acorn knop" is associated with the output of Huguenot metalworkers of the period.

7¾in (19.5cm) high

$750-850   **DN**

A pair of George II paktong candlesticks, each with a detachable foliate nozzle, above a turned tapering stem and a shaped stepped foot, with pseudo hallmarks on the nozzle and base, the base also stamped "RJB."

ca. 1740-50   9½in (24.2cm) high

$5,300-5,900   **WW**

A pair of 18th/early-19thC brass pricket candlesticks, with dished drip pans on baluster stems and triform bases.

11in (28cm) high

$450-600   **L&T**

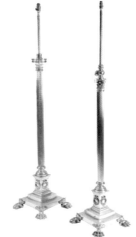

A pair of early Victorian patinated and gilt-bronze luster patent candle lamps, possibly by Palmer & Co. of London, with a registration lozenge, one shade damaged.

17½in (44.5cm) high

$260-330   **WW**

A pair of 19thC gilt-bronze candlesticks, in the manner of Etienne Martincourt, in Louis XVI style, each fluted and acanthus-cast nozzle descending to swagged stems with ram monopodia, cast in the style of Atheniennes.

8¾in (22cm) high

$1,700-2,100   **DN**

A pair of late-19thC brass Corinthian column standard lamps, above a ribbed stem and a wreath-decorated stepped base with lion's paw feet.

63¼in (160.6cm) and 70in (178cm) high

$1,100-1,250   **WW**

A pair of Victorian brass candlesticks, with ejectors, each with a trumpet socket, above a faceted and beehive-turned stem, the bases stamped "England RD 223580."

ca. 1890-1900   14in (35.3cm) high

$260-400   **WW**

A mid-18thC English or German engraved copper tea kettle, once probably silvered, body with hunting scenes and with a bird-form finial, stand with spirit burner and mask-pierced aprons between scrolling legs.

13½in (34cm) high

$400-550 **DN**

A Regency toleware kettle and stand, probably Pontypool, body painted with flowers and birds, raised on a scrolled stand with shell feet, the handle with fragments of straw work.

Toleware, any object of japanned (varnished) tinplate or pewter. The term is derived from the French name for such objects, "tôle peinte." The tinplate sheets of iron or steel dipped in molten tin or pewter (an alloy of tin and copper) were worked into a variety of domestic and decorative items, such as teapots, trays, urns, and candlesticks. The objects were then japanned with a varnish that differed from area to area but was generally based on a mixture of linseed oil, driers, and colors. Principal centers for the production of tolewares were Pontypool and Usk in England; Zeist and Hoorn in Holland; Paris; and, in the United States, Pennsylvania. The trade began in Europe in the first half of the 18thC, a little later in the United States, and had all but ceased by the end of the 19thC.

ca. 1810 *11¾in (30cm) high*

$450-600 **DN**

A large Victorian copper kettle, with a swing handle, a brass finial, and a hinged-lidded spout.

10¾in (27.5cm) high

$100-160 **WW**

A early-19thC Regency copper samovar, with Atlas supporting the globe on his neck and shoulders, with a pull-off cover, with a brass tap and a green-stained ivory ball handle.

12½in (32.2cm) high

$850-1,000 **WW**

A graduated set of eight Victorian copper haystack measures, each inscribed with a measurement: 4 gallon, 2 gallon, 1 gallon, half gallon, quart, 1 pint, half pint, gill, with coats of arms and initials "V R" and "H R."

16¼in (41.3cm) highest

$600-750 **WW**

A pair of English brass casters, of silver form, each with toupie finial, with minor marks.

ca. 1720 *9in (23cm) high*

$1,000-1,100 **DN**

A late George III copper and brass-mounted plate warmer, with swing handle and cabriole legs.

ca. 1800 *17¾in (45cm) high*

$800-900 **DN**

A pair of French cast-iron urns, attributed to Barbezat & Cie, Val d'Osne, in Neoclassical style, each with twin handles rising from the shoulder and descending past a floral relief-cast body to a waisted underside, on domed and foliate-cast stems with circular bases.

The Barbezat Foundry was established in 1836 and specialized in "ornamental works, vases, and statues for houses, gardens, and churches." The company exhibited its cast-iron wares at the Great Exhibition, including at the London edition in 1862. The present model with its distinctive scrolled handles was produced by the foundry during the second half of the 19thC.

ca. 1875 *26½in (67cm) high*

$2,600-4,000 **DN**

A 19thC Dutch brass and copper log bin, with a riveted body and with a pair of handles.

19¼in (48.9cm) diam

$210-260 **WW**

A large copper log bin, with a pair of wrought-iron handles.

34½in (87.3cm) diam

$750-850 **WW**

A New York pewter mug, bearing the touch of Frederick Bassett, old repairs on base.
ca. 1780   *4½in (11.5cm) high*
$1,200-1,450   POOK

A Philadelphia pewter mug, bearing the touch of Robert Palethorp Jr., a few dents.
ca. 1820   *5½in (14cm) high*
$400-550   POOK

A Philadelphia pewter water pitcher, bearing the touch of William McQuilken.
ca. 1850   *10in (25.5cm) high*
$550-600   POOK

A 19thC New York pewter flagon, bearing the touch of Boardman & Hart, a few dents.
11in (28cm) high
$100-110   POOK

A pair of pewter chalices, Albany, New York, bearing the touch of Peter Young.
ca. 1790   *8½in (21.5cm) high*
$7,500-8,500   POOK

A pair of pewter oil lamps, Dorchester, Massachusetts, bearing the touch of Roswell Gleason.
ca. 1840   *8in (20.5cm) high*
$850-1,000   POOK

A Philadelphia pewter sugar bowl and cover, attributed to William Will.
ca. 1780   *4¾in (12cm) high*
$4,000-4,600   POOK

A rare Middletown, Connecticut, pewter basin, bearing the touch of Stephen Barnes, good condition, no apparent damages or repairs.
ca. 1800   *10¼in (26cm) diam*
$900-1,050   POOK

A Providence, Rhode Island, pewter porringer, bearing the touch of William Billings.
ca. 1800 5½in (14cm) diam
$900-1,050   POOK

A pair of early-19thC Philadelphia pewter dishes, bearing the touch of Blakeslee Barnes, one with heavier wear and worn mark.
11¼in (28.5cm) diam
$170-210   POOK

Judith Picks

Antique dog collars, especially in silver and other metals, have become increasingly collectible, and especially so if they come with historically significant or emotionally appealing provenance. Probably the epitome of the latter, at least thus far, is the brass collar that had belonged to Boatswain, the early-19thC Romantic poet Lord Byron's much-loved Newfoundland, for whom, after Boatswain's death in 1808, he wrote "Epitaph to a Dog." When it came up for auction just under four years ago, it sold for $24,000! My interest in antique dog collars is, however, a little more personal. I've been on the lookout for one for our beloved Russian black terrier, Vladimir, for ages, but thus far just haven't found one big enough!

A George IV silver dog collar, with reeded bands, with a padlock and hallmarked for Charles Reily and George Storer.

3in (7.5cm) diam

$750-850   WW

A Victorian brass and nickel dog collar, with an engraved floral band, with a leather-lined interior, inscribed "C. B. E. WRIGHT Esq."

5¼in (13.5cm) diam

$1,600-1,800   WW

A Victorian brown leather and brass-studded dog collar, with a brass plaque indistinctly inscribed with the owner's name.

7in (17cm) diam

$1,200-1,450   WW

A Victorian nickel dog collar, of chain form, with a lock and key, inscribed "W. ANDREWS WESTON UNDERWOOD."

4¾in (12cm) diam

$260-400   WW

A 19thC nickel dog collar, with studded decoration and dogtooth edging, with a brass padlock, stamped "METALO NICKEL."

7in (18cm) diam

$260-330   WW

A brown leather and brass-studded dog collar, with a vacant plaque.

$400-450

A Victorian brown leather dog collar, decorated with brass and nickel studs, applied with a plaque inscribed "STRATTON THE HAVEN LONG CRENDON THAME OXON."

9½in (24cm) diam

$750-800

8¼in (21cm) diam

WW

A leather and brass-mounted dog collar, decorated with rosettes, studs, and lozenges.

8¼in (21cm) diam

$450-550   WW

A late-19thC/early-20thC Welsh nickel dog collar, with studded decoration, marked "METALO NICKEL" and inscribed "JONES BRYNGLAS CAERPHILLY."

6in(15cm) diam

$800-900   WW

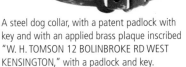

A steel dog collar, with a patent padlock with key and with an applied brass plaque inscribed "W. H. TOMSON 12 BOLINBROKE RD WEST KENSINGTON," with a padlock and key.

6in (15cm) diam

$260-330   WW

ESSENTIAL REFERENCE—VINAIGRETTES

A popular accessory among well-to-do ladies and gentlemen during the 18thC and 19thC—a period of almost universal poor drainage in cities, towns, and villages—vinaigrettes were small, tightly lidded boxes designed to contain a sponge soaked in aromatic vinegar or perfume for warding off unpleasant odors and, it was thought, protecting against disease.

- Most vinaigrettes are rectangular in shape, although some are oval, and some are in "novelty" forms, such as thimbles, barrels, bells, beehives, eggs, urns, and even fish.
- The majority of vinaigrettes were fashioned from silver, but some were of gold, and other materials, such as enamel and mother-of-pearl, were sometimes used for decorative embellishment.
- To prevent corrosion, particularly from vinegar, the interiors of vinaigrettes were often gilded.
- Many of the originally most prestigious, and now most collectible, vinaigrettes are "castle tops," their lids finely embossed with topographical scenes, including well-known castles, abbeys, or country houses, and framed within often-elaborate foliate borders.
- The biggest maker of "castle-top" vinaigrettes was the silversmiths Nathanial Mills (1746-1840) and his son, also Nathanial Mills (1811-73). Their workshop in Birmingham produced numerous examples, primarily intended as high-quality tourist souvenirs, mostly with views of famous buildings, such as Balmoral and Warwick castles and Abbotsford house, from all over the British Isles.

A George III silver-gilt vinaigrette, by Thomas Willmore, Birmingham, engraved decoration, the interior with a simple pierced grille.

1800   *1¼in (2.8cm) long 0.5oz*

$260-330   WW

A George III silver vinaigrette, by Joseph Taylor, Birmingham, with engraved checkerboard decoration, the interior with a hinged filigree grille.

1802   *¾in (2cm) long 0.2oz*

$350-400   WW

A George III silver vinaigrette, by Phipps and Robinson, London, of nutmeg grater form, engraved with a Classical maiden, the interior silver-gilt pierced and engraved, engraved with initials.

1802   *1½in (4cm) wide 1oz*

$800-850   WW

A George III silver vinaigrette, by Matthew Linwood, Birmingham, engraved with a man smoking a pipe and walking his dog, the interior with a silver-gilt pierced and embossed grille with a basket of fruit and flowers and foliate scroll decoration.

1809   *1¼in (2.9cm) long 0.5oz*

$1,100-1,250   WW

A George III silver egg vinaigrette, by Samuel Meriton, London, the cover opens to reveal a pull-out pierced silver-gilt grille, inside that is a further egg with a pull-off cover, length-engraved decoration, the interior with a pierced and engraved grille.

1794   *1½in (4cm) long 3/8oz*

$550-650   WW

A George III silver-gilt vinaigrette, by Wardell & Kempson, Birmingham, of watchcase form, engraved foliate decoration, the interior with a hinged pierced and engraved foliate-scroll grille.

1814   *1¼in (3cm) diam 0.5oz*

$1,000-1,100   WW

A George III silver-gilt vinaigrette, by Samuel Pemberton, Birmingham, with a chased panel of vine leaves and grapes, the interior with a pierced and engraved grille.

1817   1½in (4cm) wide 1oz

$550-650   **WW**

A George IV silver-gilt and bloodstone vinaigrette, by John Shaw, Birmingham, the cover and base with bloodstone panels, the sides with reeded decoration, foliate-scroll borders, the interior with an engraved and pierced grille.

1820   1¼in (2.8cm) long

$1,050-1,200   **WW**

A George IV silver-gilt vinaigrette, by John Reily, London, engine-turned decoration, the cover applied with a micro-mosaic panel of a dancing couple, the interior with a pierced and engraved grille, in a modern Asprey case, old crack on panel.

1821   1¾in (4.5cm) long 1½oz

$4,000-5,300   **WW**

A George III silver purse vinaigrette, by John Shaw, Birmingham, the front with a simulated strap and a shield cartouche, initialed, the interior with a pierced and engraved grille.

1819   1¼in (2.8cm) long 0.5oz

$450-600   **WW**

A George IV silver-gilt vinaigrette, by William Ellerby, London, with engine-turned decoration, with a vacant cartouche, foliate-scroll thumbpiece, the interior with a pierced and engraved grille of berries and leaves.

1827   1½in (4.2cm) long 1.1oz

$350-400   **WW**

A 19thC gold vinaigrette, engine-turned decoration, the interior with a hinged, pierced grille, unmarked.

ca. 1830   1in (2.5cm) diam 0.4oz

$800-900   **WW**

A 19thC silver-gilt vinaigrette, with an agate panel with a fern, the base with a bloodstone panel, the interior with a pierced and engraved silver-gilt grille, hinge pin damaged, with a ring attachment, unmarked.

ca. 1830   1¼in (3.5cm) long

$600-650   **WW**

A William IV silver vinaigrette, by Thomas Shaw, Birmingham, with engraved decoration, and with initials, the interior with a silver-gilt pierced and embossed grille.

1833   *1in (2.4cm) long 0.2oz*

$260-330   **WW**

Judith Picks

Fortunately, and unlike many of our Georgian and Victorian forebears, I've never felt the need to carry about my person when out and about an aromatic vinegar- or perfume-soaked sponge to ward off unpleasant odors, or even disease, from an inadequate public sewerage system. However, I've long had a fondness for the small decorative boxes—vinaigrettes—designed to hold such sponges, particularly if they are the impressed and engraved "castle-top" silver versions, and especially if, as in this 1935 example by Joseph Willmore of Birmingham, the "top" in question is a view of Abbotsford House, in the Scottish Borders.

A Borderer myself, I was born in Galashiels, just a few miles down the road from Melrose, where, overlooking the Tweed River, Abbotsford House still stands. Purchased by the famous historical novelist and poet Sir Walter Scott in 1811, it was substantially expanded by him between then and

1824 in the castlelike, Gothic-esque, Scottish Baronial Style.

It wasn't until I was 14 or 15 years old that I first got to see Abbotsford's interiors, which include a huge library, a collection of ancient furniture, arms and armor, and numerous other relics and curiosities connected with Scottish history. Although mightily impressive (and highly recommended), my fondest memories are of being regularly taken there by my parents during the weekends—in my preteen years in the late 1950s and early 1960s—to play and run around in Abbotsford's extensive and wonderful gardens.

Altogether fond memories, and ones I much enjoyed reexperiencing firsthand when, back in 2009, I returned to film with the BBC Antiques Roadshow.

A William IV silver "castle-top" vinaigrette, by Joseph Willmore, Birmingham, cover with a scene of Abbotsford House, the interior with a pierced and engraved silver-gilt grille, foliate-scroll border, the underside with a vacant cartouche.

1835   *1¾in (4.7cm) wide 1.5oz*

$1,300-1,800   **WW**

An early-19thC gold-mounted citrine vinaigrette, the cover with foliate-scroll decoration, and with an agate panel, the interior with an engraved and pierced grille, unmarked.

1840   *1¼in (3.4cm) high*

$3,300-4,000   **WW**

A Victorian silver "castle-top" vinaigrette, by Nathaniel Mills, Birmingham, cover with a scene of York Minster, the underside with a vacant shield cartouche, the interior with a pierced and engraved silver-gilt grille.

1842   *2in (4.8cm) wide 1.3oz*

$2,600-3,300   **WW**

A Victorian silver "castle-top" vinaigrette, engraved with a scene of St. Paul's Cathedral, by Nathaniel Mills, Birmingham, the interior with a pierced and engraved silver-gilt grille.

1843   *1½in (4cm) long 0.6oz*

$600-750   **WW**

A Victorian silver and parcel-gilt vinaigrette, engraved with a wickerwork pattern and opening to reveal a pierced grille, maker's mark "ES," Birmingham.

1843   *1¼in (3cm) wide*

$260-400   **WHP**

A Victorian silver vinaigrette, by Nathaniel Mills, Birmingham, engraved with a river scene with sailing boats, a bridge, and a townscape behind, the interior with a pierced and engraved silver-gilt grille, engine-turned sides and base, with a vacant shield cartouche.

1845   *1½in (3.7cm) wide 0.7oz*

$2,200-2,600   **WW**

OBJETS DE VERTU

CLOSER LOOK—SILVER VINAIGRETTE

This vinaigrette is by Nathaniel Mills, the younger (1811-73), who took over the business from his father, also Nathaniel (1746-1840), who had registered his first mark in 1803.

It is unusually engraved with a lake scene with a steamship, the background with buildings on a hillside, possibly Osborne House.

The interior with a pierced and engraved silver-gilt foliate scroll grille.

It has scroll borders, engine-turned sides and base, with a vacant shield cartouche.

A Victorian silver vinaigrette, Birmingham.

1847 1½in (3.5cm) wide 0.5oz

$4,600-5,300 WW

A Victorian silver vinaigrette, by Edward Smith, Birmingham, the cover with a crest of two shaking hands, the interior with a silver-gilt pierced and engraved grille.

The crest is that of Alexander, Buchanan, Haulton, and others.

1848 1½in (4.2cm) long 0.8oz

$260-330 WW

A Victorian silver "castle-top" vinaigrette, by Nathaniel Mills, Birmingham, cover with a raised view of Kenilworth Castle, the interior with a silver-gilt pierced and engraved grille, the sides and base with reeded and engine-turned tartan decoration, the base with a vacant cartouche.

1851 1½in (4cm) wide 0.9oz

$2,000-2,600 WW

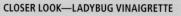

A Victorian silver and agate vinaigrette, by James Fenton, Birmingham, set with various colored stones, the underside with banded agate panels, the interior with a pierced and engraved silver-gilt grille, no apparent date letter.

1¼in (3.2cm) wide

$1,100-1,250 WW

CLOSER LOOK—LADYBUG VINAIGRETTE

This is a rare unmarked silver and enamel ladybug vinaigrette.

Although of a late date, this is a rare, complex and desirable example.

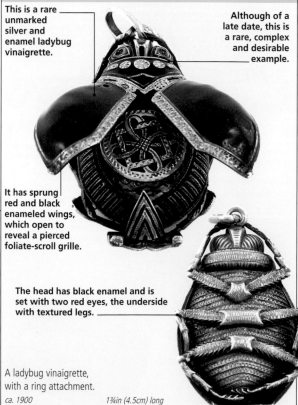

It has sprung red and black enameled wings, which open to reveal a pierced foliate-scroll grille.

The head has black enamel and is set with two red eyes, the underside with textured legs.

A Victorian novelty silver vinaigrette, by Henry Dee, London, one hinged end opens to reveal a pierced silver-gilt grille, the other opens to reveal a compartment, with a ring attachment.

1869 1¼in (3cm) long 0.7oz

$850-1,000 WW

A ladybug vinaigrette, with a ring attachment.

ca. 1900 1¾in (4.5cm) long

$3,300-4,600 WW

ESSENTIAL REFERENCE—SNUFF

Fermented, dried, ground (to a fine powder), and flavored tobacco, snuff was "discovered" some 500 years ago in North America by Christopher Columbus, who encountered the Carib indians inhaling it as a stimulant and as a remedy for ailments, such as toothache.

- Transported back to Europe, it was taken up by royalty and the aristocracy as a fashionable luxury—its medicinal properties now also valued for the alleviation of gout.
- More significantly, during the 17thC and 18thC, taking snuff acquired the status of a ritual involving studied movements of the wrist and hand—the socially aspirant nouveau riche of the 18thC could even attend private classes to receive instruction on the etiquettes of administering the powder.
- During the 19thC, thanks to increased production and reduced cost, the habit spread to the middle and lower classes. However, this popularization, with its attendant loss of exclusivity and gradual diminishment of ritual, resulted in taking snuff falling out of fashion among the aristocracy. Moreover, by the outbreak of World War I, it had also been supplanted among the general population by an even more addictive method of consuming tobacco: cigarette smoking.
- Since World War I, the use of snuff has been largely confined to a relatively small number of "connoisseurs." However, the four previous centuries of taking snuff have bequeathed a considerable legacy to the late-20thC collector—in the form of the huge variety of boxes used to store the powder at home and carry it about the person.

A William and Mary silver spice/snuffbox, engraved decoration, engraved "VNIS MALCREIENVIE," maker's mark "PR."
ca. 1690　　*1¼in (3cm) wide 0.2oz*
$1,200-1,450　　**WW**

A George II silver snuffbox, by Peter Wirgman, London, the cover figural scene of a water nymph and cherub, in an architectural setting, Rococo scroll border, gilded interior.
1746　　*2½in (6.5cm) long 2.2oz*
$550-650　　**WW**

An 18thC Dutch silver and agate snuffbox, by John Francois Biese (Biezer), Schoovnhoven, the hinged cover with a plain panel and crimped border, gilded interior.
1764　　*¼in (8.2cm) wide 2.5oz*
$650-800　　**WW**

A George II silver table snuffbox, by Gundry Roode, London, modeled as a book, the ribbed spine engraved with formal motifs, the hinged cover with a later armorial within a Rococo cartouche, the reverse side with a crest.

The later arms are those of Sebright, probably for Edward Amherst Sebright, third son of Sir John Sebright, 6th Bt. of Beechwood. During the Peninsular War he commanded 2/1st Foot Guards from March 10–April 1811.
1731　　*4½in (11.4cm) high 7.9oz*
$5,500-6,500　　**WW**

An 18thC French gold snuffbox, Paris, the center with a two-color gold rosette, and rope-work border, on an engine-turned and dot ground, the interior of the cover with a worn inscription, maker's mark partially worn.
1783-89　　*3in (7.5cm) diam 115.4g*
$6,000-6,600　　**WW**

A pair of 19thC tortoiseshell portrait-miniature snuffboxes, with one depicting Archduke Francis II, the other his wife.
3½in (9cm) diam
$1,300-1,800　　**TEN**

A late-18th/early-19thC Swiss gold snuffbox, painted in multicolor enamel, the top containing an oval miniature with the sides depicting nautical scenes, in a Wartski case.
3½in (9cm) wide
$16,000-20,000　　**LOCK**

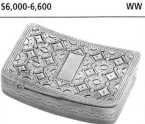

A George III silver snuffbox, by Joseph Willmore, Birmingham, engraved decoration.
1814　　*1½in (3.8cm) wide 0.5oz*
$350-400　　**WW**

A George IV silver raised-relief snuffbox, by Nathaniel Mills, Birmingham, cast with a scene from antiquity of King Solomon meeting the Queen of Sheba, engine-turned base with a vacant cartouche, gilded interior.

1828   *3in (7.6cm) wide 4oz*

$1,300-1,800   **WW**

A William IV silver "castle-top" snuffbox, by Taylor and Perry, Birmingham, the cover with a scene of Newstead Abbey, engine-turned sides and base, in a fitted case.

Newstead Abbey was formerly the home of Lord Byron.

1835   *3¼in (8.2cm) wide 3.3oz*

$4,000-4,600   **WW**

A Victorian Scottish "castle-top" snuffbox, by Alexander Graham Wighton, Edinburgh, cover with a scene of Abbotsford House within a landscape setting with fishermen, gilded interior, in a fitted case, the inside of the cover inscribed "Dr. William Bruce, from a sincere friend in grateful remembrance of his unremitting attention during a long and dangerous illness Smyrna, May 1840."

This box was probably exhibited by Wighton at the 1851 Great Exhibition, and it was known as the Waverley snuffbox. Abbotsford House was the home of the Scottish novelist Sir Walter Scott.

1839   *3¼in (8.5cm) wide 4.3oz*

$4,600-5,900   **WW**

A large silver-gilt engraved "castle-top" table snuffbox, by John Linnit, London, the cover engraved with a view of the original Licensed Victuallers' School in Kennington, London, the underside of the base engraved with the names of the Trustees and Committee men.

Licensed Victuallers' School was founded in 1803 by the Society of Licensed Victuallers. The School was originally in Kennington, and then moved to Slough in 1922 and to Ascot in 1989.

1839   *5¼in (13.5cm) wide 16.3oz*

$3,300-4,600   **WW**

A 19thC French gold- and silver-mounted tortoiseshell snuffbox, with carved textured decoration, with simulated straps and padlock, silver hinge, the padlock with a French control mark, one strap missing.

3in (7.8cm) wide

$1,050-1,200   **WW**

A late-19thC silver-plate-mounted ram's horn table snuff mull, by Walker & Hall, Sheffield, with double curled horns and dog finial on lid.

22½in (57cm) wide

$2,000-2,600   **L&T**

A 19thC papier-mâché Thames Tunnel souvenir snuffbox, decorated with shipping and warehouses above a cross section of the tunnel, with cracks and losses on the rim of the cover, minor damages to image.

3½in (9cm) diam

$300-350   **CHEF**

A Victorian silver embossed "castle-top" card case, by Frederick Marson, Birmingham, embossed with York Minster with foliate-scroll decoration on a mat background, the reverse with a vacant cartouche.

1845 4in (10.2cm) long 2.4oz
$4,000-4,600 **WW**

A Victorian silver embossed "castle-top" card case, by Frederick Marson, Birmingham, embossed the Houses of Parliament, the reverse with a cartouche engraved "E.M.B" below a crown.

1845 4in (10.2cm) long 2.4oz
$1,600-2,100 **WW**

An early-Victorian silver "castle-top" card case, by Nathaniel Mills, Birmingham, decorated in relief with St. Paul's Cathedral, the reverse engraved with a monogram beneath a coronet, some wear.

1844 4in (10cm) long 2oz 8dwt
$1,100-1,250 **TEN**

A Victorian silver engraved "castle-top" card case, by Nathaniel Mills, Birmingham, engraved with an unidentified scene, with bands of engine-turned decoration, the reverse with an initialed cartouche.

1849 3in (8.5cm) long 1.3oz
$1,300-1,800 **WW**

A Victorian silver "castle-top" card case, by Nathaniel Mills, Birmingham, with a view of The Law Courts of Dublin with the Liffey River, the reverse with similar decoration, and with an inscribed cartouche.

1849 3½in (9cm) long 1.5oz
$3,300-4,000 **WW**

A Victorian silver-shaped "castle-top" card case, by Nathaniel Mills, Birmingham, embossed with the east end of Bath Abbey, the cartouche engraved Wells, date letter overstruck by town mark, in a leather-covered case.

4in (10cm) long
$4,000-5,300 **DN**

An early-Victorian silver "castle-top" card case, by David Pettifer, Birmingham, with a view of Windsor Castle from the river, with the reverse with monogrammed shield cartouche.

1857. 4in (10 cm) high 1.9 oz
$1,300-1,800 **FELL**

A Victorian silver "castle-top" card case, by Alfred Taylor, Birmingham, engraved with the east end of Bath Abbey, the reverse with a cartouche with an armorial, in a leather-covered case from Wright & Co., 16 Milsom St., Bath, light scratches, leather case worn.

1856 4in (10cm) long
$2,400-2,900 **DN**

A Victorian silver "castle-top" card case, by George Unite, with view of Osborne House, the reverse with a vacant cartouche, Birmingham.

1863 4in (10cm) long 2.1oz
$1,600-2,100 **WW**

An Edwardian silver and enamel visiting card case, by W G Keight, Birmingham, enameled with a brown trout, in a later Tessier box.

1903 3¼in (8.3cm) long 1.2oz
$850-1,000 **WW**

A George III silver-gilt toothpick box, engraved foliate decoration, on a reeded background, the interior velvet-lined, unmarked.

ca. 1780   *4in (9.5cm) long 1.2oz*

$200-260   **WW**

A George III gold-mounted blonde tortoiseshell toothpick box, the hinged cover with a cartouche of a young lady under glass.

ca. 1790   *4in (10cm) long*

$800-850   **WW**

A George III tortoiseshell toothpick box, shield cartouche form, inlaid with mother-of-pearl decoration, bright-cut borders, and with a shield cartouche with a monogram.

ca. 1790   *3in (8.4cm) long*

$1,050-1,200   **WW**

A George III gold-mounted blonde tortoiseshell toothpick box, the cover with inlaid decoration, with a vacant cartouche.

ca. 1790   *4in (10.2cm) long*

$260-400   **WW**

A George III gilt-metal and silver-mounted blonde tortoiseshell toothpick box, with an inlaid border and with a centered initialed cartouche, with painted seaweed decoration, the interior with a mirror, the interior base velvet lined.

ca. 1790   *3.5in (9.2cm) long*

$350-450   **WW**

A George III silver toothpick box, by Samuel Pemberton, Birmingham, with bright-cut sun ray decoration, the interior with the original mirror (cracked), velvet-lined interior, with a toothpick.

1790   *3in (8.3cm) long 1oz*

$1,000-1,100   **WW**

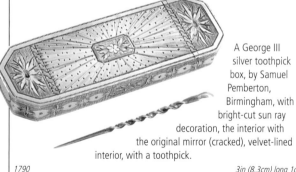

A George III silver-mounted tortoiseshell toothpick box, the cover with inlaid borders and an oval cartouche initialed, the interior with a later mirror and velvet lining, unmarked.

ca. 1790   *3in (8cm) long*

$350-400   **WW**

A George III satinwood toothpick box, the hinged cover set with a Wedgwood Jasperware panel, with a cut-steel border, the interior with the original mirror.

ca. 1800   *3¾in (9.5cm) long*

$650-800   **WW**

A George III silver toothpick box, in the manner of Phipps and Robinson, bright-cut decoration, the cover with an oval cartouche of braided hair under glass, velvet-lined interior, the inside of the cover with a mirror, unmarked.

ca. 1790-1800   *3in (8cm) long 1.1oz.*

$450-550   **WW**

An Austrian silver and enamel toothpick box, maker's mark "NA," the cover enameled with a palace on a lake, the sides with enameled decoration, the ends with filigree decoration and set with red stones.

3in (7.4cm) long

$450-550   **WW**

ESSENTIAL REFERENCE—VESTA CASES/MATCH SAFES

In 1832, in England, William Newton patented the first "strike anywhere" friction matches. Comprising a wax stem with embedded cotton threads and a tip of phosphorus, he named them after the Roman goddess of fire and the hearth, Vesta. The small boxes—called vesta cases in England, but known as match safes in the United States—were introduced soon after and rapidly became an essential, and often status-indicating, accessory of the Victorian and Edwardian era.

● Primarily designed to protect "strike anywhere" matches from accidental combustion, and featuring a ribbed surface (usually on the underside) for striking the matches, match safes were produced in three different types: "pocket" (the most numerous); "table" (larger than "pocket," and placed on convenient surfaces around the home); and "go-to-bed" (rarer, and mostly joined to a candlestick holder).

● In addition to much-favored silver, materials used to make match safes ranged from gold, brass, tin, gunmetal, and gold to bone, tortoiseshell, ceramics, and wood. Popular shapes, as well as square, rectangular, oval, and round, included diverse "novelty" forms, such as human heads, hearts, or limbs; birds and fish; boots and shoes; sporting equipment, and musical instruments.

● Favored decorative techniques applied to the cases included, as well as simple engraving, repoussé, guilloché, cloisonné, and enameling—the latter often employed on the flat surfaces of geometric-shaped cases to create sophisticated pictorial imagery.

An Austrian silver and enamel match safe, by G .A. Scheid, Vienna, the hinged cover enameled with a first-class round-trip ticket from Monte Carlo to Nice, the reverse enameled with a scene of the Nice coastline.
2¼in (5.3cm) wide 2.4oz
$3,300-4,600 WW

A Victorian silver and enamel match safe, by S. Mordan and Co, London, enameled with a pack of hounds, hinged end, chips on enamel.
1894 2in (5.7cm) long 1.3oz
$1,050-1,200 WW

A late-Victorian silver and enamel match safe, by William Neale, Chester, enameled with flowers, with a ring attachment.
1888 2in (5.5cm) long 0.9oz.
$600-750 WW

A Victorian novelty silver match safe, by Joseph Fray, Chester, modeled as a barrel, with coopered and textured decoration, hinged cover with a striker.
1885 1¼in (3.3cm) long 0.4oz
$600-750 WW

A late-Victorian silver and enamel match safe, by Saunders and Shepherd, Birmingham, the front enameled with the scene of a wounded soldier carrying his gun, and written "A Gentleman in Khaki," with a ring attachment.

This item has Boer War interest. "A Gentleman in Khaki" comes from a line in the Rudyard Kipling poem, "The Absent Minded Beggar."

A Victorian novelty silver match safe, by Howard James, Birmingham, of horseshoe form, engine-turned decoration, hinged cover, with a lighting cord and ring attachment.
1894 2½in (6cm) long 1.3oz
$260-400 WW

A Victorian novelty silver golf club sealing wax holder/match safe/stamp case, by Samuel Jacob, London, modeled as a wood, the head for matches, with a hinged cover, with a stamp holder, and with a striker for matches, the tapering stem with a pull-off cover and with a hole for a match.

Provenance: Lionel de Rothschild (1882-1942), Edmund de Rothschild (1916-2009), The Trustees of Exbury House.
1895 11¾in (29.5cm) high 2.1oz
$5,300-6,600 WW

1899 2in (5cm) long 1.1oz.
$550-650 WW

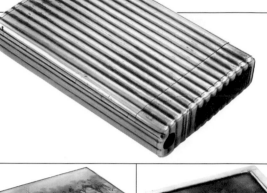

An Austrian silver cigarette case and match safe, by G. A. Scheid, fluted decoration, gilded interior, with a vesta compartment.

3¾in (9..3cm) long 5.5oz

$200-260   **WW**

A Royal presentation silver cigarette case and accompanying letter from George VI to Lionel Logue, the case by The Goldsmiths and Silversmiths Company, London, engine-turned decoration, applied with the Royal Cipher of George VI in gold, gilded interior. With the letter dated May 17, 1937, and written from Windsor Castle, reads:

My dear Logue
The Queen and I have just viewed the film of our Coronation, and I could not wait to send you a few lines to thank you again for your hard work in helping me prepare for the great day. You know how anxious I was to get my responses right in the abbey, the poor rehearsal adding greatly to my anxiety, but my mind was finally set at ease tonight. Not a moments hesitation or mistake.
The same cannot be said of the Bishops of course, nor the pen I used to sign the Oath: the ink got all over my fingers, but fortunately one can hardly make it out. The success was due to your expert supervision and unfailing patience with me over recent months, and I truly don't know how I could have done it without you. I want you to know how grateful I am, not only for your invaluable help with my speech, but for your devoted friendship and encouragement, and I hope you will accept this small gift as a token of my appreciation.
Yours very sincerely
George R.I

As a speech therapist, Logue worked with the Duke from the late-1920s into the mid-1940s. Before ascending the throne as George VI, the Duke of York dreaded public speaking, because of a severe stammer, his closing speech at the British Empire Exhibition at Wembley on October 31, 1925, proved an ordeal for speaker and listeners alike. The Duke resolved to find some way to manage his stammer, and engaged Logue in 1926. Diagnosing poor coordination between the Duke's larynx and thoracic diaphragm, Logue prescribed a daily hour of vocal exercises. Logue's treatment gave the Duke the confidence to relax and avoid tension-induced muscle spasms. As a result, he only occasionally stammered.

1936   *5in (12.8cm) long 5.7oz*

$110,000-120,000   **WW**

An Edwardian silver cigarette box, by William Hornby, London, the hinged cover with a scene of a Hunt meet, set under glass, plain thumbpiece, wood lined.

1901   *6in (16cm) long*

$850-1,000   **WW**

An Edwardian silver cigarette box and match safe, by William Wright, London, set with print of a hunting scene under glass, wood-lined interior, the reverse applied with a metal striker.

1901   *4¼in (11cm) wide*

$600-750   **WW**

An Edwardian silver double cigarette box, by William Comyns, London, the front with a later presentation inscription.

1902   *9¾in (24.8cm) long*

$400-450   **WW**

A silver and enamel cigarette case, by William Neale Limited, Birmingham, the front later enameled with a fishing scene of an angler on a riverbank, engine-turned base.

1932   *3¾in (9.5cm) long 3.5oz*

$450-550   **WW**

A 9ct-yellow gold cigarette case, having diagonal ridged decoration, maker's mark "JC," London, personalized inscription reads "SW to Robert M. Peacock, Bedford, 1941."

1934   *4¼in (10.8cm) wide 5.1oz*

$2,600-4,000   **WHP**

A presentation silver cigar box, by Garrard and Co, London, the cover engraved with a scene of a Minaret and building in Aden, the front with a presentation inscription, on four scroll feet, wood lined.

1958   *12½in (31.5cm) wide*

$1,600-2,100   **WW**

ESSENTIAL REFERENCE—NUTMEG

Antique nutmeg graters, whether fashioned in carved wood or silver, or even gold, are eminently collectible, but what's the allure of the cooking and "medicinal" ingredient without which they wouldn't exist?

- Nutmeg is a pungent, slightly sweet-tasting spice, grated or ground into a powder from the dried seeds of the fragrant nutmeg tree "Myristica fragans," and used to flavor all kinds of foods and dishes, and some beverages, too.
- The earliest use of nutmeg has been traced back some 3,500 years to the Banda Islands, part of the larger Maluku Islands group, in Indonesia. While the use of nutmeg had spread to India by the 6thC AD, and gradually thereafter via Constantinople into Europe, these islands were the only source of production until the 19thC.
- For centuries, the Indonesian location of nutmeg was known only to Arab traders, but, by the early 16thC, European sea-faring nations began invading the Banda Islands to control the production and supply. Initially, Portugal partially succeeded, but they were supplanted in the 17thC by the Dutch East India Company.
- During the late-18thC and early-19thC Napoleonic wars, the British invaded and temporarily took control of the Banda Islands from the Dutch and began transplanting the nutmeg trees to be grown in other locations—initially Sri Lanka, Penang, Bencoolen, and Singapore, and thereafter to other British colonies, notably Zanzibar and Grenada—thereby ending the Bandanese monopoly.

A William and Mary silver nutmeg grater, with a pull-off cover engraved with a tulip, the body with engraved decoration, the removable grater also marked, the base scratch initialed "B.W," maker's mark of "TK," probably for Thomas Kedder, London.
ca. 1690   *2¼in (5.6cm) long 0.5oz*
$850-1,000   **WW**

A late-17thC silver nutmeg grater, maker's mark only "I.F," teardrop form, the hinged cover and base engraved with a tulip with feather-edge borders, the interior with a steel grater.
ca. 1690   *2¼in (5.5cm) long 2.5oz*
$2,400-2,900   **WW**

A George III Scottish silver nutmeg grater, by Patrick Robertson, Edinburgh, the pull-off cover with initials under a coronet, the side with a sliding panel that reveals the steel grater.
ca. 1790   *2.5in (6.2cm) long 1.1oz*
$850-1,000   **WW**

A George III silver nutmeg grater, by Phipps and Robinson, London, the hinged cover with a reeded border and ball finial, the cover opens to reveal a hinged side, bright-cut decoration, on a rectangular foot, initialed.
1790   *2¾in (7cm) high 1.4oz*
$2,000-2,600   **WW**

A George III silver nutmeg grater, by Samuel Pemberton, Birmingham, pull-off cover opens to reveal a grater, engraved decoration, pull-off base.
1790   *1½in (3.5cm) high 0.4oz*
$800-850   **WW**

A George III silver nutmeg grater, by Thomas Meriton, London, with bands of reeded decoration, the screw-off cover opening to reveal the steel grater, monogrammed.

1797   *2in (4.8cm) high 0.7oz*

$550-650   **WW**

A George III silver nutmeg grater, by William Parker, London, the hinged cover with a baluster finial and reeded border, hinged front, on a raised rectangular foot with canted corners.

1800   *2¾in (6.8cm) high 1.3oz*

$1,600-2,100   **WW**

A George III silver nutmeg grater, by Samuel Pemberton, Birmingham, bright-cut borders, the domed cover pulls off to reveal the grater.

1800   *1¼in (3.3cm) wide 0.5oz*

$550-650   **WW**

A George III silver nutmeg grater, by Phipps and Robinson, London, the hinged cover with a crowned "G," and engraved foliate decoration, hinged base.

A Victorian silver nutmeg grater, by George Unite, Birmingham, of melon form, with panels of chased foliate and plain decoration, the hinged cover opens to reveal a grater.

1809   *2¼in (5.3cm) wide 1.3oz*

$650-800   **WW**

1848   *1½in (3.8cm) long 0.9oz*

$1,600-2,100   **WW**

A Staffordshire enamel etui, painted with figures promenading before stately buildings at the water's edge, with ships being loaded, with contents, some restoration.

ca. 1765-70   *4in (10.3cm) high*
$750-800   **WW**

A South Staffordshire snuffbox, with unusual gilt motifs of fruit and leaves within yellow and brown panels, reserved on a pink linen or gingham ground with a flower garland.

ca. 1770   *3½in (9cm) wide*
$350-400   **WW**

A South Staffordshire enamel bonbonnière, modeled as a lemon with slightly dimpled texture, some restoration.

ca. 1770   *1½in (4cm) high*
$600-750   **WW**

A small South Staffordshire enamel apple bonbonnière, with a hinged metal mount, some restoration.

ca. 1770   *1½in (3.5cm) high*
$180-240   **WW**

A rare South Staffordshire enamel bonbonnière, modeled as a pickle or small cucumber, with raised black dots on a green ground, grading to yellow as it tapers to the end.

ca. 1770-80   *2¼in (5.8cm) wide*
$1,300-1,800   **WW**

A Staffordshire enamel table snuffbox, painted with a sleeping girl being teased by two children as their mother stands by, a cow looking on, some cracking.

ca. 1770   *3¾in (9.7cm) wide*
$350-400   **WW**

A rare late-18thC South Staffordshire gilt-metal and pink enamel spy glass nécessaire, with Rococo gold cartouche painted with rural scenes, sliding covers on the eyepiece on detachable cover and body, containing scissors, a penknife with steel blade and chased with insect decoration on the gilt-metal body, two bodkins, one with snuff spoon, and a pair of tweezers.

5¼in (13cm) high
$3,300-4,000   **WW**

A pair of Staffordshire enamel candlesticks, painted with scenes of sheep amid trees and Classical ruins, the stems and detachable drip pans decorated with flowers, some damages and repairs.

ca. 1770   *12¼in (31cm) high*
$650-800   **WW**

A pair of Staffordshire enamel candlesticks, printed and colored with figures on horseback and tending cattle in landscapes, some damages.

ca. 1770   *9in (23.2cm) high*
$800-900   **WW**

An English enamel snuffbox, painted with figures in a harbor moving bales and barrels toward a pulley in the distance, the sides with vignettes of buildings and trees, echoed in the interior.
ca. 1760-70   *2½in (6cm) diam*
$650-800   **WW**

An English enamel table snuffbox, printed and colored with a shepherd playing the bagpipes to his companion, a dog and sheep standing by, the sides with flower sprays, with restoration.
ca. 1760-70   *3½in (9cm) wide*
$200-260   **WW**

An English enamel walnut bonbonnière, the molded body with striations of brown on a buff ground, some restoration.
ca. 1770-80   *1¾in (4.5cm) wide*
$550-600   **WW**

An enamel etui, painted with bucolic scenes of a shepherd with his flock and a girl carrying a basket on her head, the reverse with panels of flowers.
ca. 1770-80   *4¾in (12.2cm) high*
$260-330   **WW**

A late-18th/early-19thC English enamel commemorative patch box, painted in black with a ship at sail, the base colored a pale blue, with internal mirror, titled "Nelson and Victory," restoration.
1½in (4cm) wide
$260-330   **WW**

A late-18th/early-19thC English enamel patch box, of Lord Nelson interest, painted with HMS "Victory" at sail, within a border of white dots, on a blue ground, restoration.
1½in (4cm) wide
$260-330   **WW**

A silver-mounted enamel purse, maker's mark worn, Birmingham, enameled with a gentleman playing his lute to a sitting lady, with a chain attachment.
1906   *3in (8.5cm) long*
$600-750   **WW**

A silver gilt and enameled box, the lid enameled with a Classical figure of a lady with a cherub, London.
1919   *1.5in (3.5cm) long 19.5 gms*
$450-550   **BELL**

An Austrian silver-gilt and enamel bell push, of egg form, with a mother-of-pearl push button, with two bands of white enamel decoration, with import marks for London, importer's mark of Gourdel Vales & Co.
1911   *2½in (6cm) long*
$550-650   **WW**

A Charles II silver-gilt scent flask, of "pilgrim bottle" form, with detachable cork, engraved with a figure playing a musical instrument on one side and a dog's mask on the other among scrolling-leaf decoration and diamond pattern.

2¼in (5.5cm) high

$5,300-5,900 **WW**

A late-18thC cut-glass scent bottle, with a silver-colored metal screw stopper, gilded probably in the London atelier of James Giles, with flower sprays and a basket of flowers, inscribed "Gage D'amitie."

4¾in (12cm) high

$800-850 **WW**

A George III silver-gilt scent bottle vinaigrette, by Joseph Willmore, Birmingham, engraved foliate decoration, opens to reveal a glass scent bottle.

1809 *1¾in (4.5cm) high 0.4oz*

$850-1,000 **WW**

A Georgian tortoiseshell-cased scent bottle, the case with hinged arched cover and raised steel decoration, the scent bottle with gilt highlights, screw-off yellow metal cap and stopper beneath.

2in (5cm) high

$1,600-2,100 **CHOR**

A Georgian cut-glass scent bottle, with stopper, initialed "L.F.S."

4in (10cm) long

$130-180 **JN**

A Victorian silver-gilt-mounted ceramic scent bottle, by S. Mordan, London, decorated with roses and butterflies, push button plain hinged cover, with a chain and ring attachment.

1873 *3in (7.5cm) high*

$650-800 **WW**

A novelty silver-mounted fish scent bottle, by S. Mordan and Co., London, the screw-off cover modeled as the tail, with scale decoration.

1884 *6¼in (16cm) long*

$1,300-1,800 **WW**

A pair of Victorian silver-gilt-mounted glass scent bottles, by George Heath, London, retailed by H. Lewis and Co. New Bond Street, London, the mounts formed and engraved with flowers, the hinged covers initialed, with stoppers.

1890 *5¼in (13cm) high*

$2,000-2,600 **WW**

An Edwardian novelty silver owl scent bottle, by S. Mordan and Co, Chester, the screw-off cover modeled as an owl's head with textured feathers and set with glass eyes.

1906 *2¼in (5.5cm) long*

$1,300-1,800 **WW**

A late-17thC silver-mounted black shagreen covered aide-memoire, with stud-work borders, the interior with a slate tablet and a long stylus.

ca. 1680   *5¼in (13.7cm) high*

$650-800   **WW**

A late-17thC silver-mounted black shagreen aide-memoire case, the mounts with engraved flowers, the front with a lock, the end with a compartment for a writing implement, unmarked.

ca. 1680   *3¾in (9.3cm) high*

$1,100-1,250   **WW**

A Victorian silver-gilt aide-memoire, by Henry Dee, retailed by Thornhill, 144 New Bond Street, leather front and base, applied with a crowned monogram, London.

1869 3in (7cm) long

$550-650   **WW**

A Victorian 15ct-gold-mounted red leather aide-memoire, by Thomas De La Rue, London, the interior with two wallet compartments, stamped "Albert F. Calvert, Royston, Eton Avenue, N.W," with a gold pencil, Chester.

Albert F. Calvert was Managing Director of Consolidated Gold Mines of W. Australia.

1891   *4¾in (12cm) high*

$400-550   **WW**

A late-19thC Tartanware aide-memoire, decorated with two tartans, with a gilt-metal clasp and a bone, metal-tipped pencil, gilded leather spine, the silk-lined interior with a pocket.

4in (10cm) high

$200-260   **WW**

A 19thC French silver, silver-gilt and niello-work aide-memoire, the front applied with a gold cartouche with initials below a crown, silk-lined interior, with a pencil.

ca. 1880   *3¾in (9.5cm) long 3oz*

$650-800   **WW**

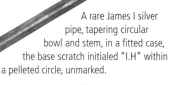

A rare James I silver pipe, tapering circular bowl and stem, in a fitted case, the base scratch initialed "I.H" within a pelleted circle, unmarked.

This pipe is written up and illustrated in "Apollo" magazine, "A rare James I silver Pipe," by Electius, Vol LXI, March 1955.

ca. 1620   *6¾in (17.2cm) long 1.3oz*

$6,000-7,500   **WW**

A Republic of Canada commemorative walking stick, with a natural wood shaft with horn ferrule and embossed white metal pommel, engraved "C. Dale/Navy Island Niagara River."

Navy Island lies in the Niagara River, 2¾ miles (4.5km) above the Horseshoe Falls, between Ontario and New York. Long a strategic military outpost and center of shipbuilding, in 1837 it was the home of the Rebellion of 1837, and self-proclaimed "Republic of Canada" led by William Lyon MacKenzie and 200 of his supporters, who sought independence from British rule. Under continuing threat, MacKenzie abandoned the island in early 1838, escaping with his followers to Buffalo, where he was taken prisoner. The island is now a Canadian National Historic site, since 1921, in recognition of it's shipbuilding and attempted Canadian Republic history.

ca. 1838   *35½in (90cm) long*

$1,300-1,800   **L&T**

A George V silver dance purse, by F.D. Long, Birmingham, decorated with foliate-engraved panels, with tan leather interior and attached finger ring and chain.

1916   *5in (12cm) wide 5.1oz*

$200-260   **CHEF**

A novelty silver butt marker cane handle, by Hilliard and Thomason, Birmingham, opens to reveal 10 numbered ivorine pegs.
1899   *4¼in (10.5cm) high*
$1,800-2,400   **WW**

An Edwardian silver butt marker, by Harry Akerman, London, retailed by Thornhill, Bond Street, patent no. 20128, modeled as a powder flask, with nine numbered ivory balls.
1902   *2¼in (5.8cm) long*
$2,100-2,600   **WW**

An Edwardian silver combination butt marker, by J. C. Vickery, London, with ivory pegs, the other end with a whistle.
1903   *3in (7.3cm) long 0.9oz*
$1,250-1,450   **WW**

A silver butt marker, by George Unite, Chester, with a fan mechanism and eight numbered ivory pegs.
1910   *2¼in (5.3cm) long 1.5oz*
$600-750   **WW**

A silver butt marker, by George Unite, Birmingham, with eight hinged and sprung holders with numbered ivory pegs, the cover initialed "D.M."
1922   *3in (7.8cm) wide 1.5oz*
$1,250-1,450   **WW**

A silver butt marker, by Asprey and Co., Chester, the cover opens to reveal three hinged sections, each containing three numbered ivory pegs.
1912   *4in (10.2cm) long 1.5oz*
$1,100-1,250   **WW**

A silver butt marker, by Asprey and Co, London, with eight numbered ivory pegs.
1925   *2¼in (5.8cm) wide 1.4oz*
$850-1,000   **WW**

An Asprey novelty 9 ct gold and oxidised metal cartridge butt marker, the base inscribed "Asprey's Cartridge Place Finder, Patent Applied For," with a 6 in a triangle and inscribed "Loaded by Asprey, Smokeless."
                2½in (6.2cm) high closed
$2,200-2,600   **WW**

A Victorian silver and enamel game counter, by Thomas Johnson, London, with six turning markers, and six enameled dials from 0-30 for hare, rabbits, grouse, partridge, pheasants, and woodcock, engraved with the initial "H" under a coronet.

1888   *2½in (6cm) wide*

$3,300-4,000   **WW**

An early-Victorian bone or ivory toggle fob seal, inscribed "Execn of S. D., Aug V., 1843, C.P. Makr" and the base with "T. I. B," with a brass suspension ring.

The initials "S. D." on this toggle relate to Sarah Dazley (1819-1843), the first and only woman to be publicly hanged at Bedford Gaol. She was known as the Potton Poisoner after she was convicted of murdering, by arsenic poisoning, her second husband William Dazley. She was also suspected of, but not tried for, murdering her first husband and son, Simeon and Jonah Mead, in 1840. She was executed on August 5, 1843, on the New Drop in front of thousands of onlookers and was the last person to be publicly hanged at Bedford Gaol.

1in (3.2cm) high

$3,300-4,000   **WW**

A silver-mounted green hardstone desk paper clip, by S. Mordan, Chester, horseshoe form.

1912   *5in (12cm) long*

$550-650   **WW**

A late-19th/early-20thC 9ct-gold donkey novelty stick pin, with a naturalistic donkey's head with textured fur on a plain gold pin, light surface marks.

head 1¼in (2.9cm) high 0.2oz

$400-550   **SWO**

A late-Victorian silver playing cards box, by Grey and Co, London, the sides set with the Queen of Hearts and Jack of Diamonds under glass, the ends with the Aces of Spades and Clubs, red leather-lined interior, on bracket feet.

1899   *4¼in (11cm) wide*

$1,300-1,800   **WW**

A Victorian novelty silver port light inkwell, by Samuel Jacobs, London, the light with a hinged cover and hinged loop attachment, with a glass liner.

1900   *4in (10cm) high*

$550-600   **WW**

A William IV silver table bell, by J and J Angell, London, engraved with a crest.

1830   *5¼in (13.5cm) high 7.1oz*

$2,600-3,300   **WW**

An Edwardian novelty silver suffragette pepper pot, by Saunders and Shepherd, Chester, modeled as a lady wearing a bonnet, and holding two placards faintly inscribed on ivorine "VOTES FOR WOMEN," the reverse with "WE CAN MAKE THINGS HOT FOR YOU."

1908   *3¼in (8.3cm) high 1.5oz*

$1,600-2,100   **WW**

An Edwardian silver photograph frame, by J Aitkin & Son, Birmingham, embossed with birds and foliate decoration.

1904   *12½in (32cm) high*

$600-750   **WW**

An Edwardian novelty silver bulldog pincushion, by Adie & Lovekin Ltd, Birmingham.
1905   *2in (5.2cm) high*
$450-550   **WW**

An Edwardian novelty silver pig and cart pincushion, by Cohen and Charles, with mother-of-pearl bowl, Birmingham.
1905   *5.5in (14.2cm) long*
$400-550   **WW**

An Edwardian silver novelty rabbit pincushion, by H. Matthews, Birmingham, date letter worn.
2¾in (6.8cm) long
$600-650   **WW**

An Edwardian novelty silver fox pincushion, maker's mark worn, Birmingham.
1905   *2½in (6.3cm) long*
$550-650   **WW**

An Edwardian novelty silver camel pincushion, by Adie and Lovekin Limited, Birmingham.
1906   *2.5in (6.5cm) high*
$450-550   **WW**

An Edwardian novelty silver elephant pincushion, by Adie and Lovekin, Birmingham.
1906   *2¾in (6.8cm) long*
$260-330   **WW**

An Edwardian novelty silver turtle pincushion, by Saunders and Shepherd, Birmingham.
1906   *2in (4.8cm) long*
$450-600   **WW**

An unusual novelty silver stag pincushion, by Adie and Lovekin, Birmingham, modeled in a standing position, on an oval base.
1911   *1½in (3.8cm) high*
$1,050-1,200   **WW**

An Edwardian novelty silver hedgehog pincushion, by Adie and Lovekin, Birmingham.
1906   *1¾in (4.4cm) long*
$550-650   **WW**

An Edwardian novelty silver frog pincushion, by Adie and Lovekin, Birmingham.
1907   *2¼in (5.6cm) long*
$450-600   **WW**

An Edwardian novelty silver rabbit pincushion, by Adie and Lovekin, Birmingham, with textured fur decoration and set with red eyes.

1907   *2¼in (5.8cm) long*

$600-650   **WW**

An Edwardian novelty silver pincushion, by H. V. Pithey and Co, Birmingham, modeled as a muzzled teddy bear, with movable arms and legs.

1908   *2½in (6cm) high*

$550-650   **WW**

An Edwardian novelty silver roller-skate pincushion, by Serle and Co., Birmingham.

1909   *2¾in (7cm) long*

$550-600   **WW**

A novelty silver cat pincushion, by W J Myatt & Co, with green glass eyes, Birmingham.

1911   *3in (7.8cm.) long*

$750-800   **WW**

An Edwardian novelty silver duck pincushion, by Crisford and Norris, with red glass eyes, Birmingham.

1922   *2in (5.5cm) long*

$400-450   **WW**

A silver mounted hat pincushion, by Tiffany & Co.

5¾in (14.5cm) diam

$160-240   **WHP**

An 18thC English gold bodkin case, with foliate strapwork on a mat ground.

2½in (6.7cm) high

$1,050-1,200   **WW**

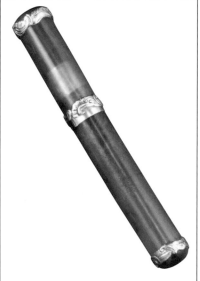

An 18thC gold-mounted agate bodkin holder, of cylindrical form, the detachable cover with scroll mounts.

3¼in (8cm) high

$800-900   **WW**

A mid-18thC English bodkin case, the taper-shaped oval bloodstone case with gold foliate-scroll cage work overall and with a posy on the rim "De mon amour gage" ("Of my love pledge"), diamond thumbpiece and the bloodstone base terminal engraved with an intaglio with a cupid within "tout pour vous" ("everything for you").

4in (9.8cm) high

$2,000-2,600   **WW**

ESSENTIAL REFERENCE—SAMPSON MORDAN

Sampson Mordan (1790–1843) was a British silversmith and a coinventor of the first patented mechanical pencil. He had been an apprentice of the inventor and locksmith Joseph Bramah, who patented the first elastic ink reservoir for a fountain pen.

● In 1822, Mordan and his coinventor John Isaac Hawkins filed the first patent in Great Britain for a metal pencil with an internal mechanism for propelling the graphite "lead" shaft forward during use.

● Mordan then entered into a business partnership with Gabriel Riddle, an established stationer. From 1823 to 1837, they manufactured and sold silver mechanical pencils with the marking "SMGR." After this Mordan continued to sell his silver pencils as S. Mordan & Co., adding many other types of silver and gold items to his product line. Mordan is well known for his whimsical pencils, as witnessed by many of the examples here. Upon Mordan's death in 1843, his sons Sampson and Augustus inherited the firm. S. Mordan & Co. continued to make silverware and brass postal scales until 1941, when their factory was destroyed by bombs during the London Blitz.

A Victorian novelty gold slide-action pencil, by S. Mordan, modeled as a pistol being held by a gauntleted hand and fist, with a registration lozenge.

1845   *1¾in (4.5cm) long*

$800-850   **WW**

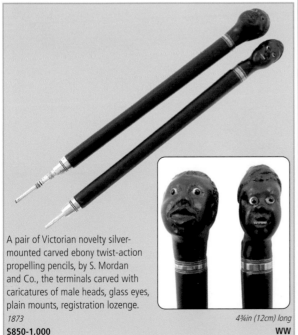

A pair of Victorian novelty silver-mounted carved ebony twist-action propelling pencils, by S. Mordan and Co., the terminals carved with caricatures of male heads, glass eyes, plain mounts, registration lozenge.

1873   *4¾in (12cm) long*

$850-1,000   **WW**

A Victorian gold traveling pen and pencil, by S. Mordan and Co., engine-turned decoration, the end pulls out and then reverses for use, screw-off terminal with a lead reservoir, with an F. Mordan gold nib, initialed.

ca. 1860   4¼in (10.8cm) long closed 0.6oz

$600-750   **WW**

A Victorian gold combination pen and pencil, by S. Mordan and Co., engine-turned decoration, the end with a screw-off cap, and twist-action pencil, the reverse twist operates the pen, marked with a design lozenge, the terminal initialed.

1869   3¼in (8.5cm) long closed 0.9oz

$600-750   **WW**

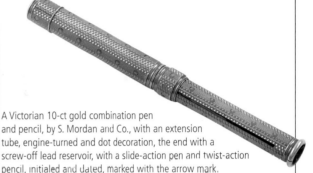

A Victorian 10-ct gold combination pen and pencil, by S. Mordan and Co., with an extension tube, engine-turned and dot decoration, the end with a screw-off lead reservoir, with a slide-action pen and twist-action pencil, initialed and dated, marked with the arrow mark.

ca. 1870   3¼in (8.6cm) long closed 0.6oz

$350-400   **WW**

A Victorian 10-ct gold-mounted hardstone dip pen, by S. Mordan, fluted mount with a slide-action operated nib holder, with a F. Mordan's 10/ gold nib.

ca. 1870   6¼in (16cm) long

$1,050-1,200   **WW**

A Victorian 10-ct gold combination pen and pencil, by S. Mordan and Co., with an extension tube, engine-turned and dot decoration, the end with a screw-off lead reservoir, with a slide-action pen and pencil, marked with the arrow mark.

ca. 1870   3in (7.6cm) long closed 0.7oz

$260-330   **WW**

A Victorian novelty silver cat propelling pencil, by S. Mordan and Co., the cat in a standing position, mechanism not working.

ca. 1880   2½in (6.5cm) long 0.4oz

$450-550   **WW**

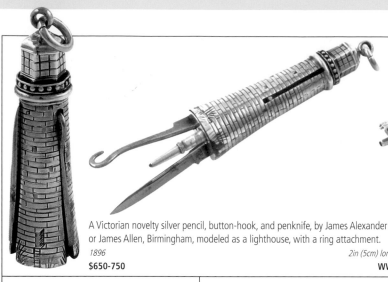

A Victorian novelty silver pencil, button-hook, and penknife, by James Alexander or James Allen, Birmingham, modeled as a lighthouse, with a ring attachment.

1896   *2in (5cm) long*

$650-750   **WW**

A Victorian novelty silver pencil, by Leuchars and Son, modeled as a shrimp, with a ring attachment, with a registration lozenge.

The KB Collection of Pencils.

1879   *2.5in (6.8cm) long*

$1,600-2,000   **WW**

A silver and enamel egg pencil, possibly Russian, also marked with a French import mark, modeled as an egg, with a ring attachment.

The KB Collection of Pencils.

(1.2cm) long

$400-550   **WW**

A Victorian novelty gold pencil, one end with a pencil, the other with a Bramah key, and with a four-sided seal with colored stone matrices, with a ring attachment, unmarked.

The KB Collection of Pencils.

(5.5cm) long

$350-450   **WW**

A Victorian novelty gold and enamel pencil, modeled as a cross, with blue and white enamel decoration, with a ring attachment, retailed by Jenner and Knewstub.

The KB Collection of Pencils.

ca. 1880   *(4.1cm) long*

$650-800   **WW**

A Victorian novelty gold and enamel slide-action pencil, modeled as a pistol, with two-color enamel decoration and engraved foliate scrolls, the end of the handle set with a citrine, with a ring attachment, unmarked.

2in (5cm) long

$350-400   **WW**

A Victorian novelty silver propelling pencil, modeled as a rowing boat, with dark blue enameled oars, with a rudder and a ring attachment, unmarked.

1½in (4cm) long

$600-650   **WW**

A 19thC French gold and enamel propelling pencil, marked on ring, enameled with a courting couple on a swing.

2¼in (5.5cm) long

$650-800   **WW**

ESSENTIAL REFERENCE—BLUE JOHN

Blue John, a rare and precious color-banded form of fluorspar, is mined in Castleton, Derbyshire. The mineral's unusual name is said to derive from the French "bleu jaune" which translates to "blue yellow," referring to its lustrous jewel tones. Another, more vernacular theory is that the term "Blue John" was used by miners to distinguish it from zinc ore, known as "Black Jack." Although prized for their rarity and decorative appeal, fluorspars, such as Blue John, have long been appreciated for their more functional qualities. The Roman poet Martial, writing toward the end of the 1stC AD, for example, claimed that wine tasted better when consumed from a "murrine" cup. "Murra" has been identified with fluorspar, and was introduced to the Romans by Pompey the Great after his expeditions in the East (possibly a variety found in Persia, present-day Iran) ca. 62 AD. Due to its fragility, fluorspar is often heated with a coating of (pine) resin to stabilize the crystals after the mineral is mined. This longstanding manufacturing process may have accounted for the added aroma referred to by Martial. The mineral was so popular in ancient Rome that, as naturalist and historian Pliny tells us, Emperor Nero himself apparently paid one million sesterces for a cup. Two Roman drinking vessels made of similar fluorspars are held in the collection of the British Museum (the Barber Cup and the Crawford Cup). The present urns date from a time when Blue John was at the height of its popularity, with makers, such as Matthew Boulton and Robert Adam, incorporating the fluorspar into their decadent works of art and society commissions.

A pair of late George III Blue John urns, in Neoclassical style, the ovoid bodies with domed integral covers and ball finials, on square-section slate bases, with minor marks, knocks, and scratches, the coloring of the purple banding being vibrant.

8½in (21.5cm) high

$20,000-26,000   DN

One of a pair of early-19thC Derbyshire Blue John urns, each with a turned finial, above an alabaster gadrooned body inlaid with Blue John fluting, on a bronze foot and an Ashford black marble plinth base.

9¼in (23.5cm) high

$15,000-21,000 the pair   WW

A late George III Blue John campana urn, the flared and part-lobed sectional body comprising two different veins of Blue John, on a stepped Derbyshire Ashford black marble base, with various chips on the everted rim, two sections of the slate base have been restored, possible repair to socle of vase.

The campana shape of the present urn harks back to Greek and Roman antiquities, which were fashionable ornaments in the late Georgian interior.

10in (25cm) high

$3,300-4,600   DN

A 19thC Derbyshire Blue John tazza, the U-shaped bowl on a turned stem and domed foot, the underside with the remains of a printed trade label "...ROYAL MUSEUM MATLOCK-BATH."

6¼in (16cm) high

$2,000-2,600   WW

An early-19thC Derbyshire Blue John urn, of campana shape, on an Ashford black marble plinth.

6¾in (16.9cm) high

$2,100-2,600   WW

A 19thC Derbyshire Blue John urn, of ovoid shape, with a button finial and on a stepped Ashford black marble plinth.

8in (20.2cm) high

$1,100-1,250   WW

A pair of 19thC French banded amethyst, quartz, and ormolu-mounted pot pourri urns and covers, each domed cover with a pierced guilloche rim cast with flower heads, descending to ovoid bodies festooned with fruiting vine and cast with twin-satyr mask handles, above a waisted socle and square-section plinth cast with imbricated laurel, with usual minor marks, knocks, and scuffs, the gilding is a little rubbed overall, one of the vases has a horizontal split.

With its striking colors and intricate figuring, amethyst quartz was used by the finest bronziers and furniture makers throughout the late 18thC and the 19thC. While the material was evidently used by important makers in England, these examples are more probable French in origin. Interestingly, the wreath finial and pierced rim adorned with flower heads share distinct similarities with Meissen shapes of the late 19thC.

14½in (37cm) high

$26,000-33,000   DN

A pair of early-19thC Regency bronze and Siena marble urns, the stepped-plinth bases with bronze collars.

13¾in (35cm) high

$1,100-1,250   **L&T**

A pair of 19thC Grand Tour bronze and Siena marble urns, of low campana form with foliate-cast handles, on square marble plinths and bases.

7¼in (18.5cm) high

$800-850   **L&T**

A pair of 19thC marble obelisks, each surmounted with a ball finial and raised on four small balls and a stepped base.

15¾in (40cm) high

$1,000-1,100   **CHEF**

A pair of late-19th/20thC black and white marble obelisks.

17¼in (43.5cm) high

$800-900   **CHEF**

A pair of 20thC amethyst quartz veneered and marble-mounted obelisks, the plinths inset with a marmo nero Belgio reserve on each side, with minor marks, scratches.

26¾in (68cm) high

$2,100-2,600   **DN**

A 19thC Italian Grand Tour giallo antico marble souvenir, in the form of the Temple of Vespasian, on a black marble base with a canted corner, general wear.

14½in (37cm) high

$5,300-6,600   **SWO**

A late Regency panorama, with a continuous hand-colored engraved view after Henry Alken "To Epsom, a Ludicrous Amusement consisting of Modern Costume, Characters, Equipages and Horsemanship," depicting a procession to the horse races, with various figures, horses, coaches, and carriages, within a drum case, with a turned lignum vitae lid and an ebonized handle, the printed sheet extends to 157½in (400cm) long.

4¼in (11cm) high

$800-900   **WW**

ESSENTIAL REFERENCE—DUNHILL

The Dunhill company was founded in 1893 by Alfred Dunhill, who, having taken over his father's saddlery, shifted focus to the production of luxury car accessories. However, in 1905, following the success of Dunhill's "Windshield Pipe" (a pipe designed to be smoked while driving or cycling), Dunhill refocused again on the tobacco industry, and its vintage smoking accessories—match safes and, especially, lighters—that remain particularly sought after today.

● During the 20thC, Dunhill produced lighters in many different designs and materials. Highly collectible examples include "Rollagas" types, with fluted ignition cylinders, in gold or silver, or embellished with shagreen or enamel panels. Their "novelty" lighters, such as the examples with inset watches, are also much in demand. However, it is their now-iconic "Aquarium" lighters that have become the most desirable.

● Introduced in the 1950s, "Aquarium" lighters featured clear Lucite side panels, hand-carved with reverse-intaglio and hand-painted aquatic imagery—never identical and of varying complexity—and the chief designers and engravers were Ben Shillingford, and Margaret and Allan Bennett.

● "Aquarium" lighters were produced in four descending sizes: "giant" (16oz; 450g); "half-giant"; "standard'; and "service." They were available with curved lift arms and bases in either gold-, silver-, or chrome plate, and they were fueled with gasoliine rather than butane (which didn't come into common usage until the 1960s).

● The well-documented list of prestigious users of "Aquarium" lighter included, most famously, the cigar-smoking Sir Winston Churchill, who permanently kept one on his desk at Chartwell, his country residence.

A British Jumbo lighter, by Dunhill, of alligator, shagreen, and silver plate, signed on underside "Dunhill Made in England Patent No. 390107" and to top "Dunhill."
ca. 1940   *4in (10cm) high*
$2,200-2,600   DRA

A 9ct-gold Rolls Royce lighter, with London hallmarks.
1931   *2¼in (5.5cm) high 1.6oz*
$26,000-33,000   WW

A Parker Beacon (Dunhill) electroplated watch lighter, the dial, with "Swiss made," inscribed "Beacon/Parker," base stamped "Licensed English Patent 143752/ Made in Switzerland/Lights in a Flash."

The Parker Beacon Company was established by Dunhill in 1928 as a subsidiary brand. Most of their lighters, as this one, were produced under their 143752 Unique Patent, manufactured by "La Nationale." They were never sold through Dunhill's Duke Street store, but promoted directly in France and north America.
2in (5.2cm) high
$260-400   WW

A Dunhill Aquarium table lighter, designed by Margaret Bennett, the Perspex panels reverse-painted with two exotic fish above a stone cave on one side, the other with a single fish swimming, cast marks.
4in (9.5cm) wide
$6,000-7,500   WW

A French table lighter with clock, by Cartier, of platinum finish and black lacquer, quartz movement, case signed "Cartier," No. 0210/1000, Swiss Made, maker's mark, this work is number 210 from the edition of 1,000, with fitted box and certificate.
ca. 2000   *4¼in (11cm) high*
$2,200-2,600   DRA

A French Jéroboam lighter, by S. T. Dupont, of brass and silver-plated brass, signed "S.T. Dupont Paris Made in France 12HAA78."
ca. 1975   *4in (10cm) high*
$2,600-3,300   DRA

ESSENTIAL REFERENCE—GARDNER PORCELAIN FACTORY

In ca. 1766, English banker Francis Gardner established a porcelain factory at Verbilki, near Moscow—the first privately owned porcelain factory in Russia. By the mid-1770s, the quality of its wares began to match those produced at the Imperial factory in St Petersburg to the extent that it began to receive numerous commissions from the Russian Imperial Court and the Russian nobility. Its most prestigious productions were the huge and magnificent services commissioned for royal banquets. Output of dinner (and tea) wares continued during the 19thC, and were augmented with well-modeled and brightly painted figures of tradesmen, craft workers, and diverse other Russian characters. After the Russian Revolution (1917-23), the factory was nationalized, renamed after the nearby town of Dmitrov, and during the Soviet era produced both mass-produced wares and individual pieces of high quality. Following the fall of Communism, the factory's original name, Gardner, was reinstated.

A Gardner porcelain figure of a street vodka seller, underglaze blue "G," the cover of barrel broken and reattached, thumb of right hand repaired.

ca. 1840-60   *9¾in (25cm) high*
$260-400   **M&K**

A mid-19thC Russian porcelain figure of a Sbiten vendor, Gardner factory, Moscow, blue "G" mark, some restoration.

7½in (19cm) high
$900-1,050   **WW**

A Russian porcelain figure of a peasant, Kornilov Factory, raised on a gilt C-scroll base, red painted factory mark.

ca. 1860   *7in (18cm) high*
$2,400-2,900   **BELL**

A mid-20thC Russian porcelain figure of an Inuit school girl, Lomonosov factory, iron-red factory mark.

7¾in (19.5cm) high
$150-180   **WW**

A Russian porcelain figure of a cobbler, Popov Factory, Moscow, mending a bast shoe, wearing a red-trimmed kosovorotka, blue Cyrillic mark, minor faults.

Bast shoes are made from bast—fiber taken from the bark of trees, such as linden. They are a kind of basket, woven and fitted to the shape of a foot. Bast shoes are an obsolete traditional footwear of the forest areas of Northern Europe. They were easy to manufacture, but not durable.

ca. 1850   *6in (15cm) high*
$600-750   **WW**

A rare Russian porcelain Natalina Danko figure of a female worker, with a pick and spade at her feet, possibly used as an inkwell, signed, some damage.

ca. 1920   *5in (12cm) high*
$70,000-90,000   **GYM**

A St Petersburg Imperial Porcelain Factory charger, from the Kremlin Service, red inventory number verso and Imperil cypher for Nicholas I (1825-55).

Fedor Solntsev (1801-92) was the main decorator of Kremlin interiors for Czar Nicholas I and was asked to study the vast collections, which culminated in a six volume work "Antiquities of the Russian State." The porcelain service commissioned from the Imperial porcelain works for the Kremlin Palace is based on drawings Solntsev made for this work, namely the cloisonné enamel and gold plates and dishes from the collections of the Kremlin Armoury, made for Czar Alexis (1645-76), father of Peter the Great.

ca. 1837-38   *13in (33cm) diam*
$5,300-6,600   **DN**

A Soviet porcelain plate, from the "Rose and Carnation" service, State Porcelain Manufactory, the center painted in black with a rose and carnation in a shallow bowl, after a design by S. Chekhonin, dated.

1922
$3,300-4,000   **BELL**

An early-19thC Russian silver snuffbox, Moscow, possibly by Jonas Berstron, the base chased with arms and a helmet, the cover with a silver-gilt relief of the bust of Alexander I, under glass.

1816   *2¼in (5.8cm) wide 1.9oz*

$550-650   **WW**

A 19thC Russian silver-gilt and niello-work toothpick box, Moscow, assay master V. Savinkov, maker possibly F. Verkhotsev, the hinged cover and base with checkered niello decoration, the cover with a plain shield cartouche.

1856   *2.5in (6.3cm) long 0.8oz*

$260-400   **WW**

A Russian silver cigarette box, modeled as a wooden cigar/cigarette box, with simulated wood effect, and with simulated paper labels and straps, inscribed, maker's mark possibly that of M. Ivanov, assay master unknown, St Petersburg.

1876   *5¼in (13.2cm) long 8.5oz*

$2,000-2,600   **WW**

ESSENTIAL REFERENCE—GENERAL LYUBOVISTKY

In 1905, General Julian V. Lyubovitsky retired from the army to become a member of the State Council of Imperial Russia, the upper house to the State Duma following the October Manifesto. It is most probable that this figure was given to him in that year to mark the culmination of an immensely successful military career and, therefore, serves as a key insight into the figures behind the Russian Imperial political structure in the critical years before 1917. He was responsible for much of the peacetime training of the Imperial army and probably played an important role in the selection of the Mosin-Nagant, featured prominently in this figure, as the standard Russian service rifle. Lyubovitsky completed his education at the 2nd Cadet Corps on June 10, 1855, in time to serve in the Crimean war of 1853-56. By 1881, following the Russo-Turkish War of 1877-78 and having risen rapidly through the ranks to Major General, Lyubovitsky was highly decorated with the Order of St. Anne, 1st class, the Order of St. George, 3rd and 4th class, the Order of St. Vladimir, 2nd and 3rd class and the Order of St. Stanislas, 1st class. Promoted to General of the Infantry in 1899, he was awarded the Order of St. Alexander Nevsky in 1902 at the age of 66.

A Russian silver presentation equestrian figure, Grachev, St Petersburg, 84 standard, cast as a cavalry soldier with drawn saber and Mosin-Nagant rifle slung from his shoulder, on a stepped marble plinth, applied with two plaques engraved in Cyrillic, the first "To the Commander of the 9th Battalion/The General of the Infantry/Julius Viktorovich/Lyubovitsky/9th Cavalry Division," the second with a list of senior officers.

1899-1908   *16½in (42cm) high*

$18,000-24,000   **ROS**

A Russian silver and guilloche enamel bonbonnière, with gold and cabochon sapphire thumb piece, the cover with a portrait medallion of Catherine II, with inscription "Her Imperial Highness Catherine II, Empress of All Russias" in Cyrillic, marked beneath "K. Faberge" workmaster's mark "AR," imperial warrant, kokoshnik mark 88.

1899-1908   *2¾in (7.1cm) diam*

$8,000-9,000   **NA**

A 19thC Russian silver and niello-work snuffbox, decorated with palatial-style buildings, the sides with a geometric pattern, an unknown maker's mark stamped inside, with the Moscow assay mark.

3in (7.5cm) wide 2.8oz

$400-550   **DAWS**

A Russian silver eyeglasses case, by Fabergé, workmaster's mark of Henrik Wigstrom, St Petersburg, the sprung-hinged cover with a cabochon sapphire thumbpiece.

1908-17   *4½in (11.5cm) long 3oz*

$3,300-4,000   **WW**

A pair of 19thC Russian cast-silver stirrup cups, by Samuel Arndt, St Petersburg, modeled as a fox with a front paw raised and a dog with paws raised, one with a French import mark.

ca. 1860   *3in (7.5cm) high 9.3oz*

$10,000-11,000   **WW**

ESSENTIAL REFERENCE—FABERGÉ

Fabergé was founded in St Petersburg, Russia, in 1842 by Gustav Fabergé, a goldsmith of French extraction. The company was later taken over by his two sons, Peter Carl and Agathon Fabergé.

- The House of Fabergé produced a wide range of innovative and outstandingly beautiful items, including cigarette cases, boxes, mantel clocks, picture frames, animal sculptures, flower carvings, and jewelry. It is best known, however, for its exquisite jeweled enamel Easter eggs.
- Carl Fabergé attracted the attention of Czar Alexander III in 1882 at the Pan-Russian Exhibition in Moscow, and from 1885 the House of Fabergé held the title of "Supplier to the Court of His Imperial Majesty."
- At the height of production, the House of Fabergé employed nearly 500 people, including talented designers and craftsmen, such as Michael Perchin, Henrik Wigstrom, Feodor Ruckert, and Erik Kollin.

- The House of Fabergé was forced to close in 1918, following the Russian Revolution.

A Fabergé nephrite, rock crystal, mother-of-pearl, and various-color gold miniature model of a sedan chair, marked with the "Kokoshnik" and "56" on one foot and workmaster's initials "M.N "for Mikhail Perchin, St Petersburg, on another foot, scratched inventory number "5885" on base, with import marks for "George Stockwell, London, 1928" on one gold side panel below window.

ca. 1899-1903   *3in (7.8cm) high*

$650,000-800,000   **COTS**

A 19thC spinach green nephrite jade desk seal, possibly Russian, in the form of a boot, the matrix engraved with a sea monster.

3in (7.5cm) high

$450-600   **WW**

A late-19thC Russian black lacquer papier-mâché tea caddy, by Vishniakov, painted with peasant figures sitting at a table drinking and playing music.

5½in (14cm) wide

$260-400   **WW**

A Russian bronze group of a peddler with his pack horse, by Evgeny Lanceray (1848-86), cast by Chopin, the naturalistic base signed in Cyrillic "E. Nahcepe," with foundry mark and the date "1875."

7in (18cm) long

$6,000-6,600   **WW**

A Russian bronze group of an Aleutian, by Vasilii Grachev (1831-1905), the base signed in Cyrillic "LBP Grachev" and with foundry mark "Fabr C.F. Woerffel."

6½in (16.7cm) high

$6,000-6,600   **WW**

A cloisonné enamel pot, possibly Russian, decorated with floral and foliate motifs, marked "84" in interior alongside a further possible maker's mark "AK."

1½in (4cm) diam 1.1oz

$450-550   **FELL**

A Russian cloisonné-enameled tea strainer, the border decorated with floral and foliate motifs, detailed.

84½in (12cm) long 1.8oz

$600-650   **BELL**

ESSENTIAL REFERENCE—RUSSIAN ICONS

Often, albeit not always, small in size, the religious paintings known as "icons" began to appear in Russia following its conversion to Orthodox Christianity in AD 988. Typically painted on wood, or cloth on wood, invested with elaborate religious symbolism, and hung or stood in both churches and domestic abodes, they were for more than 600 years almost exclusively styled on the models established by Byzantine art that emanated from the city of Constantinople. However, in the mid-17thC, following a schism in the Russian Orthodox Church, an alternative stylistic approach emerged: while subject matter—notably the Virgin Mary, Jesus, and numerous saints—remained the same, on the one hand, the "Old Believers" maintained the highly stylized imagery of traditional icons, and, on the other, under the new State Church, a fusion of Russian stylization and Western European realism developed, similar to contemporary Catholic religious art, and has essentially endured to this day.

A pair of silver-gilt and enamel wedding icons of the Mother of God and Christ Pantocrator, frames enriched with champlevé and cloisonné scrolling foliate motifs, maker's mark Cyrillic "IR," St Petersburg, stamped with anchors for St Petersburg, 84 standard.

1896   6¼in (15.8cm) high

$15,000-18,000   SWO

A 19thC Russian icon of the Kazan Mother of God, in a metal oklad with applied halos.

12¼in (31cm) high

$550-650   L&T

A late-19th/early-20thC Russian icon of Saint John the Baptist and the Saints, identified as Saint Euphrosynus of Pskov, Saint Sophia of Rome, Saint Thecla, Saint John of Rilsk, the daughters of Saint Sophia, Saint Liubov, Saint Vera, Saint Nadezhda, Saint Anna, Saint Elizabeth, Saint Kosmas, Saint Damian, Saint Michael, Saint Theodore, Saint Mitrophan of Voronezh, Saint Zachariah, Saint John, and Saint Nicholas the Wonder Worker, tempera on board, with gilded and tooled gesso ground.

18in (45cm) wide

$16,000-21,000   ROS

A parcel-gilt and cloisonné enamel icon of Christ Pantocrator, red velvet on the reverse, maker's mark Cyrillic "E. Tch," possibly Moscow, 84 standard, slight damage.

1899-1908   9in (22.5cm) high

$2,600-4,000   SWO

A miniature silver-gilt icon of Saint Andrew of Crete, his silver-gilt vestments repoussé and chased with geometric motifs, red velvet on the reverse and suspension loop, marked "Morozov" with the Imperial Warrant, maker's Cyrillic initials "IG," St Petersburg, 84 standard.

1908-17   3½in (9.2cm) high

$2,600-4,000   SWO

A parcel-gilt, silver and jeweled icon of Christ Pantocrator, the oklad with trailing foliate motifs on borders further enriched at the corners with cabochon red stones, modern red textile on the reverse, maker's mark Cyrillic "S Zh," Moscow, 84 standard.

1908-17   12¼in (31.4cm) high

$46,000-53,000   SWO

GLASS

A heavy baluster glass, with a bell bowl, on a baluster stem with cushion knop enclosing a large tear above a folded conical foot.

ca. 1710   *6½in (16.5cm) high*

$1,600-2,100   **WW**

A baluster wine glass, the funnel bowl on a baluster stem with cushion knop on a folded foot.

ca. 1715   *5¼in (13.4cm) high*

$2,600-3,300   **WW**

A rare baluster wine glass, with rounded funnel bowl, on a baluster stem with half knop over a cushion and angular knop, raised on an unusual terraced foot, a small foot-rim chip.

ca. 1725   *6in (15cm) high*

$3,300-4,000   **WW**

A small baluster wine glass, the rounded funnel bowl on a slender baluster stem with centered knop.

ca. 1740   *5½in (14.2cm) high*

$800-850   **WW**

A balustroid wine glass, on a stem with inverted baluster knop at the base, enclosing a long tear and with annulated knop at the base of the bowl, on a folded conical foot.

ca. 1740   *6¾in (17cm) high*

$850-1,000   **WW**

A wine glass, the base of the bell bowl enclosing a large tear, on a thick plain stem above a folded foot.

ca. 1740   *6¼in (16cm) high*

$400-450   **WW**

A balustroid wine glass, the bell bowl raised on a plain stem with a beaded swelling knop above a folded foot.

ca. 1740   *6½in (16.4cm) high*

$550-650   **WW**

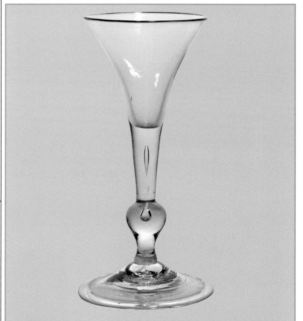

A balustroid wine glass, of "Kit Kat" or "Kit-cat" type, the drawn trumpet bowl on a plain stem enclosing a long tear above an inverted baluster knop above a folded foot.

The Kit-cat Club was composed of a group of influential men pledged to uphold the "Glorious Revolution" of 1688 and the Protestant succession. Founded by Somers, the Lord Chancellor and the publisher Tonson, the club began meeting in Christopher Cat's tavern near Temple Bar, and took its name from his mutton pies known as Kit-cats. The association of the term "Kit-cat" with a particular form of glass comes from a painting done by Sir Godfrey Kneller as part of a set he did in the 1697 to 1721 period. The painting showed six members of the club gathered around a table, enjoying their wine from glasses of the form discussed here.

ca. 1740   *6¼in (15.7cm) high*

$1,050-1,200   **WW**

A mid-18thC Newcastle light baluster glass, with a bell bowl on a slender baluster stem with a teared ball knop above.

6¾in (17.2cm) high

$850-1,000 WW

A privateer wine glass, on an opaque twist stem and conical foot, the bucket bowl engraved with a ship and the words "Success to the Dreadnought Privateer," the stem repaired with a metal sheath.

The "Dreadnought" was a Bristol ship granted a letter of marque on March 22, 1757, to its four owners: John Harbord, Jonah Thomas, Samuel Thomas, and William Wasbrough. A diary written by the ship's unnamed surgeon on a four-month cruise under the captaincy of James Leisman is in the Bristol Archives after it was donated by an American family in 2013. The diary discusses life with a crew of 120 men and details the capture of a French ship called "Lyon," which was traveling from Domingo to Bordeaux.

ca. 1757

$4,600-5,300

6¼in (15.5cm) high

WW

A wine glass, the ogee bowl raised on an opaque-twist stem, with centered knop above a conical foot.

ca. 1760 *6in (15cm) high*

$260-400 WW

A colored-twist wine glass, with a bell bowl raised on a stem enclosing blue, red, green, and white threads, a 2mm chip on the edge of the foot.

ca. 1760 *6½in (16.2cm) high.*

$2,400-2,900 WW

A wine glass, with a rounded funnel bowl engraved with a band of flowers, on a dense airtwist stem, above a high domed foot.

ca. 1760 *6¼in (16cm) high*

$550-650 WW

A wine glass, the ogee bowl molded with a honeycomb design on the base, raised on a double-series airtwist stem.

ca. 1760-65 *6in (15cm) high*

$400-550 WW

An enameled wine glass, possibly by Anthony Taylor, the funnel bowl enameled in white and yellow with Masonic symbols, on a double-series opaque-twist stem on a conical foot.

See Simon Cottle, "The Other Beilbys: British Enameled Glass of the Eighteenth Century," Apollo, October 1986, pp. 315-327 for a discussion of this style of decoration and the work of Anthony Taylor in Newcastle-upon-Tyne.

ca. 1765 *6in (15.2cm) high*

$2,100-2,600 WW

A Beilby wine glass, the bell bowl enameled in white with fruiting grapevine, raised on a double-series opaque-twist stem above a conical foot.

ca. 1770 *6¾in (17cm) high*

$4,600-5,900 WW

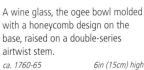

A pan-topped wine glass, engraved with a band of honeysuckle and other flowers, on a double-series airtwist stem, a small chip on the foot.

ca. 1760 *8in (20.6cm) high*

$400-550 WW

GLASS

CLOSER LOOK—FAÇON DE VENISE GOBLET

The wide, shallow bowl is molded with vertical fluting, and its exterior diamond-point engraved with repeated floral stems.

Birdlike wings flank the stem in clear and turquoise glass, the latter configured in C-scroll shapes also derived from Classical antiquity via the Renaissance.

The hollow stem is of baluster shape, and additionally knopped columnar form developed during the Renaissance.

Echoing the leaf decoration on the bowl, the foot is diamond-point engraved around its circumference with a foliate band.

A 17th/18thC Venetian or Dutch "façon de Venise" winged goblet.

5in (12.8cm) high

$16,000-21,000 **WW**

A plain stemmed goblet, of drawn-trumpet form, the plain stem with large tear inclusion and on a folded conical foot.

ca. 1740 *10in (25cm) high*

$850-1,000 **DN**

A Dutch-engraved light baluster goblet, on a baluster stem enclosing large tears around a centered disk knop above a folded helmet foot, the funnel bowl engraved with a ship at sail flying a flag bearing the lion of the country of Holland, inscribed "T Welvaren Vant Vaderlant" ("Prosperity to the Father Land").

ca. 1745-50 *8¾in (22cm) high*

$8,500-10,000 **WW**

A Dutch-engraved "Newcastle" type-goblet, the funnel bowl engraved with a drinking scene entitled "Absente Vrinde," on a stem with annular and other knops on a plain conical foot.

Illustrated: W. A. Thorpe, "A History of English and Irish Glass, pl. CI, 3."

ca. 1750 *7¼in (18.6cm) high*

$5,300-5,900 **WW**

A wine glass or goblet, with a rounded funnel bowl raised on a knopped dense airtwist stem, above a folded helmet foot.

ca. 1760 *7¼in (18.5cm) high*

$600-650 **WW**

A Dutch-engraved light baluster goblet, the funnel bowl engraved with two ships at sail, flying long pennants, inscribed "De Nobele Zeevaart" ("The Noble Shipping"), raised on a "Newcastle"-type baluster stem with a beaded knop above a conical foot, a section of the rim broken and reattached.

ca. 1765 *8¾in (22.2cm) high*

$650-800 **WW**

A Bohemian glass goblet, the bowl engraved with a fox hunt, on a faceted baluster stem, the octagonal foot engraved with "den 20: ten October 1845."

1845 *8½in (21.5cm) high*

$550-650 **WW**

A mid-18thC German pale amethyst-tint facet-stemmed goblet and a cover, possibly Saxon or Thuringian, the funnel bowl with faceted lower section, on a multi-knopped faceted stem and a domed foot.

19¾in (50cm) high

$1,300-1,700 **DN**

A "dwarf" ale glass, the drawn trumpet bowl with spiral molding, on a spiral stem on a folded conical foot.

ca. 1740   *5½in (13.8cm) high*

$1,250-1,450   **WW**

A rare armorial ale glass, the ogee bowl enameled with a coat of arms and ears of barley, on a double-series opaque-twist stem on a conical foot, a tiny chip on the foot.

ca. 1760   *7¼in (18.3cm) high*

$6,500-8,000   **WW**

An ale glass, of possible Jacobite significance, on an opaque-twist stem above a conical foot, the round funnel bowl engraved with a daffodil and "Mrs A Gof."

ca. 1760   *7¼in (18.5cm) high*

$3,300-4,000   **WW**

An ale glass, the round funnel bowl gilded in the atelier of James Giles with ears of barley and two insects, on a double-series opaque-twist stem.

ca. 1765-70   *7½in (18.8cm) high*

$2,600-4,000   **WW**

A "ratafia" glass, the drawn bowl with a band of vertical molded flutes, on a double-series opaque-twist stem on a conical foot.

ca. 1755-60   *7½in (19.3cm) high*

$850-1,000   **WW**

A "ratafia" glass, with a drawn trumpet bowl engraved with flowers, on a plain stem on a folded foot.

ca. 1750-60   *7¼in (18.6cm) high*

$600-650   **WW**

ESSENTIAL REFERENCE—BEILBY GLASS

One of five siblings—four brothers and a sister—William Beilby was born in 1740 in Durham, and subsequently sent in his teens by his father to apprentice in enameling and drawing in Birmingham. After the failure of his father's goldsmith and jewelry business, the whole family moved in 1757 to Newcastle-upon-Tyne, where there was an already thriving glass industry. After initially working as enamelers for local glassmakers, William and his sister Mary (who William had taught to paint in enamels at their family workshop), and initially under the commercial guidance of brother Ralph, an engraver by training, began to work in their own right.

Working on plain glass vessels purchased from local glasshouses, they became increasingly known for their heraldic decoration (especially coats of arms and crests), which was usually commissioned and often, due to the aspirations and vanity of some clients, fictitious rather than authentically heraldic! Other notable subject matter, again mostly commissioned, was commemorations of particular events, such as the launching of ships or the elections of lord mayors, and picturesque landscapes were also produced. Stylistically, their decoration can be collectively described as highly individual and a distinctive English interpretation of the then-prevailing and flamboyant Rococo style.

Although sister Mary is known to have had a stroke in 1774, William continued working until 1778, by which time fashions in glassware had moved on from the curvaceous Rococo to the more austere and rectilinear Neoclassical style. Having given up their workshop, left Newcastle, and retired to Fife, in Scotland, Mary died in 1797 and William in 1819.

A Beilby ale glass, the funnel bowl enameled with hops and barley, on a double-series opaque-twist stem on a conical foot, traces of gilding on the rim.

ca. 1765   *7in (17.8cm) high*

$8,000-9,000   **WW**

GLASS

A heavy dram glass, raised on a thick firing foot, the bowl engraved "Beef and Liberty."

A number of Beefsteak Clubs were established in the first half of the 18thC, the most notable (and enduring) being the "Sublime Society of Beef Steaks" in 1735 by John Rich, then manager of the Theatre Royal, Covent Garden. Meetings were held every Saturday between November and June, at which all members were required to wear the club's uniform, including buttons inscribed "Beef and Liberty." Steaks were served with onions and potatoes; the only second course offered was toasted cheese.

ca. 1750
$3,300-4,000   WW

ESSENTIAL REFERENCE—DRAM GLASSES

In terms of their shape or form, dram glasses in most respects are to other drinking glasses similar to the difference in fine art between portrait miniatures and life-size or even larger portraits—they are simply smaller versions. You will therefore encounter similar variations in bowl and stem shapes as you will on their larger counterparts, albeit the stems on drams are, in addition to being shorter, generally plainer, and you will also encounter similar forms of decoration, such as engraving or enameling.

Essentially intended to serve liquor in suitably small measure (given the strength of the alcohol), their collective name is derived from an apothecaries' unit of mass or volume that has its origins in Classical Greco-Roman times, and, by the 18thC, equated to around 1/8th of a fluid ounce (3.5ml)—a measurement that has varied both then and subsequently in time and place, and one that has become most strongly associated with whiskey (hence the Scottish-in-origin phrase "a wee dram of whisky").

It is also worth noting that you will sometimes encounter the description "dram or firing glass." Strictly speaking, the latter refers to ceremonial liquor glasses of dramlike size that, after a group toast has been raised and drunk, are slammed in unison on the table, producing a sound reminiscent of a volley of muskets, hence not only the name "firing," but also the modern-day equivalent: the stem- and footless "shot" glass.

A small wine or dram glass, with a drawn-trumpet bowl on a thick airtwist stem.

ca. 1750-60   *4¼in (10.5cm) high*
$450-550   WW

A rare Beilby firing glass, the bowl enameled with flowers, on a double series opaque-twist stem on a thick stepped foot, the foot broken and reattached.

ca. 1765   *4in (10.2cm) high*
$1,300-1,700   WW

A firing or dram glass, with a funnel bowl on a double-series opaque-twist stem on a thick foot.

ca. 1760   *4in (10cm) high*
$450-550   WW

An enameled dram or firing glass, possibly by Anthony Taylor, enameled with Masonic symbols in white edged in red, raised on a plain stem above a terraced foot.

ca. 1770   *3¼in (8.7cm) high*
$2,000-2,600   WW

A commemorative glass beaker, engraved with a ship at sail and inscribed "Every Man did his Duty" and "HMS Royal Sovereign," the reverse with "Cape Trafalgar 1805."

HMS "Royal Sovereign" was launched in 1786 and was part of Admiral Howe's fleet on the Glorious First of June. Under the command of Admiral Collingwood, she led the second column of ships at the Battle of Trafalgar while Nelson's column led the other. When news reached Collingwood of Nelson's death, he took charge of the fleet but had to transfer to HMS "Euryalus" due to the damage suffered on the "Royal Sovereign."

1805   *4½in (11.3cm) high*
$2,000-2,600   WW

A cordial glass, on a plain stem on a domed foot, the funnel bowl engraved with a sunflower.

ca. 1740-50   *6¾in (17cm) high*
$1,050-1,200   WW

A rare waisted beaker or dram glass, enameled with Masonic symbols and a foliate border.

Illustrated: "Apollo" magazine, October 1986, Simon Cottle, "The Other Beilbys: British Enamelled Glass of the 18th Century," p. 323, fig. 17.Cf. James Rush, "The Ingenious Beilbys," p. 113, fig.65 for a similar glass in the Corning Museum.

A Beilby tumbler or beaker, enameled in white with two exotic birds above foliage and a balustrade.

ca. 1765   *4in (10cm) high*

$10,000-11,000   **WW**

ca. 1765   *3in (7.9cm) high*

$11,000-13,000   **WW**

A rare Beilby beaker or tumbler, enameled with an insect and auricula about the inscription "And the Coal Trade."

ca. 1765   *3¾in (9.6cm) high*

$17,000-21,000   **WW**

A green glass tumbler or beaker, gilded in the atelier of James Giles with an exotic bird in a landscape.

ca. 1765   *3¾in (9.5cm) high*

$4,000-5,300   **WW**

A glass rummer or tumbler, engraved with "Glorious Memory of Duke William."

ca. 1770   *3¼in (8.7cm) high*

$850-1,000   **WW**

A tall "coin" tankard, engraved with hops and barley around the initials "JJ," the hollow stem enclosing a coin dated 1787, on a domed and folded foot.

ca. 1790   *8in (20.6cm) high*

$1,500-1,800   **WW**

An unusual Venetian glass loving cup or puzzle glass, probably 19thC, the deep bowl with a centered spiral straw rising to two mouthpieces formed as horses, on a short stem with crimped knop above a folded foot.

12in (30.5cm) high

$450-600   **WW**

An English wine bottle, of shaft-and-globe type, with shallow kick-in base, the surface degraded.

ca. 1660-70   *8in (20.5cm) high*
$2,100-2,600   **WW**

An English glass wine bottle, of squat-mallet form, signs of degradation.

ca. 1720   *6¾in (17cm) high*
$400-550   **WW**

A sealed onion bottle, recovered from the wreck of the Dutch East Indiaman "Hollandia," wrecked 1743, cork in-situ and retaining original contents, with good iridescence.

     7in (18cm) high
$2,200-2,600   **CM**

A sealed wine bottle, the squat-mallet form with string rim and kick-in base, with a seal inscribed "R Shutt 1810."

1810   *9¾in (24.7cm) high*
$1,600-2,100   **WW**

A Jacobite decanter and stopper, engraved with a rose and trailing foliage, the opposing side with a fanciful bird.

11¾in (30cm) high
$600-750   **CHEF**

A magnum Beer decanter and stopper, engraved on one side with a bottle ticket suspended from a chain and labeled "Beer" encircled with hops, the reverse with two birds, the faceted stopper engraved.

ca. 1765   *13½in (34.2cm) high*
$3,300-4,000   **WW**

A pair of glass decanters and stoppers, engraved with a band of stars between narrow borders with polished ovals.

ca. 1790   *11½in (29.5cm) high*
$1,300-1,700   **WW**

A green glass decanter and stopper, the mallet form decorated with a gilt label inscribed "Shrub."

ca. 1800   *9½in (24cm) high*
$650-800   **WW**

A pair of 19thC ships decanters and stoppers, the ribbed necks above hobnail-cut bands, one with an associated stopper.

9in (23cm) high
$350-400   **CHEF**

A glass taperstick, with inverted pedestal stem above a panel molded foot.

ca. 1750   *5in (12.8cm) high*

$800-850   **WW**

A George III pedestal glass candlestick, the candle nozzle on a wrythen support and fluted tapering stem.

8¾in (22cm) high

$800-850   **CHEF**

A large 15th/16thC "façon de Venise" footed bowl, molded on the underside of the bowl with 12 ribs, trailed with two bands of blue glass to the exterior rim, raised on a ribbed spreading foot applied with a ring of pinkish glass.

10¼in (26cm) diam

$8,500-10,000   **WW**

A late-16th/17thC "façon de Venise" tazza, the bowl with molded ribs and everted rim, set on a hollow inverted-baluster stem.

6¼in (16.1cm) high

$1,300-1,700   **WW**

A pair of Bristol "Non-such" blue glass rinsers, decorated probably by Isaac Jacobs, with elaborate gilt borders.

ca. 1805   *4¼in (11cm) high*

$1,050-1,200   **WW**

A 19thC "Bristol" blue glass bowl.

8¾in (22cm) diam

$850-1,000   **SWO**

A Swiss stained and leaded glass figural panel, the centered panel dated 1607, depicting three Landsknechte, inside a probably later arrangement of circular sections with two further stained roundels, later fitted to a stained wood light-box frame.

While Swiss mercenary guards were a popular theme for Wappenscheibe (armorial panels), the arrangement of three figures is unusual. The compositional arrangement of guards on a geometrically demarcated podium, and the handling of the sprawling landscape in subtle yellow tones in the upper reserve, show distinct similarities to late-16thC and early-17thC panels from the Bern region of Switzerland.

ca. 1607   *36¾in (93cm) high*

$1,600-2,100   **DN**

Judith Picks

Glass is a fragile medium, and the delicate, almost birdlike form of this "façon de Venise" carafe makes it appear even more so, which only adds to my naive but ever-undiminished sense of wonderment that a glass vessel made for use as long ago as the second half of the 16thC has somehow survived in one piece up to now. Well, thank goodness for that, because this really is a special carafe. Not only is it rare, its also a particularly refined form further enhanced by its opulent rich blue, imperial purple, and gilt decoration. With the latter depicting, in addition to lion masks, double-headed eagles—symbols of the then Austrian-centered Holy Roman Empire—it really is a most regal and desirable object, which does much to explain not only why it was subsequently owned by the Rothschild family during the 19thC and 20thC, but also its not inconsiderable value today.

An Italian "façon de Venise" carafe or ewer, the body with cold-painted gilt and wash-enamel decoration, including double-headed eagles and other mythical scaly creatures, on a conical foot beneath another gilt knop.

ca. 1560-90   *8in (20.3cm) high*

$26,000-33,000   **WW**

GLASS

A Baccarat spaced paperweight, set with six rings of canes around a centered similar ring.

ca. 1850   *2¾in (7cm) diam*

$260-330   **WW**

A Baccarat flower paperweight, set with a primrose, edged with 11 leaves.

ca. 1850   *3in (7.3cm) diam*

$550-650   **WW**

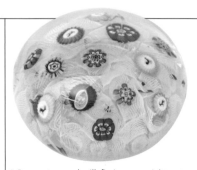

A Baccarat spaced millefiori paperweight, set with 13 canes, including a stag, dog, goat, and cockerel, signed.

1848   *2½in (6.3cm) diam*

$850-1,000   **WW**

A Baccarat spaced millefiori paperweight, with 13 canes, including Gridel silhouette canes of a stag, dog, horse, monkey, and cockerel, signed.

1848   *2¼in (5.5cm) diam*

$1,300-1,700   **WW**

A Clichy swirl paperweight, set with spiraling canes around a centered pastry-mold cane.

ca. 1850   *2½in (6.5cm) diam*

$350-400   **WW**

A large Clichy spaced paperweight, set with colorful canes, including two Clichy roses.

ca. 1850   *3in (7.5cm) diam*

$850-1,000   **WW**

A 19thC Richardson millefiori paperweight.

                              3¼in (8.5cm) diam

$210-260   **WW**

A St. Louis fruit paperweight, set with a pear, two apples, and three cherries on a latticino ground.

ca. 1850   *2½in (6cm) diam*

$550-600   **WW**

A St. Louis fruit paperweight, enclosing a spray of pears and cherries on a white latticino ground, including date and signature cane.

1953   *3in (7.5cm) diam*

$400-450   **WW**

A lampworked and polished clear glass paperweight, by Paul Stankard, USA, features squash and squash blossom, murrine artist's initial on edge "S."

ca. 1990   *3¼in (8cm) diam*

$1,500-1,800   **DRA**

A 19thC Russian glass millefiori paperweight.

                              3in (7.5cm) diam

$240-290   **WW**

ESSENTIAL REFERENCE - CANDLESTICKS

Candles—the word is derived from the Latin "candere," meaning "to shine"—provided an essential source of artificial lighting for thousands of years. The devices used to safely secure candles while burning—candlesticks—have ranged from the purely functional to the highly decorative, and it is the aesthetically pleasing aspects of both the latter and of candlelight that does much to explain why candles are still often used today, despite being technologically superseded from the late 19thC by the advent of electricity and the electric lightbulb.

- Most antique domestic candlesticks found today were made from the 18thC onward; many made prior to that have not survived, being melted down for either money (silver) or munitions (brass).
- The simplest forms comprise a base (wood or metal) with a spike (metal, often iron) on top of which is pushed the base of the candle. Mostly, but not exclusively confined to ecclesiastical use, they are known as "pricket" candlesticks.
- The vast majority of candlesticks, however, secure the candle in a nozzle, socket, or cup (also known as a "sconce"), which sits on top of a columnar stem; to catch molten wax, a circular drip pan either flares out from the rim of the nozzle or is located beneath it (and as such is sometimes referred to as a "bobeche").
- Rising from a broader geometric-shaped base, the columnar stem is often augmented at intervals with one or more decorative, protruding circular rings known as "knops."
- While sometimes made singularly, and sometimes in sets of four or more, most candlesticks were made in pairs.

A pair of 18thC bronze candlesticks, each on triform knopped stems and scroll feet.

13in (33cm) high

$200-260   CHEF

A pair of Regency patinated and gilt-bronze candlesticks, raised on dolphin stems, with the usual minor marks, knocks, and scuffs.

ca. 1815   *7¼in (18.5cm) high*

$1,300-1,700   DN

An 18thC/19thC pair of Italian gilt and painted terra-cotta angel candlesticks, in Renaissance-revival style, each with a halo and holding a chalice, probably Venetian.

21¼in (54cm) high

$3,300-4,600   WW

A pair of early-19thC French patinated and gilt-bronze figural twin-light candelabra, each with a cherub holding an urn, issuing scrolling leaves hung with beads, on a marble socle applied with a cartouche, on a rosso antico base.

18in (45.5cm) high

$1,600-2,000   WW

A pair of early-19thC French Empire gilt-bronze candelabra, with three outscrolling arms, molded with masks and on slender columns.

18¾in (47.5cm) high

$1,300-1,800   L&T

A pair of early-19thC Regency Siena marble and bronze candelabra, of patinated and gilt bronze, with single stiff sconces, four scrolling arms, and slender columns, on scrolled triform bases.

22¾in (58cm) high

$2,000-2,600   L&T

A pair of early-19thC French Charles X patinated and gilt-bronze candelabra, with centered nozzles and three further nozzles on leaf-scroll arms, on plain tapering columns raised on scroll-foliate supports and tripartite bases.

20¼in (51.5cm) high

$750-850   L&T

A pair of French "Empire" patinated and gilt-bronze candelabra, each with a winged figure of Victory, standing on a sphere, supporting a basket of fruit and flowers, plinth bases, decorated with a dancing cherub and stamped twice "J T."

ca. 1830-40   *22¾in (58.2cm) high*

$2,600-4,000   WW

A pair of George IV brass candlesticks, after a design by Rundell, Bridge and Rundell, each with a leaf-decorated socket above a triform base modeled with three swans, numbered "2" and "3," later drilled for electricity.

6¾in (17.1cm) high

$1,000-1,100 WW

A pair of Empire luster candlesticks, on three-leg supports, the drip tray hung with prismatic drops.

13in (33cm) high

$1,100-1,250 CHOR

A pair of 19thC malachite and gilt-bronze candlesticks, the gilt sconces above baluster columns, raised on hexagonal domed feet.

12½in (32cm) high

$1,300-1,800 L&T

Two pairs of mid-19thC French pricket candlesticks, with reeded columns, triform bases, and paw feet.

22¾in (58cm) and 25¼in (64cm) high

$600-750 SWO

A pair of 19thC French patinated and gilt-bronze candelabra, each with a centered candle sconce with an eagle finial insert and three further candle sconces, above tapered reeded columns with chain-draped elephant masks and lily-cast bases on tripod lion paw supports and plinths.

19in (48.5cm) high

$550-800 L&T

A pair of 19thC French bronze and ormolu figural candelabra, the three arms supported on flying Sphinx masks held by figures of Apollo and a female companion, bases cast with Classical figures in relief on white marble bases.

24½in (62cm) high

$1,250-1,450 CHEF

A pair of 19thC French gilt-bronze and marble candlesticks, with foliate sconces amid flowers in a marble urn supported by three cockerels, raised on circular plinth bases with bun feet.

13½in (34cm) high

$650-800 CHEF

A pair of 19thC American mirrored tin candle sconces, with scratches on reflective surface underneath glass.

10in (25.5cm) high

$1,050-1,200 POOK

A pair of late-19thC Samson Derby-style porcelain and gilt-bronze figural candelabra, modeled as a musician and companion in 18thC dress accompanied by dogs and sheep, set in gilt-bronze bases issuing branches with three candle nozzles, underglaze blue marks.

18¼in (46.5cm) high

$850-1,000 L&T

A small 18thC Dutch brass chandelier, with a centered knopped baluster stem issuing seven scrolled candle arms with urn candle nozzles and drip trays.

15¾in (40cm) high

$800-900   **L&T**

A French Restauration patinated and gilt-bronze eight-light chandelier, the corona decorated with palmettes above a laurel leaf band, the underside with a cone pendant.

51in (130cm) high

$2,600-4,000   **WW**

One of a pair of late-19thC French Rococo-style gilt-bronze eight-light chandeliers, each ornately worked with scrolling foliage and two putti, probably refinished, some arms loose.

56in (142cm) high

$3,300-4,000 the pair   **SWO**

A 19thC folk art red-painted tole chandelier, possibly French, with six scroll arms and a spinning top-shape stem.

26¾in (68cm) high

$850-1,000   **WW**

One of a pair of early-20thC silvered-brass eight-light "Knole" chandeliers, the turned stem decorated with cherub masks and strapwork, with scroll branches and a cone pendant, possibly by Lenygon & Co.

23in (57.8cm) high

$8,000-9,000 the pair   **WW**

An early-20thC French Louis XVI-style gilt-bronze 2-tier, 16-light chandelier, with cast stylized foliate decoration, scrolled arms, and a pineapple terminal.

41in (104cm) high

$850-1,000   **SWO**

An early-20thC French gilt-bronze six-light chandelier, in Rococo taste, with swirling acanthus branches issuing around a centered inverted baluster stem cast with flower heads and further foliage.

31¼in (79cm) high

$2,600-4,000   **DN**

An early-19thC Empire alabaster and patinated, gilt-bronze mounted pendant ceiling light, later refitted, the body surmounted by a gallery cast with anthemia and lion-mask mounts, suspended from foliate cast chains and rising to a conforming corona, with acanthus-carved terminal.

37in (94cm) high

$2,200-2,600   **DN**

A 20thC Murano chandelier, having eight lights on scrolled arms, colored glass flowers and leaves.

48in (122cm) high

$4,600-5,300   **SWO**

A Murano glass chandelier, clear glass with blue highlights, the eight arms interspersed with scrolling brackets, three shades reattached.

35½in (90cm) high

$1,050-1,200   **SWO**

LIGHTING

A late-19th/early-20thC pair of French verdigris-patinated copper and glazed hanging lanterns, the tops cast with castellated galleries and descending to circlets cast with anthemia, minor marks, knocks, and scuffs.

33in (84cm) high

$5,300-6,600 DN

A pair of mid-19thC copper and iron lanterns, with tapered glazed sides and pointed finials, mounted on cast-iron arm supports.

49¼in (125cm) high

$1,200-1,600 L&T

A George III-style green glass hanging lantern, the metal suspension band with mythical beast finials, surface wear on glass.

16¼in (41cm) high

$350-400 SWO

A 19thC Spanish iron lantern, the six lights within an ornate frame with gilt-painted, stylized foliage, "leaves" missing on one upright.

65in (165cm) high

$1,700-2,400 SWO

An early-19thC Regency iron hall lantern, with glazed sides and a foliate- and flower-cast corona.

20½in (52cm) high

$1,300-2,000 L&T

A 19thC American punched tin carry lantern, glass panes replaced.

14in (35.5cm) high

$260-330 POOK

A late Victorian bronze hall lantern, with a verdigris finish, with reeded supports applied with leaves and scrolls, with pierced-fret decoration and bearded satyr masks, with bevelled etched glass panels.

37in (94cm) high

$1,300-1,800 WW

A Victorian Hinks patent brass lantern, with a lobed ventilator and pierced detail, now converted to electricity, inscribed "Patented 1858 & 1860 James Hinks Birmingham," with tarnish and wear, glass replaced, alteration, general wear.

23¾in (60cm) high

$400-450 SWO

A pair of late-19thC brass and glass girandole oil wall lights, attributed to F. Osler, each with an original cut-glass shade and reservoir fitted with a Messengers No. 2 patent fitting, and on a pierced scrolling brass support and velvet-framed mirrored back.

24½in (62cm) high

$1,700-2,100 SWO

A pair of 19C silver-plated carriage lamps, with engraved and pierced decoration, the internal candle holder stamped "J. Knape, Estd. 1851, Burnley."

ca. 1870-80 *29in (73.5cm) high*

$7,500-8,500 WW

A pair of 19thC patinated and gilt-bronze hurricane lamps, modeled as Atlas carrying the lanterns upon his shoulders.

24½in (62cm) high

$2,000-2,600 CHEF

A Regency bronze Argand lamp, in the manner of Thomas Messenger, in the form of a Classical lidded urn with a wild boar terminal.

8in (21.7cm) high

$1,000-1,100 WW

A pair of George IV bronze table lamps, the stems decorated with acanthus leaves and flaming torches, above further bands of lappets and a triform base with three eagles, lion's paw feet and scrolling leaves and palmettes, possibly originally candelabra bases, later fitted with three lights and with shades.

ca. 1825   *26½in (67.5cm) high*
$11,000-13,000   **WW**

A cut-glass oil lamp, with an etched glass floral shade.

29½in (75cm) high
$350-400   **WHP**

A pair of Regency patinated and gilt-bronze lamps, converted from candlesticks.

ca. 1820   *12½in (32cm) high*
$1,300-2,000   **L&T**

A late-19thC Aesthetic Movement French faience and gilt-bronze-mounted table lamp, by Joseph-Theodore Deck, in Orientaliste taste and in typical Persian blue color, with "THD" monogram on the body, the base of the mount inscribed "GAGNEAU 115 RUE LAFAYETTE CI DEVANT R.D'ENGIEN/12842," metal areas with wear, probably gilded overall, although it has largely worn off the top mount.

There was clearly a relationship between Deck and the firm of Gagneau, because many examples of Deck pieces with mounts by Gagneau have appeared.

19¼in (49cm) high
$2,200-2,600   **DN**

A pair of early-19thC Regency bronze and ormolu candlestick lamps, in the form of fluted columns surmounted with urns, the ormolu with acanthus leaf, scroll and foliate designs.

15½in (39.5cm) high
$1,300-2,000   **L&T**

A pair of 19thC French patinated and gilt-bronze moderator lamps, mounted with lion's masks and lion monopodia, converted to electricity.

17¼in (44cm) high
$2,000-2,600   **L&T**

A pair of 19thC French patinated and gilt-bronze table lamps, in Louis XVI style, with dolphin handles and laurel leaf decoration.

19in (48.1cm) high
$5,300-5,900   **WW**

A 19thC Cornish red serpentine table lamp.

20in (51cm) high
$800-900   **L&T**

A pair of 19thC French cobalt-glazed porcelain and gilt-bronze mounted lamps, with twin swan-neck handles and foliate swags.

21in (53cm) high
$900-1,050   **L&T**

A pair of late-19thC Scandinavian gilt-bronze, cobalt glass and marble urns, with twin snake and acanthus handles on cobalt bodies.

18¼in (46cm) high
$6,000-7,500   **L&T**

ESSENTIAL REFERENCE—GEORGIAN JEWELRY

- In terms of Georgian jewelry history, the period spanned from 1714 to 1830, encompassing the reign of George I, George II, George III, and George IV. There were many stylistic changes taking place throughout the Georgian period. The early Georgian era encompassed the Baroque style, which featured intricate designs and symmetry. Despite being delicate, these designs were still bold and large in contrast to the Rococo style that followed. Rococo jewelry was more curvaceous and asymmetrical, yet still had many motifs in common with the Baroque style, such as bows, flowers, ribbons, and leaves.

- During both of these stylistic periods, the historical site of Pompeii was being excavated (ca. 1740), which resulted in a surge of Classical Roman imagery, such as laurels, grapevines, leaves, and keys with an emphasis on geometric, more rectilinear designs. This style is usually referred to as "Neoclassical."

- Another factor that contributed to this Neoclassical style was the fact that Napoleon had been at war in Egypt. This lead to the popularity of Egyptian motifs, such as pyramids and papyrus leaves, on Georgian jewelry.

- For the privileged, this period saw an increase in evening pursuits, because improvements in the manufacture of candles gave rise to brighter lighting. Balls of magnificent proportions were the perfect time to parade precious gems. Women often wore pearls, garnets, moss agate, or colored gems or paste in daytime. The most formal evening events, courts, balls, and receptions were the only appropriate times to wear precious jewelry. Consequently, diamonds found new favor. Mines opened in Golconda, India, and Brazil began to produce stones in the 1720s, resulting in diamonds becoming more readily available.

A Portuguese or Iberian emerald and diamond stomacher brooch, with silver petals rub set with rose-cut diamonds on a gold crimped edge, with detachable swags at each side, a detachable pendant below an oval frame and giardinetti articulated pendant center, all set with emeralds and diamonds, tested as 18ct gold and silver, replacement "C" catch, tarnish on reverse.

A stomacher, sometimes called a "devant de corsage," is a piece of jewelry worn on the center panel of the bodice of a dress. In the 18th and 19thC, stomachers became conspicuous, impressive pieces of jewelry to be worn with formal court gowns.

ca. 1750-80   6¼in (15.6cm) long
$8,000-9,000   SWO

A 18ct-gold garnet-set star brooch/pendant, possibly French, with a foil-backed Dutch rose-cut garnets, dome-back settings with a concealed hook-style bale, replacement revolver clasp, modern brooch fitting, with a case by "Garrard & Co. Ltd., 1123 Regent Street, W1."

ca. 1800   1¾in (4.6cm) wide 0.49oz
$2,000-2,600   SWO

A late Georgian diamond-set flower brooch/pendant, with an old European-cut diamond in a cut-down collet at the center, surrounded by old Swiss-cut diamonds, all in silver cut-down collets, a curved and textured gold stem, set in silver and backed in gold, with a fold-down hinged bale and detachable brooch fitting, tested as silver backed in 14-15ct gold.

1½in (3.5cm) high 0.2oz
$2,000-2,600   SWO

A Georgian foiled topaz and split-pearl brooch, with a later brooch fitting, tested as 9ct gold, a very small chip on the tip of one kite facet.

¾in (2cm) wide 0.1oz
$550-650   SWO

An early-19thC amethyst and seed-pearl brooch, in a yellow gold openwork foliate mount highlighted with small amethysts, one missing.

1½in (3.5cm) wide
$260-400   WW

A pair of George III rose-cut diamond pendeloque earrings, suspending detachable rose-cut diamond drops within a diamond-set laurel border in silver.

1¾in (4.3cm) high
$17,000-21,000   WW

A pair of 18ct-gold Catalan foiled hessonite garnet earrings, Roman set with a cushion-shaped garnet, hand engraved fleur-de-lis decoration, a trefoil of garnets, Roman set with garnets and a detachable pear-shaped boss below, with a detachable trefoil of garnets below, hinged Continental fittings, some gemstones deficient, tarnished.

ca. 1800   5¼in (13.2cm) long 1.4oz
$6,000-6,600   SWO

A George III diamond-set memorial ring, the stylized urn set with rose-cut diamonds on blue glass ground, within a border of old cushion-shaped diamonds in silver and gold.

Size T 1/2
$6,000-6,600   WW

ESSENTIAL REFERENCE—NATHANIEL MARCHANT

Antiquary, collector, dealer, painter, and draftsman, Nathaniel Marchant (1739-1816) was, above all of these, one of the greatest of English gem engravers.

- **A multiple prize winner of Society of Arts competitions in intaglio engraving in the early-1760s, he left for Rome in 1772 to study at first hand the fine and decorative arts of Classical Antiquity.**
- **Notable positions held on his return from Rome to London included: "Sculptor of Gems" to the Prince of Wales (1789); "Associate of the Royal Academy" (1791); "Engraver at the Mint" (1797); "Chief Engraver to His Majesty" (1799); and "Engraver at the Stamp Office" (1800).**
- **Much of his most important work was documented in his "Catalogue of One Hundred Impressions from Gems engraved by Nathanial Marchant," published in 1792. Many included were copied from Antiquity, while others were portraits of contemporaries or adaptations of well-known paintings.**

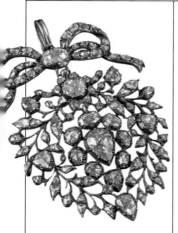

An agate and gold cameo ring, by Nathaniel Marchant, of a Classical female bust, signed "MARCHANT," unlike many Marchant pieces, which are signed in mirror writing, this cameo ring is signed in block capitals.

¾in (2cm) wide

$70,000-80,000   **TEN**

A late-Renaissance ruby and pearl necklace, with table-cut rubies and with black and white enamel decoration, with a portrait miniature of a saint and pearl drops, the seed-pearl necklace set with table-cut rubies and blue enamel decoration.

ca. 1680   *19in (48cm) long*

$7,500-8,500   **WW**

An 18thC enameled portrait miniature necklace, earrings, and pair of clasps, cased suite, the necklace with a series of hand-painted portrait miniatures, with foiled rubies, emeralds, and quartz, later case, surface marks on the enamel, two replacement gem-set links toward the back of the necklace, later scrolls and chain.

Pendant drop 2¾in (7cm)

$11,000-12,000   **SWO**

A Georgian 9ct-gold and paste-set glazed locket, with a lock of hair in the compartment, with a border of old Swiss-cut paste, in silver-cut down collets, some wear.

1½in (3.6cm) high 0.25oz

$600-750   **SWO**

A Georgian 9ct-gold heart-shaped split-pearl glazed locket, with a giardinetti surmount, with a sulfide figure of a lady, damage on the nacre of one split pearl.

Locket 1in (2.3cm) high 0.13oz

$1,000-1,100   **SWO**

A late Georgian gilt-metal cameo ring, with hand-carved lava cameos and one coral cameo, all rub set on plain rubover flat-backed collets, surface wear.

Finger size K

$450-600   **SWO**

A George III diamond-set pendant, with a diamond-set bow, with rose-cut diamonds.

2¼in (5.5cm) high

$8,000-9,000   **WW**

A George III garnet-set gold necklace and earrings, the necklace suspending an articulated garnet-set cross pendant, the earrings set with garnets.

Necklace 14½in (36.5cm) long

$7,500-8,500   **WW**

A Georgian foil-backed, flat-cut garnet eternity-style ring, one garnet deficient, tested 6-8ct gold, some deterioration to the foil.

Finger size P ¼in (0.5cm) wide

$1,600-2,000   **SWO**

CLOSER LOOK—NEOCLASSICAL PENDANT

A variant of the silica mineral chalcedony, carnelian is a semiprecious gemstone employed in or as jewelry since the Early Neolithic period. Of reddish hue—ranging from a pale pinkish orange to a deep rusty brown—it has traditionally symbolized strength, passion, love, and desire.

The smaller figure, accompanied by two attendants, is Cupid disguised as Ascanius—in Greek mythology the son of Trojan prince Aeneas and Creusa, daughter of King Priam. He's depicted presenting gifts to a sitting Dido (also with an attendant) and first queen of the Phoenician city-state of Carthage.

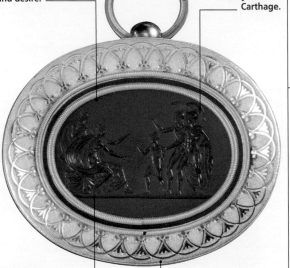

Although engraving in intaglio strictly translates as cutting a design into and beneath a surface, in relation to gemstones it also describes carving designs in relief—in other words, proud of the surface, as here.

The gold pendant frame, by Luigi Mascaelli (1804-1825), features highly stylized floral motifs—bellflowers—set within interlaced loops of arcading, and surrounding inner borders with twin rows of corn kernellike beading.

An early-19thC gold frame pendant with carnelian intaglio depicting figures from Classical Antiquity, believed to have been from the collection of Prince Stanislas Poniatowski.

2¼in (5.5cm) wide

$13,000-16,000   **WW**

A Regency acrostic gold brooch pendant, designed as a quiver of arrows and set with a ruby, emerald, garnet, amethyst, ruby, and diamond spelling "REGARD," with engraved decoration.

1½in (3.8cm) long

$2,000-2,600   **WW**

A Regency brooch, the flower heads, thistles, and leaves in three-color gold, in a Harvey & Gore case.

2¼in (5.6cm) wide

$1,600-2,000   **WW**

A Regency gold brooch, designed as a butterfly sitting on a heart, set with a pear-shaped topaz and turquoise in gold, glazed locket compartment on the reverse containing braided hair, hinged brooch pin.

1in (2.7cm) high

$2,100-2,600   **WW**

A Regency gold bracelet, the clasp set with pink topazes and a green stone within gold filigree surround.

6½in (16.5cm) long 1.1oz

$2,600-3,300   **WW**

A pair of Regency gold cannetille emerald and pink topaz bracelets, some damage, in original leather-covered case.

1820   *7¼in (18.5cm) long 2.3oz*

$6,500-8,000   **DN**

A pair of Regency carved coral pendant earring drops, dot-textured gold caps with cannetille flower head and eyelet tops, one petal bent, fittings deficient.

2¼in (5.3cm) long 0.18oz

$550-650   **SWO**

An early-19thC seed-pearl choker necklace.

13¾in (35cm) long

$2,100-2,600   **WW**

A Victorian citrine and seed-pearl brooch, in yellow gold.

1½in (4cm) wide

$650-800 **WW**

A 19thC carved amethyst cameo brooch, with bust of a woman, with pierced gold frame with black enamel border, with fitted case.

1¾in (4.5cm) high

$1,500-2,000 **WW**

A Victorian coral and diamond brooch, set with coral cabochons within stylized ivy leaves and a border of old cushion-shaped diamonds in silver and gold, with fitted case.

3¼in (8cm) wide

$1,500-2,000 **WW**

A Victorian ruby and diamond brooch, in silver and gold, detachable brooch fitting on reverse.

1½in (3.8cm) high

$1,700-2,100 **WW**

A Victorian dragonfly brooch, the body formed from a cabochon emerald and kite-shaped rubies with diamond and ruby wings and ruby cabochon eyes in silver and gold.

2¾in (7cm) wide

$3,300-4,000 **WW**

A Victorian cherub brooch, the carved moonstone head set above rose-cut diamond wings in silver on gold.

1½in (3.5cm) wide

$2,200-2,600 **WW**

A 19thC rose-cut diamond brooch, designed as a snowflake and set overall with graduated rose-cut diamonds, settings in silver on gold.

1½in (4cm) wide

$2,000-2,600 **WW**

A Victorian 9ct-gold, amethyst, and citrine pansy brooch, light surface marks on the gemstones, tarnish in areas.

1¼in (3.2cm) wide 0.2oz

$400-450 **SWO**

A Victorian 9ct-gold gem-set fly or insect brooch, with a demantoid garnet-set thorax and bouton-shaped pearl abdomen, the wings grain set with old eight-cut diamonds and rub-set diamond eyes, case by "R.S. Rowell, 115 High St. Oxford."

1¼in (3.3cm) long 0.08oz

$400-550 **SWO**

A mid-19thC lozenge brooch, with a gray button pearl within a border of diamond fleur-de-lis, emeralds, and a further border of diamonds quartered with rubies in yellow gold, suspending pearl and diamond drops, in a Harvey & Gore case.

1¾in (4.7cm) high

$6,000-7,500 **WW**

A Victorian 18ct-gold, aquamarine and garnet knot brooch, with gilt-metal pin and "C" catch.

1¼in (3.5cm) wide 0.1oz

$210-260 **SWO**

A Victorian Archaeological Revival gold and enamel brooch, an applied ram in the center, with Etruscan-style applied wire and bead decoration, original "C" catch.

ca. 1860   1¼in (3.3cm) diam 0.4oz

$1,000-1,100 **SWO**

A Victorian Etruscan Revival 15ct-gold and diamond dumbbell bar brooch, with an old European-cut diamond, with a bloomed ground and outer row of beads, with metal pin.

ca. 1870   2in (5.2cm) wide 0.2oz

$450-600 **SWO**

A Victorian bee brooch, the wings set with rose-cut diamonds and coral beads, the body set with tiger's eyes, seed-pearl eyes, on a gold bar brooch with a tiger's-eye terminal.

2¼in (5.7cm) wide

$450-550 **WW**

A 19thC gold brooch of openwork design and centered with a seed pearl, with gold pellet "millefiori" decoration.

1½in (3.8cm) wide 0.3oz

$400-550 **WW**

A Victorian brooch/pendant, set with graduated old cushion-shaped diamonds in silver on gold, with folding pendant loop.

1½in (3.7cm) high

$8,500-9,000 **WW**

A Victorian heart brooch, centered with rose-cut diamonds within a surround of blue and white enamel decoration, with outer border set with rose-cut diamonds in silver on gold.

1in (2.6cm) high

$1,050-1,200 **WW**

An enamel, moonstone, and diamond brooch, by Carlo Giuliano, of stylized peacock tail design, with enamel decoration, with cabochon moonstone "eyes" and rose-cut diamonds in gold, maker's mark "CG," with a case by Wartski.

Carlo Giuliano (1831–95) was a goldsmith and jeweler operating in London from 1860. He started work in Naples for Alessandro Castellani and was sent to London to establish a branch of the Casa Castellani. He left Castellani's employment in the early-1860s and, in turn, worked for Robert Phillips, Harry Emanuel, Hunt & Roskell, and Hancocks & Co, all leading London jewelers. In 1875, he set out on his own, starting a retail outlet at 115 Piccadilly, and specializing in Renaissance-style design.

ca. 1885   2½in (6.2cm) wide

$6,000-6,600 **WW**

A 19thC Indian Pertabgarh yellow metal brooch, depicting a male figure, his attendant, a peacock, goat, and dog in vivid green enamel, within a filigree border.

1¾in (4.3cm) wide 0.5oz

$400-550   WHP

A late-19thC gold brooch, centered with blister pearls within a border of 12 emeralds and with surround of rose-cut diamonds and seed-pearls.

2¼in (5.5cm) wide

$600-750   WW

A late-Victorian brooch, the cushion-shaped aquamarine set within a border of seed pearls in yellow gold, in a Harvey & Gore case.

2¼in (5.3cm) wide

$6,500-8,000   WW

A late-Victorian bee brooch, pavé set with old circular-cut diamonds, with seven graduated oval-shaped rubies to the body, in silver and gold.

1½in (3.8cm) wide

$8,000-9,000   WW

A late-19thC ruby and diamond square brooch, with a pair of loops set with caliber-cut rubies in silver and gold.

1¼in (3.3cm) wide

$3,300-4,000   WW

A Victorian India star, later mounted as a brooch, with a cushion-cut diamond, with four split pearls at the compass points, each ray grain set with old Swiss-cut diamonds, with a pearl, peg set at each end, 9ct gold, with a case by "Bengie, 61 High Street, Cowes."

1½in (3.6cm) wide 0.2oz

$650-800   SWO

A late-Victorian 15ct-gold bar brooch, with a centered cushion-cut diamond, claw set at a border of cushion-shaped old Swiss-cut and old eight-cut diamonds, one small eight-cut diamond replacement.

1½in (4.2cm) wide 0.17oz

$750-850   SWO

A late-Victorian 18ct-gold brooch, with an outer row of graduated circular mixed-cut rubies, claw set at a scalloped bezel, with an interior row of graduated rose-cut and old Swiss-cut diamonds, in silver and backed in gold, with a detachable brooch fitting, with a case, damaged, by "Le Roy et Fils, to The Queen, 57 New Bond Street, London."

1½in (3.7cm) diam 0.3oz

$2,600-3,300   SWO

A Victorian 18ct-gold brooch, with a mixed-cut amethyst, a Rococo scrolling lozenge-shaped frame with clamshells at the compass points and flower heads on a textured ground, tarnish on the front.

ca. 1840   1½in (3.8cm) wide 0.3oz

$260-400   SWO

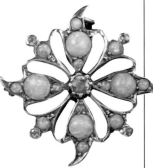

A late-Victorian gold brooch, set with cabochon opals and circular-cut green garnets in gold.

1in (2.5cm) wide 0.1oz

$400-550   WW

JEWELRY

CLOSER LOOK—VICTORIAN NECKLACE

The looped-ribbon centerpiece, the heart-shaped pendant drop, and sections of the chain are decorated with guilloché enameling, a technique in which a metal ground with a mechanically engraved (engine-turned) repeat geometric design is covered with a translucent enamel—here, royal blue in color and with contrasting solid white enamel borders—that allows for the underlying pattern to subtly shimmer through.

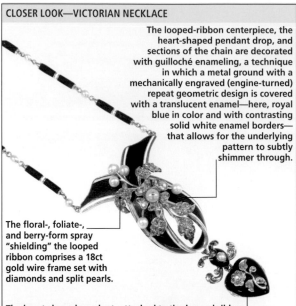

The floral-, foliate-, and berry-form spray "shielding" the looped ribbon comprises a 18ct gold wire frame set with diamonds and split pearls.

The heart-shaped pendant, attached to the looped ribbon via a small pearl-set, guilloché-enameled shield with gold, scrolling acanthus leaf "wings," is, in fact, a detachable locket, intended to house a keepsake, such as a lock of hair of a loved one.

A Victorian enamel, gold, pearl, and diamond-set necklace with pendant drop.

Centerpiece: 3in (7.5cm) long.

$3,300-4,600 SWO

A Victorian 18ct-gold fringe necklace, with smoky quartz, topaz, opal, emerald, sapphire, ruby, and turquoise, claw set in a fluted collet with a mixed-cut white sapphire, a fringe of three seed pearls below each gemstone, on a seed pearl necklace, clasp 15ct gold.

ca. 1890 *14½in (37cm) long 1oz*

$2,200-2,600 SWO

A Victorian fringe necklace, the gold necklace suspending graduated floral seed-pearl clusters in silver and gold, with case.

15½in (39cm) long

$1,000-1,100 WW

A 19thC Austro-Hungarian Egyptian Revival gold brooch/pendant, by Carl Bacher, the eagle with a carved cabochon sapphire set with diamonds in the form of a scarab, with blue and white enamel, with a fine-link gold chain and enamel lotus bale and a seed-pearl set, fine-link gold necklace, signed "CB" on reverse and control mark.

necklace 15¾in (40cm) long

$7,500-8,500 WW

A 19thC collar necklace, with openwork and scrolling links, with applied foliate decoration and set with oval and cushion-shaped rubies and emeralds in gold.

13¾in (35cm) long 3.7oz

$3,300-4,000 WW

A Victorian 9ct-gold pendant, with an oval cabochon garnet, rub set at a twisted wire border, glazed locket verso.

pendant ¾in (1.8cm) high 0.1oz

$550-650 SWO

A late-Victorian silver, backed in 18ct-gold necklace, milligrain set with graduated old-cut diamonds, a cushion-cut green tourmaline, with blade edge bars set with seed pearls, a pink tourmaline and diamond pendant drop below, set with a pink tourmaline on plain back chain.

ca. 1890 *2in (5.2cm) long 0.2oz*

$1,050-1,200 SWO

A late-Victorian 9ct-gold necklace, grain set and rub- et with split pearls, a detachable star pendant drop.

ca. 1900 *16¼in (41.5cm) long 0.5oz*

$850-1,000 SWO

A late-Victorian18ct-gold necklace, with a carved emerald pippin pendant drop and emerald beads, strung on gold wire, between pairs of graduated semi-baroque pearls, a larger carved emerald bead pendant in the center.

17¾in (45cm) long 1oz

$3,300-4,600 SWO

ESSENTIAL REFERENCE—19THC EGYPTIAN REVIVAL

Western civilization has had an enduring fascination with the architecture, art, and ornament of ancient Egypt—one that began during the Classical Roman era of Julius Caesar and Anthony and Cleopatra, and has enjoyed a number of significant revivals since, notably during the late 18thC and early 19thC.

- A revival of interest in Egyptian artifacts had been gradually gathering a head of steam during the course of the 18thC, largely fueled by archaeological excavations of Roman sites, but it wasn't until after Napoleon's military campaigns against the British in Egypt itself that the impact on Western decorative arts began to be truly felt.

- The French Emperor was accompanied by many artists and writers to document his enterprise for posterity. Numerous accounts were subsequently produced, but the most influential of these was Baron Denon's "Voyage dans la Basse et Haute-Egypte." Published in 1802, its illustrations resulted in classic Egyptian motifs, such as sphinx heads, crocodiles, palms and palmettes, lotus, scarabs, and hieroglyphics—collectively known as "Egyptiennerie"—appearing in architecture, furnishings, and other decorative artifacts, notably jewelry, throughout much of Europe during the early 19thC.

- The English navy under Admiral Nelson's annihilation of the French fleet at the Battle of the Nile in 1798 gave a notable "patriotic" impetus to "Egyptian style" in Great Britain.

- While the fashion for Egyptian imagery began to wane around 1830, it was to enjoy an even greater revival—"Tutmania"—just under a century later, following the discovery in 1922 of Tutankhamen's tomb.

A 19thC Egyptian Revival gold pendant, designed as lotus flowers with polychrome enamel, suspending five lapis-lazuli beads, centered with two lapis-lazuli beads, case by Fred Leighton.

3in (7.5cm) high

$4,600-5,300   **WW**

A 19thC amethyst-mounted cruciform pendant, with seed-pearl mounts in yellow gold.

2½in (6.5cm) high

$750-850   **WW**

A late-Victorian pendant/brooch, centered with an old cushion-shaped diamond weighing 1.20cts, with laurel motif set with old cushion-shaped diamonds, with diamond drop, with diamonds on the fleur-de-lis bale, in silver on gold.

2¾in (6.8cm) high

$8,000-9,000   **WW**

A Victorian garnet and seed-pearl cross pendant, in repoussé yellow gold mount.

4½in (11.5cm) high

$1,300-1,600   **WW**

A late-Victorian 18ct-gold cartouche-shaped brooch/pendant, with an old European-cut diamond, with a pair of smaller cushion-cut diamonds, grain set with graduated split pearls and two cushion-cut diamonds, an old European cut diamond claw set above.

ca. 1890   *2½in (6.2cm) long 0.3oz*

$1,050-1,200   **SWO**

A Victorian 9ct-gold fringe pendant/brooch, with a cabochon garnet, an outer row of plain beads, with a detachable reel-and-bale with repoussé decoration and a fold-down catch on the side, glazed locket verso with brooch pin and "C" catch.

ca. 1860   *4in (9.8cm) high 1oz*

$2,900-3,700   **SWO**

A Victorian Etruscan Revival 9ct-gold and turquoise set fringe pendant, a "V"-shaped bale and glazed locket verso.

ca. 1860   *2½in (6.1cm) high 0.2oz*

$650-800   **SWO**

A Victorian silver and 9ct-gold brooch/pendant, with an oval cabochon ruby, Dutch rose-cut diamonds and graduated rose-cut diamond-set leaves, with oval cabochon rubies, with later hinged yellow gold bale, marked "750," with a modern hinged bale.

1½in (4cm) high 0.17oz

$2,000-2,600   **SWO**

A Victorian brooch/pendant, the amethyst set within a surround of graduated old circular-cut diamonds and graduated seed pearls in silver on gold, with folding pendant loop.

1¼in (3cm) wide

$3,300-4,000 **WW**

A late-Victorian brooch/pendant, the cushion-shaped amethyst set with a surround of rose-cut diamonds, in silver and gold, in a Harvey & Gore case.

1½in (4cm) wide

$6,000-6,600 **WW**

A Victorian 15ct-gold bombé pendant, pavé set with turquoise cabochons.

1¼in (3.6cm) high 0.2oz

$600-750 **SWO**

A Victorian 15ct-gold locket, with a row of split pearls, glazed locket verso and "V" bale.

1½in (4.1cm) high 0.2oz

$750-850 **SWO**

A late-Victorian locket/pendant, the bloodstone applied with a diamond and pearl star within a border of graduated seed pearls, suspended from a bloodstone and seed-pearl bale in yellow gold.

2¼in (5.8cm) high

$1,600-2,000 **WW**

A Victorian gold locket/pendant, with a cross set with diamonds, seed pearls, and a ruby, with pellet decoration and suspended from a bow, glazed locket compartment on reverse.

2¼in (5.5cm) high

$1,300-1,800 **WW**

A Victorian 18ct-gold choker, with cabochon opals, with old European-cut white sapphires on each side, and cabochon opals on each end, each gemstone bar strung to a row of seed pearls between gold eyelets in a three-row, seed-pearl back chain, with an opal and white sapphire box clasp.

14in (35.5cm) long 1.6oz

$2,000-2,600 **SWO**

One of a pair of Victorian gold bracelets/necklaces, with a centered row of flat disks with a bead center and applied wire hoop, on a concealed box clasp, marked "15."

ca. 1870 *7¾in (19.5cm) 8¼in (21cm) long 16oz*

$2,600-4,000 the pair **SWO**

A Victorian 15ct-gold heart pendant, grain set with split pearls, with an open ribbon and bow bale, on a glazed locket verso.

1¼in (3.1cm) high 0.1oz

$1,050-1,200   SWO

A Victorian pendant, with an oval cabochon moonstone, grain set with rose-cut diamonds, a pearl drop below, and "V" bale, grain set with rose-cut diamonds, all set in silver, backed in gold, possibly Dutch import mark.

2½in (6.6cm) high 0.3oz

$1,300-1,800   SWO

A Victorian brooch/pendant, centered with a cushion-shaped diamond, with further diamonds at the strapwork mount, quartered with diamond-set foliate motifs in silver and gold.

1¾in (4.7cm) high

$6,000-6,600   WW

A late-Victorian 15ct-gold cushion-shaped hinged locket, with a glazed interior with frames, photograph, and a lock of hair, with a monogram and inscription on the front cover "Dear Rosalind" and verso "Not gone from memory, not gone from love, but gone to a father's home above, grant her o'lord thy perfect place."

$600-650

1¼in (3cm) high excluding bale 0.6oz

SWO

A Victorian gold Maltese cross pendant, set with a centered diamond-set star, with four further diamonds within pellet gold borders, with fitted case.

pendant 2½in (6.2cm) high

$3,300-4,000   WW

A Victorian 9ct-hinged locket of book form, with hand-engraved covers and spine, with a hinged lock to reveal four locket compartments, two with the original oval frames, glazing deficient, light surface wear at the corners and spine, some ripples on one photograph surround, areas of tarnish.

1in (2.4cm) high 0.4oz

$600-750   SWO

An early-19thC Italian 18ct-gold-cased circular hardstone cameo pendant, by Giuseppe Girometti, with a carved relief profile of a bacchante, a white agate profile with carved bloodstone vine leaves and grapes in her hair in a bloodstone ground, with a bloodstone verso depicting a relief four-petalld rose, with a matching textured bale, possibly Rome 1810, marks indistinct, cameo signed on the front lower right, "GIROMETTI," with a fitted case, unsigned, cameo dirty, the separate layers are natural and not bonded/composite.

Giuseppe Girometti (1780-1851) was a highly regarded gem engraver and sculptor at the Vatican, for popes Pius VII, Leo XII, and Gregory VI and the Papal Mint until about 1850. His son Pietro Girometti (1811-1959) followed in his father's footsteps to become an admired medal and cameo engraver.

2in (5cm) high 0.9oz

$26,000-33,000   SWO

An early-Victorian 15ct-gold three-stone foiled garnet and quartz ring, with a case by Parkhouse & Wyatt, Southampton.

Finger size K ½in 0.05oz

$260-400 **SWO**

A Victorian 18ct-gold turquoise and diamond oval cluster, later mounted as a ring, possibly a later under-bezel and shank.

Finger size K 0.1oz

$600-750 **SWO**

A late-Victorian 18ct-gold ring, with diamond-set shoulders, an oval mixed-cut ruby, with a border of cushion-cut and cushion-shaped old European-cut diamonds, plain underbezel with a cushion-cut diamond, ruby 2.

Finger size K-L 0.6oz

$6,000-6,600 **SWO**

A late-Victorian 18ct-gold ring, London, with a cabochon opal, an old Swiss-cut diamond.

1897 *Finger size M½ 0.1oz*

$400-450 **SWO**

A Victorian 18ct-gold ring, oval cabochon opals with pairs of old brilliant-cut diamonds, wear to claws, minor abrasions to opals.

1897 *Finger size L 0.1oz*

$850-1,000 **SWO**

A Victorian 18ct-gold ring, with old European-cut and old eight-cut diamonds, and cushion-cut rubies, surface marks on mount, the diamonds 0.20ct total.

1888 *Finger size V 0.2oz*

$600-750 **SWO**

A late-Victorian ring, with five emerald-cut rubies set in gold on the carved pierced shank.

Accompanied by report number 2203525737 dated August 28, 2019, from GIA, stating the rubies and are natural rubies with no indications of heat treatment. Origin: Burma (Myanmar.)

Finger size M

$33,000-40,000 **WW**

A Victorian cluster ring, the navette-shaped opal cabochon set within a surround of rose-cut diamonds in silver on gold.

Finger size Q

$1,050-1,200 **WW**

A 19thC-gold and enamel scarf ring, with a painted fox head, inscribed "IV Essex 1869" on verso.

1in (2.5cm) wide

$260-330 **DAWS**

A pair of 19thC Spanish Catalan 18ct-gold earrings, a cushion-shaped flat-cut garnet, plaque below set with flat-cut foiled garnets with a detachable pear-shaped pendant drop below, historic repairs on the reverse.

3½in (9cm) high 1.05oz

$3,300-4,000 **SWO**

A pair of early-Victorian 18ct-gold repoussé Rococo-style earrings, with blue and red paste, later hook fittings, marks possibly "B*S18," pinholes and a split to the centered plaque.

ca. 1840 *2½in (6.5cm) high 0.15oz*

$600-650 **SWO**

A pair of 19thC enamel and gem-set gold drop earrings, the enamels decorated with putti and with mother-of-pearl backing, with emeralds, garnets, and seed pearls in gold, shepherd's hook fittings, with case.

2¼in (5.8cm) high

$4,000-4,600 **WW**

A Victorian 9ct-gold Archaeological Revival Etruscan-style crossover hinged bangle, with a case by "H L Brown & Son, 65 Market Place, Sheffield and 90-90A Regent Street, London."
ca. 1870   *2¼in (5.6cm) wide 0.65oz*
$1,050-1,300   **SWO**

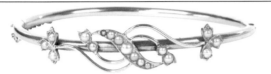

A Victorian 15ct-gold hinged bangle, grain set with split pearls, with 9ct-gold safety chain, bangle not completely round.
                              2¼in (5.6cm) diam 0.3oz
$450-550   **SWO**

A Victorian 15ct-gold shield-form hinged bangle, with an old European-cut diamond, star set at the center of a raised flat boss, light surface marks.
ca. 1860   *2¼in (5.6cm) diam 0.8oz*
$1,050-1,300   **SWO**

A Victorian lapis lazuli and gold bracelet, with a larger lapis lazuli bead on each terminal in gold.
8¼in (21cm) long
$1,600-2,000   **WW**

A late-Victorian 9ct-gold bracelet, with cushion- and oval-shaped mixed-cut amethysts, all four claw set in plain collets.
                              7in (18.2cm) long 1.3oz
$1,050-1,300   **SWO**

A 19thC Etruscan Revival ram's-head gold bangle, the head textured with realistic wool, the tapered bangle with cannetille work, hinged opening.

Etruscan Revival jewelry reflects the fascination of Victorian women with the Etruscans, who lived on the west coast of Italy between 700 BC and 300 BC. The discovery of Etruscan tombs in the 19thC inspired many Etruscan Revival jewelry collections in yellow gold.

2½in (6cm) diam Estimate:
$11,000-12,000   **WW**

A Victorian 9ct-gold hinged bangle, with an oval cabochon garnet, with white enamel dot border, applied gold beads, and a twisted wire frame.
ca. 1860   *2¼in (5.5cm) diam 0.5oz*
$1,300-1,700   **SWO**

A Victorian Scottish 9ct-gold bracelet, with specimen agate plaques, alternating with pairs of hexagonal batons with fitted end caps.
                              7¾in (19.9cm) long 1.6oz
$1,300-1,800   **SWO**

A late-Victorian hollow, 9ct-gold expanding bracelet, with a centerpiece of turquoise and split pearls, hollow Bismark chain with a split pearl or cabochon on the first three links, surface marks.
7in (18cm) long 0.6oz
$550-650   **SWO**

JEWELRY

An Edwardian necklace, set with sapphires, garnets, amethysts, and zircons in yellow gold collets on a fancy-link yellow gold necklace.

15in (38cm) long

$6,000-7,500   WW

An Edwardian 15ct-yellow gold, peridot, and pearl pendant/brooch.

1¼in (3cm) wide 0.21oz

$450-600   DAWS

An Edwardian platinum négligée pendant, grain set with old European- and Swiss-cut diamonds, two drops below, set with Swiss-cut diamonds and seed pearls.

1¾in (4.7cm) drop 0.2oz

$900-1,050   SWO

An Edwardian amethyst and diamond heart pendant, in silver and gold, on fine-link gold neck chain set with seed pearls.

Pendant 2in (5.2cm) high

$750-800   WW

An Edwardian amethyst, paste, and blister pearl necklace, with a girandole-style centerpiece, 9ct gold, areas of strain to the chain, a fully drilled blister pearl.

3¾in (9.7cm) wide 1.1oz

$260-400   SWO

An Edwardian gold pendant, an oval peridot and split-pearl cluster in the center, marked "9," wear to chain, minor surface marks.

2½in (6.5cm) wide 0.17oz

$450-600   SWO

An Edwardian 9ct-gold amethyst and split-pearl pendant, suspended in a diagonal grid layout between the leaves.

ca. 1910   2¼in (5.9cm) high 0.2oz

$750-850   SWO

An Edwardian 9ct-gold necklace, with amethyst, zircons, citrines, tourmalines, and spinels, all set in gold-spectacle settings, surface marks, later clasp, crown facet edge wear to some of the gemstones.

16in (40.5cm) long 0.5oz

$850-1,000   SWO

An Edwardian 15ct-gold spider and fly necklace, the fly pendant with cabochon ruby-set thorax, suspending a spider drop with an oval mixed-cut green tourmaline, with a mixed-cut aquamarine above, pendant possibly missing a bar between the fly and the spider.

pendant 1¼in (3.4cm) long 0.1oz

$800-900   SWO

An Edwardian 15ct-gold aquamarine and split-pearl pendant, minor surface marks on gold.

pendant 2in (5.1cm) long 0.1oz

$260-400   SWO

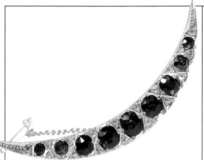

An Edwardian 9ct-gold brooch, with sapphires, between pairs of old eight-cut diamonds, gold later rhodium plated.

ca. 1910   *2¼in (5.6cm) long 0.2oz*

$800-900   **SWO**

An Edwardian 15ct-gold diamond and split-pearl flower-head brooch, minor surface marks/scratches to metal.

1in (2.7cm) diam 0.1oz

$350-400   **SWO**

An Edwardian gold butterfly brooch, set with solid white opal wings, a ruby and boulder opal body, with case.

2½in (6cm) wide

$3,300-4,000   **WW**

An Edwardian bow brooch, with old cushion-shaped diamonds and a line of graduated diamonds with a pendant loop in platinum.

1¾in (4.7cm) wide

$4,000-5,300   **WW**

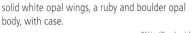

An Edwardian ring, the marquise-shaped diamond set within emeralds and diamonds in platinum and gold.

Finger size S

$7,500-8,500   **WW**

A rose gold ring, with mixed-cut sapphires and old European-cut diamonds, with a French remark for preowned golds.

ca. 1910   *Finger size M½ 0.2oz*

$2,200-2,600   **SWO**

An Edwardian 18ct-white gold brooch, with a cabochon opal, with cushion-shaped Swiss-cut diamonds, marks on the mount.

There is a good play of color on the opal—green, mauve, orange, dark orange, red, surface reaching dehydration line; surface dimple deliberately left when the opal was polished.

2¼in (5.3cm) wide 0.5oz

$2,000-2,600   **SWO**

An Edwardian 18ct-gold opal and diamond seven-stone ring, abrasions on the opals.

1905   *Finger size Q 0.13oz*

$400-450   **SWO**

An Edwardian 18ct-gold yellow topaz ring, scratches on mount.

1908   *Finger size N-O 0.2oz*

$850-1,000   **SWO**

An Edwardian 15ct-gold bracelet, mixed-cut amethysts, spectacle set, alternating with links, peg set on the center with a pearl.

6¾in (17.2cm) long 0.4oz

$1,300-1,800   **SWO**

An Edwardian seed pearl-and-diamond laurel design gold bangle.

2¼in (5.7cm) diam

$750-850   **WW**

An Edwardian 9ct-gold and turquoise-set gate bracelet.

7¾in (19.8cm) long 0.6oz

$600-750   **SWO**

JEWELRY

An Art Nouveau gold necklace, with pearls.

14¼in (36cm) long

$850-1,000   **WW**

An Art Nouveau gold and enamel butterfly bracelet, by Carreras, the gold panels each with a different butterfly motif among foliage on frosted-glass ground, the four butterflies and two further insects each decorated with plique-à-jour and cloisonné polychrome enamel, signed with applied gold plaque on reverse "E de A. Carreras Barcelona," in a case marked "Antigua Joyeria Carreras Paseo Gracia 30 calle Fernando 44 Bakcalona."

The Carreras were the oldest family of Spanish jewelers founded by Francesco d'Assis Carreras Duran (1797-1862) in Barcelona. The firm created magnificent jewels in a very traditional style for clients from across the Iberian peninsula. At the start of the 20thC, influenced by the House of Masriera, the workshop began to follow a more modernistic current in a style called "Modernisme," Barcelona's own version of Art Nouveau. For more information on Carreras, please refer to "Dictionnaire International Bijou," p. 108.

ca. 1905   *7½in (19cm) long*

$90,000-100,000   **WW**

An early-20thC brooch/pendant, with graduated old circular-cut diamonds and caliber-cut emeralds, suspending an articulated pear-shaped diamond in platinum and gold, detachable brooch fitting on reverse.

2¼in (5.5cm) high

$22,000-26,000   **WW**

A French Art Nouveau carved horn pendant, by George Pierre, with a carved poppy with a pierced outer frame.

George Pierre was one of the main designers and carvers of horn jewelry in the Art Nouveau period in France. His pieces are very collectible, especially this one with the beautifully carved poppy.

ca. 1910   *4¼in (10.8cm) high*

$550-650   **SWO**

An Art Nouveau Continental pearl and diamond bar brooch, with a centered bust of a lady with flowing hair, whiplash stems on each side, old Swiss-cut and old eight-cut diamonds, with three graduated pearl and diamond pendant drops below, marked "585," dirt and tarnish on the settings, original pin and "C" catch, maker's mark illegible.

1¼in (3.3cm) wide 0.2oz

$1,050-1,200   **SWO**

An Art Nouveau 18ct-gold diamond, ivory, and enamel brooch/pendant, later converted from a ring, possibly by Luis Masriera, with an ivory cameo habillé depicting a woman in profile, with later pendant bale, brooch pin, and visor catch, unsigned.

1¾in (4.5cm) high 0.6oz

$2,600-3,300   **SWO**

A Belle Époque 18ct-gold brooch, with old European-cut diamonds, all milligrain set with diamonds on a blade edge bar ground and an outer frame of old Swiss-cut diamonds, faced with platinum.

1½in (4.2cm) wide 0.2oz

$1,300-1,800   **SWO**

An Art Nouveau carved horn buckle, with a carved and painted dragonfly, unsigned.

4½in (11.4cm) wide 0.8oz

$200-260   **SWO**

A pair of early-20thC platinum and diamond drop earrings, an old European-cut or Swiss-cut diamond, knife edge bar below and terminating with a larger old European-cut diamond, with later screw fittings, tested as approximately platinum, screw fittings later replacements, Swiss-cut diamond possibly a replacement, very slight wear.

¾in (1.9cm) long 0.1oz

$750-850   **SWO**

Judith Picks

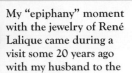

My "epiphany" moment with the jewelry of René Lalique came during a visit some 20 years ago with my husband to the Gulbenkian Museum in Lisbon, Portugal. A long-time admirer of Lalique glass, I had hitherto not fully appreciated the exquisite composition and craftsmanship of his jewelry—oil magnate and philanthropist Calouste Gulbenkian's wonderful collection of pieces instantly remedied that!

Lalique (1860-1945) had undergone a traditional jeweler's apprenticeship in Paris, working during the late 1870s and 1880s within the "diamond set" conventions of the time, but, following an intensive period of technical research into enamel and glass, he created in the mid-1890s a radically new vocabulary of materials, style, and ornament. Instead of relying on the intrinsic value of diamonds for desirability, albeit occasionally using them, Lalique's Art Nouveau pieces employed instead colored and molded glass and enamel, bleached and carved horn, and colorful semiprecious stones, such as opal. Combined with a simplicity and asymmetry of design (partly inspired by Lalique's love of Japanese art), together with often-unusual imagery derived from nature—from sycamore seeds and grasshoppers to serpents and wasps—and/or with sensual, mostly feminine, human forms, they were met initially with Parisian and, soon thereafter, international acclaim.

Sadly, Lalique stopped designing and making jewelry in 1914, turning his full attention to glass. However, as reflected in the prices his pieces command, the esteem in which they were originally held endures to this day.

An Art Nouveau Lalique belt buckle, as a female face within an oxydized pierced quatrefoil frame as billowing hair, with a blue enamel headband, stamped "LALIQUE," minor wear.

3in (7.5cm) wide 78.6grms

$33,000-40,000   **TEN**

A silver brooch converted from a buckle, design no.14, formed with two heart-shaped palmette sections and set with a labradorite cabochon, cracked, stamped "826S G.I." and with maker's mark.

1904-08   3.5in (9cm) wide

$650-800   **WW**

A Murrle Bennett & Co. 9ct-gold bar brooch, cast with Art Nouveau flower, enameled in blue and green and set with mother-of-pearl, stamped marks "9ct MB&Co."

1¾in (4.5cm) wide

$210-260   **WW**

A Charles Horner silver and enamel brooch, the Egyptian-inspired brooch modeled as a winged scarab, enameled in shades of green, blue, and red, stamped marks "CH Chester."

1905   1¾in (4.5cm) wide

$210-260   **WW**

An Art Nouveau Charles Horner silver and enamel brooch, pierced and cast with entwined stylized foliage, enameled green and blue, stamped marks "Chester 1908."

1¼in (3cm) wide

$210-260   **WW**

An Edwardian Art Nouveau silver and enamel pendant, by William Haseler, Birmingham, wirework and blue/green and purple enamel decoration, with a chain.

1908   1in (2.5cm) high

$400-450   **WW**

An Edwardian Art Nouveau silver and enamel necklace, by Charles Horner, Chester, with blue/green enamel decoration and centered white enamel circular, with two drops, in a later case.

Charles Horner (1837-96) was an English jeweler and founder of the Charles Horner of Halifax jewelry company. He founded the company in the 1860s and produced silver jewelry and accessories. Among his more famous jewelry were Art Nouveau enamel pendants and necklaces. Most pieces by this company have silver hallmarks and Charles Horner's trademark C.H. The company went into voluntary liquidation in 1984.

1909   1in (2.3cm) diam

$550-650   **WW**

A Norwegian silver-gilt enamel pendant, by Marius Hammer.

Marius Hammer, Bergen 1847-1927.

ca. 1910 Centerpiece 1¾in (4.7cm) high 0.2oz

$550-650   **SWO**

An Art Nouveau, gold, turquoise, and opal necklace, with pearl drops, marked "9C," one of the drops a later imitation pearl replacement.

15in (38cm) long 0.3oz

$850-1,000   **SWO**

JEWELRY

ESSENTIAL REFERENCE—THE ARTS AND CRAFTS MOVEMENT

The Arts and Crafts movement originated in England in the early 1860s as a reaction to the increasing industriali`ed mass production of decorative artifacts, and an attendant overornamentation and loss of quality. By way of remedy, it's leading advocates, such as designer William Morris and art critic John Ruskin, promoted a return to traditional, handmade standards of craftsmanship and design.

● Although starting in England, the Arts and Crafts movement proved influential throughout Great Britain, and much of Europe and the United States, during the course of the second half of the 19thC and well into the 20thC.

● Favored forms and motifs included flora and fauna, both often indigenous to the place of design; ancient Celtic devices, notably interlaced knots; hearts; and allegories from the Bible and literature.

● Favored materials included silver, copper, and pewter instead of more expensive gold. Colors enameled also featured strongly, notably plique-a-jour, as did more naturalistic gems, such as turquoise, pearls, and cabochons, instead of cut stones.

● Most Arts and Crafts jewelry was designed at a time when earrings were not particularly fashionable, hence the abundance of necklaces, brooches, buckles, and hair slides.

● For the first time in the decorative arts, women were much to the fore in not only the making but also the design of Arts and Crafts jewelry. Notable names to look for include: May Morris (younger daughter of William Morris); Phoebe Traquair; Edith (and Nelson) Dawson; Jessie M. King (especially for Liberty & Co.); and Georgina (and Arthur) Gaskin.

An Arts and Crafts 15ct-gold-mounted turquoise brooch, attributed to Archibald Knox for Liberty & Co., a shield-form plaque with an open whiplash on each top corner, with a hammered finish and an oval cabochon turquoise, rub set on the center with pin and "C" catch, natural surface-reaching inclusions in the turquoise.

ca. 1900   ¾in (1.8cm) high 0.1oz
$600-750   **SWO**

An Arts and Crafts citrine and silver brooch, by Sibyl Dunlop, signed "S Dunlop."

1½in (4cm) wide
$800-900   **WW**

An Arts and Crafts silver and polychrome enamel brooch, attributed to Jessie King, with an enamel floral plaque and wirework and pellet decoration.

ca. 1900   2½in (6.2cm) wide
$260-400   **WW**

An Arts and Crafts silver brooch, of stylized wreath form set with amethyst, moonstone, and turquoise in silver.

1¾in (4.5cm) wide
$600-750   **WW**

An Arts and Crafts silver pendant, possibly by Edith Stewart, the fine-link silver neck chain set with two chalcedony cabochons suspending a further chalcedony pendant within silver laurel surround.

15in (38cm) long
$600-750   **WW**

An Arts and Crafts silver and enamel pendant, by William H. Haseler, the heart-shaped pendant decorated with polychrome enamel, on an oval-link neck chain, maker's mark on reverse.

1in (2.4cm) wide
$600-750   **WW**

An Arts and Crafts moonstone and enamel pendant, by Archibald Knox, the moonstone cabochon within abstract surround decorated with green enamel and suspending a further moonstone cabochon, on gilt-metal neck chain, unsigned but attributed, with box.

Pendant 2¾in (6.9cm) long
$6,500-7,500   **WW**

A pair of Arts and Crafts drop earrings, attributed to Dorrie Nossiter, one earring suspending a green stone bead and the other a pink tourmaline bead, set with seed pearls, emeralds, and pink tourmalines.

2½in (6cm) high
$2,600-3,300   **WW**

A pair of Arts and Crafts silver and 9ct-gold drop earrings, attributed to Bernard Instone, a leaf-and-vine top section with a claw-set blister pearl suspended below, and a cabochon cornelian with an incised leaf-and-vine cap, suspended at the bottom, a trefoil cluster of incised leaves on the back, with gold hook fittings, tarnished, one eyelet above a blister pearl slightly bent.

ca. 1920   2¼in (5.5cm) long 0.2oz
$260-400   **SWO**

An Art Deco platinum opal and diamond plaque brooch, with a cabochon opal, with pierced and arched beads, with old eight-cut diamonds, on a pin-and-lever catch, case by "R.H. Phillips, Goldsmith & Jeweller, Chesterfield," some marks on the opal, the lever catch may be a replacement.

ca. 1930   *1½in (3.5cm) long 0.1z*

$2,600-3,300   **SWO**

An early-20thC American pansy brooch pendant, centered with an old circular-cut diamond, the petals pavé set with circular-cut Montana sapphires, the borders highlighted with small rose-cut diamonds in white gold, with French import marks.

2in (5.1cm) high

$15,000-18,000   **WW**

An Art Deco platinum jade, diamond, and black enamel clip brooch, by Cartier, signed Cartier London.

1½in (3.5cm) wide

$11,000-13,000   **WW**

An early-20thC 9ct-gold pearl and diamond bar brooch.

2¼in (5.6cm) long 0.2oz

$260-330   **SWO**

A French Art Deco platinum, 18ct-gold, rock crystal, onyx, and diamond brooch, a frosted, rock crystal hoop with a matching section at each side, with old Swiss-cut and old eight-cut diamonds, lines of caliber-cut cabochon onyx on each side with lines of graduated diamonds, hand engraved with laurel garlands, and a pin and visor catch, french poinçon, small guarantee mark, fitted case by "Alfred Hamsy, Joallier, 277 rue St Honoré, Paris-Cannes."

ca. 1925   *2½in (6cm) wide 0.5oz*

$6,000-6,600   **SWO**

An Art Deco Continental 18ct-white gold, diamond, and synthetic sapphire plaque brooch, with an old brilliant-cut diamond, with a pierced scalloped navette-shaped plaque, milligrain set with graduated eight-cut diamonds, a spaced linear border of baguette-cut synthetic sapphires with a waved outer edge, set with diamonds, on a pin and visor catch, possible damages.

ca. 1925   *2¼in (5.8cm) wide 0.3oz*

$1,300-2,000   **SWO**

An Art Deco-style 18ct-white gold plaque brooch, a row of three graduated brilliant-cut diamonds, all rub set in plain collets on a brilliant-cut diamond-set frame, grain set with lines of brilliant-cut diamonds.

2¼in (5.4cm) wide 0.4oz

$1,300-1,600   **SWO**

An 18ct-white gold diamond-set bow brooch, with eight cut diamonds, marked "18ct & PLAT," scratches on gold.

ca. 1925   *2¼in (5.5cm) long 0.1oz*

$550-650   **SWO**

An Art Deco, gold, ruby, and diamond bar brooch, with step-cut rubies, possibly synthetic, set in white metal, on a yellow metal tapering bar, possibly French eagle poinçoin for 18ct gold.

2in (5.1cm) long 0.1oz

$210-260   **SWO**

An Art Deco American blue zircon ring, with a synthetic sapphire and diamond mount.

ca. 1930   *Finger size O 0.2oz*

$750-850   **SWO**

An Art Deco Continental silver diamond-set fingerline plaque ring, three larger old Swiss-cut diamonds, with smaller old Swiss-cut diamonds.

ca. 1920   *Finger size P ¾in (1.8cm) high 0.09oz*

$600-750   **SWO**

An Art Deco platinum bombé ring, with an old European-cut diamond, with a row of old Swiss-cut diamonds, with a border onyx, with caliber-cut synthetic rubies, later half shank 18ct gold.

ca. 1930   *Finger size L½ Head ¾in (2.1cm) wide 0.1oz*

$1,300-1,700   **SWO**

An Art Deco tourmaline and diamond ring, the emerald-cut pink tourmaline set within single-cut diamond border and shoulders in platinum.

Finger size P

$6,000-7,500   **WW**

A platinum Art Deco ring set with 15 brilliant-cut diamonds totaling approximately 0.50ct.

Finger size T 37oz

$1,050-1,100   **LOCK**

An Art Deco 18ct-rose gold, ruby, and diamond dress ring, with princess-cut rubies and pavé-set diamonds.

Finger size P 0.36oz

$1,600-2,100   **LOCK**

An Art Deco platinum ring, possibly American, three emerald-cut diamonds, box setting with milligrain-set old brilliant-cut diamonds, with caliber-cut synthetic sapphires, with a border of old brilliant-cut diamonds.

ca. 1930   *Finger size L-M head ¾in (1.8cm) high 0.1oz*

$1,300-1,800   **SWO**

An Art Deco plaque ring, with an acorn set with a diamond, with further diamonds and caliber-cut rubies in a surround of blue enamel, with decoration in platinum and white gold.

Finger size K 1/2

$1,050-1,300   **WW**

A diamond, sapphire, and onyx ring, in the Art Deco style, with a brilliant-cut diamond of 0.50 ct, within a border of faceted black onyx, and a border of caliber-set sapphires, the shank stamped "750."

Finger size N 1/2. 0.15oz

$1,800-2,400   **DAWS**

An Art Deco-style synthetic sapphire, synthetic ruby, and diamond harem ring.

ca. 1950   *Finger size M ½in (1.1cm) wide 0.1oz*

$550-650   **SWO**

An 18ct-yellow gold bracelet, with filigree decoration, set with sapphire and rubies.

7½in (19cm) long 1.2oz

$1,700-2,100   **LOCK**

A Continental Art Deco platinum and 18ct-gold sapphire and diamond bracelet, with old eight-cut diamonds, with a French-cut sapphire and pairs of old eight-cut diamonds, possibly French, sapphires are possibly synthetic.

7in (17.8cm) long 0.1oz

$6,000-7,500   **SWO**

An Art Deco platinum and diamond bracelet, the centered pavé-set, old brilliant-cut diamond circular plaque set with a hexagonal-cut diamond within lines of baguette-cut diamonds at the cardinal points, the strap with cut diamonds, the main diamond 1.20 ct, remaining diamonds 17.35 ct, maker's marks "E.J." for Edouard Jeandy, French assay marks.

ca. 1930   *7¼in (18.7cm) long*

$20,000-21,000   **WW**

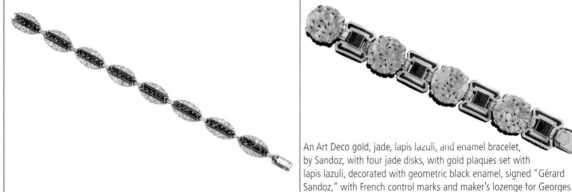

A French Art Deco platinum, sapphire, and diamond bracelet, with French control marks, maker's lozenge.

7in (18cm) long

$13,000-15,000   **WW**

An Art Deco gold, jade, lapis lazuli, and enamel bracelet, by Sandoz, with four jade disks, with gold plaques set with lapis lazuli, decorated with geometric black enamel, signed "Gérard Sandoz," with French control marks and maker's lozenge for Georges Lenfant, in case signed Gustave Sandoz, 10 Rue Royale, Paris.

This has the added advantage of an original gouache drawing.

ca. 1925   *7in (18cm) long 2.2oz*

$33,000-40,000   **WW**

An American Art Deco diamond and onyx plaque pendant, with a brilliant-cut diamond, set with old eight-cut and old brilliant-cut diamonds, with an 18ct-white gold chain, seems to be a brooch later converted to a pendant, center diamond probably a replacement.

2¼in (5.4cm) high including bale 0.7oz

$1,300-2,000   **SWO**

A French Art Deco diamond-set platinum pendant clip, centered with a baguette-shaped diamond, with pavé-set round brilliant-cut and baguette-shaped diamond borders, obscured maker's lozenge (possibly initials OP or OD), French import marks.

1¾in (4.5cm) high

$13,000-16,000   **WW**

A pair of early-20thC silver and moss agate mounted cuff links, by AL Ltd., Birmingham, of oval form.

1926

$25-40   **WHP**

A pair of Art Deco chain-link cuff links, with engine-turned decoration on white engine-turned borders, marked 18ct and 8PT.

½in (1.3cm) diam 0.2oz

$550-600   **SWO**

ESSENTIAL REFERENCE—GEORG JENSEN

When Georg Jensen (1866-1935) died, he was saluted by the "New York Herald" as "the greatest silversmith of the last 300 years." The silversmithy he founded in his native Copenhagen in 1904 continues to produce exquisite silver jewelry (and hollowware) to this day.

● Early Jensen pieces drew heavily on the organic shapes and motifs favored by the contemporary Arts and Crafts and Art Nouveau movements. They were, however, far from derivative—Jensen fused a sculptor's strength and freedom of line with a silversmith's feeling for the malleability of the metal to create a distinctive style all of his own.

● Aside from exceptional standards of design and craftsmanship, on-going commercial success also resided in always being at the cutting edge, or even ahead of the curve, on the style front—from Arts and Crafts and Art Nouveau through Neo-classical Revival and Art Deco to Organ Modernism, Postmodernism, and beyond.

● The Jensen company's policy of always encouraging innovative young designers has also contributed substantially to their commercial success. Pieces designed by, for example, Johan Rohde (Modernist), Harald Nielsen (Art Deco), Sigvard Bernadotte (Functionalsim), Arno Malinowski (see Footnote p. 434), Henning Koppel (Organic Modernism), and Viviianna Torun Bülow-Hübe (Postmodern) are particularly desirable.

A Georg Jensen silver brooch, designed by Arno Malinowski, model no.276, pierced and cast with a cockerel, stamped marks.

1½in (4cm) square

$260-330   WW

A Georg Jensen silver brooch, model no.238, pierced and cast with an exotic bird of paradise, stamped marks.

1½in (4cm) wide

$200-260   WW

A Georg Jensen silver brooch, designed by Arno Malinowski, model no.239, pierced and cast with a bird flying, stamped marks.

1½in (4cm) long

$350-400   WW

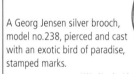

A Georg Jensen silver brooch, designed by Arno Malinowski, model no.257, pierced and cast with a dolphin and bulrushes, stamped marks.

1¾in (4.5cm) wide

$260-330   WW

A Georg Jensen silver brooch, designed by Arno Malinowski, model no.251, pierced and cast with two dolphins, stamped marks.

1½in (4cm) long

$260-330   WW

A Georg Jensen silver brooch, designed by Hugo Liisberg, model no.300, pierced and cast with a duck flying past bulrushes, stamped marks.

1¾in (4.5cm) long

$260-330   WW

A Georg Jensen silver brooch, designed by Arno Malinowski, model no.251, pierced and cast with two dolphins and foliage, stamped marks.

Born in 1899 and trained at the Royal Danish Academy of Fine Arts from 1919-1922, Arno Malinowski was, in addition to being a successful sculptor and ceramicist, an internationally lauded silver designer who worked with the Georg Jensen company from 1936-44, and again from 1949-65. He's perhaps best known for an enamel-on-silver "Kingmark" emblem, initially created in 1940 to celebrate the 70th birthday of King Christian X, and that was worn on pins and cuff links by many Danes throughout World War II as a symbol of resistance to Nazi occupation. Most of his jewelry designs, however, incorporate floral and fauna imagery—deer, horses, cockerels, and, as here, dolphins being prominent among the latter.

1½in (4cm) wide

$350-400   WW

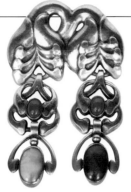

A Georg Jensen silver brooch, designed by Arno Malinowski, model no.231, cast with double flower with two pendulous drops, each set with stones, stamped marks.

2¾in (7cm) long

$550-650   **WW**

A Georg Jensen silver brooch, designed by Gudmund Hentze, model no.98, set with four green chrysoprase cabochon, with three silver drops set with amber cabochon, stamped marks.

3¼in (8.5cm) long

$850-1,000   **WW**

A Georg Jensen silver brooch, designed by Georg Jensen, model no.236, pierced and cast in relief with two flower heads inside scroll tendril border, set with two green chrysoprase and centered amber stone, stamped marks.

1½in (4cm) diam

$650-800   **WW**

A Georg Jensen silver and labradorite brooch, designed by Georg Jensen, model no.236, pierced and cast with two bellflowers, set with labradorite stones, stamped marks.

1½in (4cm) wide

$450-600   **WW**

A Georg Jensen silver necklace, designed by Arno Malinowski, model no.93, pierced and cast with two birds and an ear of corn, stamped marks.

2in (5cm) long

$400-450   **WW**

A Georg Jensen silver necklace, designed by Arno Malinowski, model no.97, pierced and cast with a bird flying among foliage, stamped marks.

1½in (4cm) long

$350-400   **WW**

A Georg Jensen silver necklace, designed by Arno Malinowski, model no.96, pierced and cast with a deer with stylized flowers, stamped marks.

1½in (4cm) wide

$400-450   **WW**

A Georg Jensen silver necklace, designed by Arno Malinowski, model no.105, pierced and cast with two butterflies, stamped marks.

2in (5cm) diam

$260-330   **WW**

A Georg Jensen silver bracelet, model no.16, alternate flower head and scroll links, each set with blue labradorite stone, stamped marks.

18cm. long

$1,300-2,000   **WW**

An 18ct-yellow gold brooch, by Deakin & Francis, Birmingham, retailed by Garrard, set with six sapphires and small diamonds.

1959   *2in (5.2cm) long 0.4oz*
$650-800   **WHP**

An 18ct-gold two-color ruby and diamond bow brooch, a centered spray cluster with graduated circular mixed-cut rubies, with graduated Swiss-cut diamonds, the looped bow with a textured finish, one diamond with a chip.

ca. 1950   *2¼in (5.8cm) high 0.6oz*
$800-900   **SWO**

A Continental gold and platinum, diamond-set bow brooch, with a centered white diamond knot, pavé set with old eight-cut and old Swiss-cut diamonds, with scattered old brilliant-cut diamonds, marked "PT 950".

ca. 1945-55   *1½in (4.2cm) wide 0.8oz*
$1,100-1,250   **SWO**

A fluted 18ct-gold bracelet, by Cartier, the eight links of lobed scallop form, signed Cartier, numbered "16511."

ca. 1940   *6¾in (17.5cm) long 4.8oz*
$11,000-12,000   **WW**

A 9ct-gold ruby and diamond bracelet, by Sannit and Stein, with a detachable brooch centerpiece, with a centered row of claw-set brilliant-cut diamonds and mixed-cut rubies.

ca. 1960   *7¾in (19.7cm) long 2oz*
$1,300-1,700   **SWO**

A 9ct-gold jade bracelet, with jade cabochons, probably nephrite, with a leaf and scrolled-ribbon frame on each setting, joined by pairs of jump rings to a concealed box clasp, tarnished.

ca. 1950   *½in (1.2cm) wide 0.4oz*
$1,600-2,000   **SWO**

An Italian 18ct-gold bracelet, hollow links joined by wire rings to a concealed box clasp, marked "750," Italian official marks 1944 to 1968, for Verona, some wear.

ca. 1950   *8¼in (21.1cm) long 1.5oz*
$2,000-2,600   **SWO**

A 18ct-yellow gold prunt ring, in the manner of Joseph Marchak, set with a cabochon turquoise and 10 small diamonds within a naturalistic setting.

ca. 1970   *Size K 0.6oz*
$1,600-2,000   **WHP**

A 9ct-gold emerald, ruby, and sapphire-set hinged bangle, with a pierced foliate top half, a mixed-cut emerald, four claw set in the center, with scattered gemstones on each side.

ca. 1970   *2¼in (5.7cm) wide 0.4oz*
$600-750   **SWO**

A yellow metal pendant, in the manner of Joseph Marchak, set with an oval turquoise and 12 small diamonds in a crosshatched setting.

ca. 1970   *2½in (6.2cm) long 1oz*
$1,300-1,450   **WHP**

An 18ct Cartier ring, set with an oval blue chalcedony cabochon in a four claw mount, with box and certificate of valuation.

Cartier was founded in 1847 in Paris by the jeweler Louis-François Cartier, who in 1899 handed over the company to his three sons. They would establish the company internationally, not least by making the Cartier name a favorite among the kings and queens of Europe and the seriously wealthy.

Finger size O 0.6oz

$2,200-2,600   **LOCK**

A diamond and sapphire ring, centered with a round brilliant-cut diamond of approximately 2.20 ct, within a border of sapphires, the white metal mount inset with diamond accents.

Finger size J 0.16oz

$6,500-8,000   **DAWS**

An 18ct-white gold ring, black diamond and two brilliant-cut white diamonds in an inline setting, centered stone 0.5 ct.

Finger size M 0.1oz

$1,100-1,250   **WHP**

An 18ct-yellow gold three-stone ring, set with fine color oval sapphire measuring approximately ⅜ x ⁵⁄₁₆in (10x8mm), with single diamond each side, approximate 0.15 ct each.

Finger size M 0.11oz

$800-900   **LOCK**

A 14ct-white gold ring, set with a pear drop, double-cabochon-cut emerald within a border of small diamonds, the split band set with further diamonds, centered stone 10.67 ct.

Finger size O 0.3oz

$1,800-2,100   **WHP**

A white metal crossover ring, set with a brilliant-cut diamond in a three-claw setting, the shoulders and setting set with smaller diamonds in channel settings, centered stone 0.75 ct.

Finger size L 0.2oz

$900-1,050   **WHP**

An 18ct-white gold and diamond, three-stone crossover design ring, with diamond-set shoulders, weight of principal stones 0.30 ct.

Finger size L 0.13oz

$350-400   **LOCK**

An American gold and cabochon red gem-set college ring, detailed "Bel Air High School" and to the shoulders "Loyal Forever Highlanders," detailed "10 K."

Finger ring size V 0.5oz

$600-650   **BELL**

A 15ct-gold three-row panther-link bracelet, a series of step-cut amethysts, each one four-claw set in a pierced collet, sections of panther link chain between, to a box clasp with a safety chain, light surface scratches to the amethysts.

7in (17.9cm) long 0.6oz

$750-850 **SWO**

A 15ct-gold, diamond and sapphire bracelet, with cluster links with an old European-cut diamond, with a surround of Swiss-cut sapphires, alternating with openwork "X" links, set with old European- and rose-cut diamonds, curb links on a swivel clasp, some wear on the silver settings, tarnished.

8¼in (21.2cm) long 0.4oz

$1,100-1,250 **SWO**

A 9ct-gold garnet and blister-pearl gate bracelet, alternating oval mixed-cut garnets and blister pearls, rub set to a plain collet at the center of the gate links, with a concealed box clasp and safety chain.

8¼in (20.9cm) long 0.5oz

$750-850 **SWO**

An 18ct-white gold three-row panther-link bracelet with diamond-set links, diamond weight 7.0ct, with box clasp and foldover safety catch.

7½in (19cm) long 1.1oz

$4,000-4,600 **LOCK**

A 14ct-white gold bracelet, set with sapphire and diamond in three-row design with hidden box clasp and safety catch.

7¼in (18.5cm) long 29g

$1,050-1,300 **LOCK**

ESSENTIAL REFERENCE—ILIAS LALAOUNIS

Ilias Lalaounis (October 4, 1920– December 3, 2013) was a pioneer of Greek jewelry and an internationally renowned goldsmith. He is especially known for his collections inspired by Greek history. In 1990, he became the only jeweler ever to be inducted into the Académie des Beaux-Arts.

- **Lalaounis provoked a sensation with his collection "Blow Up" (1970), draping the human body in gold jewelry inspired by Minoan civilization. The following year he organized an international exhibition of jewelry in Athens, joined by Van Cleef, Bulgari, Rene Kern, and Harry Winston. In 1976, he had one of his most important commissions, which would prove to be one of the most inspiring for his portfolio. Empress Farah of Iran commissioned Lalaounis to create a collection of jewelry inspired by Persian art, which went on display at the Imperial Palace in Tehran.**
- **The jewel, for Ilias Lalaounis, is not a simple decorative object; instead, it carries a message, is an expression of inner life, a link with the distant past, a symbol and a memory.**
- **In 1994, he founded the Ilias Lalaounis Jewelry Museum, located under the Acropolis, in the center of Athens. The permanent exhibition displays jewelry and micro-sculptures from 45 collections, designed by Lalaounis in the period 1940-92.**

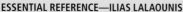

An emerald, ruby, and diamond hinged bangle, by Ilias Lalaounis, the hinged openwork bangle of crossover design, each end modeled as a lion's head, set with six graduated oval cabochon emeralds and circular-cut diamonds, with a box and tongue clasp unhallmarked, maker's mark for Ilias Lalaouni, stamped "Greece K18," with a black pouch.

2.7oz

$6,000-6,600 **BELL**

A 9ct-gold pendant cross, by Allan Christensen, Petworth, the 11 various colored gemstones, including two differing colored zircons and two amethysts, with a gold circular link neckchain, on a bolt-ring clasp.

0.8oz

$800-900 **BELL**

An American gold and platinum, diamond- and emerald-set frog pendant, by S. McTeigue, the white frog, pavé set with brilliant-cut and eight-cut diamonds with faceted emerald eyes, sitting on a lily pad with a textured and incised ground, on an 18ct-gold trace chain with a side-lever clasp, signed on the lily pad "S-McT," marked "PLAT 18k."

Pendant 1¼in (3cm) long chain 18in (45.7cm) long 0.4oz

$1,600-2,100 **SWO**

An 18ct-yellow gold "open and shut" en-tremblant flower clip, by Cartier, the closed bud opening to reveal diamond-, sapphire-, ruby-, and emerald-set stamens, signed and indistinctly numbered "(?)016637," cased.

2¾in (7cm) long 1.1oz

$3,300-4,000 **WHP**

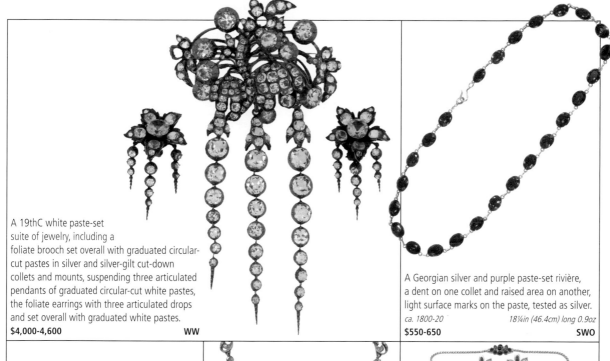

A 19thC white paste-set suite of jewelry, including a foliate brooch set overall with graduated circular-cut pastes in silver and silver-gilt cut-down collets and mounts, suspending three articulated pendants of graduated circular-cut white pastes, the foliate earrings with three articulated drops and set overall with graduated white pastes.

$4,000-4,600 WW

A Georgian silver and purple paste-set rivière, a dent on one collet and raised area on another, light surface marks on the paste, tested as silver.

ca. 1800-20 *18¼in (46.4cm) long 0.9oz*

$550-650 SWO

A Regency gilt-metal and paste en-tremblant tiara or headdress, paste-set daisy cluster heads and ferns, wheat ears, vine leaves, and bunches of grapes, some deficiencies.

ca. 1810-30

$1,250-1,450 SWO

A suite of paste-set jewelry, including a necklace with Saint Esprit dove pendant and drop earrings, set with graduated circular-cut white pastes in silver closed-back settings, with case.

$450-550 WW

A gold-plated necklace and earrings set, by Gonthiez Frères for Carven, detailed with faux pearls and blue and coral glasscabochons, signed "CARVEN DEPOSÉ 3093" and "CARVEN MODELE DEPOSÉ 2129."

1977 Necklace 20¾in (52.5cm) long Earrings 1½in (4cm) wide

$400-550 GRV

A pair of rhodium-plated flawed emerald crystal and colorless rhinestone earrings, by Marcel Boucher, signed "BOUCHER 7940E" and a copyright symbol.

ca. 1960s *1½in (4cm) long*

$260-400 GRV

A chrome-plated, black and orange enamel with orange glass beads brickwork design necklace, by Jakob Bengel, unsigned.

ca. 1930s *16½in (42cm) long*

$550-650 GRV

A Chanel gold-plated "Madame Coco" brooch, in the form of a female figure, with pin-and-visor catch, signed "Chanel, Made in France," pin bent, visor catch a little stiff, wear on gold plating in raised areas.

2½in (6.1cm) high

$400-550 SWO

JEWELRY

A Chanel gold-plated circular brooch, a raised Chanel storefront and "31 rue Cambon Paris, Chanel" in a plain ground, with textured frame, with pin-and-roller catch, signed "Chanel, Made in France, 1150," surface marks/scratches.

2¼in (5.3cm) diam

$210-260 **SWO**

A pair of gold-plated coral Gripoix poured glass and rhinestone earrings, by Chanel, signed "CHANEL."

ca. 1950s *1½in (3.5cm) long*

$650-800 **GRV**

A white metal pendant, by Robert Goossens for Chanel, detailed with faux pearl, poured glass beads, and rhinestones, unsigned.

ca. 1950s

$800-1,050 **GRV**

A gold-plated glass, enamel, and rhinestone elephant brooch, by Ciner, signed "CINER."

The Ciner Manufacturing Company was founded in New York in 1892 by Emanuel Ciner. Initially a maker of precious jewelry, from the early 1930s it also began to produce upmarket costume pieces. While their early pieces are often unmarked, after 1945 most are signed "Ciner."

ca. 1960s *2in (4.75cm) long*

$200-260 **GRV**

A gilded metal multistrand, multifaceted glass bead necklace, by Coppola e Toppo, signed "Made in Italy by Coppola e Toppo."

ca. 1960s *16½in (42cm) long*

$900-1,200 **GRV**

A rhodium-plated parrot brooch, by Coro, detailed with rhinestones, enamel and lucite, signed "Coro."

ca. 1940s *2¾in (7cm) long*

$260-330 **GRV**

A brass and white Galalith sea-horse design bangle and dress clip set, by Jean Painleve, unsigned.

ca. 1930s Bangle 2½in (6.5cm) diam Clips 1½in (4cm) high

$350-400 **GRV**

A gold-plated collar, by Givenchy, featuring a design inspired by ears of wheat, signed "Givenchy Paris New York."

ca. 1980s

$350-450 **GRV**

ESSENTIAL REFERENCE—CHRISTIAN DIOR

Born 1905 in Normandy, Christian Dior opened "Maison Dior" in Paris in 1946. His first haute-couture collection, "New Look," in 1947, took the postwar world of fashion by storm and it and subsequent twice-yearly collections elevated Dior to the preeminent arbiter of taste on both sides of the Atlantic in the late 1940s and 50s—a status underpinned by not only his costume, but also his inextricably linked costume jewelry.

- Most of Dior's earliest costume jewelry designs were exclusively couture pieces made for particular outfits or individual clients, such as Bette Davis and Marilyn Monroe, but his later pieces were produced under license in far greater numbers for sale through exclusive retail outlets.
- Eminent costume jewelers commissioned and/or licensed to design and/or make jewelry under the Dior brand included Henry Shreiner and Kramer, in the United States; Mitchell Maer, in Britain; Henkel & Grosse, in Germany; and Josette Gripoix and Robert Goossens, in France.
- Dior jewelry draws for inspiration on a wide range of historical styles, but is almost invariably given a "modern" twist by the incorporation of unusual pastes and stones—most notably the iridescent, polychromatic aurora borealis rhinestones Dior developed with Swarovski in 1955. Indian, Asian, and Middle Eastern influence is often at the fore, but so is an extensive use of floral motifs in reflection of Christian Dior's personal love of French gardens and countryside.
- After Christian Dior's death in 1957, Maison Dior continued by head designers, including: Yves Saint Laurent (1957), March Bohan (1960), Gianfranco Ferré (1989), and "enfant terrible" John Galliano (1996).

A rhodium-plated brooch and earrings set, by Christian Dior, detailed with ruby red crystals and aurora borealis rhinestones, made in Germany for Dior by Henkel and Grossé and designed by parurier Francis Winter, signed "Christian Dior 1958" and a copyright symbol.
1958   *Brooch 3½in (9cm) long Earrings 2¼in (5.5cm) long*
$1,200-1,450   **GRV**

A gold-plated pendant necklace, by Christian Dior, detailed with turquoise glass cabochons and colorless rhinestones, signed "Christian Dior" and "FOREIGN."
ca. 1950s   *16¼in (41cm) long*
$1,050-1,300   **GRV**

A Christian Dior rhodium-plated necklace, made in Germany for Dior by Henkel and Grossé and designed by parurier Francis Winter, set with rhinestones featuring a design of ribbons and flowers, signed "Christian Dior" and a copyright symbol.
1957   *16¼in (41cm) long*
$1,300-1,600   **GRV**

A gold-plated etched cuff bracelet, by Christian Dior, detailed with red glass cabochons, signed "Christian Dior," "Germany," "1968."
1968   *2½in (6cm) diam*
$600-750   **GRV**

A rhodium-plated necklace, bracelet, brooch, and earrings set, by Mitchel Maer for Christian Dior, detailed with gray glass cabochons and colorless rhinestones, signed "Christian Dior by Mitchel Maer."
1952-56
$1,300-1,700   **GRV**

A pair of gold vermeil, faux pearl, glass cabochon, and rhinestone earrings, by Mitchel Maer for Christian Dior, signed "Christian Dior by Mitchel Maer."
1952-56   *2in (5cm) high*
$550-650   **GRV**

A gold-plated green and red glass cabochon and bead cape brooch, by Christian Dior, made in Germany for Dior by Henkel and Grossé, signed "Christian Dior 1964 Made in Germany" and a copyright symbol.
1964   *5½in (14cm) wide*
$550-800   **GRV**

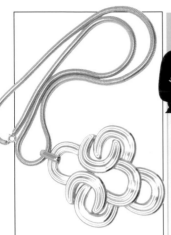

A gold plate and enamel statement pendant necklace, by Grossé, signed "Grossé," a copyright symbol, "Made in Germany" and "1971."

1971   *30in (76cm) long*
$200-260   **GRV**

A white metal, blue and colorless glass, and colorless rhinestone tasseled dress clip, by Miriam Haskell, unsigned.

ca. 1940s   *3¼in (8.5cm) high*
$260-400   **GRV**

Judith Picks

My love affair with Joseff of Hollywood jewelry, which flared some 20 years ago, when I wrote my first book on costume jewelry, burns just as brightly today as it did back then. My passion for so many of his pieces, of which I have gradually acquired—sometimes to the consternation of my husband—a reasonable collection, is explained by a number of things.

It's partly to do with the historical authenticity of so many of Eugene Joseff's designs, dating from Classical Antiquity through the Middle Ages and the Renaissance via the Georgian and Victorian eras to late-19thC Art Nouveau and 20thC Modernism and Art Deco. And it's also to do with that historical authenticity enabling Joseff to supply his costume jewelry to the movie industry, almost from it's inception through it's "golden age" and beyond. The

A Russian gold necklace, by Joseff of Hollywood, detailed with snake motifs and a red glass cabochon, signed "Joseff."

ca. 1960s   *17¾in (45cm) long*
$550-650   **GRV**

list of movies "costume-jeweled" by Joseff is beyond impressive and include: "A Star is Born" (1936); "The Wizard of Oz" and "Gone With The Wind" (both 1939); "Casablanca" (1942); "Easter Parade" (1949); "Singing in the Rain" (1952); "To Catch a Thief" (1955); "Ben Hur" (1959); "Breakfast at Tiffany's (1961); and "My Fair Lady" (1964), to name but a few! And, of course, the fact that the pieces were worn by movie stars, such as Greta Garbo, Vivian Leigh, Grace Kelly, and Elizabeth Taylor, only adds to the sense of glamour!

I'm lucky enough to own a Joseff Egyptian snake necklace like the one shown here, and it's matching earrings (not shown). Their design was inspired by pieces found in Tutankhamen's tomb in 1922, and the originals were worn by Elizabeth Taylor in the Hollywood epic "Cleopatra," in 1963. So, I'm in exalted company here!

A rhodium-plated floral design collar necklace, by Jomaz, detailed with aquamarine crystals and colorless rhinestones, signed "Jomaz" and a copyright symbol.

ca. 1950s
$550-650   **GRV**

A pair of Russian gold statement coin earrings, by Joseff of Hollywood, detailed with East Asian-inspired designs, signed "Joseff."

ca. 1940s   *5½in (14cm) long*
$200-330   **GRV**

A 935 silver, ruby, and colorless paste bracelet and ring set, by Knoll and Pregizer, in its original box, signed "935 and KP."

ca. 1920s   *Bracelet 7in (18cm) long Ring UK size L 1/2*
$1,600-2,000   **GRV**

A pair of 935 silver with black and colorless paste drop earrings, by Knoll and Pregizer, signed "SILVER," "935," and "KP."

ca. 1920s   *2in (5cm) long*
$600-750   **GRV**

A pair of gold-plated faux pearl, velvet, and rhinestone statement heart earrings, by Christian Lacroix, signed "CL," "CHRISTIAN LACROIX," and "Made in France."

ca. 1990s   *2½in (6.5cm) long*
$400-550   **GRV**

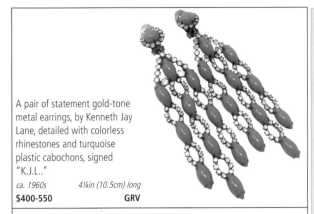

A pair of statement gold-tone metal earrings, by Kenneth Jay Lane, detailed with colorless rhinestones and turquoise plastic cabochons, signed "K.J.L.."

ca. 1960s   *4¼in (10.5cm) long*
$400-550   **GRV**

A carved horn bee design brooch, by P. Lucas, signed "P. Lucas."

ca. 1900
$350-400   **GRV**

A brass, enamel, and glass brooch, by Neiger Brothers, detailed with scenes and motifs of ancient Egypt, made in Czechoslovakia, unsigned.

ca. 1920s   *2¼in (5.5cm) wide*
$260-400   **GRV**

A sterling silver-plated, flexible gauntlet bracelet, by Napier, designed by Eugene Bertoli, detailed with pink resin cabochons, signed "NAPIER PAT. PEND."

Founded in the 1870s as E. A. Bliss Co., and renamed in 1922, the American Napier company is known for both its cutting-edge designs for domestic silver artifacts and for its jewelry. In the 1920s and early 30s, they designed necklaces, bracelets, and earrings in a range of styles, including Victorian Revival, Egyptian Revival, and Art Deco. After concentrating on silver giftware in the late 1930s and the 1940s, Napier refocused on jewelry during the 1950s and beyond, again producing a wide range of styles, but especially simple, modern, geometric, and floral designs. Their distinctive, often "chunky," sterling silver bracelets from that period, as in this example embellished with pink resin cabochons, are particularly sought after. Although under ownership of the Jones Apparel Group, Napier brand jewelry is still made today.

1955   *6¼in (16cm) high*
$350-400   **GRV**

A pair of gilded metal and glass bell-and-bow design earrings, by Louis Rousselet, signed "Made in France."

ca. 1940s   *1½in (4cm) long*
$200-260   **GRV**

A gunmetal tone necklace, by Yves Saint Laurent, detailed with gold plate, enamel, and glass cabochons, signed "YSL."

ca. 1980s   *18¼in (46cm) long*
$550-650   **GRV**

A pair of gold-plated "Rive Gauche" drop earrings, by Yves Saint Laurent, a pear-shaped glass drop with articulated foliate bell cap, surmounted with an oval glass cabochon, with clip fittings, marked "Yves Saint Laurent, rive gauche, Made in France," some wear.

3in (7.6cm) long 1.7oz
$450-600   **SWO**

A rhodium-plated bracelet, by Schreiber and Hiller, detailed with channel-set colorless and emerald green pastes, made in Germany, signed "D.R.G.M" and the patent number "1138525."

ca. 1930s   *2½in (6cm) diam*
$260-400   **GRV**

ESSENTIAL REFERENCE—TRIFARI

Trifari was founded in the 1910s by Gustavo Trifari, the Italian-immigrant son of a Napoli goldsmith. Trifari partnered with sales managers Leo Krussman and Carl Fishel to form Trifari, Krussman and Fishel in 1925, the brand commonly known as Trifari today. Trifari jewelry is marked with "Jewels by Trifari," "TKF" "Trifari."

- Beginning in the 1930s, Trifari worked with Broadway and Hollywood producers to produce designs for famous actors. But the true success of Trifari jewelry is credited to French designer Alfred Philippe, the company's chief designer from 1930 until 1968—his invisible settings for stones adding a high level of craftsmanship to the jewelry.

- Trifari pieces often imitated the look of fine jewelry, using sterling silver or vermeil, a gold-plated finish, alongside other faux materials, such as paste gemstones and imitation moonstone, chalcedony, and pearls. Among Philippe's contributions are the Trifari Crown brooches from the 1930s to the 1950s. These crowns were so popular that Trifari incorporated a crown into its signature mark ca. 1937. Many of the Trifari Crown pins feature eye-catching, brightly colored cabochons. Trifari's Jelly Belly brooches depicting seals, poodles, roosters, and other miniature animals appeared in the 1940s. Each animal's "belly" consists of a solid Lucite "pearl" with settings of sterling silver or gold plate. Poodles are especially rare and desirable.

- During World War II, Trifari was unable to use metal in its products due to rationing. This forced Trifari to switch to sterling silver. Postwar, Trifari wanted to go back to less costly, maintenance-free metal, but its audience was now used to silver.

- Trifari was now so accepted that, by 1953, Mamie Eisenhower wore costume jewelry to the inaugural ball. To match the First Lady's pink satin gown, embellished with 2,000 rhinestones, Philippe designed an "orientique" pearl choker necklace with matching bracelet and earrings, each with eight pearls.

A rhodium plated ruby red crystal and colorless paste dress clip, designed by Alfred Philippe, by KTF Trifari, signed "KTF."
ca. 1930s
$600-750   **GRV**

A carved butterscotch Bakelite floral bangle, unsigned.
ca. 1940s   *2½in (6cm) diam*
$400-550   **GRV**

A white metal, colorless paste and coral pressed-glass dress clip, unsigned.
ca. 1930s   *2¾in (7cm) long*
$260-330   **GRV**

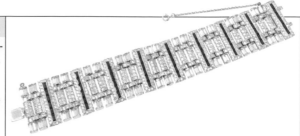

A rhodium-plated wide statement bracelet, by KTF Trifari, detailed with ruby red and colorless paste stones, signed "KTF."
ca. 1930s   *6¾in (17.25cm) long*
$1,050-1,200   **GRV**

A gold-tone metal statement ring, by Vendôme, detailed with colorless rhinestones and multicolored glass cabochons, signed "Vendôme."
ca. 1960s   *Adjustable size*
$130-200   **GRV**

A pair of white metal, paste, and pressed Carnelian glass hoop earrings, made in Czechoslovakia, unsigned.
ca. 1920s   *2in (5cm) long*
$200-260   **GRV**

A French 800 silver and enamel Egyptian Revival design bracelet, signed "800."
ca. 1920s   *6¾in (17cm) long*
$400-450   **GRV**

An Egyptian Revival brass bracelet, detailed with 13 scarablike tortoise beetles, unsigned.

Fueled by a series of archaeological excavations during the late 19th and early 20thC, culminating in the discovery in 1922 of the young pharaoh Tutankhamun's tomb—the "holy grail" of Egyptology—the 1920s and early 1930s witnessed a major Egyptian Revival across the decorative arts. Fashionable forms and motifs employed included pyramids, sphinxes, pharoahic figures, lotus flowers, and, as in this necklace, scarabs. In the Egyptian vocabulary of ornamen, the scarab beetle represented rebirth and regeneration—its habit of rolling dung into a ball was considered a symbolic reflection of the Egyptian god Ra rolling the sun across the sky every day.
ca. 1920s   *6¾in (17.25cm) long*
$350-400   **GRV**

ESSENTIAL REFERENCE—FIREPLACE SURROUNDS

Chimneypieces—nowadays more commonly referred to as fireplace surrounds—began to appear in the late- 5thC as consequence of the gradual transition from open hearths, placed in the center or near one end of a room, to the enclosed wall hearth. While smoke from the former had channeled smoke via a hood or canopy up through a hole in the roof, the latter could more efficiently disperse it via a flue concealed in the wall rising up to and out of a rooftop chimney above —a development given fiscal incentive, following the Reformation, by the abolition of a tax imposed by the Papacy on the building of chimneys!

● During the first half of the 16thC, especially in Great Britain, the new enclosed fireplaces were mostly treated, architecturally and decoratively, as little more than part of a paneled wall. However, as Renaissance ideas on architecture and design permeated throughout Europe, the fireplace became a more substantial feature in its own right. More specifically, the Italians devised a basic form—one that has survived to this day—that comprised a projecting chimney breast with a decorative fireplace surround framing the hearth.

● Made from materials as diverse as marble and other stones, plaster, wood, and, from the 19thC, cast iron, the basic architectural configuration of fireplace surrounds has remained fairly constant, and comprises a pair of columnar-like supports rising on eaach side of the hearth to support a lintel-like frieze spanning the top of it; above that there is often, but not always, a mantel, and over it there can be a decorative over-mantel (sometimes, from the 18thC, incorporating a mirror). What has often changed, however, has been the decorative forms and motifs of the fireplace surround, almost invariably following the major style movements: from late Renaissance and Baroque, through Rococo, Neoclassicism, Regency, and Empire to Victorian, Arts and Crafts, Art Nouveau, Art Deco, Modernism, and beyond.

A mid-18thC gray-painted wood fireplace surround, later repainted, with marks, scratches, old chips, and splits. opening

Opening 37½in (95.5cm) high

$1,800-2,400   DN

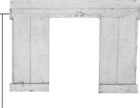

A mid-18thC cream-painted wood fireplace surround, later repainted, with marks, scratches, and abrasions, two later supporting strips of wood on back.

63½in (161cm) wide

$850-1,000   DN

A late-18thC George III pine fireplace surround, the entablature with carved ribbon-tied swags and fluted panels, the sides with urns above pilasters with ribbon-tied drape motifs.

74¾in (190cm) wide

$1,250-1,450   L&T

A mid/late-18thC George III carved pine chimneypiece, the breakfront mantel and acanthus-carved border above the main frieze carved with flower heads within roundel frames, the shell-and-dart carved surround flanked by terminals incorporating scrolls and meandering foliage.

66½in (169cm) wide

$2,600-4,000   DN

CLOSER LOOK—MARBLE AND SCAGLIOLA FIREPLACE SURROUND

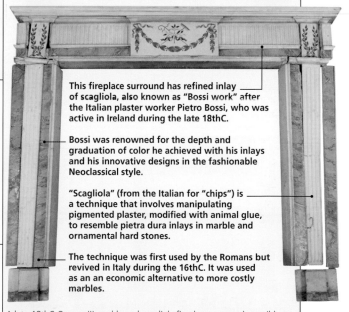

This fireplace surround has refined inlay of scagliola, also known as "Bossi work" after the Italian plaster worker Pietro Bossi, who was active in Ireland during the late 18thC.

Bossi was renowned for the depth and graduation of color he achieved with his inlays and his innovative designs in the fashionable Neoclassical style.

"Scagliola" (from the Italian for "chips") is a technique that involves manipulating pigmented plaster, modified with animal glue, to resemble pietra dura inlays in marble and ornamental hard stones.

The technique was first used by the Romans but revived in Italy during the 16thC. It was used as an an economic alternative to more costly marbles.

A late-18thC George III marble and scagliola fireplace surround, possibly Dublin, in the manner of Pietro Bossi, the fluted frieze with inlay of laurel swags and a ribbon tied trophy, flanked by conforming projecting jambs inset with simulated Siena, with losses and damages to the Siena scagliola, including areas of significant looseness and detachment.

69¼in (176cm) wide

$26,000-33,000   DN

An early-19thC pine and gesso fireplace surround, the frieze with entwined thistles and roses, palm fronds, urns, and floral swags, with recessed panel pilasters.

62½in (159cm) wide

$1,200-1,600   L&T

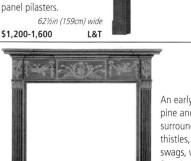

An early-19thC Scottish stripped pine and gesso fireplace surround, the frieze with roses, thistles, and birds in floral swags, with acanthus-capped fluted pilasters.

59¾in (152cm) wide

$1,700-2,100   L&T

An early-19thC Regency pine and gesso fireplace surround, the bead-molded cornice above a frieze with a Classical scene flanked by panels with gryphons and urns, with fluted pilaster legs.

73¼in (186cm) wide

$1,050-13,000   **L&T**

An early-19thC Regency pine and gesso fireplace surround, the frieze with centered flowering urn and fruiting vine pilasters capped by figures.

73¼in (186cm) wide

$1,000-1,200   **L&T**

A mid-19thC carved pine chimneypiece, in George III style, the tablet-molded frieze carved with acanthus and C scrolls, the shaped pilasters with foliate-carved borders and terminating in scroll-carved motifs, centered by patera.

72¼in (183cm) wide

$1,000-1,200   **DN**

A 19thC carved pine fireplace surround/chimneypiece, in George II style, the breakfront mantel above leaf, ovolo, and dentil moldings, the frieze decorated with ribbon-tied oak leaves, with scrolling fruit and flowers.

77¼in (195.8cm) wide

$6,000-6,600   **WW**

A 19thC variegated gray marble bolection-molded chimneypiece, piece is in five sections, expected minor chips and nibbles on edges, some dirt deposited in the creases of the marble.

51¼in (130cm) wide

$4,600-5,900   **DN**

A late-19thC carved pine fireplace surround/ chimneypiece, in George II style, with egg-and-dart and Greek-key moldings, the frieze centered with a basket of flowers, flanked by ribbon-tied swags of fruit and flowers, with conforming garlands on the jambs.

60¼in (153.1cm) wide

$2,600-4,000   **WW**

A late-19thC carved pine fireplace surround/ chimneypiece, in Adam style, the centered tablet with a pair of griffins flanking a centered urn, with scrolling leaves and husks issuing from ram's heads.

62¼in (158cm) wide

$2,000-2,600   **WW**

A 20thC stone composition fireplace surround, in George II taste, the frieze with borders of egg-and-dart and acanthus, flanked by conforming jambs terminating in articulated volute scrolls.

54¼in (138cm) wide

$2,600-4,000   **DN**

A Charles II wrought iron and brass fire grate, basket surmounted by bulbous brass terminals.

ca. 1680   *39¾in (101cm) wide*

$1,300-1,800   DN

An 18thC wrought iron fire grate, the basket incorporating two adjustable fire jack arms.

49¼in (125cm) wide

$2,000-2,600   DN

An 18thC Scottish George III cast iron hob grate, cast with thistles, harps, and roses, with a relief portrait of George III flanked by a pair of heraldic lions.

35in (89cm) wide

$2,000-2,600   L&T

ESSENTIAL REFERENCE—GEORGE BULLOCK

George Bullock (1777-1818) was an influential Regency period modeler, sculptor, cabinetmaker, and furniture designer.

- **George Bullock was born in Birmingham, where his mother ran an exhibition of wax models in the late 1790s. His brother, William Bullock, opened a museum of curiosities in the city in 1800. He moved it to Liverpool the next year, and George went with him.**
- **By 1804, George Bullock had left his brother's museum and gone into business with a looking-glass maker called William Stoakes. They advertised themselves as "Cabinet Makers, General Furnishers and Marble Workers," trading from a showroom called the "Grecian Rooms" in Bold Street, Liverpool. Around 1806, Bullock dissolved his partnership with Stoakes and took over the Mona marble quarries at Llanvechell on the island of Anglesey. The marble was shipped to Liverpool, where it was used for chimneypieces and other decorations. A contemporary guide to Liverpool described his Grecian Rooms as offering "an extensive assortment of elegant and fashionable furniture; also, statues, figures, tripods, candelabra, antique lamps, sphinxes, griffins, &c., in marble, bronze, and artificial stone."**
- **Following the success of his company, he moved to London in 1813. He had an illustrious clientele, including the Duke of Atholl at Blair Castle, the Earl of Mansfield at Scone Castle, Sir Walter Scott at Abbotsford, and also supplied the furnishings for Napoleon's exile home on the Island of St. Helena. He was celebrated for his remarkable craftsmanship, his use of exotic woods, and design influenced from the Neoclassical, Gothic, Jacobean, and Elizabethan styles.**

An early-19thC Regency cast iron and brass fire grate, in the manner of George Bullock, with a long two-bar toothed grate raised on reeded scroll legs with brass paw feet.

46½in (118cm) wide

$4,600-5,900   L&T

A late-18thC Georgian Sheffield-plated and iron register grate, the grate enclosed by cast iron panels outlined with Sheffield-plated mounts with punched decoration, the center plaque inscribed "Bickley & Larner 2 Berners St."

The British Museum has a trade card [D,2.236] for Bickley & Lardner, "metal tradesman, stove grate makers, and furnishing ironmongers," which lists them as makers of "Compleat Sets of Kitchen Furniture of Copper, Iron, Double Block Tin &c" and "Ranges with Ovens, Boilers, Ironing Stoves &c." They were located at 2 Berners Street, Oxford Street. A comparable grate of similar proportions, by the same maker, is in the Yellow Drawing Room at Wimpole Hall, designed by Sir John Soane.

54in (137cm) wide

$2,900-3,400   L&T

An early-19thC Regency brass grate, the three-bar grate enclosed by steel panels mounted with foliate clasped rods terminating in laurel wreath mounted end blocks.

42½in (108cm) high

$4,000-5,300   L&T

An early-19thC Regency Egyptian Revival steel register grate, with an angled three-bar grate flanked by Eyptian figures, the side panels with bands of concentric roundels.

36¾in (93cm) high

$2,000-2,600   L&T

An early-19thC cast iron fire grate, surmounted with brass acanthus leaves and finials, lion masks, on lion paw feet, iron pitted with some rust.

33in (84cm) high

$1,700-2,100   CHEF

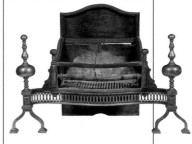

A 19thC Georgian iron and brass firebasket, the fireback above a serpentine grate and pierced brass grill flanked by baluster finials.

37in (94cm) wide

$2,000-2,600   L&T

A Regency brass-mounted, polished steel, and cast iron fire grate, in the manner of George Bullock, the centered railed basket flanked by cabriole-shaped uprights headed by wing mounts and terminating in cast lion paw feet.

This example, particularly its protruding jambs with applied gilt mounts and paw feet, resembles the design of a Bullock fire grate that was gifted by Matthew Boulton to his son Matthew Robinson Boulton to furnish his home at Tew Park, Great Tew, Oxfordshire. In the collection at Tew, there is also an unsigned drawing attributed to Bullock inscribed "Plan of Stove in Dining room and Oak Study," which depicts the distinctive grate.

ca. 1820   *40¼in (102cm) wide*
$1,200-1,600   DN

An early-19thC late Regency cast iron fire grate, the fireback panel with scrolled edge, above an open basket grate, raised on fluted and blocked feet.

29½in (75cm) high
$800-900   L&T

A 19thC brass and cast iron fire grate, in George III Adam taste, the arched backplate descending to a three-rail serpentine basket with urn finials, ball surround, and above a pierced frieze with foliage and paterae, flanked by square-section front uprights with further conforming urn mounts, with minor marks, knocks, losses to small sections of foliate decoration on the frieze.

41¼in (105cm) wide
$3,300-4,000   DN

A late-19thC Georgian-style brass and iron firegrate, the arched backplate cast with an urn relief, above a serpentine grate and pierced grille, flanked by tapered supports with punch-decorated motifs and urn finials.

35¾in (91cm) wide
$600-750   L&T

A wrought iron basket firegrate, of oval concentric tapering form and with scroll handles.

24¾in (62.5cm) wide
$600-750   WW

An early George III engraved steel fender, of adjustable design, the pierced fretwork decoration depicting scrolling foliate branches and engraved with foliate motifs and with Tudor rose terminals, the frieze centered by a stylized dolphin heraldic crest flanked by mythical creatures.

ca. 1760   *34in (86cm) wide*
$1,300-1,600   DN

A George III Irish cut-steel fire fender, the D-shaped front with lyre and geometric design.

41¾in (106cm) wide
$850-1,000   SWO

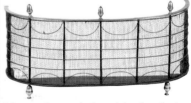

A Regency brass and wirework bowfront fender, with turned acorn finials and swag decoration.

ca. 1820 34in (86cm) wide
$1,050-1,200   WW

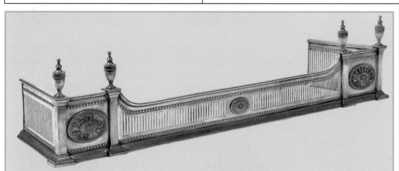

An unusual late-18th/early-19thC paktong fire fender, possibly Chinese Export, in the manner of designs by Robert Adam, the pierced frieze centered by a stylized patera terminal, flanked on each side by a large flower-head patera, surmounted overall by four urn finials, the usual minor marks, knocks, and scuffs overall, some polish residue on the rear.

Paktong, a name derived from the Chinese word meaning "white copper," is a rare nontarnishing alloy of copper, nickel, and tin or zinc. Also known as "Tutenag" or "India metal" on account of its importation by the East India Trading Companies, it originated in China. It first arrived in London in the 1720s, but it was developed by the Chinese much earlier. The principal advantage of paktong is that while resembling silver, unlike silver, it is unaffected by atmospheric conditions,and can be easily cast, hammered, and polished. Its unusual qualities were especially suited to such purposes as chimney furniture, a fact well recognized in 18thC Europe and from ca. 1750 a limited number of items, including grates, are known to have been made in England from this material.

47¾in (121cm) wide
$6,500-8,000   DN

An early-20thC brass and leather-upholstered club fender, the padded seat above tubular uprights and a molded plinth.

71¼in (181cm) wide

$1,600-2,000   DN

A 20thC brass and green leather-upholstered club fender, in Victorian style, the L-shaped seats with brass-studded edges, above columnar supports and a molded plinth base, usual minor marks, knocks, scuffs, and scratches.

87½in (222cm) wide

$4,600-5,900   DN

A 20thC brass-framed club fender.

46½in (118cm) wide

$1,100-1,250   L&T

A 19thC bronze fireguard, the back decorated with guilloche bands, the pierced front decorated with leaves, flowers, and an urn.

29¾in (75.4cm) high

$1,500-2,000   WW

A pair of rare Jacobean iron columnar andirons, the fluted uprights descending to panels cast with lozenges and twin-scrolled legs, with billet bars to rear.

ca. 1605   25½in (65cm) high

$1,300-1,800   DN

A pair of 17thC English brass and wrought iron firedogs, with brass disk finials descending to pierced supports with splayed legs.

The present andirons are loosely of Haddon Hall type. These firedogs with elaborately engraved disk finials were much copied after their rediscovery in the 19thC, and their design appealed to makers in the Arts and Crafts movement, such as Alfred Bucknall.

16¼in (41cm) high

$400-550   DN

A pair of late-18thC Louis XV chinoiserie gilt-bronze chenets, each with a sitting figure in Asian dress, above a shaped foliate base cast with rocaille and oak leaves, with brass billet bars on rear.

These chenets exemplify the popularity of Chinoiserie themes during the 18thC, and many renowned bronziers, including Jacques Caffieri ,are known to have included figures in Asian costume in their designs.

14¼in (36cm) wide

$850-1,000   DN

A pair of heavy gilt-bronze firedogs, modeled as lions triumphant, by A.W.N. Pugin for Alton Towers, each figure holding a scroll inscribed with the the Earl of Shrewsbury's family armorial motto "Prest d'Accomplir," some wear.

Provenance: Commissioned by John Talbot, 16th Earl of Shrewsbury, 16th Earl of Waterford (1791–1852) from A.W.N. Pugin for Alton Towers, Staffordshire. In 1831, the Talbots' principal residence in Heythrop burned down. The 16th Earl then came to live at Alton permanently, employing the renowned Gothic Revival architect Augustus Pugin to design a new entrance hall, banqueting hall, and various other rooms, renaming the property Alton Towers. A surviving stone fireplace, designed by Pugin, in the Dining Hall of Alton Towers is carved with a triumphant lion and the motto "Prest d'Accomplir" in identical Gothicized script to these firedogs.

In November 1918, the 20th Earl of Shrewsbury decided to sell off the majority of the Alton Towers estate and contents by auction. The countess continued to live on the estate for another two years after the earl died in 1921.

19in (48.5cm) high

$26,000-33,000   GORL

A pair of late-18thC Italian tall wrought iron firedogs, each with writhen ball finials and twist-turned supports, with expected wear.

42½in (108cm) high

$400-550   SWO

A pair of rare American sea-horse andirons, by William Wallace Denslow for Roycroft, of wrought and cast iron.

ca. 1902   22½in (57cm) high

$12,000-15,000   DRA

A pair of 19thC bronze fire irons, with lions and flaming urns on fluted half columns, the bases with swags.

14½in (37cm) wide

$650-800   **L&T**

A pair of 19thC brass chenets, depicting lions holding shields, on scrolling openwork bases.

19¾in (50cm)

$600-750   **L&T**

A pair of polished steel firedogs, by Ernest Gimson (1864-1919), made by Alfred Bucknell at Sapperton.

As a student in 1888, Gimson drew a pair of 17thC firedogs at Haddon Hall, Derbyshire and subsequently designed his own interpretation in 1904 or 1905. Two pairs were made in his smithy in brass by Bucknell, one for Earl Bathurst at Pinbury Park, Gloucestershire, and one for the Gimson family, now at the New Walk Museum, Leicester. A third pair was made at the same time in wrought iron for Sir Lionel Phillips of Tylney Hall, Hampshire.

ca. 1904-10   *28in (70.5cm) high*

$90,000-100,000   **MAL**

A set of Regency steel fire tools, comprising shovel, poker, and tongs, each with a writhen shaft and faceted grip, the openwork shovel of tulip form.

ca. 1815   *Tallest implement 32in (81cm) long*

$850-1,000   **DN**

A set of early-19thC English steel fire tools, comprising pierced tulip-form shovel, poker, and tongs, cast with faceted grips.

Shovel 30in (76cm) long

$1,600-2,000   **DN**

A set of William IV or early-Victorian brass and steel-mounted fire tools, comprising shovel, poker, and tongs, the grips cast with outscrolled acanthus leaves and a cabochon finial, the tulip-form shovel with openwork oak spray motif.

ca. 1835   *Tallest implement 32in (81cm) long*

$2,100-2,600   **DN**

A 19thC Dutch painted wood dummy board, depicting a child playing golf, usually attributed to a painting by Aelbert Cuyp.

For long attributed to Aelbert Cuyp (1620-91), but recently reappraised as more probably being by Bartholomeus van der Helst (ca. 1613–70), the original late-1650s painting that inspired the portrait on this 19thC Dutch dummy board depicts a young child playing golf by the shore. Golf, or "kolf," as it was known then, was a popular game in the Low Countries from the 14thC onward among adults and children. It was also long thought the subject of the painting was a girl. However, a better understanding of dress codes in 17thC Holland, in which it was customary for boys six and under to wear gowns, indicates that this is almost certainly a boy "kolfer."

42in (107cm) high

$1,250-1,450   **WW**

Two painted dummy boards, the painted decoration 17thC, oak supports 19thC, each canvas depicting a child and laid down on oak.

The taller one 40½in (103cm) high

$2,200-2,600   **DN**

An unusual Victorian painted cast iron elephant and castle doorstop.

12in (31cm) high

$650-800   **WW**

A Victorian cast iron heraldic doorstop, in the form of a chained greyhound with its paw resting on a shield, painted black with parcel gilt decoration.

18in (45.4cm) high

$850-1,000   **WW**

A Victorian painted cast iron heraldic doorstop, in the form of a rampant lion, on a scroll decorated base.

15in (38.3cm) high

$180-240   **WW**

A Victorian serpentine doorstop, probably Cornish, with a brass ring handle.

11in (27.8cm) high

$120-160   **WW**

A late-Victorian black-painted cast iron stickstand, decorated with scrolling leaves, with three divisions and a lift-out tray, with two registration lozenges.

29in (78.3cm) high

$200-260   **WW**

A Victorian bell-shaped doorstop, with a ball handle and a knopped stem.

22in (56.5cm) high

$170-220   **WW**

A Victorian brass doorstop, in the form of a wheatsheaf, the wreath handle above a rope-twist stem and a weighted base.

16in (40.3cm) high

$170-210   **WW**

A Victorian brass ship doorstop, in the form of "H.M.S. "Victory," with a serpent handle and a rope-twist stem.

This item has Nelson collectors interest.

15.5in (39.7cm) high

$210-260   **WW**

A late-19thC Aesthetic Movement brass door porter, attributed to Thomas Jeckyll for Robbins & Co., the semi-conical weighted base with stylized roundel and geometric decoration, handle twisted and repaired halfway down, solder visible from reverse.

Thomas Jeckyll (1827-81) was a Norwich architect and designer, best known for his metalwork designs and furniture, both influenced by Japanese design. He is best remembered for designing the "Peacock Room" at 49 Princes Gate, London.

15¾in (40cm) high

$600-750   **SWO**

An early-20thC brass fox's head doorstop, by Peerage, the handle in the form of a riding whip, with a cast iron weighted base, stamped "Peerage England 19476."

18in (45.3cm) high

$1,300-1,800   **WW**

A early-20thC brass bacchanalian cherub doorstop, by Peerage, the leaf scroll handle above a winged putto holding a grapevine, the cast iron weighted base stamped "Peerage England 16170."

19¼in (48.9cm) high

$850-1,000   **WW**

A Victorian painted cast iron boot scraper, by Kenrick and Sons, with parcel-gilt decoration, modeled with a pair of Egyptian sphinxes, with impressed marks "A Kenrick & Sons No. 614."

9in (23cm) high

$350-400   **WW**

A late-Victorian cast iron umbrella stand, designed by Dr. Christopher Dresser, decorated with stylized sunflowers and foliage, stamped "No 261," lacking drip trays.

29in (74cm) high

$475-550   **WW**

A Victorian black cast-metal umbrella and stick stand, in the manner of Coalbrookdale.

$130-200   **WHP**

A 19thC Coalbrookdale-type patent cast iron stick stand, the column in the form of a stork, the top as rustic branches and ivy leaves, with a drop pan and bearing registration lozenges, repainted.

29½in (75cm) high

$450-550   **SWO**

A late-19thC cast iron stick stand, with eight circular divisions, with turned finials, pierced open ends, and two lift-out trays.

25¾in (65.3cm)

$200-260   **WW**

A late-19th/early-20thC brass stick stand, with six divisions, a cast iron base, and a lift-out metal liner.

22¾in (57.5cm) high

$600-650   **WW**

A late-19thC Victorian tin lithograph coal scuttle, with brass handle and panel of woman and children.

20in (51cm) high

$300-350   **POOK**

ESSENTIAL REFERENCE—COALBROOKDALE

Founded by Abraham Darby, ca. 1709, in Coalbrookdale village in Shropshire, the Coalbrookdale Company was a prime mover in the start up of the Industrial Revolution. Today, it is more widely known for it's highly collectible, Victorian cast iron garden furniture.

- The technological innovation that underpinned the company's expansion and helped launch the Industrial Revolution was to use locally mined coking coal, which contained much lower than average levels of sulfur, to smelt iron ore, resulting in stronger, more durable iron which could be molded (cast) into more complex shapes than hitherto.
- Initially producing such goods as cooking pots and kettles, the company expanded during the 18thC into cast iron rails for the new railroads, cylinders for steam engines, and, iconically, the world's first cast iron bridge (at nearby Ironbridge) in 1780.
- During the 19thC, the fashion for architectural cast iron, notably balconies, boomed, and was employed in the construction of the Crystal Palace for the Great Exhibition of 1851—Coalbrookdale exhibited a pair of ceremonial gates at the latter that were subsequently installed at one of the entrances to London's Hyde Park.
- The hugely expanded range of Coalbrookdale's domestic artifacts, exported around the world and evidenced by their colossal 1,032 page catalog of 1875, included stoves, ranges, cast iron beds, hallstands (some designed by Christopher Dresser), tables, chairs, and, as here, benches.
- The Victorian taste for eclectic revival styles created a huge demand for furniture in the Gothic, Rococo, and Classical styles, and for garden furniture these were mostly configured with naturalistic plant-form imagery. Notable among these were "Fern and Blackberry," "Lily of the Valley," "Horse Chestnut," "Nasturtium," and "Passion Flower."

An early-19thC late Regency green painted wrought iron bench, with a reeded toprail above lozenge and scroll back, on scrolling arm supports, slatted seat, raised on legs terminating in protruding feet.

60¾in (154cm) wide

$2,600-3,300   L&T

A Regency wrought iron strap-work garden bench, black painted with open slats, with repairs.

62½in (159cm) wide

$1,000-1,100   CHEF

A 19thC Regency painted wrought iron garden bench, the double-arch open back above a bar seat, on splayed legs with an arched stretcher.

6¾in (171cm) wide

$1,200-1,450   L&T

A Victorian painted cast iron "Nasturtium" pattern garden seat, by Coalbrookdale, the back with a registration lozenge and stamped "C. B. Dale & Co.," with a wooden slatted seat.

54in (137.5cm) wide

$3,300-4,000   WW

A Victorian cast iron seat, in "Squirrel and Grape" pattern, with slatted hardwood seat and back.

62in (157.5cm) wide

$900-1,050   HT

A 19thC Victorian cast iron "Medallion" pattern garden bench, probably Coalbrookdale, the pierced back and arms with vines and birds and a centered relief roundel depicting a Classical figure, unmarked.

72½in (184cm) wide

$1,600-2,000   L&T

A Victorian painted cast iron "Fern and Blackberry" pattern garden seat, by Coalbrookdale, indistinctly signed, with a wooden slatted seat.

60in (153cm) wide

$2,000-2,600   WW

One of a pair of 19thC Carron foundry cast iron garden benches, with pierced arcaded backs with Rococo details, on foliate-cast scroll legs.

64¼in (163cm) wide

$6,000-7,500   L&T

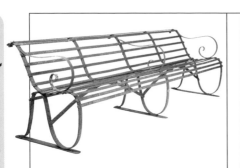

A late-19thC wrought iron garden bench, with a slatted back and seat, with scroll supports.

109½in (278cm) wide

$1,700-2,100   **WW**

A pair of architectural gates, of wrought iron.

ca. 1940   *79in (201cm) high*

$2,000-2,600   **DRA**

A Regency white-painted wrought iron wirework tree seat, of slatted construction and with arched backrests.

ca. 1815   *69in (175cm) diam*

$2,600-4,000   **DN**

A late-17th/early-18thC carved, veined white marble cistern, on a waisted oval section socle, with marks, knocks, scratches, and abrasions.

28in (71cm) wide

$7,500-8,000   **DN**

A pair of Victorian terra-cotta models of the Warwick vase, in the manner of Mark Henry Blanchard, with a grapevine frieze, the body decorated with busts, torches, and a lion's pelt, with stiff leaves and a beaded socle, rectangular plinths, decorated with ram's masks supporting swags of fruit and flowers, on a molded stepped base.

60in (153cm) high

$12,000-15,000   **WW**

A 19thC Blashfield-type terra-cotta garden urn and base, the shallow urn on a lotus-molded pedestal and square foot, on a square plinth base.

John Marriott Blashfield (1811–82) was a property developer and mosaic floor and ornamental terra-cotta manufacturer. He originally worked for the cement makers Wyatt, Parker and & Co in Millwall, but moved the business to Stamford in Lincolnshire in 1858, when it was renamed The Stamford Terracotta Company. As a result of the popularity of terra-cotta pieces at the Great Exhibition of 1851, he turned increasingly toward the manufacture of garden furniture, parapets, and urns. With the reconstruction of the Crystal Palace at Sydenham in 1854, Blashfield was awarded the contract to cast a series of colossal terra-cotta statues representing Australia, California, Birmingham ,and Sheffield by John Bell for display in the sculpture gallery at Crystal Palace. In 1859, terra-cotta production was transferred from London to Stamford, Lincolnshire, in order to exploit the local Jurassic clays, which were particularly suitable for terra-cotta production. The Wharf Road works were considerably larger than Blashfield's London premises and in the 1861 census he was calling himself "Terra Cotta Manufacturer and Pottery Company" and was employing 46 men and 13 boys.

43in (109cm) high

$6,500-8,000   **L&T**

A Victorian sandstone urn, the shallow bowl with broad fluted rim, on waisted socle and base.

46.5in (118cm) high

$6,500-8,000   **HT**

A pair of 19thC white-painted cast iron urns and stands, with a egg-and-dart molded rim above gadrooned body on fluted spreading base, the molded plinths centered by laurel wreaths.

46½in (118cm) high

$1,600-2,100   **L&T**

ESSENTIAL REFERENCE—THE BORGHESE VASE

The Borghese Vase is a monumental bell-shaped kylix sculpted from Pentelic marble. It was made in the second half of the 1st century BC in Greece as a lavish garden ornament for the Roman market. The vase was discovered in 1566 in the gardens of Sallust in Rome, along with a Silenus with Infant Bacchus, and, by 1645, the vase was in the Borghese Villa. On September 27, 1807, it was acquired by Napoleon Bonapart, sent to Paris, and placed in the Louvre museum, where it has remained since 1811. It is one of the most influential and admired Greek sculptural vases and was frequently copied in the 18thC with bronze reductions by Zoffoli and Righetti and other examples produced by Wedgwood and Coade. The present vases, with their finely sculpted frieze, copy the original closely, with their depiction of Bacchanalian revelry with Dionysus supporting a drunken Silenus, an engraving of which was published by Giovanni Battista Piranesi of his "Vasi, candelabra, cippi, sarcophagi, tripodi, Lucerne, ed ornamenti disegnati, pls. 109, 110" in 1778. However, other parts of their design borrow stylistically from the Medici vase that was first discovered in 1598 at the Villa Medici and then transferred in 1780 to the Uffizi. The use of bronze and marble in vases such as these is rare; for comparison, a related pair of Medici vases now in the Frick Collection by Luigi Valadier (1726-85) for Madame du Barry, employ the use of porphyry, gilt bronze, and marble. However, the present combination was more common for urns and candelabra in the Louis XVI period and echo the work of the celebrated bronzier Francois Remond.

A pair of rare French Louis XVI ormolu-mounted white marble vases, after the Borghese Vase, with chased frieze depicting in relief the thiasus, an ecstatic Bacchanalian procession with Dionysus draped with a panther skin and playing the aulos accompanied by Ariadne and various figures playing musical instruments, with Dionysus supporting a drunken Silenus, who is falling down, reaching for a spilled flagon of wine, and Dionysus holding a thyrsus with a panther at his feet, above a gadrooned body with applied stiff leaves and bulrush decoration and a pair of leaf-wrapped handles, above a laurel and berry stem and an acanthus-decorated socle with an outer laurel wreath, on a square plinth and a later leaf scroll decorated base with lion's paw feet.

ca. 1790   17½in (44.7cm) high
$170,000-210,000   WW

A pair of 19thC Scottish fireclay garden urns, of campana form with leaf tip-molded rims and part-lobed bodies, with loop handles, on socle bases.

37½in (95cm) high
$2,400-2,900   L&T

A pair of 19thC white and polychrome-painted cast iron urns, with gadrooned rims above the main body decorated with swags of fruit, twin handles, on molded and fluted spreading base and hexagonal shaped plinth.

3¾in (60cm) high
$1,100-1,250   L&T

A pair of 19thC white-painted cast iron urns and stands, each with egg-and-dart rim, reeded body on fluted spreading base, raised on platform.

39½in (100cm) high
$1,800-2,400   L&T

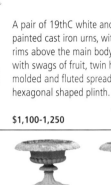

A pair of 19thC Garnkirk "Eglinton" fireclay garden urns and plinths, with relief-molded friezes with medieval figures, on square panel plinths stamped "GARNKIRK."

54¼in (138cm) high
$1,700-2,100   L&T

A pair of large 19thC Garnkirk fireclay garden urns and plinths, in the form of lotus flowers, raised on square plinths with molded shield sides, stamped "GARNKIRK" on the foot.

44in (112cm) high
$2,000-2,600   L&T

A pair of Compton Pottery-type terra-cotta urns, carved in the manner of Archibald Knox, with Celtic motifs, one with wear and minor losses, one restored.

ca. 1900   16¼in (41cm) high
$850-1,000   SWO

A pair of 20thC Indian sandstone planters, of Gothic design, each frieze with quatrefoil detail, with wear and weathering.

27½in (70cm) high
$1,700-2,100   SWO

ESSENTIAL REFERENCE—JAN CLAUDIUS DE COCK

Jan Claudius de Cock (1667-1735) was born in Antwerp and became a sculptor, draftsman, and writer. He trained during the early 1680s in the workshop of Peeter Verbrugghen the Elder, and after his death in 1686 continued to work with Peeter the Younger, joining the Guild in 1688-89 and gaining his independence in 1691. In 1693, he went to Holland to work on the Palace of Breda for King William III, Stadtholder of the Netherlands, making portrait busts of members of the House of Orange. By 1697-98, De Cock had returned to Antwerp, where he established a large workshop of assistants who helped produce his vast oeuvre of sacred and profane subjects on both a small and a monumental scale. As well as being influenced by the later Antwerp school of the Verbrugghen family, he admired antique art and the sculpture of François Duquesnoy (1597-1643). The present statues are close in style and spirit to the secular statuary that De Cock produced for gardens, courtyards, and stairwells in Dutch and Flemish houses in the 18thC. This is probably an allegory of Africa from a set of the Four Continents. One of the figures clearly represents the Infant Hercules with the club that he was to use in his Labors, slaying a variety of horrible monsters, while the little girl perhaps held the standard symbol of Omphale, a distaff, in her left hand—the piercing in her clenched fist indicates that this was perhaps fashioned in metal for the sake of durability. In a rare moment of weakness, the hero surrendered the club, a symbol of his machismo, in exchange for her ("girly") distaff to show how much he was in love with her. The fact that she is now weeping and that both have their proper symbolic attributes returned may refer to the end of the brief love affair. The fact that the present pair is neither signed nor dated may be a reflection of the fact that they are not finished; there is an uncarved wedge of marble behind the ankles of the infant Omphale.

A pair of late-17th/early-18thC Flemish carved marble allegorical figures, attributed to Jan Claudius De Cock, possibly representing Day and Night, one in the form of the Infant Hercules holding a club, the other as a young girl, possibly Omphale, weeping and holding probably a torch in her left hand, now missing.

Figures 36¼in (91.8cm) and 35¾in (90.5cm) high
Plinths 27in (68.7cm) high

$22,000-26,000 WW

One of a pair of late-19thC octagonal bronze and glass gate post lanterns, the lights with frosted glass panel sides and pointed finials, on cast iron open hexagonal bases.

57in (145cm) high
$2,400-2,900 L&T

A 19thC Italian or French marble column, the detachable rotating top above a turned stem and an octagonal base.

44in (111.5cm) high
$550-650 WW

A pair of 20thC Indian sandstone garden troughs, the panels decorated in relief with stylized floral motifs, each raised on two rectangular blocks, with general wear.

40¼in (102cm) wide
$650-800 SWO

A pair of composite stone "pineapple" garden finials.

17¾in (45cm) high
$550-650 WW

An early-20thC lead fountain, cast as a naked boy standing on an escallop shell supported by three dolphins.

30in (76cm) high
$1,300-2,000 HT

A pair of early-19thC portoro and white marble columns, the white marble capitals carved with acanthus, scrolls, and thistles, on columns.

78in (198cm) high
$2,600-4,000 L&T

A 19thC white marble bust of Clytie, upon a turned cylindrical pedestal base.

"Clytie" after the nymph turned into a flower for unrequited love of the sun god Helios.

bust 27½in (70cm) high
$5,300-6,600 CHEF

A 20thC white marble figure emblematic of "Fall," life size, depicting a draped young woman holding bunches of grapes and vines, with a further cluster of grapes in her hair, unsigned.

66½in (169cm) high
$5,300-6,600 L&T

A 19thC swell-bodied copper Ethan Allen horse weather vane, retaining an old verdigris surface, with a couple of bullet holes.

34in (86.5cm) wide

$2,100-2,600   **POOK**

A 19thC swell-bodied copper bull weather vane, the front in cast zinc, bar replaced, repairs on legs, one horn replaced.

26in (66cm) wide

$4,600-5,900   **POOK**

A 19thC Cushing & White full bodied copper horse and sulky weather vane, retaining its original makers plaque and old weathered surface, bullet hole on front leg.

26in (66cm) wide

$2,600-4,000   **POOK**

An unusual 19thC copper weather vane, modeled as a masted gun ship.

23in (60cm) wide

$400-550   **APAR**

A late-19thC handmade folk art copper-over wood whale weather vane, with iron seam along back, retaining an old tarred black surface.

34in (86.5cm) long

$15,000-20,000   **POOK**

A 19thC sheet tin running horse weather vane, with directional arrow, wear consistent with age and use.

40½in (103cm) long

$650-800   **POOK**

A late-19th/early-20thC American sporting dog copper weather vane, in the form of a setter, the hollow body in low relief.

32¼in (82cm) long

$1,050-13,000   **L&T**

An early-20thC Pennsylvania painted weather vane, with a carved wood figure atop a wood horse wrapped in sheet metal, old white surface, lacking reins, repaired splits on arms.

26in (66cm) high

$12,000-15,000   **POOK**

An early-20thC swell-bodied copper running fox weather vane, with traces of gilding.

27in (68.5cm) wide

$8,500-10,000   **POOK**

ESSENTIAL REFERENCE—PERSIAN RUGS

From around the mid-19thC a significant revival of interest in Persian weaving began, primarily generated by a Western fashion for "exotic" Middle Eastern and Eastern designs and fabrics.

- The main centers of production were Tabriz, Mashad, Isfahan, Kashan, Kirman, Heriz, and Seneh.
- The most significant carpet-producing Persian tribes were the Ashfar, the Kashgai, and the Khamseh.
- Towns generally specialized in the production of carpets and rugs, typically fine woven with wool on cotton, or occasionally silk on silk. Patterns tended to the curvilinear, featuring flowers and foliage.
- Villages and tribal regions mainly produced rugs and smaller items, such as bags, in wool on wool; carpets are fairly rare. Designs are generally individual and often geometric and/or stylized.
- Fine tribal rugs dating from before ca. 1900 are particularly sought after.

A late-19th/early-20thC Bakhtiari carpet, West Persia, the red field with allover indigo-and-ivory tree cartouche pattern, within red tree and foliate border.

130¾in (332cm) long

$4,000-5,300   **L&T**

A Bidjar carpet, of Garrus design, the blue field decorated throughout with stylized foliate branches and flowers in an asymmetric design, within an ocher border decorated with flower heads issuing palmettes, within floral decorated blue guard stripes.

The design originates with the weavers of Kirman in the 17thC, who designed a series of carpets with fields covered with interlocking arabesques enclosing floral sprays. In common with other Kirman designs, a close variant on this design began to be woven in North West Persia in the 18thC. By the 19thC, it was so well associated with the North West that it was given the name Garrus, a small weaving center near Bijar, although it was not exclusively woven there. One of the best-known carpets from this group, inscribed as being the work of Garrus and dated 1794, was formerly in the McMullan Collection, now in the Metropolitan Museum of Art, New York. The rich colors and elegant design lent itself to the demands of the European interior designers, particularly in the second half of the 19thC, and, as a result, many examples are found in country houses in Great Britain and western Europe.

251¼in (638cm) long

$7,500-8,500   **DN**

A Bidjar carpet, of Garrus design, the dark blue field decorated with an asymmetric design incorporating stylized foliate branches and flower heads, the madder border decorated with flower heads and geometricized leaves, within multiple guard stripes.

195.25in (496cm) long

$6,000-7,500   **DN**

A Feraghan carpet, the cream field decorated with an overall design of flowering foliage, within madder borders decorated with patera and multiple guard stripes.

287½in (730cm) long

$16,000-20,000   **DN**

A Ghom silk carpet, Centered Iran.

ca. 1980   *116¼in (295cm) long*

$6,000-6,600   **TEN**

A Hereke silk carpet, the centered medallion within an ivory ground, a few stains.

111½in (283cm) long

$1,050-1,200   **CHEF**

A Heriz carpet, of typical design with centered medallion on a madder ground.

192.25in (488cm) long

$4,000-4,600   **CHEF**

An early-20thC Heriz carpet, North West Persia, the brick red field with large indigo and salmon pink medallion, ivory, pink, and indigo spandrels, within indigo turtle palmette and vine border.

130¾in (332cm) long

$4,000-4,600   **L&T**

A Heriz carpet, the blue field decorated with stylized flower heads linked by geometric branches.

137¾in (350cm) long

$6,500-8,000 **DN**

A Heriz low-pile carpet, North West Persia, of hand-knotted wool, with a madder field, medallion with pendant of interlinking arabesques and vines with palmettes and flower heads, with a turtle palmette border.

ca. 1880
186in (472cm) long

$26,000-33,000 **DRA**

An Isfahan carpet, the blue field centered by a sectional medallion, within scrolling branches of flowers and intertwined borders.

166¼in (422cm) long

$2,100-2,600 **DN**

A Kashan carpet, the red field decorated with an overall design incorporating scrolling foliate motifs, birds, and animals, within a similarly decorated blue border, some wear overall, fringing has been trimmed down.

165in (419cm) long

$4,600-5,900 **DN**

A late-19th/early-20thC Kashan carpet, Central Persia, the indigo field with red-and-ivory medallion, red and blue spandrels, within indigo palmette and foliate border.

139in (353cm) long

$2,600-3,300 **L&T**

A 20thC Persian Kashan carpet, the red ground with a centered medallion and foliate ground within a banded border.

218½in (555cm) long

$4,600-5,300 **SWO**

A Kelim carpet, the geometric design formed by a palette of warm colors.

114¼in (290cm) long

$2,600-3,300 **CHEF**

A 20thC Khorassan carpet, East Persia, the purple field with bird-filled tree and foliate pattern, within indigo palmette and foliate border.

203½in (517cm) long

$4,000-5,300 **L&T**

A Kirman carpet, by Master Weaver Rashid Farrokhi, the blue field decorated with geometricized and foliate terminals, within a red border and multiple guard stripes.

198½in (504cm) long

$11,000-13,000 **DN**

A Kirman carpet, with boteh-decorated centered field, within conforming borders and madder guard stripes, signed "Azimi."

156¾in (398cm) long

$6,000-7,500   DN

A 20thC Meshed carpet, North East Persia, the blue field with red medallion, similar spandrels, within indigo foliate border, signature on one end.

132¼in (336cm) long

$750-850   L&T

A late-19th/early-20thC Qashqai Maharlu carpet, Khamseh area, South West Persia.

199¼in (506cm) long

$7,500-8,500   WW

A Qum silk carpet, of French inspired style, the pale field decorated with flowers within scroll-framed cartouches.

117¾in (299cm) long

$6,000-6,600   DN

A Saroukh Carpet, West Iran, the ivory field with scrolling floral vines and twin urns issuing flowers enclosed by raspberry borders of meandering vines flanked by ivory guard stripes.

ca. 1960   *137¾in (350cm) long*

$1,600-2,000   TEN

A 20thC Semnan carpet, Central Persia, signature on one end.

193in (490cm) long

$4,600-5,300   L&T

A Serapi carpet, the red field decorated with a centered medallion surrounded by varying stylized foliate motifs, within polychrome spandrels, the dark blue borders decorated profusely with meandering vines and flower heads.

137½in (349cm) long

$4,600-5,900   DN

A late-19th/early-20thC Serapi carpet, North West Persia.

220in (559cm) long

$17,000-21,000   WW

A Serapi carpet, decorated with stylized foliate and floral motifs, the cream medallion within a madder field and cornered by blue spandrels, the madder border decorated with blue and cream flowers.

153.5in (390cm) long

$4,000-5,300   DN

A late-19thC Sultanabad carpet, West Persia, the indigo field with stylized foliate "Mustafavi" pattern, within rust stylized foliate vine border.

244in (620cm) long

$6,500-8,000   **L&T**

A 20thC Sultanabad carpet, the cream ground with bold floral design within floral borders.

118¼in (300cm) long

$6,500-8,000   **SWO**

An early-20thC Saruk Dervish pictorial tiger or leopard rug, with an inscription and partial date, Central Persia.

48¾in (124cm) wide

$3,300-4,600   **WW**

A Tabriz carpet, the cream field of Shah Abbas design with columns of large palmettes and vines enclosed by indigo borders of meandering vines flanked by guard stripes.

ca. 1950
145¾in (370cm) long

$3,300-4,600   **TEN**

An early/mid-20thC Tabriz "Benlian" Carpet, North West Persia, the green field with red medallion surrounded by four smaller medallions, similar spandrels, within yellow and indigo cusped border, star signatures on two corners.

164.5in (418cm) long

$8,000-9,000   **L&T**

An early-20thC Tabriz carpet, North West Persia, signature on one end.

149¾in (380cm) long

$6,000-6,600   **L&T**

A mid/late-20thC Tabriz carpet, with circular cream medallion with foliate pendants, blue spandrels, within indigo cartouche border.

176.5in (448cm) long

$4,000-5,300   **L&T**

A Tabriz carpet, signed Javan Amir Khiz, the madder field decorated with an overall design incorporating palmettes and stylized foliate terminals in tones of cream and blue, within an ocher border and guard stripes, some wear patches of wear.

170½in (433cm) long

$6,000-6,600   **DN**

A Tabriz carpet, decorated with flower heads, herati, and foliate motifs.

155½in (395cm) long

$4,000-4,600 DN

A Tehran vase carpet, worked with an array of urns with flowers, birds, trees, and scrolling foliage, North Persia.

ca. 1910 *79¾in (202.5cm) wide*

$2,600-4,000 WW

A late-19th/early-20thC Varamin carpet, Central Persia, the ivory field with palmette and bird-filled lattice pattern, within red palmette and bird border.

119¾in (304cm) long

$2,000-2,600 L&T

ESSENTIAL REFERENCE—ZIEGLER CARPETS

In 1883, Ziegler and Co., of Manchester, England, established a Persian carpet manufactory in Sultanabad (now Arak), in Iran. Their intention was to adapt traditional Middle Eastern rug and carpet designs to satisfy more "restrained" Western tastes. For this reason, they employed designers from some of the then-new Western department stores, such as B. Altman and Company, of New York, and Liberty, of London, to rework standard Persian colors, patterns, and motifs. The reworked designs were then produced using newly developed dying techniques in conjunction with Ziegler's modern looms—the latter worked by highly skilled, locally recruited craftsmen. The resulting rugs and carpets were characterized by bold, allover patterns with softer, more subtle palettes than their more vibrant traditional Persian counterparts.

A late-19thC Ziegler carpet, with an ivory ground, Arak Sultanabad, West Persia.

175.25in (445cm) wide

$13,000-16,000 WW

A late-19thC Ziegler Mahal carpet, Arak Sultanabad, of Mina-Khani style design.

214in (544cm) long

$2,600-3,300 WW

A late-19thC Ziegler Mahal carpet, North West Persia.

270in (686cm) long

$7,500-8,000 WW

A late-19thC Ziegler Mahal carpet, North West Persia.

159½in (405cm) long

$17,000-21,000 WW

A Ziegler Mahal carpet, the madder field with flower-head design, cornered by navy spandrels.

204¾in (520cm) long

$4,000-5,300 DN

A late-20thC North West Persian runner, the reddish pink field with allover herati pattern, within narrow stylized ivory border.

303in (770cm) long

$4,600-5,300 L&T

ESSENTIAL REFERENCE—KAZAK RUGS

Compared to that of the rugs from the northern and eastern Caucasus, the wool pile of rugs made in the Kazak district of the western Caucasus is both longer and usually much more loosely woven, which results in more open designs with bolder, less detailed motifs. The designs are primarily based on classic Persian and Anatolian forms, and good examples exhibit a fine balance between scale and color contrast. The best examples incorporate colors that are bright and vibrant, but not brash or conflicting with each other. For example, some rugs made after ca. 1880 with early chemical dyes exhibit notably bright but harsh colors—especially oranges and purples—that don't harmonize well with traditional natural colors. It's also worthy of note that traditional and often-used shades of brown and charcoal are prone to natural oxidation due to iron in the dyestuff, giving an appearance of being "worn." However, if the supporting pile remains sound, this is not considered by collectors to be a flaw.

An early-20thC Alpan Kuba rug, East Caucasus, the indigo field with allover red medallion and harshang pattern, within red geometric border.

82¾in (210cm) long

$1,200-1,450 L&T

A late-19th/early-20thC Kazak rug, South Caucasus, the plain red field with hexagonal indigo medallion, suspending pendants, and flanked by triangles, within double indigo geometric borders.

87½in (222cm) long

$1,500-1,800 L&T

A late-19th/early-20thC Gendje prayer rug, South Caucasus, the field with polychrome lattice pattern, cream mihrab panel, within double-cross and skittle borders.

74½in (189cm) long

$1,000-1,250 L&T

A late-19th/early-20thC Kazak runner, South Caucasus, the rust red field with six polychrome medallions, within ivory harshang border.

133in (338cm) long

$1,200-1,450 L&T

An early/mid-20thC German Tetex carpet, of Caucasian style, the abrash red field with column of four lozenge medallions, within indigo S and rosette border.

157½in (400cm) long

$1,200-1,450 L&T

A good Shirvan/Akstafa runner, the four medallions within an indigo field.

ca. 1900 *112¼in (285cm) long*

$2,200-2,600 CHEF

TEXTILES

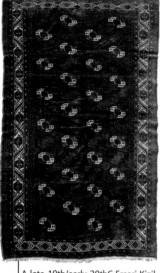

A late-19th/early-20thC Ersari Kizil Ayak carpet, Turkmenistan.

150½in (382cm) long

$600-750   **L&T**

A late-19th/early-20thC Khotan carpet, East Turkestan, the red field with vases and other objects, within olive green object and floral border.

104in (264cm) long

$2,600-3,300   **L&T**

A Turkoman silk carpet, the polychrome field of tessellating design, within a blue border, madder and ocher guard stripes.

114¼in (290cm) long

$2,100-2,600   **DN**

A first half 20thC Turkish Ushak carpet, with a Tree of Life design, West Anatolia.

151in (383.5cm) wide

$2,600-3,300   **WW**

ESSENTIAL REFERENCE—USHAK CARPETS

Ushak in Western Turkey had been a center of rug making since at least the 15thC. The town is credited with the creation of many iconic Turkish designs, such as "Lottos" and "Holbeins"—named as such due to their appearance in paintings by those artists in the early 16thC—and is also known for its large "medallion" and "star" rugs, influenced by Ottoman court designs.

After the 17thC, the market waned in Europe, and rug production in Ushak went into decline. However, demand returned in the mid-19thC, following a revived Western fashion for "exotic" Eastern designs, but because the town no longer had sufficient skilled weavers left to meet the demand, it turned to neighboring towns and villages for help. Weavers from the latter had a more tribal style, using larger knots and longer pile on all-wool foundations. Consequently, 19thC Ushak rugs are a fusion of tribal styles and older Ushak designs, and some also incorporate simplified, Persian-style floral patterns. Also, sizewise, most rugs from this period were woven to fit European and American rooms.

A late-19th/early-20thC Ushak carpet, West Anatolia, the plain orange field with olive green lozenge medallion, within camel hooked totem border.

137¾in (350cm) long

$4,000-4,600   **L&T**

A late-19thC Ushak "Turkey" carpet, West Anatolia, the red field with columns of palmettes and cruciform motifs, within red rosette and vine border.

213¼in (542cm) long

$1,300-1,800   **L&T**

A 20thC Ushak carpet, of William Morris design.

163¾in (416cm) long

$7,500-8,000   **DN**

A large Ottoman cover, of Kashmir wool, tamboured throughout in silks with pagodas and striped tents, embellished with silver metal strips.

ca. 1800   *79in (200.5cm) long*

$4,600-5,300   **WW**

A late-19thC French Aubusson rug.

112¼in (285cm) long

$2,600-3,300   BELL

An Aubusson-style wool carpet.

137¾in (350cm) long

$550-650   CHOR

A Donegal carpet, in Ushak style.

161.5in (410cm) long

$1,800-2,400   DN

ESSENTIAL REFERENCE—AUBUSSON CARPETS

In ca. 1740, Aubusson, in central southern France, already famous for its tapestries, began production of piled carpets. Initially, they were mostly copies of oriental carpets, such as Ushaks, but, from ca. 1750, they were increasingly in the style of the great Savonnerie factory at Chaillot, near Paris. Indeed, from ca. 1760 old "cartoons" (tapestry designs) from Savonnerie were often employed.

● Unlike Savonnerie, Aubusson wasn't specifically a factory but instead comprised craftsmen spread throughout the city in independent workshops, working either on their own account or producing piecework. Moreover, although they worked in the Savonnerie style, Aubusson weaves were looser, less dense, and often woven with coarsely spun wool, making the designs less crisp and regular.

● In 1771, in order to create more employment for the tapestry weavers, Aubusson began to weave "tapis-ras" (flat-woven carpets made using the tapestry technique), and it is for this type of carpet that Aubusson became best known, although the designs were still often copies of Savonnerie. While production ceased during the French Revolution, it gradually revived thereafter and continued throughout the 19thC, with Aubusson producing increasingly larger numbers of "tapis-ras," in fashionable and diverse prevailing styles, to supply the growing middle class.

A mid-19thC Aubusson carpet, in Turkish style, decorated with stylized floral foliage throughout, the centered Herati motif within a cream medallion, the crimson field surrounded by stylized lotus heads, within a cream border, some wear overall.

Probably acquired by Francis Richard Charles Guy Greville, 5th Earl of Warwick (1853-1924) for "Queen Anne's Bedroom," part of the State Apartments at Warwick Castle. Warwick Castle is one of the most important and impressive medieval castles in Great Britain, which, from the 17thC, was converted from a fortification into a residence by the Greville family, Barons Brooke, later Earls of Warwick.

332½in (845cm) long

$9,000-10,500   DN

A late-19th/early-20thC Donegal carpet, North West Ireland.

119¼in (303cm) long

$2,000-2,600   L&T

An early/mid-20thC Tetex carpet, Germany, of Tabriz style, original label on reverse.

130in (330cm) long

$1,500-1,800   L&T

A late-19thC Amritsar carpet, North India, the red field with allover herati pattern, within ivory herati border.

311¼in (790cm) long

$9,000-10,500   L&T

A late-19thC Amritsar carpet, North India, the ivory field with Herati pattern, within red stylized palmette and vine border.

223¼in (567cm) wide

$9,000-12,000   L&T

A mid-19thC Pondicherry carpet, South East India, the ivory field with allover floral pineapple and grape "chintz" pattern, within blue rose cartouche border, with a strip section, possibly removed from a pendant carpet.

Little has been written on the history of the carpet industry of South East India beyond noting that it is the oldest center of carpet weaving in India, with weavers arriving from Persia some time before 1550. Western interest in Indian carpets was aroused by the impressive examples displayed at the Great Exhibition of 1851.

Carpet 256in (650cm) long Strip 236¼in (600cm) long

$15,000-18,000   **L&T**

An Indian Oushak-style wool carpet, from the "Gazani Collection" by The Bokara Rug Company, New Jersey, the cream ground with centered floral lozenge and overall floral and scrolling foliate decoration, within a Herati-style border with flower heads on the angles.

221in (561cm) long

$800-900   **MART**

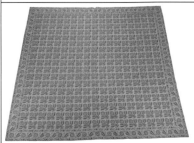

A 20thC Indian carpet, the field with foliate designs on a pale ground.

121in (307cm) long

$2,600-3,300   **SWO**

An Indo-Portuguese embroidered carpet, worked in twisted silks with a border of peonies and lions, with gilt embellishments, the field with a centered circular medallion.

ca. 1800   103½in (263cm) long

$6,000-7,500   **WW**

A Portuguese needlepoint carpet, some minor wear on edges.

100½in (255cm) long

$4,000-4,600   **DN**

A Spanish Cuenca carpet, decorated with stylized foliate motifs, figures, and animals.

111½in (283cm) long

$1,800-2,400   **DN**

A mid-20thC Swedish flat-weave rug, woven with geometric motifs.

94½in (240cm) long

$2,000-2,600   **SWO**

A North American centennial hook rug, worked with a stars-and-tripes shield within "Centennial 1776-1876" and red, white, and blue stars, maple frame, with wear and losses.

1876   34¾in (88cm) wide

$1,600-2,100   **SWO**

A late-16th/early-17thC Flemish "Game Park" tapestry, possibly Oudenaarde, with an elegant lady and attendant picking flowers in the foreground, before a group of huntsmen with horses and hounds, in a wooded landscape, within borders woven with vignettes of sitting women, musicians, and putti, surrounded by fruiting and flowering vases and scrolling foliage, later backed.

This tapestry, with its sprawling verdant grounds and broad, intricate border type, is typical of Flemish tapestry at the turn of the 17thC.

$10,000-11,000   DN

A mid-17thC Brussels figural tapestry "The Feeding of the Chickens," after Jacob Jordaens (1593-1678), "Scenes from Country Life" series, possibly workshop of Jacob Geubels II, depicting a pastoral maiden scattering grains from a basket, surrounded by animals, including a hound, peacock, and chickens, within an elaborate vaulted architectural setting flanked by masks and columns, the lower selvedge with "B*B" Brussels town mark, later backed, two horizontal tears.

Antwerp-born painter Jacob Jordaens followed in the footsteps of Rubens and Van Dyck as the city's leading artist during the 17thC. While he completed numerous mythological and religious commissions, including for the Swedish and English Royal courts, he is most well known for his exuberant genre scenes, characterized by a strong sense of realism. These qualities translate to "Scenes from Country Life" tapestry series, which Jordaens is suspected to have designed during the 1620s or 1630s.

148¾in (378cm) high
$16,000-20,000   DN

ESSENTIAL REFERENCE—VERDURE TAPESTRIES

While it is known that tapestry production began on a small scale in Europe around the 12thC, following the introduction of weaving techniques from the East, and while it is well documented that tapestry production flourished, especially in France and the Low Countries, from the 14thC to the 17thC, it isn't exactly clear where or, indeed, when "verdure" tapestries were first produced. It can, however, be stated with certainty that they had been acknowledged as a distinct form or style of tapestry by the 16thC.

Derived from the French word "vert," meaning "green," verdure tapestries were characterized by the prominent green tones of their subject matter: lush foliate and floral imagery, mostly presented, certainly initially, in idyllic forest and woodland scenes. However, as their popularity grew, more complex landscapes were portrayed, incorporating, for example, lakes, formal gardens, buildings (such as châteaux and follies), and, especially, fauna—with the latter often depicted in hunting scenes. Long popular—they are collectible today—their production gradually declined during the course of the 18thC and 19thC, following the development of a more economical medium for decorating a room—wallpaper.

A 17thC Flemish verdure tapestry, woven with various birds, including a pair of herons and a parrot, in a wooded river landscape with a bridge, in the distance an abbey and various buildings, with a ribbon-tied fruit and foliage border.

161in (409.5)cm wide
$6,000-6,600   WW

A late-16th/early-17thC Flemish Classical tapestry, probably Oudenaarde, with a general in Roman attire and soldiers, one shield emblazoned with an armorial of crescent moons and a star, with a landscape with animals and hunting figures, later backed.

108in (274cm) wide
$12,000-15,000   DN

A 17thC Flemish verdure tapestry, with trees and with a castle in the distance.

99¾in (253cm) wide
$7,500-8,500   WW

A late-17thC Flemish verdure tapestry, woven with a bird amid trees, buildings, and hills in the background.

90¼in (229cm) wide
$4,600-5,900   L&T

A late-17thC Flemish verdure tapestry, with a centered fountain and further architectural elements, backed, the tapestry bears the usual minor marks, border appears to be associated.

120in (305cm) wide
$26,000-33,000   DN

A late-17th/early-18thC Flemish mythological tapestry, Oudenarde, depicting the "Judgment of Paris," with Mercury holding an apple before the shepherd Paris and the three goddesses, Hera, Athena, and Aphrodite, depicted as queens, sitting in thrones with peacocks, before a Classical palace.

108¼in (275cm) wide

$7,500-8,500   WW

An early-18thC Flemish mythological tapestry, with Eurydice bitten by a snake, probably Antwerp, the three maidens in the foreground portrayed gathering flowers in a landscape before a distant architectural background, the border woven with foliage, trophies, lambrequin, exotic birds, and fleur-de-lis.

119¾in (304cm) high

$11,000-12,000   DN

An early-18thC Flemish verdure tapestry, with two hunters and hounds in a woodland setting, within a floral border woven with roses and other flower heads, with minor marks, selvedges later.

134in (340cm) wide

$11,000-12,000   DN

A late-17th/early-18thC Flemish mythological tapestry, of Dido and Aeneas, probably Bruges, depicting Dido in a gold dress and blue mantle approaching Aeneas, who reclines beneath an olive tree, wearing a flowing red cloak, Dido's head turned with her gaze to the viewer, accompanied by Cupid, who bears an open jewel casket, a carriage drawn by three stamping horses on the left, within flower borders with bead, and reel slips marked with cartouches, a horn, and a hunter's bag.

A clever and enterprising woman and founding Queen of Carthage, the enduring figure of Dido is best known from Virgil's account in his epic poem "Aeneid." Depicting the legend of Trojan hero Aeneas, the story recalls Aeneas and his crew being washed ashore and seeking refuge from Dido and her people. At the hands of Venus and Cupid, a passionate love affair soon ensues between the pair. The affair comes to an abrupt end after Aeneas is met by Mercury, who reminds him of his destiny as Trojan hero and future founder of Rome; he quickly departs in the night with his men, leaving behind a heartbroken Dido. Unable to cope, Dido burns all that reminded her of Aeneas and kills herself; a tragic act which provokes eternal strife between Aeneas's people and her own. This tapestry depicts an early scene in which Cupid, at the request of Venus, disguises himself as Aeneas's young son to offer gifts to Dido in return for refuge and shelter. Accepting, Dido cradles Cupid who begins to weaken her sworn fidelity to her late husband, thus revealing her newfound love for Aeneas.

148in (376cm) wide

$13,000-18,000   L&T

An early-18thC Flemish tapestry panel, possibly Lille, with a hawk, parrot, and chickens in a garden with rose bushes, a pond, later backed.

66¼in (168cm) high

$6,500-8,000   DN

An 18thC Continental "Teniers" tapestry, possibly Brussels, emblematic of Spring and fertility, depicting a shepherd with sheep, a milkmaid milking a cow, and figures in the background, the textile is restored overall, the selvedges are associated.

The milkmaid sitting prominently in the foreground is a recurring feature in genre tapestries of milking scenes after Teniers. The unusual composition of the present tapestry may also have been influenced by the "months" tapestries from the workshops of Gilles, Urbanus, and Jan Leyniers, woven during the late-17th/18thC. In this series, the month of June is rendered as a sheep-shearing scene.

106¾in (271cm) wide

$8,500-10,000   DN

A late-17thC Louis XIV Aubusson historical tapestry, with Dido and Aeneas, possibly after the designs by Giovanni Francesco Romanelli (Italian 1610-62), the top border centered by a Baronial coat of arms.

This tapestry may depict an episode from the story of Dido and Aeneas, one of the tales from Ovid's "Heroides", which revolved around legendary historical and mythological women and was a popular subject for tapestry weavers in France and Flanders alike. That series is said to follow Romanelli's influential cartoons, which were used for tapestries by the Flemish workshop of Michiel Wauters.

104in (264cm) high

$8,000-9,000   DN

An early-18thC Aubusson verdure tapestry, with Orpheus enchanting the animals, portrayed playing the lyre in a landscape with exotic birds, a vista of a formal garden beyond.

93¾in (238cm) high

$8,000-9,000   DN

An early-18thC French "Teniers" tapestry fragment, possibly Aubusson, with two rustic musicians standing on barrels, later backed.

This panel probably took its inspiration from the rustic country celebrations painted by David Teniers the Younger, which provided popular source material for tapestry manufacture during the late-17th and 18thC.

73¾in (187cm) high

$7,500-8,500   DN

A mid-18thC Louis XV Aubusson mythological tapestry, by Antoine Grellet, of Niobe and her Children, with Apollo and Artemis firing arrows at the figures in the centered field, with weaver's mark "AUBUSSON A. GRELLET."

According to Homer's "Iliad," Niobe had six sons and six daughters and boasted of her progenitive superiority to Leto, who had only two children, the twin deities Apollo and Artemis. As punishment for her pride, Apollo killed all Niobe's sons and Artemis killed all her daughters. Weaver Antoine Grellet is recorded in the Aubusson workshops during the middle of the 18thC.

206¼in (524cm) wide

$16,000-20,000   DN

A late-18thC French Aubusson pastoral tapestry, with a mother and child and reclining hunter in a landscape.

106¼in (270cm) high

$2,600-3,300   DN

A late-18thC Louis XVI Aubusson portico tapestry, in the manner of Jean-Baptiste Huet, woven in wool and silk, the centered trophy with military attributes, surrounded by a floral garland and suspended from a ribbon, flanked by flowering columns, with a scene of an eagle attacking a hare below, later backed.

104in (264cm) high

$6,500-8,000   DN

A late-18thC Louis XVI Aubusson Draperies tapestry, with Watteauesque figures in a garden, backed.

95¾in (243cm) wide

$6,500-8,000   DN

TEXTILES

A mid-18thC ivory silk and embroidered coverlet, possibly Spitalfields, in England, worked in colored and metallic threads, with centered basket of flowers, including tulips, roses, and peonies, flanked by borders with further baskets, swags, and entwined exotic flowers, palm trees, and sheaves of wheat, with a paper label for the "PANTECHNICON BELGRAVE SQUARE," stamped "THE DUKE OF LEEDS."

This coverlet may originate from the renowned silk workshops of Spitalfields. Spitalfields became the center of the silk industry after the Revocation of the Edict of Nantes by Louis XIV of France in 1685, which resulted in many French protestants fleeing to escape persecution for their religion, and settling in England. They brought with them the knowledge of their trades, including silk weaving, and set up their workshops in Spitalfields in London and surrounding areas, soon attracting demand from both London's aristocracy and burgeoning merchant classes for dress and furnishing fabrics. A ca. 1752-53 dress ascribed to the Spitalfields workshops, designed for "Lady Mayoress" Ann Fanshawe, now features in the Museum of London. The clustered arrangement of flowers can also be likened to the designs of Anna-Maria Garthwaite (1690-1763), whose botanical studies in watercolor provided patterns for the most fashionable fabrics. The Pantechnicon, for which the coverlet bears a tag, was a large repository for luxury goods in Belgravia, functioning in part as a picture retailer and furniture merchant, and as a storage warehouse. It was mostly destroyed by fire in 1874. The stamped title on the label may indicate that this coverlet was once property of the Dukes of Leeds, whose seats during the 18th and 19thC included Kiveton Hall, and Hornby Castle.

103½in (263cm) long

$10,000-11,000   **DN**

A George III folk art woolwork and watercolor picture, depicting a farmyard scene, with a watermill and attendant figures, in a glazed giltwood frame.

15in (38.5cm) wide

$550-650   **WW**

An Elizabethan chalice cover, embroidered with flowers and foliate decoration, with centered cross.

9½in (24cm) wide

$650-800   **CHOR**

A 17thC Christening cloth, with needlework decoration of flower heads.

31¼in (79cm) wide

$800-900   **CHOR**

An 18th/19thC needlework panel, worked with lovers in a garden, original frame.

14¼in (36cm) wide

$1,300-1,800   **SWO**

A Georgian needlework map, depicting England and Wales, by Sarah Powell, Beech Hill, with a later walnut and gilt frame.

1802   *21 x 28in (53 x 42cm)*

$260-400   **WHP**

An 18thC needlework panel, depicting Apollo with attendants, framed.

35¾in (91cm) high

$600-650   **L&T**

A Victorian Colonial India velvet-embroidered three-fold floor screen, each fold with 2 panels with appliqué silk needlework depicting roses, thistles, shamrocks, and lilies, the same on the reverse for 12 panels total, in an ebonized frame, bearing a brass plaque engraved "THIS EMBROIDERY CAME OFF THE DAIS ERECTED AT DELHI/ FROM WHICH/ QUEEN VICTORIA WAS PROCLAIMED EMPRESS OF INDIA/ 1877."

On January 1, 1877, the 1st Earl of Lytton, Viceroy of India, read a proclamation declaring Queen Victoria as Empress of India at the Delhi Durbar, to a mass assembly of dignitaries, maharajas, and nawabs, held on the vast plain of Coronation Park in Delhi. These needlework panels were located on the centered hexagonal tentlike pavilion, or shamiana, positioned at the frieze in a band above bannerettes encircling the upper tentlike cover, some 35 feet (10.5m) above the ground. Lytton insisted that no Indian imagery or designs were to be used in the decorative theme for the event, although he did allow for the Indian lotus to accompany the English rose, Scottish thistle, and Irish shamrock on the frieze, all represented here.

ca. 1870s   *69in (175cm) wide*

$15,000-18,000   **L&T**

A German band sampler, worked in silks on linen, with pattern bands, birds, flowers, baskets, animals, and number and alphabet series, with religious motifs and subjects, and a cartouche with initials and date, some designs taken from Johann Sibmacher's pattern book.

1746 *63in (160cm) high*

$1,800-2,400 L&T

A German band sampler, worked in silks on a linen ground edged with silk ribbons, depicting pattern bands, alphabet and number series, birds, trees, flowers, religious motifs, tools, a building and people, with initials and date, in a modern frame.

1776 *41in (104cm) high*

$900-1,050 L&T

A German band sampler, worked in silk on linen, with alphabet and number series, birds, animals, people, and religious subjects, with various initials and dates

1786 and 1810 *41¼in (105cm) high*

$1,500-2,000 L&T

An 18thC German band sampler, worked in silks on linen, with alphabet and number series, religious figures and symbols, trees, animals, birds, and people, some designs taken from Johann Sibmacher's pattern book, in a modern frame.

53¼in (135cm) high

$800-900 L&T

Judith Picks

Unlike so many needlework samplers, this is unsigned, and therefore, sadly, its needle worker is consigned to anonymity. However, that doesn't detract from its pleasingly bold floral composition— with a quintessentially English Tudor rose at its heart—which somehow contrives to be both obviously stylized and yet at the same time hint in some of its detail at the naturalistic. This "transitional" quality can perhaps be attributed to changing fashions in floral decoration in Great Britain and Europe at the time of its making: the mid-18thC, during which there began a gradual move away from the stylistic and often exotic floral imagery—notably flowers of Chinese and Indian origin, such as chrysanthemums and peonies—favored earlier in the century, toward more detailed and naturalistic renditions of less complex (and often indigenous and wild) species, such as larkspurs, poppies, and cornflowers.

A mid-18thC George III needlework sampler, worked in silks on a linen ground, depicting a flowering plant and Tudor rose, framed and glazed.

17¼in (44cm) high

$200-260 DN

An early-18thC English wool and silk needlework band sampler, embroidered on a linen ground, with a garden scene with figures and a flowering tree, above alphabets and a Biblical verse, framed and glazed.

21in (53.5cm) long

$1,050-1,200 DN

A George IV needlework sampler, worked with a house, birds, and foliage by Jane Eliza and dated, framed.

1829 *14½in (36.5cm) high*

$450-600 CHEF

A schoolgirl needlework sampler, worked with a verse above a fruit basket and field with pine trees, birds, stags, rabbits, and dogs, signed "ELIZABETH BURFOOT FINISHED THIS WORK 1832 AGED 12 YEARS," in a period rosewood frame.

1832 *16¼in (41cm) high*

$450-600 L&T

A silk on gauze crewelwork sampler, Fitzwilliam, New Hampshire, by Harriet Hayden, with a maiden under a tree, with a basket of flowers, sheep, and trees, with trailing vines and flowers, dated.

This sampler is accompanied by Harriet F. Hayden documents that include photos, history, etc.

1817   *16¼in (41.5cm) wide*

$11,000-12,000   **POOK**

A silk on gauze sampler, Harrisburg, Pennsylvania, by Elizabeth Over at the Mrs. Leah Meguier School, with a centered panel and a tomb, inscribed "Charlotte Weeping," with bowed figure, tree, urn, and bushes, with a trailing vine border, all with a border of 18 panels, with children playing, bees, an ark, a dove, a songbird, strawberries, and birds, with Elizabeth Over documents, dated.

1819   *16½in (42cm) wide*

$20,000-26,000   **POOK**

A Victorian sampler, by Susanah Winnenton Prior, nine years of age, dated, elaborately decorated with birds, trees, and foliage, framed and glazed, dated.

1844   *sampler 15¾in (40cm) high*

$300-400   **LOCK**

A late-19thC Pennsylvania floral appliqué quilt, small stains.

88in (223.5cm) square

$550-650   **POOK**

CLOSER LOOK—ITALIAN VELVET APPLIQUÉ COVER

Traditionally woven from silk, wool, or cotton, velvets have been produced for drapery since the Middle Ages, and they were particularly prized for the way the brightness and sheen of their color varied, depending on the angle at which light strikes their pile. Some of the finest Italian velvets were made in Genoa.

The border decoration is scrolling acanthus leaves and flowers. A recurring motif in the decorative arts since Classical Antiquity, the acanthus is traditionally a symbol of enduring life or immortality.

A pieced and appliqué alphabet quilt, light staining, dated.

1901   *87in (221cm) wide*

$550-650   **POOK**

Putto (plural: putti) was a small, chubby infant derived from both angelic spirits (cherubs) and also the attendants of Cupid or Eros, and was used extensively from the Renaissance to the end of the 19thC as a decorative motif, usually depicted playing among foliage or supporting festoons, swags or, as here, crowns.

Sitting beneath a crown of flowers and thorns, the infant Jesus is accompanied by a lamb and holds a serpent-entwined staff—the former symbolizing innocence and purity, suffering and triumph; the latter, via association with the Greek deity Asciepius, healing and medicine.

A large ca. 1700 (and later) Italian appliquéd cover of red velvet.

95in (242cm) long

A late-19thC patchwork quilt, with hexagonal design of geometric pattern on a red ground.

102½in (260cm) long

$350-450   **CHOR**

A patchwork quilt, of square floral panels within a continuous floral border.

102½in (260cm) wide

$450-600   **CHOR**

$4,600-5,900   **WW**

Audubon, John James, "The Birds Of America," third? edition, published in New York by Roe Lockwood & Son, 8vo edition, issued by J. W. Audubon, 500 hand-finished color plates, seven volumes.
1861
$18,000-24,000   **L&T**

Armstrong, Alexander, "A Personal Narrative of the Discovery of the North-West Passage," first edition, London, published by Hurst & Blackett, 8vo, tinted lithograph frontispiece, folding route map, publisher's cloth, spine ends bumped and nicked.
1857
$2,600-4,000   **CHEF**

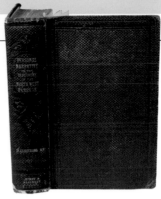

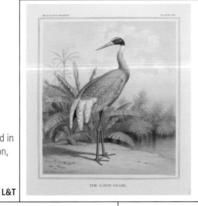

Blaauw, Frans Ernst, "A Monograph Of The Cranes," first edition, published by R. H. Porter, folio, out of series of 170 produced, 22 chromolithographed plates, original green printed cloth gilt.
1897
$6,000-7,500   **L&T**

Blome, Richard, "Britannia: Or, A Geographical Description of the Kingdoms of England, Scotland, and Ireland," London, folio, title (trimmed and laid down) folding plan of London and Westminster (laid down), plan of London (laid down), five folding engraved general maps (of six, lacking general map of Britain), 44 double-page engraved county maps, with 24pp. of engraved coats-of-arms, rebacked calf.
1673
$3,300-4,000   **CHEF**

Brant, Sebastian, "Stultifera Navis Mortalium… Jacob Locher, Basle Henricpetri," 12mo., later speckled calf gilt, crudely hand-colored woodcut on title and further colored woodcuts in text.
1572
$1,600-2,100   **CHOR**

Camden, William, "Annales of the History of the most Renowned and Victorious Princesse Elizabeth, Late Queen of England," 3rd edition, London, published Thomas Harper for Benjamin Fisher, folio, engraved portrait frontispiece, recased and rebacked old calf, bound with Prynne, W, "Hidden Workes of Darkenes," 1645, frontispiece by Hollar, staining.
1635
$1,500-1,800   **CHEF**

Chandler, Richard, "Travels in Greece: Or an Account of a Tour made at the Expense of the Society of Dilettanti," first edition, Oxford, 4to, seven engraved maps and plans by Kitchin, including two folding, contemporary calf, rebacked.
1776
$1,600-2,100   **CHEF**

Chaucer, Geoffrey, "Works," folio, lacking title with imprint, Aiii and Aiv of Prologue, the other Prologue leaves present but repaired with some loss of text, including "The Caunterburie Tales" woodcut title, bound in mid-20thC, full vellum with some damaged leaves.
1561
$5,300-5,900   **CHEF**

Darwin, Charles, "The Descent of Man," first edition, London, published by John Murray, two vols., 8vo, first issue with errata on verso of Vol. II, and other issue points, named "Clements R. Markham" on head of both titles, 16pp.

Provenance: Markham family Sir Clements Robert Markham KCB FRS, was an English geographer, explorer, and writer.

1871

$1,500-2,000   CHEF

Dibdin, Charles, "Observations on a Tour Through Almost the Whole of England…," two2 vols., n.d. [1801-02], aquatint plates and vignettes in sepia, folding table and map, 4to., cont. half-calf gilt.

$600-750   CHOR

La Bibia,

Durone, Francesco, "La Bibia," (Geneva), folio, cont. calf with initials "IW" on upper cover.

1562

$1,600-2,000   CHOR

Elliot, Daniel Giraud, "A Monograph of the Tetraoninae, or Family of the Grouse," published in New York for the author, large folio, five original parts in four volumes, 27 hand-colored lithographs, original green printed boards.

1864-65

12,000-14,000   L&T

Fuller, Thomas, "A Pisgah-Sight of Palestine and the confines thereof, with the history of the Old and New Testament acted thereon," first edition, London, printed by J. F. for John Williams, folio, engraved frontispiece and title, folding map and 27 double-page maps and plates, contemporary calf with modern reback.

1650

$2,600-3,300   CHEF

Gerard, John, "The Herball or General Historie of Plantes," first edition, London, published by John Norton, thick folio, with woodcut arms on verso, engraved portrait, numerous woodcuts in text, additional illustration bound in after X2, all in 20thC sprinkled calf.

1597

$2,600-4,000   CHEF

Machiavelli, N, "The Works of the famous Nicholas Machiavel," London, published by John Starkey, Charles Harper, and John Amery, small folio, contemporary calf, head of spine chipped.

1680

$2,600-3,300   CHEF

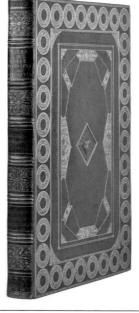

Mayer, Luigi, "Views in Egypt, Palastine and other Parts of the Ottoman Empire," London: R. Bowyer, 1801-1804-1803. Folio (18¼ x 12½in/465 x 318mm), three parts in one volume, 96 hand-colored aquatint plates, 19thC green straight-grained morocco, gilt-tooled with a border of disks surrounding a centered cottage-roof type pattern, in a custom-made case.

$13,000-18,000   L&T

Owen, Richard, "An Account of the War in India, Between the English & French, on the Coast of Coromandel, from the Year 1750 to the Year 1761," 2nd edition, printed for T. Jefferys, nine folding engraved maps, plans and views, recent half-calf gilt, green label to spine, 8vo.
1762
$550-650   LOCK

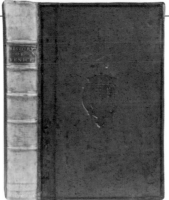

Paruta, Paulo, "The History of Venice," London, for Abel Roper and Henry Herringman, small 4to, title in red and black, two armorial bookplates of the Marquis of Stafford, rebacked speckled calf.
1658
$1,050-1,200   CHEF

Richardson, Sir John, "Arctic Searching Expedition: A Journal of a Boat-Voyage through Rupert's Land and the Arctic Sea, in search of the Discovery Ships under Command of Sir John Franklin …," published by Longman, Brown, two vols., 8vo, hand-colored folding map with small tear, 10 chromolithograph plates, publisher's cloth, one spine with slight tear.
1851
$1,700-2,100   CHEF

Roberts, David, "The Holy Land, Syria, Idumea, Arabia, Egypt, & Nubia," six vols. in three, London, published by Day & Son, small 4to, tinted lithograph titles and plates, two maps, contemporary morocco gilt, all edges gilt.
1855-56
$6,000-6,600   CHEF

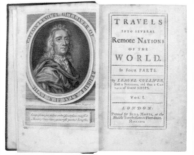

Sancho, Ignatius, "Letters of the late…An African," two vols., 12mo., cont. calf, label of vol 2 defective.
1782
$6,000-7,500   CHOR

Stow, John, "A Survey of the Cities of London and Westminster," corrected, improved and very much enlarged by John Strype, folio, two vol., 70 engraved plates, maps, and plans, including frontispieces, rebacked panel calf, worn.
1720
$4,000-4,600   CHEF

Swift, Jonathan, "Travels into Several Remote Nations of the World," volume 1, First Edition, volume 2, Second Edition, with "Political Tracts," two vols, 8vo, cont calf.
1726 and 1738, respectively
$2,600-4,000   CHOR

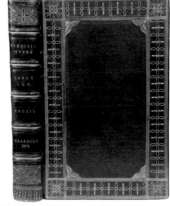

Virgil, "Works" Glasgow, Foulis, two vols. in one, folio.
1778
$4,000-5,300   CHEF

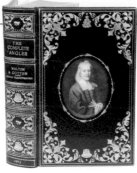

Walton & Cotton, "The Complete Angler," second edition, London, published by Samuel Bagster, 8vo, extra-illustrated, in morocco gilt Cosway-style binding with miniature oval portrait of Walton inset in upper cover, bound by Bayntun Riviere.
1815
$3,300-4,000   CHEF

Wierix, Hieronymus, late-16th/early-17thC volume containing 12 small engraved plates (scenes from the life of Christ), with dedication to Serenmis. P.P. Margaretae, Isabellae, Catarinae, n.d., 8vo., old sheep gilt.
$750-850   CHOR

Whittman, William, "Travels in Turkey, Asia-Minor, Syria, and Across the Desert into Egypt," 22 engraved plates, including 16 hand-colored, one-hand colored plan, folding map, and Turkish firman plate. 4to., cont. calf gilt, spine worn.
1803
$1,700-2,100   CHOR

Wood, Robert, "The Ruins of Palmyra otherwise Tedmore in the Desart," London, large folio, thick paper, 57 engraved plates, including folding panoramic view by Thomas Major, three pages of inscriptions, contemporary calf (rebacked).
1753
$8,000-9,000   CHEF

Churchill, Sir Winston, "My African Journey," first edition, published by Hodder and Stoughton, 8vo, frontispiece, 49 plates and maps, original pictorial cloth.
1908
$2,000-2,600   L&T

Fleming, Ian, "Casino Royale," first edition, published by Jonathan Cape, first impression with first state dust jacket without the "Sunday Times" review overprinted on the front flap, 8vo, dust jacket not price clipped.
1953
$46,000-53,000   L&T

Fleming, Ian, "For Your Eyes Only," first edition, published by Jonathan Cape, first impression [Gilbert A8a 1.1], 8vo, original black cloth gilt with eye motif on upper cover, dust jacket not price clipped.
1960
$600-750   L&T

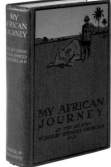

Fleming, Ian, "Moonraker," first edition, published by Jonathan Cape, first impression, State B, Binding B [Gilbert A3a 1.3], dus -jacket not price clipped, some damp staining.
1955
$6,000-6,600   L&T

Orwell, George [Eric Arthur Blair], "Nineteen Eighty-Four," first edition, published by Secker & Warburg, 8vo, original pale green cloth, dust wrapper with newspaper review of TV version of 1984 pasted on verso, book with inscription.
1949
$1,050-1,200   **L&T**

Wilde, Oscar, "A House of Pomegranates," illustrated by Jessie M. King, published by Methuen & Co, 4to, tipped in color plates, a clean copy in publisher's blue cloth, front board very slightly bowed, minor mark on lower board.
1915
$1,000-1,100   **CHEF**

ESSENTIAL REFERENCE—J. K. ROWLING

J. K. Rowling's Harry Potter books have become a modern classic of children's literature, with first edition, first impression copies of Rowling's first book being truly rare: 500 hardback copies were produced, with around 300 of these being given to libraries and schools. This would leave a maximum of 200 copies of the book in possible circulation in fine, non ex-library condition. The actual number is prbably far lower. Only a handful of first edition, first impression books were then inscribed by J. K. Rowling for friends, acquaintances, and family members. This copy is one such work. It is notable that this book was offered for sale in Edinburgh— widely regarded as the "home of Harry Potter." The boy wizard was dreamed up by Rowling on a delayed rail service between Manchester and London's King's Cross Station, however Rowling has said: "… Edinburgh is very much home for me and is the place where Harry evolved over seven books and many, many hours of writing in its cafés." Similarities can also be found between Edinburgh's many imposing independent schools and Hogwarts School of Witchcraft and Wizardry. Most notably, George Heriot's School and Fettes College, with its impressive centered spire, both strongly reflect the baronial architectural style of Hogwarts. In the past, Rowling has said that she imagines Hogwarts to be in Scotland, a claim corroborated by the Harry Potter movies, where the Hogwarts Express is seen diving over the iconic Glenfinnan Viaduct.

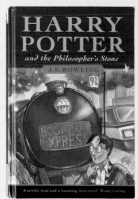

Rowling, J. K., "Harry Potter and the Philosopher's Stone," first edition, published by Bloomsbury, hardback, first impression with the "10 9 8 7 6 5 4 3 2 1" numberline on the publisher's imprint page and "1 wand" listed twice on p. 53, inscribed and signed by J. K. Rowling on the front free endpaper: "6-9-97 For James, Kate and Laura, with best wishes, J. K. Rowling," original pictorial boards.
1997
$170,000-240,000   **L&T**

'Grimm's Fairy Tales," De Luxe limited edition, No.648 of 750, illustrated and signed by Arthur Rackham, large Qto, gilt titled and illustrated vellum binding, tipped in color plates by Rackham.
1909
$750-850   **WHP**

'The Dandy Monster Comic no.1," published by D C Thomson & Co Ltd, unnamed, slight edge and corner wear.
1939
$1,800-2,400   **CHEF**

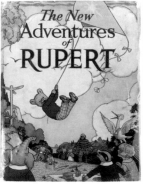

"The New Adventures of Rupert," first edition of the first Rupert Annual, Qto, red cloth with black titling and illustration of Rupert reading, dust wrapper.
1936
$1,700-2,100   **WHP**

"The Beano Book no.2," published by D C Thomson & Co Ltd, unnamed, contents a little browned.
1941
$6,000-6,600   **CHEF**

Blaeu, Jansson, (1596-1673), "Wallia Principatus Vulgo Wales," color engraved map.

19¼in (49cm) wide

$450-550 **CHOR**

Braun and Hogenberg, map of London, "Londinum Feracissimi Angliae Regni Metropolis," engraved plan with hand color, Latin text verso, with Westminster spelt "Westmuster."

ca. 1572-74 *20in (51cm) wide*

$8,500-10,000 **CHEF**

Homan, J. B., "Magnae Britanniae pars Meridionalis in qua Regnum Angliae," an early-18thC hand-colored engraved map of Great Britain.

$210-260 **CHEF**

Ortelius, Abraham (1527-98), "Americae Sive Novi Orbis Nova Destriptio," copper map of the Americas, a later pressing, hand-colored, reframed.

This map was first published in Antwerp the year before the Spanish Armada, as Francis Drake was "singeing the King of Spain's beard" by sacking Cadiz.

19¼in (49cm) long

$1,500-2,000 **SWO**

Saxton, C. and Lea, P., "Sommersetshire," hand-colored map of Somerset with inset town plan of Bath.

ca. 1693 *20in (51cm) wide*

$650-800 **CHEF**

A 17thC map of Lincolnshire, by John Speed, (1552-1629), "The Countie and Citie of Lyncolne," hand-colored copper engraving on laid/chain-lined paper bearing manufacturer's watermark, featuring ships and sea monsters, heraldic shields, and inset view of Lincoln, Hondius (signed in plate), Bassett & Chiswell, English text on verso, framed and glazed on recto and verso.

20in (51cm) wide

$450-600 **HAN**

Speed, John, "The Countie Pallatine of Lancaster, Described and Divided into Hundreds," hand-colored engraved map for George Humble, with inset town plan of Lancaster, eight portraits of Plantagenet kings and queens, framed, English text verso.

ca. 1627 *20¼in (51.5cm) wide*

$1,300-2,000 **CHEF**

Norden, John and Speed, John, "Sussex Described," hand-colored engraved map with inset town plan of Chichester, published by Bassett and Chiswell, English text verso.

ca. 1676 *20½in (52cm) wide*

$400-450 **CHEF**

Judith Picks

Every once in a while an item appears that, at first glance, makes me simply say "wow, just wow," and then, on further inspection, has me thinking this might just be the best example I've ever seen. Well, this remarkable, early-18thC English doll checked both of those boxes, and more besides.

First, her provenance is impeccable. She has been handed down through subsequent generations of the same family, who purchased her ca. 1735. Second, for a young lady now approaching 300 years old, she, her daintily ringleted, human-hair wig, and her costume are all in remarkably fine condition. Third, condition aside, the costume is exquisite; from the hand-woven brocade gown with appliqués of tiny silver beading to the lace fichu and delicately embroidered apron, from the silk shoes and complementarily accented hat to the extraordinary hand-painted silk reticule she holds in her right hand.

Yes, fourth, those hands, each with separately carved wooden fingers and thumb, are as elegant as her slender, oval, wooden face with finely shaped nose, piercing black enamel eyes, arched brows, subtly blushed cheeks, small mouth, defined little chin, long slender neck, defined bosom, and tiny waist are refined. Fifth, and not to be underestimated, is her "luxe" size—she stands just over 27in (just under 70cm) tall—which only adds to a distinct aristocratic, bordering-on-regal presence. And sixth—just a small something but one that not only literally personifies her but also absolutely confirms her as my all-time, out-and-out favorite—they found tucked inside her hat (and now safely stored in her wooden keepsake box) a piece of ragged paper that, in faded ink script, simply states her appropriately distinctive name: "Miss Timber."

Oh, and then, of course, there's the considerable price she fetched at auction, which goes to show I'm by no means alone in my admiration!

An English doll, with one-piece carved wooden head and torso, cloth upper arms, wooden lower arms and hands, dowel-jointed hips and knees, and shapely lower legs, and with original brunette human-hair wig, costume, and accessories.

ca. 1735   27¼in (69cm) high
$160,000-210,000   **THE**

A painted wooden German Grodnertal doll, the gesso face with finely painted features, peg-jointed at shoulders, elbows, hips, and knees, gesso lower arms and legs, with painted red shoes.

ca. 1820   5¼in (13cm) high
$4,000-4,600   **C&T**

A Heinrich Handwerke bisque-head doll, with sleepy eyes, open mouth with teeth, natural brown hair wig, composition body, and ball joints.

19in (48cm) high
$130-200   **CHOR**

A Heubach Koppeldorf 342.410 bisque-head doll, with sleepy eyes, open mouth with teeth and tongue, natural brown hair, composition body and limbs.

13¼in (33.5cm) high
$130-200   **CHOR**

An Emile Jumeau bisque-head E.J Bebe doll, size 6, with fixed, blue glass paper-weight eyes, closed mouth, pierced ears with blue glass drop earrings, with her original cork and leather pate and long blonde wig, on an eight-ball jointed wood and composition body with fixed wrists and blue "Jumeau Medaille, D'or, Paris" stamp on rear, marked "E.J Depose," incised 6, E J.

ca. 1880   18in (46cm) high
$6,000-6,600   **C&T**

A Jumeau size 1 bisque shoulder-head fashion doll, with fixed blue glass eyes, closed mouth, pierced ears with blue bead earrings, and blonde wig, swivel head, and on a kid leather body, incised1.

ca. 1870   10¼in (26cm) high
$1,300-1,600   **C&T**

A closed-mouth Tete Jumeau bisque-head Bebe, size 10, with fixed, brown glass paper-weight eyes, pierced ears, and original auburn wig, on a fully jointed wood and composition body with swivel wrists, and original size 10 leather Jumeau shoes with "bumble bee" stamp.

ca. 1890   22¼in (56cm) high
$3,300-4,600   **C&T**

TOYS & MODELS

An early-20thC SFJB (Societe Francaise de Fabrication de Bebes et Jouets) bisque-headed doll, with sleeping brown glass eyes and open mouth showing two upper teeth, head stamped "247 10."

20½in (52cm) long

$600-650   **WHP**

A bisque-head doll with sleepy eyes, by Simon & Halbig 34, for Kammer Reinhart, with open mouth with teeth, composition body, and ball jointed limbs.

$200-260   **CHOR**

An 1890s Simon & Halbig DEP 719 bisque shoulder-head doll, with swivel neck, with weighted blue glass eyes, closed mouth, and dimple to chin, on a jointed kid leather body with bisque lower arms, original silk two-piece gown with lace trim, incised "S&H 719 DEP."

17¾in (45cm) high

$1,000-1,100   **C&T**

A Simon & Halbig 122 bisque-head baby doll, with weighted brown glass eyes, real lashes, open mouth with two upper teeth, original brown wig, and on a composition baby body.

ca. 1910 1   *3in (33cm) high*

$550-650   **C&T**

An outstanding and rare French A.T Andre Thuillier bisque-head Bebe doll, size 7, the bisque head with fixed, blue glass paper-weight eyes, dark eyeliner, accented nostrils, and painted closed mouth with hint of smile, pierced ears, original blonde wig and cork pate, on an original early carved wooden fully jointed body with swivel wrists and ball joints to elbows and hips, incised A 7 T.

1880   *17in (43cm) high*

$33,000-40,000   **C&T**

A Deans Rag Book 40' Mascot doll, with molded, painted face, wool braided pigtails and drop-skirt velvet, and wool dress, label present.

$150-180   **LOCK**

A rare pair of French carton moule "seaside" dolls, with carved and painted papier-maché features, with later glass dome.

During the early-1800s, the Emperor Napoleon reinstated the gabelle, a highly unpopular tax on salt that brought much poverty to the northwest regions of France, which were not granted exemptions. Salt workers here, or paludiers, were exploited for their goods, only to see them being sold for high markups in other regions. Yet the picturesque scenes of coastal France continued to bring many wealthy visitors, prompting locals to make souvenirs from shells and other items foraged from their shorelines. These charming dolls, often referred to as "Les Poupée du Paludier," were lavish in their decoration but reflected the traditional costume of the impoverished Breton paludiers.

ca. 1800   *13¼in (33.5cm) high*

$2,600-3,300   **L&T**

A rare Harwin World War I felt Ally Scottish infantryman, with black boot button eyes, painted ginger hair, jointed limbs, integral khaki felt jacket and undershorts, oil-cloth boots, khaki felt spats, tartan socks and kilt, balding sporran, and a matched Glengarry.

14in (36cm) high

$1,300-1,800   **SAS**

A 1890s German Moritz Gottschalk blue roof doll's house, model 2556/2 in original condition, front opens in one wing to two rooms on two levels, with original wall and floor papers and maroon silk drapes on first floor, with an original fireplace, couch, and other pieces.

31in (79cm) high

$6,000-6,600 **C&T**

A painted wood dollhouse, symmetrically modeled as a typical property from the Georgian period, doors enclosing the six rooms separated by hall stairs and landings, the interior decorated with chinoiserie wallpaper, with marks, knocks, scratches, abrasions.

ca. 1830 *45¾in (116cm) wide*

$4,600-5,900 **DN**

A German red roof, wooden doll's house, with brick-paper facade, front door with steps to veranda, gable, and front opening to reveal two rooms with original papers, repainted roof and other restoration.

23in (58.5cm) high

$200-260 **SAS**

A G. & J. Lines "The Clock House" doll's house, no.34, timbered on left and clock dormer with working clock, front opening in the middle to reveal four rooms with fireplaces and range, original interior papers, some restoration.

G. & J. Lines was founded by Joseph and George Lines in the 1870s. The company produced dollhouses from ca. 1895. Joseph Lines's son established Lines Brothers in 1919, selling modern-style dollhouses under the name Triang from the mid-1920s. When Joseph Lines died in the early 1930s, Lines Brothers acquired the G. & J. Lines trade name and marks. Lines Brothers went into liquidation in 1971.

ca. 1910 *32in (81.5cm) high*

$200-260 **SAS**

An early-20thC doll's house, the red brick house with balcony supported on pillars and fireplaces and a staircase inside.

43¼in (110cm) high

$850-1,000

CHOR

A late 19thC half-tester bed, with 18thC silk curtains, bedding including a patchwork quilt, with on headboard "A present to Miss Belfield, daughter of Captain Belfield. J.P. 'Malmains,' Frenchay, near Bristol in commemoration of her Majesty's Jubilee 21st Jne 1887."

22in (56cm) high

$750-850 **SAS**

A miniature antique dollhouse furniture model of a chest-on-stand, walnut veneered.

6½in (16.4cm) high

$350-400 **DAWS**

A miniature antique dollhouse Georgian breakfront bookcase, with molded pediment with finial and floral marquetry inlay, diamond glazing bar doors opening to reveal a shelved interior, above frieze drawers and cupboards with painted ovals in the Sheraton taste, raised on spade feet.

8¾in (21.8cm) high

$350-400 **DAWS**

A mid-19thC sewing etui, for a child or a doll in the form of a natural walnut, probably French, with gilded hinged mount and accessories, lined in silk and velvet, the interior with scissors, thimble, faceted glass scent bottle, and needle case.

1¾in (4.8cm) long

$350-400 **MART**

Judith Picks

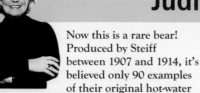

Now this is a rare bear! Produced by Steiff between 1907 and 1914, it's believed only 90 examples of their original hot-water bottle Teddy Bear were made. There has been speculation that the particularly cold winter in Europe in 1907 may have inspired their creation, and that their limited sales and production may have been due to a consumer perception that hot water in its internal, screw-capped tin canister might, in close proximity to an inquisitive child, not such a good idea! What can be in no doubt, however, is their appeal to collectors today—to the extent that in recent years Steiff have produced a replica limited edition. This splendid example, however, is very much an original and, despite a little thinning to the golden mohair on the front of the body, it is in particularly good condition.

A Steiff hot-water bottle Teddy Bear, with boot-button eyes, swivel head, jointed elongated limbs with felt pads, hump, front opening with brass hooks, lined in brown cotton with cotton wadding insulation, original tin canister with screw cap on each end, and small size FF underscored button in left ear. Also with an old leather suitcase, in which the bear has been stored, and in which is written: "Mrs Marshall and E.J. Marshall. 47 Croft Lane, Bromborough, Wirral, Cheshire."

ca. 1907   20in (51cm) high
$10,000-11,000   SAS

A Steiff cinnamon mohair teddy bear, "George," with black boot-button eyes, swivel head, jointed elongated limbs with felt pads, hump, growler, patched holes on muzzle, replaced hand pads, and repaired feet pads.

George was the childhood toy of German-born Augusta (Gussy), who went on to marry Donald and moved to Northern Rhodesia to work on the new railroad. They had four children who all played with George. Ruth (third generation owner) moved to London in the early-1960s as a young adult and George came with her. The story continues with a return to Africa, where George lived on the banks of the Zambezi for many years before a return to London to live with the fourth generation before finding a new home with Sue—this bear appears in an article written by Sue Pearson for "200 Years of Childhood" magazine.

A rare Steiff center-seam teddy bear, black boot-button eyes, swivel head, jointed limbs with remains of felt pads, hump, and inoperative growler, pads recovered.

ca. 1908   25in (63.5cm) high
$4,600-5,300   SAS

A rare Steiff black mohair teddy bear, with boot-button eyes, swivel head, jointed elongated limbs, original feet pads, hump, inoperative growler, hand pads replaced, some wear.

Seen by some as the Holy Grail of Steiff collecting, the black Steiff teddy bear is highly sought after; perhaps the most famous examples are those that are believed to have been sold in the UK during 1912, in response to the Titanic disaster; this example is not one of those, but one of few that have appeared on the market during the last 40 years, which are believed to be a special short order, a sample or just a quirk of the production line from around 1908 to 1910.

1908-10   13½in (34cm) high
$6,500-8,000   SAS

1907-08   24½in (62.5cm) high
$2,600-3,300   SAS

An early Steiff cinnamon mohair teddy bear, with black boot-button eyes, swivel head, jointed elongated limbs with felt pads, card-lined feet, hump, inoperative growler, and FF underscored button unusually on the back of the left ear.

ca. 1909   20in (51cm) high
$4,000-4,600   SAS

A rare German Steiff mohair Roly Poly Teddy Bear, golden mohair bear with black boot-button eyes, stitched nose and mouth, swivel head, jointed at the shoulders and with stitched claws, the body with rattle, button on left ear, some general wear, sparse areas mainly on back of body.

ca. 1910   5in (13cm) high
$6,000-6,600   C&T

An early Steiff center-seam teddy bear, boot-button eyes, swivel head, jointed elongated limbs, hump, inoperative growler, FF underscored button, some wear, staining on chest.

24in (61cm) high
$2,000-2,600   SAS

An early Steiff center-seam teddy bear, black boot-button eyes, swivel head, jointed limbs, hump, inoperative growler, FF underscored button, some wear, staining on chest.

24in (61cm) high

$2,000-2,600   **SAS**

A Steiff limited edition replica 1953 Zotty bear, boxed.

29½in (75cm) high

$165-400   **WHP**

An early Chad Valley teddy bear, clear and black glass eyes, swivel head, jointed limbs, hump, inoperative growler, pink map of Britain celluloid-covered label, general wear.

19½in (49.5cm) high

$350-400   **SAS**

A 1920's Chad Valley mohair plush bear, moveable jointed head, arms, and legs, Chad Valley button on upper chest.

17in (43cm) high

$200-260   **LOCK**

A Farnell World War I "soldier" teddy bear, black glass pinhead eyes, pipe-cleaner ears, swivel head, pin jointed limbs.

3¾in (9.5cm) high

$650-800   **SAS**

A Farnell teddy bear, "Pricey," clear and black glass eyes, swivel head, jointed elongated limbs with large card-lined feet, hump, and inoperative growler, hand pads replaced, slight wear, with a watercolor of Pricey in Sue's garden signed "PW 92."

From the Sue Pearson Collection. His unusual name, Pricey, came from a visit to an antique shop, where Sue discovered this Farnell with no price tag; asking the dealer how much he was, he sucked his teeth and said "he's pricey, madam " and the name stuck! Pricey, appears on the cover and page 6 of "Miller's Teddy Bears A Complete Collector's Guide" by Sue Pearson. He also accompanied Sue on many trips and TV programs, the latest being in 2017 with Alan Titchmarsh on "Masterpiece," an antique quiz show.

ca. 1920   *26in (66cm) high*

$2,400-2,900   **SAS**

A 1930s Schuco mohair teddy bear perfume bottle, with rare gold-jeweled eyes, black painted metal-framed glasses, black stitched nose and mouth, metal-framed jointed body, and removable head to reveal glass bottle with stopper, some general wear.

4¾in (12cm) high

$450-550   **SAS**

A rare Terrys teddy bear, clear and black oily glass eyes, swivel head, jointed limbs with cloth pads, card-lined feet, hump, and inoperative growler, slight wear.

1915   *19in (48.5cm) high*

$1,200-1,300   **SAS**

A Dinky Toys, Pre-War 28D, Delivery Van "Oxo," type 1, no signs of fatigue.

$7,500-8,000 LSK

A Dinky Toys, Pre-War 28K, Delivery Van "Marsh and Baxter Sausages," little playwear.

Dinky Toys was the brand name for a range of die-cast miniature vehicles produced by Meccano Ltd. They were made in England from 1934 to 1979, at a factory in Binns Road in Liverpool. Dinky Toys were among the most popular die-cast vehicles ever made, predating other popular die-cast marques, including Corgi and Matchbox.

$2,900-3,700 LSK

A Dinky No.30a Chrysler Airflow Saloon (sedan), unboxed.

$400-550 LSK

A Dinky No.30a Chrysler Airflow Saloon (sedan), rare color, chip on rear split window divider.

$650-800 LSK

A Dinky No.33d Mechanical Horse and Box Van Trailer "Hornby Trains British & Guaranteed," a few chips on body.

$900-1,050 LSK

A Dinky No.33r Mechanical Horse and Box Van Trailer, in "LNER" livery, with a few chips and marks, unboxed.

$400-550 LSK

A Dinky Toys 100 Lady Penelopes FAB 1 From TV series "Thunderbirds," in rarer fluorescent pink body, flying lady motif to the front is missing, in original box.

$650-800 LSK

A Dinky Toys, No.111 Triumph TR2 Sports.

$200-260 LSK

A Dinky Toys No.186 Mercedes Benz 220SE, rare variation with red interior, in original cardboard box.

$400-500 LSK

A rare Dinky Toys No.431 guy 4-ton "lorry," or truck, in later cardboard box.

$2,600-3,300 LSK

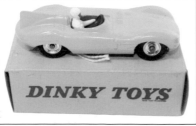

A Dinky Toys No.238 Jaguar D-type racing car, in the original box, some graffiti, vehicle with blemish on door.

$550-650 LSK

A Dinky Toys No.433 guy flat truck, in original late issue cardboard box, box grubby.
$450-550 LSK

A Dinky Toys No.502 Foden flat truck, with first type cab, in original box.
$450-600 LSK

A Dinky Toys No.503 Foden flat truck with tailboard, some rub marks, in original box.
$1,000-1,050 LSK

A Dinky Toys No.503 Foden (1st Type) Flat Truck with Tailboard, in original cardboard labeled box.
$1,050-1,200 LSK

A Dinky Toys No.511 4-ton guy "lorry," or truck, in original box.
$260-400 LSK

A Dinky Toys South African issue No.519 Simca 1000, in original South African script cardboard box.
$1,200-1,300 LSK

An original issue of the French Dinky No.570a Peugeot J7 "Autoroutes," in original cardboard box with sliding tray interior.
$1,000-1,100 LSK

A Dinky Toys No.903 Foden flat truck with tailboard, rare issue with 2nd type cab, in original box.
$850-1,000 LSK

A Dinky Toys No.920 "Heinz 57 Varieties" guy delivery van, in original cardboard box, vehicle has paint loss below rear doors.
$2,600-3,300 LSK

A Dinky Supertoys No.923 Big Bedford van, with the rare "Heinz Tomato Ketchup 57 Varieties" livery, in box with the Ketchup bottle logo.
$850-1,000 LSK

A Dinky toys No.941 Mobilgas 14-ton gas tanker, in original box.
$260-400 LSK

A Dinky Toys No.944 "Shell BP" fuel tanker, in original picture box.
$400-550 LSK

A Corgi Toys car, no.261 "Special Agent 007 James Bonds Aston Martin D.B.5," with secret instructions, two ejecting men, in original box.

In 1956, the Mettoy Company, which was founded in Northampton, England, in the mid-1930s by German emigreé Philip Ullman, launched the Corgi range of small die-cast toys. An immediate commercial success, their vehicles incorporated new features such as plastic windows, spring suspension (from 1959), doors and hoods that opened, and folding seats (from 1963). That success endured through the 1960s until the late-1970s, and was given considerable impetus by the company pioneering movie and television tie-ins—the best-known example being the James Bond Aston Martin D.B.5. Subsequent to Mettoy going into receivership in 1983, Corgi has had a management buyout, a takeover by Mattel (in 1992), another management buyout (in 1995), which resulted in the creation of a new company, Corgi Classics Limited, and the purchase of the latter by Hornby in 2008.
$550-650   LOCK

A Corgi Toys Gift Set, No40, "The Avengers," figures missing umbrellas, with original insert, in original box.
$350-400   LOCK

A Corgi Toys No.315 Simca 1000 Competition Model, in original cardboard box, with leaflet.
$200-260   LSK

A Corgi Toys No.359 Army Field Kitchen, with standing figure, in original cardboard box.
$300-350   LSK

A Spot-On Models by Triang No.107 Jaguar XKSS sedan, in original box with leaflet and wooden packing section.

"Spot-On" was a range of die-cast models made by the international toy and model manufacturer Lines Brothers (brand name Tri-ang) at their Castlereagh site, Belfast, from 1959-67. Supported by car-related accessories, such as roadside signs, garages, and gas stations, the primary "Spot-On" products were cars, trucks, and buses. A mixture of die-cast metal and injection-molded plastic, produced in a variety of often rich colors, and with features such as "Flexomatic" suspension and electric headlamps, they were of high quality—one of the best known is their London Transport "Routemaster" bus (1963)—and remain eminently collectible.
$450-550   LSK

A Corgi Toys No.485 The BMC Mini Countryman Surfing Model, in original cardboard box.
$260-330   LSK

A Spot-On Models by Triang No.112 Jensen 541, with original nonpicture box.
$450-550   LSK

A Spot-On Models by Triang, model No.113 Aston Martin DB Mk3, in original box with owners' club leaflet and collectors card.
$350-400   LSK

A Spot-On Models by Triang No.156 Mulliner Coach, box has some graffiti on lid face.
$1,500-1,800   LSK

A Spot-On Models by Triang No.215 Daimler SP250 V8 Sports Car, in original box with leaflets.
$400-450   LSK

A Black Rat Models model No. BRM011 1/50 scale hand-built metal and resin model of a Caterpillar 631D scraper cab, in original box.

$750-800 LSK

A Britains No. 127F model farm series diecast model of a Fordson Major tractor, in original box and with driver.

$260-330 LSK

A Cross RC (radio controlled) 1/12 scale kit for a 6x6 UC6 crawling truck, as issued, in original box.

$650-800 LSK

A Exoto Racing Legends 1/18 scale model of a 1964-65 Cobrid Daytona, as issued, in original box.

$260-400 LSK

A GMP Model No. G1804101 1/18 scale limited edition model of a Ferrari 330 P4, as issued, in original box.

$450-550 LSK

A Matchbox 1-75 Series No.27 Bedford Articulated Low-Loader, in original box.

$650-800 LSK

A rare issue Matchbox Superfast Series No.45 Ford Group 6, a few chips, in 1st issue Superfast box.

$3,300-4,000 LSK

A Matchbox Models of Yesteryear Y6 1916 AEC "Y" type truck, "Osram Lamps."

This is a 1961 replica of a 1916 "Osram Lamps" vehicle. It sold for two shillings and three pence in 1961. It is so sought after because it has plastic wheels, which were only used on a few examples at the end of the production run. If it had the more common metal wheels, it would be worth about $25.

$7,500-8,000 VEC

A Pocher kit No. K51 boxed 1/8 scale plastic, white metal, and leather kit for a Ferrari Testarossa, in original box.

$650-800 LSK

A Shackleton mechanical and clockwork Foden flatbed truck, in original box with leaflet, wrench, and key.

$850-1,000 LSK

TOYS & MODELS

A Meccano No. 6 outfit, green cabinet, complete.
ca. 1930-31
$900-1,050   **LSK**

A Meccano No.10 outfit, green cabinet, blue/gold, appears complete and used.
ca. 1938
$900-1,050
                                  LSK

An early-20thC carved and painted wood horse-and-cart group of forest toys, attributed to Frank Whittington.

Frank Whittington (1876-1973) established a toy-making firm at the end of World War I in the New Forest, England, making carved animals and people, inspired by his surroundings and from regular trips to London Zoo and the Natural History Museum. Originally making the toys from home, the demand became such that in 1922 he built a factory on the edge of the New Forest (Brockenhurst). The popularity of the figures rose when Queen Mary ordered two dozen Noah's Arks after seeing them at the British Industries Fairs during the interwar period.

20in (51cm) long
$1,050-1,200   **WW**

An original Action Man 1966-69 painted head Action man German Storm Trooper figure, in first issue uniform.
$200-260   **LSK**

A KO of Japan tinplate and clockwork Planet Robbie the Robot, with sparking action, missing red visor.
$165-450   **LSK**

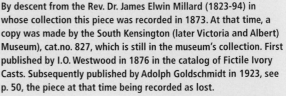

A medieval walrus ivory checkers piece, carved to illustrate Aesop's fable of the "Fox and the Stork," probably Northern France, probably second half of the 12thC.

By descent from the Rev. Dr. James Elwin Millard (1823-94) in whose collection this piece was recorded in 1873. At that time, a copy was made by the South Kensington (later Victoria and Albert) Museum, cat.no. 827, which is still in the museum's collection. First published by I.O. Westwood in 1876 in the catalog of Fictile Ivory Casts. Subsequently published by Adolph Goldschmidt in 1923, see p. 50, the piece at that time being recorded as lost.

2.5in (5.75cm) wide
$70,000-80,000   **LC**

An early Victorian bone spelling alphabet, in a mahogany case, the interior with 27 divisions containing 149 bone letters.
ca. 1840   *10¼in (26cm) wide*
$550-650   **WW**

A traveling chess set, with 32 white and red-stained ivory pieces, with a board in a mahogany folding box, top inscribed "C Oman."
All pieces ½in (1.5cm) high
$450-600   **CHOR**

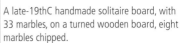

A late-19thC handmade solitaire board, with 33 marbles, on a turned wooden board, eight marbles chipped.
12¼in (31cm) wide
$1,200-1,450   **SAS**

A 7¼in-gauge live-steam locomotive, with half-cab giving access to firebox, regulator, and associated cab fittings, with transport trolley.
$3,300-4,000   **LSK**

A 7¼in-gauge live-steam 0-6-0 saddle tank locomotive, No. 05 "Holmside," removable cab roof for access to regulator and boiler fittings.
$8,500-10,000   **LSK**

A Gauge-1 live-steam spirit-fired model of a British Railway K1 locomotive and tender, with "62006" on cabsides and "British Railways" on tender, with burner and removable cab roof for access to backhead fittings, hand-operated water feed tender, with a wooden carry case.
$2,100-2,600   **LSK**

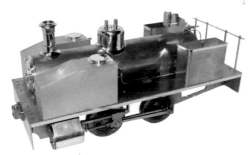

A Reeves Castings, 5in-gauge Dougal 0-4-0 Welshpool tank locomotive, unpainted.
$3,300-4,000   **LSK**

A Gauge-1 live-steam spirit-fired model of a British Railways BR 0-6-0 Locomotive and tender, with "1691" on cabsides and "British Railways" tender, in a wooden carry case.
$2,000-2,600   **LSK**

A gauge-1 live-steam model of the British Railway 4-6-2 tender locomotive "No 60007" "Sir Nigel Gresley," made by Aster Hobby Co., Inc for Fulgurex (built up), with other usual fittings. The model has never been steamed, with its original box, instructions, tools, and a display case with fitted track.

18¼in (46cm) long

$6,500-8,000   **DN**

A 2½in-gauge live-steam LMS No.4547 Class 4F locomotive and tender, with "LMS" tender and "4547" on cabsides, with access to backhead controls, controls as expected.
$1,300-1,800   **LSK**

A scratch built 2½in-gauge live-steam 4-4-2 Atlantic locomotive and tender, "GNR," coal fired.
$1,700-2,100   **LSK**

A 2½i- gauge live-steam coal-fired 4-6-2 locomotive and tender, access to backhead controls, six-wheel tender with hand-operated water feed tender.
$1,600-2,100   **LSK**

A gauge-1 live-steam model of the British Railways 4-6-2 tender locomotive "No 46232" "Duchess of Montrose," built by Bassett-Lowke, the locomotive with fitted pressure gauge, water sight-glass, regulator, whistle, fluted motion, and fitted smoke deflectors.

ca. 1980

$6,000-6,600

DN

A Bassett-Lowke Super Enterprise live-steam loco and tender, 4-6-0 "Southern 851" green.

$550-650

LSK

A Bassett-Lowke 8V DC electric "Royal Scot" engine and tender, in original box and with instructions.

$450-600

LSK

A Bassett Lowke gauge-1 0-4-0 clockwork locomotive, London & North East Railway renumbered "114."

$350-400

LSK

A Märklin for Bassett-Lowke O-gauge 4-6-0 Loco and Tender, Great Western "King George V" No.6000, 3-rail Electric 12V DC, Brunswick Green, drop link couplings, with center rail pickups, front cylinder linkage replaced.

$3,300-4,000

LSK

A Hornby Dublo 3235 4-6-2 West Country "Dorchester" loco and tender, with oiling instruction leaflet, and instructions.

$260-400

LSK

A Hornby O-gauge "Princess Elizabeth" 4-6-2 electric loco and six-wheeled tender, engine no.6201, cased.

$1,100-1,250

WHP

A Wrenn Railways W2261A Royal Scot class engine and tender, LMS post-war lined black No. 6160 "Queen Victoria's Rifleman," only ca. 200 made.

$260-400

LSK

An exhibition-quality model of a 3½in -gauge Class 47xx Great Western Railway Heavy Freight 2-8-0 tender locomotive "No 4707," built by Mr. L. E. G. Parker, the silver soldered copper boiler having fittings, including safety valve, clack, and others valves, six-wheel tender with leaf springs, hand-operated brakes, filler cap and vents, tool boxes, steps, hand and lamp irons, with applied cab side plate "4707."

50½in (128cm) long

$11,000-12,000

DN

A German tinplate clockwork model of an ocean liner, by Bing, with a long working motor, decks with three funnels and lifeboats, with rigged masts, and with printed Bing mark "Bavaria," with 14 small figures and a winding key.
ca. 1915-20   *39½in (100.5cm) long*
$8,500-10,000   **WW**

A German tinplate clockwork model of an ocean liner, by Carette, with four funnels and lifeboats, with rigged masts and a winding key.
ca. 1912-14   *24in (61cm) long*
$6,000-6,600   **WW**

A rare German tinplate display model of an ocean liner, by Marklin, of a twin-funnel liner titled "Columbus."

This tinplate liner would have been used for display purposes by shipping agents and travel firms.
ca. 1912-18   *38½in (98cm) long*
$8,500-10,000   **WW**

A model "Riva Super Aquarama" launch, by Authentic Models BV, on a wood stand.
25½in (65cm) long
$800-900   **SWO**

An exhibition standard working model of the Brixham trawler "Valerian (Holly)," built in ½ inch to 1 foot scale, the model built from drawings by Harold A Underhill.
48in (122cm) long
$1,800-2,100   **DN**

A period sailing pond yacht.
48in (122cm) long
$1,050-1,200   **DN**

A Clyde Craft Pond Yacht, named "Endeavour," hull has been damaged and repaired.
Clyde Craft Ltd produced yachts during the 1950s and 1960s in Busby, Glasgow.
$100-110   **LOCK**

An early-20thC Clinker-built pond yacht, on a later stand, mast is a mid-20thC poor-quality replacement.
78¾in (200cm) high with mast
$260-400   **CHEF**

A 19thC museum standard model of an early British live steam agricultural traction engine, the copper boiler with fittings, including water sight glass, steam pressure gauge, regulator, steel firebox door, operators standing with safety sides, lever-and-crank linkage with rod-and-bevel gear steering mechanism, twin simple cylinders with under-type motion, gear-driven water pump with clack valve fitted, safety, Watts design speed governor.

This is a rare model of "The Farmer Friend," designed in 1849 by R. Willis and promoted by Ransomes and May, who became Ransomes, Sims and Jefferies.

23¼in (59cm) long
$9,000-10,500   DN

A freelance 4-inch scale model of an agricultural traction engine, having single cylinder with steam chest on side, driver-operated cylinder drain cocks, steam safety valve, brass whistle, ratchet-operated lubricating system, steel boiler with fitted steam pressure gauge, water sight glass, firebox door, water tender with drain tap, built by Mr. B. B. Judge of Lincolnshire.

1989.
$7,500-8,500   DN

A precision-built 1-inch scale live-steam model of a Road Roller Engine, by Maxwell Hemmens, with spirit-fired copper boiler, pressure gauge, solid flywheel, whistle, pressure safety valve, and water pump, with instruction manual.

1995   22½in (57cm) long
$4,000-4,600   CHEF

A precision built 1-inch scale live-steam model of a Traction Engine, by Maxwell Hemmens, with spirit-fired copper boiler, pressure gauge, pressure safety valve, and water pump, with instruction manual.

1995   19in (48cm) long
$3,300-4,000   CHEF

A precision-built 1-inch scale live-steam model of a Showman's Engine, by Maxwell Hemmens.

1995   22in (56cm) long
$4,000-4,600   CHEF

A 2-inch scale live-steam Fowler A7 Road Locomotive Traction Engine, based on MJ Engineering Drawings, with "John Fowler of Leeds" on Smokebox door, single cylinder, free running example.

1999   34in (86.5cm) long
$6,500-8,000   LSK

A precision-built live-steam model of a York-Bolton mill engine, by Maxwell Hemmens, mounted on a hardwood base with brass plaque.

1997   13¾in (35cm) high
$1,700-2,100   CHEF

A model of a Stuart Turner Victoria Mill Engine, with copper boiler and water tank, fitted with 7-inch six-spoke flywheel, usual gauges and fittings.
$850-1,000   LSK

A diorama model of a Foster of Lincoln Threshing Machine, in approximate 1½-inch scale with working parts, toolbox, ladder, and figures with sheaves of corn together with a Foster elevator on transportation wheels, the machinery being driven by a Robey Portable steam engine having blued steel cladding on boiler with detailed rivet work, single cylinder mounted on the top of the boiler with steam inlet control, steam pressure gauge, safety valve, motion and fitted speed governor, chimney rest bracket, hand-operated brake gear with wooden brake blocks, eccentric-driven water pump on side, a pair of wooden horse shafts and two heavy horses in full leather working harness with farm workers in foreground, the whole model set on plinth bases and was built by Mr. C. W. Glenworth of Louth.
$8,000-9,000   DN

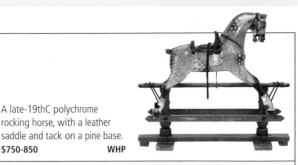

A late-19thC polychrome rocking horse, with a leather saddle and tack on a pine base.
$750-850 WHP

An early-20thC wooden rocking horse, probably by Ayres, dapple gray, unrestored, on a pine base.

51¼in (130cm) high

$2,000-2,600 BELL

An early-20thC rocking horse, of small size, dapple gray with glass eyes and hair tail.

39¾in (101cm) high

$450-600 L&T

An FH Ayres dapple gray rocking horse, bearing stencil "6 C.S.S.A " on pine cruciform base, ears chipped, mane mostly missing.

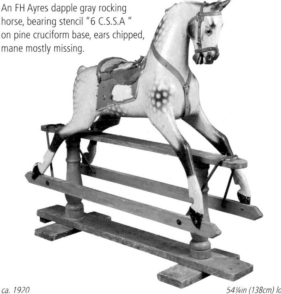

An early-20thC Triang rocking horse, on a sled base, in stripped condition.

35¾in (91cm) wide

$600-750 CHEF

ca. 1970

54¼in (138cm) long

$1,500-1,800 CHEF

A 20thC dapple gray, painted wood rocking horse, on stand.

51¼in (130cm) long

$800-900 CHEF

A Relko wooden rocking horse, by Cookham Dean of England, with glass eyes, horse hair mane and tail, and leather saddle and bridle, on a walnut swing frame.

49in (124.5cm) high

$1,500-1,800 MART

A Sapele wood rocking horse, made by Timber and Thread, hand-carved by Frank E. Lord, limited edition number 37 of 40, the swing stand with applied "Timber and Thread" plaque.

1997 *40in (101.6cm) high*

$750-850 MART

A 19thC French velocipede tricycle, the body in the form of a galloping horse on a cast-metal frame, with hand pedals and foot steering.

$550-650 WHP

A Dan mask, Ivory Coast, of carved wood and fiber, with a vegetable fiber coiffure and glossy black patina, on a custom-made mount.

9in (23cm) high

$1,500-1,800   **L&T**

A Zulu zoomorphic dance staff/snuffkerrie, South Africa, the bovine head snuff container with inlaid pewter and two miniature kerries as horns.

32in (81cm) high

$12,000-15,000   **WW**

An early Ewe cloth, Togo/Eastern Ghana, of strip-woven cotton.

119¾in (304cm) long

$2,900-3,700   **L&T**

A Tetela mask, Democratic Republic of Congo, of carved wood, pigment, feather,s and woven fiber, white wash with incised geometric grooves colored in red and black pigment.

20in (51cm) high

$2,600-3,300   **L&T**

ESSENTIAL REFERENCE—UMHALLA'S PIPE

Originally belonging to Umhalla, a Xhosa prince, it was gifted in 1853 during the Eighth Kaffir (Xhosa) War. Umhalla was a son of Cheif Mhala, who was a prominent figure in the Xhosa War, resisting British aggression and fighting to retain control of his land. Following the end of the conflict, he was later sentenced to death, which was later reduced to 20 years hard labor on Robben Island. Prince Umhalla himself, probably born in the late 1830s, was one of a select group of Xhosa royal children chosen to be sent to Cape Town in 1850, immediately prior to the outbreak of the war, as part of the British strategy to "assimilate" local power centers into the colonial economy and structures. It was during this period that Umhalla met the young Rev. Francis Fleming at a Xhosa Kraal. Umhalla and Fleming struck up a friendship, with Umhalla promising his pipe as a gift to Reverend F. Fleming. Shortly after their meeting, the Xhosa War broke out and the two did not meet again until three years later, in August 1853, when Umhalla, remembering his promise, gifted the pipe to Fleming. In later life, Umhalla remained a respected senior member of the Xhosa tribe. In 1878, he became one the first citizens in Cape Colony to be charged with treason for refusing to favor the Colonial War against the Ngqika Xhosa of Ngcayecibi. After this period, he worked in the Cape Colony legal system and went on to edit the first Xhosa-language newspaper. He was also noted as being one of the finest cricket players in South Africa.

Umhalla's pipe, South Africa, carved wood and inlaid pewter, with a 19thC label, reading "Umhalla's Pipe.

6½in (16.2cm) long

$1,500-1,800   **L&T**

A Ewe man's cloth, Eastern Ghana or Togo, of cotton, in weft-faced-style with a checkerboard pattern.

125¼in (318cm) long

$8,000-9,000   **L&T**

A Songhay Arkila Jenngo, Mali, of wool and cotton weave, dyed using vegetal and mineral pigments.

This Arkilla Jenngo, traditionally produced by Songhay-speaking weavers using a double-heddle backstrap loom. Among the seminomadic peoples of the Sahel, intended for use as a tent divider or marriage-bed curtain.

173¼in (440cm) long

$3,300-4,000   **L&T**

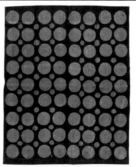

A Yoruba Adire textile, Nigeria, of dyed cotton.

80¼in (204cm) long

$4,000-4,600   **L&T**

A carved and polished green serpentine figure, by Joseph Ndandarika (Shona 1940-91), "After Bathing," Zimbabwe, the nude female figure shown reclining against a rock, signed.

1990   *18½in (47cm) high*

$2,000-2,600   **L&T**

ESSENTIAL REFERENCE—KAROO ASHEVAK

Art Gallery of Ontario curator Wanda Nanibush explains that Karoo Ashevak's art was shaped by scary stories of otherworldly monsters told to him at bedtime: "and then as he got older and he started carving, it's like these stories kind of shifted in his mind and they became much more loving and funny to him."

● Noted both for his humor as much as for the originality and skill of his art, "Spirit" is highly emblematic of Ashevak's work. The subject's face appears animated—either in surprise, fear, or wonder—yet this specter from another world is wearing mittens. The figure before us is thus rendered human and of this earth, almost charming, and in need of protecting from the cold.

● Ashevak's career was cut short by his death in 1974, one year after a solo show in New York City earned him major recognition in the United States and Canada. He had been sculpting for only four years, making this work a special find for collectors.

A whalebone carving, "Shaman with Mittens," by Karoo Ashevak (1940-74), Spence Bay/Taloyoak.

12in (30.5cm) wide

$24,000-29,000　　　　**WAD**

A stone figure, "Woman with Bucket," by Joe Talirunili (1893-1976), Povungnituk/Puvirnituq, signed in Roman.

8in (20.3cm) high

$4,600-5,900　　**WAD**

A stone figure, "Hunter with Harpoon," by Joe Talirunili (1893-1976), Povungnituk/Puvirnituq, signed in Roman, disk number inscribed.

8¼in (21cm) high

$7,500-8,500　　**WAD**

A stone figure, "Sitting Man," by John Tiktak, R.C.A. (1916-81), Rankin Inlet/Kangiqliniq, signed in syllabics.

ca. 1964　　8½in (21.6cm) high

$9,000-10,500　　**WAD**

A stone figure, "Undressing" by Davidialuk Alasua Amittu (1910-76), Povungnituk/Puvirnituq, discknumber inscribed.

9¾in (24.8cm) high

$4,000-4,600　　**WAD**

A Markosie Papigatok Inuit, "Raven Man," Kinngait, Dorset Island, of carved steatite, the standing shaman wearing a raven headdress.

6in (15cm) high

$850-1,000　　**L&T**

A Mosesee Pootoogook Inuit, "Hunter Throwing," Kinngait, Dorset Island, of carved green steatite, caribou antler, and seal gut.

6in (15cm) high

$750-850　　**L&T**

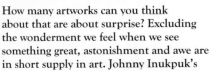

Judith Picks

How many artworks can you think about that are about surprise? Excluding the wonderment we feel when we see something great, astonishment and awe are in short supply in art. Johnny Inukpuk's "Girl Uncovers a Hibernating Bear" immediately startles, sending a thrill through the viewer as we imagine ourselves stumbling upon a sleeping predator. Adding to the suspense—yikes—the bear's eyes are open! What would we do? And more important, what happens next?

Inukpuk's sculpture is akin to a movie still, a paused moment in an action film or a chase sequence. The artist has rendered his subject in great detail, outlining the strands of her braided hair, the fringe on her coat, the creases on her skin. Her hands are larger than life, drawing attention to their surprised gesture. Inukpuk's model for this carving is proabably his wife Mary, identifiable by her cleft lip, which is visible in this sculpture. Perhaps this was created to depict a particular episode in Mary's life, making this sculpture somewhat of a family album, or perhaps the most exquisite response to a familiar question: "how was your day, honey?

A stone figure, "Girl Uncovers A Hibernating Bear," by Johnny Inukpuk, R.C.A. (1911-2007), Port Harrison/Inukjuak, signed in syllabics, disk number inscribed.

ca. 1970　　17in (43.2cm) high

$24,000-29,000　　**WAD**

An early-19thC Inuit bow, Pacific, Alaskacedar, with a channeled ridge on the flat side and with intricately woven sinew to the back.

Collected by British artist Frederick Whymper (1838-1901), who arrived in Victoria from England in 1862 on a sketching tour of northern British Columbia. In 1863, he joined as an artist the Vancouver Island Exploring Expedition and in November 1864 an exhibition of 33 of his drawings was held in Victoria. In 1865, Whymper joined as an artist the Russian-American Telegraph project, which intended to construct a telegraph line linking the United States and Europe through British Columbia, Alaska, and Siberia. In 1867, the project was abandoned and Whymper returned to England and published his narrative, "Travel and Adventure in the Territory of Alaska."

53¾in (136.6cm) long

$3,300-4,000   WW

A 19thC Inuit child's parka, Alaska, of seal gut, sealskin, seal fur, and red and natural fiber.

20in (51cm) high

$7,500-8,500   WW

A 19thC Inuit standing figure, Alaska, of walrus ivory, on a stand.

2¼in (5.3cm) high

$2,600-3,300   WW

An Inuit polar bear, Canada, of carved and polished soapstone, signed in syllabics and dated "70."

8¼in (21.2cm) long

$900-1,050   L&T

An Inuit polar bear amulet, Alaska, of walrus ivory with baleen.

4¼in (11cm) long

$2,600-4,000   WW

A stonecut print, "Dream," by Kenojuak Ashevak, C.C., R.C.A. (1927-2013), Cape Dorset/Kinngait, 28/50.

There is something fitting about Kenojuak, the grande dame of Inuit Art, representing her dreams in sharp relief. While the rest of us stumble around in the haze, Kenojuak's crystalline vision appears to have extended deep into her subconscious. It is reported that Kenojuak would only rarely lift her hand off of the surface on which she was drawing, so assured was she in her composition, line, and vision. This is evident in the sinuous lines of the animals, notably the fluidity of the birds at the top of the composition, which seems to stretch across the sky as if in slow motion. The viewer is left wondering if they are observing the artist within her dream—perhaps represented by the centered figure dressed in an amaut—or are seeing through her eyes.

1963   *22in (55.9cm) wide*

$12,000-15,000   WAD

A stonecut print, "Vision of Autumn," by Kenojuak Ashevak, C.C., R.C.A. (1927-2013), Cape Dorset/Kinngait, 43/50, work is framed.

1960   *19in (48.3cm) wide*

$13,000-16,000   WAD

A stonecut and stencil print, "Figure in Striped Clothing," by Jessie Oonark, O.C., R.C.A. (1906-85), Baker Lake/Qamani'tuaq, 21/48.

Oonark takes the rich pattern work on the traditional amaut and stylizes it even further, rendering it as one would a Modernist composition. For an image that tends nearly toward abstraction, Oonark incorporates several grounding details, including the traditional face tattoo of an Inuit woman. A prime example of the artist's ability to translate common objects into symbols, the woman's crescent-shaped ulu knife is used as a motif on both sides of the subject's face. Oonark's signature use of symmetry is displayed here, and a clear link to the artist's famous "Big Woman" print can be seen.

1971   *24in (61cm) high*

$16,000-20,000   WAD

A stonecut print, "Running Rabbit," by Pudlo Pudlat (1916-92), Cape Dorset/Kinngait, light wrinkling on the paper, work is unframed, 20/50.

1963   *25in (63.5cm) high*

$6,000-6,600   WAD

An early-20thC Apache beaded front pouch, Southwest North America, of buckskin, colored glass beads, and tin cones.

11¾in (30cm) high

$1,050-1,200 **WW**

A 19thC Apache saddle bag, Southwest North America, raw hide, red and blue dyed cotton, with traces of a red/brown pigment.

82¾in (210cm) long

$2,600-4,000 **WW**

CLOSER LOOK—ARAPAHO BAG

The Arapaho were a nomadic tribe of hunter gatherers who lived in the plains of Central U.S.A. They moved around following the buffalo herds.

The flap is leather decorated with a stitched design, with a large silver button.

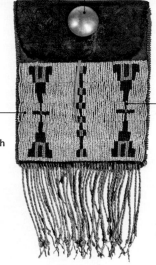

This is an early beaded commercial leather dispatch bag from ca. 1880.

The bag is decorated on the front and sides with multicolored abstract geometric devices, the back with one panel of beadwork at the bottom.

A Plains bag, Arapaho.

12in (30.5cm) long

$3,300-4,000 **SK**

An Apache bow case and quiver, Plains, of buckskin, colored glass beads and cloth, the strap with stars and strips, a crescent moon and a circle motif, with a bow having sinew bound ends, with five pigment-decorated arrows with steel tips.

Bow 39¼in (99.5cm) long

$6,000-6,600 **WW**

A Blackfoot pipe bag, Plains, of buckskin and colored glass beads.

This bag was owned by Chief Calf Child, a headman of the Canadian Blackfoot in Alberta, during the early 20thC.

ca. 1890 *35¾in (91cm) long*

$2,600-4,000 **WW**

An 1870s Plains Cree beaded hide pipe bag, of soft hide, the top edge of scalloped form with beaded edging, each side with a beaded panel, one with a multicolored thunderbird surrounded by floral devices.

Provenance: Collected by Frederick Myers (1847-1900). Myers served in the Union Army and later fought in the Indian Campaigns. He served as teamster, quartermaster, and then quartermaster sergeant in the 7th Cavalry, Company I, from 1873 to 1883, and 6th Calvary, Company K, from 1883 to 1893. He was awarded a Congressional Medal of Honor in 1891: "For conspicuous gallantry and intrepidity above and beyond the call of duty in action with the enemy at White River, South Dakota, January 1, 1891. With five men repelled a superior force of the enemy and held his position against their repeated efforts to recapture it."

27¾in (70.5cm) long

$22,000-26,000 **SK**

An early-19thC Great Lakes beaded cloth bag, of red trade cloth with silk edging, the centered finger-woven wool panel beaded with a diamond pattern and lightning devices on the side.

19in (48.5cm) long

$6,000-6,600 **SK**

A pair of Maliseet moccasins, Northeast North America, of moose hide, cloth, velvet, and colored glass beads, with trailing floral and scallop decoration.

ca. 1860 *10¼in (26cm) long*

$1,800-2,400 **WW**

A Navajo Germantown rug, Southwest North America.

73¾in (187cm) long

$2,400-2,900 **WW**

ESSENTIAL REFERENCE—GERMANTOWN BLANKETS

Germantown blankets were Navajo textiles woven from the early 1860s to 1910, with the bulk of the weavings made from 1885-90. The name of these blankets comes from the yarn used that came from wool mills in the region of Germantown, Pennsylvania. This yarn was shipped to the Navajo reservation, where the weavers would buy at the trading post. Germantown yarns gave the weavers a wide choice of colors that they hadn't had before: bright pinks and greens, dark greens, reds, yellows, and purples.

Having access to these yarns sparked a creative outburst in the Navajo weaving community of the period and resulted in highly skilled textiles that are highly prized by collectors. Note that Germantown blankets preceded the making of Navajo rugs and were woven almost exclusively for the tourist trade. These vintage Navajo blankets are too delicate to put on the floor; instead, these textiles were draped on beds, worn, or hung on walls.

A Navajo Germantown rug, Southwest North America, with an eye-dazzler serrated diamond lattice design.

80¾in (205cm) long

$2,600-4,000   **WW**

A Navajo rug, Crystal Trading Post, New Mexico, of flat-woven natural churro wool.

ca. 1910   *72in (183cm) long*

$1,000-1,100   **L&T**

A late-19thC Navajo Germantown weaving, with stacked concentric flat diamonds and geometric designs.

69in (175.5cm) long

$12,000-13,000   **SK**

A Haida totem pole, Northwest Coast, argillite with a whale, a raven and a bear, with a wood base. **Haida Gwaii "Islands of the Haida people" is an archipelago located 34–78 miles (55–125km) off the northern Pacific coast of Canada. The islands are separated from the mainland on the east by the shallow Hecate Strait. Queen Charlotte Sound lies to the south, with Vancouver Island beyond.**

9¾in (24.5cm) high

$1,800-2,400   **WW**

A Northwest Coast Argillite Platter, Haida, rim decorated with inlay shell triangles, the interior carved with a mythological subject in the form of a sea monster with a human holding its tail and jaw, surrounded by totemic heads, a fish, and raven.

16½in (42cm) diam

$6,000-7,500   **SK**

A 19thC Northwest Coast polychrome model canoe, Haida, with a full-bodied prow figure of a crouching man, paint decorated in black and red.

32in (81.5cm) long

$10,000-11,000   **SK**

A Northwest Coast ceremonial helmet mask, Kwakwaka'wakw, a wolf mask, traces of pigments, and pierced for attachment, missing some attachments.

19in (48.5cm) long

$8,500-10,000   **SK**

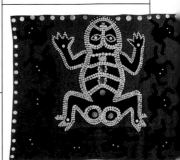

An early-20thC Northwest Coast button blanket, on an early wool blanket, with a centered frog, surrounded by 10 frogs in black fabric.

44in (112cm) wide

$4,000-4,600   **SK**

A late-19thC Northwest Coast Chilkat blanket, Tlingit, woven of mountain goat wool and cedar bark, classic form representing a whale diving, the lateral fields represent a raven sitting, with minor color fading.

54in (137cm) wide

$70,000-80,000   **SK**

A Northwest Coast wood mask, with abalone shell inlays, with a wood split at chin, and blackened on right side.

16¼in (41.5cm) high

$6,000-6,600   SK

An 1880s Plains quilled-wood stem with Catlinite pipe bowl, wood stem decorated with quillwork depicting a butterfly, a turtle, feathers, and a buffalo head, with T-type catlinite bowl.

24¼in (61.5cm) long

$2,600-3,300   SK

A late-19thC Sioux pipe bag, Plains, of buckskin, colored glass beads, rawhide, dyed quill, tin cones, and dyed horse hair.

31¼in (79cm) long

$800-900   WW

A Western Sioux fully beaded vest, Plains, buckskin with lazy stitch of a white ground with geometric designs.

ca. 1880   *23¼in (59cm) long*

$4,000-4,600   WW

ESSENTIAL REFERENCE—MOCCASINS

Moccasins were an important element to complete a Plains Indian outfit. The traditional, side-seam moccasins were soft soled and made from a single piece of hide. In the mid-19thC, hard rawhide soles became more common on moccasins across the Plains. This style might have been introduced from European footwear. After the arrival of the horse, women on the Southern Plains began to combine their moccasins and leggings. These high-top moccasins would be decorated with beads, like traditional moccasins, as well as fringe, tin cones, and metal tacks.

Fully beaded moccasins, also called burial moccasins, were worn by the living and the dead. Some wore them to show their wealth as horse owners. The beaded soles implied they always rode horses and did not need to walk. Others were made for the dead. Women would spend several days beading moccasins and other items to honor their loved ones. Finally, Native Americans on reservations sold beaded items to collectors. These, like those made for the dead, show no wear on the soles, because they were placed on display and not worn.

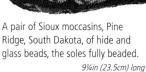

A pair of Western Sioux moccasins, Plains, of buckskin and colored glass and cut-brass beads in lazy stitch with geometric designs.

ca. 1900   *9½in (24cm) long*

$1,600-2,100   WW

A pair of Sioux moccasins, Pine Ridge, South Dakota, of hide and glass beads, the soles fully beaded.

9¼in (23.5cm) long

$550-650   L&T

A late-19thC Plains beaded hide moccasins, Sioux, with rawhide soles, soft sides, long beaded bifurcated tongues with tin cones, and multicolored beaded designs, with bead loss and stitching damage at heels.

10½in (26.5cm) long

$6,500-8,000   SK

A Southwest Polychrome Konin or Supai Katsina, Third Mesa style, hand-carved from cottonwood with white case mask with feathers on top, the feathers replaced.

Katsina 8in (20.5cm) high

$7,500-8,500   SK

A pair of Native American beaded hide moccasins, geometrically decorated.

ca. 1900   *10¼in (26cm) long*

$800-900   LSK

TRIBAL ART

A ceremonial wooden dance paddle, Austral Islands, with intricate carving throughout, the paddle blade with dual rows of ceremonial dancing figures.

39in (99cm) high

$4,600-5,900   **L&T**

A 19thC Admiralty Islands ceremonial ladle, Melanesia, coconut, wood, nut paste, and pigment, the handle carved as a figure.

11in (28cm) high

$1,700-2,400   **WW**

A 19thC Nukuoro coconut-grating stool, Caroline Islands, a serrated piece of shell was originally attached to the front/head of the stool, and a split coconut is rubbed along the sharp edge to shred the meat, with age cracks.

22½in (57cm) wide

$3,300-4,000   **SK**

A Fiji throwing club, "i ula tavatava," Melanesia, with a ribbed head with a dotted dome, a zigzag carved grip with a concave terminal.

15¾in (40cm) long

$1,600-2,100   **WW**

A 19thC Fijian kava bowl, Tanoa, of hardwood, possibly vesi, with a woven sennit cord, traces of kava on the interior, with age cracks.

17in (43cm) diam

$1,700-2,100   **SK**

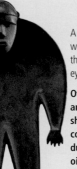

A figural Kava bowl, Daveniyaqona, Fiji, of carved wood, the bowl in the form of a shallow figure with the head in high relief, the lips subtly parted, the eyes hollow, kava deposits on the hands and feet.

Of exceptional rarity, less than 10 Daveniyaqona are known to exist. Carved in the form of a shallow figure, they were used for both the consumption of kava (yaqona) by priests during religious rites and to hold sacred oil. In Fiji, the consumption of kava would accompany important socialpolitical events and religious ceremonies. The Daveniyaqona dish was specifically associated with the burau drinking rites, whereby a highly concentrated solution was poured into the bowl without the usual dilution using water. The kava was then consumed by priests using a straw also known as a burau. The strength of the resulting reaction enabled powerful forces to enter the priest's bodies, allowing communion with ancestor spirits. The complex shapes of bowls used for such rituals are also known in the form of birds and turtles; however, the sheer scarcity of the anthropomorphic type suggests they were produced at a single center. The present example shows a deep dark patination indicative of use, with wear to the rim, attachment lug, and extended heels on the reverse. Kava deposits are present from pooling at the hands and feet of the figure. The brooding face and formidable build combined with the flowing curves create a powerful and arresting visage. The parted lips and hollow eyes seem to suggest a trance, echoing the context of its original use.

10½in (26.5cm) high

$90,000-110,000   **L&T**

A Marquesas Islands bone ornament, "ivi po'o," Polynesia, carved as a tiki with the remains of a red pigment on the eyes and lips, the back with a tiki face, shoulder blades, and buttocks.

1½in (4cm) high

$6,500-8,000   **WW**

A Sepik River amulet figure, Papua New Guinea, with a reddish pigment and remains of natural fiber around the left arm, on a base.

5½in (14cm) high

$1,050-1,300   **WW**

A Wosera standing female figure, Papua New Guinea, with a red ground pigment and with gray, black, and white pigment over, including a ringlet necklace, on a wood base.

49in (124.5cm) high

$1,600-2,100   **WW**

A 19th/20thC Papua New Guinea headrest, North Coast, with a pair of supports and an inverted lizard with another on its tail and mouth, each supporting an ancestor mask, with remains of paint.

16in (40.5cm) long

$1,300-1,600   **WW**

A 19thC Aboriginal leangle club, Western Victoria, Australia, the blade with a hand-written label "Tomahawk Rev J. Waddington."

24¼in (61.5cm) long

$2,600-3,300   WW

An Aboriginal shield, Australia, with painted pigment and dot decoration, the integral handle missing.

27¾in (70.5cm) long

$650-800   WW

An Aboriginal churinga, Central Desert, Australia.

36¼in (91.8cm) long

$5,300-5,900   WW

A 19thC Aboriginal narrow shield, Western Victoria, Australia, with carved linear decoration.

34½in (87.5cm) long

$8,000-9,000   WW

An Aboriginal churinga, Australia, of stone with carved circles and parallel linear symbols, with ocher pigment.

9½in (24cm) long

$2,400-2,900   WW

A Maori child's taiaha staff, New Zealand, carved with head and tongue profile and a pointed terminal.

37¼in (94.7cm) long

$350-400   WW

A 19thC Maori tinder box, New Zealand, the hollowed out interior having the remains of red pigment, the exterior with allover carved linear and feathered designs, the lift-off lid with a carved relief tiki head handle and the ends with further tiki heads, with inset halitosis shell eyes.

12½in (32cm) long

$6,000-7,500   WW

A Maori Patu, New Zealand, of spermwhale panbone, carved with worn ribbing on the butt of the handle, a rounded concave suspension hole and teardrop-shaped blade, deep patination indicative of extensive age and use.

19¾in (50.1cm) long

$8,500-10,000   L&T

A Maori pendant, Hei Tiki, New Zealand, of carved nephrite and pāua shell, the head angled and arms shown held to the legs, eye inlaid with shell, the reverse with an old label reading "Artefact from New Zealand Maori."

The old label on the reverse is suggestive of an early-19thC collection date.

2½in (6cm) high

$6,000-6,600   L&T

A late-17thC Brescian Miquelet-lock long-barreled pistol, the barrel chiseled with Classical figures.

36in (91.5cm) long

$7,500-8,500   **SWO**

A pair of 18thC double-barrel box-lock flintlock pistols, by Williams of London, signed, wear on the surface gilding/lacquer of the barrels.

13in (33cm) long

$8,000-9,000   **SWO**

A cased pair of late-18thC flintlock full-stock dueling pistols, by P. Bond, signed "P. Bond" with sliding safety catches, set triggers, and engraved with trophies of arms, in mahogany case with label for "William Bond, 43 Cornhill, London," with accessories, including a bullet mold, loading rod, and three-way flask.

case 14½in (37cm) wide

$11,000-13,000   **SWO**

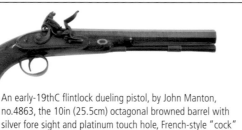

An early-19thC flintlock dueling pistol, by John Manton, no.4863, the 10in (25.5cm) octagonal browned barrel with silver fore sight and platinum touch hole, French-style "cock" and sliding safety, signed.

15½in (39.5cm) long

$4,000-4,600   **SWO**

A cased pair of early-19thC turn-over barrel percussion pistols, by Joseph Lang, with turn-off barrels, "Lang's patent turn-over system no.48," the actions unusually engraved with shooting scenes and dogs, with Cuban mahogany case, with a loading tool, bullet mold, oil bottle, and three-way flask.

Joseph Lang married the daughter of James Purdey.

case 6in (15cm) wide

$10,000-11,000   **SWO**

A cased pair of 40-bore percussion dueling pistols, by H. W. Mortimer of London, with County Down registration "D-N 11529" on the side, with original horn-tipped ramrods below, with checkered walnut butts, in the original mahogany case with various accessories.

ca. 1830   *pistols 15½in (39cm) long*

$6,500-8,000   **LSK**

A pair of 19thC percussion officer's pistols, by Mabson, having 7in (18cm) sighted octagonal barrels with engraved gold-lined breeches, border and scroll-engraved back-action bolted locks signed, one of the locks holds only at full cock, old repair to forestock of one.

12¼in (31cm) long

$1,100-1,250   **LSK**

A 19thC Sea Service percussion belt pistol, the 6in (15cm) barrel with inspection stamps with ramrod below, the lockplate stamped with a crown over "VR Tower 1840."

1840   *11½in (29cm) long*

$550-650   **LSK**

A Hopkins & Allen Ranger No.2 five-shot rim-fire pocket pistol, signed, sheath trigger, M.O.P two-piece grips.

6¾in (17.2cm) long

$400-450   **MART**

A 16-bore double-barreled rifled pin-fire Westley Richards Howdah pistol, with patent top-lever sidelock action, signed along the top rib "170 New Bond Street, London," surface rusting on the barrels.

13½in (34cm) long

$3,300-4,000   **SWO**

A pair of 19thC box-lock percussion pocket pistols, the checkered mahogany grips with white metal escutcheons and shell-carved butts.

6¼in (16cm) long

$1,100-1,250   **LSK**

A pair of 19thC box-lock percussion pocket pistols, by Durs Egg.

6in (15cm) long

$600-650   **LSK**

An early-19thC six-shot percussion pepperbox revolver, by M & J Pattison.

8in (20cm) long

$6,000-7,500   SWO

A French percussion rifled revolver, by Devisme A. Paris, model 1855, with blued barrel and frame on the Thouvenin system, signed, in original oak case with powder flask, bullet mold, and percussion cap box, a handwritten loading instruction is pasted into the lid.

$2,000-2,600   L&T

An Adams percussion five-shot double action cap-and-ball revolver, serial number B4414 and patent number 19922R, with engraved blued action, with sliding safety locking the cylinder, engraved on top of the barrel "DEANE & SON, NO. 50 KING WILLIAM ST, LONDON BRIDGE" in original case with powder flask, bullet mold, and oil bottle.

ca. 1860

$4,000-5,300   L&T

A Colt model 1849 pocket percussion six-shot revolver, serial number 203144, 5in (12.5cm) barrel with Hartford address, some knocks and age marks.

1862   *10in (25cm) long*

$1,700-2,100   CHEF

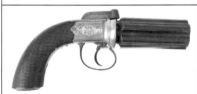

A 19thC self-cocking bar hammer-action percussion six-shot pepperbox revolver, the 3½in (8.5cm) barrels with alternating crown over "G" or "V" ciphers, the tang marked "W. Smith Lisle St London."

9in (23cm) long

$1,000-1,100   LSK

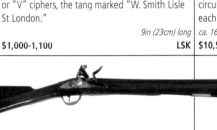

A rare German seven-barreled flintlock volley rifle, by Valtin (Valentin) Muth, Zerbst, with a static circular arrangement of hexagonal 13mm-caliber barrels fitted with treaded trunnions beneath, each barrel with hexagonal bore additions.

ca. 1680

$10,500-12,000   BELL

A late-18thC Indian service steel-barreled flintlock musketoon, by Brander & Potts, London, the lock named "Carnatic" and with military stamps repeated on the barrel, original ramrod and brass furniture.

HMS "Carnatic" was a 74-gun 3rd rate ship of the line of the Royal Navy, which was launched in 1783. The British East India Company commissioned "Carnatic" and presented the ship to the Royal Navy in 1815, whereupon the Navy renamed her the HMS "Captain," which went on to serve for a further 10 years.

38¼in (97cm) long

$6,000-7,500   SWO

A flintlock blunderbuss, the brass barrel stamped "HMS AJAX 24" and "GR" cipher, restocked.

33in (84cm) long

$1,050-1,200   CHEF

A BSA .177 caliber under-lever air rifle, numbered CS48638.

ca. 1931   *43½in (110.8cm) long*

$350-400   MART

An 18thC Continental sword, having a 31in (79cm) spearpoint blade, the brass guard with clamshell languet with faux antler handle and brass ball pommel.

37in (94cm) long

$550-650 **LSK**

A French sword, the 32in (81cm) triangular blade with remains of gilt etching and marked to the forte IGB for "Johann Clemens Boegel," in a leather scabbard.

ca. 1800 *37¾in (96cm) long*

$350-400 **LSK**

A stirrup-hilted light cavalry officer's saber, with a checkered ivory grip and curved single-edged blade with original brass-mounted leather scabbard.

ca. 1803 *31in (78.5cm) long*

$650-800 **L&T**

A British Cavalry Trooper's sword, the 35in (89cm) curved fullered blade marked "V.W." with Liege inspection mark, in a steel scabbard.

1821 *41in (104cm) long*

$600-650 **LSK**

A George VI London Scottish Regiment 1831-pattern Scottish broad sword, the 32in (82cm) double-edged blade with single center fuller etched with the Strike Sure crest and thistles, marked on the forte "By Appointment to His Late Majesty King George V, Wilkinson Sword Co. Ltd London," numbered "68021."

1831 *38½in (98cm) long*

$1,100-1,200 **LSK**

An 1821-pattern light cavalry presentation sword, blade also etched with "VR" cipher, marked "Reeves and Greaves Manufacturers," in a steel scabbard.

41in (104cm) long

$1,500-1,800 **LOC**

A Victorian Court sword, the 31½in (80cm) blade etched with a crowned "VR" cipher, marked on the forte "Parfitt Roberts & Parfitt, Jermyn St, London," having a clamshell languet with applied crowned "VR" cipher within wreath with wire-bound grip and crown pommel with bullion knot.

36¼in (92cm) long

$750-850 **LSK**

A 19thC Lifeguard's Officer's dress sword, with an 31½in (80cm) blade with brass hilt and wire-bound grip, in a brass-mounted leather scabbard.

37¾in (96cm) long

$1,300-1,800 **LSK**

A 19thC Lifeguard's Officer's dress sword, the 31½in (80cm) blade marked (faintly) on the forte "Andrews Pall Mall," having a brass boat-shaped hilt, in a brass-mounted leather scabbard.

37¾in (96cm) long

$550-600 **LSK**

A Fairbairn-Sykes 1st Pattern Commando fighting knife, the 6¾in (17cm) double-edged spearpoint blade marked on the ricasso "The F-S Fighting Knife" and "Wilkinson Sword Co Ltd London" with a shaped oval crossguard with checkered nickel grip, in a nickel-mounted leather sheath with Newey Pat. button.

11¾in (30cm) long

$2,600-4,000 LSK

An early-19thC Naval dirk, with a 6in (15cm) blade with plain crossguard and ring-turned ivory handle.

9in (23cm) long

$450-600 LSK

A Victorian cast silver-plate dagger and scabbard.

12in (30.5cm) long

$260-330 MART

A Crimea medal (1854-56) with Sebastopol clasp, naming in flowing script "Gunner John Harris J? Troop Royal Horse Artillery "

$350-400 LSK

A Queen's Sudan medal (1896-97), naming poorly erased.

$170-210 LSK

A King's South Africa medal, with South Africa 1901 and 1902 clasps, naming "4000 DMR: A. WELHAM ESSEX REGT."

Private Welham was killed in action at Driefontein on March 10, 1900.

1901-02

$90-110 LSK

A Queen's South Africa medal, 2nd type reverse with ghost dates, having Wittebergen, Johannesburg and Relief of Kimberley clasps, naming "3138 PTE. T. GROUNDS, 12: R. LANCERS."

1899-1902

$200-260 LSK

A George V Military medal, naming "33792 PTE. B. HODGKISS. 2/ YORK.R."

$400-450 LSK

An Indian Distinguished Service medal, of George V Kaisar-I-Hind type, naming "2454 TR - DFDR. MIR MUHAMMAD. 71_G. C. C."

Troop Dafader Mir Muhammad of the 71st Government Camel Corps was awarded the I.D.S.M. on May 5, 1922, for Gallantry and Distinguished conduct in the field while serving with the Waziristan force.

$1,050-1,200 LSK

An E.R. II General Service medal (1918-62), with Canal Zone clasp, naming "21126081 CFN E C HODDER REME," boxed.

$260-330 LSK

"WOMEN'S SOCIAL AND POLITICAL UNION MEDAL FOR VALOUR OF THE SUFFRAGETTE SELINA MARTIN," 1909 silver medal, ⅞in (22mm), obverse engraved HUNGER STRIKE, reverse engraved SELINA MARTIN, hallmarked Birmingham 1909, the reverse of the two enameled bars engraved "FED BY FORCE 17.9.09 and FED BY FORCE 21.12.09," the plain suspender bar engraved AUGUST 20TH 1909, the plain brooch-bar engraved "FOR VALOUR, reverse impressed TOYE 57 THEOBALDS RD LONDON," original silk ribbon, in the original green plush-lined purple morocco case of issue, the ivory silk lining on the underside of the lid inscribed in gilt "This medal was presented to Selina Martin by the WSPU in recognition of a gallant action whereby through endurance to the last extremity of hunger and hardship a great principle of political justice was vindicated."

$46,000-53,000 M&K

A Greek red-figure two-handled krater (wine vessel), Apulian region, one side with a lady wearing her chiton and sacchos, offering food to a man, the opposing side with two figures, one holding a staff.

ca. 300-275 BC   *11¾in (30cm) high*

$4,000-5,300   **CHEF**

An Ancient Egyptian faience bottle, probably Dynasty XVIII.

ca. 1550-1292 BC   *3in (7.5cm) high*

$3,300-4,000   **L&T**

A Late Period Egyptian faience Shabti, with a full frontal column of hieroglyphics, on a mount.

ca. 664-332 BC   *6¼in (15.5cm) high*

$6,000-7,500   **L&T**

A 6th/5thC-BC Attic black-figure skyphos, each side decorated with a male figure and a ram with attendants.

10in (25.5cm) wide

$1,700-2,100   **WW**

An early-5thC-BC Attic black-figure kylix, painted with grazing deer amid predators and swooping birds.

11½in (29cm) diam

$6,000-7,500   **L&T**

A carved cornelian intaglio ring, probably Roman, the oval, of faintly banded cornelian, depicting the head of a man, possibly an Emperor.

Some experts believe the face on the ring is that of Mark Anthony.

size S

$70,000-80,000   **CHEF**

A 1stC-AD Roman glass measuring pitcher, Modiolus, small trailed handle at the midsection.

5¼in (12.9cm) tall

$8,500-10,000   **L&T**

A Roman marble torso of Venus, with remnants of the folds of her garment, on a custom-made mount.

ca. 2ndC AD   *16½in (42cm) high*

$8,500-10,000   **L&T**

A large Western Asiatic bronze ibex figure, Near East, late 2nd Millennium BC-early 1st Millennium BC.

13in (33cm) high

$33,000-40,000   **L&T**

MUSICAL INSTRUMENTS

A George III mahogany square piano, by John Broadwood & Son, the case inlaid with stringing and purpleheart-and-satinwood banding, with applied gilt-brass paterae, signed, with ivory naturals and ebony accidentals, dated "1794 Patent."

62.5in (159cm) wide

$3,300-4,000 **WW**

A Henri Selmer 80 Super Action Series II gold-lacquered brass saxophone, with mother-of-pearl keys, serial no. N. 537878, in a fitted case.

$2,400-2,900 **LOCK**

A Henri Selmer Mark VII gold-laquered brass saxophone, with mother-of-pearl keys, serial no. M. 245682, in a fitted case.

$2,600-3,300 **LOCK**

An early-19thC English giltwood and gesso black-lacquered and brass harp, by Sebastian Erards, the brasswork stamped "Sebastian Erards Patent No.259, 18 Great Marlborough Street, London," the sound board decorated with putti and mythological scenes.

67in (170cm) high

$6,500-8,000 **TEN**

A late-18th/early-19thC English cello, with a later case.

back 28¾in (73cm) long

$8,500-10,000 **WHP**

A Martin Vintage Series D-18VS acoustic guitar, serial no. 11****7, of typical dreadnought form in a natural finish with a faux tortoiseshell pickguard and slotted headstock, with original fitted hard case, surface scratches, and knocks.

2006 *neck 1¾in (4.4cm) wide*

$2,600-3,300 **SWO**

A German violin, by Louis Lowendall, Dresden, the two-piece curly maple back stamped "DRESDEN" and "REGISTERED" and painted with a portrait of the violinist Ludwig Spohr, the button with a Registration stamp and number 390660, the back of the scroll branded "LOWENDALL'S ARTIST VIOLIN," with a bow stamped "GERMANY" and branded initials "ACHM," in a case with extra keys, frets, strings, and tailpiece.

Ludwig Spohr (1784-1859) was a German composer, violinist, and conductor. Highly regarded during his lifetime, he toured extensively through Europe and made six tours of England, beginning in 1820. He composed more than 150 works in the Romantic style, but he fell into obscurity for most of the 20thC, albeit he has experienced something of a rediscovery over the last few decades.

1883 *bow 29¼in (74cm) long*

$2,000-2,600 **L&T**

ESSENTIAL REFERENCE—MARTIN GUITARS

C. F. Martin & Company (usually referred to as just Martin) was founded in New York City, in 1833, by German immigrant guitar maker Christian Frederick Martin, and in 1839 it relocated to its current location: Nazareth, Pennsylvania. Although it has made mandolins, ukuleles, basses, and electric guitars, Martin is best known for its production of high-quality steel-strung acoustic and nylon-strung classical guitars. During the 20thC and 21stC, almost every professional guitarist of note—from Elvis Presley and Curt Cobain to Eric Clapton and John Mayer—has at some point played a Martin, whether live or in the recording studio, and they have also been referenced in many popular songs. A particularly notable example of the latter was Robbie Robertson of The Band's explanation that the opening line of their iconic song "The Weight"—"I pulled into Nazareth, was feelin' about half past dead"—was inspired by the "C F Martin & Co., Nazareth PA" stamp on his 1951 Martin D-28.

A 1923 C. F. Martin & Co. 0-42 acoustic guitar, made in THE USA, serial no. 18992, back and sides of Brazilian rosewood, later lacquering, later hard case, probable neck reset.

$15,000-18,000 **GHOU**

A 1967 Gibson Johnny Smith archtop electric guitar, made in the USA, serial no. 876720, the potentiometers all date to 1966, case is ca. 1980.

One of only 7 dual pickup Johnny Smith archtop shipped in 1967, and 1 of only 20 made up until that year.

$10,000-11,000 **GHOU**

A 1974 Gibson Les Paul Custom 20th Anniversary electric guitar, made in the USA, serial no. 3xxxx3, ebony finish, ebony fretboard, mild wear.

$6,500-8,000 GHOU

A 1996 Gibson J200 acoustic guitar, made in the USA, serial no. 9xxx6xx7, back and sides in maple, top is natural spruce, rosewood fretboard, in original hard case with tags.

$6,000-7,500 GHOU

A 2006 Gibson Hummingbird electro-acoustic guitar, made in the USA, serial no. 03416008, mahogany finish on the back and sides with amber-burst top, rosewood fretboard, original hard case.

$2,600-4,000 GHOU

A Fender Stories Collection Eric Johnson signature 1954 "Virginia" Stratocaster electric guitar, serial no. VA****2, in two-tone sunburst, original tweed hard case.

$2,600-3,300 SWO

A 2001 Fender Custom Shop 1969 Stratocaster Relic electric guitar, made in the USA, serial no. R08665, with Olympic white relic finish, maple fretboard.

$3,300-4,600 GHOU

A 2016 Fender Custom Shop Limited Edition '62 Stratocaster Journeyman Relic electric guitar, made in the USA, serial no. CZ5xxxx2, sunburst relic finish, rosewood fretboard.

$3,300-4,000 GHOU

A 2010 Rickenbacker 330/12 Fireglo 12-string guitar, serial no. 10 2***3, in original hard case with a Levy suede guitar strap.
2010

$2,000-2,600 SWO

A 2002 Rickenbacker 360 semihollow-body electric guitar, made in the USA, serial no. 0226686, Blue Boy finish, rosewood fretboard, in original hard case.

$3,300-4,000 GHOU

A unique 1983 Anthony Zemaitis hollow-body electric guitar, made in England, orange finish, ebony fretboard, with custom-made wooden hard case.

This unique Gretsch-inspired Zemaitis guitar was handmade for Rod Claydon in 1983 and includes his name engraved onto the truss rod cover and on the internal label, with a signed and stamped statement of authenticity from Keith Smart, chairman of the Zemaitis Guitar Owners Club.

$8,500-10,000 GHOU

A David Beckham red Manchester United No.7 home jersey, from playing Deportivo La Coruna in the UEFA Champions League Quarter-Finals, played at Estadio Riazor, on April 2, 2002.

Manchester United defeated Deportivo La Coruna 2-0 in this first leg of the quarter-final match, with Beckham scoring the first goal.
$2,600-3,300   GBA

A Johan Cruyff Barcelona No.9 jersey, from the 1976 UEFA Cup Semi-Final second-leg match against Liverpool at Anfield, April 14.

Liverpool beat Barcelona 1-1 and won the tie 2-1 on aggregate, reaching the Final, where they beat Bruges 4-3 on aggregate. Hendrik Johannes Cruijff (Johan Cruyff, 1947-2016), widely regarded as one of the greatest and most prolific soccer players of the 20thC, enjoyed a playing career spanning 20 years from 1964 until 1984, during which he made 514 club appearances, scoring 290 goals for teams including Ajax, Barcelona, and Feyenoord. He represented the Netherlands on 48 occasions, scoring 33 goals.
$13,000-15,000   GBA

A Eusebio S.L. Benfica No.10 jersey, signed by Eusebio and dated "1.12.1992" (Dec. 1, 1992) on the occasion of a tribute to Eusebio at Estadio da Luz. The shirt was put through a washing machine and the white collar and cuffs have been affected by color run.

Eusebio played for S.L. Benfica from 1961 to 1975, making 301 appearances, scoring 315 goals.
ca. 1971
$3,300-4,000   GBA

A Steven Gerrard signed red Liverpool No.8 home jersey, match-worn, from Gerrard's testimonial match against Olympiacos, August 3, 2013.

Liverpool beat Olympiacos 2-0.
$4,000-4,600   GBA

A Ray Kennedy red Liverpool No.5 match-worn jersey, from the club's League Championship-winning season 1976-77.
$4,000-4,600   GBA

A George Best (Manchester United & Northern Ireland) 1970s match-worn Adidas black-and-green pair of boots, with a signed Letter of Provenance, with a pair of George Best 1970s Manchester United blue training shorts with supporting photos, with George Best memorabilia comprising an official match program for Manchester United vs. Ipswich Town, December 29, 1973 (Best's last Manchester United home match), an England vs. Northern Ireland official match program, November 10, with original ticket, an official match program of Manchester United vs. West Bromwich Albion November 30, 2005, special edition titled "Farewell George 1946-2005," a George Best signed Northampton Town vs. Manchester United program FAC5, February 7, 1970, the famous game in which Best scored six goals, Northern Ireland vs. Holland program, October 12, 1977, Best's last international appearance, a scanned copy of a George Best and Pele dual-signed NASL color photo, and an original George Best Manchester United A&BC 1968 collector's card.
$5,300-6,600   GBA

A Diego Maradona navy and gold Boca Juniors No.10 home jersey.
ca. 1996
$1,700-2,100   GBA

A Roberto Rivelino yellow Brazil No.10 home jersey, worn playing against Scotland at Hampden Park on June 30, 1973.

Brazil defeated Scotland 1-0, with an own goal by Derek Johnstone.
$4,000-5,300   GBA

An Official 1938 FIFA World Cup tournament program, "Revue De La Coupe Du Monde Football," published by Kossuth, Paris, a 48-page program in French.
$4,400-5,300   GBA

An official souvenir program from Manchester United's 1952 Canadian tour match against Montreal All Stars at Delorimier Stadium, Quebec, May 13, 12-page program with center-spread lineups, tour schedule, English League results, Montreal and District Soccer League results, little wear.
$10,000-10,500   GBA

An England cap, awarded to Billy Wright for the international match vs. Sweden played at Arsenal FC's Highbury ground in season 1947-48, embroidered with the three lions emblem, "THE FOOTBALL ASSOCIATION, SWEDEN 1947-48," the interior with "BILLY WRIGHT."

England beat Sweden 4-2 at Highbury, November 19, 1947. William "Billy" Ambrose Wright (1924-94) made 105 appearances for England between 1946 and 1951, scoring three goals.
$4,400-5,300   GBA

A rare 1915 FA Cup Semi-Final steward's ticket, for Everton vs. Chelsea at Villa Park, March 27, 1915, yellow card printed "No.1 Entrance Door F Witton Lane" in black.

Chelsea beat Everton 2-0 before being defeated 3-0 in the Final by Sheffield United. The Final, played at Old Trafford, was known as the "Khaki Cup" due to the large number of uniformed soldiers in attendance.
1915
$1,600-2,100   GBA

SPORTING ANTIQUES

A London 1908 Olympic Judges participant's silver medal, designed by Sir Edgar Bertram Mackenall; obverse, Winged Victory, reverse, Quadriga in a chariot race; stamped "Vaughton" on the edge, in a contemporary case.

1908   *1.5oz*
$600-750   **LSK**

A London 1908 Olympic Games competitor's medal in white metal and blue enamel, the pin back numbered 1462 and stamped "Vaughton Birm."

1908   *1¼in (3cm) diam*
$650-800   **LSK**

A 1924 Paris Olympic gilt-metal and red-enameled competitor's badge, screw back numbered 9785.

1924   *1½in (3.5cm) wide*
$240-290   **LSK**

A London 1908 Olympic Games silver prize medal for Freestyle Middleweight Wrestling, awarded to the British competitor George de Relwyskow, designed by Bertram MacKennal, rim engraved "VAUGHTON, SECOND PRIZE MIDDLE WRESTLING (C.AS C)," by Vaughton & Sons, in original case.

George de Relwyskow was the youngest winner of an Olympic gold medal for wrestling—a record that stood for nearly 70 years. He took up wrestling as a means of keeping fit while training as an artist and designer in London, and he represented Great Britain in the 1908 Olympics.

1¼in (3.3cm) diam 0.7oz
$4,400-5,300   **GBA**

A 2012 London Olympic Games torch lantern, type 6 brass and glass lantern with internal mesh and oil reservoir, with two applied plaques, one engraved with "LONDON 2012" emblem and "OLYMPIC TORCH RELAY," the other "THE PROTECTOR LAMP & LIGHTING CO LTD ECCLES, TYPE 6."

The lantern was used to safely transport the Olympic flame from Athens to Great Britain, prior to the flame being carried, via a 70-day torch procession throughout the country, to the Olympic Stadium in London for the 2012 Olympics. It was made and patented by a British firm—The Protector Lamp & Lighting Company Ltd., of Eccles, Manchester—whose lanterns had been used for this prestigious purpose for the previous 30 years.

A London 2012 Olympic Games bearer's torch, with Tom Daley-autographed "shard," designed by Edward Barber and Jay Osgerby, inner and outer aluminum-alloy skin, perforated by 8,000 circles representing the total number of torch bearers in the London 2012 Relay, and also allowing a high level of transparency, including viewing of the burner system, in cardboard carrying case, with the original Certificate of Authenticity.

31½in (80cm) long 28.2oz
$4,000-5,300   **GBA**

10in (25cm) high
$3,300-4,600   **GBA**

A Hardy "Perfect" fishing reel, with brass foot, rim tension adjuster, and ivorine winder, marked "Hardy Bros Ltd, Alnwick, Patent 'Perfect' reel."

4in (10cm) diam
$600-650   **LC**

A Hardy 'The Perfect' drum alloy fly reel, Duplicated Mark II, ebonite handle, nickel tension adjuster to rim, nickel line guide, in original cardboard box and cover.

3½in (9cm) diam
$600-650   **DN**

A Hardy "Perfect" fishing reel, with ebonized winder, brass foot, and rim tension adjuster, marked "Hardy Bros Ltd, Pat Nos 24245 & 9261."

3¼in (8.5cm) diam
$400-550   **LC**

A Hardy "Perfect" brass-faced fishing reel, brass faced with alloy back, with a rod-in-hand logo and stamped "Hardy's Pat Perfect Reel," with a chunky ivorine winder, brass foot, and rim tension adjuster, in a fitted leather case.

3¼in (8.5cm) diam
$650-800   **LC**

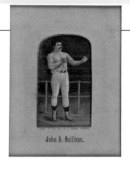

A Stevengraph of the great boxer John L. Sullivan, John L. Sullivan information verso, framed and glazed.

Stevengraphs were 19thC images woven in pure silk and were produced by Thomas Stevens of Coventry, England.

1888   *8in (20.4cm) high*
$350-400   **MART**

A Yorkshire Rugby Football Union 15ct gold medal, the reverse reading "England v. Yorkshire at Huddersfield Feby.25, 1893," hallmarked "F&S 15.625 Birmingham, 1892."

                              0.5oz
$800-900   **LOCK**

A 1960 Great Britain Rugby League cap, awarded to Alex Murphy OBE from the two fixtures against France, December 11, 1960, and January 28, 1961, mounted above a team photograph with typed note signed by Alex Murphy, framed and glazed.

Great Britain beat France 21-0 at Stadium Municipal, Bordeaux, on December 11, 1960, and 27-8 at St. Helens on January 28, 1961. Alex Murphy made 27 appearances for Great Britain between 1958 and 1971, scoring 48 points.

                    20in (51cm) high
$1,300-1,800   **GBA**

A Sean Fitzpatrick signed New Zealand All Blacks centenary shirt, signed "1892-1992."

Sean Brian Thomas Fitzpatrick ONZM (born June 4, 1963, in Auckland) is widely regarded as one of the finest rugby union players ever to come from New Zealand. In 1992, Fitzpatrick was awarded the captaincy of the All Blacks, a position he held until his retirement from test rugby. He made his 92nd and final test appearance on November 29, 1997 as a substitute in the 42–7 victory against Wales at Wembley Stadium.

$350-400   **GBA**

A 1936 All England Club Wimbledon Tennis Championships Men's Singles winner's gold medal, awarded to Fred Perry for his victory over Gottfried von Cramm, hallmarked 18ct., Birmingham 1936 by Joseph Moore, inscribed "ALL ENGLAND CLUB WIMBLEDON," reverse inscribed "LAWN TENNIS COMPETITION 1936 FRED PERRY."

Fred Perry defended his 1935 Wimbledon title against Gottfried von Cramm, winning 6-1, 6-1, 6-0.

                    1½in (3.7cm) diam 1oz
$33,000-40,000   **GBA**

A Muhammad Ali-signed pair of vintage red leather "Golden Gloves" boxing gloves.

$1,100-1,250   **GBA**

A Muhammad Ali-signed Adidas boxing boot, signed in black marker pen "MUHAMMAD ALI, AKA CASSIUS CLAY."

$1,700-2,400   **GBA**

A tilt-headed lawn tennis racquet, by Henry Malings of Frances Street, Woolwich, the convex wedge stamped with maker's stamp, some wear to stringing, head, and handle.

ca. 1875
$4,400-5,300   **GBA**

A New York Yankees team-signed baseball, including 23 player signatures with all 9 Hall of Fame players, including Babe Ruth, Earle Combs, Bill Dickey, Lou Gehrig, Lefty Gomez, Tony Lazzeri, Herb Pennock, Red Ruffing, and Joe Sewell, all on a Spalding no. 3RC "Babe Ruth" Home Run Special baseball, with a bold Babe Ruth signature on the sweet spot.

The Yankees won the World Series in a four-game sweep of the Chicago Cubs that year and was made famous by Babe Ruth's legendary "called shot" homerun in game 3.

1932
$15000-18,000   **POOK**

A signed red cricket ball and photograph (not shown), of England cricket legend Sir Ian Botham, the photo a Test Match action shot.

              photo 10in (25.5cm) high
$350-400   **GBA**

A Tiger Woods signed color photograph, mounted.

              15¾in (40cm) high
$350-400   **GBA**

A Tom Morris of St Andrews scare-neck long-nose putter, hickory shaft.

ca. 1870
$1,100-1,250   **GBA**

DECORATIVE ARTS MARKET

Decorative Arts pieces have seen a steep rise in prices of high-end, rare items and less dramatic increases in mid- to low-end goods.

Clarice Cliff is still popular, particularly rare shapes and patterns, such as the teapot on p. 514. The high-quality William de Morgan luster-glazed wares also continue to command high prices.

Many of the Doulton wares are simply now considered unfashionable. In addition, demand for works by the Barlows and Frank Butler has been sluggish. However, George Tinworth pieces depicting mice and frogs remain very much in demand. Also much in demand are Doulton pieces with experimental glazes—especially anything unusual that is lustered or flambéed. Demand for Royal Doulton figures has fallen dramatically and only the prototypes, limited production, and rare colorways are fetching good money.

Martin Brothers continue to be strong in the current marketplace. They are not to everyone's taste, but the Wally birds and the unique grotesque dog jar and cover (see p. 529) command high prices.

Moorcroft will command high prices if the pattern and shape are rare, but the more common patterns are stagnant in the market. Wedgwood Fairyland lustre ceramics continue to be on a roll, particularly in the United Sates, Canada, and Australia—rare patterns, unusual colorways, and experimental or trial pieces are highly contested.

The Ohio school, meanwhile, including Rookwood and Roseville, has had a better year, with more exciting pieces coming onto the market. George Ohr-glazed earthenware vases continue to excite, with more exceptional pieces coming onto the market.

With Art Nouveau glass, it is the big names that continue to sell: Gallé, Tiffany, Loetz, and Daum. Lalique, in particular, has had an exceptional year, with "new to the market" pieces coming to auction.

Silver from the 20thC has continued to sell well, especially pieces by Charles Robert Ashbee and Omar Ramsden, as have rare and unusual Liberty pieces, particularly those that were designed by Archibald Knox.

George Jensen silver has a strong collectors' market, particularly the pre-1945 examples and those designed by Jensen himself, and by Johan Rohde, Harald Neilson, and Arno Malinowski.

Bronze and ivory figures by Demêtre Chiparus, Bruno Zach, Josef Lorenzl, and Ferdinand Preiss perform well if they are rare, iconic, and exceptional.

The sale of early-20thC furniture has been unremarkable, although when something fresh and with good provenance appears on the market, so do the collectors. Charles Rennie Mackintosh continues to have a strong following.

Top Left: A Georg Jensen sterling silver "Grape" bowl, model 296A, marked to underside.

1930-39   *15in (38cm) wide 62.9 oz*

$10,000-14,000   **DRA**

Above: An Lenci earthenware figure, titled "Dopo Lo Studio," by Abel Jacopi, modeled as a young girl sitting, eating an apple with a book by her side, signed "Lenci - Made in Italy Turino."

11½in (29cm) high

$7,500-8,500   **FLD**

ESSENTIAL REFERENCE—CLARICE CLIFF

Clarice Cliff's (1899-1972) status as one of the most eminent Art Deco ceramics designers is long established, although her fame and success in the 1930s are perhaps still hard to fully appreciate now, because at that time there was really no such thing as a "career woman."

● She started at A. J. Wilkinson in 1916 as an enameler, and by the mid-1920s Wilkinson had given her her own studio: the Newport Pottery. Her Bizarre range was launched in 1927, and her Fantasque range shortly afterward.

● A true innovator, it was her ability to conceive not only the eye-catching patterns, but also the often-distinctive ceramic shapes those patterns were to decorate, that elevated her above other contemporary ceramics designers.

● Her bold, brightly colored patterns were hand painted by a group of dedicated decorators, mostly women, who became known as the "Bizarre Girls."

● The demand for Clarice Cliff ceramics remains particularly strong, with rare shapes, such "Yo-Yo" vases, and rare patterns, such as the "Applique" range or "May Avenue," being especially sought after.

A rare Clarice Cliff Bizarre "Applique Garden" cake plate, printed and painted factory marks, impressed date mark.
1930   *9in (23cm) diam*
$1,300-1,700   **WW**

A Clarice Cliff Bizarre "Applique Lugano" bowl, octagonal, painted in colors, the interior banded red, black, and yellow, printed factory marks, light wear.
8in (20.5cm) diam
$1,000-1,100   **WW**

A Clarice Cliff Fantasque Bizarre "Berries" plate, impressed marks, impressed date mark.
1931   *10in (25.5cm) diam*
$350-450   **WW**

A Clarice Cliff Bonjour sugar sifter, "Farmhouse," printed factory marks.
5¼in (13cm) high
$550-650   **WW**

A pair of Clarice Cliff Bizarre Fantasque "Balloon Trees" candlesticks, black printed marks, minor paint rubbing, hairline on one top.
8in (20.5cm) high
$1,050-1,200   **DN**

A Clarice Cliff Bizarre conical sugar sifter, "Blue Firs," printed factory marks, minor nicks on foot rim.
5½in (14cm) high
$1,050-1,200   **WW**

A rare Clarice Cliff Bizarre 362 "Football" vase, printed factory marks, hairline on top rim.
8in (20.5cm) high
$2,200-2,600   **WW**

A Clarice Cliff Fantasque Bizarre Stamford "Circle Tree" teapot and cover, printed factory marks.
4¾in (12cm) high
$6,000-7,500   **WW**

A Clarice Cliff Fantasque Bizarre bowl, "Circle Tree," printed factory marks.
9in (23cm) diam
$550-600   **WW**

A pair of Clarice Cliff "Football" vases, shape 361, hand painted with abstract line and block design with panels of stylized nets, large "Bizarre" mark, a small white patch on the lip of petal.

ca. 1929

$10,000-11,000   **FLD**

A Clarice Cliff Fantasque Bizarre "House and Bridge" plate, printed factory marks.

10in (25.5cm) diam

$550-650   **WW**

A Clarice Cliff ribbed charger, "Inspiration Aster," hand-painted "Inspiration Bizarre" mark.

ca. 1930   *18in (45cm) wide*

$2,600-4,000   **FLD**

A large Clarice Cliff umbrella stand, "Inspiration Caprice," hand-written ocher "Inspiration" and printed "Bizarre" back stamp.

ca. 1930   *24in (61cm) high*

$4,000-4,600   **FLD**

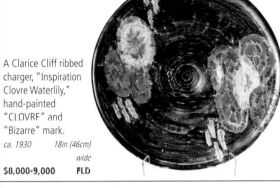

A Clarice Cliff ribbed charger, "Inspiration Clovre Waterlily," hand-painted "CLOVRE" and "Bizarre" mark.

ca. 1930   *18in (46cm) wide*

$8,000-9,000   **FLD**

A Clarice Cliff "Inspiration Knight Errant" vase, shape 356, hand painted with a knight on horseback on a castle wall, hand painted "INSPIRATION" and "Bizarre" mark.

ca. 1930   *7in (18cm) high*

$3,300-4,000   **FLD**

A Clarice Cliff umbrella stand, "Inspiration Clovre Tulip," hand painted "CLOVRE" and "Bizarre" mark, the stand has been reattached, the repair is partial.

ca. 1930   *24in (61cm) high*

$2,600-3,300   **FLD**

A Clarice Cliff conical-shaped sugar sifter, "Lorna," painted with a stylized cottage and bridge landscape, large script signature.

ca. 1936   *5½in (14cm) high*

$550-650   **FLD**

A rare Clarice Cliff "May Avenue" single-handle "Isis" vase, printed factory marks.

9¾in (24.5cm) high

$8,500-9,000   **WW**

A Clarice Cliff "Lotus" jug, "Original Bizarre," unmarked.

ca. 1928   *11¾in (29.5cm) high*

$1,300-1,800   **FLD**

A Clarice Cliff "Lotus" jug, "Original Bizarre," hand-painted rust red "Bizarre by Clarice Cliff" mark.

ca. 1928   *11¾in (29.5cm) high*

$1,600-2,000   **FLD**

A Clarice Cliff "Pastel Autumn" posy vase, shape 515, hand painted with a stylized tree and cottage landscape, "Bizarre" mark.

ca. 1930   *4¾in (12cm) high*

$2,000-2,600   **FLD**

A Clarice Cliff conical sugar sifter, "Pastel Melon," hand painted with a band of geometric fruit.

ca. 1932   *5½in (14cm) high*

$1,050-1,200   **FLD**

A rare Clarice Cliff Fantasque Bizarre "Red Gardenia" ribbed charger, printed factory marks.

18in (45.5cm) diam

$4,600-5,300   **WW**

A pair of Clarice Cliff Bizarre vases, "Red Gardenia," shape no.186, printed factory marks.

5¾in (14.5cm) high

$800-900   **WW**

A ribbed Clarice Cliff wall charger, "Rudyard," painted with a stylized tree landscape, small professional restoration on the rim.

ca. 1932   *13in (33cm) wide*

$750-850   **FLD**

CLOSER LOOK—CLARICE CLIFF LOTUS PITCHER

Underpinning virtually all of Clarice Cliff's numerous and diverse patterns is a bright palette of colors including, as here, reds, oranges, yellows, blues, and greens, often dynamically contrasted with greas or blacks, and encapsulating the sense of fun and spirit of Art Deco.

One of a number of different shaped pitchers produced by Clarice Cliff, this example, known as a "Lotus" pitcher, has a traditional baluster form and a single loop handle, instead of a twin handle, like some of her "Lotus" pitchers.

A Clarice Cliff Bizarre "Athens," "Sunray" pitcher, printed factory marks, flat chip on foot rim.

7in (18cm) high

$550-650   **WW**

Reflecting contemporary fashions in fine art, the hand-painted decoration comprises primarily linear and other geometric forms, with the latter including panels of netlike crosshatching, which signify the sporting activity that gives this abstract pattern its name: "Tennis."

A Clarice Cliff "Lotus" pitcher ("Isis" size), with "Tennis" pattern hand painted in an abstract block-and-line design with panels of stylized nets, "Bizarre" mark.

ca. 1930   *10in (25.5cm) high*

$8,000-9,000   **FLD**

A Clarice Cliff "Lotus" pitcher ("Isis" size), "Umbrellas," hand painted with repeat panels of starburst motifs, Fantasque mark, professional restoration on the upper rim.

ca. 1930   *10in (25cm) high*

$900-1,050   **FLD**

A Clarice Cliff "Lotus" pitcher, "Viscaria," with hand painted stylized tree landscape, "Bizarre" mark.

ca. 1934   *11½in (29cm) high*

$650-800   **FLD**

ESSENTIAL REFERENCE—COWAN POTTERY

The Cowan Pottery was founded by Reginald Guy Cowan (1884-1957) in Lakewood, Ohio, in 1912, moved to Rocky River, Ohio, in 1920, and continued production until 1931, when it was bankrupted by adverse financial consequences of the Great Depression. Most of the pottery's early pieces were designed by Cowan himself, and largely consisted of inexpensive, slip-cast earthenware figures with mat monochrome glazes. However, several students studying at the nearby artistically progressive and influential Cleveland Institute of Arts, along with a number of independent designers, also worked for the pottery, and it is the latter's work—especially the pieces made in limited editions made from ca. 1927 onward—that is the most collectible.

● Stylistically, some Cowan pieces show a distinctly Austrian influence, while others, particularly the work of Paul Manship, are sculptural. In contrast, the designs of Waylande Gregory are often Neoclassical in inspiration, although Gregory also produced limited-edition figures relating to contemporary dance (including Burlesque). Others notable artists and designers include Arthur Eugene Baggs, Edris Eckhardt, Raoul Josset, Herman Matzen, Frank N. Wilcox, and Viktor Schreckengost—the latter designing what is probably Cowan's most famous piece: the "Jazz" punch bowl. Originally commissioned in 1930 by Eleanor Roosevelt to commemorate Franklin D. Roosevelt's second inauguration as Governor of New York, the bowl depicts scenes of New York City on New Year's Eve, is glazed in "Egyptian Blue," and encapsulates the Art Deco style of the early 1930s.

A Cowan Pottery rare glazed earthenware figure of a beaten dog, by Waylande Gregory, incised signature, impressed manufacturer's mark on underside "Cowan."

An example of this form is held in the permanent collection of The Cleveland Museum of Art. This work is one of only a few known examples.

ca. 1931   *12in (30cm) wide*
$10,000-11,000   **DRA**

A pair of Cowan Pottery glazed earthenware bookends, by Albert Drexler Jacobson, impressed manufacturer's mark "Cowan."

1929   *5in (13cm) high*
$7,500-8,000   **DRA**

A Cowan Pottery sgraffito-decorated glazed earthenware vase, with fish, by Viktor Schreckengost, faint impressed manufacturer's mark on underside.

ca. 1931   *6¾in (17cm) high*
$5,300-6,600   **DRA**

A Cowan Pottery drypoint-decorated glazed earthenware vase, with fish, by Viktor Schreckengost, impressed manufacturer's mark on underside "Cowan."

ca. 1931   *6¾in (17cm) high*
$6,000-6,600   **DRA**

A Cowan Pottery unique glazed stoneware vase, with airplanes, by Paul Bogatay, incised signature "PB" and impressed manufacturer's mark on underside "Cowan."

1930   *9in (23cm) wide*
$4,600-5,300   **DRA**

A Cowan Pottery "Danse Moderne Jazz" plate, by Viktor Schreckengost, of glazed earthenware, impressed manufacturer's mark on underside "Cowan."

ca. 1931   *11½in (29cm) diam*
$6,500-8,000   **DRA**

A Cowan Pottery covered vase with stand, by Viktor Schreckengost, of drypoint-decorated glazed earthenware, impressed manufacturer's mark on underside of vase and stand "Cowan."

This work is particularly rare, because few examples retain their original lid and stand.

ca. 1931   *8¼in (21cm) high*
$4,000-4,600   **DRA**

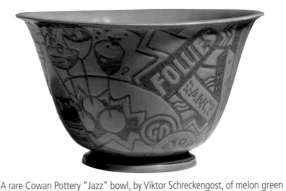

A rare Cowan Pottery "Jazz" bowl, by Viktor Schreckengost, of melon green glazed earthenware, incised signature near base "Viktor Schreckengost."

The "Jazz" bowl was initially commissioned by Eleanor Roosevelt in 1930, but Schreckengost would ultimately make three versions; the present example is the third version, known as the "Poor Man's Bowl."

ca. 1931   *13¼in (34cm) diam*
$33,000-40,000   **DRA**

A William De Morgan ruby luster charger, "Cupid and Psyche" pattern, with Morris & Co. retailer's label "MORRIS & COMPANY/ 17 ST GEORGE STREET, HANOVER SQUARE/ R.337/ Luster DISH/ VASE & COVER/ CG Y Y £8."

ca. 1880   *14in (35.5cm) diam*

$6,500-8,000   **L&T**

Judith Picks

Just by looking at this shallow dish or charger by William De Morgan (1839-1917) it's easy to see why he was a hugely successful and influential pioneer of the mid-to-late-19thC Arts and Crafts movement. The subject matter and its composition—an eagle with wings raised defending its nest of eggs—is well suited to the shape of the charger. Indeed, it's a characteristic of de Morgan's work that imagery is never incongruously applied to the shape or form of the underlying object but, instead, almost organically complements it. There's also the small matter of the energy and

artistic finesse evident in the depiction of the flora and fauna, which although stylized appears naturalistic as well. And then there's the palette De Morgan has employed. Colors and combinations of are always ultimately a matter of personal taste, but these lustrous soft reds and golds, highlighted with glimpses of a white ground, really command and sustain my attention.

A William de Morgan "Frightened Bird" double-luster shallow dish or charger, the reverse with heart-shaped leaf border, impressed "17" at center, and with "Morris & Company, 17 George St, Hanover Sq. W.1."

1890s   *14¼in (36cm) diam*

$46,000-53,000   **MART**

A William De Morgan ruby luster jar and cover, with exotic birds and foliage, impressed Sands End mark on base, bears Morris & Co. retailer's label and "£20."

ca. 1890   *12½in (32cm) high*

$8,500-9,000   **L&T**

A William de Morgan ruby luster glazed earthenware "Persian" vase, signed and numbered toonunderside "D.M. Fulham J.J. 5 22/8."

ca. 1890   *8¾in (22cm) high*

$13,000-15,000   **DRA**

A William de Morgan "Galleon" large charger, with a galleon at full sail, bordered by shells, the broad, flattened rim painted with a frieze of cherub winds blowing toward the galleon, each with a dove in flight, unsigned, restoration on rim.

ca. 1890   *17½in (44.2cm) diam*

$9,000-10,500   **MART**

A William De Morgan ceramic dish, by Charles Passenger, decorated with a galleon in a harbor with figures and fish within a stylized Persian-type scroll border, monogrammed "CP" on reverse, painted marks.

8½in (21.5cm) diam

$4,000-4,600   **DUK**

A William De Morgan pottery vase, painted with mythical birds with snakes in their beaks, among scrolling foliage, impressed tulip mark.

10¼in (26cm) high

$13,000-16,000   **WW**

A William De Morgan charger, painted with a hoopoe bird, unsigned.

14¼in (36cm) diam

$6,500-8,000   **WW**

A William de Morgan "Persian" charger, by Charles Passenger, Fulham period (1898-1907), painted with four tulips, within a stylized floral border, signed "W.De. Morgan.&.Co.Fulham" and with initials "c.p."

13½in (34cm) diam

$8,500-9,000   **MART**

A William De Morgan "Persian Flowers" pattern tile, Merton Abbey period, impressed mark, in a mahogany frame, chips on two corners, crazing throughout.

ca. 1882-88   *10in (25cm) wide*

$2,200-2,600   SWO

A William De Morgan Merton Abbey period "Omnia Vanitas" ("Strutting Peacock") tile, impressed factory mark.

6¼in (15.5cm) wide

$5,300-6,600   WW

A rare William De Morgan Merton Abbey tile, painted with the wind blowing a sailing ship on a calm sea, impressed mark.

6¼in (15.5cm) wide

$7,500-8,500   WW

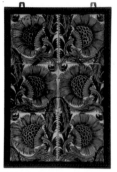

A William De Morgan six BBB tile panel, Early Fulham period, impressed factory marks, minor old restoration.

each tile 6¼in (15.5cm) wide

$7,500-8,000   WW

A William De Morgan "Chicago" pattern tile, Early Fulham period, impressed with "Sand's End" mark, chips on the corners, crazing throughout.

ca. 1888-97   *8in (20cm) wide*

$4,000-4,600   SWO

A William De Morgan "Partridge" tile, Late Fulham period, impressed factory mark, minor glaze loss.

6¼in (15.5cm) wide

$3,300-4,000   WW

A William De Morgan luster "Long-tongued Beast" tile, Late Fulham period, painted in blue and silver luster on a white ground with red luster grasses, impressed factory mark, drilled.

6in (15cm) wide

$6,500-8,000   WW

A William De Morgan "Lynx" tile, Late Fulham period, impressed factory mark.

6¼in (15.5cm) wide

$3,300-4,000   WW

A William De Morgan Pottery triple-luster tile, Late Fulham period, painted with a cockerel crowing, impressed Late Fulham period De Morgan, Iles and Passenger brothers factory mark.

6¼in (16cm) square

$8,500-9,000   WW

A William De Morgan "Galleon" three-tile panel, Late Fulham period, painted with a Classical long ship sailing on a calm sea, a large eaglelike bird attacking from the stern side and being repelled by archers, another vessel sailing on the horizon, impressed factory mark, the front tile a modern replacement by Myra MacDonnell at Froyle Tiles, middle tile museum restored, minor chips.

each tile 8in (20.5cm) wide

$9,000-10,500   WW

A Doulton Lambeth stoneware menu holder, "Mouse Musician," by George Tinworth, modeled as a mouse playing the harp accompanied by another on the piano, impressed Doulton mark "1886" and incised "GT" monogram, professionally restored on feet of piano playing mouse, dated.

1886   *3¼in (8.5cm) high*
$2,400-2,900   **WW**

A Doulton Burslem velum figure, "Mephistopheles & Marguerite," with gilded decoration, some slight wear.

12in (30.5cm) high
$1,000-1,100   **PSA**

A Doulton Lambeth stoneware eagle ewer, attributed to Mark V. Marshall, the rim mounted with a silver collar, by Brockwell & Son, London, and marked "Regd 228737."

1894   *13in (33cm) high*
$1,300-1,800   **SWO**

A Doulton Lambeth stoneware model of a sitting bear holding a honey pot.

3¾in (9.5cm) high
$240-290   **PSA**

ESSENTIAL REFERENCE—DOULTON LAMBETH

The Doulton Factory was founded in Lambeth, London, in 1815 by John Doulton, Martha Jones, and John Watts, and initially focused production on stoneware bottles and storage jars.

- When John Doulton's son Henry joined the firm in 1835, the business began to rapidly expand, making and supplying drainpipes and water filters to many cities, both in the United Kingdom and overseas.
- The commercial success of Doulton's sanitary wares let them switch their focus to decorative wares, both domestic and architectural, and in 1863 they began to work with students at and graduates of the Lambeth School of Art; by the 1880s, they were employing more than 200 artists and designers, many of them women.
- Artists and designers of particular note include the Tinworth brothers, Arthur and George, and the Barlow siblings, Hannah, Arthur, and Florence, and Mark Marshall, while significant styles embraced included Arts and Crafts, Moorish, and Art Nouveau.
- In 1901, Doulton received a Royal Warrant from the Crown, and thereafter became known as Royal Doulton.

A rare Doulton Lambeth "The Menagerie" mantel clock, by George Tinworth, depicting two mice playing a three-card trick, a wheel of fortune with another two mice, front and center is the entrance to the wild beast show, on each side is a mice band playing different instruments, a total of 20 mice, one parrot and one monkey, inscribed on the front face and each side is

a lion, tiger, a rhinoceros and a stork, incised artist initials on front right side, the timepiece made by W. Thornhill and Co. 144 and 145 New Bond St. London.

9¾in (24.5cm) high
$21,000-26,000   **WHTL**

A pair of Doulton Lambeth stoneware vases, by Hannah Barlow, decorated with a girl feeding horses and cattle.

10in (25.5cm) high
$1,300-1,800   **PSA**

A late-19thC/early-20thC Doulton Lambeth vase, by Florence Barlow, decorated with stylized birds.

11¾in (30cm) high
$260-400   **WHP**

A late-19thC Doulton Lambeth vase, by Hannah Barlow, incised with goats, some damage.

11¾in (30cm) high
$260-400   **WHP**

A pair of Doulton Lambeth stoneware jardinières on stands, with winged beast supports, all stamped "Doulton, Lambeth," restored and with further chips.

ca. 1870   *36½in (92.5cm) high*
$750-850   **SWO**

An early-Art Deco Royal Doulton figure, "The Bather" HN687, designed by Leslie Harradine, printed and painted marks.

8in (20cm) high

$550-650   **WW**

A Royal Doulton figurine, "A Wandering Minstrel," model no.HN1224, hairline crack on base, dated.

1927

$650-800   **PSA**

A Royal Doulton figurine, "Geisha," model no.HN1234, dated.

1927

$900-1,050   **PSA**

A Royal Doulton figurine, "Pamela," model no.HN1469, impressed date.

1931

$260-400   **PSA**

A Royal Doulton prototype figure, of a sitting gentleman playing a clarinet, impressed model no.1489.

ca. 1950   *7¾in (19.5cm) high*

$2,000-2,600   **PSA**

A Royal Doulton figurine, "Sonia," model no.HN1738, early model dated.

1936

$450-600   **PSA**

A Royal Doulton figurine, "Eleanor," model no.HN1754, by Harry Allen, early model dated.

1936

$400-500   **PSA**

A Royal Doulton figurine, "Reflections," model no.HN1848, early model dated.

1938

$260-400   **PSA**

A Royal Doulton figurine, "Dawn," model no.HN1858, early model with headdress, dated.

1938

$600-750   **PSA**

A Royal Doulton figurine, "Kate Hardcastle," model no.HN2028.

$260-400   **PSA**

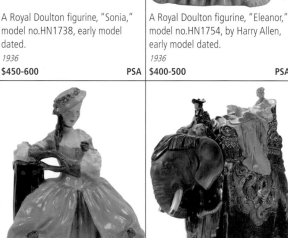

A Royal Doulton large prestige figurine, "Princess Badoura," no.HN2081, early version signed by painter "P. Smith."

21¾in (55cm) high

$5,300-5,900   **PSA**

A Royal Doulton large prestige figurine, "Matador and the Bull," model no.HN2324.

27¼in (69cm) long

$2,000-2,600   **PSA**

A Royal Doulton "The Palio Knight" porcelain equestrian figurine, model no.HN2428, limited edition no.9 of 500, on a mahogany plinth, with certificate.

19¼in (49cm) high

$1,000-1,100   BELL

A Royal Doulton prototype figure, of a farmer taking a drink, impressed model no.3409.

9¼in (23.5cm) high

$1,200-1,600   PSA

A Royal Doulton prestige model, "Charge of the Light Brigade," HN no.3718, designed and modeled by Alan Maslankowski.

17in (43cm) high

$4,000-4,600   PSA

A Royal Doulton limited-edition character figure, from the Stuarts series, King James I, HN3822.

$260-400   PSA

A Royal Doulton figurine, "The Sketch Girl," of a Victorian street seller with tray of dolls and toys, impressed date.

1924

$450-600   PSA

A Royal Doulton prototype figure, of a lady in a red dress, "not for resale" back stamp and block number 2997 on base.

$550-650   PSA

A Royal Doulton advertising figurine, "Grossmith's Tsang Ihang."

12¼in (31cm) high

$600-650   PSA

A Royal Doulton advertising figure, "Beefeater The Illustrated London News," printed factory mark.

7¾in (19.5cm) high

$210-260   WW

A Royal Doulton character jug, "Hatless Drake," D6115, a rare hatless version with unusual hint of yellow color on muff.

$1,100-1,250   PSA

A Royal Doulton character jug, "Winston Churchill," model no.D6170, in unusual cream colorway, no back stamp.

$1,600-2,100   PSA

A Royal Doulton character jug, "Field Marshall Smuts," model no.D6198.

$600-650   PSA

A Royal Doulton character jug, blue "Pearly Boy," D6207.

ca. 1947

$2,600-3,300   PSA

A Royal Doulton character jug, "Clark Gable," D6709, made for the Celebrity Collection 1983 and rejected because of licensing issues and removed from sale.

$2,000-2,600 PSA

A Royal Doulton character jug, "The Guardsman," model no.D6755, painted in a different color of black tunic with gold and silver highlights, minor glaze issues on bearskin.

$260-330 PSA

A Royal Doulton character jug, "Alfred Hitchcock," model no.D6987 with rare pink shower curtain.

$300-350 PSA

A Royal Doulton character jug, "Clint Eastwood," designed in 2005 as part of the "Celebrity Film Star" collection but not put into production.

$4,000-4,600 PSA

A rare large Royal Doulton prototype character jug, "The Witch," modeled in the 1980s by William K Harper, "not for resale" back stamp.

$5,300-6,600 PSA

A Royal Doulton prototype character jug, "The Wizard," modeled in the 1980s by William K. Harper, "not for resale" back stamp.

$5,300-6,600 PSA

A Royal Doulton rare large model of a mallard duck, model no.HN1198, dated.

1939 *14½in (37cm) high*

$450-600 PSA

A Royal Doulton prestige model of a sitting fox, model no.HN2634.

10¼in (26cm) high

$850-900 PSA

A Royal Doulton model of a sitting fox, in rare khaki green glaze.

1920s *10in (25.5cm) high*

$600-650 PSA

A Royal Doulton model of a flambé sitting bulldog.

ca. 1927 *6in (15cm) high*

$800-900 PSA

A Royal Doulton model of a sailor bulldog, medium size, dated.

1941 *4½in (11.5cm) high*

$800-900 PSA

A Royal Doulton flambé model of a penguin chick, on a marble dish.

5¼in (13.5cm) high

$260-330 PSA

A Goldscheider Pottery large "Egyptian Dancer" figurine, designed by Josef Lorenzl, model no.5281, impressed and printed marks.

See Ora Pinhas, "Goldscheider Pottery," Richard Dennis Publications, pp.108-109, for six examples of this figure illustrated in different colors.

18¼in (46.5cm) high

$4,000-5,300   **WW**

A Goldscheider Pottery figure of a dancer, modeled by Josef Lorenzl, printed marks and "Lorenzl," completely restored and painted.

16in (40.5cm) high

$2,000-2,600   **SWO**

CLOSER LOOK—GOLDSCHEIDER DANCER

The notably slender shoulders and arms of the dancer are characteristic of figures designed by Josef Lorenzl and serve to emphasize the angular elegance of her posture.

Just on their own, the dancer's close-fitting cloche (bell-like) hat and her partly revealed bobbed hairstyle beneath instantly denote contemporary late Jazz Age and Art Deco fashion.

The diaphanous costume daringly leaving little of the dancer's body to the imagination is also typical of Lorenzl, as are the exquisitely modeled folds and patterns of the "fabric."

Slightly elongating the slim lower legs of the dancer, while posing her in heels on the balls of her feet and raising her on a slightly domed plinth further enhances the dynamic elegance of the composition.

A Goldscheider Pottery model of a dancer (no.5940), designed by Josef Lorenzl, with impressed factory marks.

17¼in (44cm) high

$10,500-12,000   **WW**

A Goldscheider Pottery figure of a lady, designed by Josef Lorenzl, stamped "6211/252/19" with a printed mark, small chips on the base.

15½in (39.5cm) high

$1,050-1,200   **SWO**

An Art Deco Goldscheider Pottery figure, by Stefan Dakon, model 7897, impressed mark, professionally restored break in her skirt.

9in (23cm) high

$750-850   **FLD**

A Goldscheider porcelain dancer, by Joseph Lorenzl, model 7582, with painted and impressed factory marks, tiny glaze chip in skirt, some crazing lines in glaze.

13¼in (33.75cm) high

$800-900   **MART**

A mid-to-late-1930s Goldscheider painted terra-cotta wall mask of a lady, model no.6911, printed mark, with adhesive label.

10¼in (26cm) high

$550-650   **DN**

A Goldscheider pottery wall mask, No.7089/65, impressed and printed marks.

11½in (29.5cm) high

$850-1,000   **SWO**

A Goldscheider pottery wall mask, No. 6775, with original silvered label, impressed number and printed marks.

10½in (26.5cm) high

$850-1,000   **SWO**

A Goldscheider pottery wall mask, No. 6911, impressed and printed marks, with original silver label.

1885-1935   *10½in (26.5cm) high*

$850-1,000   **SWO**

A Grueby two-color vase, with leaves and buds, impressed manufacturer's mark, with lotus symbol, incised signature on underside "H."

1898-1910   *10¼in (26cm) high*

$21,000-26,000   DRA

A Grueby glazed earthenware vase, with irises, impressed manufacturer's mark, with lotus symbol, incised unidentified artist cipher and number "178."

1898-1910   *11½in (29cm) high*

$26,000-33,000   DRA

A Grueby glazed earthenware vase, by George P. Kendrick, impressed manufacturer's mark on underside, with lotus symbol, impressed number to underside "34."

This form is colloquially referred to as a Kendrick vase and is one of his best-known designs, which were made in many variations, some reticulated, some with handles.

1898-1910   *12in (30cm) high*

$20,000-26,000   DRA

A Grueby glazed earthenware vase, with jack-in-the-pulpits, by Wilhelmina Post, impressed manufacturer's mark on underside "Grueby Pottery Boston USA" with lotus symbol, incised signature on underside "WP."

ca. 1909   *12in (30cm) high*

$26,000-33,000   DRA

ESSENTIAL REFERENCE—GRUEBY

The Grueby Faience Company was established in 1894 in Revere, Massachusetts, by William Henry Grueby (1867-1925), and produced architectural tiles and art pottery.

- One of the primary decorative techniques Grueby employed in the decoration of its pictorial tiles was "cuerda seca" ("dry cord," in Spanish), in which thin bands of waxy resin were used to separate different colored glazes during firing.
- Inspired by the simplicity of Japanese ceramics and the distinctive mat glazes found on some French ceramics, Grueby's art pottery, most notably its vases, were typically of organic form with stylized foliate decoration, and the majority were finished in a matte, cucumber green glaze.
- In addition to its art pottery and tiles, Grueby also entered into a partnership with Tiffany Studios to produce lamp bases.
- After considerable commercial success, Grueby began to struggle against increasing mass-market competition, was declared bankrupt in 1909, and finally closed in 1920.

A Grueby glazed earthenware vase, partly obscured die-stamped Grueby, early straight-line mark to underside.

ca. 1898   *9in (23cm) high*

$46,000-53,000   DRA

A Grueby glazed earthenware vase, by George P. Kendrick, model 84, impressed manufacturer's mark and model number on underside, with lotus symbol.

1898-1910   *11½in (29cm) high*

$33,000-40,000   DRA

A rare Grueby glazed earthenware vase, impressed manufacturer's mark on underside, with lotus symbol and incised unidentified artist's cipher.

1898-1910   *16in (41cm) high*

$53,000-59,000   DRA

A Grueby glazed earthenware vase, with leaves and buds, impressed "Grueby Faience Co. Boston" and numbered "194," incised signature on underside "ET."

An example of this form was exhibited by Grueby at the Paris Exposition Universelle in 1900.

1898-1910   *9in (23cm) diam*

$40,000-46,000   DRA

A Grueby glazed earthenware, leaded glass, and brass table lamp, by Ellen Farrington, with a period shade in the style of Tiffany Studios, impressed manufacturer's mark, incised initials "E.R.F.."

ca. 1905   *20in (51cm) high*

$33,000-40,000   DRA

A Lenci figure of "Polka-dot lady," in a hat with dog.

14in (36cm) high

$450-600 PSA

Judith Picks

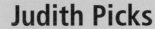

Founded in Turin, Italy, in 1919 by Helen (Elena) Konig Scavini and her husband Enrico, the Lenci factory was named as an acronym of the company's motto: "Ludus Est Nobis Constanter Industria." This translates as "Play Is Our Constant Work," and to my mind is a modus operandi almost invariably evident in their highly collectible ceramic figures of young women produced from ca. 1928 and well into the 1930s. Quintessential female-figural Art Deco, there's a stylish playfulness to their composition that manages to convey, through a mixture of posture and chic couture, both a sense of female emancipation and, at the same time, an endearing innocence or purity of spirit—the latter, here, subtly enhanced by the engagement of the young lady with a delicate little bird at her feet.

An early-1930s Lenci Pottery figure of a stylish young woman, "Janetti," with a small bird at her feet, designed by Helen Konig Scavini.

16in (40cm) high

$12,000-15,000 WW

A Lenci pottery group of mermaid and child on the back of a tortoise, "Mamma Sirena," by Helen Konig Scavini, marked "Lenci, Made in Italy Torino VIII. XI."

ca. 1930 *13½in (34cm) high*

$3,300-4,000 CHOR

A Lenci "Nella" figure, modeled by Helen König Scavini, as a lady sitting on a bench, the reverse forming a box with a cover surmounted with a frog, inscribed "Lenci/Made in Italy 8.3.93?" with star, restored extensively.

9in (23cm) high

$3,300-4,000 SWO

A Lenci figure "La Modista—Il Cappellino," designed by Helen Konig Scavini, a version without a hatbox or dog, inscribed "Lenci Torino Italy 8-3-33 XI," left leg glued crudely below the knee, chips.

1933 *13½in (34.5cm) high*

$6,000-6,600 SWO

A Lenci earthenware figure, by Helen Konig Scavini, titled "Primo Romanzo," signed, professional restoration on the hand.

ca. 1932

$6,000-7,500 FLD

A Lenci earthenware figure, titled "Nudino," by Helen Konig Scavini, modeled as a female nude in kneeling pose wearing a large wide-brim hat.

7½in (19cm) high

$2,600-3,300 FLD

A Lenci earthenware figure, titled "Dopo Lo Studio," by Abel Jacopi, modeled as a young girl sitting, eating an apple with a book by her side, signed "Lenci - Made in Italy Turino."

11½in (29cm) high

$7,500-8,500 FLD

DECORATIVE ARTS

ESSENTIAL REFERENCE—MARTIN BROTHERS

Starting out in 1873 with just a kiln at their family home in Fulham, London, Martin Brothers moved into an old soap works in Southhall, London, in 1877, where production continued until 1923. They used salt-glazed stoneware to make their hand-crafted and distinctive designs, with each of the four brothers taking on a different role in the business: Robert Wallace Martin modeled the figures—the grotesques and face pitchers were chiefly his work; Walter threw the pots; Edwin painted and decorated them; and Charles, the youngest, ran their retail store and gallery in Holborn, London—often hiding his favorite pots to prevent them from being purchased!

A Martin Brothers glazed stoneware bird tobacco jar, by Robert Wallace Martin, incised signature and date on base "RW Martin London 1881" and on head "RW Martin."

1881   *13¾in (35cm) high*

$46,000-53,000   **DRA**

A Martin Brothers stoneware bird jar and cover, by Robert Wallace Martin, bird with upcast knowing look, etched "R W Martin & Bros, London & Southall," firing cracks on neck of body.

5¾in (14.5cm) high

$26,000-33,000   **WW**

A Martin Brothers stoneware bird jar and cover, by Robert Wallace Martin, on ebonized wooden base, incised "Martin Bros London & Southall."

10½in (26.5cm) high

$53,000-66,000   **WW**

A Martin Brothers stoneware bird jar and cover, by Robert Wallace Martin, on ebonized wood base, incised "R W Martin & Brothers London & Southall" on head and "Martin Bros London" on base, small chip on rim of inner rim of head.

11¼in (28.5cm) high

$46,000-53,000   **WW**

A Martin Brothers "The Wise Owl" stoneware bird jar and cover, by Robert Wallace Martin, one eye remaining vigilantly open, incised "R W Martin Sc, London 11 1884" on base and "c R W Martin & Brothers London & Southall 11 1884" on cover, repaired damages, dated.

1884   *11¾in (30cm) high*

$33,000-40,000   **WW**

A Martin Brothers salt-glazed stoneware bird tobacco jar, by Robert W. Martin, on an ebonized wood base, incised "Martin Bros. London + Southall 9-1898."

1898   *11in (28cm) high*

$40,000-53,000   **DRA**

A Martin Brothers salt-glazed stoneware tall bird tobacco jar, by Robert W. Martin, on an ebonized wood base, head and base incised "Martin Bros. London + Southall 9-1898."

1898   *14in (35.5cm) high*

$60,000-70,000   **DRA**

A Martin Brothers salt-glazed stoneware tall bird tobacco jar, by Robert W. Martin, on an ebonized wood base, head incised "R.W. Martin + Bros. London + Southall 2-1889," based incised "Martin Bros. London + Southall 2-1899."

1899   *14in (35.5cm) high*

$60,000-70,000   **DRA**

Judith Picks

The desirability of Martin Brother's delightfully eccentric, late-19thC and early-20thC, salt-glazed stoneware bird jars is now long established and, judging by the considerable price this splendid example recently fetched at auction in the United States, shows no signs whatsoever of abating. It's easy to understand why. It's in some part due to the fact that the colors employed—a muted palette of cream, gray, brown, blue, and yellow developed by brother Walter Frazer Martin (1857-1912)—is particularly pleasing to the eye, but above all its due to their quirky modeling by brother Robert Wallace Martin (1843-1923), a trained sculptor who had studied at the Lambeth School of Art. More specifically, it's their remarkably "human" anthropomorphic expressions—ranging from the supercilious to the solemn and, here, stern and concerned disapproval—that will always be at the heart of their enduring appeal.

A Martin Brothers salt-glazed stoneware bird tobacco jar, by Robert W. Martin, incised "RW Martin+Brothers, London+Southall, 11-1900."

1900   *13¾in (35cm) high*

$53,000-66,000   **DRA**

A Martin Brothers salt-glazed stoneware barrister bird tobacco jar, by Robert W. Martin, on an ebonized wood base, incised "Martin Bros. London + Southall 6-1903."

1903   *9¼in (23.5cm) high*

$20,000-26,000   **DRA**

A pair of small Martin Brothers "The Barrister and his Defendant" stoneware birds, by Robert Wallace Martin, the barrister leaning forward to whisper to the recoiling client, on ebonized wooden bases, incised "R W Martin & Bros," and the defendant with "Southall 1914."

tallest 3¾in (9.5cm) high

$26,000-33,000   **WW**

CLOSER LOOK—MARTIN BROTHERS JAR

As with their better-known bird figures, the primary focus of the composition and modeling of this Martin Brothers figure is its endearing yet slightly disturbing anthropomorphic face, in this case that of a grotesque dog with smiling eyes and equally smiling toothy grin.

Mottled "orange peel" salt glazes in muted shades of yellow, brown, and black are combined to create a "naturalistic" skin tone.

Also as with many other Martin figures, it's all too easy to forget they're not simply decorative sculptures but are also functional; the removable head serves as the cover for the hollow storage jar body.

The modeling of the paws—four toes each at the front, four toes and a big toe each at the back—echoes the dog-human anthropomorphism of the head.

A unique Martin Brothers stoneware grotesque dog jar and cover, by Robert Wallace Martin, incised on neck and underside of base "11-1884 R W Martin London & Southall."

1884   *9in (23cm) high*

$60,000-70,000   **WW**

A Martin Brothers salt-glazed stoneware small triple-bird tobacco jar, by Robert W. Martin, on an ebonized wood base, heads and base incised "R.W. Martin and Bro. London + Southall 29.1.1914."

1914   *7¼in (18.5cm) high*

$53,000-66,000   **DRA**

A Martin Brothers salt-glazed stoneware double-face pitcher, incised signature and date on underside "Martin Bros London + Southall 6-1897."

1897   *9¾in (25cm) high*

$13,000-18,000   **DRA**

A Martin Brothers stoneware spoon warmer, by Robert Wallace Martin, impressed "R W Martin" stamp, incised "R W Martin London & Southall," one toe glued.

5¼in (13.5cm) high

$26,000-33,000   **WW**

A Martin Brothers stoneware "Birdman" jar and cover, by Robert Wallace Martin, on ebonized wood base, incised "R W Martin & Bros, London & Southall" on neck, base incised "7-12-1907 R W Martin & Bros, London & Southall."

9¼in (23.5cm) high

$46,000-53,000   **WW**

A Martin Brothers vase, decorated with grotesque fish, eels, and octopus, marked "R.W Martin Bros London & Southall," dated.

1888   *20½in (52cm) high*

$33,000-40,000   **K&O**

A Martin Brothers earthenware "Dragon" vase, by Edwin and Walter Martin, incised and painted with fighting dragons, incised "1 1898 Martin Bros London & Southall," repaired damage and losses, dated.

1898   *17¾in (45cm) high*

$7,500-8,000   **WW**

A William Moorcroft for James MacIntyre miniature ewer, "Poppy Garland" pattern, printed mark, and underglaze green monogram.

ca. 1903   *2½in (6.5cm) high*

$1,000-1,100   **K&O**

A William Moorcroft for James MacIntyre miniature vase, stippled orange "Poppy" pattern, printed mark and underglaze green monogram.

ca. 1904   *3in (7.5cm) high*

$1,600-2,100   **K&O**

A William Moorcroft for James MacIntyre miniature vase, "Yellow Poppy and Rose" panel pattern, printed mark and underglaze green monogram.

ca. 1908   *3in (7.5cm) high*

$1,600-2,100   **K&O**

An early-20thC Moorcroft Florian baluster table lamp, by William Moorcroft for Liberty, general wear, with later mounts and shade.

17¾in (45cm) high

$2,000-2,600   **SWO**

A William Moorcroft miniature vase, "Cornflower" pattern, impressed marks and underglaze green monogram.

ca. 1914   *3in (7.5cm) high*

$1,500-1,800   **K&O**

A Moorcroft Pottery "Revived Cornflower" or "Brown Chrysanthemum" vase, designed by William Moorcroft, impressed marks, painted green signature and date.

1915   *15¾in (40cm) high*

$6,000-6,600   **WW**

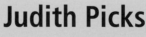

A Moorcroft Pottery "Claremont" plate, designed by William Moorcroft, with Shreve silver mount, painted "W Moorcroft Shreve & Company San Francisco," fine hairline crack on rim.

8½in (21.5cm) diam

$1,050-1,300   **WW**

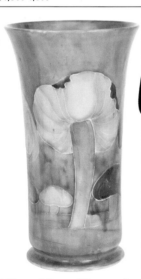

A Moorcroft Pottery "Claremont" vase, designed by William Moorcroft, probably retailed by Liberty & Co, printed regd mark and painted green signature.

9¾in (24.5cm) high

$4,000-4,600   **WW**

Judith Picks

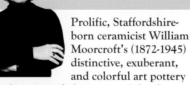

Prolific, Staffordshire-born ceramicist William Moorcroft's (1872-1945) distinctive, exuberant, and colorful art pottery has long appealed to me, and the sheer diversity of his designs means almost all tastes are catered for. This particular example, typically applied to a traditional form—a wall charger—is one of my favorites, and is the product (one of many) of the artistically and commercially successful collaboration between Moorcraft and Liberty & Co. of Regent St, London. Commissioners, retailers and, indeed, arbiters of innovative and tasteful design since the late 19thC, Liberty's sold this charger, along with other flat and hollow wares in the same range, under the grand title of "Claremont," which, understandably, had a more desirable "ring" to it than simply "Toadstool"—the fungal forms depicted at the heart of Moorcroft's composition.

A Moorcroft Pottery "Claremont" wall charger, designed by William Moorcroft, retailed by Liberty & Co., printed Liberty mark, painted green signature.

11¾in (30cm) diam

$4,000-4,600   **WW**

A Moorcroft Pottery "Cornflower" jardinière, designed by William Moorcroft, painted green signature.

3½in (9cm) high

$1,500-1,800 **WW**

A Moorcroft "Eventide" vase, with a blue signature, stamped marks and numbered, crazing on the body.

6in (15cm) high

$750-850 **SWO**

A Moorcroft Pottery "Flambé Chevrons" vase, shouldered form, painted with bands of chevrons bordering columns, in blue and ocher under a red flambé glaze, impressed marks, painted blue signature.

8¼in (21cm) high

$1,500-2,000 **WW**

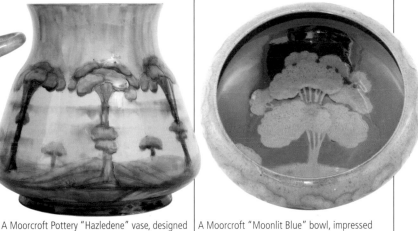

A Moorcroft Pottery "Hazledene" jardinière, designed by William Moorcroft, painted with a band of trees with a winding path in the foreground, painted green signature, impressed marks, professional restoration to a hairline crack.

8¼in (21cm) high

$4,000-4,600 **WW**

A Moorcroft Pottery "Hazledene" vase, designed by William Moorcroft and retailed by Liberty & Co, footed, painted green signature, printed "Liberty & Co" mark.

10in (25cm) high

$2,100-2,600 **WW**

A Moorcroft "Moonlit Blue" bowl, impressed marks "198" and green signature, crazing.

8¾in (22cm) diam

$750-850 **SWO**

A Moorcroft Pottery "Pansy" baluster vase, designed by William Moorcroft, painted in shades of blue, purple, yellow, and green on a white ground, impressed marks, painted green signature.

13½in (34.5cm) high

$4,000-4,600 **WW**

A William Moorcroft "Pomegranate" cookie jar (or biscuit barrel) and cover, impressed marks, blue facsimile signature, crazing.

6¾in (17.5cm) high

$800-900 **SWO**

A Moorcroft banded vase, with the "Honesty" pattern, impressed factory marks, blue painted signature.

ca. 1925 *9¾in (24.5cm) high*

$600-650 **BELL**

A Newcomb College Pottery glazed earthenware vase, with tall pines and full moon, by Sadie Irvine, signed, dated, and numbered on underside "NC/JM/OP58/325/SI."

1925   9¼in (23cm) high

$13,000-15,000   DRA

An early Newcomb College Pottery glazed earthenware vase, by Harriet Joor, impressed manufacturer's mark on underside "NC JM W," glazed signature and number on underside "JH KK24."

1903   9in (23cm) high

$8,000-9,000   DRA

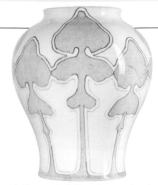

An early Newcomb College Pottery glazed earthenware vase, with stylized leaves, by Katherine Kopman, glazed signature on underside "KK" with impressed "U."

ca. 1902   6¾in (17cm) high

$6,000-6,600   DRA

An early Newcomb College Pottery glazed earthenware vase, with stylized arrowroot, by Desiree Roman, signed, dated, and numbered on underside "NC/JM/U/ C87/D.R.."

1901   8¾in (22cm) high

$8,000-9,000   DRA

CLOSER LOOK—NEWCOMB COLLEGE POTTERY VASE

The shapes of Newcomb College wares—here, a squat ovoid—were mostly inspired by the soft, curvaceous forms of both indigenous rustic and traditional Asian pottery.

Prior to ca. 1910, Newcomb College wares mostly featured a distinctive color palette of yellows, blues, greens, and black, which in some cases, as here, were contrasted against an ivory ground.

Located in New Orleans, Newcomb pottery specialized in imagery of the flora and fauna indigenous to the southern United States. Typical flora included tobacco and cotton plants, blossoms, and, as here, cacti.

In addition to marks denoting the pottery, the artist, and the date, the underside of Newcomb College wares originally bore a label declaring that the "Designs are not Duplicated."

An early Newcomb College Pottery glazed earthenware vase, with cactus blossoms, by Marie Ross, stamped on underside "NC JM U" with incised signature "M Ross" and glazed number "X33."

1903   6in (15cm) high

$13,000-15,000   DRA

An early Newcomb College Pottery glazed earthenware vase, with irises, by Anna Frances Simpson, signed, dated, and numbered on underside "NC/JM/CZ76/Q/AFS."

1909   10¼in (26cm) high

$16,000-20,000   DRA

A Newcomb College Pottery glazed earthenware vase, with live oaks and Spanish moss, by Anna Frances Simpson, signed, dated and numbered on underside "NC/SG27/49/JH/AFS."

1930   6in (15cm) high

$10,000-11,000   DRA

A Newcomb College Pottery scenic glazed earthenware vase, with full moon, by Anna Frances Simpson, impressed manufacturer's mark, date, and number on underside "NC QG55 JM 77" with incised signature "AFS."

1927   7in (18cm) high

$6,500-8,000   DRA

A Newcomb College Pottery Transitional glazed earthenware plaque, glazed manufacturer's mark on lower left "NC," impressed date on verso "JH43."

1918   9¾in (25cm) high

$8,000-9,000   DRA

ESSENTIAL REFERENCE—GEORGE OHR

Eccentric in both behavior and appearance, George Ohr (1857-1918) was born in Biloxi, Mississippi, where he first worked as a blacksmith, then a file cutter, and then a tinker, before becoming a sailor. However, in 1879 his childhood friend Joseph Meyer invited him to New Orleans to learn the art and craft of pottery.

Subsequently, back in Biloxi, Ohr established his own pottery, digging his own clay from the banks of the Tchoutacabouffa River, shaping vessels—mostly hollow wares—and then "misshaping" (folding, denting, crumpling, twisting, and squashing) them into unique forms. Their eccentricity wasn't, however, confined to just their shapes. Ohr called all his pots his "mud babies," and his workshop the "Pot-Ohr-E." Indeed, he referred to himself at any given time as either "Geoerge Ohr M.D. (Mud Dauber)" or "George Ohr P.M. (Pot Maker)"; or "The Unequaled Variety Potter"; "The Pot-Ohr"; or, and best known nowadays, "The Mad Pottery of Biloxi."

Many examples of George Ohr's work are now displayed at the Ohr-O'Keefe Museum of Art (designed by Frank Gehry) in Biloxi, while those privately owned continue to change hands at increasingly high prices.

A George Ohr glazed earthenware vase, featuring a deep in-body twist and an indigo, yellow, and pink sponged-on glaze, impressed signature "G.E. Ohr, Biloxi, Miss."
1897-1900   *7in (18cm) high*
$33,000-40,000   **DRA**

A George Ohr glazed earthenware vase, featuring an in-body twist and purple and blue sponged-on glazes with an orange interior, impressed signature on underside "G.E. Ohr, Biloxi, Miss."
1897-1900   *4¼in (11cm) high*
$26,000-40,000   **DRA**

A George Ohr glazed earthenware vase, two ribbon handles, and a green and gunmetal glaze, impressed signature "G.E. Ohr Biloxi, Miss."
1897-1900   *8in (20cm) high*
$40,000-53,000   **DRA**

A George Ohr scroddled bisque earthenware vase, with an asymmetrical pinched and lobed rim, incised signature "GE Ohr," dated and inscribed on body "Mary had a little lamb and George has a pot ohr E Amen Dec 25 1906."
1906   *6¼in (16cm) wide*
$26,000-33,000   **DRA**

A George Ohr glazed earthenware vase, with a double spout, an in-body twist, two ribbon handles, and a green and ocher speckled glaze, impressed signature "G.E. Ohr Biloxi."
1895-96   *4½in (11cm) high*
$20,000-26,000   **DRA**

A George Ohr glazed earthenware vase, with an in-body twist, ruffled rim, and brown and ocher glazes, impressed signature "Geo. E. Ohr Biloxi, Miss."
1895-96   *5½in (14cm) high*
$33,000-40,000   **DRA**

A George Ohr glazed earthenware "Snake" vase, featuring a snake, lobed rim, an in-body twist, and a green glaze with blue speckling, impressed signature on underside "G. E. Ohr, Biloxi."
1895-96   *4in (10cm) high*
$100,000-110,000   **DRA**

A George Ohr glazed earthenware vase, with a quatrefoil rim and a raspberry and turquoise mottled glaze, impressed signature "G.E. Ohr."
1897-1900   *4½in (11cm) diam*
$26,000-33,000   **DRA**

CLOSER LOOK—GEORGE OHR VASE

The rim is everted and pinched into an irregular wavelike form. Similarly irregular and organic variations on this found on other Ohr pots include pinched or twisted pleats and folded petal-like forms.

In-body twisting is a signature Ohr technique found on many, albeit not all, of his vessels. This is a particularly deep, vigorously executed, and overtly sculptural example.

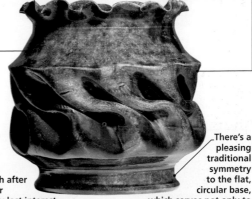

There's a pleasing traditional symmetry to the flat, circular base, which serves not only to provide stability for the pot, but also, simply by way of contrast, accentuate the avant-garde nature of the modeling above it.

Although after 1900 Ohr gradually lost interest in glazing his pieces, this pot displays the mottled and speckled combinations of glazes—here, predominantly greens, orange, and indigo—he preferred to use prior to that.

A George Ohr glazed earthenware vase, with a pinched rim, an in-body twist, and indigo glaze, incised signature on underside "Ohr Biloxi."
ca. 1900   *6in (15cm) high*
$110,000-120,000   **DRA**

DECORATIVE ARTS

ESSENTIAL REFERENCE—ROOKWOOD

The Rookwood Pottery was founded in 1880 in Cincinnati, Ohio, by Maria Longworth Nichols Storer (1849-1932), who had trained as a ceramics painter and been especially inspired by the Japanese art and French ceramics she had seen at the Centennial Exposition in Philadelphia in 1876.

Rookwood soon established itself as one of the most important art potteries in the country—by the 1920s it was employing some 200 people—and became known in particular for its innovative glazes. These included: "Standard Glaze" (yellow-tinted, high gloss, and often used over floral and foliate imagery); "Iris" (clear and colorless); "Sea Green" (clear but green tinted); "Ariel Blue" (clear but blue tinted); "Vellum" (mat and used over underglaze decoration, especially floral and scenic); and "Ombroso" (brown or black mat, and used on incised pieces).

Despite also having commercial success with architectural pottery, notably ceramic tiles, Rookwood suffered badly during the Great Depression and filed for bankruptcy in 1941. Subsequently, however, the company has changed hands and location a number of times since, and currently has a production studio back in Cincinnati.

A Rookwood Pottery dull finish glazed earthenware flask, by Edward Cranch, impressed signature, date, and number on underside "Cranch Rookwood 1884 85."

1884   *6¾in (17cm) high*
$8,000-9,000   **DRA**

A rare Rookwood Pottery and Tiffany Studios "Sea Green" glazed earthenware lamp, by Kataro Shirayamadani, patinated copper, leaded slag glass, and patinated metal, impressed signature, date, and number "Flame mark/I/S1647" with artist cipher, impressed manufacturer's mark on inner edge of shade "Tiffany Studios New York."

The base features decoration of cattleya orchids with leaves in metal overlay with a rare variation of the Tiffany Studios Vine Border shade with a single pink blossom. The leaf overlay was probably completed by Japanese metal worker R. Ito.

1901   *14¼in (36cm) high*
$65,000-70,000   **DRA**

A Rookwood Pottery glazed earthenware vase, with squeeze-bag "Sea Green" decoration, by Artus Van Briggle, impressed manufacturer's mark, date, and number on underside "Flame mark 735D G," trial marks, seconded mark, and incised artist's initials "AVB."

1898   *7in (18cm) high*
$4,600-5,300   **DRA**

A Rookwood Pottery glazed earthenware "Standard Glaze" Native American portrait vase, by Grace Young, featuring a portrait of Shavehead from the Aarapahoe tribe, incised title on underside "Shavehead - Arapahoe," impressed manufacturer's mark "Flame mark/886B."

1899   *12½in (32cm) high*
$9,000-10,500   **DRA**

A Rookwood Pottery "Relief Iris" glazed earthenware vase, with poppies, by William Purcell McDonald, impressed signature, date, and number "Flame mark/S1565/C/WMD."

1900   *14¼in (36cm) high*
$53,000-59,000   **DRA**

A Rookwood Pottery glazed earthenware "Modeled Mat" vase, with geese, by Kataro Shirayamadani, impressed manufacturer's mark, date and number on underside "Flame mark I 832B" with incised artist cipher.

1901   *10½in (27cm) high*
$20,000-22,000   **DRA**

A Rookwood Pottery "Iris Glaze" earthenware plaque, "Steamboat on the Ocean," by Sturgis Laurence, incised signature on lower left "SL," impressed signature, date, and number on verso "Flame mark/III/X1168X."

1903   *13¾in (35cm) wide*
$12,000-15,000   **DRA**

A Rookwood Pottery "Iris Glaze" earthenware vase, with flying geese, by Albert R. Valentien, impressed signature, date, and number "Flame mark/IV/614B/A.R. Valentien."

1904   *14¼in (36cm) high*
$18,000-24,000   **DRA**

A Rookwood Pottery "Dark Iris Glaze" earthenware vase, with herons and cattails, by Kataro Shirayamadani, impressed signature, date, and number "Flame mark/VII/942B" with artist cipher.

1907   *8¼in (21cm) high*
$18,000-24,000   **DRA**

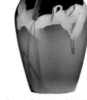

A Rookwood Pottery earthenware "Iris Glaze" vase, with ducks, by Carl Schmidt, impressed manufacturer's mark, date, and number "Flame mark VIII 907 D W" with circular incised artist's cipher.

1908   *10½in (27cm) high*
$3,300-4,000   **DRA**

A Rookwood Pottery banded "Iris Glaze" earthenware vase, by Kataro Shirayamadani, with white cranes flying over a snowy forest, impressed signature, date, and number "Flame mark/X/951B" with artist cipher.

1910   *11¾in (30cm) high*
$22,000-26,000   **DRA**

A Rookwood Pottery "French Red" glazed porcelain vase, with forsythia, by Sara Sax, impressed signature, date, and number, "Flame mark/XXII/2040D/SX," partial original paper label.

1922   *9½in (24cm) high*
$13,000-18,000   **DRA**

A Rookwood Pottery glazed porcelain vellum plaque, "Schooner," by Carl Schmidt, with original frame, glazed signature to lower right "C. Schmidt," impressed signature and date on verso "Flame mark/XXIV."

1924   *12in (30cm) high*
$12,000-13,000   **DRA**

ESSENTIAL REFERENCE—ROSEVILLE

The Roseville Pottery was founded in Roseville, Ohio, in 1890. It initially produced utilitarian wares and launched its first Art Pottery range, "Rozane," in 1900. Frederick Hurten Rhead (1880-1942), son of Frederick Rhead and brother of Charlotte Rhead, worked at Roseville 1904-08 and created several ranges, including the popular "Della Robbia." Other notable designers included Frank Ferrell and glaze maker George Kraus. In 1908, Roseville introduced several mass-produced, molded ranges, many of which were inspired by forms from nature. The pottery closed in 1954.

A Rookwood Pottery glazed porcelain vellum plaque, "Mountains Over Lake," by Fred Rothenbusch, impressed signature and date on verso "Flame mark/XXXV."

1935   *15¾in (40cm) wide*
$13,000-16,000   **DRA**

A Roseville Pottery reticulated Della Robbia glazed earthenware vase, with daffodils, by Frederick Hurten Rhead, incised signature to body "M.F."

1906 07   *11½in (29cm) high*
$15,000-17,000   **DRA**

A Roseville Pottery glazed earthenware Della Robbia vase, with stylized flora, by Frederick Hurten Rhead, incised signature on body "E.C.," remnant of paper manufacturer's label.

1906-07   *11½in (29cm) high*
$11,000-13,000   **DRA**

A Roseville Pottery glazed earthenware umbrella stand, with peacock, by Frederick Hurten Rhead, with squeeze-bag decoration, glazed decorators" initials on body "HR" and "PL."

"HR" stands for Harry Rhead, Frederick Rhead's brother.

ca. 1908   *20½in (52cm) high*
$26,000-32,000   **DRA**

A Roseville Pottery glazed earthenware Carnelian II vase.

ca. 1926   *13½in (34cm) high*
$5,300-6,600   **DRA**

A Ruskin Pottery high-fired stoneware vase, by William Howson Taylor, the mushroom glazed stocky body with sang-de-boeuf splashes with green and turquoise spots, impressed factory mark and date.

1905   *6¼in (16cm) high*

$6,500-8,000   **WW**

Judith Picks

I'd be more than happy to give this Ruskin Pottery stoneware vase room in my house. It appeals to my sensibilities on a number of grounds. First and foremost, I simply love the shape—of shouldered form with elongated cylindrical neck and everted rim and, like most Ruskin pieces, inspired in this respect by traditional Chinese ceramics. Ultimately, however, it's the decoration of this time-honored form that really appeals to me. Founder (in 1898, in West Smethwick, near Birmingham) of the Ruskin Pottery, William Howson Taylor (1876-1935) energetically pursued the study of innovative glazing techniques—including luster, crystalline, and high-fired glazes in diverse colors—and mastered the complex techniques employed in the application of, for example, soufflé and flambé glazes. In this case, he's covered the vase in a running sang-de-boeuf glaze over a mottled ground and highlighted it in a sky blue—an abstract composition that, in my mind's eye, magically transforms stoneware into metal.

A Ruskin Pottery high-fired stoneware vase, by William Howson Taylor, with impressed marks.

ca. 1909   *11½in (29cm) high*

$4,600-5,300   **WW**

A high fired Ruskin Pottery vase, decorated in a tonal lavender and blue glaze with copper green spotting and various sweeps of color, impressed West Smethwick mark and dated, an old slither bruise on foot rim with several fleabite pieces missing.

1908   *9¼in (23.5cm) high*

$1,700-2,600   **FLD**

A Ruskin Pottery high-fired stoneware vase, by William Howson Taylor, in a mottled moss green soufflé glaze, impressed "WHT" monogram, shape no. 231.

The remains of a paper label on the base of the vase proudly alludes to the occasion of the pottery winning the Grand Prize at the St. Louis International Exhibition in 1904.

4¼in (11cm) high

$850-1,000   **WW**

A Ruskin Pottery high-fired stoneware solifleur vase, by William Howson Taylor, covered in a sang-de-boeuf glaze with lavender patches, unsigned.

5½in (14cm) high

$450-600   **WW**

A Ruskin Pottery high-fired stoneware vase, by William Howson Taylor, covered in a running sang de boeuf glaze over silver gray, unsigned.

10in (25.5cm) high

$850-1,000   **WW**

A Ruskin Pottery high-fired stoneware vase, by William Howson Taylor, apple green speckled glaze with sang-de-boeuf patches and fissuring, impressed factory mark and date.

1910   *10in (25cm) high*

$3,300-4,000   **WW**

A high fired Ruskin Pottery vase, decorated in a sang-de-beouf with light fissuring and deep red patches, impressed mark and dated, several open air bubbles in the firing.

1922   *8¾in (22cm) high*

$2,000-2,600   **FLD**

A Ruskin Pottery high-fired stoneware vase, by William Howson Taylor, covered in sang-de-boeuf and purple glaze with turquoise splashes, impressed factory mark and date.

1926   *5¾in (14.5cm) high*

$1,600-1,800   **WW**

ESSENTIAL REFERENCE—FAIRYLAND LUSTRE

Wedgwood's highly distinctive Fairyland Lustre range was designed 1915-29 by Daisy Makeig-Jones (1818-1945).

● Makeig-Jones had studied at the Torquay School of Art, before becoming a tableware painter and designer at Wedgwood in 1909.

● She decorated her Fairyland Lustre series with colorful scenes of fantastical lands and magical kingdoms, featuring goblins, sprites, spirits, and other supernatural beings.

● Initially popular both during and after World War I, they had fallen out of fashion by the late 1920s, only to enjoy a notable revival among collectors during the last quarter of the 20thC, which, reflected in the high prices rarer patterns command, endures to this day.

A Wedgwood Fairyland lustre vase and cover, designed by Daisy Makeig-Jones, "Jewelled Tree" pattern, gilt-printed "Portland Vase" mark, painted "Z4968."

ca. 1920   *11½in (29cm) high*

$5,300-6,600   **M&K**

A Wedgwood "Flame" Fairyland lustre vase, designed by Daisy Makeig-Jones, "Pillar" pattern, gilt-printed "Portland Vase" mark, painted "Z5360/1."

ca. 1920   *14in (35.5cm) high*

$5,300-6,600   **M&K**

A Wedgwood Fairyland lustre "Malfrey" pot and cover, designed by Daisy Makeig-Jones, "Ghostly Wood" pattern, the cover with the "Owls of Wisdom" pattern, incised 2312, gilt-printed "Portland Vase" mark.

ca. 1920   *13in (35cm) high*

$26,000-40,000   **M&K**

A Wedgwood Fairyland lustre "Elves in a Pine Tree" plaque, designed by Daisy Makeig-Jones, inside orange luster border, in original ebonized wood frame, printed factory mark.

10½in (26.5cm) high

$3,300-4,000   **WW**

A Wedgwood Fairyland lustre Lincoln "Rainbow" plate, designed by Daisy Makeig-Jones, decorated with figures in a mystical landscape, the rim with dragon creatures among flower and foliage, highlighted in gilt, printed "Wedgwood" mark.

10¾in (27.5cm) diam

$4,600 5,300   **WW**

A rare Wedgwood luster "Malfrey" pot and cover, designed by Daisy Makeig-Jones, with Japanese floral mon on the shoulder, inside the cover and base of the vase a gilt spider's web design, printed Wedgwood mark.

7½in (19cm) high

$5,300-6,600   **WW**

A Wedgwood Fairyland lustre "Malfrey" pot and cover, "Bubbles II," designed by Daisy Makeig-Jones, pattern no. Z52557, the cover decorated with a spider, the interior printed in gilt with four elves, printed and painted marks, small chip on the rim of the cover.

7¼in (18.5cm) high

$17,000-21,000   **WW**

A Wedgwood Fairyland lustre pillar vase, "Torches," designed by Daisy Makeig-Jones, pattern Z4968, printed factory mark, painted "Z4968."

11¼in (28.5cm) high

$5,300-6,600   **WW**

A pair of Wedgwood Fairyland lustre covered vases, "Ghostly Wood," designed by Daisy Makeig-Jones, printed Wedgwood mark, painted "Z4968."

15in (38cm) high

$40,000-53,000   **WW**

DECORATIVE ARTS

An Arequipa glazed squeeze-bag-decorated earthenware vase, with leaves, by Frederick Hurten Rhead, signed "Arequipa California 2128."

1911-13   *8¼in (21cm) high*

$20,000-26,000   **DRA**

A Beswick "Girl in Red Jacket and Brown Breaches."

$3,300-4,000   **PSA**

A Bing & Grøndahl porcelain vase, by Fanny Garde (1855-1928), with blackberries, flowers, and leaves, blue "B & G," "485," and "F Garde."

6¼in (16cm) high

$1,500-1,800   **SWO**

A Burgess & Leigh charger, by Charlotte Rhead, decorated with three swans on a pond with lilies.

14in (36cm) diam

$6,000-6,600   **PSA**

A Burmantoft's Faience jardinière and stand, probably designed by Joseph Walmsley, with two peacocks displaying in a formal garden landscape, impressed and painted marks, minor glaze loss.

40½in (103cm) high

$5,300-6,600   **WW**

A Carlton Ware Handcraft vase, "Peach Melba" pattern no.3448, ovoid, printed and painted marks.

7in (17.5cm) high

$160-240   **WW**

An Aesthetic movement Chelsea Keramic Art Works glazed earthenware vase, by George W. Fenety, impressed mark "CKAW" with incised artist signature "GWF."

ca. 1880   *7¾in (20cm) high*

$5,300-6,600   **DRA**

A Dedham crackle-glazed stoneware vase, with flowers, by Hugh C. Robertson, incised signature on underside "Dedham Pottery BM HCR."

1896-1908   *9in (23cm) high*

$16,000-20,000   **DRA**

A Della Robbia Pottery vase, by Hannah Jones and Charles Collis, incised with stylized flower and foliage panels, incised mark, and Lloyd, painted artist monograms.

15½in (39cm) high

$2,600-3,300   **WW**

A Dennis Chinaworks "Adele" vase, designed by Sally Tuffin, decorated by Vanessa Thompson, thrown by Rory Mcleod, with a portrait of Adele Bloh-Bauer after the portrait by Gustav Klimt in 1907, painted marks, "WW16," dated.

2019   *13½in (34.5cm) high*

$2,400-2,900   **WW**

An Essevi figure of a mother and child, "Il figlio dell'amore," by Sandro Vacchetti, inscribed "Essevi Made in Italy Torino nil Figlio dell'Amore di Sandro Vacchetti 29-9-938 XVI I," both legs restored.

11¾in (30cm) high

$2,600-3,300   **SWO**

A rare Fulper floor vase, sky flambé glazed earthenware, stamped manufacturer's mark on underside "Fulper."

ca. 1915   *34¼in (87cm) high*

$13,000-18,000   **DRA**

A Hancock & Sons Morris Ware vase, by George Cartlidge.

9½in (24cm) high

$400-500   **PSA**

A George Jones majolica game pie tureen, cover and liner, modeled with two boar hunting scenes, impressed and painted pattern numbers, minor glaze flakes.

ca. 1875   *12¼in (31cm) wide*

$5,300-5,900   **TEN**

A George Jones majolica tazza, a stag and doe on the base with a small rabbit peeping out of its burrow, black registration diamond, some restoration.

ca. 1871   *10½in (26.5cm) high*

$3,300-4,000   **WW**

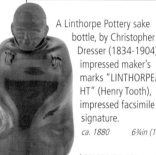

A Linthorpe Pottery sake bottle, by Christopher Dresser (1834-1904), impressed maker's marks "LINTHORPE/ HT" (Henry Tooth), impressed facsimile signature.

ca. 1880   *6¾in (17cm) high*

$29,000-34,000   **L&T**

A Linthorpe Pottery jardinière, designed by Christopher Dresser, in the Egyptian style, stamped "2297," crack on the base.

11in (28cm) diam

$400-500   **SWO**

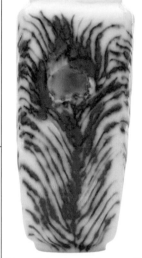

A Losanti glazed porcelain vase, with peacock feathers, by Mary Louise McLaughlin, incised signature and number on underside "MCL 333."

1899-1904   *6in (15cm) high*

$13,000-18,000   **DRA**

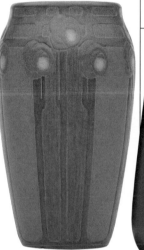

A Marblehead glazed earthenware vase, by Arthur Hennessey and Sarah Tutt, featuring crisp, deeply carved conventionalized flowers, impressed manufacturer's mark on underside "MP" with ship symbol, incised signature on underside "HT."

This rare vase is one of only four known examples. The stylized design of the flowers may have been influenced by Charles Rennie Mackintosh's famous rose design, also referred to as Mackintosh Rose.

ca. 1910   *6¾in (17cm) high*

$190,000-200,000   **DRA**

A Marblehead glazed earthenware vase, with crouching panthers in low relief, impressed manufacturer's mark on underside "MP" with ship symbol.

The panther design is most often seen on a green background, this example in blue is particularly rare and perfectly fired. An example of this form and decoration is held in the permanent collection of The Metropolitan Museum of Art.

1908-20   *6¾in (17cm) high*

$60,000-70,000   **DRA**

A Maw & Co. earthenware luster charger, painted with a galleon at full sail with three fish below, the chamfered edge with Vitruvian scrolling, inscribed "Maw & Co. Ltd. Jackfield Salop 1897," with artist's monogram "AP," some minor wear.

1897   *19¾in (50cm) diam*

$4,000-4,600   **SWO**

A Merrimac glazed earthenware vase, with stylized flowers, impressed manufacturer's mark on underside "Merrimac" with sturgeon.

1900-08   *7½in (19cm) high*

$9,000-10,500   **DRA**

A Midwinter Pottery vase, designed by Jessie Tait, tube line decorated, printed factory marks.

9in (23cm) high

$260-400   **WW**

A Minton's Pottery wall charger, "The Butterfly Collector," by William S. Coleman, in original ebonized wood and gilded frame, signed, minor oxidization to paint.

22½in (57cm) diam

$24,000-29,000   **WW**

A rare Morris and Co tile, designed by Edward Burne-Jones, "Cinderella-The Slipper Fits," painted in colors unmarked, minor rim chips.

6in (14.5cm) square

$2,000-2,600   **WW**

A Richard Parkinson Pottery plate, designed by Susan Parkinson, with a stylized chess pawn figure, impressed marks.

9in (22cm) diam

$550-600   **WW**

A Pewabic Pottery iridescent glazed earthenware baluster vase, impressed manufacturer's mark on underside "Pewabic Detroit."

1915-30   *11½in (29cm) high*

$3,300-4,000   **DRA**

A Pilkington's Lancastrian luster vase, by Gordon Forsyth (1879-1952), decorated with a frieze of lions, painted artist's and date ciphers on the base, impressed factory monogram and marks "IX/ENGLAND," dated.

1909   *13¼in (33.5cm) high*

$15,000-20,000   **L&T**

A Poole Pottery "Leaping Deer" ovoid vase, designed by Truda Carter, painted by Doris Marshall, "TZ" pattern, impressed mark, painted pattern, and artist cipher.

5in (12.5cm) high

$550-650   **WW**

A Carter's Poole Pottery tile, probably designed by Edward Bawden, painted with Poole Pots and a leaping gazelle bookend, unsigned.

5¼in (13.5cm) square

$650-800   **WW**

A Rhead Pottery mirror-black glazed earthenware vase, by Frederick Hurten Rhead, impressed potter-at-wheel mark on underside.

1914-17   *10¼in (26cm) high*

$3,300-4,000   **DRA**

An Adelaide Robineau glazed porcelain centerpiece, this unique work featuring 5 large and 19 small hand-carved frogs, carved signature and date on underside "AR 1926."

The "New York Times" made mention of this work in a 1990 article about the Japanese aesthetic influence on American art pottery.

1926   *13in (33cm) diam*

$60,000-70,000   **DRA**

A Rörstrand carved and reticulated glazed porcelain floor vase, by Karl Lindstrom, stamped triple crown manufacturer's mark on underside "Rörstrand" with artist's initials "KL," incised number on underside "12854" with impressed number "85."

ca. 1900   *25in (63cm) high*

$6,000-6,600   **DRA**

A Royal Copenhagen porcelain vase, decorated with floral swags within gilt-band borders of anthemion and scrolling foliage, on a gilt domed foot and applied with two burnished gilt dolphin handles, green printed factory mark with blue wave.

ca. 1923   *16½in (42cm) high*

$2,600-3,300   **DN**

A Royal Dux Art Deco figure, of a nude lady sitting on draped stool, impressed no 2895, restoration on end of thumb.

19in (48cm) high

$850-1,000   **PSA**

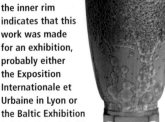

A Sèvres crystalline-glazed porcelain and gilt-bronze floor vase, incised number on inner edge of rim "L139PN" with exhibition decal label "S1914DN."

The incised number on the inner rim indicates that this work was made for an exhibition, probably either the Exposition Internationale et Urbaine in Lyon or the Baltic Exhibition in Malmö, both held in 1914.

1914   *39½in (100cm) high*

$20,000-26,000   **DRA**

A Teco Pottery glazed earthenware vase, model 310, by Fritz Albert, impressed manufacturer's mark and model number to underside "Teco 310."

ca. 1905   *18in (46cm) high*

$53,000-59,000   **DRA**

A Tiffany Studios glazed porcelain moss green Favrile pottery vase with water lilies, incised signature and number on underside "LCT L.C. Tiffany Favrile Pottery P1177."

ca. 1901   *8¾in (22cm) high*

$10,500-12,000   **DRA**

A Tiffany Studios glazed earthenware Favrile pottery artichoke vase, incised signature on underside "LCT" and etched "L.C. Tiffany Favrile Pottery P1328."

1904-14   *5½in (14cm) high*

$8,500-9,000   **DRA**

A Troika Pottery large "Wheel" vase, by Avril Bennett, painted "Troika Cornwall England" and artist cipher.

12½in (32cm) high

$1,050-1,200   **WW**

A University City crystalline-glazed porcelain gourd vase, by Taxile Doat.

This work was probably created during Doat's tenure at University City, however it is also possible that is was completed prior while he was in France.

1912-14   *9in (23cm) high*

$55,000-63,000   **DRA**

A Van Briggle glazed earthenware vase, with morning glories, by Artus Van Briggle, incised signature, date, and number on underside "AA Van Briggle 1903 III 208" with remnants of original price tag.

1903   *11¾in (30cm) high*

$15,000-17,000   **DRA**

A Walrath Pottery glazed earthenware vase, with stylized flowers, by Frederick Walrath, incised signature on underside.

1908-18   *8¾in (22cm) high*

$16,000-20,000   **DRA**

A Weller Pottery glazed earthenware floor vase, with chrysanthemums, by Jacques Sicard, glazed signature near base "Weller Sicard."

1903-17   *20½in (52cm) high*

$5,300-5,900   **DRA**

A Wemyss Pottery pig, retailed by Thomas Goode & Sons, impressed mark, painted Thomas Goode mark, chip on ear.

17in (43cm) wide

$1,000-1,050   **WW**

A T. J. Wheatley & Co. glazed earthenware vase, incised signature, date and number on underside "T. J. W. & Co. No. 22 Pat 14128 1880."

1880   *12in (30cm) high*

$6,500-8,000   **DRA**

A Winton Ware "Fantasy" luster vase and cover, by A. G. Harley Jones, with Art Deco maidens in an Arabian setting, stamped with "A G Harley Jones" gilt mark, rubbing on gilt areas.

10¾in (27cm) high

$350-400   **SWO**

A Jugendstil/Art Nouveau Zsolnay vase, by Sandor Apati Abt, applied mark on the base and impressed 6184 23, rubbing on the gilding.

8¾in (22cm) high

$4,600-5,300   **FLD**

ESSENTIAL REFERENCE—DAUM

The Daum glassworks was founded in 1878 in Nancy, France, by Jean Daum, and rose to prominence in the 1890s under Jean's two sons, Auguste and Antonin. Drawing on imagery from nature, and inspired by Asian and Far Eastern art, the contemporary Art Nouveau movement, and, especially, the work of Emile Gallé, they introduced their cameo glass at the Chicago World Fair in 1893. In addition to their cameo work, in which multiple layers of glass are carved to create a design in low-relief, the Daum brothers also employed a range of other techniques, including acid-etching, pâté-de-verre (in which crushed glass is packed into molds and fused in a kiln), and "intercalaire" (in which powdered glass is sealed between layers of glass). In the late 1920s and the 1930s, Daum embraced the Art Deco style, and the company is still active today.

A late-19thC Daum vase, with gentians, of acid-etched, enameled, and gilt-cameo glass, gilt signature on underside "Daum Nancy" with Croix de Lorraine.

9½in (24cm) high
$9,000-10,500   **DRA**

A Daum acid-etched cameo glass vase, relief decorated with purple flowers against a mottled orange ground, signed "Daum Nancy France."

ca. 1900   *11¼in (28.3cm) high*
$1,000-1,100   **BELL**

A Daum acid-etched, enameled, and gilt glass vase with bees, gilt signature on underside "Daum Nancy" with Croix de Lorraine.

ca. 1900   *4in (10cm) diam*
$6,000-6,600   **DRA**

A Daum vase, with poppies, of acid-etched, fire-polished, and wheel-carved opalescent cameo glass and martelé surface, etched signature on underside "Daum Nancy" with Croix de Lorraine.

ca. 1900   *5¾in (15cm) diam*
$2,100-2,600   **DRA**

An Art Nouveau Daum Nancy cameo glass vase, mottled yellow glass body cased with fruiting blackberry sprays in blue, acid-cast "Daum Nancy" mark.

5in (12.5cm) high
$3,300-4,000   **WW**

A Daum vase, with snowdrops, of acid-etched, padded, and wheel-carved cameo glass, etched signature on underside "Daum Nancy" with Croix de Lorraine.

ca. 1900   *7in (18cm) high*
$9,000-10,500   **DRA**

A Daum cameo glass bowl, with a mottled ground cut with flowers, marked "Daum Nancy France," wear on base, blown bubbles on base and side of body.

8in (20cm) diam
$750-850   **SWO**

A Daum cameo glass vase, the mottled green ground overpainted with trees, signed "Daum Nancy," ground foot.

8in (20cm) high
$3,300-4,000   **SWO**

A Daum acid-etched glass vase with gazelles, incised signature on base "Daum Nancy France" with Croix de Lorraine. **This work's combination of size, color, and quality of acid-etching makes it an especially fine and rare example.**

ca. 1930   *13½in (34cm) high*
$8,500-9,000   **DRA**

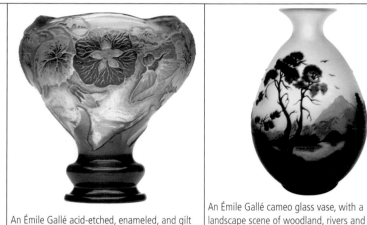

An Émile Gallé acid-etched and wheel-carved cameo glass marquetry vase, with crocuses, incised signature on body "Gallé."
ca. 1900   *8in (20cm) high*
$13,000-18,000   **DRA**

An Émile Gallé acid-etched, enameled, and gilt cameo glass coupe, with nasturtiums, cameo signature on body "Gallé."
ca. 1900   *8in (20cm) high*
$7,500-8,000   **DRA**

An Émile Gallé cameo glass vase, with a landscape scene of woodland, rivers and mountains, and birds in flight, cameo signature on body.
ca. 1900   *8¾in (22cm) high*
$2,600-4,000   **FLD**

An Art Nouveau Émile Gallé cameo glass vase, cameo decorated with berried foliage, cameo signature.
4in (9.5cm) high
$400-450   **WW**

A pair of Émile Gallé pomegranate sconces, of acid-etched cameo glass, patinated bronze and enameled metal, paper manufacturer's label on back of one "Emile Gallé Nancy Paris," signature on each shade in cameo "Gallé."
ca. 1910   *11in (28cm) wide*
$12,000-13,000   **DRA**

An early-20thC Émile Gallé acid-etched cameo glass vase, with clematis, signed in cameo on body "Gallé."
11½in (29cm) high
$5,300-6,600   **DRA**

A Gallé floral cameo glass vase, acid-etched with multiheaded flowers, with cameo signature, nibbles and scratches on the base.
15¾in (40cm) high
$1,800-2,400   **SWO**

An Art Nouveau Émile Gallé cameo glass vase, cased in ocher, cameo decorated with wild flowers and foliage, cameo signature.
13in (34cm) high
$750-850   **WW**

An Émile Gallé mountain landscape cameo vase, signed "Galle," scuffing in places, remnants of white on the rim.
10¼in (26cm) high
$2,600-3,300   **SWO**

An early-20thC Émile Gallé cameo glass vase, cased in ruby over a graduated amber and clear ground, cut with dog roses, with internal polishing and cameo signature.
9¼in (23.5cm) high
$1,600-2,100   **FLD**

ESSENTIAL REFERENCE—LALIQUE

René Lalique (1860-1945) was an eminent and influential designer who worked largely in the Art Nouveau and then the Art Deco styles. He started out as a jewelry designer and then opened his first glassworks in 1908. The Lalique glassworks produced items as diverse as vases, chargers, screens, lamps, car mascots, lights, and fountains, which were primarily mold blown or pressed, and of frosted white, opalescent glass. Colored pieces are rarer, and therefore can command higher prices, while pieces made by the "cire perdu" (lost wax) technique are rarer still, and thus the most eagerly sought after. Many of Lalique's designs continued in production after his death, with pre-1945 pieces tending to be marked "R. Lalique, France," and post-1945 pieces mostly marked just "Lalique, France."

A Lalique "Archers" vase, no.893, cased butterscotch and white stained, molded "R. LALIQUE."

1921   *10½in (26.8cm) high*

$18,000-24,000   **L&T**

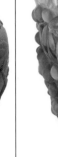

A Lalique "Archers" vase, no.893, deep amber, engraved "R. Lalique France No. 893."

1921   *10½in (26.7cm) high*

$12,000-13,000   **L&T**

A Lalique "Avallon" blue-stained vase, decorated with birds and berries, model no.986, wheel-carved mark on base "R. LALIQUE."

ca. 1927   *6in (15cm) high*

$1,600-2,100   **CHOR**

A Lalique "Biches" vase, no.1082, cobalt blue and white stained, stenciled "R. LALIQUE FRANCE."

1932   *6½in (16.5cm) high*

$7,500-8,000   **L&T**

A Lalique "Dahlias" vase, no.938, clear, frosted, blue stained, and black enameled, intaglio "R. LALIQUE."

1923   *4¾in (12cm) high*

$5,300-6,600   **L&T**

A Lalique "Davos" vase, no.1079, burnt umber, stenciled "R. LALIQUE FRANCE," a small polished nick on the rim edge of the base.

1932   *11½in (29cm) high*

$16,000-21,000   **L&T**

A Lalique "Escargot" vase, no.931, electric blue, molded "R. LALIQUE" twice, later engraved "R. Lalique France."

1920   *8½in (21.3cm) high*

$18,000-24,000   **L&T**

A Lalique "Farandole" vase, no.1052, cobalt blue, stenciled "R. LALIQUE," engraved "France."

1930   *7¼in (18.5cm) high*

$13,000-18,000   **L&T**

A Lalique cased opalescent glass vase, designed by Rene Lalique, "Formose" no.934, with blue staining, molded "R. Lalique."

7in (17cm) high

$6,500-8,000 WW

A Lalique "Formose" vase, of green glass with white patina, etched signature on underside "R. Lalique France."

1924 *6¾in (17cm) high*

$6,500-8,000 DRA

A Lalique "Frise Aigles" vase, clear, frosted, and gray stained, wheel-engraved "R. LALIQUE."

1911 *12¼in (31cm) high*

$15,000-17,000 L&T

A Lalique "Gui" vase, no.948, teal green, molded "R. LALIQUE," engraved "Lalique."

1920 *6¾in (17cm) high*

$5,300-6,600 L&T

A Lalique "Malesherbes" vase, by René Lalique, etched signature on underside "R. Lalique France No. 7014."

1927 *9in (23cm) high*

$6,500-7,500 DRA

A Lalique "Milan" vase, no.1029, cobalt blue, stenciled "R. LALIQUE," engraved "France."

1929 *11in (28cm) high*

$29,000-37,000 L&T

A Lalique "Lierre" vase, no.1041, cobalt blue, stenciled "R. LALIQUE FRANCE."

1930 *6¾in (17cm) high*

$3,300-4,000 L&T

A Lalique "Monnaie du Pape" vase, etched with a design of honesty leaves, molded "R. Lalique" mark.

1914 *9in (23cm) high*

$2,600-3,300 CHOR

Judith Picks

It wouldn't be entirely true to state that when it comes to Lalique "black is the new black," because in many respects that's usually been the case. Rare colors have always commanded a considerable premium among collectors of Lalique, and black glass is among the rarest. Designed in 1929, this Lalique "Montargis" vase is a case in point. Although named after a commune in the Loiret department of north-central France, its repeat trapezoid motif decoration was purportedly inspired by a Native American basket-weave pattern—a distinctive and elegant geometric design, applied to an equally pleasing angular ovoid form, that's quintessential late-1920s and 1930s Art Deco style. Since its introduction, it has been produced in a limited number of "colorways"—including frosted and clear, frosted and pale blue patinated, and, as here, frosted and polished black—and it is the latter that is the rarest and most desirable to the extent that, when they do come onto the market, they can command anything between five and ten times the price of the others!

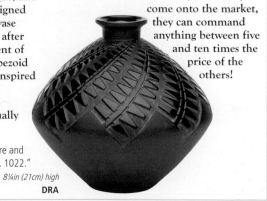

A Lalique "Montargis" vase, etched signature and number on underside "R. Lalique France No. 1022."

1929 *8¼in (21cm) high*

$26,000-33,000 DRA

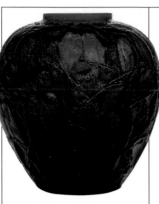

A Lalique "Perruches" vase, no.876, deep amber and white stained, intaglio "R. LALIQUE," molded "R. LALIQUE."
1919   *10¼in (25.8cm) high*
$24,000-29,000   **L&T**

A Lalique "Perruches" vase, no.876, cased opalescent and blue stained, intaglio "R. LALIQUE," molded "R. LALIQUE."
1919   *10in (25.5cm) high*
$40,000-46,000   **L&T**

A Lalique "Quatre Masques" vase, no.878, frosted and sepia stained, engraved "R. Lalique France."
1911   *11½in (29cm) high*
$16,000-20,000   **L&T**

A Lalique "Serpent" vase, no.896, clear, frosted, and gray stained, intaglio "R. LALIQUE."
1924   *10½in (26.7cm) high*
$40,000-46,000   **L&T**

A Lalique "Six Danseuses" lamp and shade, no.2179, clear and frosted, base stenciled "R. LALIQUE."
1931   *10¼in (26cm) high*
$12,000-15,000   **L&T**

A Lalique "Terpsichore" vase, no. 10-911, clear and frosted, stenciled "R. LALIQUE FRANCE."
1937   *12¾in (32.3cm) high*
$17,000-21,000   **L&T**

A Lalique "Tourbillons" vase, no.973, on a patinated bronze base, stenciled "R. LALIQUE FRANCE."
1926   *8¾in (22.2cm) high*
$9,000-10,500   **L&T**

A Lalique "Tuileries" vase, no.1053, cobalt blue, stenciled "R. LALIQUE."
1930   *10¾in (27.8cm) high*
$12,000-15,000   **L&T**

A Lalique "Coq Nain" car mascot, no.1135, topaz, molded "R. LALIQUE FRANCE."
1928   *8in (20.3cm) high*
$2,600-3,300   **L&T**

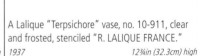

A Lalique "Victoire" car mascot, no.1147, on later ebonized mount, molded "R. LALIQUE FRANCE."
1928   *10¼in (26cm) long*
$10,500-12,000   **L&T**

ESSENTIAL REFERENCE—LOETZ

In 1836, in Klostermüle, Bohemia, Johann Baptist Eisner founded a glassworks that, in 1840, was acquired by glass entrepreneur and maker Johann Loetz. Upon his death in 1851, the factory was taken over by his widow, Susanne Gerstner-Loetz, and became known as Loetz Witwe (Loetz Widow) until 1879. At this point, the factory was taken over by Loetz's grandson, Max Ritter von Spaun, the name returned to just Loetz, and it began to expand significantly to the point that, by the late 19thC and during the early 20thC, it had become one of the greatest and most influential glassworks of central Europe. Fueling this, primarily in the Art Nouveau style, were organic forms, innovative techniques and finishes (notably iridescence), and the bold use of color by designers, such von Spaun, Franz Hofstätter, Maria Kirschner, Michael Powolny, Koloman Moser, and Josef Hoffmann. The Loetz factory finally closed in 1947.

A Loetz hand-blown glass "Phänomen" vase, (Gre 8058).
ca. 1899　　　*10in (25cm) high*
$4,000-4,600　　　**DRA**

A Loetz hand-blown glass and brass "Phänomen" candleholder, (Gre 358).
ca. 1900　　　*7½in (19cm) high*
$4,000-5,300　　　**DRA**

A Loetz "Phänomen" hand-blown glass vase, (Gre 6893), etched signature on underside "Loetz Austria."
ca. 1898　　　*9¾in (25cm) high*
$1,700-2,100　　　**DRA**

A Loetz hand-blown glass vase (Ausf 102), with applied details.
ca. 1900　　　*6¾in (17cm) high*
$4,600-5,300　　　**DRA**

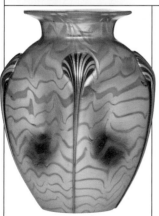

A Loetz hand-blown glass "Phänomen" vase, (Gre 1/78), etched signature on underside "Loetz Austria."
ca. 1901　　　*6in (15cm) high*
$4,000-4,600　　　**DRA**

A Loetz "Phänomen" hand-blown glass vase, (Gre 1/78), etched on underside "Loetz Austria."
ca. 1901　　　*8in (20cm) high*
$4,600-5,300　　　**DRA**

A Loetz May-Green "Cytisus" hand-blown glass vase.
ca. 1902　　　*7in (18cm) diam*
$2,000-2,600　　　**DRA**

A Loetz hand-blown glass "Tango" vase, by Michael Powolny.
ca. 1914　　　*7¼in (18cm) high*
$1,700-2,100　　　**DRA**

A Moncrieff's Monart Ware cloisonné vase, shape L, scarlet red liner, surface decorated with luster, white crackled design, collection label on base.

9¾in (24.5cm) high

$650-800   **WW**

A rare Moncrieff's Monart Ware surface decorated vase, model AVD31, applied collection paper label.

10in (25.5cm) high

$1,600-2,100   **WW**

A Moncrieff's Monart Ware glass table lamp, with metal fittings, unsigned.

11in (28cm) high

$2,600-3,300   **WW**

A 1930s Monart glass vase, shape JF.

11½in (29cm) high

$550-650   **FLD**

A 1930s Monart glass box and cover, shape DC, retains original paper label.

5½in (14cm) diam

$750-850   **FLD**

A 1930s Monart glass vase, shape OF, with vertical pull-up pattern over an opal interior.

11in (28cm) high

$800-850   **FLD**

A 1930s Monart glass vase, shape EA, decorated with gray enamel paisley swirls over a mottled celadon ground.

11½in (29cm) high

$1,300-1,800   **FLD**

A 1930s Monart stoneware cloisonné glass vase, shape MF, retains part of original paper label.

9½in (24cm) high

$1,600-2,100   **FLD**

A 1930s Monart cloisonné stoneware glass vase, shape C.

8in (20cm) high

$800-900   **FLD**

A 1930s Monart "Paisley Shawl" glass vase, shape FA.

9½in (24cm) high

$1,200-1,600   **FLD**

A 1930s Monart stoneware glass vase, shape A, with mottled silver diagonal bands over the mottled ocher ground.

9in (23cm) high

$1,300-1,800   **FLD**

A Tiffany Studios hand-blown Favrile glass vase, etched signature on underside "L.C.T. E1801."

ca. 1896   *12½in (32cm) high*

$24,000-29,000   **DRA**

A Tiffany Studios vase, with leaves and vines, of hand-blown Favrile glass, featuring a rare color combination with black on the exterior and blue and purple on the interior, etched signature and number to underside "L.C.T. o435."

ca. 1896   *7¼in (18cm) high*

$4,000-5,300   **DRA**

A Tiffany Studios paperweight vase, of hand-blown Favrile glass, numbered on underside "U5175."

ca. 1900   *4in (10cm) high*

$8,000-9,000   **DRA**

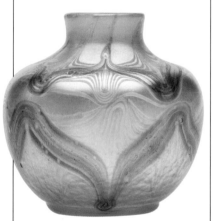

A Tiffany Studios vase, of hand-blown Favrile glass, etched signature and number on underside "L.C.T. Q9313."

ca. 1902   *3¾in (10cm) high*

$3,300-4,000   **DRA**

A Tiffany Studios vase, of hand-blown Favrile glass, etched signature and number on underside "L.C.T. Q6035."

ca. 1902   *7¼in (18cm) high*

$3,300-4,000   **DRA**

A Tiffany Studios miniature hand-blown Favrile glass vase, etched signature on underside "L.C.T. T3291."

ca. 1903   *2½in (6cm) high*

$2,000-2,600   **DRA**

A Tiffany Studios floriform vase, of hand-blown Favrile glass, etched signature on underside "L.C.T. Favrile."

ca. 1910   *14½in (37cm) high*

$1,700-2,600   **DRA**

A rare Tiffany Studios "Aquamarine" vase, of internally decorated hand-blown Favrile glass, etched signature and number on underside "L.C.T. 1610J."

ca. 1915   *10½in (27cm) high*

$16,000-21,000   **DRA**

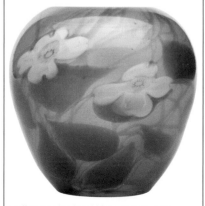

A Tiffany Studios hand-blown Favrile glass paperweight vase, etched signature on underside "L.C. Tiffany Favrile 3580P."

ca. 1921   *4¾in (12cm) high*

$6,500-8,000   **DRA**

DECORATIVE ARTS

A Gabriel Argy-Rousseau pâte-de-verre glass "Fern" coupe, catalog no.27.19, the twin handles modeled as fern fronds, signed in the cast "G. Argy-Rousseau" on the rim.

8in (20cm) wide

$6,000-7,500   **WW**

A Gabriel Argy-Rousseau pâte-de-verre glass vase, "Primroses," signed "G. Argy-Rousseau" on side and "France" on base.

6¾in (17.2cm) high

$5,300-6,600   **WW**

A Charles Catteau glass vase, produced by Scallmont, Belgium, signed.

ca. 1925   *8¾in (22cm) high*

$160-210   **BELL**

A rare and tall James Couper and Sons Clutha glass "Propeller" vase, designed by Dr. Christopher Dresser, acid-etched Liberty Lotus flower mark on base.

11in (28.5cm) high

$10,000-11,000   **WW**

An Art Nouveau Guerchet silver-mounted enameled glass vase, the silver foot cast in low relief with foliage spray rising to overlay the body with violet flower stems, the glass body enameled with violets, highlighted in gilt, stamped "Guerchet" on foot.

4¾in (12cm) high

$1,300-1,800   **WW**

An Islamic-style gilded and enameled Bohemian glass vase, by Fritz Heckert, with three calligraphic Kufic script roundels, inscribed "F. H. 504/11 arab I."

ca. 1895   *8in (20cm) high*

$900-1,050   **SWO**

An Art Nouveau Kralik iridescent molded glass bowl, mounted with pewter mounts, the handles formed as leaves, unsigned, worn base rim on the pewter.

10¼in (26cm) diam

$450-600   **SWO**

An early-20thC Kralik glass vase, on an iron stand, base rusted.

12½in (32cm) high

$400-450   **SWO**

A Moser amber glass vase, engraved with a stag and tree, etched mark, in a fitted box.

14in (35.5cm) high

$550-650   **CHOR**

An ARS Murano glass Aquarium vase, by Elio Raffaeli, depicting fish and an octopus amit coral, seaweed, and bubbles, etched "ARS" mark and script artist's mark on base.

11½in (29.25cm) high

$1,300-1,800   **MART**

A James Powell & Sons Whitefriars Mount Carmel sea green glass vase, applied with blue threaded decoration, unsigned.

Wendy Evans "Whitefriars Glass Museum of London," p. 272, bottom right illustration includes a line drawing of a comparable vase found in a tomb at Mount Carmel and another in the British Museum (Bungay), which inspired this Powell design.

5in (12.5cm) high

$850-1,000   **WW**

A James Powell & Sons Whitefriars Minoan glass vase, unsigned.

8¾in (22cm) high

$350-450   **WW**

A 1920s Charles Schneider "Rubaniers" glass vase, with stylized hanging garlands, etched mark, "Le Verre Francais" on underside.

11½in (29cm) wide

$600-750 BELL

A Quezel hand-blown glass vase, etched signature on underside "Quezel J 392."

ca. 1910 *8¼in (21cm) high*

$2,600-3,300 DRA

A Quezel hand-blown glass "Jack-in-the-Pulpit" vase, etched signature on underside "Quezel V 19."

ca. 1910 *13¾in (35cm) high*

$4,600-5,300 DRA

A Schneider glass tazza, with a mottled orange and yellow bowl and stem, with purple pronts, etched "Schneider France."

7in (18cm) diam

$1,200-1,600 SWO

A Steuben Shelton vase, of acid-etched gold aurene over alabaster glass.

ca. 1928 *11¾in (30cm) high*

$6,000-6,600 DRA

A Steuben sculptured Chrysanthemum vase, of acid-etched opal over green cintra glass, acid-etched manufacturer's mark near base "Steuben" with fleur-de-lis.

ca. 1925 *13in (33cm) high*

$4,600-5,300 DRA

A Thomas Webb (Stourbridge) cameo glass vase, decorated with butterflies around flowering rose sprays, the reverse with two large butterflies and a spray of heather, molded mark on the underside.

ca. 1880-90 *7¾in (19.5cm) high*

$2,100-2,600 WW

A Thomas Webb & Sons claret pitcher, wheel engraved on the front with a scene of Venus rising from the sea, the border and handle terminals with shells, the reverse with an open viewing roundel.

ca. 1880 *10¾in (27cm) high*

$4,600-5,300 CHOR

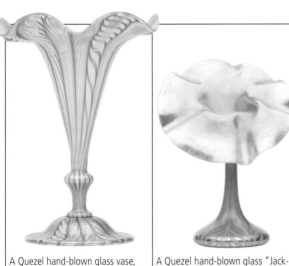

A late-19thC important cameo glass vase, by George Woodall, owned by the artist, the figure subject representing the myth of Fielea and Ariston, Cupid encouraging the maiden to sketch the silhouette of her Corinthian lover on the wall as a permanent reminder of his youthful beauty, the reverse with an artist's palette and brush, signed "Geo Woodall" and titled on the underside.

9in (23cm) high

$260,000-330,000 BON

A set of three mid-20thC American Art Deco frosted glass, silver overlay, and silver-plate mounted liquor decanters, bodies with silvered overlay and labels for "SCOTCH," "RYE," and "BOURBON," two with partial makers labels for the National Silver Deposit Ware Co., New York.

13in (33cm) high

$2,000-2,600 L&T

A pair of enameled glass decanters, enameled with mounted riders, horses, and hounds.

ca. 1930 *11in (28cm) high*

$1,600-2,100 L&T

A late-Victorian Aesthetic Movement oak hall stand, in the manner of James Shoolbred, with brass mounts, with a brass trade label, inscribed "George Davis Plymouth cabinet maker and upholsterer."

39¼in (99.5cm) high

$1,700-2,100   WW

A pair of late-19thC Aesthetic Movement gray-painted and parcel giltwood stools, probably American, marks, knocks, scratches, abrasions.

19¾in (50cm) high

$1,300-1,800   DN

An Émile Gallé "Aux Grenouilles" umbrella stand, of mahogany, fruitwood, rosewood, bronze, and tin, featuring cast-bronze frog handles, marquetry, carved panels of pond foliage, and frog leg-shaped feet, inlaid signature "Gallé."

ca. 1900   29in (74cm) high

$20,000-26,000   DRA

An Art Nouveau Émile Gallé marquetry wall shelf, marquetry inlaid with a coastal tree panel flanked by flower stems, marquetry signature Gallé.

24½in (62cm) high

$4,600-5,300   WW

A Louis Majorelle (1859-1926) marquetry and carved Coiffeuse, the mirror frame inlaid in various woods with narcissi and ferns, with shelves for candles with leaflike supports, the top inlaid with ferns and bees, having a frieze drawer with bronze handles with rose terminals.

ca. 1900   50in (125.5cm) high

$4,600-5,900   ROS

A John Pearson Liberty & Co. mahogany settle, the top centered with a copper-embossed panel of a galleon, signed "J.P 95."

64¾in (164.5cm) high

$4,000-5,300   SWO

An Eugène Gaillard pearwood and Fortuny silk upholstery settee.

ca. 1911   54in (137cm) wide

$15,000-17,000   DRA

Judith Picks

To my mind, perhaps the most admirable quality of the eminent turn-of-the 20thC Italian "Stile Liberty" (Art Nouveau) designer Carlo Bugatti (1855-1940) is the sheer distinctiveness of his work. Presented with a piece of his furniture (he also designed metalware, textiles, and ceramics), it's almost impossible to think it might have been conceived by anyone else. Bugatti drew for inspiration on nature, on traditional Moorish, Egyptian, and Japanese vocabularies of art and ornament, and also on the writings of the 19thC French architect Eugène Viollet-le-Duc (1814-79), and I think it's the adoption of le-Duc's ideas on the use of decorative elements to draw attention to the structure of a piece, instead of to disguise it, that underpins the uniqueness

of "Bugatti style." This splendid walnut cabinet is a case in point, in which step-cut profiles emphasize the feet and are echoed above in stepped and ebonized wooden applications on the tops of the doors and side panels above. Similarly, inlaid and hammered brass and pewter decoration emphasizes the rectangular frame of the carcass, while elaborate brass hinges pointedly reveal instead of disguise how the doors are hung, and a large, inlaid circular roundel with brass center that spans the doors further serves to emphasize the overtly geometric construction of what can only be a Bugatti cabinet.

A walnut, ebonized wood, pewter and brass inlaid, and hammered brass cabinet, by Carlo Bugatti.

ca. 1900   38in (96cm) high

$20,000-26,000   ROS

An early-20thC Art Nouveau glazed mahogany display cabinet, the raised back over an inlaid front, the glazed door set with stained glass and opalescent glass flower heads.

71in (180cm) high

$800-900   SWO

ESSENTIAL REFERENCE—BRYNMAWR FURNITURE MAKERS

Brynmawr Furniture Makers Ltd was a furniture manufacturing company established during the Great Depression as part of the "Brynmawr Experiment" in Brynmawr, Wales. Following the industrial relations general strike of 1926, Brynmawr was particularly badly affected, suffering high levels of unemployment, with attendant financial and social deprivation. In an attempt to tackle these problems, a small Quaker-led group, led by Peter Scott, arrived in Brynmawr in 1928-29, initialy to provide nutritional and medical relief supplies, and establish a system of social care, but thereafter to encourage new industries and employment. Brynmawr Furniture Makers Ltd was part of this new enterprise, which included at the outset knitting, weaving, and boot-making companies, and the factory made furniture until 1939.

An Arts and Crafts oak wardrobe, by Brynmawr Furniture Makers Ltd., opening to reveal two sections with shelves, over a hanging space with a shoe rack, with five drawers on the right-hand side, the door fixed with a mirror and tie rail, unmarked.

69¼in (176cm) high

$3,300-4,000   **SWO**

An Arthur Romney Green (1872-1945) oak refectory table.
ca. 1930   *70in (178cm) long*
$2,600-4,000   **SWO**

A walnut dressing table, designed by Stanley Webb Davies and made by craftsman Ernest John Oldcorn, signed with monograms.
1934   *64¼in (163cm) high*
$4,000-4,600   **SWO**

A Keverne Dewick oak refectory table.

In 1986, Keverne Dewick was inspired at the Cambridge Folk Festival by a man making guitars. He went on to set up with Aubrey Hammond, an Edward Barnsley-trained turner and furniture maker. He works from his workshop and studio at Alby Craft Centre in North Norfolk. This refectory table was made by him for a client in Norfolk.
150¼in (381.5cm) wide
$4,000-4,600   **SWO**

A set of seven Arts and Crafts oak dining chairs, attributed to W. R. Lethaby (1857-1931) for Morris & Co. or Liberty.

Lethaby was an influential 19thC architectural historian who worked as an assistant to Richard Norman Shaw from 1879-90.
ca. 1900
$6,000-6,600   **CHOR**

An Arts and Crafts Liberty & Co. wall-hanging bookshelf, with a stenciled motto on the front of the shelf "Choose An Author As You Choose A Friend," the cupboard with an embossed copper panel centered with a dragonfly, with a Liberty label.
ca. 1895   *31½in (80cm) wide*
$800-900   **SWO**

An Arts and Crafts oak settle, in the style of Liberty.
46in (117cm) wide
$2,000-2,600   **SWO**

A Liberty & Co. oak hall stand, the back inlaid with copper and green ceramic tile panel below a mirror.
76½in (194cm) high
$6,000-6,600   **WW**

An Austrian Arts and Crafts stool, designed by Adolf Loos.
14½in (37cm) high
$1,300-1,800   **SWO**

Judith Picks

Some "signatures" are simply grander than others—take a look at any document bearing that of, for example, Queen Elizabeth I of England (1533-1603) and you'll instantly see what I mean— and some are simply of more humble appearance, and yet are no less distinctive for that. They can also be, like the carved mouse "signature" found on the hand-crafted wooden pieces of the English, Yorkshire-born, cabinet maker Robert

"Mouseman" Thompson (1876-1955), more endearing—it purportedly originated early in his career, when he described himself as being "as poor as a church mouse." Equally endearing is the tradition it established; several of the craftsmen who trained under the "Mouseman" went on, as cabinet makers in their own right, to sign their pieces with a carved animal. They include: Malcolm "Foxman" Pipes; Wilf "Squirrelman" Hutchinson; Graham "Swanman" Duncalf; and Peter "Rabbitman."

An Arts and Crafts glazed oak bookcase, labeled "Arthur W Simpson The Handicrafts Kendal" and stamped "8919," with key.

45½in (115.5cm) high

$3,300-4,000　　SWO

A rare pair of Robert "Mouseman" Thompson oak bookends, in the form of elephants, one with a recessed carved signature of a mouse.

6¾in (17cm) high

$18,000-24,000　　LC

ESSENTIAL REFERENCE—C. F. A. VOYSEY (1857-1941)

Charles Francis Annesley Voysey, was educated at Dulwich College and was a prolific architect-designer within the Arts and Crafts Movement. An undistinguished academic at college, Voysey later claimed he became an architect because it was "the only profession for which one did not need to pass any examinations." Beginning his career in 1881, he first established himself as a designer of furniture, textiles, and wallpapers. Winning his first building commissions in 1890, he quickly earned a reputation as a master of artistic cottages and modern country houses. He paid meticulous attention to detail, designing every aspect of a project, down to the door hinges. Voysey regularly exhibited watercolor elevations of his building projects, furniture, and decorative designs at the Royal Academy, and he is celebrated today as one of the leading British designers of the turn of the 20thC. The simple design, personified by a heart motif on the back of a chair, is one of Voysey's best known furniture designs. F. C. Nielsen, who made other furniture that Voysey designed, made these chairs from 1902 in differing proportions. One tell-tale detail is the dovetail construction attaching the splat to the frame. Versions of this chair can be seen in major collections around the world with leather or rush drop-in seats. Voysey had a limited number of designs that he used, but in many of his plans for interiors, this model appears often— his mantra for his furniture being a "sense of proportion and puritanical love of simplicity."

A pair of rare Arts and Crafts oak armchairs, by C. F. A. Voysey, each with leather and studded drop-in seats, one chair is split on the splat panel above and below the heart shape, right arm has been reset.

ca. 1902　　*39½in (100.5cm) high*

$33,000-40,000　　SWO

An Arts and Crafts oak-framed throne armchair, by Arthur Simpson of Kendal, with an incised motto on the back panel "It is the mind, that makes the body rich!."

ca. 1910　　*51¼in (130cm) high*

$4,000-5,300　　SWO

A Swedish Arts and Crafts oak lounger chair, with retractable back and ottoman, reupholstered.

78¾in (200cm) long

$650-800　　SWO

A Charles Frances Annesley Voysey oak table, for the Essex and Suffolk Equitable Insurance Society, Capel House, possibly made by F. C. Nielsen.

53¼in (135cm) long

$13,000-18,000　　WW

A Peter Waals sycamore highboy.

1927　　*56¾in (144cm) high*

$6,500-8,000　　SWO

An Arts and Crafts copper wall mirror, with embossed decoration and "Omnia Vanitas" ("All is Vanity") on the panel above the mirror.

33in (84cm) high

$1,200-1,600　　SWO

ESSENTIAL REFERENCE—GUSTAV STICKLEY

Designer and furniture maker Gustav Stickley (1858-1942) was one of the leading figures in and proponents of the American Arts and Crafts Movement.

- After training at his uncle's Pennsylvania chair factory, he founded the Stickley Brothers Chair Co. with his brothers Albert and Charles, in 1883, eventually leaving to form his own company in Eastwood, New York, in 1898; the latter closed in 1915.
- Although strongly influenced by the work of William Morris and the English Arts and Crafts Movement, unlike the latter, who focused on hand-crafting, Stickley utilized machines to manufacture his original designs, which enabled him to produce them in greater numbers and be more affordable.
- At the height of his success, Stickley's furniture sold throughout the United States, promoted, in no small part, by his publication of the "Craftsman" magazine.

An early Gustav Stickley writing table, model 417, of oak, leather, and brass.

ca. 1901   *48½in (123cm) wide*

$10,000-10,500   **DRA**

A Gustav Stickley knock-down settle, model 210, of oak, rope, and linen, early red manufacturer's decal on interior of seat stretcher "Als Ik Kan Stickley" with joiner's compass.

ca. 1904   *84½in (215cm) wide*

$12,000-15,000   **DRA**

A Gustav Stickley knock-down settle, model 210, oak with vinyl upholstery, with early red manufacturer's decal on upright "Als Ik Kan Stickley" with joiner's compass.

ca. 1902   *82¼in (209cm) wide*

$16,000-18,000   **DRA**

A Gustav Stickley double-door bookcase, model 544, of oak, glass, and copper, with early red manufacturer's decal to reverse "Als Ik Kan Stickley," with joiner's compass.

ca. 1902   *61in (155cm) wide*

$5,300-6,600   **DRA**

A Gustav Stickley oak tea table, model 604, early red manufacturer's decal on underside "Als Ik Kan Gustav Stickley," with joiner's compass.

1903-04   *26¼in (67cm) high*

$2,600-3,300   **DRA**

A Gustav Stickley drop-arm Morris chair, model 369, of oak and leather, with red manufacturer's decal on leg "Als Ik Kan Gustav Stickley" with joiner's compass.

1905-12   *40¼in (102cm) high*

$4,600-5,900   **DRA**

A Gustav Stickley sideboard, model 809, of oak and copper, paper manufacturer's label on reverse "No. 809 The Craftsman Workshops Gustav Stickley Designed and Made by Gustav Stickley Eastwood, N.Y."

1905-07   *53¼in (135cm) wide*

$6,500-8,000   **DRA**

A Gustav Stickley oak and hammered copper music cabinet, model 70W, remnants of paper manufacturer's label on back "Craftsman," branded signature on back "Stickley," with joiner's compass.

1912-16   *47¼in (120cm) high*

$6,500-8,000   **DRA**

A Gustav Stickley oak and patinated brass sideboard, model 814, applied distributor's label "From the Robert Mitchell Furniture Co. Cincinnati" over remnants of paper manufacturer's label "Craftsman Trademarks Reg'd Als Ik Kan Stickley" with joiner's compass.

1912-16   *66in (168cm) wide*

$5,300-6,600   **DRA**

An L. & J.G. Stickley oak, hammered copper, and glass cabinet, model 729, with decal manufacturer's label on interior "L. & J.G. Stickley Handcraft."

1907-12   70in (178cm) high

$13,000-18,000   **DRA**

An L. & J.G. Stickley oak dining table, with eight 11-in (28cm) leaves, decal manufacturer's label on underside "The Work of L. & J.G. Stickley."

1912-20   142in (360.5cm) wide when extended

$3,300-4,000   **DRA**

An L. & J.G. Stickley drop-arm Morris chair, model 410, of oak and leather, red manufacturer's decal on reverse "L&JG Stickley Handcraft" with joiner's compass.

1906-12   39½in (100cm) high

$6,500-8,000   **DRA**

A Charles Sumner Greene and Henry Mather Greene stained mahogany and velvet rocking chair, from the Dr. William T. Bolton-T. Belle Barlow Bush House, Pasadena, carved signature on underside "His True Mark Sumner Greene."

ca. 1907   37in (94cm) high

$33,000-40,000   **DRA**

A Limbert oak library table, paper manufacturer's label on underside "Limbert Arts Crafts Furniture Made in Grand Rapids Michigan."

ca. 1906   35¾in (91cm) wide

$2,000-2,600   **DRA**

A Limbert double-door bookcase, model 356, of oak, glass, and brass, applied manufacturer's label on verso "Limberts Arts and Crafts Furniture Trademark Made in Grand Rapids and Holland."

ca. 1910   51½in (131cm) wide

$20,000-26,000   **DRA**

A Frank Lloyd Wright oak and leather chair, from the Francis Little House, Peoria.

1913-15   30in (76cm) high

$8,000-9,000   **DRA**

A Charles Rohlfs oak chair, with carved signature and date on underside "R 1902."

1902   44in (112cm) high

$9,000-10,500   **DRA**

A Roycroft oak, leaded glass, and copper cabinet, model 55, carved orb and cross mark on escutcheon plate.

ca. 1905   40in (102cm) high

$21,000-26,000   **DRA**

A Roycroft Morris chair, model 43, of oak, leather, and enameled metal, incised manufacturer's mark on front of seat "Roycroft."

ca. 1906   42½in (108cm) high

$13,000-15,000   **DRA**

An Alvar Aalto "Tank" model 400 armchair, with original brown zigzag seat and back, stamped "105" on the underside.

1936   *26¾in (68cm) high*

$4,600-5,900   **SWO**

An Alvar Aalto 1930s Finnish Type 21 chair, of molded plywood with orange paint, Finmar label.

$3,300-4,600   **CHOR**

A Ruth Campbell vanity and stool, of lacquered wood, mirrored glass, upholstery, gilt metal, and brass, the vanity featuring two drawers, painted signature and date on stool "Ruth Campbell 1928."

1928   *68¼in (173cm) high*

$6,500-8,000   **DRA**

ESSENTIAL REFERENCE—JULES LELEU

Jules Leleu (1883-1961) was born into a family of artisans and artists in Boulogne-sur-Mer in Northern France and was one of the fathers of French Art Deco design. Although he "never achieved the international fame of Jacques-Émile Ruhlmann, Jean Michel Frank, or Le Corbusier," the "New York Times" once wrote, "he was just as successful and probably more prolific than his better-known contemporaries." Leleu exhibited at the prestigious Exposition des Arts Decoratifs in 1925, for which he designed the chairs for the Grand Salon and the Music Room, both part of the French Embassy Exhibition, and also exhibited a complete suite of furniture in his own space on the Esplanade des Invalides. He won a Grand Prize at the 1925 Exposition, and one of his pieces was purchased by the Metropolitan Museum in New York City. Often compared with the furniture designs of Ruhlmann, Leleu's chairs, tables, and cabinets emphasized simple shapes, exotic woods and marquetry, inlaid ivory, and other embellishments. Because these techniques had been brought to France from Asia, Leleu employed Asian craftspeople for this work. Hamanaka, one of the great masters of lacquer work, and the famed Jean Dunand, who had learned the skills from Hamanaka, collaborated with Leleu on pieces where lacquer was an element. Leleu was prolific and was constantly evolving and developing his styles. The awards that he won brought him many important clients and commissions, including the ocean liners "Ile de France" and the famed and ill-fated "Normandie." Among other important commissions were a dining room for the Elysée Palace, and, later on, the Grand Salon des Ambassadeurs at La Societé des Nations in Geneva, called the Salon Leleu, and is still in existence.

An Art Deco burl-walnut veneer cocktail cabinet, probably Epstein, of L'Odeon form, with two center twin-door fitted cabinets, the top compartment with electric light, fitted with suite of glasses, decanters, cocktail shaker, and tray, unsigned, one glass missing.

60¼in (153cm) high

$5,300-6,600   **WW**

An Art Deco walnut and bird's-eye maple cocktail cabinet, probably by Epstein, some knocks on the edges.

63in (160cm) high

$4,600-5,900   **SWO**

An Art Deco Jules Leleu sycamore parquetry cabinet, with four cupboards, inlaid with pewter, flanked with plain capitals and columns, stamped "21667" and signed on one of the center doors, knocked edges, one bronze capital missing, no keys.

74½in (189.5cm) wide

$3,300-4,600   **SWO**

An Art Deco Jules Leleu "Feux d'artifice" ("Fireworks") rosewood and marquetry commode, inlaid with rosewood, ebony, and mother-of-pearl marquetry flowers, some veneer losses.

74¾in (190cm) wide

$80,000-90,000   **SWO**

An Art Deco Jules Leleu rosewood and marquetry cocktail cabinet, the stepped top over a parquetry and marquetry inlaid fall-front cupboard, with ebony and mother-of-pearl flowers, enclosing a blonde wood and mirrored interior, signed and stamped "23997."

52½in (133.5cm) high

$7,500-8,500   **SWO**

A Bruno Mathsson lounge chair, model 36, for Firma Karl Mathsson, of beech, birch, and webbing, decal manufacturer's labels "Bruno Mathsson Firma Karl Mathsson Made in - Värnamo - Sweden" and "Bruno Mathsson Mobler."

ca. 1936   *60in (152cm) long*

$3,300-4,600   **DRA**

An Art Deco G. Pion patinated wrought iron table, the frame with inset black-veined marble top and lower shelf, stamped "G Pion, SGDC."

30in (76cm) high

$750-850   WW

An Art Deco macassar ebony games table, in the manner of Émile-Jacques Ruhlmann, the baize-inset top over four pull-out slides, raised on silvered reeded baluster legs.

37in (94cm) wide

$2,600-4,000   SWO

An "Egyptomania" gilt metal-mounted hardwood chair, after an 18th Dynasty model found in the tomb of Tutankhamun, bone-inlaid and parcel gilt, with a carved panel of the god Heh above a double-curved seat with uraei styles and intertwined plants between tapestry lion-paw feet.

On November 5, 1922, Howard Carter, leader of Lord Carnarvon's archaeological expedition, discovered the location of the tomb of the Egyptian pharaoh Tutankhamun. Although some tomb robbing was evident, it remains the best preserved and most complete tomb in the Valley of the Kings. News of Carter's discoveries—which consisted not only of the mummified pharoah himself, but also a wealth of decorative objects and furniture that were kept with him for use in the afterlife—quickly spread, resulting in a resurgence in popularity for all things Egyptian. Harry Burton, the only photographer granted access to the tomb and whose archive is held by the Griffith Institute at the Ashmolean Museum, Oxford, made it possible to circulate images of what they found. This is a copy of models the team discovered, which are illustrated and discussed in Hollis S Baker, "Furniture in the Ancient World," London, 1966, pp. 75-84.

ca. 1925   *20in (50cm) wide*

$17,000-24,000   SWO

A Peter Waals small ebony and macassar desk-top cabinet, with painted decoration by Louise Powell, with shallow domed top, twin hinged ebony doors set with macassar panels painted with simple foliate band and center red flower wreath, opening to nine small drawers, all with painted white and red flower panels, the interior of the doors profusely painted with red flowers, on sleigh feet, one drawer with paper label No.L92 in the catalog of C.H. St J.Hornby.

Provenance: Charles Harold St John Hornby (1867-1946), Chantmarle House, Dorset. St John Hornby, as he was widely known, was both a successful businessman and a private printer. In 1919, Hornby bought Chantmarle in Dorset, a fine but remodeled house that had started life out as a manor house for the monks of Milton Abbey in the 13thC. It was here that Hornby commissioned the Barnsleys, Powells, and Waals to furnish his new house, and an article in "Country Life" of July 7, 1950, shows a number of pieces of furniture by both Ernest and Sidney Barnsley as well as a set of plates by the Powells illustrating aspects of Hornby's life and interests. The same article also states "The products of the Gimson-Barnsley school are little heard of today, but by breaking with traditional forms and concentrating on simplicity of design, fine finish, and beautiful woods, they anticipated in their hand-made pieces several of the ideals of later designers who have accepted the aid of the machine."

18in (46cm) wide.

$33,000-40,000   WW

A pair of Art Deco Waring & Gillows beech, yew, and upholstered saloon armchairs, from Cunard White Line liner RMS "Mauretania II."

$450-600   WHP

An Art Deco walnut corner dressing table.

68¼in (173cm) wide

$450-600   SWO

A French Art Deco lacquered "Japonesque" four-fold screen, of cloud design, painted with lillies, the reverse decorated in gilt with painted Chinese symbols with citrus fingers, lily pads, leafy bamboo, butterflies, auspicious items, and calligraphy.

84¼in (214cm) high

$17,000-24,000   DUK

An Art Deco Madagascan ebony desk, the back fitted with a bookcase enclosed with glass sliding panels, some wear, one key.

ca. 1928   *63¼in (160.5cm) wide*

$3,300-4,600   SWO

An Art Deco burl0walnut serpentine sideboard, the front opening to reveal a mirrored and shelved interior, with a glass side over a drawer, flanked with further cupboards enclosing a drawer and a shelf, repolished and restored.

70in (178cm) wide

$5,300-6,600   SWO

ESSENTIAL REFERENCE—REFORMED GOTHIC

Reformed Gothic was an Aesthetic Movement style of the 1860s and 1870s in architecture, furniture, and decorative arts that was popular in Great Britain and the United States. A rebellion against the excessive ornament of Second Empire and Rococo Revival furniture, it advocated simplicity and honesty of construction and ornament derived from nature. Unlike the Gothic Revival, it sought not to copy Gothic designs, but to adapt them, abstract them, and apply them to new forms.

● The style's leading advocates were English designers Christopher Dresser and Charles Eastlake. Eastlake's "Hints on Household Taste, Upholstery, and Other Details," published in England in 1868 and in the United States in 1872, was one of the most influential decorating manuals of the Victorian period. The Eastlake movement argued that furniture and decor in people's homes should be made by hand or by machine workers who took personal pride in their work. Eastlake lectured in the United States in 1876.

A rare Bruce Talbert Reformed Gothic brass mantel clock, probably manufactured by Cox & Co or Hart, Son, Peard & Co, unsigned.

10¾in (27cm) high

$4,000-4,600 WW

An Arts and Crafts C. F. A. Voysey (1857-1941) oak architectural clock, the dial inlaid with pewter letters "Tempus fugit," enclosing a simple clock movement with striker and pendulum, replaced movement.

The architectural form of the piece demonstrates Voysey's belief in simplicity of decoration without which, he said, "no true richness is possible."

ca. 1902   19¾in (50cm) high

$16,000-20,000 SWO

An early-20thC Arts and Crafts Thomas Justice & Sons mantel clock, of oak, patinated hammered copper, patinated meta,l and enamel, inscribed "Maneo Nemini" or "I wait for no one," metal manufacturer's label on verso.

14¾in (37cm) high

$4,000-5,300 DRA

A Liberty & Co. Tudric pewter timepiece, in the style of Archibald Knox (1864-1933), with simple French movement, stamped "Tudric" and numbered "072" on the base.

5½in (14cm) high

$2,600-3,300 APAR

A Liberty & Co. Cymric silver carriage clock, maker's mark for Liberty & Co. Ltd., Birmingham, model no. 5508, engraved with feathered and flower details.

1918   3½in (9cm) high

$3,300-4,600 SWO

A Tudric pewter and enamel clock, designed by Archibald Knox for Liberty & Co., stamped "0369," with brass key, movement stamped "Lenzkirch" and numbered 517044.

7¾in (19.3cm) high

$5,300-6,600 SWO

An Art Nouveau silver-mounted mantel clock, Birmingham.

1909   12½in (32cm) high

$1,100-1,250 SWO

An Art Deco alabaster-mounted clock, two front feet missing.

20½in (52cm) wide

$400-450 SWO

An Art Deco spelter and marble-mounted mantel clock, mounted on one side with a lady and a greyhound, inscribed "E. Bourgedi/ Doudeville," stamped on the plinth "Menneville."

21¾in (55cm) wide

$850-1,000 SWO

DECORATIVE ARTS

A Doulton Lambeth stoneware oil lamp, by Mark V Marshall, incised with a Chinese figure and dragon, impressed and incised marks.

1883   *25½in (65cm) high*
$1,300-1,800   **WW**

An Émile Gallé "Nicotiana" table lamp, of acid-etched cameo glass and bronze, signed in cameo on base and shade "Gallé."

ca. 1900   *19¼in (49cm) high*
$8,000-9,000   **DRA**

An Art Nouveau Émile Gallé cameo glass table lamp and shade, decorated with dragonflies, cameo Gallé signature on shade and base.

                          14½in (37cm) high
$6,000-7,500   **WW**

A Charles Georges Ferville Suan (1847-1925) gilt-patinated bronze table lamp, modeled as a fairy reaching up to a dragonfly.

                          18½in (47cm) high
$2,000-2,600   **WW**

An early-20thC French Art Nouveau bronze cat table lamp, with pierced shade with green glass insert.

                          16½in (42cm) high
$3,300-4,600   **L&T**

An Art Nouveau Moritz Hacker (1849-1932) electroplated table lamp, with nautilus shell shade, model no.120, unsigned.

                          13½in (34.5cm) high
$2,600-4,000   **WW**

An Art Deco Bakelite lamp, with a molded compressed spherical shade.

                          16½in (42cm) high
$260-400   **SWO**

A Donald Deskey table lamp, for Deskey-Vollmer, Inc., of chrome-plated brass and steel and lacquered wood.

1930   *14in (36cm) high*
$16,000-21,000   **DRA**

A Daum Nancy acid-etched table lamp, amber glass shade with vertical acid-etched columns, wrought iron-mount shade signed "Daum & Nancy France."

                          26½in (67cm) high
$12,000-15,000   **WW**

A 1930s chrome standard lamp, with stepped inverted shade.

                          53¼in (135cm) high
$900-1,050   **FLD**

ESSENTIAL REFERENCE—TIFFANY STUDIOS

Tiffany Studios was originally established, in 1885, as the Tiffany Glass Company. Its founder, Louis Comfort Tiffany (1848-1933) was the son of one of the founders of Tiffany & Co., and had trained as an artist in both New York and Paris, before specializing in stained glass.

- **Specializing in decorative glassware, including creating and trademarking Favrile glass in 1893, Tiffany studios made its first Tiffany lamp in 1895, conceived by Clara Driscoll, one of the in-house designers.**
- **Typically in the Art Nouveau style, Tiffany lamps mostly comprise a leaded slag glass shade supported on a patinated metal base.**
- **Popular at the time, Tiffany lamps are still highly prized by collectors today, and can command exceptionally high prices.**

A Tiffany Studios "Dragonfly" table lamp, of Favrile glass, leaded glass, patinated bronze, brass, and quartz pebbles, with a rare Pumpkin base with pebble decoration, marked on shade "Tiffany Studios New York."

ca. 1898 — *18in (46cm) high*

$120,000-130,000 — DRA

A Tiffany Studios leaded glass and acid-etched gilt-bronze "Spider" table lamp, the spider shade and finial on a mushroom base, impressed manufacturer's mark "Tiffany Studios New York 337," metal manufacturer's label on shade "Tiffany Studios New York 1424."

1899-1920 — *17¼in (44cm) high*

$26,000-40,000 — DRA

A Tiffany Studios leaded glass and patinated bronze "Tulip" table lamp, impressed manufacturer's mark "Tiffany Studios New York 333," metal manufacturer's label on shade "Tiffany Studios New York 1535."

ca. 1910 — *19in (48cm) high*

$70,000-80,000 — DRA

A Tiffany Studios and Rookwood Pottery mushroom lamp, of leaded glass, glazed earthenware, and patinated bronze, marked on shade "Tiffany Studios New York 1548-6" and on ends of light switches "Tiffany Studios," impressed illegible flame mark and number "959D" on base.

1899-1920 — *18½in (47cm) high*

$20,000-26,000 — DRA

A Tiffany Studios 12-light "Lily" table lamp, of patinated bronze and Favrile glass, featuring a "Pond Lily" base, marked on each shade "L.C.T.," marked on base "Tiffany Studios 21817" with Tiffany Glass and Decorating Company trademark "TGDCO."

1899-1920 — *20in (51cm) high*

$37,000-42,000 — DRA

A Tiffany Studios "Autumn Leaf" table lamp, of patinated bronze, leaded, and ripple glass, with a library base colloquially known as an "onion" base, marked on shade "Tiffany Studios New York" and on base "Tiffany Studios New York 26374."

1899-1920 — *34in (86cm) high*

$33,000-40,000 — DRA

A Tiffany Studios "Turtleback" tile table lamp, of patinated bronze, Favrile glass, and leaded glass, featuring a "Crutch" base with "Turtleback" band, marked on shade "Tiffany Studios New York."

1899-1920 — *22in (56cm) high*

$46,000-53,000 — DRA

A Tiffany Studios "Daffodil" table lamp, of patinated bronze and leaded glass, featuring a "Crutch" base, marked on shade "Tiffany Studios New York" and on base "Tiffany Studios 444."

1899-1920 — *22in (56cm) high*

$26,000-33,000 — DRA

DECORATIVE ARTS

ESSENTIAL REFERENCE—THE HANDEL COMPANY

Established in Meriden, Connecticut, in 1885, Eydam and Handel became The Handel Company in 1903 when founder Philip J. Handel (1866-1914) bought out his partner Adolph Eydam.

- Handel is best known for its distinctive reverse-painted or enameled glass lampshades. Typical imagery includes flowers, birds, butterflies, and scenic views—both landscapes and seascapes.
- On Philip J. Handel's death in 1914, the company passed to his wife Fannie, and then to his cousin William H. Handel, prior to ceasing production in 1936.

A Handel wooded landscape table lamp, of patinated metal and obverse and reverse-painted acid-etched glass.

1914   *23in (58cm) high*
$5,300-6,600   **DRA**

A Handel table lamp, with wooded landscape, of obverse-painted, reverse-painted, and acid-etched glass and patinated metal, signed on shade "Handel 6230," impressed manufacturer's mark on shade ring "Handel Pat'd No. 979664."

1914   *22in (56cm) high*
$8,000-9,000   **DRA**

A Handel "Aquarium" lamp with mermaid base, of reverse-painted and acid-etched glass and patinated metal, signed on shade "Handel 6393," impressed manufacturer's mark on shade ring "Handel Lamps Pat'd No. 979664."

ca. 1915   *22in (56cm) high*
$26,000-40,000   **DRA**

A Handel "Sunset Landscape" table lamp, of patinated metal and reverse-painted acid-etched glass, signed "Handel 6534," stamped manufacturer's mark on shade ring "Handel Pat'd No. 979664."

1917   *24in (61cm) high*
$4,600-5,300   **DRA**

A Dirk van Erp table lamp, of patinated hammered copper and mica, impressed open-box windmill stamp on base and on underside of shade "Dirk Van Erp San Francisco."

ca. 1920   *21½in (55cm) high*
$13,000-18,000   **DRA**

An early-20thC Quezal table lamp, of patinated metal and hand-blown glass, etched manufacturer's mark "Quezal."

16in (41cm) high
$6,500-8,000   **DRA**

An early-20thC Roycroft hammered copper, mica, and brass table lamp, impressed orb and cross mark on body.

27in (69cm) high
$15,000-17,000   **DRA**

A Roycroft table lamp, model 905, of leaded slag glass and hammered copper with applied patina, featuring a shade designed by Dard Hunter and base attributed to Victor Toothaker, impressed orb and cross mark on lamp base.

ca. 1925   *22in (56cm) high*
$22,000-26,000   **DRA**

A Fulper Vasekraft table lamp, of Cat's Eye flambé-glazed earthenware and leaded glass, stamped manufacturer's mark "Fulper," "23," "Patents Pending in United States and Canada, England, France, and Germany," and "Vasekraft" mark with potter at wheel on underside of base, shade stamped on interior "23 23 41."

ca. 1909   *18in (46cm) high*
$13,000-18,000   **DRA**

A Liberty & Co. Cymric silver three-piece coffee set, designed by Archibald Knox, all cast in low relief with Celtic knot motif, coffeepot Birmingham 1908, milk pitcher Birmingham 1912, sugar basin Birmingham 1903.

6in (15cm) high

$7,500-8,500   **WW**

A Liberty & Co. Tudric pewter and green glass claret pitcher and cover, designed by Archibald Knox, cast with stylized motifs, minor chips, wear on the base of the glass base.

ca. 1904   *8in (20cm) high*

$1,600-2,100   **SWO**

A pair of Liberty & Co. silver and enamel candlesticks, applied with silver and blue/green enamel rosettes, detachable drip pans (one unmarked), on raised square bases.

1907   *5¼in (13.5cm) high*

$2,000-2,600   **WW**

A Liberty Tudric pewter and enamel pitcher, molded with sinuous designs, with enamel cabochons, the handle woven with copper wire, stamped marks and numbered "0305," some wear.

8¼in (21cm) high

$550-650   **SWO**

A Tiffany & Co. sterling silver large "tomato" ladle, of "Lap Over Edge" pattern, handle etched, monogrammed, minor surface scratches, marked.

ca. 1880   *12¼in (31cm) long 9.7oz*

$1,050-1,200   **DRA**

A Tiffany & Co. inkstand, of hammered and etched silver, with fern decoration, two inkpots, a center compartment, and two drawers, engraved with monogram "GFS" and presentation inscription, marked "6258 4169."

George F. Shrady, MD, was a prominent New York physician and tended to Ulysses S. Grant during his last illness.

ca. 1880   *9¾in (25cm) wide 19.2oz*

$3,300-4,000   **DRA**

A late-19thC Tiffany & Co. Etruscan sterling silver paper knife, by George W. Shiebler & Co., marked "Winged (S), Sterling, 836, Tiffany & Co.."

11in (28cm) long 5.8oz

$6,000-6,600   **DRA**

A late-19thC Tiffany and Co. silver and silver-gilt pepper pot, applied with gilded dragonflies, the pull-off cover with pierced decoration and with a dragonfly finial.

Edward Moore period, 1873-91.

4¼in (10.5cm) high 1.8oz

$1,100-1,250   **WW**

A sterling silver Tiffany & Co. St. Dunstan water pitcher, marked on underside "166606 226."

ca. 1907-47   *10¾in (27cm) high 45.9oz*

$2,600-4,000   **DRA**

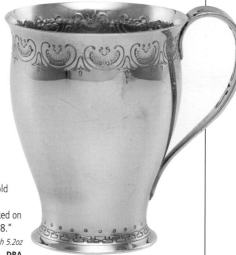

A Tiffany & Co. 18ct gold cup, with a shell and bellflower border, marked on underside "16857 7908."

1907-47   *3½in (9cm) high 5.2oz*

$9,000-10,500   **DRA**

ESSENTIAL REFERENCE—GEORG JENSEN

Born in Rådvid, the son of a Danish blacksmith and knife grinder, Georg Jensen (1866-1935) had been apprenticed as a goldsmith, graduated in sculpture, and run a failed ceramics business prior to establishing his silversmithy, the Georg Jensen Company, in Copenhagen in 1904. Some 31 years later, upon his death, the obituary in the "New York Herald" saluted him as "the greatest silversmith of the last 300 years." Initial success with jewelry soon allowed for expansion into the production of hollow ware and flatware, too, and stylistically all the great style movements of the 20thC and 21stC (the company is still operational to this day) have been embraced: Arts and Crafts, Art Nouveau, Neoclassical, Art Deco, Modernism, Organic Modernism, Postmodernism, etc., but all somehow rendered quintessentially "Jensen." Much of this can be attributed to the company always— both prior to and post Georg Jensen's death—working with brilliant and innovative designers, particularly notable examples of whom, aside from Jensen himself, include: Johan Rohde (1865-1935); Gundorph Albertus (1887-1969); Harald Nielsen (1892-1977); Henning Koppel (1918-81); and Vivianna Torun Bülow-Hübe (1927-2104), better known as just Torun.

A Georg Jensen silver cocktail shaker, designed by Gundorph Albertus, design number 572, spot-hammered decoration, the pull-off cover with a stylized geometric foliate-and-ball finial, import marks for London, importer's mark of George Stockwell.

1929   10½in (26.5cm) high 23.5oz
$6,500-8,000   **WW**

A Georg Jensen sterling silver Blossom tazza, model 2, marked on underside, also with French import marks.

1925-32   7in (18cm) high 19.5oz
$5,300-6,600   **DRA**

A Georg Jensen sterling silver "Grape" bowl, model 296A, marked on underside.

1930-39   15in (38cm) wide 62.9oz
$13,000-18,000   **DRA**

A Georg Jensen silver four-piece "Schilling" tea and coffee service with tray, designed by Johan Rohde, marked "321 A," tray marked "321 C."

1933-44   Tray 18¾in (47.5cm) wide 133.5oz
$9,000-10,500   **DRA**

A pair of Georg Jensen silver "Grape" pattern candlesticks, stamped marks, design no. 264.

post 1945   11½in (29.5cm) high 91.95oz
$12,000-15,000   **DN**

A pair of Georg Jensen silver "Grape" pattern candelabra, design no.383A, stamped marks, in mahogany Jensen cases.

post 1945   10½in (26.5cm) high 209.4oz
$40,000-46,000   **DN**

A Georg Jensen silver fish dish, drainer, and cover, design no.335C, designed by Johan Rohde in 1919, stamped marks.

post 1945   30in (76cm) long 219.4oz
$80,000-90,000   **DN**

A Georg Jensen sterling silver covered coupe, designed by Johan Rohde, model 43, marked on underside and cover.

post 1945   6¼in (16cm) high 13.5oz
$1,600-2,100   **DRA**

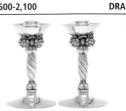

A pair of Georg Jensen sterling silver "Grape" candlesticks, model 263, marked on underside of each "Copenhagen, Denmark."

1945-77   5½in (14cm) high 21.9oz
$7,500-8,500   **DRA**

A silver Gorham Manufacturing Company Egyptian-style teapot and sugar bowl, the teapot and sugar bowl featuring decoration of sphinxes and pharaoh heads, engraved on bowl "Marian Holyoke" and on underside of bowl "from Lucy K. Tuckerman August 15 1877, 2396 7301," on plate "Marian," and on underside of plate "from Lucy K. Tuckerman, 2396 2285," with Tiffany & Co. bowl and under plate, ca. 1877.

The teapot and sugar bowl were a christening gift from Lucy Tuckerman (1858-1904) to Marian Holyoke (1877-1973).

1869-74   *Teapot 8½in (21.5cm) high 61.6oz*

$4,600-5,900   DRA

An Arts and Crafts A. E. Bonner London silver centerpiece, spot-hammered decoration, set with enamel and chrysoprase cabochons, with a center chrysoprase cabochon.

1907   *7¼in (18.4cm) diam 27.2oz*

$4,600-5,300   WW

An Arts and Crafts silver seven-piece "Country Range" tea and coffee service, comprising a teapot, coffeepot, sugar bowl, and a tray, maker's mark for Johnson, Walker & Tolhurst Ltd., London 1904, signed "L. Movio, 1904," the kettle-on-stand and hot water pot, maker's mark Godfrey, Bell & Godfrey Ltd., London 1920, signed "L. Movio."

The facsimile signature of Latino Movio (1858-1949) has been noted on chased and embossed Arts and Crafts silver pieces hallmarked between 1901 and 1907.

tray 29¾in (75.5cm) wide 288oz

$13,000-18,000   SWO

A Cymric Arts and Crafts enameled silver vase, attributed to Rex Silver, Birmingham, for Liberty and Co., with green, blue, and orange enamel berries and leaves.

1906   *5¾in (14.5cm) high*

$2,000-2,600   K&O

An Arts and Crafts H. G. Murphy London silver beer pitcher, by H. G. Murphy, in the early-18thC manner, marked with the Falcon mark.

1929   *10¾in (27.5cm) high 39.5oz*

$6,000-7,500   WW

ESSENTIAL REFERENCE—OMAR RAMSDEN & CARR

Born in Sheffield, England, Omar Ramsden (1873-1939) was an innovative and influential designer and maker of silverware. Joining forces with Alwyn Carr (1872-1940) in 1898, he established a studio in Chelsea, London, producing silverware to a high standard, and often decorated with hardstones or enamel. Pieces made by Ramsden after his partnership with Carr ended in 1919 are stamped or incised "OMAR RAMSDEN ME FECIT" ("Omar Ramsden Made Me").

An Arts and Crafts Omar Ramsden and Alwyn Carr, London silver pot and cover, embossed with grotesque masks and set with four oval chrysoprase cabochons, spot-hammered decoration, the tapering pull-off cover with a chrysoprase finial, on four pierced sinuous bracket feet, also engraved "OMAR RAMSDEN ET ALWYN CARR ME FECURUNT MXII."

1911/12   *3¾in (9.5cm) high 5.3oz*

$10,500-12,000   WW

An Arts and Crafts Omar Ramsden and Alwyn Carr, London silver bowl, spot-hammered decoration, applied with six circular bosses chased with alternate Tudor rose and fleur-de-lis decoration, inscribed "OMAR RAMSDEN ET ALWYN CARR ME FECURUNT."

1913   *5¼in (13.7cm) diam 4.1oz*

$1,500-1,800   WW

An Arts and Crafts Omar Ramsden and Alwyn Carr, London silver and enamel cigarette casket, spot-hammered decoration, the cover with a galleon on a stormy sea, interior wood-lined, the sides chased "I WAS WROUGHT FOR HARRY BALDWIN BY COMMAND OF C.M.BETTS IN THE YEAR OF OUR LORD MCMXIV," also engraved "OMAR RAMSDEN ET ALWYN CARR ME FECERUNT MCMXIV."

1914   *5½in (14cm) wide 24oz*

$7,500-8,500   WW

An Arts and Crafts Omar Ramsden, London silver caddy, with eight fluted-scroll supports and inscribed "ARS LONGA VITA BREVIS," also engraved "OMAR RAMSDEN ME FECIT."

1929   *5in (12.5cm) high 18.3oz*

$4,600-5,300   WW

An Arts and Crafts Omar Ramsden, London, silver caddy spoon spot-hammered fig-shaped bowl, the terminal with three lozenge-shaped green stone cabochons.

1935   *3½in (9cm) long 1.4oz*

$7,500-8,500   **WW**

An Arts and Crafts Omar Ramsden, London, silver goblet, spot-hammered decoration, foot with a rope-twist border and inscribed "Ann," engraved "OMAR RAMSDEN ME FECIT."

1936   *4¾in (12.2cm) high approx 5.1oz*

$2,000-2,600   **WW**

An Arts and Crafts Omar Ramsden, London, silver tazza, spot-hammered decoration, with a cast border of pineapples, grapes, and fruit, on a stem with cherub heads, inscribed "OMAR RAMSDEN ME FECIT."

1938   *5½in (14cm) high 24oz*

$2,600-4,000   **WW**

An Art Nouveau William Hutton and Son, London silver casket, spot-hammered decoration, hinges mounted with chrysoprase cabochons, wood lined.

1902   *6½in (16.5cm) wide*

$2,600-4,000   **WW**

CLOSER LOOK—WIENER WERKSTATTE BOX

The overtly geometric form (octagonal and stepped) embraces the stylistic preferences of the "machine age" that began in the late 19thC, and is also prescient (by some 20 years) of the later Art Deco style of the 1930s.

The hammered scroll forms surrounding the cover's center panel are rendered in a decidedly modern style, but as a decorative motif date back thousands of years, most notably to the Classical Greco-Roman vocabulary of ornament.

The painted panel at the center also embraces past and present: originally a Greek bishop of the 3rd-4thC AD, Saint Nicholas had by the late 19thC, because of his association with giving gifts, become increasingly associated, as Santa Claus, with the celebration of Christmas—an association that strongly indicates this box, and what it originally contained, was originally conceived as a Christmas present.

A Wiener Werkstatte silver-gilt box and cover, by Eduard Josef Wimmer Wisgrill, the cover inset with a an ivory panel painted with Saint Nicholas by E. J. Wimmer, stamped "Wiener Werkstatte" and "WW" mark, head of Diana, artist monogram on base, inside cover inscribed "8 December 1911."

1911   *5¼in (13cm) wide*

$20,000-26,000   **WW**

An Art Nouveau silver teapot, designed by Archibald Knox for Liberty, Birmingham, also stamped Cymric, ivory scroll handle.

1904   *5¼in (13.5cm) high 14.3oz*

$1,600-2,100   **WW**

A Henry Wigfull, Sheffield, sterling silver vase, with impressed touchmarks on upper edge "H.W."

1905   *12½in (32cm) high*

$5,300-6,600   **DRA**

A Cartier Art Deco box, of 14ct yellow gold and enamel, signed "Cartier 14k" with inscription.

1933   *3in (8cm) wide*

$7,500-8,500   **DRA**

A Danish Karl Gustav Hansen (1914-2002) four-piece coffee and tea service, .925 standard marks, dated.

1940   *Coffeepot 8in (20cm) high 64oz*

$5,300-6,600   **SWO**

A silver Art Deco H. G. Murphy, London, bowl and cover, spot-hammered decoration, the pull-off cover with engraved decoration, marked with the falcon mark.

1935   *4¾in (11.8cm) diam 10.6oz*
$4,000-5,300   **WW**

An Art Deco Padgett & Braham Ltd., London, silver twin-compartment cigar and cigarette box, with a center detachable cigar cutter for two sizes and match safe, with a striking strip on the front.

1940   *12½in (31.5cm) wide*
$3,300-4,000   **DN**

An Art Deco S. J. Rose, London, 9ct-gold matchbook case, engine-turned barley decoration with hand-engraved scroll beads on each outer edge.

1929   *2½in (6cm) high 1.2oz*
$800-900   **SWO**

A Josef Hoffmann hand-hammered silver centerpiece bowl, for Wiener Werkstätte, impressed designer's and manufacturer's mark to top edge "JH Wiener Werkstätte Made in Austria 900" with hallmark and "WW" with rose mark, impressed mark "Wiener Werkstätte."

ca. 1918   *10in (25cm) wide*
$33,000-40,000   **DRA**

An Austrian Josef Hoffman four-piece tea service with tray, for Wiener Werkstätte, of hand-hammered silver and ivorine, impressed manufacturer's marks, "JH Wiener Werkstätte Made in Austria 900" with rose mark and hallmark.

ca. 1920   *14½in (37cm) high*
$20,000-26,000   **DRA**

A pair of Josef Hoffmann hand-hammered silver vases, for Wiener Werkstätte, impressed manufacturer's marks on one example "WW JH Wiener Werkstätte Made in Austria 900" and on the other example "WW JH Made in Austria 900" with rose mark.

ca. 1918   *8¼in (21cm) high*
$33,000-40,000   **DRA**

A rare graduated set of Indian silver Penguin decanters, possibly Narotamdas Bhua, after a cocktail shaker design by Emil A. Schuelke for Napier, each with hinged cover and red Perspex handles, each with engraved "DH" in diamond-shaped panel, stamped "T100G."

It has been suggested that the T.100 silver mark has been used in Bombay. The markings were intended to indicate the purity of the silver, the number giving the percentage of pure silver, although tests have shown this to be optimistic. The T mark was also used in Lucknow and Bengal as well as on Cutch-style silver from Karachi.

Tallest 9¼in (23.5cm) high
$8,500-9,000   **WW**

An American Emil Schuelke silver-plated brass Penguin cocktail shaker, for Napier Company, impressed manufacturer's mark on underside "Napier."

1936   *12¼in (31cm) high*
$5,300-6,600   **DRA**

A WMF silver-plated centerpiece, decorated in the Art Nouveau manner with a pair of winged beauties with shaped blue glass liner.

6¾in (17cm) high
$400-500   **WHP**

An Arthur Cameron and Charles Robert Ashbee copper and enamel box, for The Guild of Handicrafts, the hinged cover inset with enamel panel of a standing rhinoceros by Arthur Cameron, cedar lining, enamel signed "AC" monogram.

This enamel is after the Rhinoceros woodcut by Durer dated 1515.

7in (18cm) wide

$6,500-8,000 **WW**

A Glasgow School tin wall mirror, stamped in low relief with two facing peacocks and entwined berried foliage, on wood base, unsigned.

35in (89cm) wide

$1,300-1,800 **WW**

A Liberty & Co. Arts and Crafts copper Tudric wall mirror, the plate flanked by stylized tulips, the reverse with ivorine "Liberty & Co Ltd, London" plaque.

ca. 1905 *24¾in (63cm) high*

$1,700-2,100 **BELL**

A Liberty & Co. Arts and Crafts copper Tudric wall mirror, the riveted sections of copper laid over a wooden frame, the plate flanked by stylized tulips, the reverse with ivorine "Liberty & Co Ltd, London" plaque.

ca. 1905 *24¾in (63cm) high*

$1,700-2,100 **BELL**

A Newlyn Industrial Classes patinated copper wall mirror, hammered in low relief with a frieze of scaly fish, with beveled mirror, unsigned.

15in (38cm) wide

$750-850 **WW**

An Arts and Crafts Newlyn-style copper fire screen, the center panel embossed galleon with dragon on the sail and waves beneath, in an ironwork frame.

19¼in (49cm) high

$350-400 **CHOR**

A late-19thC/early-20thC Continental giltwood sunburst mirror.

34in (86cm) diam

$2,000-2,600 **L&T**

An Arts and Crafts patinated copper wall mirror, stamped in relief with flowers and foliage, set with four Ruskin Pottery ceramic roundels, paper label on reverse.

The paper label on the reverse states the mirror was presented by the Clarion Club members 60 years ago as a wedding present, and is dated 16.1.67, implying a date of 1907.

24in (60cm) high

$1,700-2,100 **WW**

A Dirk van Erp humidor of hammered copper with applied patina, impressed closed-box windmill mark on underside "Dirk Van Erp," monogrammed "CCR."

1911-12 *10in (25cm) wide*

$6,000-6,600 **DRA**

A Karl Kipp hammered copper with applied patina three-handled vase, for Tookay Shop, impressed signature on underside "KK."

1912-15 *7¼in (18cm) high*

$4,000-4,600 **DRA**

A cocktail shaker, by The American Thermos Bottle Co., of chrome-plated steel, signed on underside "The American Thermos Bottle Co. Norwich, Conn. USA The Only Thermos Reg. US Pat. Off. Replacement Filter No. 859F Made in USA."

ca. 1935 *5½in (14cm) wide*

$2,000-2,600 **DRA**

A 19thC French bronze group of the "Education of Achilles" by Chiron, after Francois Rude (French 1784-1855).

This group was inspired by Jean-Baptiste Regnault's monumental canvas entitled "L'Education d'Achille par le centaure Chiron," which was exhibited at the Salon of 1783, and was also his morceau de réception at the Academy in the same year.

19½in (49.5cm) wide

$5,300-5,900 WW

A bi-color patinated bronze model of a nude youth, the "Sleep of Narcissus," by Claire Jeanne Roberte Colinet (French, 1880-1950), inscribed "Cla. R. Colinet" in the maquette.

Colinet was born in Brussels and trained there under Jef Lambeaux before moving to Paris in 1910, where she rose to become an important part of the Art Deco movement. Although primarily known for chryselephantine dancers, Odalisques, and Orientalist groups, for the present model, Colinet took inspiration from mythological subject matter, which makes the model a unique part of her oeuvre.

19¼in (49cm) long

$5,300-6,600 DN

A patinated bronze "Charity" figure, by Sir Alfred Gilbert MVO RA (1854-1934), on ebonized wood base, unsigned.

18¾in (47.5cm) high

$21,000-26,000 WW

A 19thC French bronze figure of a Greek warrior, after the antique, on a marble base, inscribed "F. Barbidienne," with foundry stamp.

34¼in (87cm) high

$4,600-5,300 L&T

A bronze sculpture, dark brown and medium brown patinas, "La Bacchante," by Albert Carrier-Belleuse (French 1824-87), signed "A Carriere-Belleuse" with foundry stamp "B.D. Paris Vrais Bronze," on an associated bronze socle with "Salon de Beaux Art" plaque.

24½in (62cm) high

$2,600-3,300 L&T

A late-19thC French bronze figure of Milo of Croton, after Jacques-Edme Dumont (French 1722-75), the Greek athlete depicted splitting a tree trunk.

30½in (77.5cm) high

$5,300-5,900 WW

A bronze bust of a young child, "Buste D'Enfant," after Aime Jules Dalou (French 1838-1902), cast by the Hebrard foundry, signed "Dalou," numbered "9" and with foundry mark "Cire Perdue A. A. Hebrard," on a marble plinth.

This sculpture relates to Dalou's commission to provide a marble monument celebrating Queen Victoria's children for a private chapel at Windsor Castle. This model served as a preliminary sketch for one of the figures in the monument. Both the terra-cotta maquette for the monument and the original study for "Buste d'Enfant" are currently part of the Petiti Palais Collection in Paris. This bronze was cast shortly after Dalou's death in 1902, no lifetime casts were ever made.

16in (40.8cm) high

$6,000-7,500 WW

An animalier bronze model of a stalking lion, "Lion A L'Affut," by Isidor-Jules Bonheur (French 1827-1901), cast by Peyrol, the naturalistic base signed "I. Bonheur" and stamped "Peyrol."

Bonheur was a regular Paris Salon exhibitor and the above bronze was cast by his brother-in-law, Hippolyte Peyrol.

18¼in (46.5cm) long

$4,600-5,300 WW

A carved wood sculpture, with gesso and silver-leaf patination, "Aigle, (Eagle perched)," by Wilhelm Krieger (1877-1945), incised "Prof Krieger," applied paper label "Geschenk von Prof Krieger 7 Oct 35."

24in (61cm) high

$12,000-15,000 WW

DECORATIVE ARTS

A late-19thC Austrian cold-painted bronze figure of a monkey, by Franz Bergman, impressed "FB/ Geschutz."

4¼in (11cm) high

$800-900   **L&T**

A 20thC cold-painted bronze horse and jockey, by Franz Bergmann, with Bergmann amphora mark and stamped "4928" on underside.

6¼in (16cm) long

$1,600-2,100   **L&T**

An Austrian cold-painted bronze inkwell as a song thrush on a cherry branch, by Franz Bergmann, hinged at the neck to reveal an inkwell, possibly associated, stamped "Bergmann Geschutzt 459."

ca. 1900   *9in (23cm) wide*

$1,100-1,250   **CHEF**

An early-20thC Bergman cold-painted bronze figure of an Arab Boy, stamped "B" in an urn and "GESCHUTZ 2897," wear on the painted surface.

2¾in (7cm) high

$1,000-1,100   **TEN**

CLOSER LOOK—FRANZ BERGMAN RABBIT

The cold-painted (not fired) finish is characteristically sophisticated, and the subtle gradations of the fawn and gray colors of the rabbit's coat highly naturalistic.

The sense of alertness is also conveyed not only via the posture of the rabbit, but also the naturalistic modeling of the muscle underneath the coat.

Another characteristic of Bergman animal figures is a strong sense of alertness, clearly evident here in the gaze of the rabbit's eyes.

A late-19thC Austrian cold-painted bronze sculpture of a rabbit, from the Franz Xavier Bergman (1861-1936) foundry, the underside indistinctly stamped "DEPOSE GESCHUTZT" and model number 1215.

6¼in (16cm) long

$4,600-5,900   **DN**

A late-19thC Austrian painted terra-cotta figure of a Jack Russell terrier, with inset glass eyes.

14½in (37cm) high

$600-750   **L&T**

A late-19thC/early-20thC large Austrian painted terra-cotta figure of a pug, with glass eyes and later leather collar.

20½in (52cm) high

$2,000-2,600   **L&T**

A late-19thC/early-20thC Austrian cold-painted bronze of a St. Bernard, marked "GESCHÜTZT" on the underside.

5¼in (13cm) long

$550-650   **L&T**

A late-19thC/early-20thC Austrian cold-painted bronze of a donkey, naturalistically cast and painted.

4¼in (10.5cm) long

$550-650   **L&T**

A bronze figure of a naked lady, "Danseuse a la Boule," by Lucien Charles Edward Alliot (French 1877-1956), stamped "19-50."

31¼in (79cm) high

$1,300-1,800   **SWO**

A gilt bronze and ivory figure, "The Singing Pierrot," by Robert Bousquet (1894-1917), signed "Bousquet."

15½in (39.5cm) high

$7,500-8,500   **SWO**

A patinated bronze and ivory figure, "Hooded Cloak," by Demétre Chiparus (Romanian 1886-1947) for Etling Paris, on onyx plinth, signed "H Chiparus, Etling Paris."

7¼in (18.5cm) high

$4,000-4,600   **SWO**

A patinated bronze and ivory figure, "Lazzarone," by Demétre Chiparus (1886-1947), on an onyx plinth, unsigned.

9½in (24cm) high

$4,000-4,600   **SWO**

ESSENTIAL REFERENCE—CHIPARUS

'The Dancer of Kapurthala" is believed to have been inspired by Anita Delgado (1890-1962), a flamenco dancer who captured the heart of the Maharajah of Kapurthala when he saw her perform at a café, while attending the wedding of Spain's King Alfonso XIII. They later married and she changed her name to Maharani Prem Kaur Sahiba.

Demétre Chiparus (1886-1947), was born in Drohoi, Romania, went to study in Italy with the sculptor Raffaello Romanelli, and then enrolled at the École des Beaux-Arts in Paris. The distinctive sculptures he produced, in the Art Deco style, were frequently made with bronze and ivory—a tradition that had been used in ancient Greece and commonly known as chryselephantine.

Chiparus, fascinated by the discovery of Tutankhamun's tomb and influenced by Diaghilev's Ballets Russes, was also inspired by the exotic—something that is evident in this fantastic sculpture.

An Art Deco-style figure of a dancer, "Footsteps," after Demétre Chiparus, of patinated metal and ivorine, on an onyx base.

16½in (42cm) high

$850-1,000   **CHOR**

A patinated and gilt-bronze and ivory figure, "The Dancer of Kapurthala," by Demétre Chiparus (Romanian 1886-1947), on a stepped onyx base, signed and stamped "Made in France" and numbered "35," possibly resilvered on the hat.

22½in (57cm) high

$40,000-53,000   **SWO**

A cold-painted bronze and ivory figure of a dancer, by Stefan Dakon (Austrian 1904-92), signed "Dakon," on an onyx plinth, lacking both hands.

9½in (24cm) high

$650-800   **SWO**

A patinated bronze model, "Egyptian Maiden," by Hans Harders (1871-1950), on a slate base, signed in the cast "Harders."

12¾in (32.5cm) high

$1,600-2,100   **WW**

An Art Deco bronze and ivory figure of a dancer, by Josef Lorenzl, on an onyx base, signed in cast "LORENZL," silver finish worn, head possibly reset.

1925   *7¼in (18.5cm) high*

$1,500-1,800   **SWO**

A cold-painted bronze figure of a dancer, by Josef Lorenzl, signed, on an onyx plinth, wear and rubbing.

12in (30.5cm) high

$2,400-2,900   **SWO**

A bronze and ivory sculpture, "Woman with Borzoi dog," by Josef Lorenzl (1892-1950), on an onyx base, signed, chip in ivory at base of neck.

10in (25.5cm) high

$2,600-4,000   **WW**

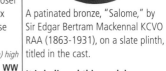

A patinated bronze, "Salome," by Sir Edgar Bertram Mackennal KCVO RAA (1863-1931), on a slate plinth, titled in the cast.

It is believed this model was exhibited at the Royal Academy in 1897.

14in (35.5cm) high

$13,000-18,000   **WW**

Judith Picks

The bronze, and bronze and ivory, figures of Joseph Lorenzl (1892-1950) are mostly of female dancers. The latter were also the favored subject matter of many of Lorenzl's contemporaries. However, there's rarely any chance of mistaking a Lorenzl dancer for one by another Art Deco sculptor. Highly stylized, and with the bronze usually either silvered or cold-painted, his fusion of elongated limbs, small breasts, slim, nude or semiclad boyish figures frozen in overtly acrobatic-athletic poses, and mostly wearing flowing scarves (as here) or waving tambourines, cymbals, or fans—employed to further enhance the sense of movement and drama— makes Lorenzl's sculptures instantly recognizable, and that's a quality that's desirable, both aesthetically and commercially.

An Art Deco cold-painted bronze figure, "Scarf Dancer," by Josef Lorenzl (Austrian 1892-1950), on an onyx plinth, signed "Lorenzl."

ca. 1930   *27in (68.5cm) high*

$16,000-21,000   **SWO**

An Art Deco gilt-bronze figure, by Georges Morin (German 1874-1950), on a marble plinth, signed.

13¾in (35cm) high

$800-900   **SWO**

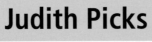

A pair of Art Deco bronze and ivory cold-painted bookends, "Wisdom" and "Poetry," by Roland Paris (Austrian 1894-1945), model numbers "2623" and "2622," on marble bases, inscribed "Roland Paris."

ca. 1925   *7in (17.5cm) high*

$4,600-5,900   **SWO**

An Art Deco ivory and cold-painted bronze of a lady, by Franz Peleska-Lunard (Austrian b.1873), signed "Peleska RuM," on a marble plinth.

10½in (26.5cm) high

$2,600-4,000   **SWO**

A cold-painted and carved ivory figure, "The First Jewelry," by Ferdinand Preiss (German 1892-1943), modeled as a girl wearing a long dress, scarf, and clogs with a heart-shaped pendant on a chain, engraved "F. Preiss," on an onyx base.

ca. 1925   *5¼in (13.7cm) high*

$1,200-1,600   **SWO**

ESSENTIAL REFERENCE—FERDINAND PREISS

One of the most esteemed and influential sculptors of the Art Deco period, Ferdinand Preiss (1882-1943) was born in Erbach, Germany. Having been apprenticed at 15 to the ivory carver Philip Wilmann, he subsequently worked for him and then elsewhere in both Germany and Italy, Preiss met Arthur Kassler in 1905, and the following year they established the firm of Preiss-Kassler in Berlin. The company name was shortened to "PK" in 1910, temporarily closed during 1914-18, before finally closing for good upon Preiss's death in 1943.

Preiss, together with other carvers and sculptors—notably Ludwig Walter, Louis Kuchler, Dorothea Charol, and Philip Lenz—employed at PK, created figures in mostly ivory, or cold-painted bronze and ivory (chryselephantine), but sometimes also in just bronze, and all were usually mounted on green or black onyx bases. While all the figures were highly naturalistic, many also had, despite being frozen in time, a stylish sense of energy and movement about them, especially those depicting contemporary sporting figures and dancers. Other subject matter included similarly contemporary and fashionable activities as diverse as smoking cigarettes, recreational bathing, and flying, as well as studies of young children, and a number of small Classical female nudes.

'Thoughts," an ivory figure, model no. 1131, by Ferdinand Preiss (1882-1943), on onyx base, signed, with dark lines across the figure and chips on two corners.

4¾in (12cm) high

$2,000-2,600   SWO

A large patinated bronze sculpture, "Sonny Boy," by Ferdinand Preiss (1882-1943), on a slate base, etched "F Preiss" on base.

11½in (29.5cm) high

$4,600-5,300   WW

An Art Deco patinated and silvered bronze figure group, by Louis Riché (French 1877-1949), a lady with borzoi dogs, signed, on a marble plinth, wear in the patinated areas, back corner restored.

24in (61cm) wide

$2,000-2,600   SWO

An Art Deco bronze and ivory sculpture, by Bruno Zach (Ukrainian-Austrian1891-1935), depicting a cold-painted female dancer in 1920s dress, on marble base, signed in cast "B ZACH," some scratches.

ca. 1925   13½in (34.3cm) high

$7,500-8,500   SWO

A cold-painted bronze figure, "Sonny Boy," by Ferdinand Preiss, on an onyx plinth, unsigned, some rubbing and wear.

11½in (29cm) high

$2,000-2,600   SWO

An Art Deco patinated spelter centerpiece of a lady, mounted with a dolphin, on a marble and onyx plinth, with chips.

27¼in (69cm) wide

$650-800   SWO

An Art Deco patinated bronze figure of a javelin thrower, on a stone plinth, signed on the base "NAO'(?), some rubbing and scratches, some chips.

23¾in (60cm) high

$1,100-1,250   SWO

An Art Deco patinated spelter figure of a panther, on a marble base, with chips in the plinth.

25½in (65cm) wide

$900-1,050   SWO

An Art Deco spelter and marble centerpiece, a sprinting man and a dog, on a marble and onyx stand, inscribed "L.Valderi," chips on the base, possible restoration of the foot.

22¼in (56.5cm) wide

$1,250-1,450   SWO

MODERN MARKET

The auction and gallery market for Modernist design has been exceptionally robust during the Covid-19 pandemic. People either cannot or do not want to travel as much. All the money saved has gone into people's homes. This has proved to be of great consequence to purveyors of 20thC design. Material such as the furniture of George Nakashima, the ceramics of Betty Woodman, and the glass of Lino Tagliapietra, was going gangbusters before the pandemic, and prices have only risen since 2020.

Why has this market been so strong for so long? Over the past half century, there has been a slow but inexorable crawl toward modernity in the minds of curators and collectors. Back in the 1960s, a lifetime or two ago, collectors were following museum leads in chasing traditional antiques—Chippendale, Duncan Phyfe, Empire, Folk Art, and Victorian work commanded top prices. But even then, as an interest in Art Deco slowly formed, we could see the evolution first of museum interest and then of collecting tastes. Arts and Crafts was an anomaly back then; I remember setting up at antiques shows with Stickley furniture and the other dealers would sneer, making such comments as, "I would use that sideboard as a workbench." Within a decade, those same dealers were mostly out of business, especially as the 1980s saw a rise in Modernist design collecting, which centered on postwar factory furniture by Herman Miller and designs by Charles and Rae Eames.

Less than a decade later, American Craft furniture began to shine. Masterworks by Wendel Castle, Albert Paley, Sam Maloof, and others, as well as Nakashima, started to command the world's attention. What's interesting is that while such furniture still enjoys broad support, the crawl toward modernity continued to include work by contemporary masters. It's a fitting irony that with Modernist collecting starting in about 1980, record prices are being set for work that wasn't even made until *after* the start of the new millennium.

Again, great design by recognized masters in very good condition is selling for big money. That inclination has continued in force, with major galleries and auction houses focusing on work by George Ohr, Toshiko Takaezu, Dale Chihuly, and Lino Tagliapietro.

The main takeaway is that the information age has meant that buyers are much better informed, with virtual visits to bricks and mortar galleries, auction halls, and dealers. Better photography, more informative descriptions, and the capacity to use comparative pricing have never been more available. And judging by the amount of decorative art being sold since early 2020, collectors and museums are both using this information to the advantage of the market. How long will this last? Are we in a bubble? I don't have a crystal ball, but stronger pricing brings out stronger pieces and, as long as that flow of better material continues, I would expect pricing to follow suit.

David Rago, of Rago-Wright-Lama Auctions

Top Left: An earthenware ceramic dish, "Quatre poissons polychromes," by Pablo Picasso.

15½in (39cm) wide

$10,500-12,000   **SWO**

Above An Italian "Agra" cabinet, by Roberto Giulio Rida, of opaline glass and brass.

2015   *31¾in (81cm) wide*

$13,000-16,000   **DRA**

ESSENTIAL REFERENCE—MARK BRAZIER-JONES

New Zealander Mark Brazier-jones (b. 1956) began his career as a furniture maker in 1983, as a founding member of the Creative Salvage Group. The group's first show of welded sculpture furniture—anarchic and experimental design made from parts of Broken Britain—was sold out, poetically described by Nick Wright in "Cut and Shut: The History of Creative Salvage"—as a mix of "sex, drugs, and cabriole legs." Paul Smith was a patron. So, too, Mario Testino, Nigel Coates, and Mick Jagger. Mark is an artist, sculptor, furniture maker, lighting designer, and engineer all wrapped into one. Today, he works an hour away from him London home, in a rustic 16thC barn in rural Hertfordshire, driving to work in one of his collection of American classics cars. "I like to buy old and make it reliable," he says.

He cites his key artistic inspirations as the Baroque, particularly the work of architect and sculptor Gian Loreno Bernini (1598-1680), and Jean Tinguely, the Swiss postwar sculptor best known for the wacky kinetic art sculptural machines he called "meta-mechanics."

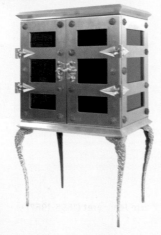

A "Cortes" cabinet on stand, by Mark Brazier-Jones (b.1956), the steel body with blue acrylic inset panels, applied bronze "sea-creature" roundels and polished bronze hinges, on naturalistically cast bronze cabriole legs, signed to the side 8/20 and dated.

1995   *68¼in (173cm) high*
$6,500-8,000   **SWO**

A Chairman's desk, by Wendell Castle, of ebonized mahogany, bubinga, anigre veneer, mahogany veneer, oak, and cherry, carved signature and date.

1992   *68¾in (175cm) high*
$6,500-8,000   **DRA**

ESSENTIAL REFERENCE—WENDELL CASTLE

Wendell Castle (1932-2018) was an American furniture artist. Castle was born in Emporia, Kansas, and is famous for his use of stack lamination, a woodworking technique he pioneered in the 1960s, which was based on a 19thC sculptural technique used for making duck decoys. Stack lamination allowed Castle for to create large blocks of wood out a series of planks, which were then carved and molded into the biomorphic shapes for which he is famous.

A dog bed, by Wendell Castle, of ebonized mahogany and satinwood, carved signature and date.

1992   *64½in (164cm) long*
$21,000-26,000   **DRA**

An "El Morro" desk and chair, by Michael Coffey, of laminated and carved African mozambique, carved signatures and date.

1973   *64in (163cm) wide*
$40,000-66,000   **DRA**

A Waring & Gillow Ltd English walnut veneer library table, designed by Serge Chermayeff, two cupboards flanking a center drawer, one internally fitted with three angled drawers, the other shelves.

61in (157cm) wide
$5,300-6,600   **WW**

A Danish writing desk, by Nanna Ditzel (1923-2005), in rosewood and oak, designed for Soren Willadsen, model number 12478.

1958   *65¾in (167cm) wide*
$6,500-8,000   **CHOR**

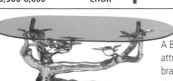

A Belgian coffee table, attributed to Willy Daro, of cast brass and glass.

ca. 1980   *46in (117cm) long*
$6,000-6,600   **DRA**

A later copy "670" lounger and "671" ottoman, designed by Charles and Ray Eames, with walnut-veneered seats and back, the headrest is worn and lightened.

armchair 39½in (100cm) high
$2,400-2,900   **SWO**

An Ercol elm and beech spindle-back "loveseat" or bench, by Lucien Ercolini.

$1,600-2,100   **WHP**

ESSENTIAL REFERENCE—VLADIMIR KAGAN

Born in Germany in 1927, Vladimir Kagan emigrated with his family to escape Nazi persecution in 1937—initially to France, and then to the United States. After studying architecture at Columbia University, he left prior to graduation in 1947 to work for and train with his father, a cabinet maker. A year later, he opened his first independent furniture store in New York City, and from 1950 he went into partnership with Hugo Dreyfuss, forming Kagan-Dreyfuss. Intent on creating furniture for everyday living, his innovative pieces fused the simplicity of line associated with Mid-Century Modern designers, such as Finn Juhl and Hans Wegner, with the organic forms of contemporaries, such as Isamu Noguchi. Kagan died in 2016, but with collectors, such as Brad Pitt, Demi Moore, Uma Thurman, and Tom Cruise, demand for his standout furniture remains unsurprisingly strong.

A floating seat and back sofa, by Vladimir Kagan for Vladimir Kagan Designs, Inc., of walnut and upholstery, upholstery manufacturer's label on underside.
ca. 1952-80   *81in (206cm) wide*
$33,000-40,000   **DRA**

A Mexican "Hand Foot" chair, by Pedro Friedeberg, of carved Mexican walnut, incised signature on base "Pedro Friedeberg."
ca. 1975   *36in (91cm) high*
$33,000-40,000   **DRA**

A Danish teak and rattan daybed, designed by Peter Hvidt & Orla Mølgaard-Nielsen for France & Søn, with replaced cushions.
80in (203cm) wide
$1,300-2,000   **SWO**

A Hammer Handle chair, by Wharton Esherick, of hickory, figured white oak and rubber-coated webbing.

This chair is the third of four variations Esherick made of the Hammer Handle chair.
ca. 1950   *31½in (80cm) high*
$22,000-26,000   **DRA**

A cabinet, model PE 40, by Paul Evans for Directional, of welded, gilt, and enameled steel and slate, welded signature and date.
1970   *96in (244cm) wide*
$53,000-59,000   **DRA**

An American Cityscape coffee table, by Paul Evans for Paul Evans Studio for Directional, of steel and chrome-plated steel, etched manufacturer's mark on base "Paul Evans."
ca. 1975   *60¼in (153cm) long*
$4,000-5,300   **DRA**

A 1950s G Plan "Librenza" sideboard, by E. Gomme, now painted midnight blue, with a glass top over three drawers, the two bi-olding cupboards mounted with "Tema e Variazioni" wallpaper, designed by Piero Fornasetti, manufactured by Cole & Son, now discontinued, on sputnik legs.
58¾in (149cm) wide
$2,400-2,900   **SWO**

ESSENTIAL REFERENCE—PIERRE JEANNERET

Pierre Jeanneret (1896-1967) was a Swiss architect who collaborated with his cousin Charles-Édouard Jeanneret (who assumed the pseudonym Le Corbusier), for about 20 years. In 1922, the Jeanneret cousins set up an architectural practice together. From 1927 to 1937, they worked together with Charlotte Perriand at the Le Corbusier-Pierre Jeanneret studio. They collaborated once again after War World II on the plans for the New town of Chandigarh in India.

Jeanneret, in collaboration with the English husband-wife team of Maxwell Fry and Jane Drew, was responsible for much of Chandigarh's large civic architecture project.

A "Puzzle" chair, designed by Arne Jacobsen, with a hide-slung seat and a stained plywood frame.
27½in (70cm) high
$1,000-1,100   **SWO**

An early sofa, by Vladimir Kagan for Kagan-Dreyfuss, Inc., of upholstery and casters.
ca. 1950   *120in (305cm) wide*
$40,000-66,000   **DRA**

A pair of French/Indian easy armchairs from Punjab Engineering College, Chandigarh, by Pierre Jeanneret, of teak, cane, and upholstery.
ca. 1955   *29½in (75cm) high*
$26,000-33,000   **DRA**

MODERN DESIGN

A Danish rosewood chest-of-drawers, designed by Kai Kristiansen.

ca. 1960   *34in (86cm) wide*

$1,600-2,100   **SWO**

A pair of Linley oak bookcases, with burl-walnut and ebony-strung doors.

110¼in (280cm) high

$6,000-7,500   **WW**

A rosewood sideboard, designed by Christian Linneberg, with sliding doors, opening to reveal an oak-lined interior, some scuffing on the stand.

88½in (225cm) wide

$2,600-4,000   **SWO**

A Dux "Pernilla 3" lounge armchair, designed by Bruno Mathsson, with a webbing seat, with a reading stand, branded "Bruno Mathsson Design Made in Sweden," replaced headrest.

67in (170cm) long

$2,600-4,000   **SWO**

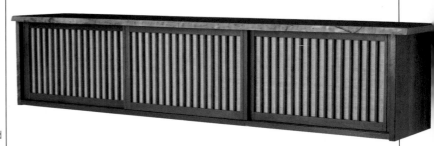

A Marshmallow sofa, by George Nelson & Associates for Herman Miller, of Alexander Girard naugahyde, enameled steel and brushed chrome-plated steel, upholstery manufacturer's label on underside "Herman Miller Inc. New York NY, Delivery Date: 6/10/60, 2789 5670 Marsh Sofa."

1956-60   *52in (132cm) wide*

$20,000-26,000   **DRA**

An American black walnut and pandanus cloth hanging wall cabinet, by George Nakashima for Nakashima Studio, signed with client name.

1960   *86¾in (220cm) wide*

$90,000-100,000   **DRA**

A tea cart, by George Nakashima for Nakashima Studio, of American black walnut, pandanus cloth, and casters, featuring two drop leaves, one drawer with dividers, and two sliding doors concealing one adjustable shelf.

It comes with a digital copy of the original drawing.

1962   *61in (155cm) wide*

$46,000-53,000   **DRA**

A Brazilian/Italian Rio chaise longue, by Oscar and Anna Maria Niemeyer, for Fasem, of lacquered wood, leather, and brass.

ca. 1978   *68in (173cm) long*

$21,000-26,000   **DRA**

A Sanso table, by Mira Nakashima for Nakashima Studio, of Claro walnut, walnut, and rosewood.

1994   *71¾in (182cm) wide*

$70,000-80,000   **DRA**

A "Rainbow Chair," by Patrick Norguet for Cappellini, acrylic-colored Lucite.

2000   *31½in (80cm) high*

$5,300-6,600   **SWO**

A Getama "Position" chair, designed by Okamura & Marquardsen.
1989 *65in (165cm) long*
$1,500-1,800 **SWO**

An Italian "Agra" cabinet, by Roberto Giulio Rida, of opaline glass and brass.

This work is from the limited edition of nine examples produced exclusively for H. M. Luther, New York.
2015 *31¾in (81cm) wide*
$13,000-16,000 **DRA**

A "Dragon's Back" table, by Albert Paley, of formed and fabricated steel, stainless steel, and glass, impressed signature and date on base "© Albert Paley 1998."

This work is from the edition of 10 and is registered in the Paley Studio Archives as number DT 1998 01.
1998 *69in (175cm) diam*
$26,000-33,000 **DRA**

A British/American mahogany cabinet, model 1/36, by I. H. Robsjohn-Gibbings for Widdicomb, featuring six drawers, fabric manufacturer's label on one drawer.
ca. 1955 *66in (168cm) wide*
$4,600-5,900 **DRA**

A desk, by Phillip Lloyd Powell, of chip-carved walnut, figured walnut, ebony, and hammered iron.
ca. 1965 *91in (231cm) wide*
$26,000-33,000 **DRA**

A 1950s "Woodpecker" chair, by Ernest Race, with teak arms, believed to be a prototype armchair.
$2,100-2,600 **WHP**

A pair of Knoll "Barcelona" lounge chairs, by Ludwig Mies van der Rohe, of leather and chrome-plated steel, label "GMC NY A 3042" and "GMC NY A 3081."
ca. 1960 *29in (74cm) high*
$6,500-8,000 **DRA**

A pair of 1970s leather upholstered boxing glove lounge chairs, by De Sede, model DS-2878.
63in (160cm) long
$7,500-8,500 **CHOR**

A surrealist gentleman's wardrobe, by Andrew Varah (1944-2012), "Umbrella Men," each door modeled as a gentleman's knee-length overcoat and boots, the center figure with a peg leg, with Brazilian rosewood, tabu, satinwood, oak, and burl oak, metal door furniture.

Varah produced about five variations of the "Umbrella Men" wardrobe between 1987 and 2003, and each example is unique. The surrealist-inspired design is inlaid with various veneers, and the gentlemen's umbrella handles act as door handles.
79¼in (201.5cm) wide
$6,500-8,000 **DN**

A pair of Getma "GE-270" teak armchairs, designed by Hans Wegner, with original back and seat cushion, branded "Getama Gedsted Denmark."
30in (76cm) high
$4,000-4,600 **SWO**

A shell-form earthenware sculpture, by Steve Buck, unsigned.

16in (40cm) high

$600-750 **WW**

An earthenware pitcher, by Simon Carroll (1964-2009), with colored glazes, signed "SPC 07."

2007 *13¾in (35cm) high*

$1,500-1,800 **CHOR**

A stoneware vase, by Hans Coper (German, 1920-1981), unmarked, restored.

9in (23cm) high

$2,600-3,300 **SWO**

'Buffalo Frog," by David Gilhooly, of glazed ceramic, impressed "Gilhooly 78."

1978 *24½in (62cm) high*

$7,500-8,500 **DRA**

A terra-cotta ewer, by Linda Gunn-Russell, with bird's-beak spout, painted and sponged with a geometric pattern, signed, dated.

1988 *16in (41.5cm) high*

$1,000-1,100 **WW**

A large sack-form raku sculpture with keyhole and staples, by Peter Hayes, incised "P Hayes 04" on slate base, dated.

2004 *27in (68cm) high*

$1,050-1,200 **WW**

A paper, clay, and slip sculpture, "Folded Megalith Form," by Ewen Henderson (1934-2000), unsigned.

early-1990s *17¾in (45cm) high*

$3,300-4,000 **WW**

'Thief of Unicycle" and "Swindler's Dream" from the Humanimals series, by Sergei Isupov, of glazed and hand-painted porcelain, signature and date on base.

2012 *17in (43cm) high*

$20,000-26,000 **DRA**

A Mo Jupp (1938-2018) standing female figure, earthenware with white slip highlights, incised marks on side of base.

31.5in (80cm) high

$3,300-4,000 **WW**

A flattened earthenware sculpture, "Head with Yellow Hair," by Christy Keeney (b. 1958), impressed artist's stamp "Keeney 1993."

1993 *15½in (39.5cm) high*

$1,000-1,100 **CHOR**

An early hand-built stoneware vase, by Jennifer Lee, speckled olive base, haloed with dark ashed bands, pale speckled rim, unsigned.

Jennifer Elizabeth Lee OBE (born 1956) is a Scottish ceramic artist with an international reputation. Lee's distinctive pots are hand-built using traditional pinch-and-coil methods. She has developed a method of coloring the pots by mixing metallic oxides into the clay before making.

9in (23cm) high

$21,000-26,000 **WW**

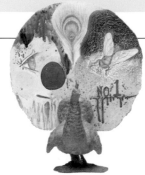

'Peacock No. 1" from the Reclamation series, by Michael Lucero, of glazed and hand-painted earthenware, reclaimed lead sculpture and wood peg, with glazed signature, title, and date "No. 1 Michael Lucero 2 18 94."

1994 *26in (66cm) high*

$4,000-5,300 DRA

"Dotty Pumpkin," by Kate Malone (b. 1959), crystalline-glazed stoneware with applied porcelain buttons, signed and dated.

2017 *6¾in (17cm) wide*

$3,300-4,000 WW

A large stoneware vessel, by John Maltby (b. 1936), with raku-glazed handle and neck and sgraffito bell-shaped base, with applied bird and cross motifs, signed "Maltby" below.

15¾in (40cm) high

$550-650 CHOR

A tall glazed earthenware bottle, by Gertrud and Otto Natzler, featuring glaze-melt fissures, slip signature on underside "Natzler," paper studio label on underside "M643."

1963 *9½in (24cm) high*

$6,000-6,600 DRA

An earthenware vase, by Magdalene Odundo, incised with band of geometric decoration, unsigned.

Dame Magdalene Anyango Namakhiya Odundo DBE (b. 1950) is a Kenyan-born British studio potter, who now lives in Farnham, Surrey. She has been chancellor of the University for the Creative Arts since 2018.

9in (23cm) high

$3,300-4,000 WW

A Richard Parkinson Pottery "Chess" wall plate, designed by Susan Parkinson, decorated with a medieval maiden, in blue on a white ground, impressed marks.

8¾in (22cm) diam

$850-1,000 WW

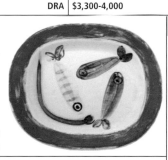

An earthenware ceramic dish, "Quatre poissons polychromes," by Pablo Picasso.

Conceived in 1947 and executed in a numbered edition of 200.

15½in (39cm) wide

$10,500-12,000 SWO

CLOSER LOOK—LUCIE RIE BOWL

In terms of form, echoes of artifacts from many cultures—Roman, Asian, Mesoamerican, and European—can be detected in Rie's work, and yet each pieces is almost instantly recognizable as a "Lucie Rie."

As her biographer Tony Birks observed, Rie's shapes are a fascinating combination of opposites: simple, yet subtly complex; economical yet luxurious; and sturdy yet frail—the latter a dynamic quality known as the "Lucie Rie Quiver."

Rie used unusually brilliant glazes for a studio potter, here an emerald green, but she also employed, most notably, peacock blue, magenta, uranium yellow, and gold.

Rie often supplemented the main glaze with bands of manganese oxide (as here) or copper carbonate that bleed from the rim to produce infinitely complex variations in texture and color.

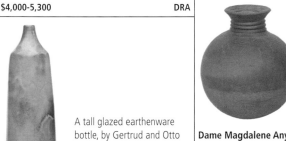

A fine, flaring conical bowl on slender foot, by Dame Lucie Rie, stoneware inlaid with green lines, with controlled golden-manganese rim and band on foot, impressed seal mark.

7¾in (19.5cm) diam

$40,000-53,000 WW

A stoneware footed bowl, by Dame Lucie Rie, with an emerald green glaze and bronzed manganese drip rim, impressed with artist's seal.

ca. 1980 *6½in (16.5cm) diam*

$40,000-66,000 CHOR

MODERN DESIGN

A glazed stoneware vase, by Phil Rogers (b.1951), with three lug handles, with a white-speckled glaze, artist's monogram mark.

11in (28cm) high

$350-450　　　　　　　　**SWO**

A ceramic wall plaque, "Mare and Foal," by Helmut Schäffenacker (1921-2010), with a design of horses in colored and luster glazes, impressed marks.

20in (51cm) high

$260-400　　　　　　　　**CHOR**

A Momo Form, by Toshiko Takaezu, of glazed stoneware, incised signature.

ca. 1985　　　*17¾in (45cm) high*

$40,000-66,000　　　　**DRA**

An untitled stack, by Peter Voulkos, of gas-fired glazed stoneware with pass-throughs and slashes, on underside "Voulkos 73," this work is registered under the Voulkos and Co. catalog number CR703.41-G.

1973　　　*33¾in (86cm) high*

$33,000-40,000　　　　**DRA**

Two porcelain beakers, by Edmund de Waal (b. 1964), pale celadon glaze with delicate crackle, impressed maker's mark.

Author of "The Hare with the Amber Eyes," Edmund de Waal's porcelain vessels range from vast installations to tiny translucent beakers. Having trained in Japan, he has incorporated elements of that country's rich tradition of ceramics, developing a distinctive style with a celadon glaze and subtle variations in texture and tone.

1995　　*4in (10.1cm) and 3¾in (9.9cm) high*

$3,300-4,000　　　　**CHOR**

A hand-built stoneware vase, by John Ward, glazed with geometric panels, impressed seal mark.

14½in (37cm) high

$8,500-9,000　　　　**WW**

A stoneware vessel, by John Ward (b. 1938), mottled cream glaze and sgraffito decoration on a ribbed body, impressed "JW" seal.

12½in (32cm) diam

$4,600-5,900　　　　**CHOR**

A hand-built stoneware vase, by John Ward (b. 1938), mat black with rust brown patches, the neck with turquoise green highlights, impressed seal mark.

14in (35.5cm) high

$7,500-8,500　　　　**WW**

A stoneware vase, by Robin Welch, painted with panels in red, bronze, and ocher on an off-white ground, impressed seal mark, exhibition paper number.

23½in (59.5cm) high

$1,050-1,200　　　　**WW**

A Whitefriars "Drunken Bricklayer" vase, designed by Geoffrey Baxter in kingfisher blue textured glass, with original paper label.

8¼in (21cm) high

$350-450 **SWO**

A postwar Textured range glass "Pyramid" vase, by Geoffrey Baxter for Whitefriars, in Tangerine, pattern 9674.

7in (17.5cm) high

$450-600 **FLD**

An untitled work, by Martin Blank, of hot-sculpted glass, of three elements, with incised signature and date "Martin Blank 2005."

2005 *40in (102cm) wide*

$9,000-10,500 **DRA**

SSargasso Sea Droplet," by Nancy Callan, of blown and etched glass.

Sargasso Sea Droplet is an exemplary droplet form, fading from green to aqua with an innovative cane pattern that Callen invented a few years ago consisting of two separate layers.

2019 *16in (41cm) high*

$13,000-18,000 **DRA**

A "Persian" group of hand-blown glass, by Dale Chihuly, composed of nine elements, with etched signature and date on two elements "Chihuly 89."

1989 *29in (74cm) wide*

$24,000-29,000 **DRA**

A "Persian and Seaform" group, by Dale Chihuly, of hand-blown glass, with 10 possibly assembled "Persian and Seaform" elements, etched signature and date, "Chihuly 90."

1990 *24½in (62cm) wide*

$23,000-26,000 **DRA**

An early "Peach Blow Blanket Cylinder," by Dale Chihuly, of hand-blown glass, etched signature and date on underside "Chihuly 76."

1976 *17in (43cm) high*

$16,000-20,000 **DRA**

A Daum glass "Masque de Verre" sculpture, designed by Jean Faucheur, etched Faucheur Daum France 122/275.

16in (40.5cm) high

$3,300-4,000 **WW**

An untitled ornamented box, by Kyohei Fujita, of blown glass, gold and silver leaf, and silver-plated metal, etched signature "Kyohei Fujita," original box.

1995 *4in (10cm) high*

$6,500-8,000 **DRA**

A pear-shaped iridescent glass vase, by Peter Layton (b.1937), etched signature, minor scuffing.

8¾in (22cm) high

$350-450 **SWO**

A segmented form, by Harvey Littleton, of hand-blown, cut, and polished glass, with etched signature and date, "© Harvey K Littleton 1987."

1987 *5in (13cm) deep*

$4,600-5,300 **DRA**

A Pulcino glass bird, designed by Alessandro Pianon, for Vistosi, set with murrine glass eyes, on copper feet, unsigned.

8in (20.5cm) high

$7,500-8,500 WW

A Pulcini glass bird, by Alessandro Pianon for Vistosi, in green with red and blue murrine canes, with further millefiori glass eyes, on copper wire feet.

ca. 1964 *12in (30.5cm) high*

$9,000-10,500 FLD

An important Masai installation, by Lino Tagliapietra, of fused glass with battuto and inciso surface and aluminum, incised signature "Lino Tagliapietra."

This work is composed of eighteen elements and is one of the artist's earliest, largest, and most intricate and colorful Masai installations.

ca. 2005 *121in (307cm) wide*

$90,000-100,000 DRA

ESSENTIAL REFERENCE—LINO TAGLIAPIETRA

Born in Murano, Italy, in 1934, Lino Tagliapietra was apprenticed at the age of 12 to glass maestro Archimede Seguso and, having worked at the Gagliano Ferro factory, and educated himself in Modern art and the history of glass, he earned the rank of "maestro" himself in 1959 at the age of 25.

Subsequently, Tagliapietra has worked with many of Murano's leading glass factories, including Venini & C; La Murrina, Effetre International (where he became artistic and technical director from 1976-89); and EOS Design nel Vetro. He has also shared techniques with the American glass maestro Dale Chihuly, given workshops at La Scuola Internazionale del Vetro (Murano), as well as taught at the Pilchuck Glass School in Washington State—with the latter generating a further and on-going exchange of ideas and techniques between Italian and American glass maestri.

Hugely innovative and internationally influential, Tagliapietra has, drawing on glassmaking techniques both ancient and modern, tended to focus since the late-1980s on creating his own, unique studio art glass.

An Italian hand-blown glass "Hopi" vessel, by Lino Tagliapietra, etched signature and date on underside "Lino Tagliapietra 2003."

2003 *15½in (39cm) high*

$26,000-33,000 DRA

A Mdina glass vase, etched mark and dated.

1976 *8½in (21.5cm) high*

$260-400 SWO

An untitled Italian vessel, by Lino Tagliapietra, of hand-blown glass and partial inciso surface, etched signature and date "Lino Tagliapietra 2000."

2000 *22½in (57cm) high*

$20,000-26,000 DRA

An Italian hand-blown glass Tessuto vase, by Lino Tagliapietra, for Effetre International, etched signature and date, "Lino Tagliapietra Effetre International 1987."

1987 *14½in (37cm) high*

$18,000-24,000 DRA

'Faviidae II," by Zoe Woods, of wheel-carved, blown glass.

From the Fothom series, "Faviidae-II" utilizes grinding and polishing techniques to explore patterns, forms, and textures that allude to ambiguous terrains.

2020 *6¼in (16cm) high*

$6,000-6,600 DRA

"Chiotto," by Toots Zynsky, of fused and thermoformed glass threads, signed on underside "Z."

2011 *11¾in (30cm) wide*

$26,000-33,000 DRA

A pair of brutalist Swedish wall lights, by Tom Ahlström and Hans Ehrlich, of iron and glass, rewired.

29½in (75cm) high

$1,300-2,000   **SWO**

A pair of sconces, by Maison Baguès, of silvered metal and cut and mirrored glass.

ca. 1940   24in (61cm) high

$5,300-6,600   **DRA**

A Tommaso Barbi table lamp, with an enameled ceramic and brass base.

ca. 1975   32½in (82.5cm) high

$1,100-1,250   **SWO**

A postmodern VeArt Glass "Leda" chandelier, by Örni Halloween for Artemide Italy, with two tiers of ruby glass branches, with 6 above 12.

1992   47¼in (120cm) diam

$4,600-5,300   **SWO**

A 1970s Georgia Jacob "Flaming Torch" table lamp, with a resin shade and marble base.

27½in (70cm) high

$260-400   **WHP**

A pair of Murano glass "Penguin" lamps, each labeled.

24in (61cm) high

$2,600-3,300   **SWO**

A Corona Lamp, by Albert Paley, of forged and fabricated steel, anodized aluminum and glass, impressed "© Albert Paley 1999 5 70 1."

This work is number 1 from the edition of 25.

1999   38in (97cm) high

$6,000-7,500   **DRA**

A chandelier, by Tommi Parzinger for Parzinger Originals, of brass, silk, glass, and enameled aluminum.

ca. 1955   33in (84cm) high

$9,000-10,500   **DRA**

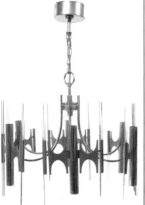

A Sciolari chandelier, gold-plated with glass rods, with original Sciolari label.

ca. 1970   27½in (70cm) high

$1,050-1,200   **SWO**

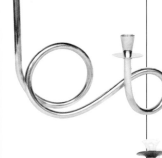

A De Vecchi J8 silver candlestick, designed by Piero De Vecchi, originally designed and made for the Eighth Milan Triennale, stamped marks.

1947   10in (25cm) high

$1,300-1,800   **WW**

A monumental Italian blown glass chandelier, attributed to Venini.

ca. 1940   55in (140cm) high

$5,300-6,600   **DRA**

A hand-blown white opaque glass lamp, atributed to Gino Vistosi (1925-80) for Murano, with yellow highlights.

11in (28cm) high

$550-650   **WHP**

A verdigris bronze, "Radiaux the Limousin Bull," by Richard Cowdy (b. 1937), on a Portland stone plinth, signed and numbered "6/11," Cowdy Foundry seal.

1983   *14¾in (37.5cm) high*

$750-850   **WW**

Two bronze figures, "Boxing Hares," by John Cox (1952-2014).

35½in (90cm) high

$4,600-5,900   **SWO**

A rare Gabriella Crespi (1922-2017) ostrich, of gilded bronze and with ostrich egg, signed.

ca. 1970   *29¼in (74cm) high*

$4,000-5,300   **SWO**

A patinated bronze bird, "Green Woodpecker," by Geoffrey Dashwood (b. 1947), signed and numbered "8/12."

1990   *9in (22.5cm) wide*

$5,300-5,900   **WW**

A polished bronze, "Pointing figure," by Bernard Meadowes (1915-2005), signed with "M" initial, numbered "1/6."

12¼in (31cm) high

$8,000-9,000   **WW**

A bronze work, "Balance," by Kees Verkade (Dutch, b.1941), numbered "3/6."

1993   *50½in (128cm) high*

$20,000-26,000   **SWO**

A disk wall sculpture by Curtis Jere (Jerry Fels and Curtis Freiler, established 1963), mixed metals, partly lacquered, signed.

ca. 1970   *35in (89cm) diam*

$1,700-2,100   **DN**

A pair of modern silver candlesticks, by Leslie Durbin, London, the stems modeled as three swimming fish, mounted on cockle bases.

1973   *3½in (8.8cm) high 10.3oz*

$1,000-1,100   **WW**

A parcel-gilt silver sauceboat, by Stuart Devlin, London, with silver-gilt pierced and textured decoration on a mat background, textured handle.

1969   *10½in (26.9cm) long 25oz*

$2,600-3,300   **WW**

An untitled (Sonambient) work, by Harry Bertoia, of beryllium copper and bronze, with a certificate of authenticity from the Harry Bertoia Foundation.

1972   *66in (168cm) high*

$90,000-100,000   **DRA**

A 1980s Chanel bouclé wool double-breasted jacket, Boutique labeled, with double Cs on gilt buttons, monogrammed silk lining.

34in (86cm) bust

$650-800 **KT**

ESSENTIAL REFERENCE—KARL LAGERFELD

Inès de La Fressange was photographed wearing this model in Paris Vogue, March 1984. It is also reproduced in "Chanel Catwalk" by Alexander Fury, p. 33, again modeled by de La Fressange. It was one of the key looks of that collection and is arguably one of Lagerfeld's most iconic and important creations ever for the House of Chanel. This dress combines the 19thC silhouette of the fashions worn by Empress Eugenie with the elaborate passementerie used on military uniforms with Coco's adoration of chains and pearls and the restrained elegance of a classic Chanel suit.

Alexander Fury considered this to be one of the most important looks for Chanel and featured it in "Chanel: The Impossible Collection," Assouline, 2019, for which he selected just 100 designs from the Chanel archives to best demonstrate the history and highlights of the House.

A Chanel couture by Karl Lagerfeld "L'Imperatrice" crinolined coatdress, labeled and numbered "63225," the basket-weave cloqué silk overdress with silver-backed gilt lion-mask buttons from neck to hem, cuffs, and the four patch pockets, the "crinoline" underskirt with matching silk front and flounces of black taffeta, with faux blister pearl and gilt chain martingale.

Spring-Summer 1984 *34in (86cm) bust*

$46,000-53,000 **KT**

An Ossie Clark for Radley lurex dress, labeled and size 12, with self-ties at waist.

1973 *36in (92cm) bust*

$1,500-1,800 **KT**

An apricot ziberline evening gown, by Jules-François Crahay for Maison Lanvin couture, labeled.

ca. 1968 *32in (81cm) bust*

$3,300-4,000 **KT**

A late-1960s/early-1970s Valentino Garavani couture wool ensemble, with velvet insertions, labeled, with a box-cut jacket with oversize hood of beaver lamb, with knee-length dress and associated vinyl belt.

34in (86cm) bust

$4,600-5,300 **KT**

A snakeskin and beaded cocktail dress, by Alexander McQueen for Givenchy couture, Look 31, the snakeskin panels (Lycodonomorphus rufulus) intersected and edged with tulle bands embroidered with a lattice of cork and wood beads, Spring-Summer 2001.

This was McQueen's final collection for Givenchy before they parted over "artistic differences" and there was no runway show.

32in (81cm) bust

$7,500-8,000 **KT**

Am early-1970s Quorum black moss crêpe ensemble, labeled.

34in (86cm) bust

$1,100-1,250 **KT**

A Vivienne Westwood "Armor" vest and cap, from the "Time Machine" collection, woven in navy with pale blue stripes, lined in ivory acetate, the school-boy cap with embroidered orb motif, red label.

Fall-Winter 1988-89 *size 40*

$4,000-5,300 **KT**

A late-1960s Del Frate Op Art monochrome printed silk faille hat, labeled, with two bunches of faux red berries and bow at rear.

20in (51cm) circum.

$130-200 **KT**

An early-1960s Dior mohair and feather hat, labeled and with Heleni Arnold retailer label.

20½in (52cm) circum.

$450-600 **KT**

A 1950s Dior feather and velvet hat, Paris, labeled with "copie" and numbered "760."

21in (53cm) circum

$650-800 **KT**

A Balenciaga "Motocross" leather classic hip crossbody bag, serial number 242803-4415 K-002123.

9in (23cm) wide

$450-600   SWO

A Chanel black chevron flap bag, calf skin leather, double "CC" black leather logo on front, gold tone chain and leather shoulder strap, authenticity number 21390377, with dust bag, with removable purse.

8¾in (22cm) wide

$3,300-4,000   SWO

An "Haut à courroies" travel bag, by Hermès, of leather, canvas, and brass, signed.

1991   21in (53cm) high

$6,000-7,500   DRA

An "Haut à courroies" travel bag, by Hermès, of brown leather and brass, signed, with original bag.

1973   22in (56cm) high

$8,000-9,000   DRA

A 1960s Paco Rabanne chain-link purse, label stamped "Paco Rabanne Paris, production RICAF, Italy, Modèle Déposé," gilt-metal and faux-tortoiseshell plastic disks.

9in (23cm) long

$2,400-2,900   KT

A Valentino Garavani "rockstud" leather purse with guitar strap, gilt metal, and hardstone.

9½in (24cm) wide

$1,600-2,100   BELL

A Louis Vuitton "Boulogne" purse, with monogram coated-canvas exterior, vachetta leather trim, zipper, and studded exterior pocket, date code DU0034, with care card, and dust bag.

11¾in (30cm) wide

$850-1,000   SWO

A 1940s bakelite purse, casket shaped with gilt-metal mounts, the hinged lid with interior mirror and with swing handle.

9in (22.5cm) wide

$200-260   CHOR

A Louis Vuitton monogrammed canvas "Keepall 50" holdall, with LV monogram canvas exterior, vachetta leather trim, gold-tone hardware, authenticity number MB0066, monogrammed.

19¾in (50cm) wide

$1,100-1,250   SWO

A Louis Vuitton monogrammed canvas cabin bag, gold-tone hardware, with front zipper and slip pockets, a side-zipped pocket.

17¾in (45cm) high

$1,250-1,450   SWO

A 20thC Louis Vuitton monogrammed leather suitcase, brass-bound corners, bearing "LV" stamps on locks, studs, and catches, lockplate stamped "Louis Vuitton, Made in France."

28in (71cm) wide

$2,000-2,600   L&T

A French suitcase, by Louis Vuitton, of vinylized canvas, leather, and brass, later customized with a hand-painted skull design, signed "Louis Vuitton LV Made in France" with paper label on interior "Louis Vuitton LV 849054.."

ca. 1945   32in (81cm) wide

$4,600-5,300   DRA

Every antique illustrated in Miller's Antiques has a letter code, which identifies the dealer or auction house that sold it. The list below is a key to these codes. In the list, auction houses are shown by the letter A and dealers by the letter D.

Inclusion in this book in no way constitutes or implies a contract or a binding offer on the part of any of our contributors to supply or sell the goods illustrated, or similar items, at the prices stated.

AB Ⓐ
ALDRIDGES OF BATH LTD.
www.aldridgesofbath.com

APAR Ⓐ
ADAM PARTRIDGE
www.adampartridge.co.uk

BELL Ⓐ
BELLMANS
www.bellmans.co.uk

BON Ⓐ
BONHAMS
www.bonhams.com

C&T Ⓐ
C&T AUCTIONEERS & VALUERS
www.candtauctions.co.uk

CHEF Ⓐ
CHEFFINS
www.cheffins.co.uk

CHOR Ⓐ
CHORLEY'S
www.chorleys.com

CM Ⓐ
CHARLES MILLER LTD.
www.charlesmillerltd.com

COTS Ⓐ
COTSWOLD AUCTION CO.
www.cotswoldauction.co.uk

DAWS Ⓐ
DAWSON'S
www.dawsonsauctions.co.uk

DN Ⓐ
DREWEATTS
www.dreweatts.com

DRA Ⓐ
RAGO ARTS
www.ragoarts.com

DUK Ⓐ
DUKE'S
www.dukes-auctions.com

FELL Ⓐ
FELLOWS
www.fellows.co.uk

FLD Ⓐ
FIELDINGS
www.fieldingsauctioneers.co.uk

GBA Ⓐ
GRAHAM BUDD
www.grahambuddauctions.co.uk

GHOU Ⓐ
GARDINER HOULGATE
www.gardinerhoulgate.co.uk

GORL Ⓐ
GORRINGE'S
www.gorringes.co.uk

GRV Ⓓ
GEMMA REDMOND VINTAGE
www.gemmaredmondvintage.co.uk

GYM Ⓐ
GOLDING YOUNG
www.goldingyoung.com

HAN Ⓐ
HANSONS
www.hansonsauctioneers.co.uk

HT Ⓐ
HARTLEYS
www.hartleysauctions.co.uk

JN Ⓐ
JOHN NICHOLSON'S
www.johnnicholsons.com

K&O Ⓐ
KINGHAMS
www.kinghamsauctioneers.com

KT Ⓐ
KERRY TAYLOR AUCTIONS
www.kerrytaylorauctions.com

L&T Ⓐ
LYON & TURNBULL
www.lyonandturnbull.com

LC Ⓐ
LAWRENCES AUCTIONEERS (CREWKERNE)
www.lawrences.co.uk

LOC Ⓐ
LOCKE & ENGLAND
www.leauction.co.uk

LOCK Ⓐ
LOCKDALES
www.lockdales.com

LSK Ⓐ
LACY SCOTT & KNIGHT
www.lsk.co.uk

M&K Ⓐ
MELLORS & KIRK
www.mellorsandkirk.com

MAB Ⓐ
MATTHEW BARTON LTD
www.olympiaauctions.com/matthew-barton-ltd

MAL Ⓐ
MALLAMS
www.mallams.co.uk

MART Ⓐ
MARTEL MAIDES AUCTIONS
www.martelmaidesauctions.com

NA Ⓐ
NORTHEAST AUCTIONS

POOK Ⓐ
POOK & POOK INC.
www.pookandpook.com

PSA Ⓐ
POTTERIES AUCTIONS
www.potteriesauctions.com

ROS Ⓐ
ROSEBERYS
www.roseberys.co.uk

SAS Ⓐ
SPECIAL AUCTION SERVICES
www.specialauctionservices.com

SK Ⓐ
SKINNER INC.
www.skinnerinc.com

SWO Ⓐ
SWORDERS
www.sworder.co.uk

TEN Ⓐ
TENNANTS
www.tennants.co.uk

THE Ⓐ
THERIAULT'S
www.theriaults.com

VEC Ⓐ
VECTIS
www.vectis.co.uk

WAD Ⓐ
WADDINGTON'S, TORONTO
www.waddingtons.ca

WHP Ⓐ
W&H PEACOCK
www.peacockauction.co.uk

WHTL Ⓐ
WHITLEY'S
www.lionandunicorn.com

WW Ⓐ
WOOLLEY & WALLIS
www.woolleyandwallis.co.uk

DIRECTORY OF AUCTIONEERS

This is a list of auctioneers that conduct regular sales. Auction houses that would like to be included in the next edition should contact us at *publisher@octopusbooks.co.uk*

ARIZONA
Old World Mail Auctions
www.oldworldauctions.com

ARKANSAS
Hanna-Whysel Auctioneers
Tel: 479 273 7770

Ponders Auctions
www.pondersauctions.com

CALIFORNIA
Bonhams & Butterfields
www.bonhams.com

I M Chait Gallery
www.chait.com

eBay, Inc.
www.ebay.com

H.R. Harmer
www.hrharmer.com

Michaan's
www.michaans.com

San Rafael Auction Gallery
www.sanrafaelauction.com

L H Selman Ltd.
www.theglassgallery.com

Slawinski Auction Co.
www.slawinski.com

Sotheby's
www.sothebys.com

NORTH CAROLINA
Robert S Brunk Auction Services Inc.
www.brunkauctions.com

Raynors' Historical Collectible Auctions
www.hcaauctions.com

SOUTH CAROLINA
Charlton Hall Galleries Inc.
www.charltonhallauctions.com

COLORADO
Pacific Auction
www.pacificauction.com

Pettigrew Auction Company
Tel: 573 796 2433

Priddy's Auction Galleries
Tel: 303 377 4411

CONNECTICUT
The Great Atlantic Auction Company
www.atlanticauctioncompany.com

Norman C Heckler & Company
www.hecklerauction.com

Lloyd Ralston Toys
www.lloydralstontoys.com

Winter Associates Inc.
www.auctionsappraisers.com

SOUTH DAKOTA
Fischer Auction Company
www.fischerauction.com

FLORIDA
Auctions Neapolitan
www.auctionsneapolitan.com

Burchard Galleries/Auctioneers
www.burchardgalleries.com

Arthur James Galleries
Tel: 561 278 2373

Kincaid Auction Company
www.kincaid.com

TreasureQuest Auction Galleries Inc.
www.tqag.com

GEORGIA
Arwood Auctions
Tel: 770 423 0110

Great Gatsby's
www.greatgatsbys.com

Red Baron's Auction Gallery
www.redbaronsantiques.com

IDAHO
The Coeur d'Alene Art Auction
www.cdaartauction.com

INDIANA
AAA Historical Auction Service
Tel: 260 493 6585

Lawson Auction Service
www.lawsonauction.com

Schrader Auction
www.schraderauction.com

Stout Auctions
www.stoutauctions.com

Strawser Auctions
www.strawserauctions.com

ILLINOIS
The Chicago Wine Company
www.tcwc.com

Hack's Auction Center
www.hacksauction.com

Leslie Hindman Inc.
www.hindmanauctions.com

Sotheby's
www.sothebys.com

Susanin's Auction
Tel: 312 832 9800

John Toomey Gallery
www.toomeyco.com

IOWA
Jackson's Auctioneers & Appraisers
www.jacksonsauction.com

Tubaugh Auctions
www.tubaughauctions.com

KENTUCKY
Hays & Associates Inc.
Tel: 502 584 4297

LOUISIANA
New Orleans Auction Galleries
www.neworleansauction.com

MAINE
Thomaston Place Auction Galleries
www.thomastonauction.com

MARYLAND
Hantman's Auctioneers & Appraisers
www.hantmans.com

Richard Opfer Auctioneering Inc.
www.opferauction.com

Sloans & Kenyon
www.sloansandkenyon.com

Theriault's
www.theriaults.com

Weschler's
www.weschlers.com

MASSACHUSETTS
Douglas Auctioneers
www.douglasauctioneers.com

Eldred's
www.eldreds.com

Grogan & Company Auctioneers
www.groganco.com

Skinner Inc.
www.skinnerinc.com

White's Auctions
www.whitesauctions.com

Willis Henry Auctions Inc.
www.willishenry.com

MICHIGAN
Frank H. Boos Gallery
Tel: 248 643 1900

DuMouchelle Art Galleries Co.
www.dumouchelles.com

MINNESOTA
Tracy Luther Auctions
www.lutherauctions.com

MISSOURI
Selkirk Auctioneers
www.selkirkauctions.com

Simmons & Company Auctioneers
www.simmonsauction.com

MONTANA
Allard Auctions
www.allardauctions.com

Stan Howe & Associates
Tel: 406 443 5658

NEW HAMPSHIRE
Paul McInnis Inc. Auction Gallery
www.paulmcinnis.com

Schmitt Horan & Co.
www.schmitt-horan.com

NEW JERSEY
Bertoia Auctions
www.bertoiaauctions.com

Nye & Co.
www.nyeandcompany.com

Rago Arts & Auction Center
www.ragoarts.com

NEW YORK
Christie's
www.christies.com

Copake Auction Inc.
www.copakeauction.com

Samuel Cottone Auctions
www.cottoneauctions.com

Doyle New York
www.doylenewyork.com

Guernsey's Auction
www.guernseys.com

Keno Auctions
www.kenoauctions.com

Mapes Auction Gallery
www.mapesauction.com

Phillips
www.phillips.com

Sotheby's
www.sothebys.com

Stair Galleries
www.stairgalleries.com

Swann Galleries
www.swanngalleries.com

OHIO
Belhorn Auction Services
www.belhorn.com

Cincinnati Art Galleries LLC.
www.cincyart.com

The Cobbs Auctioneers LLC.
www.thecobbs.com

Cowan's Historic Americana Auctions
www.cowanauctions.com

Garth's Auction Inc.
www.garths.com

Treadway Toomey
www.treadwaygallery.com

Wolf's Auction Gallery
www.wolfsgallery.com

OKLAHOMA
Buffalo Bay Auction Co.
www.buffalobayauction.com

OREGON
O'Gallery
www.ogallerie.com

PENNSYLVANIA
Noel Barrett
www.noelbarrett.com

William Bunch Auctions
www.bunchauctions.com

Concept Art Gallery
www.conceptgallery.com

Freeman's
www.freemansauction.com

Hunt Auctions
www.huntauctions.com

Pook & Pook
www.pookandpook.com

Sanford Alderfer Auction Co.
www.alderferauction.com

TENNESSEE
Kimball M Sterling Inc.
www.sterlingsold.com

TEXAS
Austin Auctions
www.austinauction.com

Dallas Auction Gallery
www.dallasauctiongallery.com

Heritage Auction Galleries
www.ha.com

VIRGINIA
Green Valley Auctions Inc.
www.greenvalleyauctions.com

Ken Farmer Auctions & Estates
www.kenfarmerllc.com

Phoebus Auction Gallery
www.phoebusauction.com

DIRECTORY OF AUCTIONEERS

CANADA

ALBERTA

Hall's Auction Services Ltd.
www.hallsauction.com

Hodgins Art Auctions Ltd.
www.hodginsauction.com

Lando Art Auctions
www.landoauctions.com

BRITISH COLUMBIA

Maynards Fine Art Auction House
www.maynards.com

Waddington's
www.waddingtons.ca

Heffel Fine Art Auction House
www.heffel.com

ONTARIO

A Touch of Class
www.atouchofclassauctions.com

Waddington's
www.waddingtons.ca

Walkers
www.walkersauctions.com

Robert Deveau Galleries
www.robertdeveaugalleries.com

Heffel Fine Art Auction House
www.heffel.com

Sotheby's
www.sothebys.com

QUEBEC

Empire Auctions
www.empireauctions.com

Iegor - Hôtel des Encans
www.iegor.net

Specialists who would like to be listed in the next edition, or have a new address or telephone number, should contact us at *publisher@octopusbooks.co.uk*. Readers should contact dealers before visiting to avoid a wasted journey.

AMERICAN PAINTINGS
James R Bakker Antiques Inc.
www.bakkerproject.com

Jeffrey W Cooley
www.cooleygallery.com

AMERICANA & FOLK ART
Augustus Decorative Arts Ltd.
www.portrait-miniatures.com

Thomas & Julia Barringer
Tel: 609 397 4474
Email: tandjb@voicenet.com

Bucks County Antique Center
Tel: 215 794 9180

Garthoeffner Gallery Antiques
www.garthoeffnerantiques.com

Allan Katz Americana
www.allankatzamericana.com

Olde Hope Antiques Inc.
www.oldehope.com

Pantry & Hearth,
www.pantryandhearth.com

J B Richardson
Tel: 203 226 0358

The Rookery Bookery
www.therookerybookery.com

Patricia Stauble Antiques
www.patriciastaubleantiques.com

Throckmorton Fine Art
www.throckmorton-nyc.com

Jeffrey Tillou Antiques
www.tillouantiques.com

ANTIQUITIES
Frank & Barbara Pollack
Tel: 847 433 2213
Email: barbarapollack@comcast.net

ARCHITECTURAL ANTIQUES
Garden Antiques
www.bi-gardenantiques.com

Cecilia B Williams
cbwantiques@gmail.com

ARMS & MILITARIA
Faganarms
www.faganarms.com

BAROMETERS
Barometer Fair
www.barometerfair.com

BOOKS
Bauman Rare Books
www.baumanrarebooks.com

CARPETS & RUGS
Karen & Ralph Disaia
Tel. 860 434 1167

Quadrifoglio Gallery
www.quadrifogliogallery.com

CERAMICS
Charles & Barbara Adams
Tel: 508 760 3290
Email: adams_2430@msn.com

Mark & Marjorie Allen
www.antiquedelft.com

Jill Fenichell
www.jillfenichellinc.com

Philip Suval, Inc
Tel: 540 373 9851

COSTUME JEWELRY
Deco Jewels Inc.
Tel: 212 253 1222

CLOCKS
Kirtland H. Crump
www.kirtlandcrumpclocks.com

Schmitt Horan & Co.
www.schmitt-horan.com

DECORATIVE ARTS
H L Chalfant Antiques
www.hlchalfant.com

Brian Cullity
www.briancullity.com

Gordon & Marjorie Davenport
Tel: 608 271 2348

Peter H Eaton Antiques
www.petereaton.com

Leah Gordon Antiques
www.leahgordon.com

Samuel Herrup Antiques
www.samuelherrup.com

High Style Deco
www.highstyledeco.com

R Jorgensen Antiques
www.rjorgensen.com

Bettina Krainin
www.bettinakraininantiques.com

William E Lohrman
Tel: 845 255 6762

Macklowe Gallery
www.macklowegallery.com

Lillian Nassau
www.lilliannassau.com

Perrault-Rago Gallery
www.ragoarts.com

Sumpter Priddy Inc.
www.sumpterpriddy.com

James L Price Antiques
www.priceantiques.com

R J G Antiques
www.rjgantiques.com

John Keith Russell Antiques Inc.
www.jkrantiques.com

Israel Sack
www.israelsack.com

Lincoln & Jean Sander
Tel: 203 938 2981
Email: sanderlr@aol.com

Kathy Schoemer American Antiques
www.kathyschoemerantiques.com

Van Tassel/Baumann American Antiques
Tel: 610 647 3339

DOLLS
Sara Bernstein Antique Dolls & Bears
www.rubylane.com/shop/sarabernstein-dolls

Theriault's
www.theriaults.com

FURNITURE
Antique Associates
www.aaawt.com

Barbara Ardizone Antiques
Tel: 860 435 3057

Artemis Gallery
www.artemisantiques.com

Boym Partners Inc.
www.boym.com

Joan R Brownstein
www.joanrbrownstein.com

Carswell Rush Berlin Inc.
www.american-antiques.net

Evergreen Antiques
www.evergreenantiques.com

Eileen Lane Antiques
www.eileenlaneantiques.com

Lost City Arts
www.lostcityarts.com

GENERAL
Alley Cat Lane Antiques
www.rubylane.com/shops/alleycatlane

Bucks County Antiques Center
Tel: 215 794 9180

Manhatten Arts & Antiques Center
www.the-maac.com

Showcase Antiques Center
www.showcaseantiquesofcny.com

South Street Antique Markets
Tel: 215 592 0256

GLASS
Brookside Art Glass
www.wpitt.com

Holsten Galleries
www.holstengalleries.com

Paul Reichwein
Tel: 717 569 7637

JEWELRY
Ark Antiques
www.arkantiques.org

Arthur Guy Kaplan
Tel: 410 752 2090

LIGHTING
Chameleon Fine Lighting
www.chameleon59.com

MARINE ANTIQUES
Hyland Granby Antiques
www.hylandgranby.com

METALWARE
Wayne & Phyllis Hilt
www.hiltpewter.com

ASIAN
Marc Matz Antiques
Tel: 617 661 6200

Mimi's Antiques
Tel: 443 250 0930

PAPERWEIGHTS
The Dunlop Collection
www.glasspaperweights.com

SILVER
Alter Silver Gallery Corp.
Tel: 212 750 1928

Chicago Silver
www.chicagosilver.com

Imperial Half Bushel
www.imperialhalfbushel.com

TEXTILES
Pandora de Balthazar
www.pandoradebalthazar.com

Colette Donovan
Tel: 978 346 0614
Email: colettedonovanantiques@comcast.net

M Finkel & Daughter
www.samplings.com

Cora Ginsburg
www.coraginsburg.com

Stephen & Carol Huber
www.antiquesamplers.com

Stephanie's Antiques
Tel: 212 633 6563

TRIBAL ART
Arte Primitivo
www.arteprimitivo.com

Marcy Burns American Indian Arts
www.marcyburns.com

Morning Star Gallery
www.morningstargallery.com

Elliott & Grace Snyder
www.elliottandgracesnyder.com

Trotta-Bono American Indian Art
www.trottabono.com

20THC DESIGN
Mix Gallery
www.mixgallery.com

Moderne Gallery
www.modernegallery.com

Modernism Gallery
www.modernisminc.com

CANADIAN SPECIALISTS

CANADIANA
The Blue Pump
Tel: 416 944 1673

Ingram Antiques & Collectibles
Tel: 416 484 4601

CERAMICS
Cynthia Findlay
www.cynthiafindlay.com

Pam Ferrazzutti Antiques
Tel: 905 639 2608

FURNITURE
Croix-Crest Antiques
Tel: 506 529 4693

Faith Grant
www.faithgrantantiques.com

Lorenz Antiques Ltd.
Tel: 416 487 2066

Maus Park Antiques
www.mausparkantiques.ca

Milord Antiques
www.milordantiques.com

Richard Rumi & Co. Antiques
www.rumiantiques.com

Shand Galleries
Tel: 416 260 9056

GENERAL
Toronto Antiques on King
www.torontoantiquesonking.com

JEWELRY
Fraleigh Jewellers
www.fraleigh.ca

Fiona Kenny Antiques
www.fionakennyantiques.com

SILVER
Richard Flensted-Holder
Tel: 416 961 3414

Louis Wine Ltd.
www.louiswine.com